One Nation
Indivisible

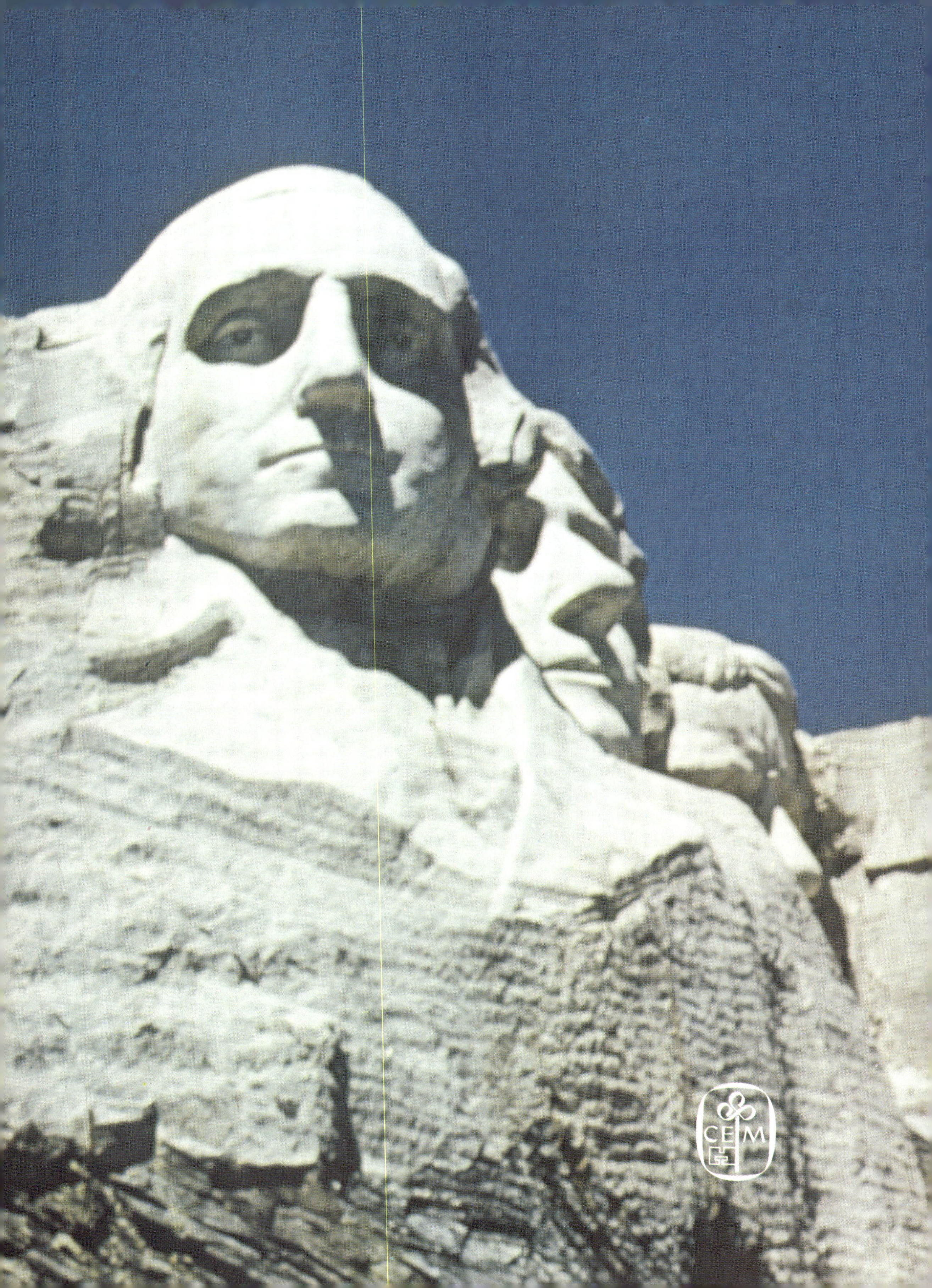

One Nation Indivisible

HELLER • POTTER

CHARLES E. MERRILL BOOKS, INC.
Columbus, Ohio

THE AUTHORS

LANDIS R. HELLER, JR., is an experienced teacher and counselor. He received his A.B. degree from Franklin and Marshall College and his M.A. from the University of Pennsylvania. Mr. Heller has taught history at the junior high school, high school, and college levels and is Chairman of the History Department at Columbus School for Girls, Columbus, Ohio. A member of the American Historical Association as well as many other professional groups, Mr. Heller is the author of numerous articles for historical journals.

NORRIS W. POTTER is a teacher of history and English at Punahou School, Honolulu, Hawaii. He received his A.B. degree from Colby College, his M.A. and Ph.D. degrees from Boston University, and is a member of Phi Beta Kappa. Dr. Potter, a Rear Admiral in the United States Naval Reserve (ret.), formerly taught at Northeastern University. He is the author of numerous articles and co-author of the text, *Hawaii: Our Island State*.

Study activities by **David Meyers**
Illustrations by **Cary**
Artifact drawings by **Vernon Mould**
Maps, charts, and graphs by **DBA Graphics, Inc.**

On the cover of this book, and on its title page, are photographs of one of the nation's great monuments, Mount Rushmore National Memorial in South Dakota. Mount Rushmore has on it four huge busts of Washington, Jefferson, Lincoln, and Theodore Roosevelt carved between 1929 and 1941 by Gutzon Borglum. The monument combines art with nature in a truly permanent way. These pictures have been chosen for the cover and title page because they symbolize the permanence and indivisibility of our nation; George Washington's bust in particular has been chosen for the cover photograph because he, perhaps more than any other American leader, is symbolic of the unity of the United States.

Copyright © 1966 by
CHARLES E. MERRILL BOOKS, INC., Columbus, Ohio 43216
All rights reserved. No part of this book may be reproduced in any form, by any method whatsoever, without permission in writing from the publisher.
Printed in the United States of America.

INTRODUCTION

One Nation Indivisible has been written to fulfill the need for an accurate, unbiased interpretation of American history for the junior high school student. Taking into account the contributions of all segments of the American population, the authors have tried to interest and involve as many students as possible in the richly varied procession of our country's history. Toward this end, the history has been carefully enlivened, including not just a catalogue of events, but a panorama of the men and women who breathed life into the past and gave freely to the growth of America. *One Nation Indivisible* includes quotations from many of our past heroes and eyewitness accounts of famous events—from the signing of the Constitution to the storming of San Juan Hill.

Written in a clear, narrative style, *One Nation Indivisible* has been geared to challenge but by no means discourage junior high school students. The text meets the requirements of standard word-count and vocabulary tests, such as the Dale-Chall checklists, for the junior high school student. The content of this book has been evaluated by outstanding historians, insuring that the latest historical research has been included in it.

Strong features of this text are its organization and study activities. Ten meaningful unit divisions have been made in the book. At the end of each of these units is a time line, a comprehensive series of individual research activities, and a group of suggested activities such as plays, panel discussions, and debates for the entire class.

Within these ten units are 31 chapters, each of which is terminated by a varied group of study activities called, collectively, "The Chapter in Perspective." Incorporated into this section are three different types of identifications, thought questions, and a unique activity called "Place Yourself in History." This latter exercise involves the student as directly as possible in the ebb and flow of history. To do this, it sets up an authentic historical situation or dilemma and asks the student to participate in it by using his imagination, outlining his own reactions and his own conclusions.

The chapters themselves are divided into sections, each of which is followed by a group of questions called "Looking Back." These exercises, which include both rote and thought questions, are ideal for daily assignments.

A special effort has been made to provide an index which covers in thorough detail both the text material and the photographs. Other appendix material contributes to the overall usefulness of *One Nation Indivisible*. The United States Constitution has been carefully annotated by an experienced college teacher with a background in Constitutional history and law. These annotations may be utilized to promote a detailed basic understanding of the Constitution. The appendices also include a list of Presidents; a list of states, state capitals and their populations; and a comprehensive listing of important events in American history. A fully annotated bibliography is divided into units which correspond with those in the book.

Photographs, original drawings, sketches of artifacts, and a full complement of maps, charts, and graphs heighten the student's interest in this book and add much to the information contained in it.

The authors wish to thank Professor G. Wallace Chessman, of the department of history, Denison University, and Mr. T. W. Kahrl of The Ohio State University for their valuable and helpful suggestions. The support and assistance of Penny Pritchard Potter and Edna Eby Heller have also contributed greatly to the completion of this text.

PREFACE to the STUDENTS

The historian is not a self-sufficient individual. He depends upon the information of specialists in other fields: the archeologist, the economist, the scientist, the geographer, and many others. Their findings are the threads with which the historian weaves the tapestry of man's progress through the ages. Since the United States is a relatively young nation, much of its history has been carefully recorded; and since it is the only nation up until the time of its founding to have been formed according to recorded plan, the materials for our American tapestry are abundant. After gathering, classifying, and analyzing available materials, the historian chooses those which are most important and useful. The choices he makes come together in a book such as this one, and, hopefully, inform you about the past of your own nation. Thomas Jefferson once said, "History, by apprizing people of the past, will enable them to judge of the future; it will qualify them as judges of the actions and designs of men; it will enable them to know ambition under every guise it may assume; and knowing it, to defeat its views." The story of *One Nation Indivisible* lies before us in this book, to inspire us, to teach us by example, and to rekindle in our minds the spirit of the great American past.

The student of history must remember that our nation is a great land mass as well as a complex of laws, ideals, and men. Look at the photographs along the margins of these two pages. In them you can gain some impression of the variety within the nation: a saguaro cactus in Arizona, a covered bridge in Indiana, Jefferson Memorial in Washington, D. C., the skyline of New York City, San Francisco's Chinatown, the Little Red Schoolhouse in New England, a lighthouse on the Maine Coast, the New York World's Fair, and the Grand Canyon. All are interesting, vital scenes that help to form the whole picture of America. Rich farmland, soaring cities, spacious plains crossed by superhighways add detail to the picture. Americans have used their land wisely at times, unwisely at other times, but the land has given America's men and their ideas a place to expand and grow.

★

More than anything else, America's people are her greatest natural resource. President Kennedy once called this country "a nation of immigrants," and it has been just that. Almost every American family had its origins elsewhere, whether those origins were in Europe, Africa, or Asia. The fear, the awe, and the unquestioned thrill of hope at coming to a new land have been experiences shared by every immigrant to American shores. While it is a harsh fact of our world that the hope has not been fulfilled for all Americans, it is important to realize that the United States still remains a nation of hope.

★

We should remember that American history is not simply a mass of tiresome detail. All history is made up of details. Some are important ones; others serve only to provide background for the main events. The events and details of American history, in all of their glory and complexity, have a direct connection with each of you in this time and in this place. They should hold the same interest for you that the history of your own family holds, because your own family is a part of American history. Perhaps your forebears are not mentioned by name in the text, but when you think of your grandfather or your great-grandfather, think of him as one of the thousands that crossed the ocean or the desert in search of new opportunity. Whether he came here ten or 300 years ago, whether he came in chains or as a colonial founder, he is still one of the American heroes who grasped the opportunity to participate in the American experience.

CONTENTS

UNIT 1
America Changes from Wilderness to Colonial Empire

1. The Discovery and Exploration of the New World — 2
2. The English Colonies Become Firmly Established — 22
3. Life and Development of the English Colonies — 45
4. England and France Battle for a Continent — 62

UNIT 2
Dissatisfaction and Rebellion Inspire a New Kind of Government

5. The Colonists Become Americans — 88
6. Americans Turn to Revolution — 104
7. These United States Adopt a Constitution — 142

UNIT 3
The American Eagle Tries Its Wings

 8. Federalists and Republicans Launch the New Government 164
 9. The United States Gains the Respect of Other Nations 181
10. Industrial and Social Developments 196

UNIT 4
American Horizons Extend and Widen

11. Jackson and the New West 226
12. How the United States Gained More Territory 239

UNIT 5
The Union Breaks Apart and Mends More Strongly

13. The Underlying Causes of Secession 262
14. A Nation at War With Itself: Civil War 284
15. The Nation Rebuilds 312

Left: the cliff palace at Mesa Verde, Colorado, is one of the oldest man-made dwellings on the North American continent, built long before Columbus' first voyage. Below: Plymouth Rock, on which the Pilgrims first stepped ashore. Right: King Charles II of England granted this colonial charter to the Carolina colony in 1663.

Plimoth Plantation Photo

UNIT 6
The Wide Open Spaces Are Filled

16.	The Awakening Industrial Giant	330
17.	The Vanishing Frontier	342
18.	The Farmer and the Land	355
19.	Immigration and the Advance of Labor	367

UNIT 7
Americans Build for a Complex Future

20.	Cultural and Social Change	382
21.	Life in City and Country	401
22.	A New Role on the World Stage	417

UNIT 8
Americans Find Ways to Solve New Problems

23.	The Progressives and the "Square Deal"	436
24.	A Challenge to the "New Freedom"	450
25.	Peacetime Problems	470

Left: Revolutionary War cannons look across the bay in historic Edenton, North Carolina. Below: Concord Bridge and Monument. Right: Fort Macon, on North Carolina's central coast.

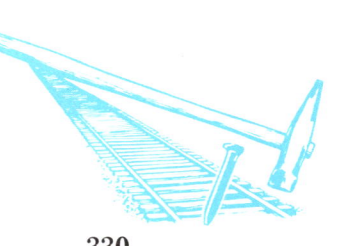

UNIT 9
America Participates in the Problems of the World

26. Recovery and the Road to War	492
27. The World in Flames	511
28. Days of Infamy and Victory	525

UNIT 10
America Flourishes in a Shrinking World

29. The Problems and Challenges of Our Times	546
30. The Uneasy Fifties	566
31. America Moves Ahead in the Sixties	579

Appendix

Annotated United States Constitution	608
Important Dates in American History	633
Annotated Bibliography	639
Presidents of the United States	651
The States of the Union	655

General Index
660

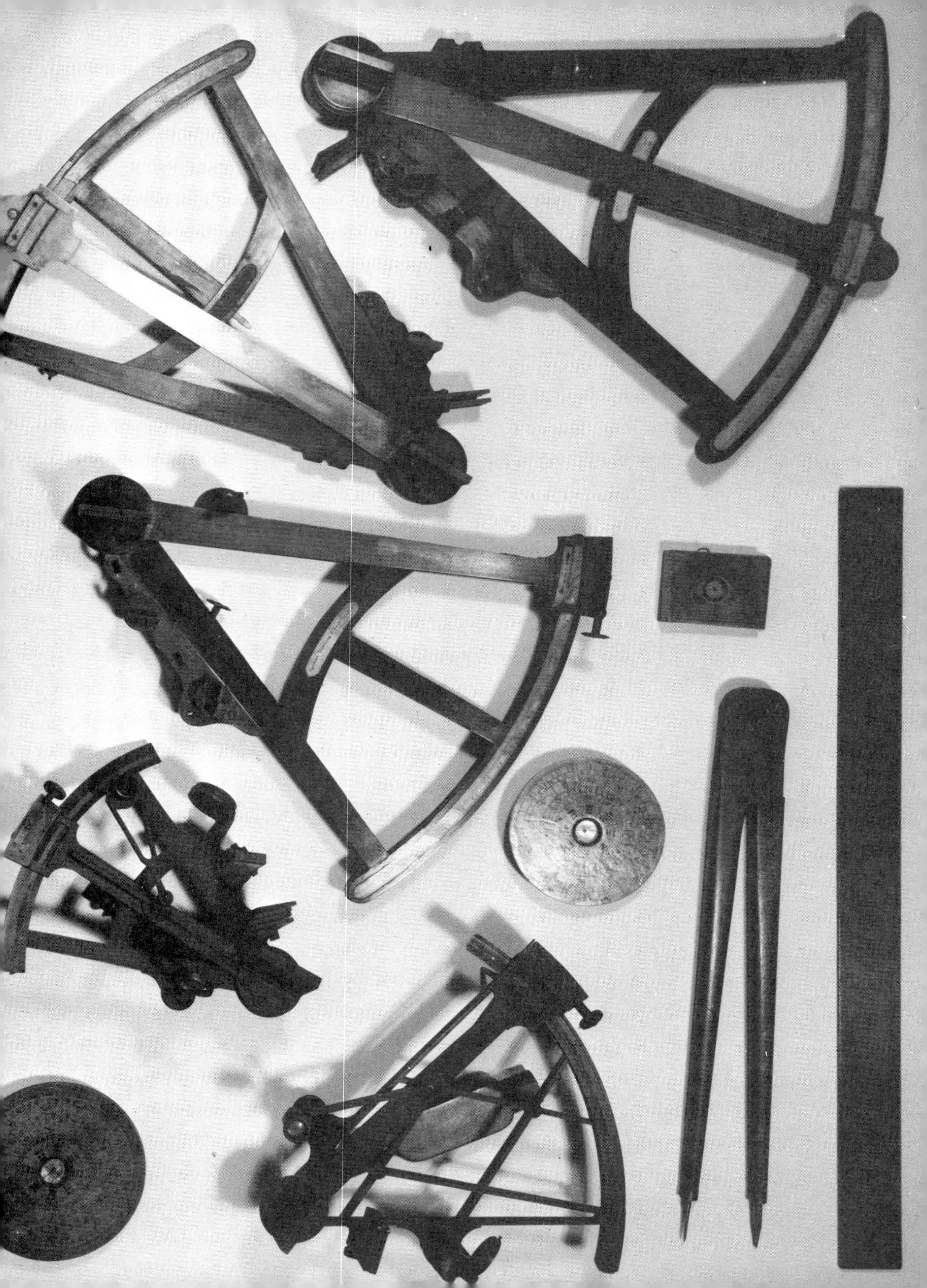

CHARTS and GRAPHS

The Thirteen Colonies Are Founded	41
Colonial Trade with England—1700-1775	47
How the Colonies Were Governed	94
Division of Public Lands	144
Congressional Powers	152
Urban and Rural Population Growth	208
	402
	600
Development of Political Parties	278
	499
Advantages of Each Side in Civil War	286
Railroad Mileage—1830-1960	345
	603
Farming Becomes Efficient	356
Working Farm Population	357
Growth in Public Education—1870-1960	387
	597
Growth in Higher Education—1870-1960	388
	597
National Park Acreage	439
Great Grandfather Had a Better Voting Record	447
Paved Road Mileage	478
	602
Growth of Labor Unions—1900-1965	497
	568
Organization of the United Nations	549
Progress in Democracy	598-599
Modern Technology Conquered the Atlantic	602
Airline Mileage—1930-1965	603
How an Amendment Is Made to the Constitution	623

Such navigational aids as the compass, the astrolabe, and the sextant (left) were the crude instruments used by ocean-going explorers for centuries. Such a modern vehicle as the Atlas rocket (right) is guided by highly complex systems of computers and other electronic machines. The great difference between the two methods of navigation is symbolic of man's progress through the years.

MAPS

Pre-Columbian Exploration and Trade Routes	6
Atlantic Explorations (1492–1610)	10
Interior Explorations	15
English Colonies in North America	30
Influence of Massachusetts on New England Settlement	43
Economic Structure of the Colonies (1700)	47
Population Growth and Territorial Expansion (1650–1750)	63
Principal Localities in the French and Indian War	73
Quebec (1759)	78
Results of the Treaty of Paris (1763)	81
The Thirteen Colonies (1775)	106
The Birth of the Revolution (1775–1775)	109
Action in Canada and Ticonderoga during the Revolution	115
Campaigns in the Middle Colonies	121
The United States after the 2nd Treaty of Paris	138
Land Claims of the Colonies Conflict (1783)	143
Northwest Territory	145
The Louisiana Purchase	176
War of 1812—The Great Lakes	184
Action on Chesapeake Bay (1814)	187
American Roads, Railroads, and Canals (1860)	202
Oregon Territory	247
Growth of the United States (1776–1867)	255
Free States, Slave States, and Territories	264
Status of United States (August 1861)	270
Confederate States of America	288
Civil War (1861–1862)	293
Civil War (1863)	296
Civil War (1864)	302

Civil War (1865)	307
Railroads to the West	346
Spanish-American War	423
The Panama Canal Zone and Central America	441
Europe (1914)	457
United States Participation in World War I	465
Europe (1941) with 1938 Boundaries	507
Japanese Conquest (1941–1942)	528
North African and Italian Campaigns (1942–1943)	531
Allied Campaigns in Europe (1944–1945)	536
War in Korea	555
Divided Indochina	560

The *U. S. S. Constitution*, the heroic ship of the War of 1812, was rebuilt by public subscription in 1925. It is now maintained at Boston Navy Yard.

National Gallery of Art—Washington, D.C.—Andrew Mellon Collection

ONE NATION INDIVISIBLE

UNIT 1

America Changes from Wilderness to Colonial Empire

1. The Discovery and Exploration of the New World

1. Europe Looks Beyond Its Borders • **2.** Spain Turns Westward • **3.** England Stakes Its Claims • **4.** France Takes an Active Interest • **5.** Europe's Claims Conflict

2. The English Colonies Become Firmly Established

1. Englishmen Look to the New World • **2.** Settlers Seek Fortunes and Freedoms in Southern Colonies • **3.** The Middle Colonies Develop a Middle Way of Life • **4.** Religious Motives Bring Settlers to New England

3. Life and Development of the English Colonies

1. The Colonies Prosper and Grow Economically • **2.** Different Environments Mold Different Ways of Life • **3.** A Sense of Unity Begins to Emerge

4. England and France Battle for a Continent

1. English Colonies Increase in Value • **2.** French Colonies Grow More Slowly • **3.** The French and the English Clash Indecisively • **4.** A Great War Decides America's Future

It was all-important that the British Colonial officials maintain good relations with the Indians of North America. Benjamin West's painting, Colonel Guy Johnson, *symbolizes this relationship. Johnson's uncle, Sir William Johnson, lived among the Indians, keeping communication between them and the British open for almost half a century.*

1 The Discovery and Exploration of the New World

Today we are living in a period of accelerated discovery, totally unlike any previous age. Already man has orbited the earth, and scientists claim that he may soon reach the moon.

In view of our rapid progress, it seems impossible that for thousands of years the broad lands on which we live were unknown. The people of the Old World went about their daily lives without knowledge of the two great continents which lay on the other side of the planet. However, Columbus' accidental discovery of America led to an exciting search for riches and adventure in the New World, which makes the story of America more thrilling than fiction.

1. Europe Looks Beyond Its Borders

Before man began to think scientifically, the people of Europe, Asia, and Africa gave little thought to the notion that there were any other continents in the world. Those who thought about the world at all thought that it was flat, and that the lands they knew lay in the middle of it, surrounded by water. In the several hundred years before Columbus' time, only the wisest geographers believed that the world was round.

In the centuries before Columbus sailed, men were acquiring information about the size and shape of the world. Men who lived in northern Europe sailed to a new land they were later to name Vinland. The crusades and the travels of Marco Polo informed Europeans of the riches to be found in the East. Portuguese sailors traveled far beyond the shores of their native land. Scientific inventions, such as the compass and other instruments, made extended navigation possible. Out of curiosity and need, Europe was ready for expansion, for new discoveries, and for explorations. The first to push these explorations forward were the brave men of the North: the Norsemen.

The Norsemen

A thousand years ago the greatest sailors in the world were the Norsemen, who lived in Norway, Sweden, and Denmark, in the north of Europe. In their long, low ships, driven by sails and oars, the Norsemen made many daring trips out onto the open waters of the Atlantic Ocean. Traveling far to the west, they discovered Iceland and Greenland. Then about the year 1000, Norsemen, led by a daring Norse sailor named Leif Ericsson, or Leif the Lucky, went still farther and reached the coast of North America. They named the new land Vinland because of the many wild grapevines growing

Norse helmets, shield. Above: Norse ship.

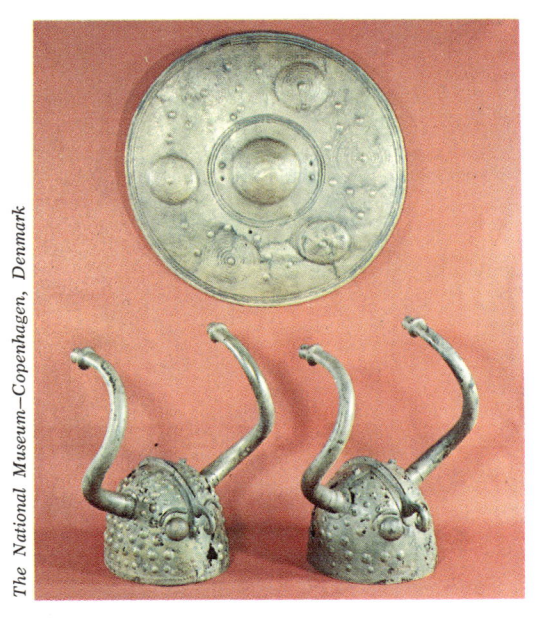

The National Museum—Copenhagen, Denmark

there. The Norsemen made attempts to found a Norse settlement in North America, but the hardships of the climate or the unfriendliness of the natives brought these attempts to an early end.

Since they did not establish colonies, the Vikings did not receive full credit for the discovery of the New World. But they did receive credit for their contributions to the later settlement of it. Their ships were the first to be seaworthy for long ocean voyages, and they established a bustling trade between Greenland and Iceland and northern Europe. The way was paved for later voyages and trade.

The Crusades

Although the people of western Europe did not follow the Norsemen in their explorations of the New World, they made many explorations and discoveries in other areas. From the eleventh to the fourteenth century, thousands of Europeans traveled to Palestine to war against the Moslems for control of the Holy Land.

3

The Crusades, as these wars were called, accomplished little of their original purpose. Christians were not prepared to fight against well-trained warriors of the Moslem world. However, these wars had a marked effect upon social and economic conditions of Europe. The Crusaders brought back with them knowledge of many new products: spices, to preserve food; drugs, to be used as medicine; precious gems, silks, china, and glassware, to change the drabness of their lives. Such luxuries were previously unknown to most of Europe. It was the sight of these treasures from distant lands that began a wave of European trade with the countries of the East.

From the time of the earliest Crusade, the trade between Europe and the East was controlled by Italian merchants, especially those of Venice and Genoa. These merchants acquired privileges of trade in the important cities of Constantinople, Antioch, and Alexandria, not only because of their nearness, but also in exchange for ships and financial assistance to the Crusaders.

Marco Polo's Travels

The Crusaders and the successful business of the Italian merchants sparked interest in Eastern trade. Marco Polo, an Italian from the city of Venice, made the long journey across the continent of Asia. He discovered the wealth of the Far East to be very great. After winning the confidence of the great Kubla Khan, the ruler of what is now Mongolia and China, he was asked to remain in that strange land to fill various governmental posts. His stay lasted seventeen years. In those years, he traveled widely, observing carefully the varied products of Eastern trade. He noted that the European prices for some of these products were exceedingly high, making it impossible for many people to purchase them. Since the original cost was only a fraction of the final sale price in the markets of Europe, a great margin of profit was being made by either the merchants or the owners of the Eastern caravans.

On Marco Polo's return to Italy, he published a book telling of his experi-

Marco Polo crosses the desert on a camel. He had first traveled eastward with his uncle when he was a boy. Later he led his own expedition. On his return to Italy, his fantastic stories were written down and influenced other explorers, such as Columbus.

ences in the Far East. In it he spoke of many things strange to Europeans: the people, the customs, the products, and the great sea to the east of China. Since the book was widely circulated in Europe, the question was naturally asked whether this sea could be the other side of the Atlantic Ocean. Many historians have thought that Columbus acquired the idea of sailing west to reach the East from reading Marco Polo's book. At the very least, we can say that Europe became aware of the enormous profits being made from the Far Eastern trade. This encouraged each of the different maritime nations —Portugal, Spain, England, and France— to look for its own route to the East.

Prince Henry's School of Navigation

Portugal was one of the nations most interested in finding the new route to the East. Prince Henry of Portugal, usually known as Prince Henry the Navigator because he founded a school of navigation, sent many ships down the western coast of Africa in the hope of finding an all-water route south of that continent to Asia. Although Prince Henry never lived to see it, in 1487, a Portuguese navigator named Bartholomew Diaz reached the southern tip of Africa, known as the Cape of Good Hope. By 1498, Vasco da Gama, also from Portugal, had sailed around the south of Africa and reached India by sea.

The Portuguese now had the trade route which they had long sought. Soon Lisbon, the capital of Portugal, became one of the busiest seaports in Europe. Vasco da Gama's discovery threatened to destroy the Mediterranean trade through Constantinople, Antioch, and Alexandria. Prince Henry's efforts in earlier years had finally borne fruit.

Columbus' small ships, the *Santa Maria*, the *Nina*, and the *Pinta* were short and broad-beamed and sailed very slowly.

Looking Back

1. How did the Norsemen contribute to the discovery and exploration of North America?
2. In what ways did the Crusades affect Europe?
3. Explain how Marco Polo influenced the affairs of Europe and Asia.
4. Show how the efforts of Henry the Navigator helped Portugal to become a leading nation.

2. Spain Turns Westward

Unlike the Portuguese, the Spanish did not send men to explore the coast of Africa in search of a new route to India. Spain, though skeptical, was willing to listen to the wild dreams of an Italian sailor. That sailor, Christopher Columbus, was obsessed with the idea that the world was round. He was convinced that the East could be reached by sailing west. Credit must be given to the Spanish for taking a chance on Columbus' seemingly wild idea and for making it possible for him to prove his theory.

The discovery by Columbus of the new lands to the west astounded the European world. In the next two centuries, thousands of Europeans sailed to the New World, some for adventure and others to settle. The Spanish led in this migration, creating an empire in the Americas that was to last for three hundred years. They founded the first colonies. Before 1600 two universities were founded; great cathedrals were built; cities were created with fine bookshops, theaters, and paved streets; large-scale farming with many agricultural crops was introduced; and new sources of wealth were found in the mining of gold and silver. Throughout the sixteenth century, the exploits of the Spanish were unmatched by other nations.

Christopher Columbus

A Sailor's Dream. Born in Genoa, Italy, about 1451, Columbus loved the sea. As a youth, he was fond of studying the crude maps and charts of those early times. It is supposed that he went to sea at an early age, probably sailing as far as Iceland. He grew up to be an accomplished sailor. He was one of the few people of his day who believed the earth to be round.

If the world were round, thought Columbus, one could surely sail west and reach Asia. Little dreaming of the great size of the earth, he believed that such a route would be shorter than the one which the Portuguese were seeking around the south of Africa.

A Voyage of Discovery. For years Columbus traveled through Europe, trying to find someone who would supply him with ships and money with which to make a voyage to the west. Everywhere he met with refusal and ridicule. At last Queen Isabella and

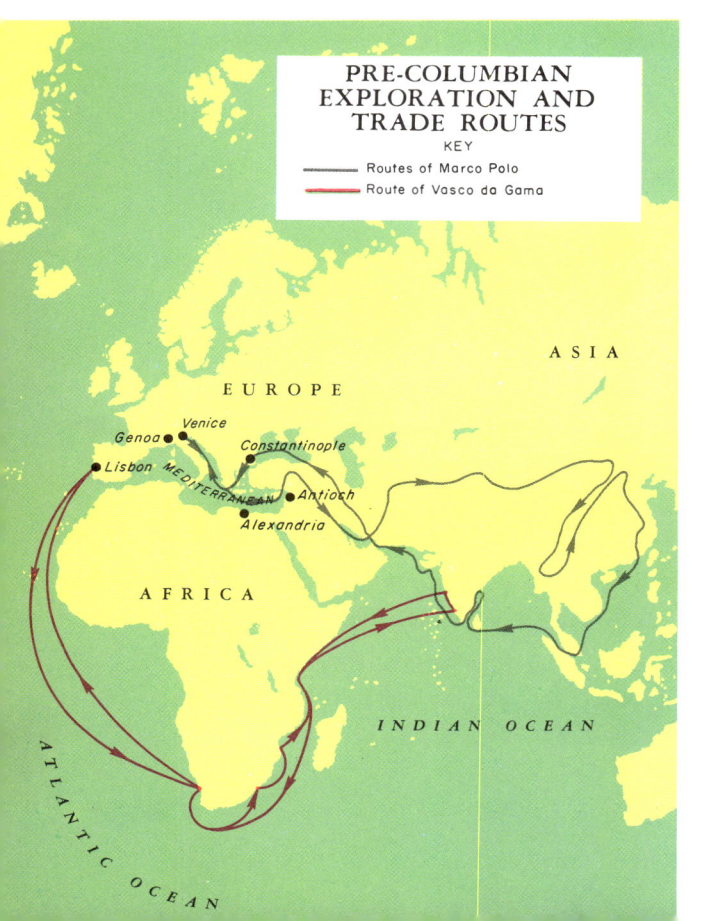

PRE-COLUMBIAN EXPLORATION AND TRADE ROUTES
KEY
Routes of Marco Polo
Route of Vasco da Gama

King Ferdinand of Spain agreed to help him and supplied him with three ships and a crew for each. On August 3, 1492, Columbus' little fleet set sail from the port of Palos, in Spain. His fleet consisted of the ships *Santa María*, *Niña*, and *Pinta*, with a combined crew of ninety men.

After a brief stop for repairs and provisions at the Canary Islands, Columbus and his three ships started west through unknown seas. Never had his men sailed so far from shore. Frightened even before the voyage began, they became more and more panic-stricken as the ships traveled farther and farther from home.

More than two months after the little fleet left Spain, it was still sailing on to the west. The discontent of the sailors had now become dangerous, and they threatened mutiny. It seemed as though the dauntless spirit of Columbus could no longer prevent the men from turning the ships around and heading home. Then, on October 12, a joyful cry of "Land!" was raised.

Columbus took tropical birds like these parrots back to Spain with him as proof that he had been to new and strange lands.

The land they saw proved to be one of the Bahama Islands. Columbus and his men went ashore and claimed the land for Spain. He had discovered the New World although he thought he had reached the shores of Asia.

Back and forth among the islands Columbus cruised, looking in vain for the rich cities of the East. At last, dis-

---

Christopher's son Ferdinand, in his biography of his father, writes of the discovery of land in this graphic fashion:

"It would have been impossible for the Admiral much longer to have held out against the numbers who opposed him; but it pleased God that, on the afternoon of Thursday the eleventh of October, such sure tokens of being near the land appeared that the men took courage and rejoiced at their good fortune as much as they had been distressed before. From the Admiral's ship a green rush was seen to float past.

"Sailors in the *Pinta* saw a cane and a staff in the water.... Those of the *Nina* saw a thorn branch with red berries.... From such signs the Admiral was certain that he was now quite near to land, and after the evening prayers he made a speech to the men, reminding them of God's mercy in granting them favorable weather for so long a voyage and now comforting them with so many tokens of success."

appointed, he returned to Spain, taking with him a few of the curious copper-skinned natives, some birds, and some fish which he had found. Because he still believed these islands to be near India, he called them the Indies, and the people whom he found living there he called Indians.

Later Voyages. The Spaniards regarded Columbus as a great hero. The next year they sent him on another voyage to the west, and in 1498 and 1502 he made his third and fourth voyages. Because he could not find the Asiatic cities which he sought, the people of Spain lost interest in him, and a few years after his last voyage the great explorer died in poverty and neglect, never knowing that he had found a new world. It is noteworthy that Columbus never set foot on the North American continent.

Further Explorations

Amerigo Vespucci. The New World to the west was not named after Columbus. In 1499, several of the men who had been with Columbus on his first and second voyages, planned an expedition of their own to the New World. With them sailed a merchant named Amerigo Vespucci. After returning to Europe, he wrote an account of his voyage which was widely circulated. A German geographer read

Balboa looks out over the wide expanse of the Pacific Ocean. Would his clothes be practical for jungle travel?

In a letter to Ferdinand and Isabella, Columbus described the admirable characteristics of the natives he found in the new world.

"They are so ingenuous and free with all they have, that no one would believe it who has not seen it; of anything that they possess, if it be asked of them, they never say no; on the contrary, they invite you to share it and show as much love as if their hearts went with it, and they are content with whatever trifle be given them, whether it be a thing of value or of petty worth. I forbade that they be given things so worthless as bits of broken crockery and of green glass and lace-points, although when they could get them, they thought they had the best jewel in the world."

8

it and suggested that the new lands to the west be called America after Amerigo Vespucci. The world accepted this idea, so our continent is named America instead of Columbia.

Ponce de Leon. In spite of the small interest which Spain showed in Columbus' voyages, it was not long before Spanish settlements were founded on the islands he called the Indies. Cuba and Puerto Rico soon became thriving colonies.

In 1513, Ponce de Leon was the governor of Puerto Rico. From the Indians he heard a strange story of a fountain. The governor, growing old and determined to find this fountain which might make him young again, immediately set out on his search with a number of followers.

Ponce de Leon's expedition sailed northwest at the beginning of Easter week. Within a few days they came upon the shore of a very warm and sunny land. They named it Florida, from the Spanish name for Easter, *Pascua florida,* meaning the "Feast of Flowers." Of course, Ponce de Leon found no Fountain of Youth, but he did find and claim this beautiful land for his country.

Balboa. The same year that Ponce de Leon discovered Florida, another Spaniard, named Balboa, started out on an exploring expedition. While living in Hispaniola (hiss-pahn-yo'lah), an island near Cuba, Balboa heard of a great sea lying to the south and west. With a party of men he set out through the jungles of the Isthmus of Panama in search of it. For days they struggled on. At last Balboa reached the top of a mountain from which he could see the broad, blue waters of a great ocean stretching away to the south and west. Balboa was the first European to view the Pacific Ocean from its American shore.

de Soto. Hernando de Soto was another Spanish explorer. He landed with men and horses on the west coast of Florida and marched inland. De Soto was cruel and greedy, but he was also brave. For hundreds of miles, he and his followers made their way through lands which no white man had ever

This detailed Aztec calendar is an example of Aztec skill in sculpture and astronomy. Cortez conquered a vital, advanced culture.

visited. For two entire years the Spaniards pressed on, always hopeful of finding gold and wealthy cities, like the legendary "Seven Cities of Cibola," to conquer, but finding only vast stretches of unbroken forest. At last they came to a mighty river, and de Soto gazed out across the broad waters of the Mississippi, the greatest river in North America.

The Spaniards built rafts, crossed to the opposite bank and pushed farther into the West, looking for gold. After months of fruitless searching, they turned back and reached again the rolling waters of the Mississippi. Here de Soto died, worn-out and disappointed.

His companions lowered his body into the waters of the great river which he had discovered.

Coronado. Another intrepid Spaniard, Coronado, governor of the Mexican province, went exploring in North America. Hearing of rich cities to the north, he set out to find them. He explored the great western plains, and a party of his followers even made their way to the Grand Canyon of the Colorado River. Coronado came upon a number of wretchedly poor Indian villages, but he found none of the wealth he sought. Disappointed, he returned to Mexico, then called New Spain. Though he had found no rich cities to conquer, he had added much to man's knowledge of the great northern continent of the New World.

Magellan. Columbus thought he had proven that the East could be reached by sailing west. Real proof that the world was round was the accomplishment of a Portuguese sea captain, Ferdinand Magellan, sailing under the flag of Spain. In 1519, Magellan set sail to explore the eastern coast of South America. Finding a passage through the southern tip of the continent, now known as the Straits of Magellan, he sailed boldly across the Pacific. Magellan himself was killed in a battle with some natives of the Philippine Islands, but his men pushed ever westward. A few of them at last reached Europe again, three years after they had started. For the first time, men had sailed around the world.

The Conquerors

Cortez. Spain sent out other exploring expeditions. One of them, commanded by a general named Cortez,

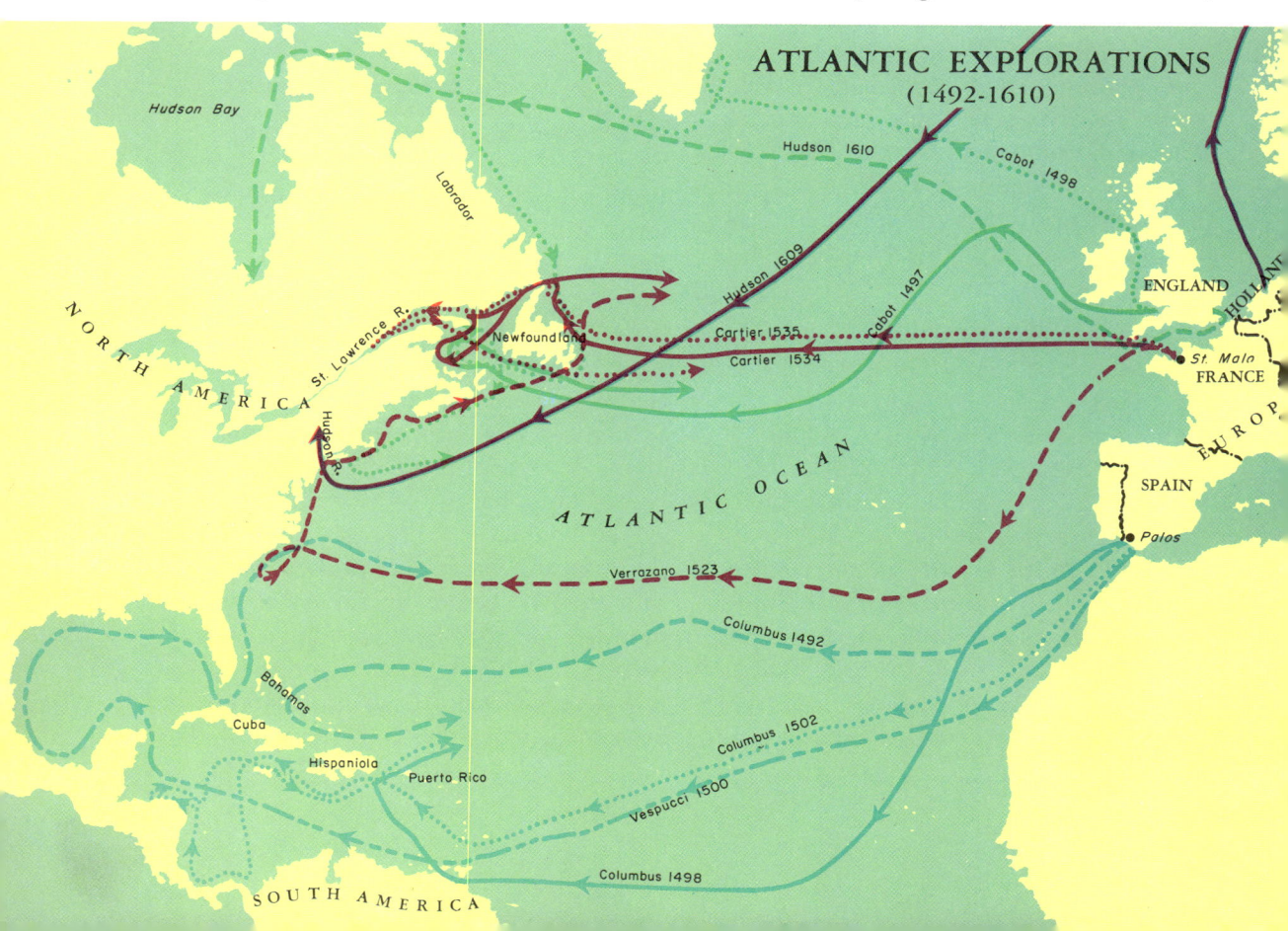

Montezuma, the Aztec ruler, welcomes Cortez to his capital city. Notice how differently they are dressed. Why?

landed in Mexico. Cortez had heard of the fabulous wealth of the Aztec Indians and was determined to investigate. When the Aztecs heard of his arrival, they believed that he was their "fair god" who had ruled their land hundreds of years ago and, upon sailing away in a large canoe, had promised to return.

The Spanish were welcomed into the Aztec capital city of Tenochtitlan (tay-nock-tee-TLAHN'). It seemed more like a fairy tale city than anything they had seen before. Great temples and buildings, irrigation systems, paved streets, many canals, skilled craftsmen, and art works convinced Cortez that this was a civilization worth capturing. The desire for plunder and the religious indignation against the Aztec custom of offering human sacrifices caused fighting to begin between the two peoples. After many bitter battles and great loss of life, Montezuma, the Aztec emperor, was imprisoned and the Aztec civilization fell. The Spanish robbed the land of its fabulous treasures of gold and silver, enslaved the Indians, and established a rule in Mexico noted for its cruelty.

Pizarro. High in the Andes Mountains in the western part of South America lived an Indian tribe known as the Incas. The Incas had vast treasures of gold, silver, and jewels. A Spaniard named Pizarro (pih-ZAHR'o) heard of their great wealth and determined to conquer them. With his Spanish army, he landed on the western coast of South America and marched inland. The Incas were not able to defend themselves against men as well armed and protected as the Spaniards were, and the cruel Spaniards mowed down thousands of Indians with their guns. The ruler, Atahualpa (ah-tah-WAHL'pah), was imprisoned. In exchange for his freedom he offered to fill a room as high as he could reach with gold. When the

California's Carmel Mission is a well preserved reminder of the days when Spain controlled western North America.

> *Cortez*
>
> After the conquest of Montezuma, the Aztec chiefs paid their tribute to Cortez in vast quantities of gold and silver plate. To this tribute Montezuma added his great hoard of ornaments, precious stones, and trinkets that were particularly valuable for their unusual craftsmanship. In our own currency, the value of the tribute amounted to six million, three hundred thousand dollars. Quite a prize! Mexico had yielded greater treasures than the combined wealth of many European kings.

room was filled with gold (an amount valued today at approximately fifteen million dollars), Pizarro, instead of releasing Atahualpa, strangled him to death before the eyes of his subjects. The country of the mighty Incas, called Peru, became another colony of Spain.

It is interesting to note that most of the Spanish leaders and explorers failed to find the things they sought. Yet their explorations were far more important than they dreamed, for they laid the basis of Spanish claim to Florida, to Mexico, to Peru, and to the western part of what is now the United States.

Looking Back

1. Discuss the theories of Columbus and the results of his voyages to the New World.
2. Show how each of the following explorers added to man's knowledge of the New World and the growing power of Spain: Vespucci, de Leon, Balboa, de Soto, Coronado, Magellan.
3. Compare the contributions to Spain by Cortez and Pizarro.
4. Which of the Spanish explorers or conquerors made the most important contribution to his nation? Explain.

3. England Stakes Its Claims

Since Spain and England were rivals in Europe, it was quite natural that they would become rivals in the New World. Five years after Columbus made his famous voyage, the English king, Henry VII, sent representatives of his nation to America to compete with the Spanish. Henry VII, always jealous of Spain, felt the honor of England was at stake if he did not surpass the Spanish.

The voyages of the English did not bring gold to their monarch, nor did they bring spices or exotic tropical foods. What the English did acquire was another kind of wealth more valuable than Spanish gold or Portuguese spices. As colonies were established, these "little Englands" supplied the much-needed raw materials for English manufacturers and became markets for manufactured goods from the mother country. These colonies also became "little Englands" in another sense. They became overseas experiments in English law, ideas of liberty, and religious freedom.

Discovery and Exploration

The Cabots. After Columbus had started a great wave of exploration to the west, John Cabot, another Italian, who was living in England at the time, was sent by Henry VII to discover lands for the English crown. In 1497, Cabot sailed westward, following a course over the North Atlantic. After many wearying weeks at sea, he at last sighted the coast of Labrador. He landed and claimed the country for England, returning home the same year. The next year, with his son Sebastian, John Cabot again visited North America, and this time explored the coast as far south as Carolina. These explorations of the Cabots were to lead later to England's claim to most of the land along the Atlantic coast of North America.

Drake. For nearly eighty years after Cabot explored the coast of North America, few Englishmen made voyages to the New World. But when Queen Elizabeth came to power, English interest in exploration and navigation was revived. In 1577, Francis Drake, a young English sea captain, set out to see how much trouble he could make for Spain in her new colonies. Spain and England had long been rivals, and, though they were not at war, Drake and his countrymen felt a keen dislike for all Spaniards.

Sailing west, Drake captured and destroyed many Spanish ships and

Drake's small maneuverable ships attack a clumsy Spanish galleon.

Henry Hudson sails his ship, the Half Moon, up the river named for him. Can you point out many differences between Hudson's ship and Drake's on the preceding page? Columbus' on page 5? How are ships different today?

seized the treasure they carried. Down the eastern coast of South America he sailed and through the Straits of Magellan into the Pacific Ocean where other Spanish ships became his prey. Drake was sure that on his return Spanish warships would be guarding the Straits or would be sent to capture him in the Atlantic.

He knew that he could not return home the way he came. Therefore, he sailed up along the western coast of North America. Then, taking on provisions and water at what is now called Drake's Bay, near San Francisco, he sailed across the broad waters of the Pacific Ocean. Nearly three years after leaving England, he returned, having sailed around the world.

Hudson. Strangely enough, it was an Englishman, Henry Hudson, who gave the Netherlands its claim to lands in North America. Twice Hudson, sailing under the English flag, had attempted to find a route to Asia around the north of Europe. In 1609, the Dutch East India Company sent him on a third expedition.

With a small crew, Hudson set out in his little vessel, the *Half Moon*. Once more he tried to find a passage around the north of Europe, but ice barred his way. He then turned back and headed westward. When he reached the American coast, he sailed south, always looking for a channel through the land to the Pacific. Finally he came to a wide, deep bay into which flowed a large river. Here, he thought, was a long-sought passage. But pushing on up the river he saw that it grew steadily narrower and more shallow, and at last he turned about and sailed back to Europe. His discovery of the splendid harbor, now New York Bay, and the river later named for him gave the Netherlands a claim to the lands bordering these waters.

The following year, Hudson made another voyage, this time with an English vessel and an English crew. Still searching for a northern route to Asia, he discovered a great bay, now known as Hudson Bay, and claimed the lands adjacent to it for England. Because Hudson would not give up his search for a passage to the Pacific and return home, his sailors mutinied and cast him adrift in an open boat with his small son and eight sick companions. Then, heartlessly, the mutinous crew set sail for Europe, leaving the little band to perish in the icy wastes of Hudson Bay. Of the returning crew, only four survived the voyage back to England.

Looking Back

1. How were the explorations of the Cabots valuable to England?

2. Show how Drake's activities helped his nation.

3. Describe the voyages of Henry Hudson showing how both England and the Netherlands benefited from them.

4. What purposes did English explorations have, and what kind of wealth did the English find?

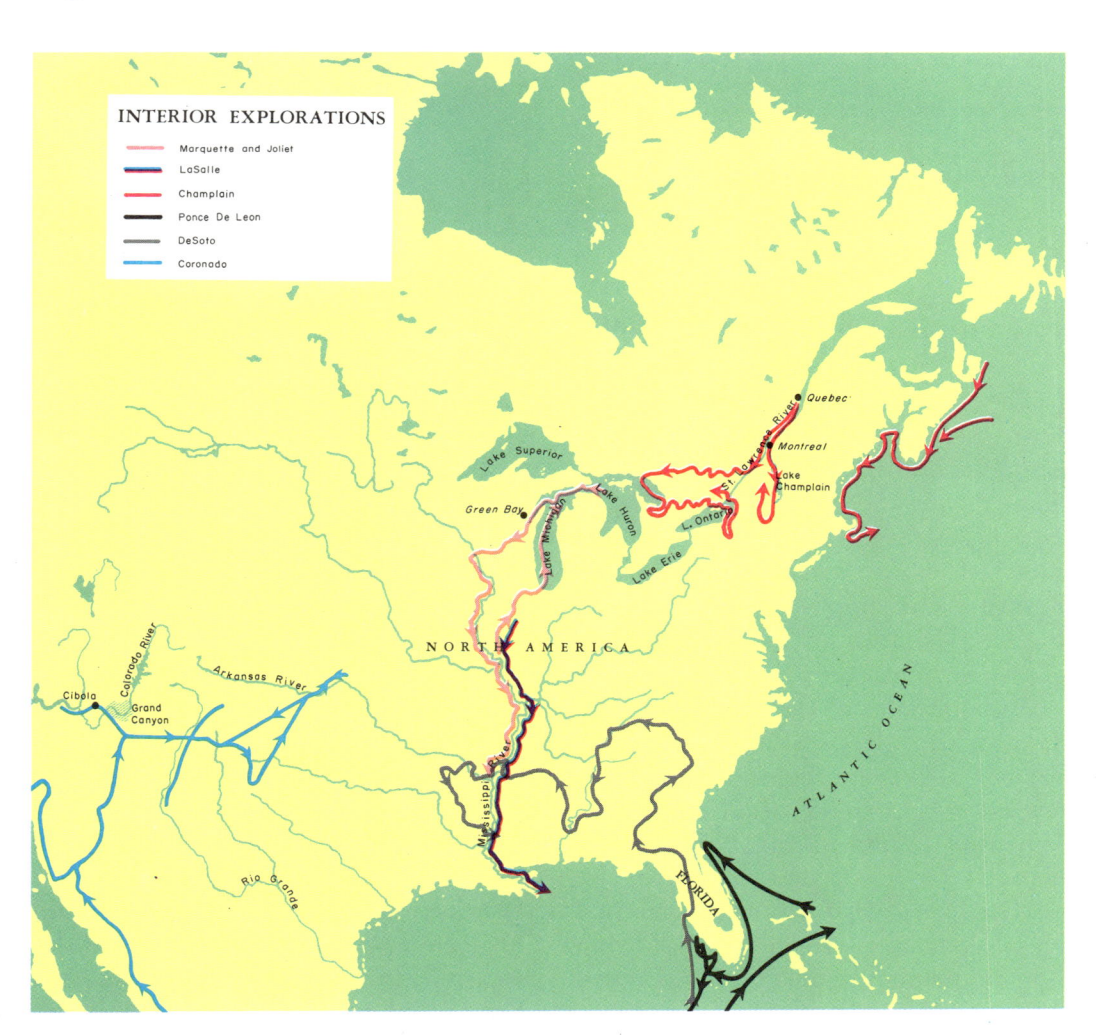

Verrazano Bridge, spanning the entrance to New York Harbor through which Verrazano was probably first to sail, is the longest suspension bridge in the world.

4. France Takes an Active Interest

The French probably first became acquainted with the New World through cod fishing off Newfoundland. Some historians believe that Frenchmen fished here before 1500. Records show that the markets of northern France were supplied with cod from the Grand Banks in the early decades of the sixteenth century.

Through tales of the fishermen or of Spanish travelers, the French king, Francis I, became interested in America. During his reign, the French sent four expeditions to the New World, one led by Verrazano and three by Cartier. These expeditions established no permanent settlements but did register permanent claims for the French in the New World.

Journeys of Exploration

Verrazano. The original French claim to the New World was based on the explorations of Giovanni Verrazano, an Italian employed by the French king. In 1523, he touched North America somewhere along the North Carolina coast and then followed the coastline north to Newfoundland. Like others before him, Verrazano hoped to find a passage through the New World by which ships could sail to the west and reach Asia.

Cartier. Jacques Cartier, a sea captain from the French city of St. Malo in Normandy, was commissioned by Francis I to make a voyage to the New World in search of new lands, gold,

16

and other riches. He explored the Gulf of St. Lawrence, claiming it for France. The two Indians who accompanied Cartier on his return to France spoke of a great inland stream. The French thought this might possibly be the long-sought passage to China.

On his second voyage, Cartier sailed up this great stream, the St. Lawrence. Although he soon realized that it was a river, and not a strait leading to the Pacific Ocean, he pressed on through the autumn and traveled as far as the present site of Montreal. He and his men were forced to spend the winter in the New World, but when spring came they sailed back to Europe.

A third expedition was led by a French nobleman, Jean Francois Roberval, who employed Cartier as the pilot. The aim of this expedition was to establish a colony. Impatient with Roberval's method of organizing his colonizing venture, Cartier departed for the St. Lawrence, expecting Roberval to follow with additional men and supplies. Jacques Cartier established a small colony nine miles from Quebec in 1541. Because of the severe winter, shortage of supplies and fear of the Indians, the colonists decided to return to France. Sailing down the St. Lawrence, Cartier met Roberval and his party of settlers who pressed on up the river. Cartier and his followers refused to go back with them.

A new colony founded by Roberval existed for a year, until he too returned to France, after which it completely disappeared. Because of Cartier's visits, France laid claim to all lands bordering the Gulf of St. Lawrence and the St. Lawrence River.

Champlain. French interest in the New World slackened after these first explorations, but it did not die out. In 1608, a Frenchman named Champlain established a settlement in North America. Landing on the shores of the St. Lawrence River, his settlers soon put up a few houses and a fort and set out to explore the surrounding country. Their settlement, called Quebec, was the first permanent French settlement in America.

Although his explorations and his settlement were a great help to France in colonizing the New World, Champlain made a mistake that was to prove most costly to the French cause. Near his settlement at Quebec lived a tribe of Algonquin Indians, who were then engaged in a war with the Iroquois Indians to the south. Champlain joined a war party of Algonquins and helped them defeat their enemy. His assistance won him the friendship of the Algonquins, but it also led to a deep hatred of the French by the much more powerful Iroquois nation. This hatred was evident again a cen-

Champlain's statue, a memorial to the greatest French colonizer, looks out over the old city of Quebec, Canada.

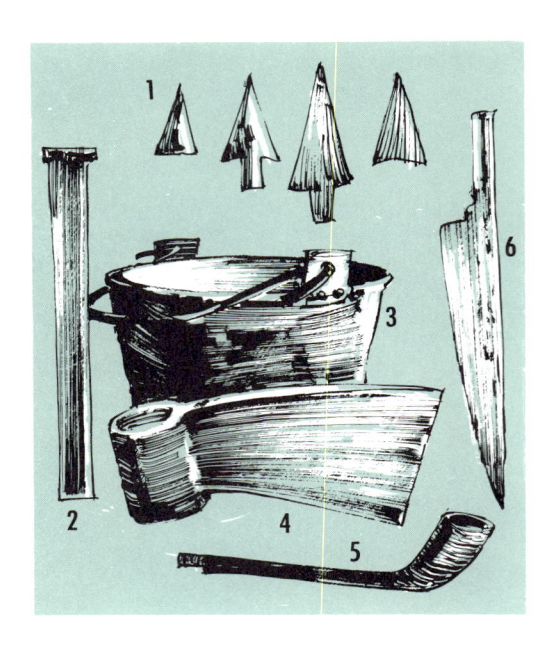

French-Indian trade goods: 1. copper arrowheads 2. a chisel 3. copper pot 4. iron axe head 5. copper pipe 6. knife blade.

tury and a half later when the Iroquois fought the French in the French and Indian War.

Marquette and Joliet. Soon after Champlain brought French settlers to the New World, French missionaries began to teach Christianity to the Indians. One of the most famous of these missionaries was Father Marquette (mahr-KETT'). Believing that the Mississippi led to the Pacific Ocean, he and a young fur trader named Louis Joliet (JOH'leh-ET) started out in 1673 to follow the river to its mouth. As they went along, they made friends with the Indians, and Marquette preached Christianity to them.

Their experiences were varied and exciting. At last they reached the point where the Arkansas River joins the Mississippi. They dared not go farther than this, for they were afraid of what they might find farther south. Since they were by then convinced that the Mississippi did not flow into the Pacific, they turned about and started north again. When they reached Green Bay, on Lake Michigan, Father Marquette was so exhausted by his travels that he decided to remain there. Joliet carried to the new French settlement of Quebec the tales of the great region they had explored.

La Salle. Joliet's report of his travels excited another Frenchman, named La Salle, who determined to explore this new land and claim it for France. After a long and difficult journey, he arrived at last at the mouth of the Mississippi. In 1682, he claimed for France all lands drained by the Mississippi River, naming the vast territory Louisiana, after the French king, Louis XIV.

Later La Salle tried to establish a French colony near the mouth of the Mississippi. Starvation and disease defeated his plans, causing the colony to fail. The great French leader was murdered by one of his own men.

The French explorers gave to their country a large and valuable part of North America. Because of their brave efforts, the entire Mississippi basin, as well as Canada, Acadia (present-day Nova Scotia), and the lands lying about the Great Lakes and the St. Lawrence, became territories of France.

Huguenots

In 1564 a band of French Protestants, or *Huguenots* (HEW'guh-nohts), came to America and landed in Florida. Since they came to stay, they brought their wives and children with them. Landing near St. Johns River, they built a settlement and a fort.

When the Spaniards found that the French were settling on what they regarded as their soil, they were very angry. A Spanish settlement, St. Augustine, was established not very far from the spot where the French had settled. A Spanish army was sent from St. Augustine to attack the French, and soon the promising little Huguenot settlement was wiped out. Although an expedition from France later fought the Spaniards, the French never again tried to establish a settlement in Florida.

Looking Back

1. What factors caused Cartier to fail in his efforts? How did he succeed?
2. Show how Marquette and Joliet helped France in the New World.
3. What great territories were claimed for France by La Salle?
4. What was the fate of French attempts to settle Florida?
5. Summarize the accomplishments of Champlain for France.

5. Europe's Claims Conflict

At the end of the period of exploration the known lands of North America were held by four nations—Spain, France, England, and the Netherlands. The Spaniards held the entire southwestern part of the continent and also the Florida peninsula. The French held a great stretch of territory running from the icy coast of Labrador through the center of North America to the mouth of the Mississippi River. The English held a narrow strip along the Atlantic coast as well as the land draining into the Hudson Bay. They also claimed land on the Pacific coast. The Dutch held land on the Atlantic coast in the vicinity of New York Bay.

The Spaniards

The Spaniards built the first settlements in the New World. In Mexico, Florida, and the southwestern part of what is now the United States, they established missions for the purpose of teaching the Indians to be Christians. Little villages grew up around many of the missions, and in time the Spanish language came to be widely used throughout these regions.

The Spaniards, however, chose not to establish colonies. They crossed the ocean in search of riches or for the purpose of teaching the heathen Indians to be Christians. They cared little for the building of cities and the establishment of industries and homes in their new lands. So those who came were mostly men—soldiers, adventurers, and missionaries—and comparatively few Spanish families moved to America. For this reason, Spain never gained a very firm foothold in North America. Only small settlements grew up around the forts, trading posts, and missions.

The French

The French made settlements all through the wilderness bordering the Great Lakes and the St. Lawrence

River. They built forts and trading posts for they had discovered that it was very profitable to buy furs from the Indians and to sell them in Europe where they would command a large price.

Like the Spaniards, the French did not establish colonies. Many Frenchmen who came to America intended to return to Europe as soon as they had made a comfortable sum of money. A few small towns were established along the St. Lawrence River, but the greater part of the French population did not live in towns. Their forts and trading posts, each manned by a small number of Frenchmen, were scattered throughout the broad French lands. From these centers, the French traders and trappers went out into the wilderness to trap fur-bearing animals and to trade with the Indians. For months at a time they lived alone in little cabins far from civilization, lacking even the comradeship of the few other white men of the post. Sometimes the Frenchmen lived with the Indians and even took Indian wives. The sparse distribution of Frenchmen in America, however, gave France a weak hold on her American possessions.

The English and the Dutch

The English and Dutch, on the other hand, brought their families to the New World and settled down to stay. Most of the settlers lived together in towns, and in time their colonies became much more densely populated than those of the French and Spanish. The English and Dutch occupied far less land, but what they held they held more firmly. And the great number of early English colonists ensured the later English ownership of much of North America.

Looking Back

1. Describe the successes and failures of the Spanish in the New World.
2. Show how French activities in the New World compared with those of the Spanish.
3. Why did the English and Dutch settlements in the New World seem to be more permanent than the French or Spanish settlements?

The Chapter in Perspective

What Do These Dates and Terms Mean?

Norsemen	Incas
Crusades	1492
1000	Huguenots
Aztecs	1608

Where Are These Places?

St. Augustine	Peru
Sts. of Magellan	Vinland
Cape of Good Hope	Quebec
St. Lawrence River	Holy Land

Who Are These People?

Marco Polo	Cortez
da Gama	Cabot
Columbus	Drake
Vespucci	Hudson
Ponce de Leon	Marquette
Balboa	Joliet
Magellan	La Salle
Champlain	Cartier

Questions for Study

1. Discuss the conditions in Europe that were favorable for a period of discovery and exploration in the New World.
2. Why is Magellan's expedition considered to be one of the greatest feats of navigation?
3. Why is Columbus considered to be both a failure and a success?
4. In what ways did European rivalries affect the discovery and exploration of the New World?
5. Compare the early settlements made in the New World by the Spanish, French, English, and Dutch.
6. For what reasons were the Indians unable to resist the early advances of the white arrivals?
7. Account for the large number of Italian explorers and the absence of Italian claims to the New World.
8. In what ways did the period of discovery and exploration affect life in Europe?
9. What geographic factors in the New World favored and hampered exploration?
10. Show how the period of discovery and exploration changed man's knowledge of the world in which he lived.

Place Yourself in History

You are an experienced sailor living in Palos, Spain. Posted outside a tavern near the waterfront you see the following notice:

Experienced crew wanted to sail to the Indies following a new westward route. Real chance for adventure, glory, and riches. Be one of the first to reach China with the royal-sponsored expedition. Report to the mate of the "Niña," "Pinta," or "Santa Maria." Sailing on August 3, 1492.
    Christopher Columbus

What would you have done? Why? Was this a chance for fame and fortune or was it an invitation to destruction and death? Was it a mad-cap scheme or the chance to be a true hero?

2
The English Colonies Become Firmly Established

As the seventeenth century dawned, England found herself claiming a great wilderness stretching along the Atlantic Coast of North America. England could not really own this land until she sent enough people to occupy it, and, luckily, there were those who wanted to go. The journey was dangerous, and when the newcomers arrived, they were faced with Indians, lack of food, and isolation from all they had once known—in some cases home and family. The pioneers who started the English colonies in North America were indeed brave adventurers.

1. Englishmen Look to the New World

Early Attempts to Found Colonies

During the reign of Queen Elizabeth (1558–1603), small ships began to make their way from the shores of England to North America. Filled with adventurous, freedom-seeking men, the ships beat their way across the stormy Atlantic. They did not always arrive safely, and when they did, the colonists in them did not always survive. Since navigation was a risky art at best, the ships sometimes reached land they had not set out for. For example, a 1585 expedition financed by Sir Humphrey Gilbert never reached the mainland but landed at Newfoundland. Gilbert's colony failed, and on the trip back to England, he was lost at sea.

Gilbert's half brother, Sir Walter Raleigh, was also interested in colonizing. In 1584 he sent out two ships which explored the coast of North America and brought back glowing descriptions of the land they had visited. The following year Raleigh sent a number of colonists to make a settlement on Roanoke Island off Virginia's shore. The colonists stayed only about a year, and when they returned to England they brought back two plants new to the English—the potato and tobacco plants. Tobacco soon became popular throughout England.

Two years later Raleigh attempted a second colony on Roanoke Island. John White was chosen governor of the colony, and here was born Virginia Dare, the first white child born in English America. Several months later, Governor White sailed to England for supplies, but his return to Roanoke was delayed for several years because of the war between Spain and England. When he did return, the settlement had completely disappeared. No one has ever been able to find out what happened to the "lost colony."

Colonization by Companies

Later colonists profited by Raleigh's and Gilbert's mistakes. Instead of being sponsored by only one man, colonies founded during the reign of James I were supported by corporations. Groups of merchants furnished funds to buy ships and supplies for colonists, who, in turn, worked for the company which sent them to North America. The corporations or companies obtained permission and rights, usually called a charter, to the land they were to colonize. For example, the Plymouth Company and the London Company (two competing English colonization companies) each received from James I ten thousand square miles of land, in overlapping areas. Settlements of the two groups were required to be at least one hundred miles apart.

The first expedition of the Plymouth Company was captured by Spanish raiders near Puerto Rico. It had been driven far off its course by unpredictable Atlantic winds. Later, the Plymouth Company founded a short-lived colony on the coast of what is now Maine. Troubled by cold weather and lack of food, the colonists made their way back to England in 1608.

The rocky coast of Maine was too forbidding and harsh a place for a successful settlement.

Looking Back

1. What was the fate of the attempts by Gilbert and Raleigh to establish settlements in the New World?
2. How did lack of navigational skill affect early voyages by the English colonizers?
3. In what ways did the corporations or companies profit from early attempts at colonization?

2. Settlers Seek Fortunes and Freedoms in Southern Colonies

Virginia — The First Successful Colony

Settlement. The Virginia colony begun by the London Company was, however, to prosper and grow. Eventually it became the beachhead for English colonial activity. At first, the one hundred colonists who landed in Virginia in 1607 did not adjust very well. Many had no idea what life in the wilderness was like. Indeed, some of the men who came had the mistaken idea that the New World was full of gold, which would be theirs for the taking. Men who had never done hard physical labor were faced with the grim necessity of cutting down trees and building their own shelters, not to mention planting and raising crops for food.

Although their settlement, which they named Jamestown in honor of King James of England, was located in an attractive spot, it was low and marshy. Mosquitoes thrived in the damp atmosphere, and diseases new to the colonists killed many of them. Indians also proved to be a problem for the new settlement of Jamestown. They resented the coming of the white man, and they did as much as they could to annoy the men of the London Company.

Captain John Smith. Fortunately for the hard-pressed colonists, there was an able leader in the colony. He was Captain John Smith, a young soldier who had no fear of hard work. Smith had been a fighter against the Turks in eastern Europe and was used to the inconvenience and hardship of being in a strange and hostile land. One of his first tasks was to impose some order on life in Jamestown. He made strict rules, and men who did not do their share of the work were denied their share of the food. Smith handled the problem of Indian attacks in two ways. First, he built a fort in which the colonists could take refuge in case of attack. Second, Smith tried, for a time successfully, to persuade the Indians to help the colonists by giving them food. However, when the Indians no longer brought food to the colonists, a ter-

A Jamestown settler tries to persuade others to work. How would Captain John Smith have handled the man sitting on the log?

Ships in James Bay unload their precious cargo —English women who would marry the men of Jamestown.

ony. Many planters grew rich selling tobacco to English merchants, and as the demands in England increased from year to year, more and more people were employed in raising and processing the crop. Finally, in 1619, one year before the Pilgrims were to land at Plymouth, the first Negroes were brought from Africa to America to work on the tobacco plantations. These early ancestors of today's American Negroes labored side by side with the white indentured servants. In some cases these Negro servants were granted their freedom after a period of time.

Since Virginia was the first colony to be settled and to prosper, a great part of the English colonial effort was expended in its direction. Thus, the first part of the history of the Southern Colonies is, in effect, a history of Virginia. Virginia was big enough, and her opportunities were great enough,

The ruins of Jamestown's first church mark the spot where John Rolfe married Pocahontas in 1614. Their marriage insured peace with the Indians for eight years.

rible period of want set in. This period became known as the "starving time." Once more the little colony was threatened with destruction. Then, when hope was almost gone, two ships arrived from England, bringing more food for the settlers and wives for the lonely men of Jamestown. Many families arrived on these two ships, and for the first time the settlement of Jamestown rang with the shouts of children.

A Growing Colony. The Virginia colony was now, seemingly, permanent. Governors were sent from England to run the colony in the best interests of the English king, and large tobacco plantations were started. Tobacco was the economic salvation of the new col-to absorb most of the colonists who arrived on the Atlantic seaboard in the first twenty years of English colonization. The ways of Virginia, her economic system, and her culture were copied and extended later in the other colonies of the South. In some cases, Carolina was one, discontented settlers from Virginia founded new colonial centers. Also, powerful men in England were granted rights to certain lands in the New World, and this gave rise to new colonies. Most colonies profited from Virginia's mistakes and copied her successes, some of which we will now learn about.

House of Burgesses. It was clear to most of the colonists that the London Company in England could not effectively make laws for the government of Virginia. Officials 3500 miles from Jamestown could have little idea about the problems of administering the new colony, so, in 1619, the colonists were permitted to elect a representative council. Known as the House of Burgesses, this council was the first elected representative body in the New World. Its members came from the numerous small settlements which were growing up throughout the Virginia Colony. The House of Burgesses was to help the governor rule and to make the laws for Virginia. Although the laws made by the House of Burgesses could be rejected by the English king, it was a great step toward self-government.

In 1624 King James I of England took away the charter given to the London Company and made Virginia a royal colony. This gave King James greater personal control of the colony. He now appointed the governors, but he still allowed the House of Burgesses a small part in making the laws.

Government of Virginia. During the next fifty years, Virginia was to grow and prosper. By 1670, 38,000 people lived there, not many by today's standards, but a great number of people for that time. All was not peaceful however. The colonists wished for rights of self-government, and those who challenged the wilderness for their livelihood were not always satisfied

Some of the most beautiful buildings in America were built before 1700. The Colonial Capitol at Williamsburg, Virginia, is one of them. It is preserved as a historical monument, along with other colonial buildings. Would it be large enough to house a modern state government?

with the rules established by the governor and approved by the king in England. Unfortunately, not all governors had the best interests of the colony at heart.

The man who was governor of Virginia in 1660, Sir William Berkeley, did not cater to the hopes and wishes of the colonists. For one thing, he opposed the establishment of free public schools, holding to the principle that ignorant men were easier to govern. He also built up a great fur trade with the Indians, primarily for his own profit. When the Indians began to massacre groups of colonists in Virginia, Berkeley did not want to punish them. It was clear that his fur trade meant more to him than the colonists.

Bacon's Rebellion. Nathaniel Bacon, a young plantation owner, took matters into his own hands. Raising a volunteer army, he went out to rout the Indians who had been causing trouble. Bacon's successful action, taken without the permission of Governor Berkeley, caused the governor to hire an army to attack Bacon's forces upon their return to the settlement. Bacon and his group of volunteers defeated Berkeley's army and drove them from Jamestown. However, soon after this, Bacon died mysteriously, either of poison or of disease, and Berkeley immediately returned to Jamestown. Once the governor's power was reestablished, he punished without mercy those who had helped defeat the Indians and revolted against his rule. When the king of England heard of Berkeley's savage behavior, the governor was recalled to England in disgrace. Other governors of Virginia were more humane and more just.

Bacon's Castle, built in 1655, was the home of Nathaniel Bacon who rebelled against Governor Berkeley's authority.

Expansion and Progress. When the government of Virginia outgrew provincial Jamestown, it moved to its new site at Williamsburg. There the royal governor not only ruled the colony politically but socially and culturally as well. The College of William and Mary, named after the English king and queen, was founded there (1693) as the second college in the thirteen colonies. The city of Williamsburg became one of the most important and colorful cities in colonial America.

Three other colonies were founded in the southern part of the North Atlantic seaboard. They were Maryland, the Carolinas, and Georgia, which was the last of the original thirteen to be founded. Maryland and the Carolinas both were adjacent to Virginia; in fact, Maryland's territory was carved out of land which had been orginally granted to Virginia and the London Company.

Berkeley Plantation, on the James River in Virginia, was originally built by Governor Berkeley, the colonial administrator of Virginia. It is preserved today with many of its original furnishings. The grounds are beautifully kept up.

Discontented settlers from Virginia founded Carolina, and some of the settlers of Maryland were members of religious groups which were not tolerated in Virginia. Since Georgia was not founded until 1733, that colony's connection with Virginia was not so strong.

Maryland — An Experiment in Tolerance

The settlement of Maryland differed from all the others because of the unusual charter granted to one of the original stockholders of the Virginia Company, the first Lord Baltimore, in 1632. Under the grant, 10,000,000 acres were to be held in "free and common soccage." In medieval times this term was used to designate an absolute authority over a given area of land. Thus, Lord Baltimore became responsible to no one. He could set up the courts, collect rents and taxes, and regulate commerce. Only two arrowheads and one-fifth of all the gold and silver found in the colony were to be sent each year to the king in payment for this gift of land. No provision was made for the people to have a voice in the governing of the colony.

Settlement. Upon the death of Lord Baltimore, the grant of the lands north of Virginia, to be called Maryland after King Charles I's wife Henrietta Maria, passed to Baltimore's son Cecilius. Cecilius, in turn, sent his brother Leonard to serve as the first governor. The first party of several hundred settlers arrived in Maryland in 1634 and immediately began bartering with the Indians for land. Evidently the colonists bartered well, for the Indians gave them land already planted with maize. Unlike neighboring Virginians, these colonists experienced neither a starving time nor a scarcity of food. By the end of the first summer, they were able to export maize to New England in exchange for fish.

Act Concerning Religion. Probably Maryland's most valuable contribution to our colonial heritage was the concept of religious toleration. As early as 1649, the legislature passed a law called the *Act Concerning Religion* or the Edict of Toleration. Although the law, which favored Catholics, did not provide complete toleration, it was a step in this direction. The law was difficult to enforce, but it did serve as a precedent for the First Amendment to the Constitution.

As we study the founding of other colonies, we can see that most people

Touro Synagogue, oldest in America, is a historical shrine in Newport, Rhode Island.

leaving England for the New World left for economic reasons. But there were other reasons also. All religions except the Anglican religion were looked on with disfavor in England. Besides the Puritans and the Pilgrims, large groups of Roman Catholics also felt the sting of religious persecution. Therefore, some colonists came to America for religious reasons. And in Maryland, the purpose of settlement was both religious and economic.

Lord Baltimore, himself a Roman Catholic, felt the colony might prove to be a haven of refuge for persecuted members of every faith, but he also hoped it would provide an income for his family. The colony proved successful both as a source of income for the man who established it and as a refuge for the settlers.

The Carolinas and the Grand Model

Founding the Colonies. In the year 1653, a few members of the Virginia Colony were dissatisfied with life in Virginia and decided to found a settlement of their own. Heading south, they settled on the banks of the Chowan River. Since they had no charter from the English government, which owned the land, the colony had little chance of survival. The formation of an English colonizing company for Carolina in 1663, however, gave new life to the effort of the Carolina colonists who had migrated from Virginia. The land granted to Lord Clarendon and his company by the English king absorbed the area which the Chowan settlers had occupied, so it became part of the new colony of Carolina.

Tryon Palace at New Bern, North Carolina, completed in 1770 as the first permanent capitol of the North Carolina colony, later served as the first state capitol.

The first band of settlers sent out by the English company arrived in 1670. They settled first on the banks of the Ashley River in the southern part of Carolina. Two years later, Charleston was founded nearby. This settlement grew slowly but surely as other colonists arrived from the mother country.

In addition to the English, some Huguenots or French Protestants came from France to escape religious persecution. They were an intelligent and hard-working group and did much to improve the colony.

Political Misfortune. With its mixture of people, its fertile soil, and its seaboard location, Carolina prospered economically. However, her political fortune was another matter. Lord Clarendon and the other men to whom the English king, Charles II, assigned the Carolina charter were chosen mainly because they were court favorites. They knew very little about governing, and in fact regarded the colony as a place to carry out their far-fetched scheme of government called the *Grand Model*. All power in this form of government was concentrated in the hands of a few noblemen, who, in turn, dictated all rules, even down to those concerning clothing styles. The colonists themselves, most of whom had come to enjoy more freedom, found their lives more restricted than they had been in England and Virginia.

For many years, the people patiently endured the straitjacket of the Grand Model, but at last they could stand it no more. A group of them appealed to the king to change their form of government. The colonists had good reasons for such a petition, as they felt great dissatisfaction toward the rule of the noblemen. Also, the two Carolina settlements were three hundred miles apart, causing them to develop along different lines. After considering the case, the king divided the colony into two parts, North Carolina and South Carolina, making each a separate royal colony under a governor appointed by the king. Under the royal governors, the Carolinas prospered.

Georgia — Last of the Thirteen

Oglethorpe's Plan. The last of the thirteen colonies to be founded in the

New World was Georgia. A British general named James Oglethorpe had watched with interest the development of the other colonies. He thought that he knew their strengths and their weaknesses, and he believed that he could found a colony better than any of the other twelve. Moreover, he was very much distressed by the fact that in Great Britain people who owed even small debts that they could not pay were being thrown into prison. He felt that if these people could be freed and taken to a new land, they might begin life over again and become fine citizens. The general was also disturbed by the persecution of Protestants in Germany. A third matter which worried him was the presence of Spanish colonies not far south of the Carolinas. If a strong colony could be founded between South Carolina and the Spanish settlements, he thought, all the northern settlers would be safer in case of trouble.

General Oglethorpe and a group of English "trustees" were granted a stretch of land in South Carolina after he had petitioned King George II for the right to colonize the area. The British government decided to make a separate colony of this land, naming it Georgia in honor of the king. At the same time, they decided to free imprisoned debtors in England to go with General Oglethorpe. In the year 1733, Oglethorpe landed with many settlers, both men and women, on the shores of the Savannah River and founded the town of Savannah.

Spanish Threat. Oglethorpe's foresight in planning a colony between the Spanish lands to the south and the British settlements along the coast to the north was soon justified. His army was well trained, and when a Spanish expedition entered Georgia, intent on wiping out the British, the Georgians defeated them so completely that they retreated into Florida and never again attempted to attack the colonies. Oglethorpe seized this opportunity to claim for Georgia much land in the northern part of Florida that had been held by the Spaniards.

Rules and Regulations. The rules and regulations established by General Oglethorpe and the Georgia Trustees were strict, although some of them had merit. For example, slavery was outlawed in the Georgia colony at first, as was intoxicating liquor. On the other hand, the colonists were denied the freedom to vote, and no Roman Catholics could hold religious services. Also, those who could not fight in the army—the elderly and all women and children—could not own land. This meant that wealth in Georgia rested solely in the hands of those eligible for military service.

As in Virginia and Carolina, settlers had come to Georgia to seek more, not less, freedom. They protested Oglethorpe's rules so bitterly that at last the laws were changed. In 1752 the king of England, George II, took over the task of appointing governors for the Georgia colony, and from that time on the colony prospered.

Unfortunately, in their haste to overcome the strict rules of Governor Oglethorpe, the colonists changed all the rules. Slavery was soon permitted in Georgia, and the liquor trade became important. The introduction of slavery into Georgia helped the colony economically at first, but many years later, the one-crop plantation system, fostered and encouraged by slavery, was to bring economic distress to Georgia and the entire South.

Looking Back

1. Discuss the early problems faced by the Jamestown settlers and show how they were overcome.
2. How was the settlement of Maryland different from the way other colonies were settled?
3. In what ways did the Grand Model affect the settlements in the Carolinas?
4. Give four reasons for the settlement of Georgia.
5. In which of the southern colonies would you have preferred to settle? Why?

3. The Middle Colonies Develop a Middle Way of Life

New York, Pennsylvania, New Jersey, and Delaware were called the Middle Colonies, because of their geographical position between the South and New England, and the Bread Colonies, because of the abundance of grain produced.

The farms were mostly medium-sized, except for some large estates in New York, with fertile soil and broad, level expanses. Land was easy to acquire. The fertility of the land, religious toleration, and democratic control brought many settlers of non-English origin, such as Germans and Irish, into the Middle Colonies. Many of them had been skilled and industrious farmers in Europe.

Side by side with agriculture, commerce flourished, especially through the excellent harbors of New York and Philadelphia. Chief exports were flour, wheat, salt beef and pork, deer skins, lumber, copper, and iron.

Throughout colonial history, both the British and the colonists recognized that whatever happened in these key colonies determined the future of the English New World possessions. They were key experiments in religious toleration; in the people's adaptation of English ideas of liberty and freedom; and, finally, in gaining wealth for both the colonies and the mother country.

New York Under Two Nations

Dutch Settlement. In 1664, England obtained another colony on the eastern coast of North America: New York. This colony was first settled by the Dutch in 1614, and from 1621 until its capture by the English it was ruled by the Dutch West India Company of the Netherlands under the name of New Netherland.

The Dutch founded many prosperous settlements along the Hudson River. The chief town, New Amsterdam, was a flourishing Dutch city of brick houses and great windmills, built on the island of Manhattan.

Surrender to the English. The English had two reasons for taking New Netherland from the Dutch. In the first place, because of the explorations of the Cabots, they decided that they owned the entire eastern coast of North America from the northern shores of New England far beyond the borders of the Carolina colony. In the second place, they noticed with alarm that the Dutch of New Netherland were becoming strong and well established. As a result, the English refused to let a powerful colony of another nation separate their New England settlements from those farther to the south. They found an excuse to seize the colony in 1664, when a war broke out in Europe between England and the Netherlands. In that year a fleet of English warships appeared in the harbor of New Amsterdam and, despite the anger of its fiery governor, Peter Stuyvesant, the little Dutch colony surrendered without firing a shot.

English Settlement. The English divided New Netherland into three colonies. To the chief colony and the settlement of New Amsterdam, they gave the name New York, in honor of the Duke of York, brother of the king of England. The other two colonies became known as New Jersey and Delaware. Almost immediately, the king turned the three colonies over to the Duke of York who was allowed to govern them as he pleased.

The Duke appointed Edmund Andros, a strong and able man, as governor of the New York colony. One of his most important acts was to form a committee for maintaining good relations between the settlers and the Indians of the area. This committee judged disputes between white men and Indians impartially. It also promoted understanding and peace, and

A Dutch building in New Amsterdam. The stair-step roofends were typical features of Dutch architecture in 1600.

the settlers of the New York colony were in much less danger of Indian attacks than ever before.

Andros, though able, was a stern man, and he made many enemies. The colonists were especially disappointed that Andros was more concerned with the financial gain of the colony than with the well-being of the colonists. After great protest by the colonists, Andros consented, with the Duke of York's permission, to form a colonial assembly. For a brief period, the Duke of York recalled Andros to England, appointing a temporary governor.

The Dominion of New England. In 1685, however, King Charles II of England died, and the Duke of York became King James II of England. He forbade the newly created colonial assembly of New York to meet, and he tried to combine all the colonies between Maine and Maryland into one

Peter Stuyvesant, fiery ruler of Dutch New Amsterdam, was furious when England attacked and captured "his" colony.

unit, to be called the *Dominion of New England* and to be ruled by a single governor—Edmund Andros. However, King James II was not destined to rule for long. He was deposed in 1688. When news of the change in English government reached the colonies, some people in Boston rebelled, seized Governor Andros, and threw him into prison. This event marked the end of the Dominion of New England.

Growth and Progress. In 1691 New York was made a royal colony. Between that date and 1750, its population grew to 80,000. Settlements were made north along the Hudson River to Albany and west through the Mohawk Valley. Because of its excellent harbor, New York, almost from its founding, was one of the most important shipping centers in the colonies.

Pennsylvania, a Home for Quakers

Like some other colonies, Pennsylvania was settled by people who left England primarily for religious reasons. The settlers of Pennsylvania were known as *Quakers*, or *Friends*, and in America they hoped to find a place to practice their religious beliefs in peace. The Quakers were different from other Protestant religions in that they did not believe in the use of force to settle disputes. This sometimes made them the objects of much ridicule in England, and it was to escape persecution that they came to America.

William Penn. The Quakers were led by William Penn, a well-educated, powerful man from a respected English family. Penn's father had been an admiral in the British navy and, as such, had much influence at court. Part of Admiral Penn's influence was, in fact, financial, because William Penn was given Pennsylvania in payment for a debt owed his father by the English king, Charles II.

In 1681, Penn sent a shipload of Quaker colonists to America. Some of them settled at New Castle, in the Delaware colony, and some at Upland, not far away in Penn's new territory. The next year Penn himself crossed the ocean with one hundred more Quakers. After a short stop in New Castle, they sailed on up the Delaware River to the point where it is joined by the Schuylkill. There they established the city of Philadelphia.

Treaty with the Indians. The Indians in Pennsylvania, naturally enough, viewed the coming of the Quakers with misgivings. But, in a meeting between the two groups, Penn told the Indians that the Quakers were lovers of peace and that they would treat the Indians fairly and be their friends. A council, made up of six white men and six Indians, was established to draw up a treaty. For their part, the Quakers agreed to buy whatever land they needed from the Indians, instead of taking it by force. The Indians, in turn, agreed to live in peace with their new Quaker neighbors. As long as Penn remained alive, his treaty with the Indians was never broken.

The Great Law. William Penn next drew up a set of laws known as the *Great Law*. It provided that all colonists should be free to worship in any way they thought best; that all male settlers who paid taxes had the right to vote; that every male member of any Christian church might hold office; that all children should begin training for some trade or useful occupation at the age of twelve; that only two crimes —murder and treason—should be punished by death; and that all prisoners should be put to work at some useful trade and if possible made into good citizens. These last two provisions are especially significant in view of the fact that, at that time, there were over two hundred crimes punishable by death in England, and no one had ever thought before of making a prison into a workshop instead of merely a place to lock up those who had done wrong.

In Germany, the Protestants were being persecuted for their religion. Many of them fled to the New World and settled in Pennsylvania, where they became known as "the Pennsylvania Dutch." The Irish Protestants, too, left their country in large num-

William Penn and his fellow Quakers meet with the Indians. In all his dealings with Indians, Penn stuck to his principles of kindness, fairness and decency. He believed in peace and good will, and his was one of the few Indian treaties that was carried out.

bers and came to Penn's colony. Both the Germans and Irish were hardworking and thrifty, and the colony quickly grew and prospered.

Delaware

The area which is now the state of Delaware was explored by both the Dutch and the English. Because of the hostility of the Indians, a small settlement made by the Dutch in 1631 was forced to disband. A few years later the Swedes settled in the Delaware Bay territory, naming it New Sweden. There they built Fort Christina, now Wilmington. Years later, the Dutch captured it, and then the English took it from the Dutch. The English changed the name of the colony to Delaware, in honor of Lord Delaware, who had explored the area for the English. Charles II, then the English king, granted Delaware, New York, and New Jersey to his brother, the Duke of York. The Duke, not wishing to be burdened with the new lands, leased Delaware to William Penn, who called it "three lower counties."

The two colonies had a cultural unity, but they also had many differences, and the people of Delaware resented the political control by the Pennsylvania Quakers. Delaware was granted a separate legislature in 1703 but did not elect its own governor until the colonies separated from England in 1776.

With the exception of Pennsylvania, few colonies had such a mixture of nationalities and religions as Delaware. Swedes, Dutch, English, French, and Scotch-Irish; Lutherans, Anglicans, Quakers, Huguenots, Presbyterians, and various German religious sects made up the population of the two colonies.

New Jersey's Complicated Past

The colony which we know now as the state of New Jersey had a complicated history. It was traded back and forth between England and Holland four times before it finally became the possession of the English crown in 1664. Even then, however, New Jersey's troubles were not over. Six different English groups or individuals, ranging from the English king to a pair of

---

Penn's Noble Experiment

If thou thinkest twice, before thou speakest once, thou wilt speak twice the better for it.

We are too apt to love Praise, but not to Deserve it.

Be not deceived with the first appearance of things, but give thyself Time to be in the right.

Have a Care therefore where there is more Sail than Ballast.

Haste makes Work which Caution prevents.

Opportunities should never be lost, because they can hardly be regained.

Refuse not to be informed: For that shows Pride or Stupidity.

—William Penn from *Some Fruits of Solitude.*

This replica of the original Mayflower *is surrounded by modern pleasure boats on its arrival from Plymouth, England.*

Quakers named Fenwicke and Byllynge, controlled the colony from 1664 until 1738. Finally in 1738, New Jersey got its own governor, which it kept until independence was declared in 1776.

Since the New Jersey colony was controlled by so many different groups, naturally many different types of people settled there. Long Island Puritans, persecuted Quakers from other colonies and from Europe, and Negro slaves from Africa were a few of the groups that originally populated the New Jersey colony.

Looking Back

1. Why did the English seek to drive the Dutch from New Amsterdam?
2. What was the fate of the Dutch settlements in the New World?
3. How did the colonists react to the Dominion of New England? Explain these reactions.
4. For what reasons did Pennsylvania enjoy a rapid growth?
5. Why can early Delaware be called a "miniature United Nations"?

4. Religious Motives Bring Settlers to New England

The first English attempt to settle in what is now called New England was unsuccessful. As we have seen, the attempt of the Plymouth Company to place colonists on the coast of what is now the state of Maine in 1608 failed. Not until 1620, when the Pilgrims arrived from England on the rocky Massachusetts coast was there a solid New England colony. The Pilgrims were nearly all *Separatists,* a group of Puritans whose beliefs brought government persecution in England. These first real settlers of New England had looked far and wide for a place to practice their religious beliefs. At first they tried to slip away to Holland where they thought they might have more freedom. More freedom to worship they did find, but they could not get good jobs in Holland, so many of them returned to England. Still persecuted in England, some decided to cross the Atlantic.

The Pilgrims of Plymouth

The Pilgrims made arrangements with the Virginia Company to found an independent colony on land owned by the corporation, and the king of England stated that he would not bother them provided they lived in peace. Land and religious freedom guaranteed, the colonists set out in the *Mayflower* from Plymouth, England, in September of 1620. It is likely that the *Mayflower* was headed for land held by the Virginia Company, but storms forced the tiny ship to seek refuge inside the tip of Cape Cod in Provincetown Harbor. From Provincetown they explored the surrounding area and in late December of 1620 landed in Plymouth where they found a fresh-water stream, cleared land, and a hill that could be protected by fortifications. The location proved to be the site of an old Indian village, but the Indians had been wiped out in a smallpox epidemic several years earlier.

Pilgrims land on the Plymouth shore in cold, rough December weather. What tasks faced them on their first day ashore?

A Struggle for Survival. The history of the settling of New England and the people who settled there is one of the most fascinating aspects of our country's founding. Had it not been for some fortunate events, the little beginning the Pilgrims made in Massachusetts might not have survived as a colony. In the first place, the Pilgrim's colony was not an "official" colony; that is, since it lay outside the lands of the Virginia Colony, and since it was not recognized by the crown, the colonists at first had no real legal basis for settlement. Also, a plague swept the colony in the first winter and killed half of the 102 *Mayflower* settlers, as well as many of the Indians throughout New England. Luckily, however, the Pilgrims gained help from an unexpected source: Indians from the surrounding areas showed them how to plant maize and to gather clams and lobsters from the waters of the Atlantic.

The Mayflower Compact. The governing of the colony was assured by one of the most amazing documents of the colonial period, the *Mayflower Compact*. In the Mayflower Compact, the Pilgrims agreed, while still aboard the little ship in Provincetown Harbor, to further their religion, enact "just and equal laws," and to do other things that would ensure the rights of colonists. This compact proved to be all that was necessary to ensure the political security of the little colony. Later the colonists gained title to the land they occupied, but they were never granted a royal charter. This lack of charter made them independent of all controls but their own, and they functioned successfully in this

The first Thanksgiving dinner in America was held sometime in the harvest season of 1621. The Pilgrims had had a terrible winter in 1620–21. Over half their number had died. After a good harvest and a warm summer, those who were left were glad to be alive. The feast, shared with the neighboring Indians, consisted of wild game and fish, vegetables and fruits, and cakes and bread baked by Pilgrim women.

way for seventy years until the Plymouth Colony was annexed to the much larger Massachusetts Bay Colony.

The Puritans of Massachusetts Bay

Founding the Colony. The Massachusetts Bay Colony got its real start in 1630. It was founded by an English company in which there were many influential Puritans. Unlike the Pilgrims, who wished to worship in an altogether different manner from the Church of England, the Puritans wished to *purify* what already was there. They wished to enact reforms within the structure of the Church of England itself.

Governor Winthrop. John Winthrop, a wealthy, educated Puritan, was chosen governor of the colony by the stockholders of the Massachusetts Bay Colony. In 1630, eleven ships carrying about one thousand settlers sailed the Atlantic and landed at Boston, which they made the capital of their colony. By 1643, the colony had mushroomed to a population of fifteen thousand.

Governor Winthrop proved to be an able administrator but a stern taskmaster. When the Puritans in England broke with the official Church of England, the Puritans in America often became as intolerant of other religions as the churchmen in England had been of the Puritans and Separatists.

Governor Winthrop believed strongly that only "good" Puritans should be tolerated in the Massachusetts Bay Colony, and his cold lack of understanding for other religious points of view drove many groups out of the colony and into other parts of New England. Thus, like Virginia and the Southern Colonies, the Massachusetts Bay Colony became the point from which other groups of settlers fanned out to found the other New England colonies: Connecticut, Rhode Island, New Hampshire, and Maine.

Connecticut — Colony with a Constitution

In 1636, some discontented Massachusetts Puritans, unable to practice their religion as they saw fit, migrated to the Connecticut Valley. Under the leadership of a minister named Thomas Hooker, the Connecticut Puritans drove their cattle and hogs through the woods to found the towns of Wethersfield, Hartford, and Windsor along the Connecticut River. The towns which Hooker's group founded were governed by a kind of constitution called the *Fundamental Orders of Connecticut*. The Connecticut settlers had many obstacles to overcome. For one thing, the Dutch had claimed the area many years before 1636, and the rights of Hooker and his band to settle there were very much in question. Also, hostile Indians occupied the whole area. But the group endured, and later, the English governor of

---

The Mayflower Compact—An agreement between Pilgrim leaders. Signed November 11, 1620 at Cape Cod

In the Name of God, Amen. We, whose names are underwritten, the Loyal Subjects of our dread Sovereign Lord King James, by the Grace of God, of Great Britain, France, and Ireland, King, Defender of the Faith, &c. Having undertaken for the Glory of God, and Advancement of the Christian Faith, and the Honour of our King and Country, a Voyage to plant the first colony in the northern Parts of Virginia; Do by these Present, solemnly and mutually in the Presence of God and one another, covenant and combine ourselves together into a civil Body Politick, for our better Ordering and Preservation, and Furtherance of the Ends aforesaid; and by Virtue hereof do enact, constitute, and frame, such just and equal Laws, Ordinances, Acts, Constitutions, and Offices, from time to time, as shall be thought most meet and convenient for the general Good of the Colony; unto which we promise all due Submission and Obedience. In witness whereof we have hereunto subscribed our names at Cape Cod the eleventh of November, in the Reign of our Sovereign Lord King James of England, France, and Ireland, the eighteenth and of Scotland, the fifty-fourth. Anno Domini, 1620.

The Thirteen Colonies Are Founded

	Colony	Date of First Established Settlement and Important early Settlements	Principal Founders	Types of Government (including dates of charter or proprietary grants and transfer to royal control)
SOUTHERN	Virginia	1607—Jamestown	London Company John Smith, Thomas Dale	Charter (1606) Royal (1624)
	Maryland	1634—St. Mary's	George Calvert (Lord Baltimore)	Proprietary (1632) Royal (1692) Proprietary (1715)
	North Carolina	1660—Albemarle	"Eight Noble Lords" including Lord Clarendon and Lord Ashley Cooper	Proprietary (1663) Royal (1729)
	South Carolina	1670—Albemarle Point, abandoned later for Charleston	"Eight Noble Lords" including Lord Clarendon and Lord Ashley Cooper	Proprietary (1663) Royal (1719)
	Georgia	1733—Savannah	James Oglethorpe	Proprietary (1732) Royal (1753)
MIDDLE	New Netherland	1624—Albany, New Amsterdam	Dutch West India Company	Under Dutch rule
	New York	See above	James, Duke of York	Proprietary (1664) Royal (1685)
	New Jersey	1623—Fort Nassau, Hoboken	Dutch West India Company Swedish South Company Lord Berkeley George Carteret	At first, under Swedish and Dutch rule Proprietary (1664) Royal (1702)
	Pennsylvania	1683—Philadelphia	Quakers; William Penn	Proprietary (1681)
	Delaware	1638—Christinaham (later Wilmington)	Swedish South Company Peter Minuit	Swedish rule, then Dutch Proprietary (1664)
NEW ENGLAND	Plymouth	1620—Plymouth	"Pilgrim Fathers" William Bradford; Myles Standish	Self-governing Joined to Massachusetts (1691)
	Maine	1623—York, Saco, Falmouth (now Portland)	Fernando Gorges	Proprietary (1629) Joined to Massachusetts (1691)
	Massachusetts	1629—Salem, Cambridge, Boston	Puritans organized into Massachusetts Bay Company John Winthrop	Charter (1629) Royal (1691)
	New Hampshire	1623—Dover, Exeter, Strawberry Bank (now Portsmouth)	John Mason, John Wheelwright	Charter (1629) Royal (1679)
	Rhode Island	1636—Providence, Newport	Roger Williams, Ann Hutchinson	Self-governing Charter (1663)
	Wethersfield, Windsor Hartford	1634—Wetherfield, Windsor, Hartford	Thomas Hooker	Self-governing Merged in Connecticut (1662)
	New Haven	1638—New Haven, Milford	John Davenport	Self-governing Merged in Connecticut (1662)
	Connecticut	(see above) Hartford, New Haven	(see above)	Charter (1662)

Puritan dress and household items were simple and functional. Lower left, a primitive toaster.

Religious Freedom in Rhode Island

Rhode Island was founded by another discontented Puritan, Roger Williams. Williams did not like the strict rules of religion put forth by Winthrop and the other governing Puritans of the Massachusetts Bay Colony. He wished to "seek the truth" about religion in his own private way, and he did not think that the church should have a hand in governing the state. Even more shocking to the Puritan elders was Williams' belief that the land occupied by the colony belonged to the Indians and not to the colonists.

All of Williams' seeking after truth and questioning caused him to be banished from the colony. He spent the winter with his friends, the Narragansett Indians, and in 1636 established the town of Providence, in present-day Rhode Island. Other colonists were expelled from the Massachusetts Bay Colony, and Williams welcomed them all with open arms. Most important, he extended to them true religious freedom. Like Maryland in the Southern Colonies and Pennsylvania in the Middle Colonies, Rhode Island became the center of religious freedom in New England.

New Hampshire and Maine, The Northern Colonies

Two men, Captain John Mason and Sir Ferdinand Gorges, owned much of the land which now makes up the states of Vermont, New Hampshire, and Maine, though they did little to develop it. Colonists from the Massachusetts Bay Colony filtered into this area, and in 1644 the New Hampshire area was incorporated, illegally,

Connecticut incorporated Hooker's people into that colony.

At the same time Hooker and his band were settling the area, a fort was being built at the mouth of the river by Englishmen who claimed the whole area as a colony. A settlement grew up around the present town of New Haven, also founded by a merchant and a Puritan minister, and this settlement and the fort constituted a valid English colony.

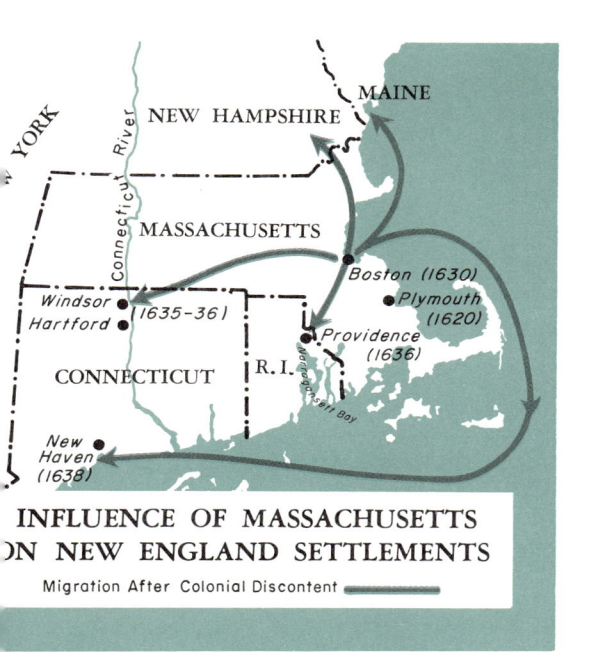

INFLUENCE OF MASSACHUSETTS ON NEW ENGLAND SETTLEMENTS
Migration After Colonial Discontent

into the Massachusetts Bay Colony. In 1668, soon after the death of Gorges, Maine was also joined to the Bay Colony, of which it remained a part from

Instruments like Roger Williams' compass and sundial were essential for wilderness travel. Williams depended on them to find his way to Rhode Island.

1691 until the early 1800's. New Hampshire later became a separate royal colony.

Among the colonies of the North, Middle, and South there were many similarities as well as differences. The colonists' right to worship as they pleased was an important reason for the settlement of the Plymouth Colony as well as for the settlement of Rhode Island and Connecticut. The first Southern colonies were inspired more by a search for new opportunity than by a search for religious freedom, although later Southern Colonies, especially Maryland, were settled by colonists seeking religious freedom. In the Middle Colonies, Pennsylvania was settled by Quakers, although New Netherland (later New York and New Jersey) was settled for commercial gain.

Actually, religious toleration existed more completely in Rhode Island than anywhere else. The Puritans of New England, for all their professed search for religious toleration, were not very tolerant of anyone who held beliefs different from their own.

Looking Back

1. What were the importance and significance of the Mayflower Compact?
2. How did the Pilgrims differ from the Puritans in their relationship to the Church of England?
3. Why did the Massachusetts Bay Colony become a "mother" of colonies?
4. How did Rhode Island come to be a haven for those suffering persecution?
5. In which of the early New England colonies would you have preferred to settle? Why?

The Chapter in Perspective

Who Are These People?

Gilbert	Oglethorpe
Raleigh	Andros
John Smith	Penn
Berkeley	Winthrop
Lord Baltimore	Roger Williams

Where Are These Places?

Roanoke Colony	Virginia
New Amsterdam	Jamestown
Hudson River	Plymouth
Massachusetts Bay Colony	

What Do These Dates and Terms Mean?

Separatists	1630
Puritans	charter
Mayflower	1649
Quakers	1619
Pilgrims	Grand Model
1620	1607

London Company
Plymouth Company
Act Concerning Religion
House of Burgesses
Dominion of New England
Fundamental Orders
Mayflower Compact

Questions for Study

1. Discuss fully the similarities and the differences that existed in the early English colonies.
2. Why did many people who sought and obtained religious freedom in the New World become intolerant of other religions?
3. Explain why the largest colonial settlements were found along the Atlantic coastline.
4. How did the early colonists attempt to govern themselves under written rules?
5. Why were the theories of Roger Williams bound to get him into conflict with the rulers of Massachusetts?
6. How do you think the average Englishman looked upon the colonies by 1732?
7. What were the chief geographic differences among the Southern, Middle, and New England colonies?
8. Show how geography influenced the economies of the early English settlements.

Place Yourself in History

You are hiding behind a tree observing strangers arriving on your shores. The new arrivals have a tremendous war canoe from which come odd-looking people in smaller canoes. The men carry sticks in their arms. All appear to be somewhat frightened and suspicious as their canoes are dragged up on the beach. These men are not like any you have seen before. You are an Indian chief witnessing the first arrival of white men on your shores.

What would you have done? How did your reaction affect the history of your native land?

Life and Development of the English Colonies

3

Generally, English colonists who settled in North America shared the same dreams of freedom, whether religious, economic, or political. In order to realize their dreams, they took great risks to come to America.

However, when they arrived, each group was faced with different problems, so that, although the dreams did not change, the methods of achieving them differed widely. For example, the colonist who settled in wintry, rocky Maine was confronted with a different set of problems from the one who settled the warm, fertile lands of South Carolina or Georgia. This led to a distinctly different development of sections of the country: the New England Colonies, the Middle Colonies, and the Southern Colonies.

1. The Colonies Prosper and Grow Economically

Since most North American English colonies were founded by corporations interested in making a profit, the colonists who were sent there were expected to send financial gains back to the mother country. In some cases, companies such as the London Company would guarantee the support of a colony until it began to export products to the mother country. In other cases, the colonists were expected to establish themselves as best they could, and think about the profits of the company that sent them whenever they could manage. And in some cases—Pennsylvania for example—a colony existed simply as a place where a new society was to be formed. However, in all cases, the colonists tried their best to make their colony prosper and grow, and the methods they used depended on their location, their social class and status, and sometimes their religion.

The Plantation System in the South

Broad lands and large fields, fertile soil, and a warm climate were key influences in the development of the South. These conditions made possible the large farms, called plantations, which extended across the Southern Colonies. Aside from planting crops to sustain their own lives, the Southern colonists were most interested in finding a profitable product which they could sell to the mother country. The first of these "cash crops" was tobacco, which the Virginia colonists began to export in 1615. In 1627, the Virginia colony sent back to the mother country half a million pounds of this weed, and it was clear that by planting a tobacco crop, a colonist could assure himself of some profit.

Tobacco, first cultivated by John Rolfe in 1612, has been a steady source of income for America for 350 years.

The One-Crop System. In the South Carolina colony and later in the Georgia colony it was soon found that rice and indigo (used in making dye) were also valuable crops. Many farmers and plantation owners concentrated on only one of these crops, hoping to gain great profits from the export of large amounts. This one-crop system caused the Southern farmers many problems. In the first place, the soil of any given plantation which concentrated on only one crop soon became exhausted and useless. Instead of fertilizing the land (chemical fertilizers were used little before 1900), planters would simply clear and plant more land. They could afford to buy land with the profits they had made from their crops in earlier years. However, from the beginning, most of the land was controlled by a very few people, and the small, independent farmer moved gradually toward the frontier.

Slave Labor. Although some small farms remained in the South, the great part of the land was taken up with plantations that needed many workers. At first, indentured servants, both Negro and white, did the work of the plantations. When the plantation owners found it inconvenient to set the servants free after their obligation was fulfilled, they encouraged the importation of slaves from Africa. African natives were captured by chieftains of enemy tribes, forced into slave ships where many of them died, and the remainder sold to planters on their arrival in America. The lives of slaves were controlled from the time they arrived in America until they died on

Colonial Trade with England 1700-1775

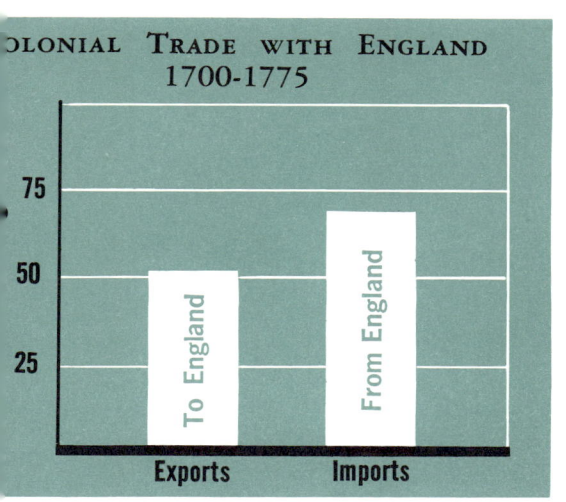

Although colonies traded secretly with other countries, most of their trade was with England. What does the graph tell you about the economic condition of the colonies?

the plantation. Such control over their labor force gave the slave owners a distinct advantage over those who used freedmen for laborers. Naturally, slave labor was relatively inexpensive, and soon even those who did not like the idea of slavery owned slaves. Slavery was widespread throughout the South after 1700.

At first the South was the most prosperous of the colonial sections of North American continent, but those who held land in the South became richer while those who were small farmers were pushed off the land. Naturally, the slaves, denied an education and unable to find jobs of their own, sank into complete dependence on "the masters." Thus the prosperity of the Southern Colonies was limited to the landed gentry or plantation owners.

New England's Diversified Economy

The land of the New England Colonies was beautiful but bleak. What land could be cultivated was often full of stones, and the mountains and rivers sliced the land into small areas, so that plantation cultivation was impossible. Also, the winters were long and hard; the wind swept down out of the north, bringing snow, and the growing season was much shorter than it was in the South. Because they could not farm so easily as the Southern colonists, the Pilgrims and Puritans had to learn to garner a living from the sea. Consequently, although

New England's flourishing coastal trade was carried on in small vessels like this one. Hand-loaded, depending on wind for power, these sturdy boats handled tons of dried fish and huge barrels of sugar and molasses.

This pillory at the Williamsburg gaol (jail) was meant to punish criminals. Those arrested for various crimes were made to stand in it night and day, rain or shine, for lengths of time that varied according to the severity of their crime.

at first farming was important in both the Northern and Southern colonies, fishing and hunting supplied much of the food in New England.

A Living from the Sea. In fact, fish became the product that the New England colonists could most effectively export to England. Unlike the Southern one-crop system, the small colonial fishing industry did not wear out the soil or the sea, and New England to this day enjoys a thriving fishing industry. Along with fishing went shipbuilding since the colonists needed small and large ships in order to fish and carry their products to Europe. So ships, along with all the things needed to sail them and make them seaworthy, like sails and ropes, became another major product of the New England Colonies.

A Flourishing Trade. Because of the ships built in New England, and because towns grew up early around the harbors there, tradesmen could ship their goods to Europe and down the Atlantic coast to the other American colonies. Boston and New Haven became flourishing centers of trade early in American history. Tradesmen sold their goods through the streets, and ships from foreign harbors spread products from Europe through the colonies. In fact, many of the early Puritan families became wealthy merchants. Nothing in the strict rules of the Puritan religion said that a man should not earn an honest dollar when he could, and much of New England was fairly prosperous early in its history.

Growing Prosperity. Although the New England Colonies did not become as prosperous in the first ten years as the Southern Colonies did, their development progressed steadily and firmly. Slavery was not practical in New England, and it went against the religious beliefs of the Puritans, although some Puritan shipbuilders and merchants took part openly in the slave trade. Also, the *economy* in the New England Colonies was *diversified,* which simply means that there were many ways to make money, whereas in the South there was only one way to become rich: through becoming a planter.

The Balanced Economy of the Middle Colonies

The colonies of New York, New Jersey, Delaware, and Pennsylvania were known as the Middle Colonies mainly because they were placed between the Southern Colonies and New England. Moreover, in many ways they were a combination of both of the other sets of colonies. In some places, there was room for broad plantations, and in these areas, large estates, owned by one man and employing many workers, sprang up. On the other hand, the Appalachian Mountains passed through the center of some of the Middle Colonies, and in the shadows of these mountains there were small farms and villages. Also, the soil of these colonies was fertile in some sections, poor in others. Finally, the weather offered opportunity for an average growing season, generally too short to raise crops like rice and indigo, but long enough to raise tobacco in some sections. As a result, there was much farming, some plantations, and, around the port of New York, thriving commerce. The Middle Colonies were aptly named, for they struck an economic balance between the extremely diverse New England area and the one-crop South.

Looking Back

1. What were the chief factors that favored the development of the plantation system in the South?
2. Discuss the advantages and disadvantages of the "one-crop system" in the South.
3. How was the labor problem of the South met?
4. What were the chief activities in the diversified economy of New England?
5. Why could it be said that the Middle Colonies had a balanced economy?

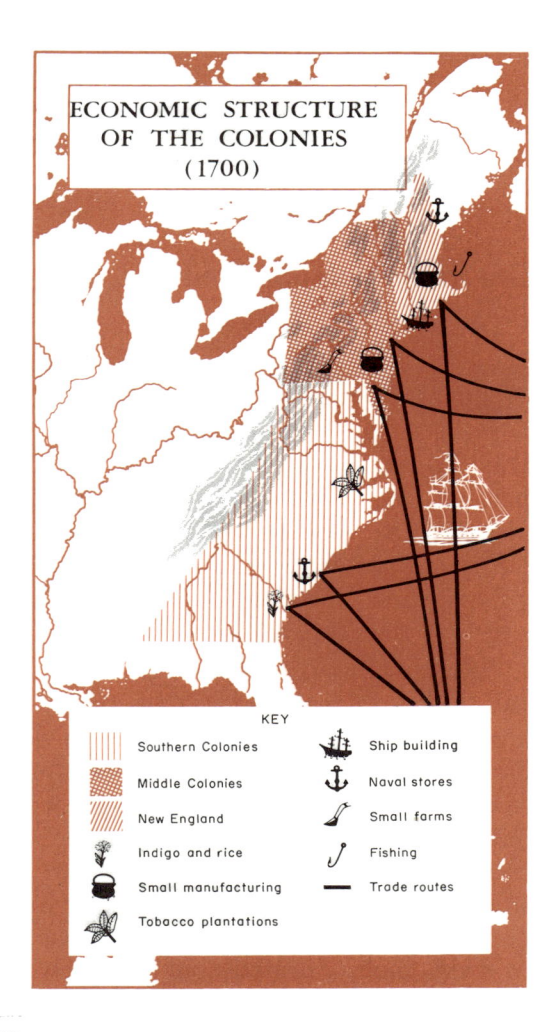

ECONOMIC STRUCTURE OF THE COLONIES (1700)

KEY
- Southern Colonies
- Middle Colonies
- New England
- Indigo and rice
- Small manufacturing
- Tobacco plantations
- Ship building
- Naval stores
- Small farms
- Fishing
- Trade routes

2. Different Environments Mold Different Ways of Life

In the same way that colonies developed along different economic lines, so did the colonists mold their ways of life according to their religion, their location and their economic status. The New Englander, faced with the need to support himself in a number of different ways, became thrifty and active. In the Southern Colonies however there developed a large gulf between rich and poor, so there is no way to describe the "typical" Southerner. And the settler in the Middle Colonies was difficult to classify also, because his way of life was part Southern, part New England; part Puritan, part Anglican. All we can do here is to list examples of the kind of life a person might have led had he lived in any of these places.

Life in the Colonial South

In the South there were as many ways of life as there were distinct groups of people. In early colonial days, groups were more strictly defined in the South than in any other part of the Thirteen Colonies. The planters, the yeomen farmers, and the Negro slaves comprised three different groups, each of which led lives different from the others. The gulf between a rich, educated, landowning planter, and a slave, uprooted from his native land by force, unable to understand most of the English language, and unfree, is unimaginable by today's standards of democracy. Yet the gulf existed. The yeoman farmer's way of life stood somewhere in between. He was not rich; but he was free. He was probably not educated; but he knew the English language, and he had come to North America by choice. Finally, although he might have been an indentured servant who owned no land, he had many opportunities to claim land to make his own way in life.

Southern Dwellings. Nowhere were the differences in Southern ways of life more apparent than they were in the types of dwellings in which the people lived. The slave was likely to live in a rather crude cabin, built of unfinished lumber or logs. In sharp contrast to the slave cabin was the large, usually well-furnished home of the slave owner. The frontier cabin of the yeoman farmer was likely not to differ markedly from the cabin of the slave. It was probably constructed of logs, and it contained numerous articles of homemade furniture, sturdy and solid, but lacking in the refine-

A late seventeenth-century American slot-back armchair. The seat was woven from splints; the legs were turned on a lathe.

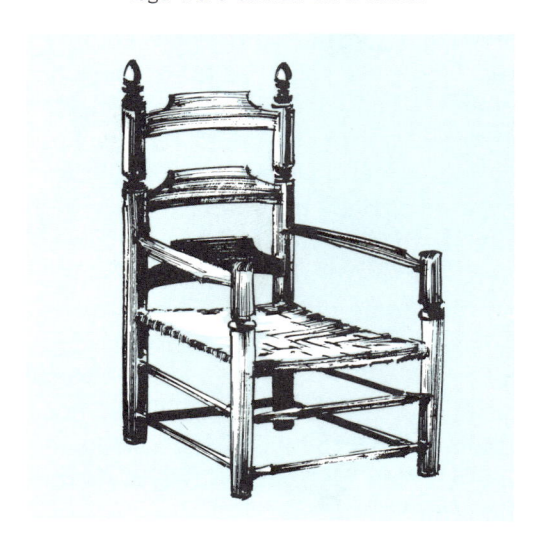

50

ment and craftsmanship of the slave owner's furniture, which often was imported from Europe. The slave cabins were furnished sparsely since slaves had little spare time to make furniture and also since they came from a land in which furniture was quite different and not so necessary.

Different Foods. The different groups followed different eating habits also. The Negro slaves, who had to adapt themselves to a new climate and new foods, usually ate filling, starchy products like rice or sweet potatoes, mainly because little else was available to them. They were given meat or fish rarely. The yeoman farmer raised much of his own food, and supplied his table with meat by hunting in the abundant forests of the frontier. Deer, quail, pheasant, wild turkeys, and fish from rivers and lakes made his diet a rustic but healthy one. The plantation owners, who copied wealthy Europeans when they could, had cooks and hunters to supply their tables with a variety of foods, both wild and domestic. Each plantation had its garden and its plot of ground for domestic animals.

Social Patterns. Entertainment and social life was varied also. Plantation owners often lived miles away from each other, and when families visited, the occasion called for a celebration. However, the life of a plantation owner was usually a lonely one. His only day-to-day associates were slaves and his own family. The slaves on the other hand at least had the small comfort of being with a large group of their own people, although slaves on a particular plantation might have come from many

When attacked, New Englanders entered blockhouses of this type for protection.

different parts of Africa's west coast. Often these transplanted Africans reverted to their tribal music and dances for entertainment, making their songs sadder when they remembered their far-off homelands and the families from which they had been separated. Perhaps the most lonely life of all was the one lived by the frontier farmer and his family. Often separated from others like him by miles of forest, he spent his time in a constant battle against the wilderness, chopping fields out of forest, and planting crops where only wild things had grown. His entertainment was the pleasure of being free and owning his land.

Exceptions to Every Rule. It is impossible to generalize about Southern colonial life. There were villages and towns in which a class of artisans and merchants grew up. By the same token there were smaller landholders who perhaps did not live much better than their slaves. And there were very wealthy plantation owners who treated their slaves quite well. Not all yeomen farmers lived in the wilderness. Some perhaps lived in coastal areas developed early in colonial times. Finally, there were some, not many, but some, free Negroes who gained their freedom as a result of their particular talents, such as medicine or entertaining. But the lives described in the preceding paragraphs are not different in kind from the lives lived by the majority of each group: slaves, farmers, and plantation owners.

Puritan Influences in New England

Although at first all colonists were faced with the same problems of hostile Indians and rugged, unsettled land, by the beginning of the eighteenth century the New Englander led an extremely different life from the Southerner. Society in New England was not divided so clearly into rich and poor, slave owner, farmer, and slave, as it was in the South. Religion also played a very important role in molding the lives of the New England colonists. Since there were mainly small farms rather than plantations in New England, small towns and villages grew up which became centers of commerce and culture. Moreover, the young man of New England was faced with a number of choices as to job and way of life. He could be a farmer, a tradesman, a fisherman, or any of a number of other things, while the Southern youth was bound in most cases to the kind of life his father had led.

The Role of the Puritan Church. The Puritan religion was the foundation for much of the behavior of the early New Englanders. As we have seen, the main colonies were founded by Puritan leaders or their followers, and the religion had great influence on colonial government. Often the first structure to be built in a New England village or town was the church. And the church was often a most uncomfortable place. Most Puritan village churches were unheated, and during the day-long Sunday services, the congregation was expected to sit up straight on hardwood benches and not make any unnecessary noises. Often young boys who dared to laugh were whipped in front of the whole congregation.

The Puritans held a very religious outlook and believed that they would be severely punished for any wrongdoing. They were so serious in fact

The interior of a Puritan church. Notice the complete lack of decoration and the uncomfortable wooden benches.

that they disapproved of most recreational activities as well as dancing and games. Work and a complete lack of enjoyment were the cornerstones of a Puritan's life. Naturally such an attitude affected the whole life of any Puritan. No author wrote anything but sermons or religious poetry. Any music but church music was forbidden. The church was the center of the Puritan's life.

Unusual Punishments. The Puritans made many strict laws to control their colonies. And they devised various punishments for those unfortunates who chanced to break a rule. For example, a drunkard might be made to sit on a wooden horse all day, holding an empty pitcher in one hand to show that he had drunk too much. People charged with being witches were hanged. However, most Puritan punishments were meant to humiliate rather than to injure permanently. The ducking stool did little more than injure a talkative woman's pride, although sometimes she did catch a severe cold. Stocks were used to punish the vagrant or the petty thief, and this kind of punishment was used throughout the colonies.

Advantages of Puritan Discipline. On the other hand, the rigorously moral life led by the Puritan gave him certain advantages. Puritans were, generally, frugal. They saved their money; they kept their homes neat and clean, and they contributed a great deal to the economic well-being of New England. Hard work and discipline made their society a stern one, but not an unhappy one. Puritans took pride and satisfaction from their neat, efficient homes, and they could always realize directly the fruits of their labors. The Puritan influence was important in the formation of a hard-working, disciplined America which was later able to make great sacrifices to win the Revolutionary War with England.

Plimoth Plantation Photo

These houses, known as "First House" and "1627 House," are identical with the original Pilgrims' homes.

Non-Puritan New England. New England life was not totally under Puritan influence however. We have seen how Roger Williams led his small band away from the strict Puritan rule into Rhode Island. Here people of all religious beliefs were welcomed. The first Jewish settlement in America was in Rhode Island in the 1600's, and Catholics, Anglicans, and other Protestants settled there also. Moreover, large cities like Boston and New Haven attracted many different types of travelers to the New World, and all of these were not necessarily drawn here for religious reasons.

Educational Beginnings. In the large communities of New England, education flourished. Harvard College was established in Cambridge, near

Massachusetts Hall at Harvard University is the oldest Harvard building still in use. Built in 1720, it is a fine example of Georgian architecture. The building now houses the president's office and still serves as a dormitory for students, its original purpose.

Boston, in 1636. Although it was founded to prepare young ministers, it was the first of a large number of American schools devoted to many different subjects. Surprisingly, as early as 1647, Massachusetts was concerned enough about the education of her children to pass a law making all villages of a certain size provide schools for their children. Boston established the Boston Latin School for young men in 1635, soon after the community was settled.

Along with the establishment of schools in the New England Colonies came the development of reading materials, textbooks, and newspapers. Naturally, Puritan families wanted their children to learn to read the Bible; and later, as settlers became more and more curious about what was going on around them, the first newspapers appeared. The first books to be published and read in the New England Colonies were religious in nature. New England farmers were also interested in the weather and crop production, so almanacs were published quite early in the history of the New England Colonies. The first one appeared in 1632 in Cambridge, Massachusetts.

The New England Primer, the earliest textbook, first published in 1690, was mainly religious in its lessons, but it did teach young children to spell and read. *The New England Primer* was the only elementary schoolbook in America for fifty years, and for one

This early schoolbook was called a "horn book." The alphabet could be seen beneath a thin layer of cow's horn.

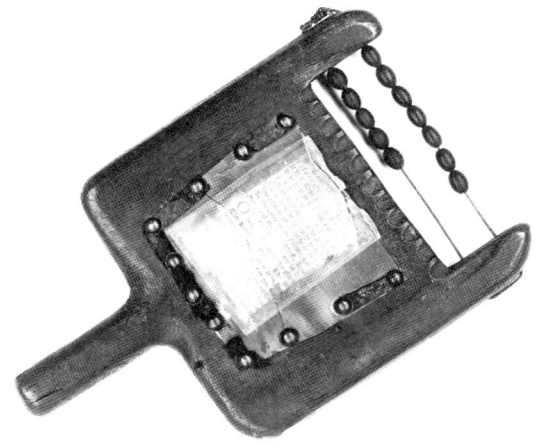

54

hundred years it occupied an important place in American education. Even if the children who learned from it were not of Puritan backgrounds, they learned to think in Puritan ways from reading the lessons in The New England Primer.

The "American Way" in the Middle Colonies

In the Southern Colonies, a person's life was determined by his particular social level whether slave, independent farmer, or planter. In New England, a person's life was guided by Puritan principles and beliefs, whether or not he was a Puritan. In the Middle Colonies, matters of religion and class played important roles in the shaping of the settlers' lives, but there were so many religions, so many classes, that it is difficult to say how the average settler in the Middle Colonies lived.

Variety is Important. If he were an ordinary Pennsylvania Quaker, he dressed, ate, and enjoyed himself in a modest manner; if he were a wealthy Quaker, he might live simply but still control great amounts of land. If he were from Maryland, perhaps he was a Catholic. He might operate a small farm or live in Baltimore where he built fast sailing ships or learned a trade. If he were a wealthy Maryland Catholic, he might live on a huge estate on Chesapeake Bay, owning slaves, eating fine foods, living much like a Carolina plantation owner. If he were of Dutch descent, he might live in a small town like the one Washington Irving described in his story, "Rip Van Winkle." Again, if he were wealthy, he might control a large estate, or, if he lived in New York City, he might be a merchant whose fortune depended upon the whims of the stormy Atlantic Ocean.

The "Melting Pot." It is certainly true that the Middle Colonies were more uniquely "American" than the other colonies early in their history. In New York City one could hear the

Shipbuilding. Construction of an early "Heel Tapper" fishing schooner in Gloucester, Mass., in the 1700's. Unlike Baltimore ships, these were slow, businesslike sailers, wide built to hold a large cargo.

accents of Holland, of Germany, of Scotland, of Ireland, and of England. Free Negroes lived in New York as early as 1650. In 1654, a group of twenty-three Portuguese Jews made their way to New York to settle. It was in the Middle Colonies, and particularly in New York when it was under Dutch rule, that the American "melting pot" had its start. Here people from various cultures, speaking various languages, came together to exchange fresh ideas, new ways of looking at things, new foods, and new beliefs.

Colonists at Work and Play

Children in colonial times had few toys, and those they had were mostly carved out of wood. Wooden dolls, tops, and hoops were common, and some of the boys had marbles. There were many games, some of which are still played to this day. Hopscotch, blind man's buff, puss-in-the-corner, marbles, and many kinds of tag were popular. The boys held contests in wrestling, boxing, foot racing, boat racing, horse racing, and swimming. Croquet and chess were played by both boys and girls, and skating and sleighing were activities enjoyed by New Englanders.

There were also frequent corn husking bees in which the young people got together and laughed and sang as they shelled the corn, and quilting parties at which the women and girls talked over the affairs of the day as they made the household quilts.

Frequently, especially in the South, finely-dressed men and women with powdered wigs performed the graceful colonial dances. Many games of cards were popular. Lawn bowling, which had been introduced in New Amsterdam by the Dutch, spread throughout the colonies and was much enjoyed. There were cockfights in which trained roosters battled to the death while the onlookers cheered their favorites and often wagered on the outcome. Weddings, birthdays, and other celebrations were usually marked by feasting and gaiety.

Where the Colonists Lived. Perhaps the wealthiest colonists were the successful Southern planters, with their broad fields of tobacco and other crops. They built the most beautiful of the colonial houses—great mansions, two or three stories high, with large, high-ceilinged rooms, many windows, and broad verandas whose roofs were

This southern plantation house was typical of the well-built homes owned by prosperous planters. Many homes like this are still preserved today.

A typical slave cabin. Made of rough lumber and poorly furnished, it was the only home many slaves knew.

supported by great square pillars. In New England, on the other hand, the colonists' houses were mainly little cottages with wide, gently sloping roofs, occasionally broken by dormer windows with many small panes of glass. The homes of the backwoods farmers were made of heavy timber covered with overlapping clapboards cut from the solid logs of the forest trees. Many had only one large room, but others had a second story, larger than the first and overhanging it. This was for defense. It enabled the owner to fire down, through holes in the floor, at Indians who attacked the house.

Colonial Furniture. The furnishings of the colonial homes differed almost as much as the houses themselves. Many of the great houses on the plantations and in the cities had finely carved oak and mahogany furniture brought from Europe. The houses of less wealthy people had American-made furniture, not so expensive as that from Europe but just as strong and just as serviceable. In the backwoods farm houses, the furniture was very rough and was usually cut from forest logs by the owner of the house himself.

The household equipment of colonial times would seem very crude to us. The fireplace was the only source of heat. Here the family gathered in cold weather, and here they did their cooking, too, for there were no stoves or gas ranges in early colonial times. It must have been difficult, indeed, to heat the colonial homes. Few of them had glass in the windows because of the great expense of importing it from Europe. For many years, oiled paper was used in the windows of the poorer homes to let the light in and keep the wind out. For light, pine torches, candles, and smoky whale oil lamps were all the colonists had. Only the wealthiest had china plates and silver knives and forks. Most of the people had to be content with pewter plates and with wooden trays called trenchers.

Colonial kitchen utensils hung from the wall. At lower right is a cheese press. Why has the frying pan a long handle?

57

What the Colonist Wore. Colonial clothes were very different from the clothes we wear today. The wealthy people wore fine costumes made of cloth imported from Europe. The men wore coats with wide collars and large buttons. Their trousers were knee breeches. White stockings were usually worn, as were low shoes with buckles. A broad-brimmed or three-cornered hat completed the costume. The women's gowns had long, full skirts that swept the ground. Some gowns were made of a heavy figured cloth called brocade and were trimmed with lace so stiffly starched that it would stand alone. Those of lesser means wore clothes of the same style but they were made of homespun cloth rather than of rich materials from Europe.

Travel and Communication. Travel and communication in the colonies were extremely slow. The mail was carried by boat or by men on horseback, and passengers were carried in stagecoaches drawn by four or six horses. It took six days for a stage coach to travel from New York to Boston and three days from New York to Philadelphia, a distance of about a hundred miles. Most of the traveling was done by day for fear of highwaymen and robbers. There would be frequent stops along the road for meals or all-night lodging at little roadside inns. In the backwoods districts, where there were no roads, the only means of travel was on foot or horseback. Travel on the water was slow, too, for the only large vessels were sailboats, wholly dependent on wind and tide.

American stagecoaches, first made in England, were impractical on rough roads. Later colonists used leather thoroughbraces instead of steel English springs to improve the ride.

A typical roadside inn, about 1760. Notice the Conestoga wagon and stagecoach in front.

Diversity Fosters Local Pride. As we have seen, life in the American colonies was varied. The New Englander had little in common with the Southerner beyond their mutual wish to make a new life for themselves in a new continent. Most colonists did not think of themselves as Americans. Rather they thought of themselves as New Yorkers, Pennsylvanians, Virginians, and so forth. All of them had great pride in their sections of the country. However, even though the colonies were different, their basic similarities united them somewhat. First of all, they were all colonies of England; most colonists spoke or tried to speak English. By 1775, the colonists began to consider their common causes, and some of the sectional feeling dropped away.

Looking Back

1. How did the economics of the South affect the social classes of the area?
2. What effect did the Puritan Church have on the people of New England?
3. By what steps did Massachusetts take the lead in developing educational opportunities for its inhabitants?
4. Justify the statement: The Middle Colonies were more uniquely "American" than the other colonies early in their history.
5. Prepare a brief report on two of the following: colonial homes; colonial furniture; colonial transportation; colonial dress.

3. A Sense of Unity Begins to Emerge

However, even today, any American feels pride in his own section of this country. Southerners are loyal to the South; New Englanders think New England is the best place to live; Californians would not trade their California homes for any other ones. What unites us now is our strong form of federal government, and what united the colonists was, finally, their similar ideas and forms of government, and the need to combine for their own survival and security.

Progress in Self-Government

The main point to be made about government of the different colonies is that eventually all the colonies found that they needed some form of representative governing body. The first colonial assembly was the Virginia House of Burgesses (a burgess was a free man elected from a given section), formed in 1619. Plymouth Colony immediately set up a popular assembly made up of all qualified freemen. Later, when there were too many qualified freemen to assemble in one building, it was decided to elect representatives. The same kind of arrangement was made in the Massachusetts Bay Colony.

Significantly, these first representative assemblies became *bicameral*, that is they consisted of two houses, an upper house and a lower house. Today, our Congress in Washington is bicameral since it consists of two houses.

Decline of English Governors' Power. At first most of the assemblies had little power to make laws. The governors of the colonies, like Berkeley of Virginia and Winthrop of Massachusetts Bay, controlled most of the lawmaking in their respective colonies. Later, however, the colonists assumed more and more responsibility for their respective affairs. When Berkeley left the governor's office of Virginia in 1677, the colonists gained great power and, in effect, were almost independent. Winthrop also was forced to concede more power to the colonists, as was Governor Andros in New York. By the time independence was declared in 1776, colonists were openly defying the powers of the royal governors in most all of the colonies.

Summing Up

Different in matters of religion and culture, similar in ideas of freedom and government, the early colonists combined their differences and their similarities to build a strong and lasting government. Most of the colonists shared common problems. They were faced with a frontier of forest and mountain along the Atlantic seaboard of North America. In all cases they were faced with diseases they had never heard of, winters the likes of which they had never known in Europe, and the enormous problem of raising food on land that had never seen a plow. Hostile Indians also proved a problem, but soon the colonists learned to become adept in the ways of the forest.

Finally, and most important, the colonists learned the necessity of governing themselves, and of learning and guaranteeing tolerance for ideas different from those they might have learned in Europe. These ideals proved to be the framework of the enduring American nation that was to develop.

Looking Back

1. By what means were strong colonial sectional feelings turned into feelings for unity?
2. How did the colonists show their early interest in self-government?
3. What are the advantages and disadvantages of a bicameral legislature?
4. Why were royal autocratic governors unpopular in the colonies?
5. What powers did most of the early assemblies possess?
6. Name some of the common problems most colonists shared.
7. In what ways did the colonies succeed in establishing different religious groups?

The Chapter in Perspective

Where Are These Places?

Harvard College
College of William and Mary

What Do These Dates and Terms Mean?

plantation system
"cash crop"
one-crop system
indentured servant
New England Primer
bicameral

Questions for Study

1. Why was agriculture a basic industry in all of the colonies?
2. In what ways was the plantation life of the South more English than typically colonial?
3. In which colonies could one find the greatest extremes in social classes? Why?
4. Which colony, in your opinion, offered the greatest opportunities to a new arrival from England in 1750? Support your choice.
5. Little mention has been made about manufacturing as an important industry in the early colonies. Explain why.
6. For what reasons was organized recreation of little interest to the typical colonist?
7. Was education as important and necessary in colonial days as it is today? Why?
8. What social, political, and economic pressures favored an early westward movement?
9. How did the natural resources and climate of the colonies affect their homes and methods of transportation?

Place Yourself in History

You are present at the auction, although you are not sure whether you wish to buy or not. The crowd is in a gay mood for the sale has been well advertised, food is free, drinks are plentiful. Folks from all over the countryside are in attendance because the new shipment presents opportunities for purchasing objects that have not been on public view before. The auctioneer strides to the front. "Friends, I have a prime hand here, just off the ship."

You are at the slave auction. Human beings—Negro slaves—are about to be sold into permanent bondage.

What are your reactions? How can you explain the reactions of those around you?

4

England and France Battle for a Continent

France and England were involved in a major struggle for world power in the early 1700's. The North American continent with its great wealth was a valuable prize in this struggle, and soon it became one of the many battlegrounds in what was truly a world war.

Most North American colonists were English. They shared English ideals and values. When the war between France and England flared up in North America there was little doubt as to which side the great majority of colonists would take.

1. English Colonies Increase in Value

When the English settlements were first started in the early 1600's, no one foresaw the exceptional growth that would occur in the next one hundred and fifty years. Although English ships did not sail back to the mother country laden with gold as the Spanish ships did, raw materials and trade from the English colonies was far more valuable. England became an empire. She needed the raw materials from the colonies to produce her manufactured goods, and she needed the people of the colonies to increase her market. By 1750 the British crown considered her lands in the New World as necessary to her economic survival and the maintenance of her role as a world power.

Rapid Growth of Population

Before 1700 the people in the English colonies were predominately English. Institutions of government, the laws, and the language clearly illustrated this. After 1700 the immigrants came from many nations. Among the largest groups to come of their own accord were the Germans. Other immigrant groups were the Scots, Irish, Dutch, Swiss, and French. Also, a sizable portion of the American colonial population was Negro Africans who, although they did not come of their own accord, nevertheless must be considered an immigrant group. It is estimated that the population of the original colonies grew from a quarter of a million in 1700 to over a million and a half in 1760.

Of course, colonial statistics did not present as accurate a picture as today's census; no specific agency existed in the 1700's to compile census figures. Estimates suggest that the New England Colonies had a population of approximately 500,000 in 1750; the Middle Colonies, 400,000; and the Southern Colonies, 700,000. Of the latter figure 300,000 were slaves.

Colonies became strong by much more than mere numbers. Rapid increase in population, however, indicated that there were many attractions in colonial life. The reports sent back to England spoke well of the living conditions in the Thirteen Colonies. Constant immigration continued; the colonists found here in the New World what they did not find in the Old. Some found religious freedom; some found political liberty. Nearly all the settlers managed to improve their economic status. With religious, political, and economic conditions so satisfactory, the colonists were ready to defend their homeland from all attempts of a foreign power to control them.

The status of political, social, and economic affairs went far toward giv-

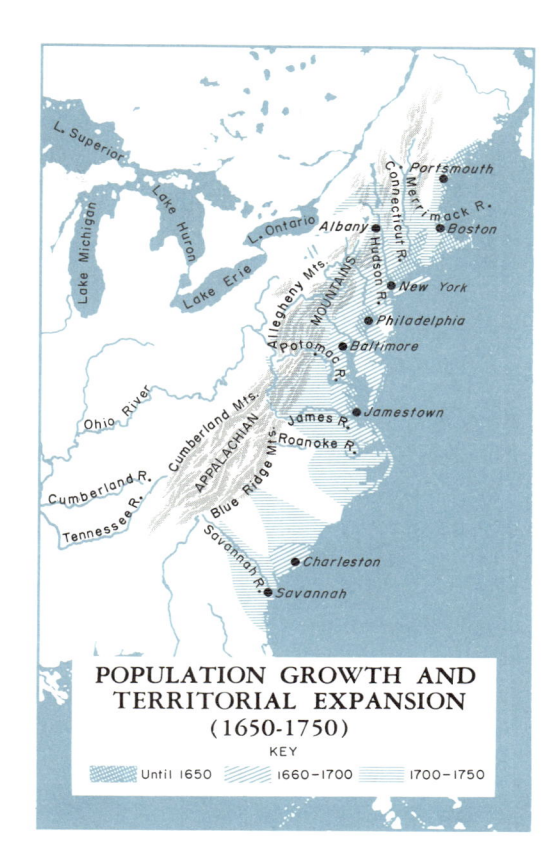

POPULATION GROWTH AND TERRITORIAL EXPANSION (1650-1750)
KEY: Until 1650 | 1660-1700 | 1700-1750

ing continued growth and strength to the varied English settlements. The colonists were sure that the French could offer them nothing better. The settlers were not here merely to trade and gain wealth. They were here to establish for themselves and for their children a new and satisfying way of life.

Westward Territorial Expansion

When the colonies were founded, only small settlements along the coastline were first established. Inland expansion was not expected by the English, the French, or the Indians. Even though the French had a claim to the eastern coast of North America through the explorations of Verrazano, no serious objection was raised when the

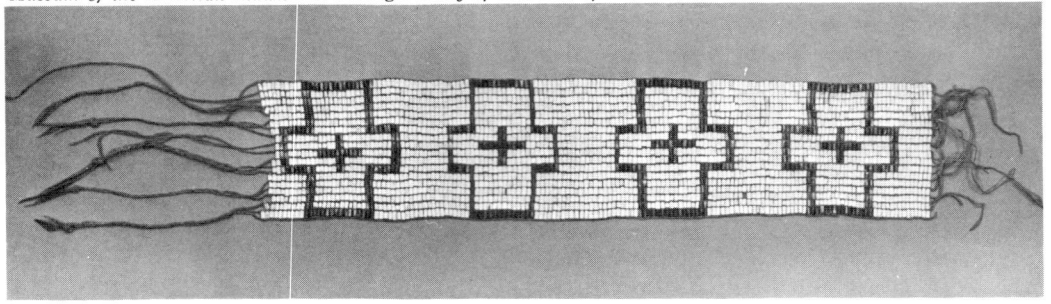

Museum of the American Indian and Carnegie Study of The Arts of The United States

A wampum belt was made from shells, usually purple and white ones. The Indians used these belts for money, for decoration, and for gifts. Indians and colonists often exchanged wampum as signs of trust.

English set up small communities. Their presence in small numbers did not appear to threaten French fur trading, since the most valuable section for trapping was not along the coast. Sometimes the Indians tried to hinder English settlements, but at other times they were friendly and helpful. Land was plentiful.

French and Indian Concern. As the population increased and the English occupied larger and larger portions of land, the French and the Indians expressed concern. At first, they merely protested, but later the bad feeling erupted into open warfare. The French knew that the English hindered their fur trading, and the Indians realized they were being crowded out of their rightful hunting grounds. Each had a justifiable cause for concern.

The French and the Indians were most disturbed by the claims of the English colonists which were based upon charters. Many of the early colonial charters granted land west to the Mississippi or even to the Pacific. Virginia, for instance, included in her original charter land now occupied by the following states: West Virginia, parts of Maryland and western Pennsylvania, Ohio, Kentucky, Indiana, Illinois, Michigan, Minnesota, and part of Wisconsin. If the English made good their claim to all this vast area, the French and the Indians would lose most of the lands they claimed.

Colonial Viewpoint. English territorial expansion was, however, inevitable. As for the colonists, they looked at the wide expanses of free land as a challenge to move into the West and take possession of this land. Most settlers wished to become land owners. Liberal land policies and a constant influx of immigrants made the occupation of western lands almost a necessity.

Many of the wealthy planters of the South owned vast acreage. For example, Robert Carter owned 300,000 acres and 1000 slaves. The William Byrd estate claimed 80,000 acres; Charles Carroll, 10,000 acres. New immigrants were forced to go west to find unoccupied land. The English colonists, as a group, looked upon the French and the Indians as hindrances to the growth and development of the colonies.

Prosperity in the Colonies

The colonies enjoyed great economic growth from 1700 to 1750. By the latter date, the colonies were enjoying the profits from an abundant overseas trade. The New World French and the merchants in England began to be jealous of American prosperity. The French considered the prospering thirteen colonies along the coast as a threat to the existence of the inland French settlements. They feared that these settlements would be swallowed up by their neighbors' wealth and vigorous growth. Back in France, the French monarch, too, realized that he had to compete against a developing nation if France was to be the leading power in North America. The English merchants saw in the prosperity of the colonies a future in which the colonists could get along without English trade.

Agricultural Surplus. The wealth and prosperity of the colonists was very noticeable to the foreigners who came here to visit or to travel. There were few beggars or paupers. Differences in wealth did exist, but nearly everyone had good food to eat, clothing to wear, and a comfortable place to live. This was probably due to the fact that a large percentage of the people were self-sufficient farmers. Even the artisans and craftsmen did some farming. In many cases, the clergy maintained farms besides taking care of their parishes. Lawyers and doctors, too, followed this pattern. The production of an abundance of food was the result. So plentiful was the supply that, by 1750, the colonists were able to ship produce to the West Indies, to England, and to Mediterranean countries. In that year, New York alone exported 80,000 barrels of flour. Other colonies shipped huge quantities of fish, salt pork and beef, grain, flour, rice, and livestock. In the South, agricultural wealth was to be found in tobacco and indigo.

Shipbuilding. Not only did the colonists export agricultural products, but they also owned and manned the ships carrying these products. The raw materials found in the forests made it possible to build ships for less than half what it would cost in Europe. New England led the other colonies in the shipbuilding industry. It is estimated that by 1760 one-third of all English ships were being built in America. This represented a production of some three hundred ships yearly. Closely connected with the industry of shipbuilding was that of manufacturing naval supplies and products needed in building and maintaining ships, such as tar, pitch, and turpentine. Since American forests yielded an abundance of white pine, fir, and oak, tons of lumber were exported to the West Indies and to southern Europe.

Fur Trade. In all the colonies the fur trade flourished. In some sections of the country, it proved to be a valuable source of income until the Revolution. Northern Colonies provided mostly beaver skins, while some Southern Colonies supplied deerskins. The white man depended on the help of the Indian in supplying these pelts. In exchange for furs, the traders offered beads, hatchets, trinkets, knives, axes, hoes, guns, and ammunition. Such objects cost the traders very little, so they made a tremendous profit from the exchange. Sometimes rum was a medium of exchange. Although most colonies passed laws against the practice of selling firearms and rum to the Indians, the laws were often ignored.

The English colonists did better than the French in the fur trade because they could buy the items of exchange more cheaply than the French. This was because so many of these items were manufactured in the Thirteen Colonies. The French had to ship most items for exchange from France.

Fishing. Fishing provided another source of wealth for the colonies. It is not surprising that the colonists, living so close to the sea, found in fishing not only a source of food but financial gain. They found an inexhaustible supply of cod, halibut, bluefish, herring, mackerel, and shad in the coastal waters. Before the fish could be sent to the markets of the West Indies or to Europe, they had to be dried and salted to prevent spoilage. Such preparation required manpower, and the trade required ships. Here again, the English colonists were in a position to do profitable business. They lived close to the sea, owned the ships, and had the necessary manpower.

Home Manufacturing. In addition to the industries connected with the forest and the sea, manufacturing raised the economic standards of the Thirteen Colonies. Although the colonists purchased many manufactured articles from the mother country, they produced a great amount of clothing, furniture, ironware, and glass in their own homes and workshops.

Cape Breton women dry fish as colonists did.

Colonial blacksmiths made andirons and all other ironwork. Notice bellows and anvil.

Looking Back

1. What factors in the colonies helped bring a rapid increase in population from 1700 to 1760?

2. In what ways did the claims and self-interests of the British, French, and Indians clash over early westward expansion?

3. Why was there an agricultural surplus in the colonies despite a rapidly growing population?

4. Why was the fur trade so vital an economic factor in colonial days?

5. Where were the chief foreign markets of the colonies other than Europe? Why?

2. French Colonies Grow More Slowly

While the British were busy building the colonies, the French were exploring the vast interior of the American continent. Occasionally the French established settlements, but they did not build colonies in the sense that the English did.

The French possessions differed from those of the English in a number of ways. New France depended on her mother country for government more than the thirteen English colonies did on England. Local self-government, which flourished in the English colonies, did not exist in New France. France governed the settlements in the New World much like the provinces in France. That is, all authority and power came from the central capital, Paris.

The French land policy also hindered the growth of the colony. In New France, as in Europe, the nobles owned immense tracts of land. Frenchmen not of noble birth paid rent in cash or labor to the lords. Such a system offered little incentive to the average settler to build homes. In contrast, the English colonists prided themselves in the homes they built, in the land they owned, and in the governments they helped to run.

Areas Claimed by France

French Exploration. During the period of European exploration, the French had been especially active. Verrazano had claimed the Atlantic seaboard of North America for France. Cartier, in search of the Northwest Passage, had discovered the St. Lawrence River. Champlain, the principal founder of New France, had explored extensively the coastal waters north of Cape Cod and the areas of the Great Lakes and Lake Champlain. Joliet and Father Marquette were the first white men to travel through the north-central part of the United States from Lake Michigan to the Mississippi River. They even sailed south on the Mississippi to what is now Arkansas. Finally, La Salle explored the central part of the continent from the Great Lakes to the mouth of the Mississippi. Although these men were better explorers and missionaries than colonizers, they did establish claims for France to more land than any other European nation could claim.

Disputed Claims. French possession of the St. Lawrence and the Great Lakes was never disputed by other nations. However, disagreements did arise concerning the rights to the Mississippi. Spain had explored the Great River and the surrounding territory before France, and so looked upon the French as intruders. When the French plainly stated that their explorers gave them claims not only to the Mississippi but to all land drained by its tributaries, conflicts developed with the English. As was mentioned earlier, many of the English colonial charters granted land west from the Atlantic coast to the Mississippi or even to the Pacific. Nowhere was this conflict of land claims more intense than in the Ohio Valley.

The French claims included parts of Virginia, Maryland, Pennsylvania, and

New York. But the English colonists consistently ignored such claims to their soil, and until the French and Indian War, they could do this. However, when the French or French-led Indians raided English settlements, claims could no longer be simply ignored but had to be resisted.

Slow Population Growth

The population of New France grew slowly. French America offered few inducements to attract settlers. Missionaries, of course, came for the purpose of spreading the Christian faith. Government officials came to perform their duties as representatives of the French king. Soldiers came to offer protection to all Frenchmen and to French property. Most of the French in the New World had, therefore, been sent out from France for specific purposes and were here in the line of duty.

A few French settlers, however, were not sent to America but came by their own choice. After they lived here for awhile, the new land in the wilds of New France or the Mississippi Valley did not seem very desirable as a permanent home. Climate and poor soil made farming difficult. The French government chose to grant land only to the nobles. The skilled craftsmen found little market for their products. These disadvantages for the middle-class French settlers caused many to turn to the fur trade in the hope of making a fortune and then returning to France.

Quebec, the first town built in French territory, grew very slowly. Other inhabited areas were scattered along the St. Lawrence River and smaller rivers. Many of the settlements, for example, Montreal and Detroit, developed from trading posts. Other settlements were villages grouped around trading posts or forts. It is estimated that the population of New France in mid-eighteenth century was approximately 60,000 people. At the same time, settlers in the thirteen English colonies numbered more than twenty times those of France.

Wealth from Furs

Louis XIV, King of France, had hoped to build strong colonies after the pattern of the English. His advisers knew that fur trading alone would not establish a strong and permanent empire. They understood the economic value of prosperous farms, and for this reason, the French government tried in vain to check the de-

The Chateau Frontenac overlooks modern-day Quebec, which has three times as many people as did all of French Canada in 1750.

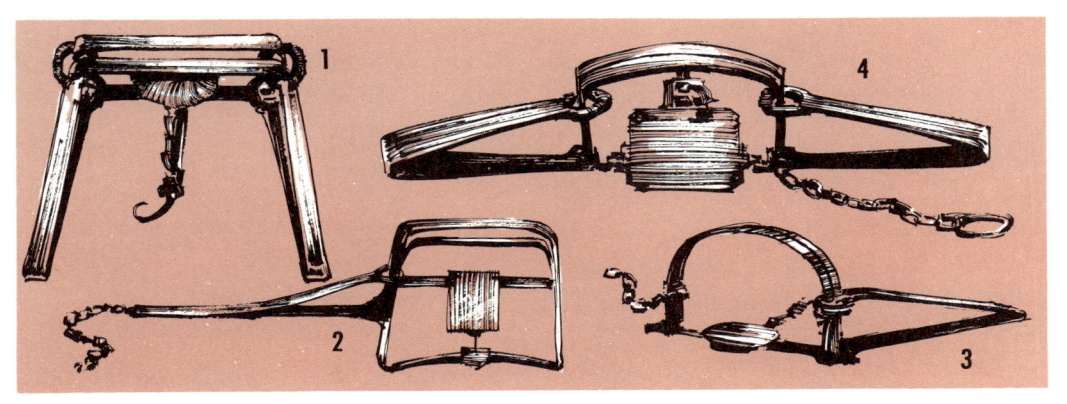

Steel traps did not become common in North America until 1750. Since they were usually made by local blacksmiths working with crude iron, their springs often snapped in cold weather. 1. 1750 beaver trap 2. fox trap 3. bear trap 4. 1820 beaver trap.

velopment of fur trading to the neglect of farming and manufacturing.

Farming and Lumbering Prove Unprofitable. The short growing season in Canada hindered successful agriculture. French colonial farms produced some wheat, rye, barley, peas, beans, flax, and hemp, since these crops did not require a long growing season. The French settlers also attempted to develop cattle and poultry farming. But, compared with the abundant production on the farms of the English colonists, French production was small.

French settlements were scattered too much to make manufacturing a source of income. Near the towns of Quebec and Montreal, a small market for lumber did develop, but to cut lumber and prepare it for shipping required many hours of hard labor. Furthermore, most settlers were not interested in such enterprises as farming and lumbering because they offered less financial return than trapping.

This widespread search for wealth from the forests, instead of farming and manufacturing, caused France to lose eventually her New World possessions. To whom did the hunting and trapping grounds really belong: the Indians, the French, or the English? This became the dispute of the century.

Flourishing Fur Trade. Despite this dispute, the fur trade flourished, and furs became the chief form of wealth. French trappers, almost constantly away from civilization, adapted well to life in the forests. Many hunters lived and trapped with the Indians, spreading out to the north, the west, and the south over the vast French territory. The life of the hunter and fur trader was a hard and rugged life. However, his furs yielded enormous profits when sold in the markets of Europe.

Montreal Fair. In fact, the success of the fur trade was due, at least partially, to the assistance of the Indians. The French gained friendship with the Indians by living with them, by intermarrying, and by trading. Each summer, the French and Indians held a great fair in Montreal. Indians arrived in fleets of canoes, several hundred in number, to sell the furs of beaver, otter, and other animals. The first day of the fair was devoted to flowery speeches by both the Indians and the French. Trading began on the second day. The French displayed articles desired by the Indians, such as blankets, knives, beads, guns, and ammunition. The Indians paid for these articles with furs.

Few spectacles in American history were more colorful than the fair at Montreal. The possibility always existed that the night before actual trading began, the Indians would somehow acquire some liquor, or "firewater" as it was very frequently called. The French benefited by such a situation, for an Indian with an excess of "firewater" was likely to place too many furs on the trading counter. However, a sober Indian drove a hard bargain, cleverly trying to get the most for the fewest furs.

Looking Back

1. In what ways did the French colonies differ from those of the British?
2. Where did the areas claimed by Spain, France, and Great Britain come into conflict?
3. Why did French population in the New World grow slowly?
4. Under what handicaps did French agriculture and manufacturing operate?
5. Compare the way the typical British and French frontiersman treated the Indians.

3. The French and the English Clash Indecisively

The English colonists in America were loyal Englishmen and the French were loyal Frenchmen. It is not surprising, therefore, that when a series of wars broke out in Europe between France and England, the French and English colonies in America also went to war. These wars between the colonies were known as the intercolonial wars.

King William's War

The first of these wars, King William's War, started in 1689. A party of Frenchmen and Canadian Indians made a surprise attack upon the little village of Schenectady (skeh-NEK'tah-dee), New York, burned the houses, and massacred men, women, and children. At almost the same time a band of Indians attacked the town of Haverhill (HAY'ver-ull) in Massachusetts. The enraged English hit back at once. A band of Boston colonists under Sir William Phips of Maine made a successful attack on the French stronghold of Port Royal in Acadia. Before their determined assaults, the fortress fell. The English held it until the end of the war in Europe, when it was restored to France by the treaty of peace.

Queen Anne's War

Another war between France and England began in 1701. In the colonies it was called Queen Anne's War. French and Indians attacked Deerfield, Massachusetts, burned the town, and killed many settlers. The English, in turn, sent shiploads of troops against the city of Quebec. The expedition ended tragically when the ships were wrecked. Many of the soldiers were drowned, and Quebec remained untaken. A second expedition, however, stormed Port Royal, as Phips and his men from Boston had done a few years before, and once more the English flag was hoisted over its walls. This time, when the war was over, England retained Port Royal and with it the entire province of Acadia, which was renamed Nova Scotia.

King George's War

A third French and British war spread to the American colonies in 1744 and was known as King George's War.

Two views of the reconstructed fort at old Port Royal. It was held by both French and English at various times.

The French used Cape Breton Island in the Gulf of St. Lawrence as a naval base. From its rocky harbors they sent out warships to capture British vessels off the New England coast. As long as Cape Breton remained in French hands, these raiders had a base from which to work, and it was almost impossible to subdue them.

Clearly, the island of Cape Breton had to be captured, even though it was defended by the strong fortress of Louisbourg, on its eastern shore. Under the leadership of Colonel Pepperell, a few thousand brave English colonists set out, traveling part way by ship and part way on foot. It was a hard and dangerous attempt. The heavy cannon had to be dragged through swamps and over ridges, and the little army was almost exhausted when it reached Louisbourg. Aided by a British fleet, Pepperell and his men besieged the stronghold, and at the end of six weeks the French surrendered on June 15, 1745. However, the treaty at the end of King George's War restored Louisbourg to the French.

Looking Back

1. For what reasons did the British colonists enter the wars against France from 1689 to 1744?

2. What were the main events and results of King Williams's War? Queen Anne's War? King George's War?

3. Find terms in the peace treaties of the above wars to indicate that the interests of their colonists in America were not of major concern to the British.

An English frontier fort, elevated so that soldiers could fire down on invaders. Cannons are arranged in corner bastions so that they could sweep the field in a crossfire.

4. A Great War Decides America's Future

The first three intercolonial, or French and Indian, wars were only echoes of greater wars in Europe. In 1754, a war began which was to be a desperate struggle between the French and British for the possession of most of North America. This was the French and Indian War, which started in America and spread to the Old World.

King William's, Queen Anne's, and King George's wars had been indecisive. Competition for world trade continued. England wanted to possess the French lands and France wanted to possess those of England. Another war was inevitable. But no one knew when either nation would finally begin it.

Danger Signals in the Ohio Valley

The rivalry of the two nations centered in the possession of the Ohio Valley. For the French, the Ohio River afforded the most convenient route from Canada to the Mississippi and New Orleans. The English hoped to settle this area, and both nations desired the Ohio fur trade.

Washington's Mission. In order to protect their lands in the West against the British, the French had built a line of forts just west of the Appalachian Mountains. Some of these forts stood on land the British colonies claimed. Irritated by the presence of French strongholds within the borders of his colony, Governor Dinwiddie of Virginia sent a messenger to the French commander to demand that the French soldiers be withdrawn. The messenger whom the governor chose was named George Washington.

When Washington delivered the governor's message to the French commander, he received an answer which could mean nothing but war. The French were not willing to leave. That being the case, Governor Dinwiddie determined to drive them out by force. Again he sent George Washington, this time with a small company of soldiers, to occupy a fort which some British frontiersmen were building not far

Ft. Necessity, rebuilt near Uniontown, Pennsylvania, is where Col. George Washington fought the French and Indians in 1754.

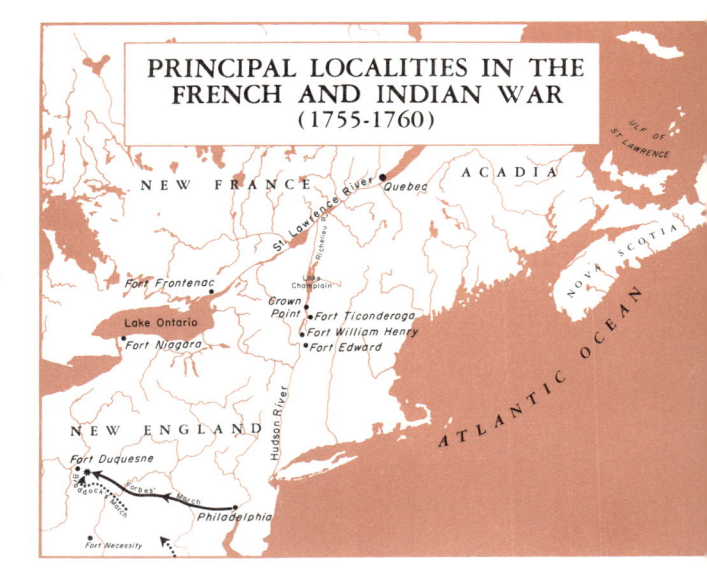

PRINCIPAL LOCALITIES IN THE FRENCH AND INDIAN WAR (1755-1760)

In general, the French controlled much of Canada, the Great Lakes, and the western Appalachian region at the beginning of the war. Why were they interested in these regions?

from the strongholds of the French. But when Washington and his men arrived at the fort, they found that the French had already occupied it and had named it Fort Duquesne (doo-KAYN').

Early Skirmishes. Washington had too few men to capture Fort Duquesne, but he soon discovered a French camp in the wilderness which he believed could be taken. Washington and his men made a surprise attack on May 24, 1754, forced the Frenchmen to surrender, and in doing so won for the British the first battle of the French and Indian War.

The French were not slow in striking back. They soon cornered Washington and his tiny army in a little, hastily constructed fort which Washington's army called Fort Necessity. After a brief siege, the English were forced to surrender and to promise that they would not try to build another fort in that area for a year. Washington had no choice but to agree to these terms. The French then released him and his men, and they journeyed sadly back to Virginia without having accomplished the job they had set out to do.

The Albany Congress. The government authorities in Britain watched the movements of the French with alarm. The British had to take definite action or all their colonies would be endangered. To prepare for action and defense, Britain summoned representatives from each of the Thirteen Colonies and from the Iroquois Indians to a conference at Albany, New York.

Delegates from seven colonies and warriors from the Iroquois nation assembled at Albany during the summer of 1754. The Iroquois, previously friends of the British and enemies of the French, were invited to the conference because the British feared that the French successes in the West might cause the Indians to take a neutral stand in the coming conflict. To wage war successfully over frontier areas in the 1750's, the aid of Indian allies was necessary. No plan to expel the French had much chance of success without the help of the Iroquois.

In Albany, the Indians complained of British land frauds; they claimed that the British took more land than they paid for. Since the Indians secured their supplies through fur trading, they resented the invasion of their hunting grounds. In particular, the area that is now New York State had been invaded by traders from Virginia and Pennsylvania. Furthermore, the Indians claimed that the entire New York frontier could not be defended from the French without more forts and more British soldiers.

The *Albany Congress*, as this conference was called, then proceeded to make recommendations to be sent to the British government. Those at the conference denounced the French, acknowledged the grievances of the Indians, recommended the building of new forts, and advised the colonists not to settle west of the Appalachian Mountains.

To carry out these recommendations, the congress adopted a plan of union for the colonies. Written primarily by Benjamin Franklin, the Albany Plan called for the colonies to unite voluntarily under one government. The government would consist of a president general to be appointed by the king and a grand council to be made up of delegates from each colony. The council would have the right to control Indian affairs, construct defenses, and levy taxes. Submitted to the colonial assemblies for their approval, the plan was rejected. The assemblies did not want to give up their right to levy taxes. Even though the plan failed, it influenced the organization of later congresses at the beginning of the Revolutionary War.

The Western Campaigns

Braddock's Defeat. In 1755 Great Britain sent troops to Virginia under General Edward Braddock. He determined to lead a powerful army of British soldiers against the French strongholds to the west. He also took with him George Washington and a small band of colonial troops. Unfortu-

Braddock's Army in full regalia, playing fifes and drums, marches through the Pennsylvania wilderness. Would it be difficult for the French and Indians to ambush them?

nately, General Braddock refused to accept Washington's advice to send out scouts, so his fine army marched into an ambush near Fort Duquesne and was badly beaten. The general himself was killed, and once more Washington was forced to lead a beaten army back to Virginia.

Indian Raids. This untimely defeat of the British forces left a 350 mile frontier open to attack by hordes of Indians, chiefly Shawnees and Delawares. These Indians wreaked havoc upon the small English settlements in the area. Many settlers were either massacred or captured. Some were tortured to death, their cabins were burned, and their property destroyed. Flight to the eastern counties offered the only protection.

After these destructive raids, the settlers, with the aid of the colonial authorities, built a string of at least a dozen forts along the Pennsylvania frontier. Many of these were manned by the colonial militia on constant patrol. Bounties were offered to the white settlers for scalping Indians. But even though the colonists tried these methods, Indian raids continued.

Second Ohio Campaign. The British did not make a second attempt to capture Fort Duquesne, the key to French strength in the Ohio Valley, until 1758, three years after General Braddock's defeat. In the meantime, England had officially declared war on France, and a new Prime Minister, William Pitt, had adopted a vigorous war policy. One objective of Pitt's policy was to oust the French from the Ohio Valley.

The British planned an expedition under the leadership of General Forbes. He commanded a force of about six thousand men including British regulars and colonial militia. The forces were to gather at Fort Bedford, some seventy miles east of Fort Duquesne. From this rallying point, a new military road, later called the Forbes Road, was built westward to the Ohio Valley.

But advance to the West was slow, because General Forbes became ill, and building a road through wilderness was difficult. When an outpost was established about fifty miles from the goal, a certain Major Grant with eight hundred men was sent to spy on the French fortifications. Disregarding his orders, he attacked the fort, only to be defeated and find himself taken prisoner.

Fall of Fort Duquesne. The French also sent out spies. As a result, the French realized that the British outnumbered them ten to one. They did not wait to be attacked but burned Fort Duquesne and fled north to the French posts on the Great Lakes.

When they arrived at what was left of Fort Duquesne, the British rebuilt it and called it Fort Pitt in honor of the new Prime Minister. General Forbes stationed a garrison of several hundred men to guard the strategic point against future French attacks. This British victory closed the Ohio Valley to the French. It also relieved a large portion of the frontier of the Indian menace.

The Power Struggle in the North

When the campaigns in the north began in 1755, the future of British America looked very uncertain. Only one victory could be claimed against the French, the battle of Lake George in upper New York State. Several months earlier General Braddock had been defeated in his attempt to capture Fort Duquesne. Expeditions against the French at Fort Niagara on Lake Ontario and against Crown Point on Lake Champlain (sham-PLAYN') had also failed.

Despite their successes, the French feared British attacks against New

Guards with authentic muskets and costumes guard the entrance to old Fort Niagara.

France, which they felt would come through one of three specific routes. One of these was over Lake Ontario and then down the St. Lawrence River. Another went north through the Champlain corridor: up the Hudson River, through Lake George and Lake Champlain, following the Richelieu (REE'shuh-LYOO') River into the St. Lawrence. A possible third route into French territory was by sea to the mouth of the St. Lawrence and on up the river.

French Advances Under Montcalm. In 1756, the very clever and capable French general, Montcalm, arrived in New France to command French forces. In his first campaign, he aimed at closing the route to New France over Lake Ontario to the English. On the lake the British had built Fort Oswego as a base for future invasions into New France. Montcalm attacked the fort suddenly, without warning, and captured 1600 prisoners and vast stores of supplies. The French now controlled the entire lake.

After this victory, Montcalm moved to the Lake Champlain area to attack Fort William Henry at the southern tip of Lake George. This fort was the most advanced post of the British route to New France through the Champlain corridor. Montcalm won here too, and the British surrendered, with the agreement that they be allowed to retire to Fort Edward, farther south. But Montcalm's Indian allies refused to allow these terms and massacred hundreds of the British prisoners. The French then burned the fort.

The capture and destruction of Fort William Henry was the high point of French military advance. Montcalm commanded about 3000 trained regulars and 12,000 French colonists and Indians. Against him, the British pledged the might of their sea and land forces. The government was willing and able to send all necessary supplies and men to win the war. France, however, had too many entanglements in Europe to do the same thing. Furthermore, the French could not compete with British naval power.

British Naval Supremacy. The supremacy of British naval strength in the closing years of the war made their victory possible. For example, it allowed them to capture again the fortress of Louisbourg at the entrance to the Gulf of St. Lawrence. General Amherst and Lord Howe, British commanders, proceeded against Louisbourg with forty warships. After a siege of many weeks, the fortress surrendered with thousands of prisoners in the summer of 1758.

When they lost Louisbourg, the French lost one of their most strategic strongholds in America. Louisbourg had been heavily fortified to guard the entrance into New France. With its entrance left unguarded, New France was open to invasion. A month later Fort Frontenac on the north side of Lake Ontario also fell to the British.

Only Fort Ticonderoga (ti-kahn-duhr-oh′gah) on Lake Champlain withstood an organized British attack. Here Montcalm maintained a clever defense. His troops felled hundreds of trees surrounding the fort, and British troops could not penetrate this jungle

This restoration of Fort Ticonderoga, on Lake Champlain in New York, is an outstanding museum of military history. The fort was a strategic stronghold both in the French and Indian War and in the Revolution. The cannons are typical of the eighteenth century.

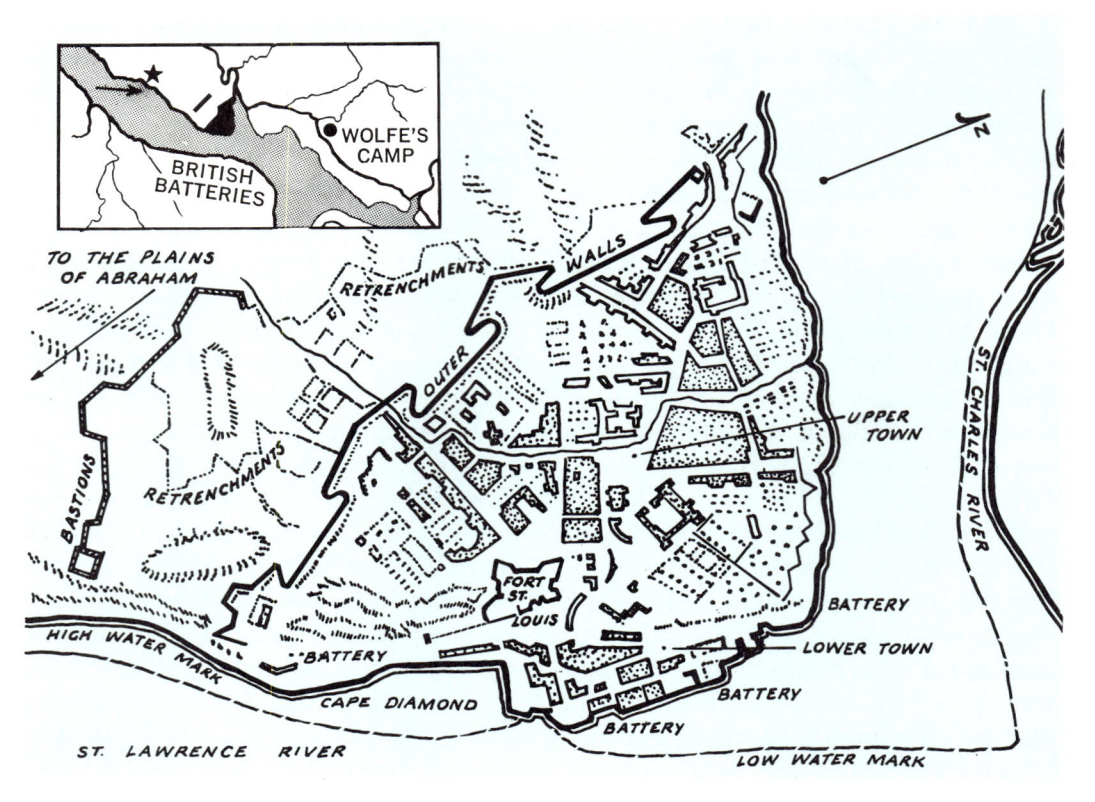

This map shows Quebec to be strongly fortified. Why, when the English had climbed the cliffs (see arrow, upper left), did they have a relatively easy time capturing the town?

to organize a successful attack. But the defense of Ticonderoga was an exception. This was 1758, a year in which the tide turned against the French. They lost Louisbourg, Fort Frontenac, and Fort Duquesne. The French knew the next attack would be against Quebec, the heart of New France.

A Year of Decision. The following year, 1759, the British government was determined to end the war by an all-out effort to defeat France. The greatest fleet of British ships up to this time (about 250) sailed for America. With the fleet sailed 30,000 men to add to the fighting forces. After years of fighting, the British were equipped to end French control of Canada.

The Fall of Quebec

English strategy against Quebec divided the British regulars and the colonial militia into three expeditions. One group, under General Wolfe, would attack Quebec by way of the St. Lawrence. Another, under General Amherst, would move north through Lake Champlain to Montreal, capturing French forts in that area along the way. The third force would first attack Fort Niagara and then proceed east along Lake Ontario to Montreal.

The Siege. The siege of Quebec began in June of 1759 and lasted all summer. The French commander, General Montcalm, did not believe that the

British would attempt to sail their fleet up the St. Lawrence, and he felt sure they could not sail beyond Quebec. French fortifications along the river, he reasoned, would hinder the passage of a fleet. Also, sailing up the St. Lawrence could be disastrous for anyone unfamiliar with the shallow areas. The location of the city of Quebec, heavily fortified on the steep cliffs three hundred feet above the river, gave the French a false feeling of security. They underestimated General Wolfe, the military genius, who commanded the British. The British were surprised to find that the French had built such excellent fortifications. The French were surprised by the size of the British invasion force.

General Wolfe sent half of his fleet up the river, passing the fortress and city of Quebec, while the other half anchored several miles downstream. Wolfe's artillery dug in on the shore opposite Quebec where their guns could hurl shells into the fortress.

General Wolfe realized as he carefully studied the physical aspects of the area that his army must somehow climb the steep cliffs to engage the French in battle. He finally planned to make a landing a mile and a half up the river from Quebec.

The Plains of Abraham. During the night, Wolfe's men embarked in small boats. A French sentry challenged them, but a British soldier replied in French that the boats were merely bringing supplies. Since the French were expecting reinforcements, they were fooled by this trick and the boats were allowed to proceed. The cliff, however, still presented an obstacle. With great difficulty, Wolfe's men scaled the steep cliffs, overpowered the guards, and assembled for battle on the Plains of Abraham, a level plateau outside the fortified city of Quebec.

When Montcalm was informed that the British had accomplished the impossible, he had no choice but to fight. Montcalm's army was larger, but the British were better trained and better disciplined.

Leader of the French

" Montcalm, still on horseback, was borne with the tide of fugitives towards the town. As he approached the walls a shot passed through his body. He kept his seat; two soldiers supported him, one on each side, and led his horse through the St. Louis gate. On the open space within, among the excited crowd, were several women, drawn, no doubt, by eagerness to know the result of the fight. One of them recognized him, saw the streaming blood, and shrieked, 'O mon Dieu! mon Dieu! le Marquis est tué!' 'It's nothing, it's nothing,' replied the death-stricken man; 'don't be troubled for me, my good friends.' "

—Francis Parkman, American Historian
1823–1893

> *Leader of the English*
>
> "Here Wolfe himself led the charge, at the head of the Louisbourg grenadiers. A shot shattered his wrist. He wrapped his handkerchief about it and kept on. Another shot struck him and he still advanced, when a third lodged in his breast. He staggered, and sat on the ground. . . . Asked if he would have a surgeon, 'There's no need,' he answered, 'it's all over with me.' A moment after, one of them cried out, 'They run; see how they run!' 'Who run?', Wolfe demanded like a man roused from sleep. 'The enemy, sir. Egad, they give way everywhere!' Then turning on his side the dying man murmured, 'Now, God be praised, I will die in peace.'"
> —Francis Parkman, American Historian 1823–1893

Much depended on the outcome of this battle: the future of North America, in fact. And yet, the British won in fifteen minutes. With the rout of Montcalm's army, New France was lost. Both Montcalm and Wolfe were mortally wounded. It was merely a question of time until all of New France would fall to the British, and the French subjects would become English subjects. This happened the following year.

Treaty of Paris, 1763

The treaty ending the French and Indian War was signed at Paris in 1763. A secret treaty signed in 1762 between France and Spain ceded all French lands west of the Mississippi River and New Orleans to Spain. The Treaty of Paris had these provisions:

Benjamin West painted this highly fanciful picture called *The Death of Wolfe*. It was painted in his London studio; his friends posed for the painting, so it is inaccurate historically.

RESULTS OF THE TREATY OF PARIS (1763)

(1) France was to cede to England all her lands in North America east of the Mississippi;
(2) France was permitted to continue ownership of St. Pierre and Miquelon, small islands off the coast of Newfoundland (owned by France to the present day);
(3) England agreed to grant religious liberty to Roman Catholics in Canada;
(4) For eighteen months after signing of the treaty, Frenchmen in Canada would be allowed to leave the country with all their possessions;
(5) Continued fishing rights were granted to French citizens in the St. Lawrence and off the coast of Newfoundland.

Looking Back

1. Summarize the part played by George Washington during the French and Indian War period.
2. Discuss the purposes and results of the Albany Congress.
3. How did the British win control of the Ohio Valley from the French?
4. Why is the battle of Quebec considered one of the most important battles in history?
5. Comment on this statement: The Treaty of Paris in 1763 decided that Great Britain and not France would be supreme in the New World.

The Chapter in Perspective

Who Are These People?

Verrazano
Cartier
Louis XIV
Phips
Pepperell
Washington
Dinwiddie
Franklin
Braddock
Pitt
Montcalm
Wolfe
Amherst

What Do These Dates and Terms Mean?

naval supplies
1689
King William's War
Queen Anne's War
1701
1744
Forbes Road

King George's War
1754
Albany Congress
French and Indian War
1763
Treaty of Paris
Plains of Abraham

Where Are These Places?

Fort Frontenac
Port Royal
Fort Pitt
Louisbourg
Ft. Duquesne

Quebec
Fort Necessity
Ft. William Henry
Acadia
Ft. Ticonderoga

Questions for Study

1. Compare the strength of the British and the French at the start of the French and Indian War.
2. Why did fewer foreigners emigrate to New France than to the British colonies?
3. What products and items came to the British colonies from the West Indies?
4. Why was it cheaper to build ships in the colonies than in England?
5. For a look into the distant past, tell why the Iroquois fought with the British against the French.
6. How did colonial participation in the wars between France and England help develop colonial confidence?
7. Who gained more from the defeat of the French—the British or the colonists? Explain.
8. What part did British naval supremacy play in the victory?
9. Show how the geography of the area involved affected the strategic importance of Ft. Royal, Ft. Pitt, Louisbourg, Quebec, Ft. Ticonderoga.
10. On a map of North America, indicate the territory included in what one historian called "one of the largest real estate deals in history" —the Treaty of Paris, 1763.

Place Yourself in History

August 7, 1752 is an important day in your life. Seven years ago, you arrived in the New World without friends, money, or prospects. You owed money for your transportation from England. After seven years of work—without pay other than room and board—you are now debt free. You are an indentured servant who has fulfilled his contract.

What are your plans for the future? Where do you plan to settle? Why? Summarize some of your experiences of the past seven years.

Expanding Your Outlook

Doing It Yourself

1. Draw a series of pictures that show the clothes, weapons, and ships of the Norsemen.
2. Imagine that you have returned from the Crusades. Report to your fellow villagers on your experiences.
3. Make a chart of the explorers using the following headings: name, country, sailed for, date, accomplishments.
4. Using a map of the world, give a report on the accomplishments of Prince Henry the Navigator.
5. Choose the explorer who in your opinion made the greatest contribution to the development of the New World. Write a biography of this man.
6. Make a model of a medieval invention that affected man's progress.
7. Make a map of the New World in 1763 indicating the land claims of European nations.
8. Make a chart of the English colonies in America listing: name, founders, date, purposes, major settlement, chief products, special achievements.
9. Present a report to the class on the development of religious freedom in the English colonies.
10. Draw a cartoon reflecting the hostility between the French and the English colonists.

Working with the Class

1. With a group of classmates, imagine you are reporters interviewing Marco Polo upon his return from the Orient. The rest of the class is your audience.
2. Choose five committees to report to the class on the contributions to the American way of life made by the Indians, Spanish, English, French, and Dutch.
3. A committee of three is visiting England to encourage settlement in the New World. Each member represents one of the major divisions: New England, the Middle Colonies, and the South. Present your views to the class.
4. To show your understanding of colonial problems, imagine that all classmates are members of either the Virginia House of Burgesses or a New England town meeting. Let the class choose a presiding officer and go into session.

5. Form a committee of those interested in colonial architecture. Make models or present pictures that show a typical New England home, a Dutch manor in New York, a rich planter's home in Virginia, and a log cabin on the frontier.
6. An international meeting is to be held in your classroom. The topic: "Life in the New World in 1763." What views might be expressed by representatives from a. Quebec, b. Boston, c. Albany, d. Philadelphia, e. Charleston, f. Mexico City, g. Rio de Janeiro, h. Buenos Aires?

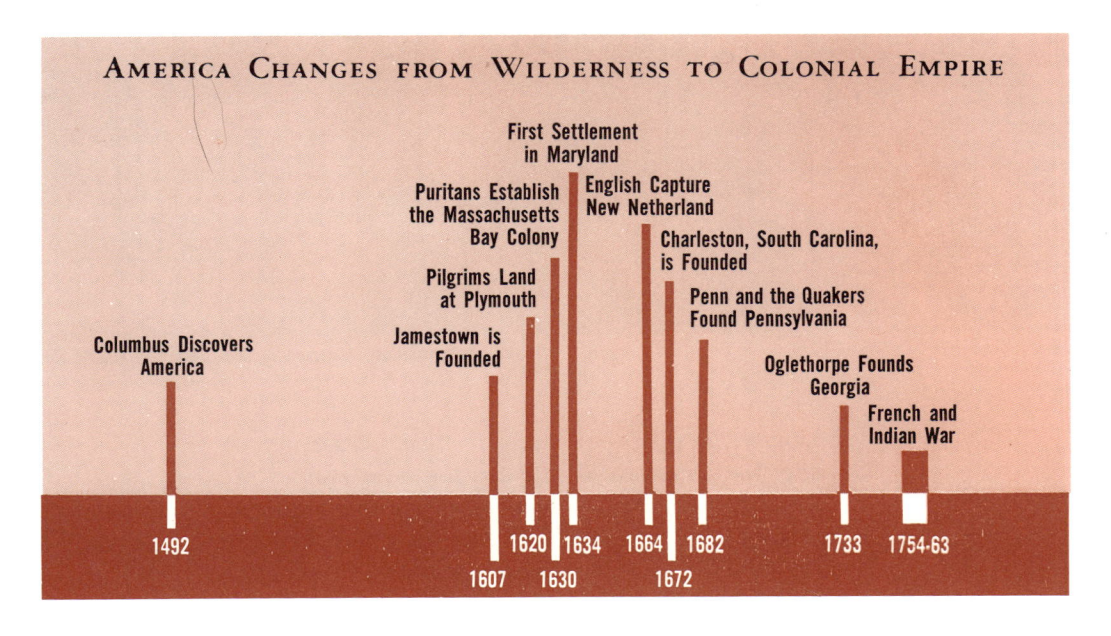

America Changes from Wilderness to Colonial Empire

1492	Columbus Discovers America
1607	Jamestown is Founded
1620	Pilgrims Land at Plymouth
1630	Puritans Establish the Massachusetts Bay Colony
1634	First Settlement in Maryland
1664	English Capture New Netherland
1672	Charleston, South Carolina, is Founded
1682	Penn and the Quakers Found Pennsylvania
1733	Oglethorpe Founds Georgia
1754-63	French and Indian War

The Metropolitan Museum of Art—Gift of John S. Kennedy, 1

Emanuel Leutze's painting called Washington Crossing the Delaware *is perhaps the most famous of the Revolutionary period. The artist captures the desperate determination of the American army. Leutze lived from 1816 to 1868, and he painted this picture 75 years after the event from written records.*

ONE NATION INDIVISIBLE

UNIT 2

Dissatisfaction and Rebellion Inspire a New Kind of Government

5. The Colonists Become Americans
1. England Changes Its Colonial Policies • **2.** The Colonists Voice Their Objections • **3.** Britain Tightens Its Control

6. Americans Turn to Revolution
1. Armed Resistance Begins • **2.** Resistance Turns to Rebellion • **3.** England Carries the War to the Middle Colonies • **4.** The Americans Advance on Land and Sea • **5.** The War in the South Proves Decisive • **6.** American Independence Becomes a Reality

7. These United States Adopt a Constitution
1. The New Nation Survives the "Critical Period" • **2.** Convention Delegates Frame a New Constitution • **3.** The Constitution of the United States

5

The Colonists Become Americans

To American shores came settlers from England, Holland, France, Spain, Sweden, and many other nations. Many forces blended these settlers into one great people. Chief among these were the hardships they faced. Fighting common enemies, such as poverty, the Indians, the French, or enduring severe British control, caused the colonists to think of themselves as Americans rather than as displaced Europeans. The story of how these many people joined together as a single nation, ready to resist foreign oppression to the utmost, is one of the most thrilling chapters in our history.

1. England Changes Its Colonial Policies

During the French and Indian War, the French predicted that if the British gained control of New France it would not be for long. This opinion existed because the colonists were, even then, changing their attitude toward British rule. As the French had predicted, the colonists did become discontented, and England's control began to slip.

The colonists themselves changed when the menace of France was removed. No longer did they need England's protection. England, too, changed her attitude toward the colonies. She expected them to do much more than they had been doing for their mother country. A distinct period of American history ended with the Peace Treaty signed in Paris in 1763.

Growth of Americanism in the Colonies

Colonial Character. At the end of the wars between the French and the British in America, the population of the British colonies was diverse and interesting. Many of the colonists were descendants of the early pioneers who bravely crossed a mighty ocean in search of a new and better life in the New World. In many cases, they had left their homes to escape religious or political oppression. They were usually people far broader and more flexible in their views than those who remained behind to be ruled by the strict customs of the Old World.

Self-Reliance and Determination. It required persistence and determination to hew homes out of the wilderness, and these qualities the settlers had. The hardships of the early years in America killed many of them, but those who survived learned courage and tolerance, were strong and healthy, and had great endurance. To these early pioneers who risked their lives to make homes on an unfriendly shore, we owe an immense debt.

Self-confidence. Continued struggles to push back the frontier and make a civilization out of wilderness developed a people who had little fear of danger and little need of the softening luxuries of Europe. Wars with the Indians taught the colonists in America how to fight. Their conflicts with settlers from other lands, however, brought about the greatest change in the British colonists.

Some of America's finest artisans and craftsmen were the early furniture makers. Using tools which they often made themselves, they designed simple, functional, and beautiful furniture, some of which still survives today. Do you recognize any of the tools in the picture?

Europe was a sea voyage of many weeks away, and the colonists had to depend largely on themselves for protection. They found that they could fight well, better in fact than the trained British troops, who were not fitted for fighting in the wilderness. The colonists also learned, through the participation of colonial militia in the French and Indian wars, that they themselves could form an effective, independent fighting unit. This led them to have confidence in their own ability.

Independent Thinking. The colonies were becoming independent in other ways. The first pioneers knew the value of education, and it was not long before schools and colleges were established in the colonies. These made it unnecessary to cross the ocean in order to get an education. Industries, too, flourished, and the colonists came to depend on Great Britain for very few of the necessities of life.

As the years went on, those who had come from Great Britain died. Their places were taken by younger generations, born in America, to whom the mother country was but a name. Only the traders and merchants had any direct contact with Europe, and most of the colonists thought little of the lands across the sea. Less and less did they regard themselves as British, separated from their homeland by a long and dangerous sea voyage. More and more did they come to think of themselves as Americans with homes in the New World and with their own interests, their own industries, and their own problems.

Different Theories of Trade and Development

A Taste of Freedom. Before 1760, the mother country had been so busy with affairs in Europe and with the wars which she was waging throughout the world that she permitted her colonies to do as they pleased. The Navigation Laws, to be sure, required Americans to ship their goods only in British ships and to import goods only from Great Britain. But these laws were not enforced, and a thriving colonial trade had grown up with the Spanish and French possessions in the West Indies. Since the colonists had some voice in the local government, they began to think of themselves as being practically self-governing. They levied their own taxes. Freedom of speech and freedom of the press were taken for granted. In short, the mother country's neglect had given the colonists a taste of freedom, and they found it very sweet.

George III's Determination. Then in the year 1760, George III became king of Great Britain. He was a man of great force and determina-

George III's tyrannical rule and ill-advised programs led to the American Revolution. He became insane in 1811.

English Monarchs	Dates of Reigns	Events in America During Reigns
Henry VII	1485–1509	Explorations of John Cabot
Henry VIII	1509–1547	Explorations of Sebastian Cabot
Edward VI	1547–1553	
Mary I	1553–1558	
Elizabeth I	1558–1603	Drake circumnavigates globe Settlements in Va. by Raleigh
James I	1603–1625	Settlement of Jamestown Voyages of Henry Hudson
Charles I	1625–1649	Charters granted to Md. and Mass.
Interregnum	1649–1660	
Charles II	1660–1685	Charters granted to Carolinas, R.I., and Conn.
James II	1685–1688	Dominion of New England
William and Mary	1688–1702	King William's War
Anne	1702–1714	Queen Anne's War
George I	1714–1727	
George II	1727–1760	King George's War French and Indian War begins
George III	1760–1820	American Revolution

tion, but he had little foresight and was unreasonably stubborn. When he ascended the throne, Britain was just finishing a long and expensive series of wars and was heavily in debt. The mother country, moreover, had acquired new lands in many parts of the world, and this new empire was rather loosely held together. King George set about to find some way of solving his country's problems and strengthening the empire.

Mercantilism. The king and his advisers at last decided on what became known as the *Mercantile Theory of Trade*. This was simply the development of the colonies for the benefit of the mother country. The king argued that Great Britain's distant lands did her little good unless she profited directly from them. All British colonies, therefore, should be required to trade only with Great Britain. They should have no industries that would compete with those of the mother country so that their markets would be opened to all British goods. They should bend their energies toward producing naval stores (pitch, hemp, and masts) and other goods which Britain needed badly. The colonists were well paid for these products. If the Mercantile Theory were put into operation, the king believed that it would strengthen the British empire by drawing the colonies closer to the mother country and increasing their dependence on her.

The King's Proclamation. In 1763, an Indian leader named Pontiac led an uprising against the British settlers. Many settlements were destroyed, and even some of the British forts were captured and their garrisons killed before Pontiac's Indians were defeated.

The king felt that no western settlements would be safe unless they were protected by a large standing army. However, he knew that it would cost a great deal of money to maintain such an army. It would be much better, he thought, if there were no British settlements west of the mountains for the Indians to attack or for the troops to defend. Consequently, in 1763, he issued a proclamation forbidding any British settlers from traveling west of the Appalachian Mountains to establish new homes and settlements.

Many of the colonists were very unhappy about the king's proclamation. They had won the western lands from the French, and they proposed to develop them as rapidly as possible. King or no king, they were going to settle in the west, and many hundreds proceeded to do so in spite of the king's proclamation. All that King George III had gained was a feeling of bitterness towards him by his American colonists. But bitterness did not all stem from the king's proclamation.

Writs of Assistance. In order to collect duties and prevent smuggling, King George III sent warships to the American coast. All vessels, both incoming and outgoing, were stopped and searched for smuggled goods. Trade began to fall off. Even worse, there now appeared in the American seaports officers of the king, armed with general search warrants called *Writs of Assistance*. Nowadays, if an officer wishes to search a house or building, he has to have a warrant, telling which house or building and for what he wishes to search. These

The colonists showed the way they felt about the Stamp Act by such cartoons as this one, encouraging colonists to paste stamps over a skull and crossbones, the symbol of piracy.

Writs of Assistance, however, gave the king's officers the right to break into any house or building and search it for smuggled goods. Many innocent people were roused out of their beds at night and had to stand helplessly by while their houses were ransacked.

Sugar and Stamp Acts. Since the king thought that the colonies existed only for the benefit of the mother country, he was determined that England should receive the greatest possible help from them. He had taxed the people of Great Britain to the limit, and he now proposed to lay a direct tax upon the American colonists. This had never been done before. The colonists were accustomed to being taxed only by their own legislatures. They had come to believe that the British government would not and could not levy additional taxes on them. But they were mistaken because in 1764, Parliament passed the American Revenue Act, sometimes called the *Sugar Act*. It was the first act enacted by Parliament specifically to raise revenue in the colonies. However, it also gave British merchants complete control of the American sugar industry. Thirty years earlier an act had been passed placing a tax on sugar imported from non-British possessions, but the government had been lax in enforcing it. However, nothing indicated to the colonists that this act of 1764 would not be enforced. Furthermore, the tax would be paid only in gold or silver coins.

The payment in "hard money" instead of paper currency was a special hardship. Since the British government had prohibited the issuing of paper money throughout the colonies, a scarcity of all kinds of currency existed.

To raise money by a tax on imports was certainly objectionable to everyone in America. But much more objectionable was the passing of an additional act to raise revenue within the colonies. Therefore, when the Stamp Act was passed by Parliament in 1765, the colonists at once prepared to resist it.

The *Stamp Act* provided that official stamps, ranging in price from a half-penny (one cent) to ten pounds ($50.00), must be placed on all business papers, pamphlets, newspapers, and legal documents in the colonies. This meant added expense to every colonist. When it was learned that part of the money gained from the stamps was to be used to support an army of 10,000 British soldiers in the colonies, the people were even more distressed. They felt that they did not need such an army, nor did they want it. Besides being expensive, many thought that it would merely be another way for the king to deprive them of their liberty.

Looking Back

1. What were the factors that led to the development of "Americanism" among the colonists? Discuss the effect of each of these factors.
2. Explain the Mercantile Theory of Trade. Show how it affected the relationship between Great Britain and her American colonies.
3. Why did the colonists dislike the king's Proclamation of 1763?
4. For what reasons did the king favor and the colonists oppose the Writs of Assistance?
5. Discuss the purposes and terms of both the Sugar and Stamp acts.

2. The Colonists Voice Their Objections

No Taxation Without Representation

Throughout the colonies there was a postwar decline in business and trade. Added taxation and regulation of money appeared to the colonists an attempt to ruin their prosperity. Town meetings were called. Heated arguments took place between those blindly loyal to the crown and those who wanted little or nothing to do with it.

The colonists felt that they had the right to participate in government and to make the laws by which they were to abide. This was one of the reasons they had come to America. Having a hand in their own government was something that had been guaranteed by their charters from the king and by long established practice since the colonies began. All Englishmen, both in England and in America, claimed representation in the lawmaking body as their right. The right to participate in government distinguished Englishmen from Frenchmen or Spaniards who did not have this right. Therefore, the colonists thought it was illegal and unfair for Parliament to pass taxation laws because the colonies were not represented in Parliament and could not be. The cry was: *taxation without representation is tyranny.*

The Parsons' Cause. In Virginia, Patrick Henry, a patriot from the back country, was pleading the colonists' cause. He was then a young and brilliant lawyer. Later he became one of the most important figures in bringing about the separation between the colonies and the mother country.

The case which brought Patrick Henry into prominence was a peculiar

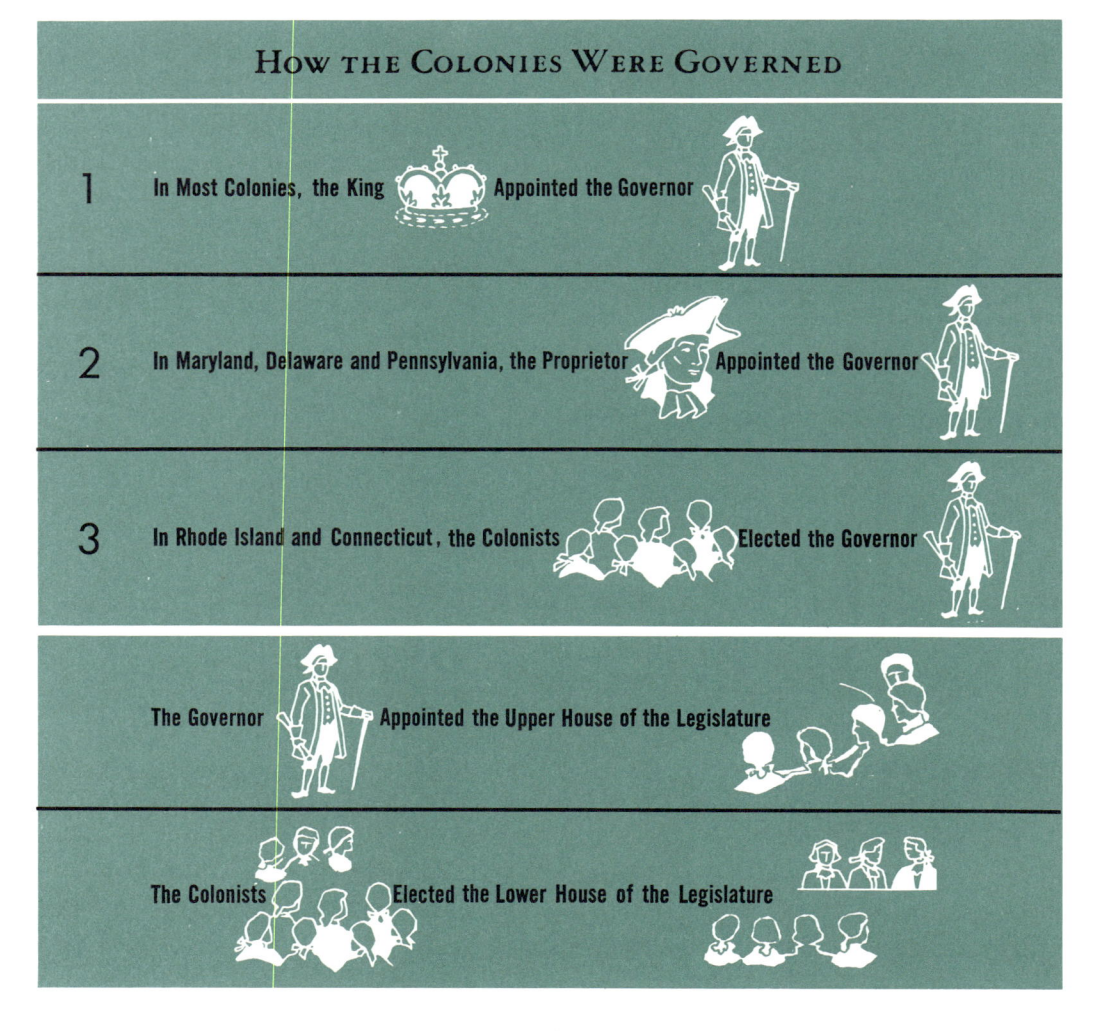

How the Colonies Were Governed

1. In Most Colonies, the King — Appointed the Governor
2. In Maryland, Delaware and Pennsylvania, the Proprietor — Appointed the Governor
3. In Rhode Island and Connecticut, the Colonists — Elected the Governor

The Governor — Appointed the Upper House of the Legislature

The Colonists — Elected the Lower House of the Legislature

one. In the late colonial period, because of the lack of currency, tobacco was often used in place of money in Virginia. During the French and Indian War, the Virginia legislature passed a law stating that the salaries of all clergymen should be paid in tobacco or in money at the rate of two cents for each pound of tobacco due each clergyman. At first this was satisfactory, but later, when the price of tobacco rose from two to six cents a pound, the clergymen felt that they were being cheated when they were given only two cents in place of a pound of tobacco. They said they were receiving only one-third as much money as was due them. News of their distress reached England, and at once the king ordered that the law be discontinued. The clergymen then began to sue for money they felt was owed them for their past services, and Patrick Henry was given the task of seeing that they did not get it.

In this "Parsons' Cause," as it was called, Patrick Henry made his first appearance in court. He attacked vigorously not only the clergymen but also the king for interfering in the affairs of the Virginia Colony. Said Henry, "A king, from being a sovereign of his people, degenerates into a tyrant, and forfeits all right to obedience" when he sets laws aside at the request of a single class of people. Many thought that Henry was too bold in his speech, but others agreed with him. More and more the feeling spread throughout the colonies that the king and the British government should not meddle in their affairs.

Nonimportation Policy. The idea of taking some united action against the policies of the British government came out of the town meetings, especially the ones in New England. One of the ways the colonists decided to act was to refuse to make the merchants in England rich by buying their products. So they decided to do without some of the things they normally bought from England. Some of these things were luxuries: fine clothes, lace, perfume; but others were necessities: guns and iron pots and kettles. The colonists hoped that British merchants, deprived of their rich American market, would complain to Parliament and get the taxes repealed.

One result of this policy of *nonimportation* was that Americans learned to manufacture for themselves things which they had formerly bought from England. Thus, domestic manufacturing in the colonies got a good start before the Revolution. For example, some manufacturing firms which still exist in

Patrick Henry, like Samuel Adams, was an agitator. His inspiring phrases kindled interest in the Revolution.

New England and elsewhere had their start in this period.

It did not take long for the English business world to feel the lack of trade. Protests eventually caused Parliament to repeal some of its most objectionable taxes. In turn, this made the colonists more bold to continue the use of the weapon of nonimportation whenever they thought necessary. Furthermore, the colonists had gained a foothold in manufacturing. The threat that it would become more than a foothold loomed large in the minds of the British legislators. Laws had to be changed or new markets found for British goods. While Britain was trying to decide what to do about the problem, colonial business was prospering.

Sons of Liberty. After the passage of the Stamp Act and other attempts to regulate colonial business, protesting colonists organized secret societies, called *Sons of Liberty.* The purpose of these societies was twofold: to discuss the general state of taxation within the colonies; and to find ways to oppose the hated Stamp Act. With almost uniform opposition to the taxes throughout the colonies, securing memberships was no problem. To join the Sons of Liberty was the patriotic thing to do. Leadership did not come from a single class of people. Some leaders were wealthy, but some were simply craftsmen: carpenters, silversmiths, or farmers.

Unfortunately, the leaders of the Sons of Liberty did not hesitate to lead their groups into violence. Everywhere, by one method or another, the Sons of Liberty tried to force the British stamp agents to resign their positions. Many agents found it necessary to resign. Those who refused to do so found their windows broken or their homes looted. Some agents were hanged in effigy. The supporters of British policies feared this organized opposition, and for good reason.

Stamp Act Congress. The activities of the Sons of Liberty were locally planned and locally carried out. But if opposition were to have any lasting effect, it had to become universal. Delegates from nine of the colonies met in New York to plan further action. This meeting was known as the *Stamp Act Congress.* It drew up a Declaration of Rights stating that, according to the charters granted them by the British rulers, American colonists possessed the same rights as all other British subjects. They felt that since they were not represented in the British Parliament, Parliament had no right to tax them. When the first of the stamps ar-

Of the many different kinds of colonial money, these are only three types issued before and during the Revolution.

Revolutionary patriots pull down a statue of King George III to get lead for bullets.

Naturally, these people violently opposed its enforcement. The colonists were not alone in opposing the Stamp Act. The British merchants, too, were against it, for trade with America was falling off to an alarming extent. The members of Parliament soon heard of the wide opposition to the act. William Pitt, later to become the Prime Minister, declared, "In my opinion, the kingdom has no right to lay a tax on the colonies. . . . I rejoice that America has resisted."

Repeal of the Stamp Act. With pressure from both sides of the Atlantic, Parliament promptly repealed the law, but added a provision stating that the British government had the right to "bind the colonies in all cases whatsoever." This provision was known as the *Declaratory Act*.

Although the colonists did not agree with the British government's theory that they had the right to control and regulate the colonies, they rejoiced

Top: Simple iron bullet mold. Middle: Molten lead ladle. Bottom: Armorer's brass mold for making six bullets at once.

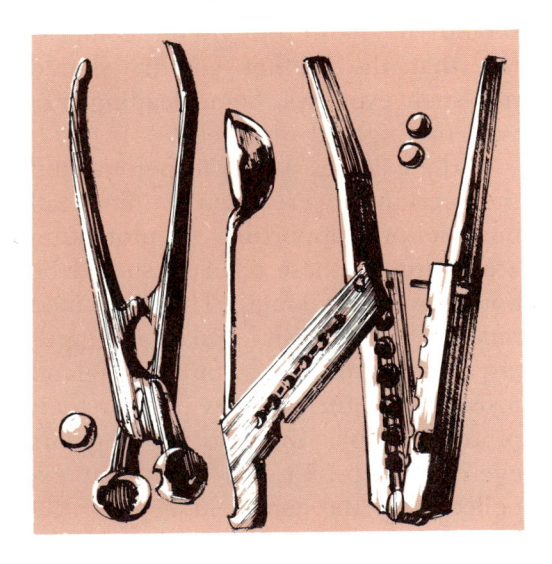

rived from Great Britain, they were promptly burned. Throughout the colonies the people pledged themselves not to buy any more goods from British merchants until Parliament should repeal the Stamp Act.

Widespread Opposition to the Stamp Act. The Stamp Act Congress had the support of the most influential people in the colonies. If the law were enforced it would mean great loss to merchants, bankers, lawyers, and publishers, who could not carry on their businesses without buying many expensive stamps.

over the repeal of the Stamp Act. The New York Assembly voted to show its appreciation in a concrete way. It ordered two leaden statues to be erected, one to honor King George III and one to honor William Pitt, the British statesman who brought about the repeal. Later, when the colonies were fighting for independence from England, the citizens of New York City pulled down the statue of George III, melting it into bullets to be fired at King George's soldiers. The statue of Pitt they did not touch.

Looking Back

1. What was the significance of Patrick Henry's handling of the Parsons' Cause?
2. Describe the "weapon" used by the colonists against unfavorable actions by Parliament. How effective was it?
3. Who were the Sons of Liberty?
4. In your opinion, was the Stamp Act Congress a success or failure? Why?
5. How did the Declaratory Act affect colonial relations with Britain?

3. Britain Tightens Its Control

The Cost of Protection

From the time of the French and Indian War until the American Revolution, a substantial group of English citizens sincerely felt that the mother country had spent too much money protecting the colonies from the Indians and the French. They did not question the fact that protection was necessary. The question was: Who should pay the bill? The colonists felt that the mother country should pay such expenses. Some leading officials in England disagreed.

If the colonies were prosperous, and they certainly were, then the financial burden of supporting a protecting army, argued these officials, should be borne by the colonies. This explained much of the English legislation regarding taxation of the colonies. England insisted that the colonies pay for their protection by the British regulars even after the French had been expelled from the continent.

The colonists believed that this was a move to repress them and to enforce the collecting of duties on imported goods. In earlier years it had been difficult for the British to prevent smuggling and to collect duties. Several times crowds mobbed the king's customs officers in Boston and other cities.

The Boston Massacre. As soon as the British soldiers arrived, quarrels began to occur between them and the colonists. In Boston, two companies of soldiers were quartered in the houses of the town. The people took every opportunity to show their unwelcome guests that they were not wanted. British soldiers on the street, with their blazing red uniforms, were called "Lobsterbacks" and sometimes were pelted with stones by groups of boys.

Serious trouble was bound to come sooner or later. One day in March, 1770, a Boston crowd surrounded a group of soldiers, taunting them and

The "Boston Massacre," as it was called, is shown in this engraving by Paul Revere. Revere's engraving is largely inaccurate since the British soldiers were outnumbered six to one but it was used as evidence to stir up colonial feeling against them. The first man to die was a Boston Negro, Crispus Attucks. He is shown lying face down in the foreground.

throwing snowballs. The exasperated soldiers fired on the crowd, killing four citizens and wounding several others. So bitter was the resentment of the people of Boston at this action that the British soldiers had to be removed for their own safety to an island in the harbor.

Committees of Correspondence. The British government's policy affected not only Massachusetts but all the British colonies in America. Samuel Adams was a member of the Massachusetts legislature who had taken a lively part in causing the repeal of the Stamp Act. He came to realize that the colonies must work together and under his leadership *Committees of Correspondence* were organized. These were groups of men in each colony who made it their business to inform the people of the other colonies, by letter, of everything of public importance that happened. Thus the news of the Boston Massacre traveled throughout all the colonies, greatly increasing the indignation against the British.

The Townshend Acts. The English Parliament passed the *Townshend Acts* which placed a duty on window glass, paper, paint, and tea—four things that the colonists could not do without. The money paid to the British government through these taxes was to be used to support the army, which was already in America, and also to pay governors, judges, and other British officers. If all these men were in Britain's pay, they would be entirely dependent on the government and would have to work for Great Britain's interests.

Like the Stamp Act, the Townshend Acts were vigorously resisted throughout the colonies. Many colonial mer-

> *The Boston Tea Party*
>
> "Last Night 3 Cargoes of Bohea Tea were emptied into the Sea. This Morning a Man of War sails.
>
> This is the most magnificent Movement of all. There is a Dignity, a Majesty, a Sublimity, in this last Effort of the Patriots, that I greatly admire. The People should never rise, without doing something to be remembered—something notable And Striking. This Destruction of the Tea is so bold, so daring, so firm, intrepid and inflexible, and it must have so important Consequences, and so lasting, that I can't but consider it an Epocha in History. . . .
>
> The Question is whether the Destruction of this Tea was necessary? I apprehend that it was absolutely and indispensably so. They could not send it back, the Governor, Admiral and Collector and Comptroller would not suffer it. . . . To let it be landed would be giving up the Principle of Taxation by Parliamentary Authority, against which the Continent have struggled for 10 years. . . ."
>
> —Excerpts from Vol. 2, *Diary and Autobiography of John Adams*, Belknap Press of Harvard University Press

chants refused to import the taxed goods. Others refused to import or use any British goods at all. Such actions were so damaging to Great Britain's trade that it was not long before Parliament repealed the Townshend Acts, leaving only a small tax on tea. This small tax was to show the colonists that, whether they liked it or not, they were still subject to British taxation.

Parliament firmly believed that because most of the Townshend duties had been removed, and because the tax on tea was very low, the Americans would be willing to pay this one remaining tax. Events were to prove that this was wrong. A number of tea ships set out from Great Britain for various American ports, but their reception was far from encouraging. In Charleston, South Carolina, the tea was landed, but was left to spoil, for no one would buy any of it and pay the tax. In New York and Philadelphia, the citizens would not allow the tea to be brought ashore. At Annapolis, the Maryland colonists set fire to the tea ship and destroyed it, together with its cargo.

The Boston Tea Party. The reception of the three Boston tea ships caused a great deal of excitement in Great Britain. When the vessels first arrived in Boston Harbor, the colonists declared that none of the tea should ever come ashore. The governor of the Massachusetts colony declared that the vessels could not leave until the cargo had been landed. Two stubborn adversaries had met, and neither wanted to move. It was plain that something must be done. Samuel Adams gathered together a large number of earnest Patriots in the Old South Meeting

House in Boston. Although they held a long and heated discussion, apparently they disagreed on what to do.

That night, however, a band of citizens dressed as Indians appeared at the water front. They manned small boats, rowed out to the three ships, and climbed aboard. Whooping like Indians, they dragged the boxes of tea up onto the decks, split them open, and dumped almost $100,000 worth of cargo into the harbor. *The Boston Tea Party* was the answer of the people of Boston to the British tax on tea.

The Intolerable Acts. When news of the Boston Tea Party reached Great Britain, the king and his supporters in Parliament were very angry. At once they passed a series of five laws which the colonists called the *Intolerable Acts*. The first of these, the Boston Port Act, closed the port of Boston to all trade until the people would admit that they were wrong and would pay for the destroyed tea. The second act deprived the people of Massachusetts of all voice in their government and placed in control officers appointed by the king. The third, known as the Administration of Justice Act, provided that any British soldier or official accused of any serious crime should be tried in Great Britain, where everything would be in his favor, instead of in the colonies. The fourth act stated that the British government had the right to quarter soldiers in the homes of the colonists. The fifth act deprived the colonists of the territory north of the Ohio River and east of the Mississippi and made this land a part of Canada. The Quebec Act, as this last provision was called, was intended to win the friendship of the French Canadians living in this territory and in Canada. By passing it, Parliament hoped to gain their help in case of serious trouble between Great Britain and her American colonies.

Colonists disguised as Indians sneak aboard a tea ship in Boston harbor. Thus began the "Boston Tea Party."

Carpenter's Hall, Philadelphia, was built in 1770 for the Carpenter's Guild. The first Continental Congress met there in 1774.

The reaction of the colonists was unmistakable. Patrick Henry, addressing the members of the Virginia legislature, expressed the feeling of thousands of patriots when he cried out: "Is life so dear, or peace so sweet, as to be purchased at the price of chains and slavery? Forbid it, Almighty God! I know not what course others may take, but, as for me, give me liberty or give me death!"

The First Continental Congress. Representatives of each of the colonies met at Philadelphia in September, 1774, to consider what was to be done. This meeting was the *First Continental Congress*. After discussing the situation, the members issued a Declaration of Rights and Grievances. In it they demanded the right to levy all taxes and petitioned the king to relieve their wrongs. In the different colonies, groups were organized whose members were to stop the buying or using of British goods until the unjust laws of Parliament had been repealed.

The declaration of the Continental Congress was ignored by the British government. The next time that a Continental Congress was called, it was for the purpose of assuming the authority of governing the colonies and organizing an army to resist the British.

Looking Back

1. In what ways did economic needs and pressures affect British legislation concerning the colonies at this time?
2. How did the Committees of Correspondence help unite the colonies?
3. What was the purpose of the Townshend Acts? What was their fate?
4. By what means did the Intolerable Acts punish the colonists and seek to strengthen the power of the British government?
5. What steps were taken by the First Continental Congress to meet its problems?

The Chapter in Perspective

Who Are These People?

George III	Patrick Henry
Pontiac	Pitt
Samuel Adams	Crispus Attucks

What Do These Dates and Terms Mean?

Navigation Laws	Declaratory Act
mercantilism	Boston Massacre
Parsons' Cause	Sons of Liberty

1764
1765
Quebec Act
Boston Tea Party
Intolerable Acts
Townshend Acts
Writs of Assistance
Stamp Act Congress
Proclamation of 1763
Declaration of Rights
First Continental Congress
Committees of Correspondence
Declaration of Rights and Grievances

1774
direct tax
Sugar Act
Stamp Act

Questions for Study

1. Account for the official change of attitude of Britain toward her American colonies after 1763.
2. How did Britain's lax enforcement of previous laws regulating colonial commerce create difficulties after 1763?
3. What arguments did the British use to justify the proclamation of 1763?
4. How did the Writs of Assistance differ from search warrants used today?
5. What were the grounds on which the colonists based their claim of "no taxation without representation"?
6. As an English citizen living in London, how would you have looked upon the Stamp Act?
7. By what actions did the colonists demonstrate a greater sense of unity from 1763 to 1774?
8. Do you feel that the different interests and views of England and the colonies could have been reconciled in 1774? If not, why? If yes, how?
9. How did the colonial coastline and available harbors favor smuggling by traders in violation of British law?
10. Which colonies were most affected by the proclamation of 1763 and the Quebec Act of 1774? Why?

Place Yourself in History

The First Continental Congress in its Declaration to England, passed the following, referring to the colonists:

> Resolved,
> That they are entitled to life, liberty and property, and they have never ceded to any sovereign power whatever, a right to dispose of either without their consent.
> That our ancestors who first settled these colonies, were at the time of their emigration from their mother country, entitled to all—the rights, liberties, and immunities of free and natural-born subjects, within the realm of England.
> That the foundation of English liberty, and of all free government, is a right in the people to participate in their legislative council....

How would you as a colonist have reacted to this declaration? Would you have supported it or condemned it as an inflamatory statement? What arguments could be made for or against the statements in the declaration in both England and the colonies?

6

Americans Turn to Revolution

When little David strode forth to fight mighty Goliath, the thousands of men in two great armies gasped in astonishment. Likewise, when an infant nation without a navy, an army, or even a government accepted the challenge of mighty Britain to do battle, the whole world wondered at its daring.

To understand how the American Revolution came about, we must realize that strained relations had existed between England and her colonies for several decades prior to the actual conflict. In fact, no less an authority than John Adams, Revolutionary leader and second President of the United States, wrote in 1818: "The Revolution was effected before the war commenced. The Revolution was in the minds and hearts of the people . . . This radical change in the principles, opinions, sentiments, and affections of the people was the real American Revolution."

1. Armed Resistance Begins

The hostile attitudes on both sides before 1775 convinced British and Americans alike that war would come sooner or later. It is probable that extremists on both sides were looking for some excuse to fight.

Advantages of the British

When it became evident that war between Great Britain and her American colonies was coming, men on both sides of the Atlantic began seriously considering what the outcome might be. At first glance, Britain seemed to have enormous advantages. First of all, the British had great wealth at their command with which to carry on a long war. The colonists, for their part, had comparatively little gold or silver.

The British, moreover, had well-organized armies and officers equal to those of any nation. At first the colonists had no army and few leaders capable of organizing and training men. Then, too, the British had factories for making guns, swords, and bayonets, as well as great shipyards for the building of warships. America, on the other hand, was not equipped to manufacture implements of war; nor did she possess cannon to arm her warships. Finally, Great Britain had the strongest navy in the world, and many ships were available to carry troops and supplies across the ocean and up and down the coast. The Americans had not a single armed naval vessel.

Other factors, too, favored the British. The population of the colonies in 1774 was only about three million. Of these, almost a third were British sympathizers, known either as *Loyalists* or *Tories*, who refused to fight against the mother country. Though the Loyalists were spread throughout the Middle and Southern Colonies, they were especially strong in New York. The colonies, moreover, were united only by the Continental Congress, which had so few powers that it could scarcely be called a government.

Advantages of the Americans

There were a few factors, however, that favored the colonists. The fight-

English warships stand off the American coast. Perhaps the greatest advantage the British held was their naval superiority. Experienced officers and sailors and well-fitted, well-armed ships like these made Britain's navy practically invincible.

THE THIRTEEN COLONIES
(1775)

ing would be in their own land, a land they knew well, whereas the British would have to find their way through unfamiliar territory. The colonists were strong, hardy men, many of whom lived the toughening life of pioneers and were in fine condition to withstand the hardships of war. Their experiences in the recent French and Indian War and in fighting Indians had schooled them in wilderness warfare. They were, therefore, prepared to give any army a fight worth remembering.

Then, too, the British were faced with the problem of transporting troops and supplies over three thousand miles of ocean. This British disadvantage could be expected to work to the benefit of the Americans. Nor were the British at home united in their feelings regarding the war. The Whigs, under the leadership of such great men as William Pitt and Edmund Burke, did much to oppose the moves of the king's followers, who were known as the Tories. This disagreement at home was an added handicap to the British. Later, when Spain, France, and the Netherlands declared war against Great Britain, American prospects brightened considerably.

Lexington and Concord

Gage's Plan. General Gage, commander of the British forces in Boston and newly appointed governor of Massachusetts, decided upon a plan to check further resistance to the authority of the crown. A Tory informant had reported that the Patriots were collecting military supplies at Con-

When the monument standing next to Concord Bridge, seen here, was dedicated in 1837, Ralph Waldo Emerson immortalized it thus:
"By the rude bridge that arched the flood,
"Their flag to April's breeze unfurled
"Here once the embattled farmers stood
"And fired the shot heard round the world."

cord, twenty-two miles northeast of Boston. General Gage was determined to destroy or capture these supplies. He also learned that two rebel leaders, Samuel Adams and John Hancock, were hiding in nearby Lexington for fear that the British authorities might prevent their attending the Continental Congress soon to meet in Philadelphia. Here, thought General Gage, was his chance to try out his plan to subdue Massachusetts by capturing the supplies and the rebel leaders. To accomplish this, it was necessary that the British maintain utmost secrecy. During the night, therefore, six hundred British soldiers left Boston to cross the Charles River to Cambridge.

The steeple of "Old North Church" in Boston glowed with its message to Paul Revere and Charles Dawes.

Patriot Preparations. While the British redcoats were secretly planning the march to Lexington and Concord, the Patriots were observing their every movement and were eavesdropping on military conversations wherever possible. Since many soldiers were lodged in private homes, such opportunities were not infrequent. Suspecting General Gage's intentions, the people of Boston made careful preparations for meeting any British move toward Concord. Signal lanterns were made ready in the tower of Old North Church. Should the redcoats travel by sea, two lanterns would be hung in the steeple; one lantern meant that the troop movement would be by land. Across the bay in Charlestown, the Patriots, when they saw the signal, could in turn carry the alarm to the surrounding countryside.

Paul Revere and Charles Dawes were selected to carry the warning rapidly and by separate routes so that Samuel Adams and John Hancock would have ample opportunity to flee to safety. When the messengers saw the two lanterns hung in the steeple, they galloped off on their swift horses to spread the alarm. In response to their shouted warnings, they gathered a growing army of colonial Patriots who had hastily drawn on their clothes and seized their guns.

The Shots "Heard 'Round the World." Before dawn, the British arrived in Lexington. But much to their surprise, the Patriots were on hand to greet them. Captain Parker, the American leader at Lexington, calmly informed his men: "Stand your ground! Don't fire unless fired upon! But if they want to have a war, let it begin

THE BIRTH OF THE REVOLUTION (1775-1776)

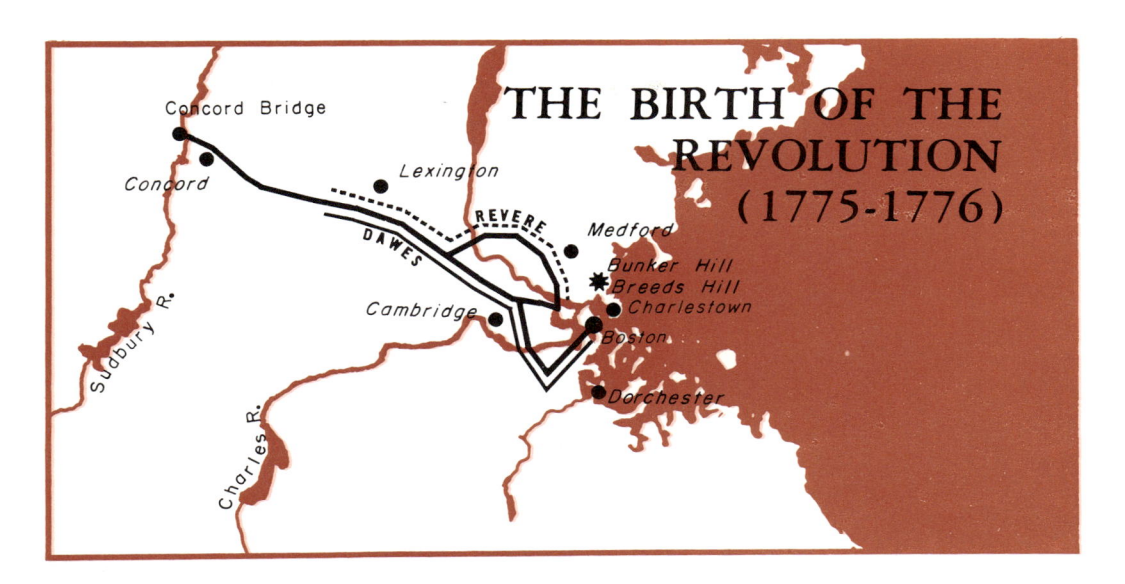

here!" Although the officers on both sides tried to avoid any shooting, a British soldier fired into the group of Patriots. In the skirmish that followed, eight Americans were killed.

From Lexington, the British troops proceeded to Concord. There isolated groups of *minutemen*, so-called because of their readiness for duty at a moment's notice, moved through the streets, between houses, and behind trees. Additional forces kept arriving from the surrounding villages and countryside. The redcoats underestimated both the capable leadership of the Patriots and the determined efforts of the entire province to preserve colonial rights.

At Lexington the Patriots, due to advance warning, had foiled the attempt to capture Adams and Hancock. Now at Concord the British searched in vain for the military supplies. The previous day the Patriots had hidden their stores against just such a search. Musket balls and cartridges had been carefully hidden in barrels in attics and covered with feathers. Gunpowder had been stored in the woods, and muskets and light cannon were buried between the furrows of plowed fields.

Rout of Redcoats. After looting and burning many buildings, the redcoats began their long trek back to Boston. The return, however, was not to be made in peace. From behind fences and walls, trees and bushes, hundreds of minutemen poured shots upon the retreating army. One after another, the redcoats fell, often without seeing any enemy at whom to fire. The British retreat became a rout.

News of the events at Lexington and Concord soon spread to the other colonies. Such an attack by British soldiers was proof that Britain was determined to subject them to tyranny. The lengthy debate had turned to open warfare, and the conflict was to last for eight long years.

The Second Continental Congress

In May, 1775, the month following the clash at Lexington and Concord, the *Second Continental Congress* met

(Above) As the British retreated from Lexington and Concord, the Patriots poured a withering rain of bullets into their column. (Below) The second Continental Congress convened in Independence Hall, Philadelphia. Why was Philadelphia a convenient meeting place?

at Independence Hall, Philadelphia. Not all of the delegates were ready for a complete break with the mother country, but desire for independence was growing. Some hoped for one more appeal to the king for redress of colonial grievances. In reply John Adams asked how wrongs could be righted when Massachusetts blood had been shed and Patriots killed.

Washington Takes Command. Congress met the immediate problem on June 15 by taking responsibility for the troops assembled around Boston. None of the Patriots wanted England to think that only the New England area was discontented. The delegates hoped to present a united front by choosing a commander-in-chief who was not a New Englander. John Adams, therefore, proposed the nomination of George Washington, who lived in Virginia. After considerable debate, Washington was unanimously chosen to command the Patriot forces. The next day he formally accepted the appointment without salary. Four major generals were selected to assist Washington.

A Declaration and a Proclamation. Congress continued in session as the voice of the colonies. Seeking foreign alliances, it invited Canada to join the American cause, while it began to court European nations for the same purpose. At home, it established a system of currency. In defense of the decision to take up arms against the mother country, Congress issued a "Declaration of Causes for Taking up Arms." The king replied by issuing a "Proclamation for Suppressing Rebellion and Sedition."

Looking Back

1. Discuss the advantages held by the British and those held by the colonists as war threatened.
2. What were Gage's goals in Lexington and Concord? Were they achieved?
3. What was the significance of the action at Lexington and Concord?
4. How did the delegates to the Second Continental Congress show that colonial sentiment was divided?
5. To what sources did the colonists turn for possible assistance?

2. Resistance Turns to Rebellion

It was at Lexington that Captain Parker had said, ". . . if they want to have a war, let it begin here." That statement seemed to express the sentiment of all New England. The hated redcoats had to be removed by whatever method necessary. After the skirmishes at Lexington and Concord, the Massachusetts Colony had authorized the raising of an army of 13,600 men. Other New England colonies promised an additional 9500 to be sent to Cambridge, a few miles from Boston.

Seeing the Patriot army assembling, the British also prepared for action. The redcoats had not been in Boston long before they realized how unwelcome they were and how difficult it would be to avoid war. Now both sides were resigned to what appeared to all to be an unavoidable conflict.

Patriot Victory at Ticonderoga

If the colonists were to carry on a war, they needed better arms and equipment. The minutemen at Lexington and Concord had opposed British muskets with nothing but their own hunting rifles. They also would need cannon and powder. An enterprising Vermont leader named Ethan Allen soon supplied these.

High above the waters of Lake Champlain stood powerful Fort Ticonderoga, which the British had taken from the French. Here were many cannon and great stores of muskets and powder, guarded by a garrison consisting of only forty-two men. Before dawn on a May day in 1775, Ethan Allen with eighty-three minutemen—the "Green Mountain Boys"—approached the fort. The sentinel was overcome before giving the alarm, and through the gate poured the Americans. Rousing the sleepy British commander, Allen demanded immediate and unconditional surrender of the fort. The commander had to give in, and the fort was captured without a battle. Cannon, powder, muskets, and shot from Fort Ticonderoga gave the Patriots such equipment as they had never had before.

Bunker Hill — A Costly British Victory

The British in Boston, meanwhile, had all that they wanted of fighting with the Massachusetts minutemen. They remained in the town where they were safe, while a great army of Americans gathered about them. The English general, Gage, bided his time and did nothing until at last reinforcements arrived, giving him an army of eight thousand men. With such a force, thought Gage, he would soon defeat the untrained colonial army.

Americans on Breed's Hill. Gage for a long time had wanted to fortify Bunker Hill, which stood across the river in Charlestown and overlooked the city of Boston. The general found it difficult, however, to catch the Americans napping. On the morning of June 17, 1775, he awoke to learn that the Americans had already entrenched themselves on the summit of Breed's Hill nearby. Clearly, the Americans must be driven from their position, or the British would shortly be forced out of Boston. General Howe was sent with a force of three thousand soldiers to capture the entrenchment.

On the top of the hill were fifteen hundred Americans. The British soldiers approaching the hill made tempting targets, and a few woodsmen in the

Men and animals bringing the cannons from Ticonderoga to Boston found it a difficult task in mid-winter.

This boulder on the village green at Lexington, Massachusetts, marks the spot where the line of Minutemen stood April 19, 1775. Captain Parker's words, "If they mean to have a war, let it begin here," were prophetic. This was indeed the first skirmish in the American Revolution.

trenches raised their rifles and brought down soldiers in the ranks. Then came the order, "Don't fire until you see the whites of their eyes," and in grim silence the minutemen waited for the attack.

The Battle of "Bunker Hill." Not until the British soldiers were close upon them did the Americans fire. When they did, their volley ripped the British ranks wide open and sent the redcoats hurrying down the hill, leaving many dead and dying on its slope.

Hastily reforming their lines, the redcoats charged back up the hill. Again the Americans withheld their fire until the British were so close that they could not miss. Again a deadly volley rang out, and once more the seasoned British soldiers were forced back.

Now the British commander, General Howe, gathered his force and led the redcoats up the hill himself. But this time no withering volley greeted him. The American ammunition was gone, and the remaining British swarmed in triumph over the top of the hill. The defenders were driven back, battling gamely to the last with rocks and clubs and the butt ends of their rifles. It was a British victory, but a very costly one, for more than a thousand English lay dead upon the hill slopes. Though fought on the slopes of Breed's Hill, the battle was misnamed the Battle of Bunker Hill.

American Occupation of Boston

Soon after the Battle of Bunker Hill, George Washington formally took command of the American army in the town of Cambridge. Then, with his forces watching the city, he waited for the arrival of the cannon that he knew were being brought from Ticonderoga.

Early in March, 1776, fifty pieces of artillery arrived, and Washington proceeded to occupy Dorchester Heights, overlooking the city of Boston. Firmly entrenched there, he gave General Howe, who had succeeded Gage in charge of the forces in Boston, the choice of leaving the city at once or having it battered to pieces about him. The rows of American guns on Dorchester Heights looked dangerous to General Howe, and he promptly ordered his men aboard their ships and departed for Nova Scotia.

The Invasion of Canada

In the meantime, two detachments of American soldiers, under Richard Montgomery and Benedict Arnold, invaded Canada. It was a long and bitter winter, and food was scarce. Long before the Patriots reached their destination, they were forced to eat their moccasins (which were made from animal skin) to keep alive! Nevertheless, they carried on in spite of all obstacles. Montgomery captured Montreal, while Arnold's little colonial army was still struggling toward Quebec.

Failure at Quebec. When at last the two joined their pitiful forces near Quebec, the strongest English fortress in America, they must have known that it would be impossible for them to take the fort. But faced with no chance of winning, the two leaders led an attack upon the walls. Montgomery fell dead, and Arnold was wounded. The British drove the American forces back and recaptured Montreal. A brave invasion attempt had failed.

An Invasion Foiled. With the coming of spring, the British were quick to follow up the American defeat in Canada. Arnold's retreating forces were followed south through the Champlain Valley by a strong British force. A fleet of British warships was launched on Lake Champlain for use in transporting the redcoats. Hastily, Benedict Arnold built a tiny fleet of American ships and set out to check the British advance. The fleets met near Valcour (VAL'koor) Island in Lake Champlain. In the fierce battle which followed, Arnold's ships were beaten and scattered, but the British fleet was also badly damaged.

It was now October, 1776, and winter was coming on. There was little time to repair the fleet and continue the invasion. Benedict Arnold, though beaten in battle, had foiled the British.

These cannons, at Fort Niagara in New York State, are typical of the ones used in the Revolution.

ACTION IN CANADA AND TICONDEROGA DURING THE REVOLUTION

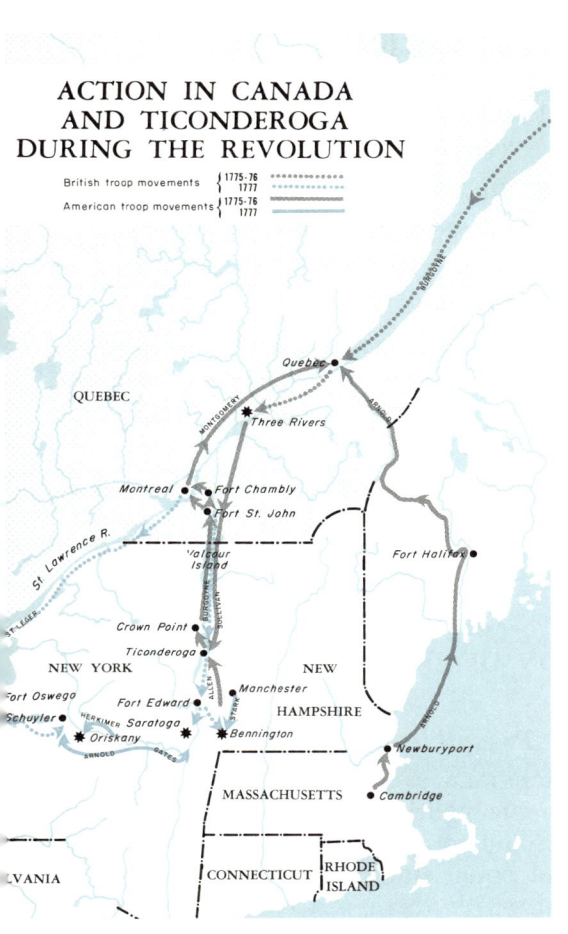

Where were most American movements directed in 1775-76? Were they successful?

The Widening Rift

Three developments, following close upon each other, drove the Americans still farther from a settlement with the British government.

Common Sense. One of these developments was the publishing of a pamphlet in Philadelphia with the thought-provoking name of *Common Sense*. The author, Thomas Paine, was an Englishman who had come to live in America. Paine boldly declared that the time for a final separation from Great Britain had arrived and that Americans must fight for their liberty. Widely read throughout the colonies, *Common Sense* did much to swing public opinion in favor of a fight to the finish.

Hessian Troops. The king's use of foreign troops was a second move destined to drive the colonies farther away from the mother country. Because the war was not popular in Great Britain, volunteers were slow in joining the ranks. At last the king was forced to hire thirty thousand soldiers from the Prince of Hesse, ruler of a German province. The use of the Hessians was an unfortunate blunder. The colonists no longer felt that they were fighting against their relatives in Great Britain but rather against the king and his hired foreign troops. Many who had previously opposed the war now joined in the fighting.

Independence Declared. The decisive event which widened the rift between the mother country and the colonies was the action taken by the Second Continental Congress. As the first year of fighting drew to a close, the feeling that the colonies should break definitely and finally from the mother country found increasing favor. In June, 1776, Richard Henry Lee of Virginia offered a resolution in the Continental Congress that "These United States are, and of right ought to be, free and independent states." John Adams seconded the resolution. A committee, headed by Thomas Jefferson of Virginia, was at once appointed to draw up a declaration of independence.

On the fourth day of July, 1776, the Continental Congress formally adopted the *Declaration of Independence*. The members present signed their names to the document, each fully aware that in so doing he was signing his own death warrant should the war for independence fail. With the signing of the Declaration of Independence, the British colonies in America ceased to exist as the property of Great Britain.

The Declaration itself follows a logical organization and consists of four parts: the preamble, a statement of the reasons for issuing the Declaration, a list of charges directed against King George III, and the actual Declaration of Independence.

Looking Back

1. In what ways did the victory at Ticonderoga aid the colonists?
2. Why was the defeat at Bunker Hill considered a victory by the colonists?
3. Account for the American victory at Boston.
4. How did the American attempt to invade Canada and the British attempt to invade the colonies from the north end in a stalemate?
5. In what way did Thomas Paine contribute to the American cause?

DECLARATION OF INDEPENDENCE

Preamble

When, in the course of human events, it becomes necessary for one people to dissolve the political bands which have connected them with another, and to assume among the powers of the earth the separate and equal station to which the laws of nature and of nature's God entitle them, a decent respect to the opinions of mankind requires that they should declare the causes which impel them to the separation.

Reasons for Declaration

We held these truths to be self-evident: That all men are created equal; that they are endowed by their Creator with certain unalienable rights; that among these are life, liberty, and the pursuit of happiness; that, to secure these rights, governments are instituted among men, deriving their just powers from the consent of the governed; that, whenever any form of government becomes destructive of these ends, it is the right of the people to alter or to abolish it, and to institute a new government, laying its foundation on such principles, and organizing its powers in such form, as to them shall seem most likely to effect their safety and happiness. Prudence, indeed, will dictate that governments long established should not be changed for light and transient causes; and, accordingly, all experience hath shown that mankind are more disposed to suffer, while evils are sufferable, than to right themselves by abolishing the forms to which they are accustomed. But when a long train of abuses and usurpations, pursuing invariably the same object, evinces a design to reduce them under absolute despotism, it is their right, it is their duty, to throw off such government, and to provide new guards for their future security. Such has been the patient sufferance of these colonies; and such is now the necessity which constrains them to alter their former systems of government. The history of the present king of Great Britain is a history of repeated injuries and usurpations, all having in direct object the establishment of an absolute tyranny over these states. To prove this, let facts be submitted to a candid world.

Charges Against the King

1. He has refused his assent to laws, the most wholesome and necessary for the public good.

2. He has forbidden his governors to pass laws of immediate and pressing importance, unless suspended in their operation till his assent should be obtained; and, when so suspended, he has utterly neglected to attend to them.

3. He has refused to pass other laws for the accommodation of large districts of people unless those people would relinquish the right of representation in the legislature—a right inestimable to them, and formidable to tyrants only.

4. He has called together legislative bodies at places unusual, uncomfortable, and distant from the depository of their public records, for the sole purpose of fatiguing them into compliance with his measures.

5. He has dissolved representative houses repeatedly for opposing, with manly firmness, his invasions on the rights of the people.

6. He has refused for a long time, after such dissolutions, to cause others to be elected; whereby the legislative powers, incapable of annihilation, have returned to the people at large for their exercise; the state, remaining, in the meantime, exposed to all the dangers of invasions from without and convulsions within.

7. He has endeavored to prevent the population of these states; for that purpose obstructing the laws for naturalization of foreigners; refusing to pass others to encourage their migration hither, and raising the conditions of new appropriations of lands.

8. He has obstructed the administration of justice by refusing his assent to laws for establishing judiciary powers.

9. He has made judges dependent on his will alone for the tenure of their offices and the amount and payment of their salaries.

10. He has erected a multitude of new offices, and sent hither swarms of officers to harass our people and eat out their substance.

11. He has kept among us, in times of peace, standing armies, without the consent of our legislatures.

12. He has affected to render the military independent of, and superior to, the civil power.

13. He has combined with others to subject us to a jurisdiction foreign to our Constitution and unacknowledged by our laws, giving his assent to their acts of pretended legislation:
    a. For quartering large bodies of armed troops among us.
    b. For protecting them, by a mock trial, from punishment for any murders which they should commit on the inhabitants of these states.
    c. For cutting off our trade with all parts of the world.
    d. For imposing taxes on us without our consent.
    e. For depriving us, in many cases, of the benefits of trial by jury.
    f. For transporting us beyond seas to be tried for pretended offenses.
    g. For abolishing the free system of English laws in a neighboring province, establishing therein an arbitrary government, and enlarging its boundaries so as to render it at once an example and fit instrument for introducing the same absolute rule into these colonies.
    h. For taking away our charters, abolishing our most valuable laws, and altering fundamentally the forms of our governments.
    i. For suspending our own legislature and declaring themselves invested with power to legislate for us in all cases whatsoever.

14. He has abdicated government here by declaring us out of his protection, and waging war against us.

15. He has plundered our seas, ravaged our coasts, burnt our towns, and destroyed the lives of our people.

16. He is at this time transporting large armies of foreign mercenaries to complete the works of death, desolation, and tyranny, already begun with circumstances of cruelty

and perfidy scarcely parallelled in the most barbarous ages, and totally unworthy the head of a civilized nation.

17. He has constrained our fellow-citizens, taken captive on the high seas, to bear arms against their country, to become the executioners of their friends and brethren, or to fall themselves by their hands.

18. He has excited domestic insurrections amongst us, and has endeavored to bring on the inhabitants of our frontiers the merciless Indian savages, whose known rule of warfare is an undistinguished destruction of all ages, sexes, and conditions.

In every stage of these oppressions we have petitioned for redress in the most humble terms; our repeated petitions have been answered only by repeated injury. A prince, whose character is thus marked by every act which may define a tyrant, is unfit to be the ruler of a free people.

Nor have we been wanting in our attentions to our British brethren. We have warned them, from time to time, of attempts by their legislature to extend an unwarrantable jurisdiction over us. We have reminded them of the circumstances of our emigration and settlement here. We have appealed to their native justice and magnanimity, and we have conjured them by the ties of our common kindred to disavow these usurpations, which would inevitably interrupt our connections and correspondence. They, too, have been deaf to the voice of justice and of consanguinity. We must, therefore, acquiesce in the necessity which denounces our separation, and hold them, as we hold the rest of mankind—enemies in war; in peace, friends.

Statement of Separation

We, therefore, the representatives of the United States of America, in general Congress assembled, appealing to the Supreme Judge of the world for the rectitude of our intentions, do, in the name and by the authority of the good people of these colonies, solemnly publish and declare that these united colonies are, and of right ought to be, free and independent states, that they are absolved from all allegiance to the British crown, and that all political connection between them and the state of Great Britain is, and ought to be, totally dissolved; and that as free and independent states, they have full power to levy war, conclude peace, contract alliances, establish commerce, and do all other acts and things which independent states may of right do. And for the support of this Declaration, with a firm reliance on the protection of Divine Providence, we mutually pledge to each other our lives, our fortunes, and our sacred honor.

Signers of the Declaration

The foregoing declaration was, by order of Congress, engrossed and signed by the following members:

John Hancock

NEW HAMPSHIRE
Josiah Bartlett
William Whipple
Matthew Thornton

MASSACHUSETTS
Samuel Adams
John Adams
Robert Treat Paine
Elbridge Gerry

RHODE ISLAND
Stephen Hopkins
William Ellery

CONNECTICUT
Roger Sherman
Samuel Huntington
William Williams
Oliver Wolcott

NEW YORK
William Floyd
Philip Livingston
Francis Lewis
Lewis Morris

NEW JERSEY
Richard Stockton
John Witherspoon
Francis Hopkinson
John Hart
Abraham Clark

PENNSYLVANIA
Robert Morris
Benjamin Rush
Benjamin Franklin
John Morton
George Clymer
James Smith
George Taylor
James Wilson
George Ross

DELAWARE
Caesar Rodney
George Read
Thomas McKean

MARYLAND
Samuel Chase
William Paca
Thomas Stone
Charles Carroll
of Carrollton

VIRGINIA
George Wythe
Richard Henry Lee
Thomas Jefferson
Benjamin Harrison
Thomas Nelson, Jun.
Francis Lightfoot Lee
Carter Braxton

NORTH CAROLINA
William Hooper
Joseph Hewes
John Penn

SOUTH CAROLINA
Edward Rutledge
Thomas Heyward, Jun.
Thomas Lynch, Jun.
Arthur Middleton

GEORGIA
Button Gwinnett
Lyman Hall
George Walton

3. England Carries the War to the Middle Colonies

British Strategy

The British brought the war into the Middle Colonies and expended their greatest efforts there for several reasons. One significant reason was the presence of a large Loyalist population in New York and Pennsylvania. Loyalists could be counted on to aid the British and to spy on the movements of Washington's army. Furthermore, there were many Quakers who for religious reasons would not fight for either side. In New England, overwhelming anti-British sentiment had hindered every plan the king's soldiers

CAMPAIGNS IN THE MIDDLE COLONIES

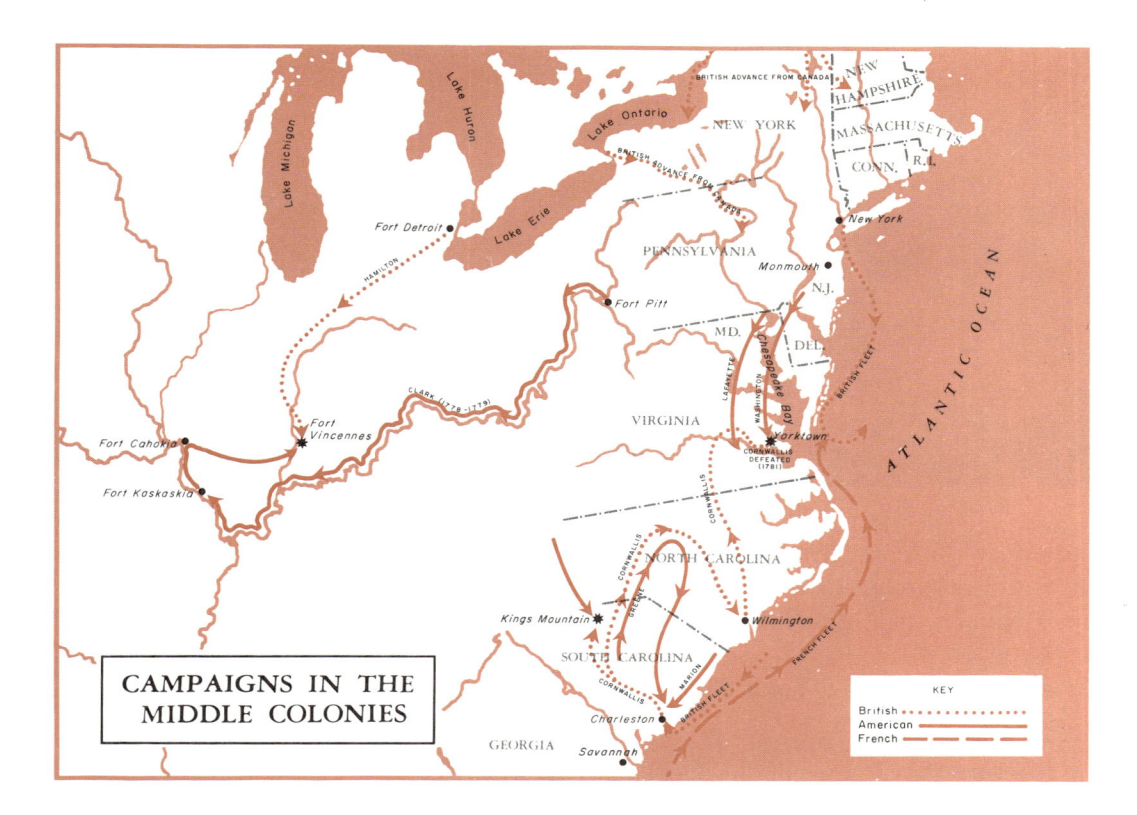

had attempted. Clearly the situation would be different in the Middle Colonies.

Importance of "Bread Colonies." Assuredly the people of the Middle Colonies were more friendly to the British. But there was another advantage of great importance to an army fighting several thousand miles away from its base of supplies. The "Bread Colonies," true to their name, would provide much-needed food supplies.

In many ways New York, Pennsylvania, New Jersey, and Delaware were the key colonies for the British. Their abundance of food was, of course, one reason. Another was the very excellent shipping facilities these colonies offered. The British had a choice of several ports to use for landing armies, as bases for naval operations, and as centers for importing supplies from England. Still another factor contributing to the strategic military importance of these colonies was their geographical position. An army occupying them could split the forces of an opposing army holding both the Northern and the Southern Colonies. Should the British maintain control of this vital section of America, the colonists would have no hope of final victory.

"Divide and Conquer." To the government in London, the plan to "divide and conquer" seemed, on paper, to be completely workable. With New York and Philadelphia in British hands, the ports closed to colonial trade, the Loyalists actively employed in aiding the king's troops, and vital food supplies cut off from the colonists, the war could not last long. What was not evident on paper was the tremendous will to fight of the

This is the first schoolhouse in which Nathan Hale ever taught. During the Revolution, Hale was sent by Washington to spy on the British lines. Posing as a teacher, he was apprehended and hanged. On the gallows Hale said, "I only regret that I have but one life to give for my country."

Connecticut Development Commission

American forces. British authorities also underestimated the "Old Fox," as they were to call Washington.

The Attack on New York City

Soon after the capture of Boston and before the signing of the Declaration of Independence, George Washington led his army to New York City. Nearby he built two forts, Fort Washington and Fort Lee, to keep the British fleet from sailing up the Hudson River.

General Howe, when he returned from Nova Scotia, landed on Long Island to find an army of nine thousand Americans entrenched on Brooklyn Heights. A small detachment of Americans which advanced to meet him was decisively defeated. It seemed certain that the American position on Brooklyn Heights would soon be taken.

But here General Howe made a serious mistake, for he postponed the capture of the Americans until the next day. This gave the colonists just the chance they needed. Under cover of fog and darkness, Washington succeeded in rescuing his army and transporting it across the river into New York City. When the British stormed Brooklyn Heights the next day, there were no defenders left to be captured.

Just as Washington had forced General Gage to abandon Boston, so General Howe now forced Washington to abandon New York.

Lee's Disobedience. Northward marched Washington and his men up the east bank of the Hudson River. Dividing his army, he left a small detachment under General Charles Lee, a former British officer, and crossed the river to Stony Point, which he fortified. Meanwhile, Lord Cornwallis, one of the British generals, was leading his forces north along the river. Both Fort Washington and Fort Lee fell before him, and it became evident that Washington's little army could not stop him. Knowing that he would need every American soldier he could get, Washington ordered Lee's forces to cross the river and join him. Lee, however, hoping to get command of the army himself, disobeyed Washington's instructions.

Washington's Retreat Across New Jersey. Without Lee's troops, Washington's only hope lay in flight, and he set out to the southwest through New Jersey toward Philadelphia. After him came Cornwallis, with his redcoats. Had Cornwallis been able to catch up with Washington during this retreat, the war would certainly have ended, but Washington was too skillful a commander to let this happen. Trees were felled across the road by the American army, bridges were burned, crops and supplies were destroyed, and everything possible was done to hamper the advance of the redcoats. Nevertheless, there were times when the front ranks of the British were less than a mile behind the fleeing Americans. It was not until Washington reached the Delaware River and crossed it with his army, taking or destroying every boat for miles up and down the stream, that the British were finally halted. Here, in December weather, Washington camped and planned his next move.

Washington's disobedient officer, General Lee, chose this time to lead his troops across the Hudson and into New Jersey. Leaving them to camp in the open, Lee took up his headquarters at a tavern some miles away. While he was there, a squad of British soldiers burst in upon him and captured him. His troops, however, pushed on without him, and at last joined Washington's forces.

American Victories at Trenton and Princeton

Washington was not a man to be satisfied by merely keeping out of the clutches of the enemy. Although his forces were greatly outnumbered and poorly trained, he determined to strike a decisive blow at Cornwallis' troops. The moves he made during the days which followed his crossing of the Delaware River have been described as

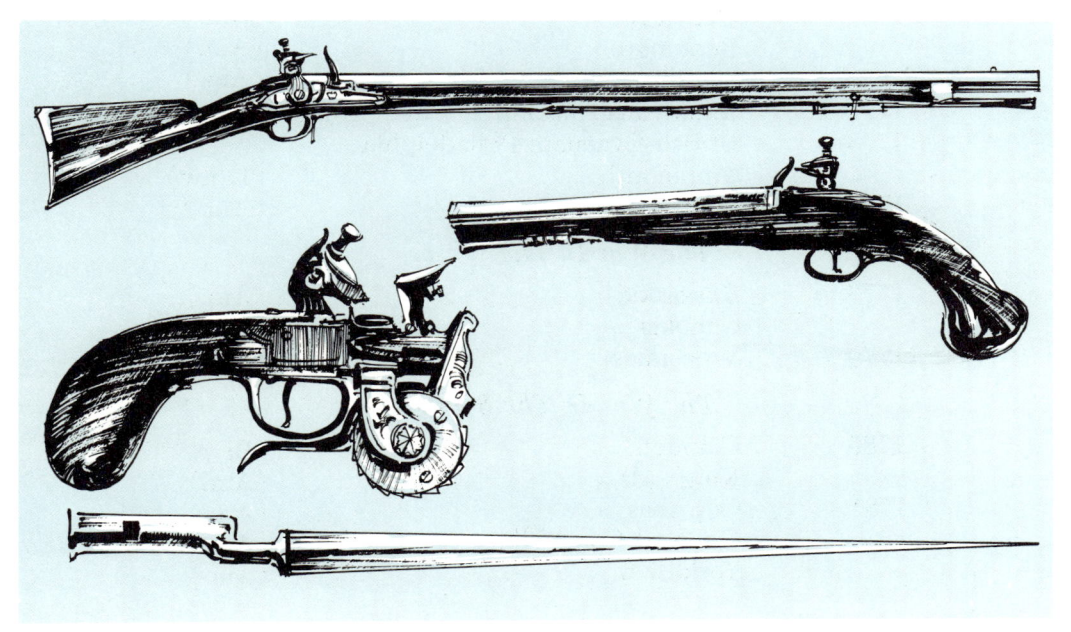

Top: "Brown Bess" rifle, used by British soldiers from 1670 to 1830. Below it is a regulation British pistol. Next is a powder tester. At bottom is a Brown Bess socket bayonet.

among the most brilliant in military history.

After following Washington to the banks of the Delaware, the British general spread his army out along the river and then left his soldiers in order to spend the Christmas holidays in New York. He planned a fine celebration, for he felt that Washington's long retreat meant that resistance was at an end and that the war was practically over.

A Christmas Surprise. Washington discovered that a large body of Hessian troops was stationed in the town of Trenton, on the other side of the river, and he determined on a surprise attack. With 2500 men, he crossed the river north of the town and marched upon the unsuspecting Hessians. The attack was sudden, and the victory complete. Roused out of their sleep, the soldiers of the king were in no condition to withstand the assault of

The War In New England and Middle Colonies

Year	Place	Victory
1775	Lexington	(Am.)
	Concord	(Am.)
	Bunker Hill	(Br.)
1776	British Evacuate Boston	
	Brooklyn Heights	(Br.)
	Trenton	(Am.)
1777	Princeton	(Am.)
	Brandywine	(Br.)
	Paoli	(Br.)
	Germantown	(Br.)
	British Occupy Philadelphia	
	Oriskany	(Am.)
	Bennington	(Am.)
	Saratoga	(Am.)
1777–1778	Americans Encamp at Valley Forge	
1778	British Evacuate Philadelphia	
	Monmouth	(Draw)
1779	Stony Point	(Am.)

The War In The West

Year	Place	Victory
1778	Kaskaskia	(Am.)
	Cahokia	(Am.)
1779	Vincennes	(Am.)

The War In The South

Year	Place	Victory
1780	Camden	(Br.)
	King's Mt.	(Am.)
1781	Cowpens	(Am.)
	Guilford Court House	(Am.)
	Yorktown	(Am.)

the Americans. After a few scattered volleys, they threw down their arms and surrendered, and Washington left the town with a thousand prisoners and many valuable stores.

Escape of the "Old Fox." When Cornwallis heard of this surprising American victory, he was much distressed and rushed back to join his troops. Leaving part of his army at Princeton, he led the rest of his soldiers out in search of the American army. By great good fortune he managed to trap Washington between the British force and the Delaware River. So sure was Cornwallis that he had his enemy at last, that he pitched camp and decided to wait until morning to bag the "Old Fox," as he called Washington.

Washington was well aware of his danger. With the British army in front of him and the river behind him, escape seemed impossible; but Washington was not a man to give up so easily. Throughout his camp, he had great fires built, and he left a few men to keep these burning brightly. Then quickly, under cover of darkness, he led his army up along the river bank and around the flank of the British army. Cornwallis never suspected what was going on, for there before him, all night long, he saw the American camp fires burning; and it never occurred to him that Washington's army was not there.

Success at Princeton. Once away from Cornwallis's men, Washington headed straight for Princeton. There he found the soldiers that Cornwallis had left behind. A desperate battle occurred. At first the Americans were driven back. Then Washington rallied his men and they fought more fiercely than ever, winning the battle and taking five hundred prisoners. In quick succession the American army had won two great victories, and had lost very few men.

Meeting a Money Crisis. Still the situation was desperate. Many of the soldiers in Washington's army had enlisted just for short periods, and the time had nearly come when they could return to their homes. The general knew that only by having plenty of money to pay them well could he keep enough soldiers with him to make resistance possible.

Two Philadelphia bankers responded nobly to Washington's appeal for help. Robert Morris, a friend of Washington's, implored his friends and business associates to contribute funds to the Revolutionary cause. Another banker, Haym Salomon, teamed with Morris to raise funds throughout the Revolutionary period. Salomon negotiated with foreign governments for loans and outright gifts, and he helped Morris raise considerable sums of money from already hard-pressed Americans. The efforts of these two men made the success of the Revolution possible.

The fifty thousand dollars that Morris raised to aid Washington's efforts at Princeton meant that the American army could continue to hold the field against the British. Washington led his army into winter quarters at Morristown with renewed hope in his heart.

British Strategy

For the British, the time had now come to begin their campaign of "divide and conquer." New York with its many Tory sympathizers would be the

British soldiers found moving equipment through blocked woodland paths impossible. Their slow progress made American victory over Burgoyne possible.

most logical place for this campaign to take place.

The British plan involved simultaneous troop movements from three directions. General Burgoyne was to come down from Canada with a large army, capturing the forts of Crown Point and Ticonderoga as he came. In the meantime, General Howe was to leave New York City and to proceed north up the Hudson until he met Burgoyne. A third army under Colonel St. Leger was to cross from Canada to Oswego and approach through the Mohawk Valley. The British command thought that the three armies would reach Albany about the same time and would join forces there, successfully dividing the colonies. It was a good plan, and had it succeeded it would without a doubt have meant the end of the Revolutionary War.

Burgoyne's Expedition. Burgoyne's army started out very successfully from Canada. Marching through the Champlain Valley, he easily captured the fortresses of Crown Point and Ticonderoga. But suddenly the picture changed. General Philip Schuyler, leading an army of American soldiers, had been busy felling trees across the path Burgoyne was to follow. The trees slowed up the British troops, but they slowed up the supply wagons even more. Finally the army became widely separated from its food supply. Since his men had to be fed, Burgoyne sent one thousand men into Vermont to get food from the town of Bennington. Instead of food, they found an American force under Colonel John Stark, who defeated them so badly that fewer than a hundred of the original thousand redcoats returned to Burgoyne; and they brought no food.

But a worse fate was to befall General Burgoyne. Proceeding southward, he came upon an American army fortified at Saratoga. At once the British attacked but were repulsed with heavy losses. Burgoyne withdrew to wait for the reinforcements that were to come with General Howe. Days went by and then weeks, and the reinforcements did not arrive. Either Howe's orders had failed to reach him, or he had decided to ignore them and follow out a plan of his own. On October 9, Burgoyne led a second assault against the Americans, and again he was badly defeated. Faced with starvation, Burgoyne held out a few more days and then on October 17 he surrendered to the American General Gates.

St. Leger's Campaign. What, meanwhile, had been happening to St. Leger? Landing his army at Oswego, the British colonel was at once joined by a great band of Tories and by many Iroquois (EAR′oh-kwoy) Indians anxious to go on the warpath. Marching southeast, he attacked and laid siege to Fort Stanwix, an American stronghold controlling the Mohawk Valley. The garrison of the fort refused to surrender, and St. Leger prepared for a long siege.

Then word reached the British that General Herkimer, a Patriot living nearby, was on his way to attack with an army he had gathered together. At once a strong force of Tories and Indians set out to defeat him. The armies met at Oriskany (or-ISS′kuh-nee), where one of the bloodiest battles of the war was fought. General Herkimer, though shot through the leg early in the fray, continued to direct his army to the very end. After hours of desperate hand-to-hand fighting in the midst of a terrific thunderstorm, the British were at last forced to withdraw.

Hearing the distant fighting, the Americans in Fort Stanwix launched their own attack on the British camp. They succeeded in capturing and bringing back enough supplies to ensure a long and stubborn resistance to the siege. Still, the attackers had not been driven away, and no further help could be expected from Herkimer's crippled army. The brave old general was himself so seriously wounded that he died a few days after the battle.

Then, hearing of Arnold's approach with the army that had forced Burgoyne to surrender, St. Leger broke camp and took his force back to Canada.

Howe's Capture of Philadelphia. Having failed to come to Burgoyne's assistance, General Howe now made a plan for himself. He decided to leave New York City and to capture Philadelphia, then the largest city in America. Across New Jersey he started with his army; but Washington so delayed and harassed his troops, without actually engaging in battle, that Howe returned to New York in disgust.

Soon, however, Howe made another attempt to reach Philadelphia, this time by sea. When his ships reached the mouth of the Delaware River, they were stopped by cannon shots from forts which Washington had erected there. Unable to go farther by boat, Howe's army was put ashore at the head of Chesapeake Bay. From there it proceeded by land.

At Brandywine Creek, Howe met resistance from the Americans. Washington's small army fought bravely but was so outnumbered that it was forced to fall back. The British continued their triumphant march, meeting with little further opposition. Howe took possession of Philadelphia in September, 1777.

These huts housed Washington's men at Valley Forge, Pennsylvania, in winter 1777–78.

But the forts at the mouth of the Delaware River still worried the British commander, and he determined to capture them. Leaving part of his forces at Germantown, near Philadelphia, he started south along the river. Here Washington saw a chance to capture or destroy a part of Howe's army. Dividing his men into four groups, Washington led a sudden attack upon the forces at Germantown, under cover of darkness and a heavy fog. At first the British gave way in great confusion. Then an accident occurred which robbed Washington of the battle. One of the four divisions of his army was lost in the fog and stumbled by mistake upon the rear of another American division. Each mistook the other for the enemy and promptly opened fire. Before the mistake was discovered, the British had rallied, and Washington's army was driven back.

General Howe found the forts at the mouth of the Delaware stronger than he had expected. For over a month they held out, and many British officers and men gave up their lives before the strongholds were at last captured and the British left in control of the Delaware River.

Winter at Valley Forge. After the battle of Germantown, General Washington gathered his forces and went into winter quarters at Valley Forge. Great was the suffering of the American army during the winter of 1778. While the enemy lived in comfort in the houses of Philadelphia, Washington's soldiers, scarcely twenty miles away, were freezing and suffering in their forlorn camp. There was little shelter for the men, and few indeed had even straw to sleep on. Over three thousand soldiers had no shoes. By midwinter, food was scarce. Sometimes whole days went by in which the soldiers had nothing at all to eat. Many deserted and returned to their homes, but a surprisingly large number remained in the American camp. They were inspired by a new pamphlet written by Thomas Paine, *The Crisis*, and by the courage and determination of their general. For the cause of liberty they willingly endured the hardships of that terrible winter.

Jealousy of Washington's Command. One of the reasons why Washington's army was not better cared for at Valley Forge was the jealousy of some of his officers and of many of the leaders in Congress. We have seen how General Charles Lee refused to help Washington and tried himself to gain command of the army. Another man, General Gates, joined in the chorus of criticism which had been leveled against the commander-in-chief, and a plot was formed to have Washington removed from the command. Fortunately, the scheme did not succeed. In time the people of the country came to realize more clearly what a great and unselfish man Washington was.

Friends in Need. In spite of the dreadful hardships, much good came from the winter at Valley Forge. A young French nobleman, Lafayette (lah-fay-ET'), and a young German, DeKalb (duh-KAHLB'), had crossed the ocean during the summer of 1777 and had joined Washington's army. Now another German, Baron von Steuben, and two Polish noblemen, Pulaski (poo-LAH'ski) and Kosciusko (kos-ee-US'koh), also joined the Americans. These men were trained European army officers, and they put Washington's soldiers through a hard and intensive campaign of military drill. As the winter wore on, the Americans came to look less and less like raw farmers and more and more like seasoned troops. By spring, Washington's army, though small, was nearly as well trained as that of his enemy.

This stone house, Washington's Command Post at Valley Forge, Pennsylvania, still stands and is open to the public.

For some time France had considered lending its active assistance to the Americans in their struggle against France's long-time enemy, England. Their defeat in the Seven Years' War still bothered Frenchmen, but they were unwilling to risk another war so soon without some indication of possible victory. The news of the American success at Saratoga was the assurance that France had awaited.

In 1778 word was relayed to the Americans that the French king had recognized their independence and was willing to send aid. Much of the credit for gaining that recognition belonged to Benjamin Franklin, now over seventy years of age, who had gone to France as a representative of the new American government. His personal success, added to the American military success, resulted in the French contribution of more than $2,000,000 to the war and the sending of many troops and a fleet of warships.

Changing Tides of Battle

Battle of Monmouth. The British army in Philadelphia was now commanded by General Clinton. Hearing that France had entered the war and fearful lest the French fleet sail up the Delaware River and cut off his supplies, Clinton abandoned Philadelphia and started to march his army to New York. At Monmouth, New Jersey, Washington's forces attacked the retreating redcoats. General Charles Lee, who had been released by the English and had rejoined Washington, nearly lost the battle by ordering a retreat when an American victory seemed certain. But Washington rallied his troops and drove Clinton's soldiers from the field.

Indian and Tory Massacres. Although the British had failed in their attempt to take all of New York, they still had allies there. The Tory leaders joined with the chief of the Iroquois to create a reign of terror for the American Patriots. Defenseless towns and villages throughout New York were captured, and men, women, and children were cruelly put to death.

Realizing that something must be done to put a stop to this horrible campaign of torture and death, Washington sent an army of 5000 men under the leadership of young General John Sullivan. Sullivan met the enemy near the present city of Elmira, New York, and after a hard-fought battle put them to flight with great loss. His marauding army continued to march through Indian country, burning forty villages of the Senecas and Cayugas (kah-YOO′gahz), both tribes of the Iroquois nation. This expedition broke the back of the Iroquois resistance.

Treason of Benedict Arnold

In 1779 there occurred an event which nearly broke Washington's heart and which brought discouragement to all patriotic Americans. Benedict Arnold, who had taken part in the invasion of Canada and the successful battle at Saratoga, had not been advanced as rapidly as he felt that he deserved to be. Then, too, Arnold's wife was sympathetic to the British cause. The combination of Arnold's disappointment and his wife's British leanings led him to the decision to betray the young nation he had helped. He agreed to assist the British in capturing the strong fortress of West Point, of which Washington had given him the command. Meeting a British spy, Major André (AHN′dray), Arnold turned over to him the plans of the fort, as well as a scheme for attacking it. Unfortunately for Arnold, André was captured before he again reached the British lines, and Arnold saved himself only by immediate flight. Although the British government did provide a sizable pension for his family and offered him a commission in the army, Benedict Arnold lived out the last twenty years of his life in disgrace.

Looking Back

1. What were the British goals in shifting the fighting to the Middle Colonies?
2. Summarize the military activities in the campaign for the control of New York City.
3. Why were the victories at Trenton and Princeton vital to the American cause?
4. Describe the "three-fold plan" of the British.
5. How can you explain the decision of the French to aid the Americans?

4. The Americans Advance on Land and Sea

In 1778, a serious danger threatened the Americans in the West. The British commander at Detroit, Colonel Henry Hamilton, was busy urging thousands of Indians to hurl a great attack against the American colonies.

Hamilton had little love for the Americans, and so eagerly did he urge the Indians to go on the warpath and collect scalps that he became known as "the hair-buyer." It was clear that if something were not done, the Indian inhabitants of the great regions to the west might strike a deadly blow at the young American nation.

The Campaign in the West

To meet this danger, George Rogers Clark, a young Virginia woodsman, gathered an army of two hundred men and set out down the Ohio River. His force was pitifully small for the task assigned him, but the spirit of leadership was so strong in young Clark that no obstacle seemed too great to be overcome. Fort Kaskaskia (kas-KASS'-key-ah), the first British stronghold which he reached, proved an easy prey, for the garrison had been withdrawn for service near Detroit. When the British garrisons at Cahokia (kah-HOH'key-ah) and Vincennes heard that the Americans were coming, they hauled down the British flag in token of surrender. It seemed that the conquest of the West would be quick and bloodless.

Colonel Hamilton, meanwhile, heard what was going on and gathered a British army of five hundred men. By forced marches he reached Vincennes before Clark could get there and reclaimed the fort for Great Britain.

Clark realized that he must do something to foil Hamilton. With 130 picked men, he set out across the flooded lands of Illinois. For sixteen days his men pushed on, sometimes up to their knees and sometimes up to their necks in the flowing ice-cold water. When at last they reached Vincennes, they were tired and weak. But George Rogers Clark never hesitated. Keeping his men concealed so that the British would not know how few there were, he demanded the instant surrender of the fort, stating that if he were forced to take it by assault all of the inhabitants would be slaughtered. Hamilton had only to lead his five hundred men out of the fort, and the much weaker Americans would have been at his mercy, but fortunately he did not know this. Frightened and undecided, he asked for a three days' truce. Clark repeated his demand for an immediate surrender. Then the British threw down their arms, the

George Rogers Clark is pictured here carrying frontier equipment: haversack, knife, sword, powderhorn and Kentucky rifle.

A complex system of pulleys and lines were used to secure a British ship's cannon. This 12-pounder was fired by igniting powder in the barrel which drove out the cannon ball.

gates of the fort were opened, and out came Hamilton's army, beaten.

Clark's forces were then aided by an extremely fortunate circumstance. A band of Indians, who had been off on a scalping party, suddenly appeared. They knew nothing of the seizing of Vincennes, and were returning from a successful raid to receive the praise of the British commander. At once Clark had the murderers killed. To the other Indians present, it taught a great lesson, for they saw Hamilton and his men standing helplessly by, unable to aid them, and they became so afraid of the Americans that the great Indian attack never occurred. Thus did George Rogers Clark win for America the western territory which Great Britain had captured from France but twenty years before.

The War on the Sea

Barry's Naval Successes. At the beginning of the war, the Americans had no navy at all, whereas Great Britain had the mightiest fleet in the world. Late in 1775, however, the little American brig *Lexington* was commissioned and was placed under the command of Captain John Barry. Early the next year, the *Lexington* succeeded in capturing the British ship *Edward*, bringing about America's first naval victory.

In 1777 Barry commanded a flotilla of little boats which attacked Howe's fleet while it was moving against Philadelphia. Though he could not prevent Howe from taking the city, he did capture some British supply ships, and the goods which he took proved very helpful to Washington's army.

Besides Barry's little fleet, Congress granted permission for privately owned ships to serve as privateers. This was done by issuing papers, called *Letters of Marque,* empowering merchant ships to act as American warships on the high seas and to capture British vessels. In spite of the privateers and the small number of American warships, Great Britain continued to rule the seas without much interference from the United States.

The "Bon Homme Richard." When France entered the war, Benjamin Franklin persuaded the French king to lend the Americans a number of warships until the end of the war. The most famous of these was named the *Bon Homme Richard,* in honor of Franklin who had written *Poor Richard's Almanac.* The *Bon Homme Richard* was old, slow, and half rotted, and some of its heaviest guns were cracked, but it was destined to gain for itself a fine place in American history.

With a few smaller ships, the *Bon Homme Richard* started out from France under the command of Captain John Paul Jones to raid the English coast and burn British shipping. After capturing a number of ships and conducting a successful raid on a British seaport, the little fleet came upon forty British merchant ships under the protection of two warships, the *Serapis* (seh-RAY′pis) and the *Countess of Scarborough.* At once the *Bon Homme Richard* engaged in a fierce combat with the larger of the two British ships, the *Serapis,* while Jones' other ships were busy subduing the *Countess of Scarborough.*

The *Serapis* was a sounder ship than the *Bon Homme Richard* and should have won easily, but the Americans made up in gallantry what they lacked in equipment. Early in the battle the two ships drifted together, and the American sailors at once bound them fast, so that the guns of each were firing point-blank into the side of the enemy. Soon a British shell carried away the *Bon Homme Richard's* flag, and at once the enemy's captain called out to know if the Americans had surrendered. "On the contrary," shouted Captain Jones, "I have just begun to fight."

At this point, one of the French ships sailed by and fired a broadside which did more damage to friends than foes. In spite of all these troubles Jones fought on, and at last, with the *Serapis* burning and the *Bon Homme Richard* sinking, the commander of the *Serapis* hauled down his flag. The victory was won. The Americans boarded the British ship, put out the fire, and sailed triumphantly into port.

Other nations received with joy the news that the British navy had lost a battle on the sea. Spain and Holland were both jealous of the British naval power, and both of these countries soon followed the example of France and America and declared war on Great Britain. The victory of Captain John Paul Jones was extremely helpful to the American cause.

Looking Back

1. How did George Rogers Clark help the American cause in the West?
2. By what means did the Americans meet the challenge of the British navy?
3. What effect did the defeats of the British navy have on other European nations?

5. The War in the South Proves Decisive

When the British were unable to defeat the colonial forces in New England or in the Middle Colonies, they turned their attention to the South. Their plan was to divide the American forces by causing Washington to keep part of his army around New York and move the other part of it to the South to stem the British advance. The British plan depended, in part, on the hope that the majority of Southern colonists would be on their side. It was true that many Southerners were loyal to the crown, but the British chose to ignore one of the realities of war: people tend to flock to the winning side.

One other assumption hurt the British cause. The British assumed that the redcoats could and would fight as fiercely as colonial soldiers. They ignored the fact that the American soldier was fighting to keep his home and family free. Often what the American soldier lacked in practiced skill, he made up in spirit and enthusiasm for his cause.

Fall of Charleston to British

The British had setbacks, too, however. In the summer of 1776, a British fleet sailed to capture Charleston, South Carolina. Little Fort Moultrie (MOL'tree) in the harbor was not very strong, but the men who defended it would not surrender. It is said that in the heat of the conflict a cannon ball from a British ship struck the flagstaff of the fort, and the flag fell to the beach outside of the walls. Quick as a flash, Sergeant Jasper, one of the defenders, leaped over the wall and

A Civil War soldier's impression of Fort Moultrie, Charleston, South Carolina.

brought back the flag, planting it firmly in place. The British could not capture the fort, and Charleston remained in American hands.

In December, 1778, a fleet of British warships appeared off the city of Savannah, Georgia, and after a brave but futile resistance, the city fell. Over a year later Charleston, South Carolina, too, was forced to surrender, and the British armies started confidently inland to make their conquest complete. The town of Camden was one of the first to be captured.

Defeat of Gates in South Carolina

In the South, General Gates, victor at Saratoga, was placed in command of the American army in June, 1780. Camden, South Carolina, a British post and supply base, was defended by only a small British force, and before the main British army under Lord Cornwallis should arrive, Gates had a fine opportunity to recapture the town. He delayed so long, however, that Cornwallis reached there ahead of him, and in the battle which followed the Americans were defeated and forced to retreat. In the battle, De Kalb, the German officer, distinguished himself by his great bravery, falling dead with eleven wounds in his body.

Redcoats Surrender at King's Mountain

After defeating the Americans at Camden, Cornwallis rested his troops, then started north to conquer the Carolinas. Everywhere he met with unexpected resistance. Small bands of Patriots under such able leaders as Marion and Sumter attacked his scouting parties, cut off his supplies, and in

King's Mountain, North Carolina, was the site of the battle which a British general described as "the first link of a chain" of British defeats.

many ways delayed his advance. Still he met no American army large enough to hinder him seriously. Coming at last into North Carolina, Cornwallis sent out more than 1000 men under the command of Major Ferguson to gather Tories to join the British army. Ferguson pushed on to the heart of a region which, he was soon to find, had few Tories but many Patriots. As his army advanced, word spread for miles around that the enemy was coming, and the patriotic woodsmen of that section seized their guns and hastened to repulse the British invaders.

Guerrilla Warfare. All too late did Ferguson realize that he was in the midst of his enemy. Sharpshooters from thickets began to pick off the soldiers in his ranks. Looking about for a place to make a stand, he selected King's Mountain, a great hill with three sloping sides and one steep cliff. "Well, boys," exulted the major, "here

> *Cornwallis' Parole*
>
> Charles Earl Cornwallis Lieutenant General (of his Brita)nnick Majesty's Forces
>
> Do acknowledge myself a Prisoner of War to the (United) States of America, & having permission from His (Excellen)cy General Washington, agreeable to Capitulation, to proceed to New York & Charlestown, or either, & to Europe.
>
> Do pledge my Faith & Word of Honor, that I will not say or do anything injurious to the said United States or Armies thereof, or their Allies, until duly exchanged; I do further promise that Whenever required, by the Commander in Chief of the American Army, or the Commissary of Prisoners for the same, I will repair to such place or places as they or either of them may require
>
> Given under my Hand at York Town 28th day of October 1781
>
> —Cornwallis

is a place from which all of the rebels cannot drive us."

But the major underestimated his enemy. Attacking from three sides at once, the woodsmen crawled up the hill, hiding always behind rocks, bushes, and trees, and keeping up a steady fire that soon began to thin the British ranks. In vain did the redcoats look for a foe at whom to shoot. In vain did Ferguson order a bayonet charge down the mountainside. The unfortunate British were mowed down with never a chance to strike at their enemy. At last Ferguson himself was killed, and his army surrendered.

General Gates had now been removed from the command of the Southern army, and Washington had appointed General Greene to take his place. Greene divided his army into two parts and threatened Cornwallis' army from both sides at once. The unhappy British commander did not know which way to turn.

The Battle of Cowpens

In January, 1781, a strong detachment from Cornwallis' army, under Colonel Tarleton, met a part of Greene's army, under Morgan and Pickens, at Cowpens, near King's Mountain. There followed a fierce battle in which the American army, pretending to retreat, drew the British into a circular trap and forced them to surrender.

The British campaign in the South had come to a standstill. Foes on every side struck and were gone before Cornwallis could rally his troops. Finally Cornwallis was forced to realize the futility of his situation.

Final Victory at Yorktown

The spring of 1781 saw the fighting turn in favor of the Americans. In the South, Greene, Marion, and Sumter struck blow after blow at Cornwallis, who, discouraged, led his army north through the Carolinas. As they crossed into Virginia, the British came upon Lafayette's forces, who retreated before them. Up through Virginia went Cornwallis, always in pursuit of an elusive army which would not offer battle. All at once the tables turned, and Lafayette, receiving reinforcements, held his ground and began to menace Cornwallis. In great alarm the British general entered the town of Yorktown, on a cape extending into Chesapeake Bay.

American-French Attack. In the meantime, French troops under General Rochambeau (roh-sham-BOH′) had landed in Connecticut. Washington met Rochambeau and arranged for a joint attack against the British in New York City. Rochambeau informed Washington that the French fleet had been sent to the West Indies to aid in a joint attack against the British either in New York or in Virginia. However, a letter arrived from French Admiral De Grasse in the West Indies saying that he would sail for Chesapeake Bay with 3000 troops and his entire fleet. The attack against New York was then canceled.

Washington and Rochambeau immediately made plans to take their armies to Virginia for a combined campaign to defeat Cornwallis at Yorktown. De Grasse and his fleet arrived first, blockading Chesapeake Bay so that no supplies or help could be brought to Cornwallis. The presence of Washington and Rochambeau in Connecticut led the British commander in New York to believe that the French and the Americans were going to attack that city while Washington and Rochambeau suddenly broke camp and rushed their armies to join Lafayette before Yorktown.

Surrender of Cornwallis. Cornwallis soon came to realize his position. Before him was an army of 16,000 Frenchmen and Americans. And the warships which now lay at anchor in Chesapeake Bay were French, cutting off escape by the sea. The situation was hopeless.

Caught in a trap, Cornwallis never had a chance. For a week he held out, while the cannon of the French fleet and the American troops played havoc with his army. On October 17, 1781, he and his men marched out and surrendered to the Americans. The fall of Yorktown practically marked the end of the war. King George III and the government of Great Britain were forced to acknowledge the independence of the United States, and our country became a free nation.

Looking Back

1. Why did the British shift their activities to the South?
2. How did their naval strength aid the British in their early victories in the South?
3. How did American victories at King's Mountain and Cowpens help shift the scene of fighting?
4. In what ways did the French contribute to the American victory at Yorktown?
5. Why was the British surrender at Yorktown of such importance to the Americans?
6. Much has been written about Francis Marion, the "Swamp Fox". How did he help defeat the British?

6. American Independence Becomes a Reality

The final victory over the mother country by its former colony amazed the world. However, the victory was by no means due alone to American strategy or American military might, significant though each of these factors was. The success of the Revolution can be attributed in part to two factors aside from the American efforts.

In the first place, the war that began with the firing of a few shots at Lexington and Concord became a world conflict. Spain, in 1779, and Holland, in 1780, joined France and the Americans in their war against Britain. In so doing they saw an opportunity to strike back at the "mistress of the seas," while they helped a struggling nation come into existence. Most of the remaining countries of Europe practiced "armed neutrality," resisting the commercial and mili-

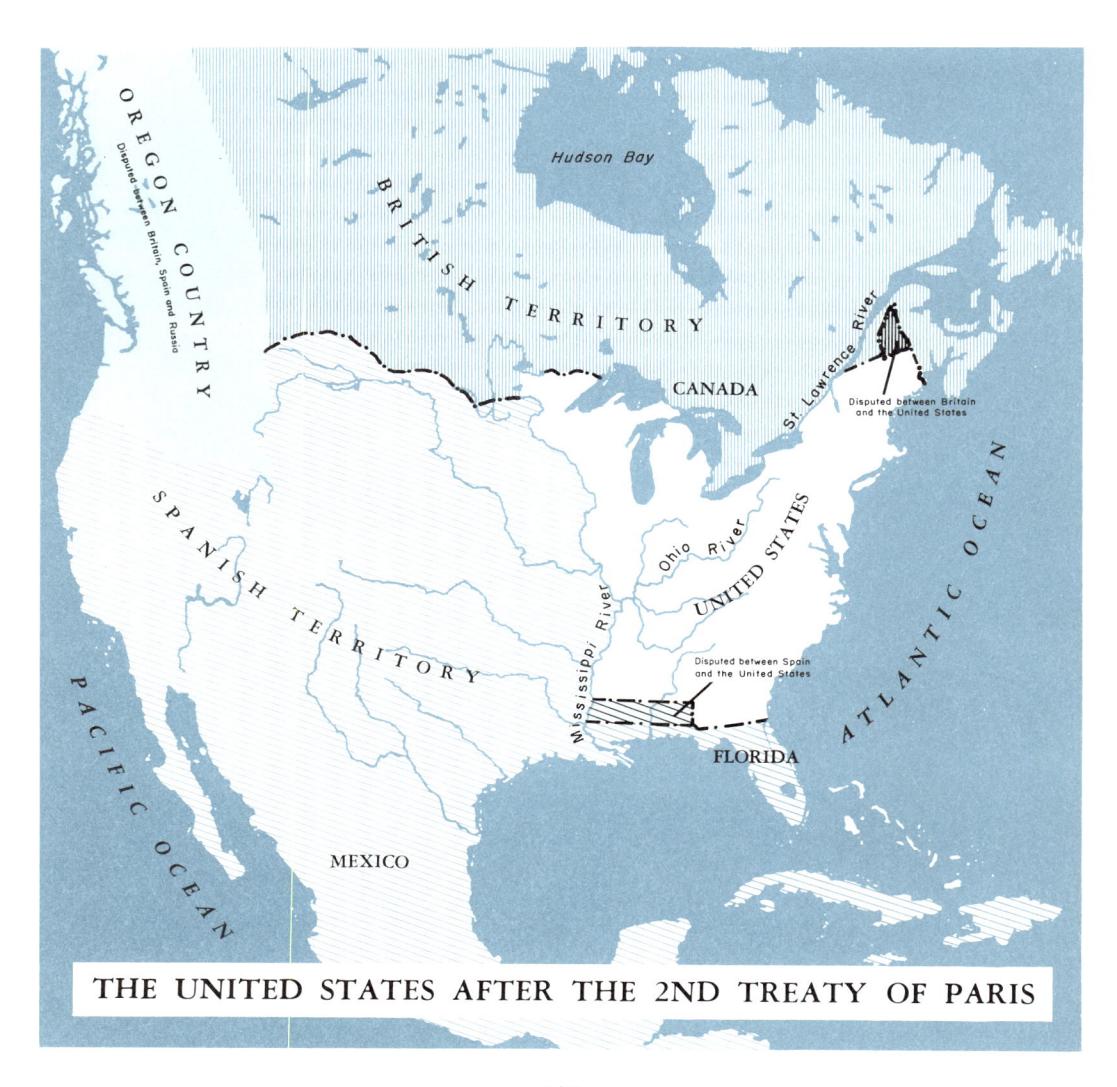

THE UNITED STATES AFTER THE 2ND TREATY OF PARIS

tary interests of England wherever possible. Thus England found herself on the defensive in Europe and Asia, as well as in the Americas.

A more direct contribution to the American victory was French aid in the form of men, money, supplies, and ships. The final victory at Yorktown would not have been possible without French cooperation.

Treaty of Paris, 1783

Negotiations. Peace negotiations began in Paris in April of 1782. Benjamin Franklin was in France as the representative of the Continental Congress at the court of Louis XVI. John Adams was in Amsterdam as the representative to Holland. These two men, with John Jay and Henry Laurens, were appointed as commissioners of the former colonies to arrange a treaty.

Terms. By the terms of the treaty, signed September 3, 1783, America gained recognition of its independence and of its claim to the lands east of the Mississippi River. British forces were to surrender all forts in the American territory. In turn, the American commissioners agreed to recommend payment of debts owed by Americans to British subjects.

Effects of the American Revolution

Ralph Waldo Emerson described the battle of Concord in his "Concord Hymn" as "the shot heard round the world." The effects of the American Revolution were widespread and were actually felt throughout the world. In England the struggle for independence caused the British to reconsider their colonial policy. The Thirteen Colonies had said that they felt an allegiance to the king but not to Parliament.

After the Revolution, England treated her colonies somewhat differently. Gradually, other colonial possessions of England with British customs, British language, and British laws were permitted to give their allegiance to the king and not to Parliament. The severe policies of George III caused Parliament to take some of his authority away from him and from future monarchs so that the king or

The Liberty Bell proclaimed American independence in 1776. It now is on display at Philadelphia's Independence Hall.

queen of England is today more revered as a symbol than an actual ruler. But there were changes in other European nations too.

The French Revolution. In France, the ideas expressed in the preamble to the Declaration of Independence became popular through lectures and writings. Frenchmen observed closely the workings of democracy. They noted that when the war was over, Washington, as head of the army, did not assume a dictatorship but returned to his estate at Mount Vernon. Liberty and freedom were offered by all the states. The prosperity of the young country also impressed the French, for in their country almost the opposite condition existed. Only the very wealthy possessed land. Only the very wealthy or the people of noble birth enjoyed the liberty and the privileges that everyone enjoyed in America. This situation within their own country and the example of the thirteen American colonies encouraged the French to start their own revolution.

A Model for the World. After the Napoleonic era, numerous revolutions occurred, patterned after the American Revolution. Many of these took place in the Spanish colonies in South America. Our southern neighbors claimed, as we had claimed in 1776, that they had the right to revolt against tyranny and attempts to destroy liberty. Even today our policy toward the new emerging nations around the world stems from the similarity between their position and ours at the time of our War for Independence.

Looking Back

1. How did the policy of "armed neutrality" by European nations favor the Americans?

2. Who were the American representatives at the Paris negotiations?

3. List the chief terms of the Treaty of Paris in 1783.

4. In what ways has Emerson's comment about "the shot heard round the world" proved to be true?

5. Which nation was the first to follow America's ideas expressed in the preamble to the Declaration of Independence? Why?

The Chapter in Perspective

Who Are These People?

Gage	Morris	Charles Lee	Kosciusko
Revere	Salomon	Cornwallis	Franklin
Ethan Allen	Lafayette	Burgoyne	George R. Clark
Arnold	DeKalb	Stark	Barry
Paine	von Steuben	Gates	John Paul Jones
Howe	Pulaski	St. Leger	Rochambeau

Where Are These Places?

Lexington	Saratoga
Concord	Oriskany
Ticonderoga	Valley Forge
Breed's Hill	Monmouth
Bunker Hill	Vincennes
Trenton	Camden
Princeton	Cowpens
Bennington	Yorktown
King's Mountain	

What Do These Dates and Terms Mean?

Loyalists	*The Crisis*
Tories	privateers
Whigs	Letters of Marque
July 4, 1776	Treaty of Paris
minutemen	*Common Sense*
1783	guerrilla warfare
Hessians	armed neutrality
Oct. 17, 1777	
Bon Homme Richard	
Declaration of Independence	

Questions for Study

1. Why were there so many Loyalists or Tories in the colonies as war began?
2. What evidence is available to indicate that the desire for independence was not unanimous among the colonists?
3. By quoting from the Declaration of Independence where possible, show that it contains several sections with special purposes.
4. List at least eight of the charges against the king listed in the Declaration of Independence. For each of these charges, give an example from history.
5. Explain why the American victory at Saratoga is considered by many to be the turning point of the war.
6. Why was the raising of money and the maintaining of an army so difficult for the Americans?
7. Why is Washington considered to have been a great general when his military victories were so few?
8. Why, in your opinion, were the American colonies able to win their independence?
9. In what ways did geographic factors contribute to an American victory in the Revolutionary War?
10. After checking the map, explain why the British three-fold plan was well conceived.

Place Yourself in History

It is midnight and you have just gone to bed, after writing two lines on a long delayed letter. Just as you are about to fall asleep, you are disturbed by shouts and the sounds of running men. As you open your window, you hear, "The British are coming!" Recrossing the room, your eyes see the neglected letter. It reads: Lexington, Massachusetts, April 18, 1775.

What do you do? Do you join the other townsmen assembling on the village green? Do you risk your life by flying in the face of authority which is oppressive to you? Do you disregard the commotion and go back to bed? Justify your actions.

7 These United States Adopt a Constitution

When the defeated British soldiers marched from Yorktown, General Washington asked his men not to cheer. Perhaps Washington realized that more difficult problems loomed ahead and the time for cheering had not yet arrived.

It must be remembered that when the Revolution ended, the United States was not a nation but a group of thirteen separate states, held together by the weak authority of the Continental Congress. Many feared that the transition from English control to a government by the people could result in tyranny with the moneyed classes gaining control. If such a situation should develop, all the gains of the Revolution might be lost.

1. The New Nation Survives the "Critical Period"

State Constitutions

To counteract the development of possible new threats to their liberties as the revolution progressed, and to be prepared for eventual independence, the colonies reconsidered their constitutions and charters. Eleven out of the thirteen drew up new constitutions to deal with the new situation. For example, the Continental Congress, the central government of the colonies, had suggested to New Hampshire that its provincial convention "establish such a form of government as in their judgement will best produce the happiness of the people and most effectually secure peace and good order in that province, during the present dispute between Great Britain and the colonies."

Rhode Island and Connecticut continued to use their colonial charters, changing those words and phrases that referred to the British government or to the king.

State and colonial constitutions written before and during the American Revolution contained provision for a strong legislative branch consisting of two houses. Since most of the power was delegated to the legislative branch, the executive branch was in a weak position. Most constitutions provided for frequent elections, but no person could vote or hold office who did not own property. Judges were appointed and could hold office as long as they maintained good behavior; that is, as long as they continued to hand down judgments and decisions that were in keeping with the colonial ideas of freedom and democracy.

The Second Continental Congress

Accomplishments. The Second Continental Congress was formed from necessity in 1775. The British colonies in America were facing war with their mother country. Thirteen separate colonies could not possibly carry on a war, and a central government of some sort was needed to keep alive the idea of union. Representatives at the Second Continental Congress had no definite powers, but they assumed the authority to declare war on Great Britain, to raise an army, and to appoint officers. To pay the soldiers they borrowed money from whatever sources and in whatever amounts they could. It was this Second Continental Congress, too, that made the terms with France when she came into the war, and that made a treaty with Great Britain when the war was over.

But a Congress alone, without definite powers, is a poor substitute for a strong government. Realizing this as

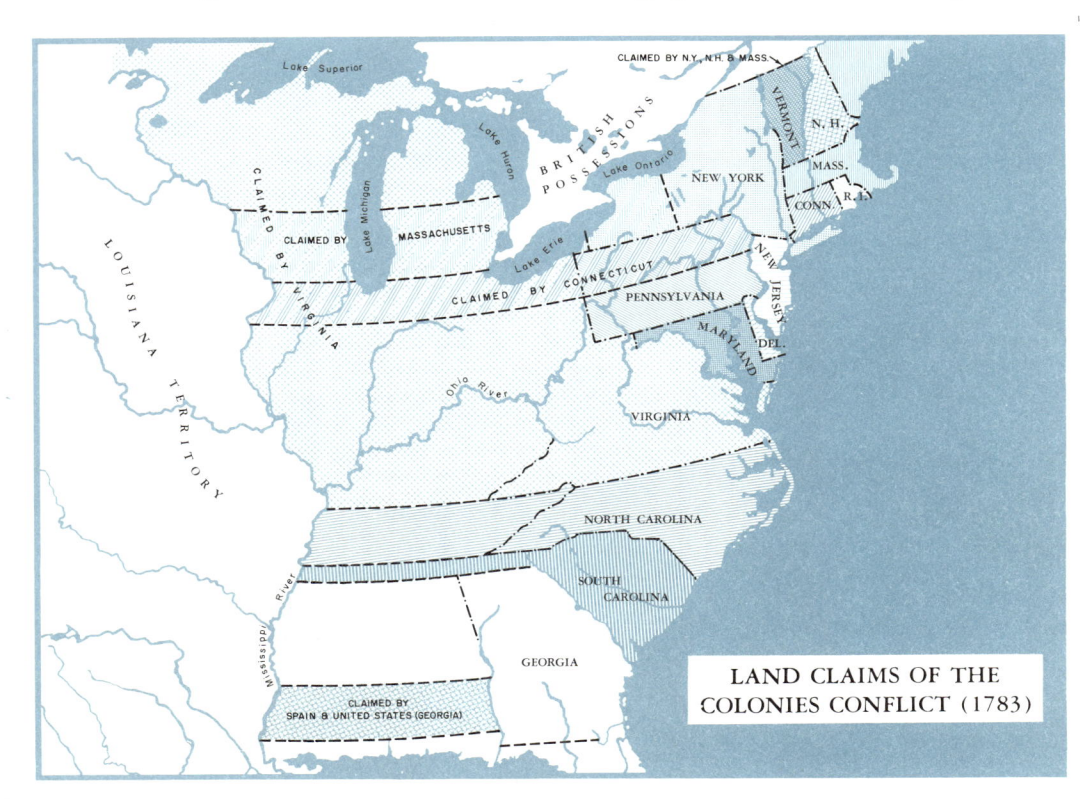

LAND CLAIMS OF THE COLONIES CONFLICT (1783)

early as 1776, the representatives drew up a constitution, known as the *Articles of Confederation,* and submitted it to all the states. Some of the states adopted the Articles promptly, but it was five years before they were adopted by all the states and thus became the basis for the government of the country.

Adoption of Articles of Confederation. Maryland was responsible for the delay in accepting the Articles. Georgia, North and South Carolina, Virginia, Connecticut, Massachusetts, and New York all claimed, on the basis of early charters, parts of the land west of the Appalachian Mountains. The legislatures of these seven states planned to use their shares of the western lands to pay their soldiers for serving in the revolution. The other states had no such resource, and Maryland claimed that since all of the states had fought for this territory, each of them had an equal right to it. Unless these lands were turned over to the nation as a whole to be used for the benefit of all of the states, Maryland would not accept the Articles of Confederation.

For a long time, the landowning states hesitated, but at last New York and Virginia offered to give up their claims. When this was done, Maryand, the last state to do so, adopted the Articles of Confederation, which then became the law of the land. In later years the other states also surrendered their claims.

Weak Government under the Articles

The Articles of Confederation proved to be an extremely feeble form of government. They made provision for a Congress which was merely an advisory body. It could make laws, but it had no power to enforce them. It could request money from the various states, but it had no means of collecting this money if the states did not choose to pay. Congress had no control over commerce and trade between the different states, or between any state and a foreign nation. The states themselves made their own tariffs and taxes with the the federal government having no power to interfere. Finally, there was nothing in the Articles of Confederation that provided for their

Immediately after the Land Ordinance of 1785, entire sections of townships were sold to interested buyers. These buyers then sold the land in smaller pieces. When it became apparent that this system encouraged land speculation, pioneers bought no more than one-eighth of a section directly from the government. How many acres was one-eighth of a section? How was education provided for?

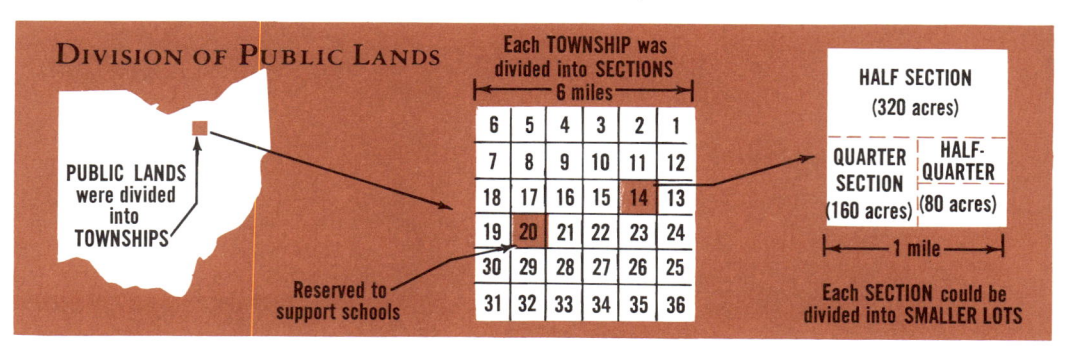

DIVISION OF PUBLIC LANDS

PUBLIC LANDS were divided into TOWNSHIPS

Each TOWNSHIP was divided into SECTIONS
6 miles

6	5	4	3	2	1
7	8	9	10	11	12
18	17	16	15	14	13
19	20	21	22	23	24
30	29	28	27	26	25
31	32	33	34	35	36

Reserved to support schools

HALF SECTION (320 acres)
QUARTER SECTION (160 acres) | HALF-QUARTER (80 acres)
1 mile
Each SECTION could be divided into SMALLER LOTS

being changed without the consent of every state.

It is easy to explain the weaknesses of the Articles. Each of the states had been a separate colony, independent of all the others. Each colonist had learned to love his colony. After the war, colonial patriotism turned to state patriotism, and the first thought of each citizen was for the importance of his state. He cared little for the weak and almost nonexistent government represented by Congress. It meant real sacrifice to give up a single one of a state's rights to the national government. As a result, the national government was granted few rights. Had the national government existed first and the states been created afterwards, such a situation would not have come about. But it did come about, and it brought extreme weakness to the central government. It is understandable that the period when the United States was governed under the Articles of Confederation (1781–1789) is often referred to as the "Critical Period."

Two Significant Laws

Land Ordinance. After the land holding states gave up their claims to the lands to the northwest, from Virginia to the Lake of the Woods, Congress found that possession of this vast area created many problems. Settlers literally swarmed into the new territory. Some organization had to be imposed on the land. The natural result was the *Land Ordinance of 1785,* which arranged for the survey and later sale of northwestern lands. Townships were to be surveyed in six mile squares. Each township was then to be divided into thirty-six sections of six hundred and forty acres each.

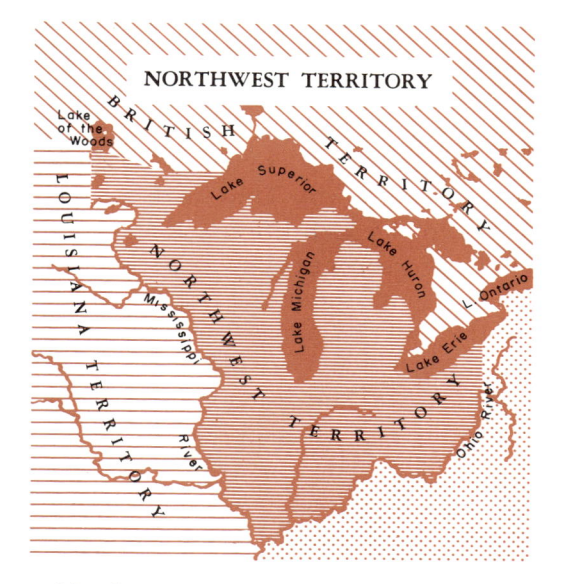

Northwest Ordinance. Of even greater importance was a law known as the *Northwest Ordinance,* the Ordinance of 1787, or the Magna Carta of the Northwest. This famous document provided for a governor, a secretary, and three judges to govern any given territory in the Northwest in its earliest stages. After the population of a particular territory grew to five thousand males over twenty-one, a two-house legislature could be elected, but all the laws passed had to be approved by Congress. As soon as the area could boast of sixty thousand inhabitants, a constitution could be drawn up, officers chosen and then that part of the Northwest could enter the Union as a state. The Ordinance specifically stated that no less than three and no more than five states were to be formed out of the Northwest territory. Not counting part of Minnesota, five new states, Ohio, Indiana, Illinois, Michigan and Wisconsin, entered the Union from the Northwest Territory.

It is interesting to note that this Ordinance in its Article III states that "schools and the means of education shall be forever encouraged." Article VI said that there would "be neither slavery nor involuntary servitude in said territory." (These words are almost identical with the Thirteenth Amendment to the Constitution that was to be passed seventy-eight years later.)

The most significant aspect of the Northwest Ordinance was the unselfishness shown by old, established states. It was surprising that the "original thirteen" decided to allow new, potentially more wealthy, states to gain equal political power. As has been pointed out, the original states did some fighting among themselves. They were jealous of each other's power, both political and economic. And one of the critical periods in American history was the period in which the newly created thirteen states tried to settle all their differences in order to build a united country.

It must have occurred to the political leaders that more states would only complicate their problems, yet they went ahead, with faith in their ideals, to ensure that new states would be admitted with powers equal to the old states. This farsighted gamble, taken by the authors of the Northwest Ordinance, is one of the most significant cornerstones of our American success story. It ensured, unselfishly, a voice in government for all the states, both large and small, old and new.

Relations with Other Countries

Foreign nations were not slow to discover the weaknesses of America. Great Britain refused to grant the newly established nation a fair share of her trade, and, in spite of anything that Congress could do, continued to hold valuable fur-trading posts in lands that she had surrendered to America. Although she had agreed to evacuate these posts in the Treaty of Paris in 1783, British agents continued to trade with the Indians in the Northwest and to incite them to raids on American settlements. Great Britain justified this by asserting that the United States did not repay fully the losses suffered by the Loyalists in the Revolution. Even the colonial ally France refused to recognize Congress as a government and would have no dealings with the new country. Spain tried to tempt the settlers who were now pouring into the Mississippi Val-

The Empress of China, shown here, brought back only trinkets and knick-knacks from her first voyage, but it started a bustling trade.

Early lighthouse lamp. Oil lamps reflected from concave mirrors on a round frame.

ley and other lands in the west to give up their allegiance to so feeble a government and become Spanish subjects. Even the Barbary pirates of Africa began to prey on American ships without fear of retaliation from Congress.

Despite the unfortunate attitude of many countries toward the infant nation in America, trade did flourish. American exports to Holland, France, and even to England increased. However, England did prevent American trade with the West Indies. Some products could not be sent at all; other products could be sent only in British ships. This had an unexpected effect upon American trade, causing businessmen to look for other markets.

An American ship, the *Empress of China*, sailed around Cape Horn to Canton, China. Profits from silks and teas were so enormous that other merchants and businessmen entered into the China trade.

In 1785, the Congress sent Thomas Jefferson to Paris and John Adams to London to investigate trade possibilities. They found it extremely difficult to obtain commercial treaties or concessions from either England or France. The British bluntly informed John Adams that no concessions would be given to the United States and that the outposts at Niagara, Oswego, Detroit, and at several other points on American soil would continue to be occupied by England unless Americans paid their debts to Englishmen. As mentioned earlier, such a provision appeared in the Treaty of Paris, 1783, but the American government found it almost impossible to enforce.

Interstate Jealousies

The Articles of Confederation made few, if any, provisions for jealousies between the individual states. When a band of people from Connecticut moved into Pennsylvania and settled in the Wyoming Valley, they were regarded as undesirable immigrants from a foreign country. Some of the Pennsylvanians even went so far as to join the Delaware Indians in making war on the newcomers. The territory that is now Vermont was caught in a three-way tug-of-war among New York, New Hampshire, and Connecticut, and many lives were lost in this quarrel before it was finally settled. Virginia and Maryland, too, quarreled bitterly over the trade rights on the Potomac River, which flowed between them.

The neighboring states of New York and New Jersey might have helped each other immensely, but each preferred its own advancement to the good will of its neighbor. Heavy duties were laid by both states on goods brought in from the other. Finally, New Jersey went to the extreme of laying a tax of hundreds of dollars upon a lighthouse which was built on her coast to guide ships into New York harbor. Such doings soon brought people to realize that the national government, and not the states, must have control over commerce and tariff.

Financial Problems

Paper Money. One of Congress's major problems was keeping the states from issuing paper money of all shapes and sizes. So many European goods were bought by Americans that the imports greatly exceeded the exports in value. These imports had to be paid for in gold and silver which went back to Europe, so before long a great shortage of metal money made itself felt in America. Most of the states began to issue paper money which had no gold or silver to back it up. This paper money soon decreased so much in value as to be practically worthless. Foreign goods could not be bought with it, and money printed in one state often would not be accepted by the people living in another.

Shays' Rebellion. Massachusetts was one state which tried to avoid the issuing of paper money. This brought troubles of another sort. With their gold and silver used up in European trade, and with no paper money, the people had no way to pay their debts or their taxes. Many were thrown into prison or were sued for sums that they could not pay because they had no common medium of exchange with which to pay.

Such a situation was bound to lead to widespread discontent and to have unfortunate results. In the western part of the state a farmer named Daniel Shays raised an army of about two thousand desperate men. They wanted to stop the suing and imprisoning of men who had no money to pay their debts! The courthouse at Worcester was surrounded and all courthouse business was stopped. Next, Shays' army marched on to Springfield with the idea of seizing the arsenal and getting guns and cannon for their protection. They failed to take the arsenal, and before long a body of militia was raised which routed Shays' men and forced the leader to flee to New Hampshire.

Such was the state of the country from the end of the Revolution until 1787. Each state government was working for itself, and the national government was so weak and had so little real power that the United States of America were anything but united.

Two Interstate Conventions

The Alexandria Convention. The rivalry between Virginia and Maryland over the navigation rights to Chesapeake Bay and the Potomac River reached a climax in 1785. By that time, both states were making ridiculous claims to the entire bay and river. They even went so far as to try to tax the cargoes of ships which were tied up at the other state's wharves. There was talk of settling the affair by an appeal to arms, but fortunately wiser heads prevailed.

At last, in 1785, a meeting was held in Alexandria, Virginia, to discuss the affair and settle it in a logical and friendly way. George Washington approved of this way of handling things, and at his suggestion the Virginia and Maryland delegates moved their meeting to his beautiful home at Mount Vernon where they continued their discussions. For this reason, the meeting is sometimes known as the *Alexandria Convention* and sometimes as the *Mount Vernon Convention*.

Although the delegates from Virginia and Maryland managed to settle their particular problems and disputes without much difficulty, it became apparent during the meeting that Pennsylvania, Delaware, and perhaps some of the other states would also be interested in having a voice in the matters under discussion. Another meeting was therefore proposed, to be held the following year in Annapolis, Maryland. All thirteen of the states were invited to send representatives.

The Meeting at Annapolis. *The Annapolis Convention*, held in 1786, was a great disappointment. On the day that the meeting was to begin, delegates from only five of the thirteen states had shown up. Five states could not decide the fate of eight others, and the delegates decided to cancel the meeting. However, one of the delegates, Alexander Hamilton of New York, suggested that a call be issued for a third meeting, to be held the following year in Philadelphia. This motion was approved. The Annapolis Convention then adjourned—and within a few hours delegates from two

The Constitution and the Declaration of Independence had to be carefully copied by clerks using writing equipment like this. Top left: a fine silver inkwell. Bottom left: a stone inkwell. Sand, used to blot the ink, was kept in a bowl like the one at top right. Quills were dipped in the ink.

other states arrived. Had these two delegates arrived earlier, it would have provided a majority and made it possible to hold an official meeting in 1786. The convention, however, had formally adjourned and was not reopened.

Looking Back

1. How did the Second Continental Congress fulfill the need for a central government in the colonies during the Revolution?
2. Why did Maryland hold up ratification of the Articles of Confederation for a long time?
3. Explain why the years 1781-1789 are often referred to as the "Critical Period."
4. List the chief terms of the Northwest Ordinance. Why was each important?
5. Shays' Rebellion was important for several reasons. What are two of them?
6. Summarize briefly the problems faced by the new nation at its start.

2. Convention Delegates Frame a New Constitution

Dissatisfaction with The Articles

In the 1780's, most Americans were dissatisfied with the Articles of Confederation. The cause of this dissatisfaction centered around economic and political problems which appeared serious enough to demand revision or amendment of the Articles.

American business, in the states and abroad, encountered all types of hindrances because of the lack of authority delegated to the central government. States themselves set up tariff barriers hindering trade. Great confusion resulted from individual states exercising control over custom duties. Aside from tariff difficulties, different types of money presented a problem. In theory, Congress had the authority to regulate the currency, but in practice, such regulation proved impossible since each state issued its own money.

Politically, the greatest problem under the Confederation seemed to be its inability to enforce laws. Congress could raise an army only if the states obeyed its request for troops. Furthermore, treaties made by the central government had to be approved as the law of the land by all the states. Since the states acted separately, Europe looked upon them as thirteen separate

Standing around a table at the Federal Convention: John Adams, William Livingston, Benjamin Franklin, Thomas Jefferson and Roger Sherman who introduced the "Connecticut Compromise".

> ### Federal Conventions
>
> Franklin, the elder statesman, at the Convention frequently expressed his concern for the success of the deliberations. Madison wrote:
>
> "Whilst the last members were signing, Dr. Franklin, looking towards the president's chair, at the back of which a rising sun happened to be painted, observed to a few members near him, that the painters had found it difficult to distinguish, in their art, a rising from a setting sun. "I have", said he, "often and often, in the course of the session, and in the vicissitudes of my hopes and fears as to its issue, looked at that behind the president, without being able to tell whether it was rising or setting; but now, at length, I have the happiness to know that it is a rising, and not a setting sun."
>
> —Madison's Debates in the Federal Convention

countries rather than an effective union. The European viewpoint was very close to the truth. Because of the inability of the Congress to exercise power, the states gave the Congress only half-hearted support.

The Federal Convention at Philadelphia

When the call was issued to all the states to send delegates to a convention in Philadelphia, sixty-two representatives were appointed. Fifty-five men assembled in Independence Hall, in the same room where eleven years before the Declaration had been written and signed. Of the fifty-five men, thirty-nine finally signed the Constitution drafted by the convention.

The instruction given to these men from their state authorities was simply to revise the Articles of Confederation. Most men felt that more than revision was needed. Even numerous amendments to the basic Articles would not meet the country's needs. But no real plan had been prearranged; discussion was the order of the day. Out of the days of debate, these patriotic representatives produced a superior document which has been changed but little in nearly two centuries of use.

The Delegates. Absent from this group were the liberals of the revolutionary period: Thomas Paine, Thomas Jefferson, Patrick Henry, John Adams, and Samuel Adams, giving conservatives the majority. Washington, universally respected and admired, was chosen as the chairman. Other outstanding leaders were Benjamin Franklin, Alexander Hamilton, James Madison, and George Mason. A great share of the credit should be given to James Madison, often called the "Father of the Constitution." He had acquired, by his wide reading, a profound and scholarly knowledge of history and politics. This can be observed in the thorough notes which he kept on the convention. All of the men had experience in government and many had studied extensively in the theories of government.

It is important to realize that the men who met at Philadelphia were not elected officials in the sense that our senators and representatives are today. In fact, they had no real authority to decide the course of the nation. Those who were sent from individual states were leaders in their own states, but they were not national leaders as yet. The conference needed the authority and prestige of a national leader, and only one man could give it that: George Washington. Washington attended the conference, taking little part in the debates, but lending his great influence and judgment to the proceedings. When the Constitution was presented to the states, George Washington's approval went a long way in promoting its ratification.

Work of the Convention. As the deliberations of the convention continued, the matter of obeying or disobeying their instructions became a grave concern of all the delegates. They had been sent to revise the Articles, not to discard them, but it was obvious that a new document was the only solution to the major problems of government. After some debate, the representatives decided to pledge themselves to complete secrecy until the work of the convention was finished. When the time came for the new document to be presented to the states and when the citizens compared it with the old Articles of Confederation, public sentiment, it was felt, would be in favor of the new Constitution.

The Constitutional Debates

As could be expected, there was much disagreement over the type of representative government that the young nation would have. Again, the states manifested their desires for power, first the large states, then the small states.

CONGRESSIONAL POWERS

Under The Constitution		Under the Confederation
1. Call on the militia (soldiers trained by each state).	in addition to	1. Declare war and make peace, and organize an army and navy.
2. Control the relations of the United States with other nations and Indian tribes.		2. Control the relations of the United States with other nations and Indian tribes.
3. Regulate trade passing from one state into another (interstate commerce) and trade with foreign nations.	in addition to	3. Regulate trade with the Indians.
4. Borrow money to pay expenses.		4. Borrow money to pay expenses.
5. Impose direct taxes to pay expenses of the central government.	instead of	5. Ask each state to raise money to pay expenses of the central government.
6. Coin all money and regulate its value.		
7. Organize courts to decide all disputes about the United States Constitution and laws, disputes between state governments, and between citizens of different states.		
8. Govern the capital city of the United States and territory not yet made into states.		
9. Make rules for naturalization of new citizens. Issue patents to inventors.		
10. Do anything else, not definitely stated, which is necessary to carry out any powers which are mentioned.		

> **Sources Used In Writing the Constitution**
> 1. British System of Government
> 2. Colonial Charters
> 3. State Constitutions
> 4. Articles of Confederation
> 5. Declaration of Independence
> 6. Ideas of Colonial leaders
> 7. Writings of English and European political thinkers

The Virginia Plan. The large states were more or less represented by Virginia, which had a large, well-established population and, at the time, a great deal of land. Edmund Randolph of Virginia presented a plan, called the *Virginia Plan*, which gave certain distinct advantages to Virginia and the other larger states. Randolph's plan provided that the representative government should be made up of men elected directly by the people, in proportion to the number of people in a state. This plan would give great advantages to states with large populations. The plan also provided that an upper house would be elected by the members of the lower house. Since large states would have more lower house members, this too would give states like Virginia a great advantage.

The New Jersey Plan. The small states also had a plan, however, and New Jersey represented their cause. William Paterson, of that state, presented a plan under which the federal legislature was to consist of only one house, represented by an equal number of members from each state. This plan would give small states an equal voice in the government, but it would give those people in larger states less power than they should have had. If a small state had only a population of a thousand and a large state had a population of ten thousand, it would be unfair for them to have an equal number of representatives as suggested by the *New Jersey Plan*. All the people would not have an equal say in the government.

The Connecticut Compromise. At last a committee was appointed, and a plan known as the *Connecticut Plan* was adopted. This provided for two houses of Congress, a lower house called the *House of Representatives* and an upper house called the *Senate*. In the House of Representatives, each state would be represented according to population. The Senate would have two representatives from each state, regardless of its size. Both the large and small states were satisfied by this compromise.

Three-fifths Compromise. Next came the question of whether or not slaves should be counted as part of the population in figuring the representation of a state. The northern states had few slaves, and the southern states had a great many. Bitter was the

> **Important Rights Guaranteed by the Constitution**
> 1. Freedom of Speech
> 2. Freedom of the Press
> 3. Freedom of Worship
> 4. Right to Assemble Peaceably
> 5. Right to Life and Liberty
> 6. Right to a speedy and public trial
> 7. Right to hold property
> 8. Right to petition the government

> *Powers Given in the Constitution*
> *Delegated Powers*—powers which only the national government can exercise.
> *Concurrent Powers*—powers shared by both national and state governments.
> *Reserved Powers*—powers expressly given to the states.
> *Prohibited Powers*—powers denied to both national and state governments.

debate on this subject, and agreement seemed unlikely. But, in the end, another compromise was made to try to satisfy both the northerners and the southerners. It was agreed that each slave would be counted as three-fifths of a person, though no slave had the right to vote. If a state had fifty thousand slaves, they would count as thirty thousand inhabitants. This was to apply both in determining the representation of that state in the House of Representatives and in portioning out its share of national taxes, which were to be divided according to population.

Commerce Debate. The third great compromise concerned commerce and the slave trade. Until 1787 the states had regulated their commerce and had levied taxes against each other, just as they would against any foreign nation. The northerners wanted Congress to have sole control of both interstate and foreign commerce, while the southerners wanted some power over commerce left with the states. Again, certain of the southern states refused to be governed by a constitution which abolished the slave trade, while many in the northern states wanted it abolished. At last a compromise was reached, by the terms of which Congress would be empowered to regulate commerce, but could not abolish the slave trade before 1808. Congress could, however, place a limited tax on each slave imported.

Ratification by the States

Federalists and Anti-Federalists. Now that the Constitution was framed, it became a question of whether or not it would be adopted by nine of the states, the number necessary to make it the law of the land. The fight over the adoption of the Constitution led to

> **The Federalist** was a series of 85 letters which appeared in a New York semi-weekly paper called the **Independent Journal.** These letters urged the New York delegation to the Constitutional Convention to ratify the Constitution. Scholars still refer to **The Federalist**, which was later published in book form, in interpreting the Constitution.

The New-York Historical Society

the forming of the first two political parties in America. Those who favored the Constitution were called the *Federalists*, and those who opposed it, the *Anti-Federalists*. For a long time, the issue was in doubt. Opinion ran strong on both sides.

In the heat of the campaign, a series of articles appeared in the press. Later they were published in a little pamphlet called *The Federalist*. Alexander Hamilton was the man who wrote most of these articles which cleverly and convincingly set forth the reasons why the Constitution should be adopted. James Madison and John Jay also contributed to *The Federalist*.

Controversy in New York. The articles supporting the Constitution were published in New York because there the argument was especially close and bitter. Hamilton was again to serve the Federalists well.

Many of the citizens who had grown weary of the domineering government of Britain feared that the Constitution would merely provide another tyranny no less terrible. King George, they feared, would be succeeded by King Congress, and taxes would be laid on them no less irksome than the Stamp Act and the Townshend Acts. It was with this proposition that Hamilton had to contend in the New York convention. So brilliantly and convincingly did he speak, and so cleverly did he point out the advantages of a central government, that at last, after ten other states had already ratified, New York ratified the Constitution and became one of the United States.

Throughout the country there was great rejoicing. To many Americans, the United States at last had the appearance of a real nation, one of which they could be proud and one that European nations would respect. New York, with its wealth and large population, was the most important link in the chain. When at last New York ratified, many cities held elaborate celebrations with parades, floats, fireworks, orations, and religious services.

Earlier, after spirited debates, Delaware, Pennsylvania, New Jersey, Georgia, Connecticut, Massachusetts, Maryland, and South Carolina had ratified, or accepted, the Constitution. When in June, 1788, the ninth state, New Hampshire, also voted to adopt it, the Constitution became the law of the United States. Soon afterwards Virginia, New York, North Carolina, and finally Rhode Island fell into line. The thirteen states, by adopting the Constitution and agreeing to abide by its terms, became, in reality, a single nation. For the first time, the United States were really united.

Looking Back

1. In what ways did the Federal Convention in Philadelphia exceed its authority?

2. How were the differences concerning representation between the large and small states settled?

3. In what way was the matter of counting slaves resolved?

4. What compromises concerning the control of commerce were reached at the Convention?

5. How did ratification of the Constitution lead to the development of political parties?

3. The Constitution of the United States

"It will be the pattern for all future constitutions and the admiration of all future ages."

—William Pitt, British Prime Minister at the time of the Constitutional Convention

"The American Constitution is the most wonderful work ever struck off at a given time by the brain and purpose of man."

—Gladstone, 19th century British Prime Minister

Probably the most unusual provision of the new government was the formation of the three departments: legislative, judicial, and executive. This was an innovation. No previous governments had tried a similar pattern. The framers felt that this threefold form of government would prevent any one branch from assuming undue power. Under its new Constitution, the government of the United States would be a government of checks and balances, for each department would check the powers of the other, and a balance of power would be maintained among the three branches. Though many powers were kept by the individual states, enough power was given to the central government to insure its respect at home and abroad and to do away with the weaknesses of the Articles of Confederation.

Preamble

"We the people of the United States, in order to form a more perfect Union, establish Justice, ensure domestic Tranquility, provide for the common defence, promote the general Welfare, and secure the Blessings of Liberty to ourselves and our Posterity, do ordain and establish this Constitution for the United States of America."

Article I

Legislative Department

Article I sets up the machinery for the creating and passing of laws to govern the country. In this article is described the process by which the average American citizen participates in government through his elected representatives and senators. It establishes rules for the election of congressmen, the terms for which they serve, and the qualifications they need in order to hold office. One of the most important things about this first part of the Constitution is the group of rules which outlines exactly the power given to Congress in relation to the other important branches of government, and to the state governments.

Article II

Executive Department

This section of the Constitution states that the "executive power shall be vested in a President of the United States of America." The manner of the election of both President and Vice-President is provided for, although election today is controlled by the Twelfth Amendment. When a President is selected, many qualifications are considered, but the Constitution requires only three.

The second section establishes the principles that the civilian overrules the military and that only Congress can declare war. Provision is made for the executive departments or cabinet posts and that the chief officer in each may be required to send to the President his written opinion on any subject relating to his department. When the President makes treaties and appoints ambassadors, they must be approved by the Senate.

Section three sets forth the policy of the President giving to Congress information on the "state of the union" or other important messages that he may judge necessary and expedient.

The last section states that the President and civil officers can be removed by "impeachment for, and conviction of, treason, bribery, or other high crimes and misdemeanors."

Article III

Judicial Department

Article III outlines the role of the third branch of the government, the judicial power. It provides for a Supreme Court to which lower courts can appeal. It allocates certain cases to local courts and other cases to be tried in the state courts. In all cases there is the guarantee of trial by jury.

Article IV

Relations of the States

Here the rights and duties of states and the rights and liabilities of citizens are set forth. The article further outlines the process for admitting new states.

Article V

The Amending Process

Article V ensures that the Constitution can be amended and states the method of such additions.

Article VI

Supreme Law of the Land

This article states that the Constitution, the laws passed by the federal government, and the treaties made by the authority of the United States shall be the supreme law of the land.

Article VII

Ratification

Article VII establishes the method for ratification of the Constitution by the states.

The Bill of Rights. In March, 1789, within two years of its adoption, the Constitution received ten amendments, which were passed in a single group and were ratified by the necessary nine states before the end of 1791. These ten amendments were all closely connected and had the common purpose of guaranteeing the citizens of the United States certain rights. Among them were the right of trial by jury, freedom of speech, freedom of the press, and religious freedom. Collectively, the ten amendments are referred to as the *Bill of Rights*.

Amendments I–X

The Bill of Rights

I. Establishes freedom of religion, press, speech, assembly, and petition.
II. Gives the right to keep and bear arms.
III. Says that no private citizen can be required to keep soldiers in his home.
IV. Frees private citizens from search of their persons, houses, papers, and effects.
V. States that an accused person is innocent until proven guilty.
VI. Grants protection of the laws to the accused.
VII. Guarantees trial by jury.
VIII. Protects citizens from excessive fines and cruel punishments.
IX. Ensures rights not stated in the Constitution.
X. Gives powers not delegated to the federal government to the states.

Amendments XI–XXIV

XI. Prohibits individuals from suing a state in federal court.

XII. Provides for separate ballots for the election of President and Vice-President.
XIII. Abolishes slavery.
XIV. Grants citizenship to all persons born or naturalized in the United States.
XV. Ensures for any male citizen the right to vote.
XVI. Gives power to Congress to collect taxes on incomes.
XVII. Establishes the direct election of senators by the people.
XVIII. Prohibits the manufacture, sale, and distribution of intoxicating liquors in the United States and its territories.
XIX. Grants to women the right to vote.
XX. Abolishes the "lame duck" sessions of Congress.
XXI. Repeals the Eighteenth Amendment.
XXII. Limits the presidential terms.
XXIII. Grants to the citizens of the District of Columbia the right to vote in presidential elections.
XXIV. Abolishes the poll tax.

The Chapter in Perspective

What Do These Dates and Terms Mean?

Articles of Confederation	1786	Virginia Plan
"Critical Period"	Alexandria Convention	New Jersey Plan
Northwest Ordinance	Annapolis Convention	Three-fifths Compromise
1785	Federal Convention	*The Federalist*
1787	Federalists	
Shays' Rebellion	anti-Federalists	

Who Are These People?

Madison   Paterson
Washington   Hamilton
Randolph   Jay

Where Are These Places?

Independence Hall   Potomac River

Questions for Study

1. Evaluate the performance of the Second Continental Congress as the functioning government of the colonies in revolt.
2. Why would you have (or have not)

supported Maryland's position regarding ratification of the Articles?
4. How did the terms of the Northwest Ordinance reflect democratic trends and an appreciation of future national problems?
5. Which foreign nation, in your opinion, presented the greatest problem during this period? Why?
6. Explain how interstate jealousies revealed the need for a stronger national government.
7. What was the real significance of Shays' Rebellion?
8. How did the Constitution seek to establish a system of checks and balances?
9. Which states were formed out of the Northwest Territory?

Place Yourself in History

It has been a long, difficult time of decision for you and your closest friend. Both of you are delegates to the convention called in New York to ratify the Constitution. Speeches and debates have been long and sharp. Tomorrow, July 26, 1788, your votes are to be cast. And yet you are uncertain. The vote will be close.

What would you have done? Would you have voted for or against ratifying the Constitution? Would the vote of you and your friend affect the final decision of the convention?

Expanding Your Outlook

Doing It Yourself

1. Prepare a speech to your class imagining you are either a. a colonial member of the Stamp Act Congress or b. a member of Parliament favoring the Stamp Act.
2. As a resident of Boston, write a letter to your cousin in London describing conditions immediately before and after the Boston Tea Party.
3. Make a series of posters that urged colonists to carry out the boycott of English goods.
4. Starting with the Stamp Act and going through the beginning of the war, list the main events under the headings: British action and colonial action. Try to show that a specific action by one side brought forth a specific reaction by the other.
5. Make a map showing the military campaigns of the Revolution and locating the sites of the major battles.
6. Write a newspaper account of conditions in the colonies after the Revolution that earned the period the title "The Critical Period."
7. Make a diagram in the form of a flight of steps leading from 1763 to independence. Each step leading to the platform of independence should be labeled.
8. Write an account of the winning of independence by the United

States as it might have appeared in a newspaper in France or Spain or England.

Working with the Class

1. Form a group to be members of the Committees of Correspondence with each member representing a different colony. Pass your communications and answers among the group. The class may wish to hear them.
2. Make the entire class members of the Constitutional Convention. Assign roles in advance and then discuss the issues in the great debates over the major compromises.
3. Plan a debate before the class on the topic: "The American Revolution Could Have Been Averted."
4. Arrange a class committee to prepare a "You Are There" program for one of the following: a. adoption of the Declaration of Independence, b. Yorktown, c. Shays' Rebellion.
5. Organize a committee to turn out a one page newspaper that might have appeared in New York in 1787.
6. Imagine that you and several classmates were opposed to colonial independence. Prepare a joint statement setting forth your views.

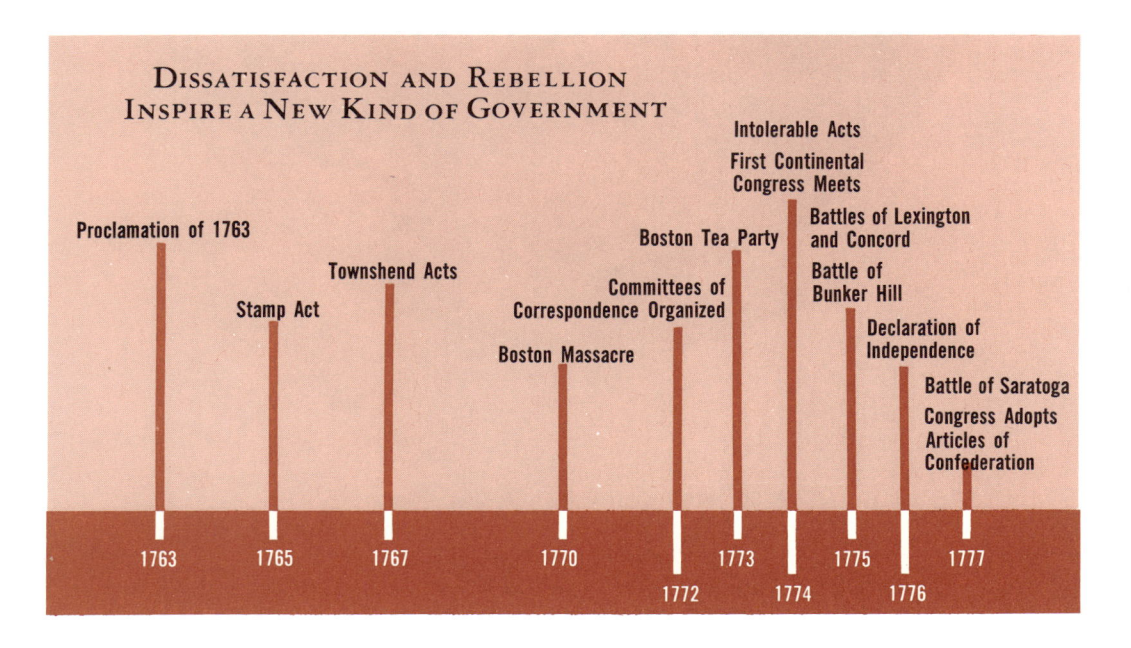

DISSATISFACTION AND REBELLION INSPIRE A NEW KIND OF GOVERNMENT

1763	Proclamation of 1763
1765	Stamp Act
1767	Townshend Acts
1770	Boston Massacre
1772	Committees of Correspondence Organized
1773	Boston Tea Party
1774	Intolerable Acts; First Continental Congress Meets
1775	Battles of Lexington and Concord; Battle of Bunker Hill
1776	Declaration of Independence
1777	Battle of Saratoga; Congress Adopts Articles of Confederation

The Home Insurance Company

W. J. Vache *painted this decorative panel in 1830 near Baltimore. It is known as the* Maritime Eagle and Shield, *and is symbolic of a young and ambitious American nation. The ship in the panel is probably the* Ohio, *a United States ship-of-the-line.*

ONE NATION INDIVISIBLE

UNIT 3

The American Eagle Tries Its Wings

8. Federalists and Republicans Launch the New Government

1. Washington Charts the Course of the New Nation • 2. Adams Serves in Troubled Times • 3. Jefferson and a New Party Steer the Nation

9. The United States Gains the Respect of Other Nations

1. The Nation Fights Once More for Independence • 2. The United States Moves Ahead Under Madison • 3. The Nation Enters an "Era of Good Feeling"

10. Industrial and Social Developments

1. American Know-How Goes into Operation • 2. The Industrial Revolution Reaches America • 3. The Government Encourages Industrial Growth • 4. The Social Revolution Brings Enlightenment

8. Federalists and Republicans Launch the New Government

The whole world watched as the new government was launched. Both Europeans and Americans believed that the American Constitution was an ambitious project, and they were doubtful that it would succeed. It took strong men to convince the people that the theories of the Constitution were practical.

One of these men was George Washington, first President of the United States, respected for his leadership in the Revolution as well as his character. Washington reluctantly accepted the Presidency as his patriotic duty, providing the government with the strong hand of a capable leader.

1. Washington Charts the Course of the New Nation

The people of the United States differed widely in their opinions of the Constitution, and as Federalists and Anti-Federalists carried on a bitter campaign before its adoption. Nevertheless, they all agreed in their admiration for George Washington. It is not surprising, therefore, that when the new form of government went into effect, the man who had led the American armies in war was chosen to lead the American people in peace. In our first election—the election of 1788—Washington was unanimously elected the first President of the United States.

Washington's Advisers

President Washington surrounded himself with a group of able advisers known as his *cabinet*. Thomas Jefferson, author of the Declaration of Independence, was selected as Secretary of State, and to him fell the duty of handling the foreign affairs of the country. General Henry Knox, an able soldier, was appointed Secretary of

War. Edmund Randolph became Attorney General. Alexander Hamilton was made Secretary of the Treasury, perhaps the most difficult office of all for the United States had no money and many debts.

To the important post of Chief Justice of the Supreme Court of the United States, Washington appointed John Jay. Jay was one of the authors of *The Federalist* and a signer of the treaty of peace with Great Britain. Under Jay five Supreme Court associate justices were given office. They were to help him try cases brought before the court. The machinery of the United States government was now ready to be set in motion.

Hamilton's Financial Policy

Taxation. Alexander Hamilton early showed real genius in handling the financial affairs of the United States. Realizing that the country could not long endure without funds, he induced Congress to pass three measures, all of which brought money into the government's treasury. One of these, the first tariff bill, placed a small duty on certain foreign goods entering our ports.

George Washington, father of our country, painted by Gilbert Stuart, American artist.

A Tonnage Act was also passed, which taxed all foreign merchant ships entering American harbors, at the rate of about fifty cents per ton. The third measure sponsored by Hamilton was a direct tax on all distilled liquors.

The Whiskey Rebellion. After a time, the tax which Congress had put on alcoholic liquors brought unpleasant results. The farmers of the backwoods region grew large quantities of corn. It was so hard to haul this corn to market that they had formed the habit of distilling it into corn whiskey which was easier to transport and to

---

The First President Writes of His Duties

"In every act of my administration, I have sought the happiness of my fellow-citizens. My system for the attainment of this object has uniformly been to overlook all personal, local, and partial considerations: to contemplate the United States, as one great whole. . . . While I feel the most lively gratitude for the many instances of approbation from my country; I can no otherwise deserve it, than by obeying the dictates of my conscience. . . ."

—From Washington's letter to the Boston Selectmen
  July 28, 1795

sell. The tax on liquors lessened the profit of the farmers, and naturally they were violently opposed to this measure. Finally, in 1794, the farmers of western Pennsylvania refused to pay the tax and severely beat the men who came to force collection. Realizing that the laws of the country must be respected, Washington at once dispatched an army to put down the *Whiskey Rebellion,* as it was called. As the army approached, the rebellion collapsed, and there was no further organized resistance to the tax.

Payment of Debts. It was Hamilton's purpose to use the money raised by the taxes to pay the country's many debts. First, there were the nations from which the United States had borrowed money during the Revolution. Then there were the debts owed by the government to those men who had lent the country money during the war and to soldiers who had served in the war. Besides all these debts of the nation, Hamilton proposed to assume and pay the debts of the different states. He foresaw that this assuming of the states' debts would result in giving the government a greater taxing power. The people to whom the states owed the money were the richest and most influential, and Hamilton was sure that they would stand back of increased taxation if it were levied for the purpose of repaying their loans.

In time, Hamilton was able to accomplish what he had set out to do. The debts of both nation and states were paid, and ever since that time the credit of the United States has been unquestioned throughout the world.

Banking and Currency. In 1791 Hamilton persuaded Congress to establish the first national bank, known as the Bank of the United States. This bank was established at Philadelphia; and there, in the following year, the first United States Mint was built to coin all types of money. Paper money was now issued, with the credit of the United States government behind it. Since faith in the government was increasing all the time, the people in all of the states accepted this currency at its face value. Unlike the old paper money issued by each state, the United States bills could be used anywhere in the country. This common medium of exchange did much to encourage interstate commerce and trade.

Rise of Political Parties

The political leaders of the country and their followers early began to divide themselves into two distinct groups. One group believed in a liberal interpretation of the powers given by the Constitution to the central government. They felt the government should not be limited to those powers specifically delegated to it by the Constitution, but should be allowed additional authority whenever needed. Hamilton was the leader of this *broad construc-*

The old lighthouse, Cape Henry, Virginia, is a symbol of the early federal government. Commissioned by Alexander Hamilton, it ended interstate disputes over lighthouse rights.

The blacksmith shop was important in Colonial America since horses were the main power source for vehicles. The blacksmith also had a thriving business in household ironwork.

tion group, and to it Washington allied himself during his first term as President. However, he was opposed to political parties as such and never would admit that he belonged to one. The other party was afraid that the government would grow too strong and would take away too many of the powers of the states. Its members felt that no powers should be allowed the central government unless specifically given it by the Constitution. Thomas Jefferson was the leader of these *strict constructionists*.

Hamilton's *broad constructionists* kept the name of *Federalists*, for they favored a strong federal government. The wealthiest and most highly educated people in the country at the time were Federalists. They were mostly merchants, manufacturers, and other city dwellers. Their idea of a proper government was one in which trained political leaders handled the important affairs of state, leaving only the less important questions to the state, county, and town governments. This took away some power from the average man, but the Federalists felt that it was given to those best fitted to govern. Jefferson's *strict constructionists*, on the other hand, favored a government in which the poor farmer as well as the influential aristocrat could participate. They adopted the name *Democratic-Republicans*.

Many farmers and people living in small towns supported the Democratic-Republican party. They were not in close touch with the central government, and they disliked seeing any powers slip out of their hands to be given to unknown lawmakers in the nation's capital. Many people who feared the way in which Hamilton was using money freely to pay the nation's debts also joined the Democratic-Republicans. Still others felt that the federal government did not give the people as much voice in affairs as they deserved. It was from this varied group of people that the Democratic-Republicans gained supporters.

Reelection of Washington

Despite the competition which had sprung up between the Federalists and the Democratic-Republicans, George Washington had no rival when, in 1792, he ran for President a second time. It is said that he was tired of public service and wanted to retire to his beautiful estate at Mount Vernon. However, he clearly saw the dangers that would threaten the infant government if his firm hand should be removed. Hamilton's financial policy, Washington felt, might never be given a fair trial if he did not accept a second term in office.

The Democratic-Republicans, in 1792, managed to gain a majority in the House of Representatives. The problems Washington encountered in working with a Congress politically opposed to him were many. And similar problems have been encountered by every President in the same situation. One of the fascinating things about the American system of government is that in spite of disagreements between a President and a Congress, the business of government goes on.

Foreign Affairs

Upheaval in Europe. The years following the American Revolution were trying ones for many European nations. Great changes were taking place in Europe. For centuries France had been ruled by kings, some of them just and some of them cruel. The people of France wanted a different form of government and, in 1789, started a revolution. The armies of Louis XVI, King of France, were ineffective in stopping the uprising when many of his soldiers joined the revolution. Uncontrolled mobs swept through the palace and seized the king and queen, who were later put to death. So great was the reaction against the old methods of government that the revolutionists did not know where to stop. They created a reign of terror which lasted for several years and claimed the lives of many thousands of people.

As soon as France became a republic, Frenchmen began to stream into other countries to preach the cause of freedom. Fearing that similar revolutions would overthrow their kings and their governments, a combination of European powers, led by Great Britain, declared war on the new French Republic.

The Proclamation of Neutrality. What was America to do? Washington was not long in doubt. To take part in the war might cost the United States her liberty. It would certainly cost the lives of thousands of Americans. So, in 1793, Washington declared that the United States would aid neither Great Britain nor France, but would remain a *neutral* country.

Both Great Britain and France were enraged by the proclamation of neutrality. The British felt that the Americans were their own blood brothers, speaking the same language, and

British officers capture a seaman on an American merchant ship. Such ships, when threatened by English men-of-war, were helpless.

The Genêt Affair. France, too, was making trouble for the United States. She sent to America, as minister, a young Frenchman named Genêt (zhe-NAY′), who began his stay by stirring up feeling against Great Britain. He wanted to lead the United States into joining the war against England.

In an interview with Washington, Genêt learned that he could expect no help from the United States, and that if he wished to remain in this country he must be careful of what he did and said. Citizen Genêt had more patriotism than wisdom. He had, too, the European notion that the American government was weak and could be easily pressured into following his ideas. So the young Frenchman proceeded to defy the President and set to work in American ports fitting out ships to prey on British merchant vessels. This was more than Washington could stand, and he at once sent word to the French government that Genêt must be asked to return to France. Genêt was ordered to return.

In spite of the trouble which the young Frenchman stirred up in the United States, he must have found many things which he liked in America. Or perhaps he was afraid of the action his own government might take against him, for he did not return to France but decided to become a citizen of the United States. He settled in a little town near Albany, New York, where he was later married, and where in time he died and was buried.

The Jay Treaty. Things could not go on as they had, and something needed to be done to relieve the oppression from abroad. At last, in 1794, Washington sent John Jay, the first

should certainly come to their aid against a foreign power. The French pointed out that only a few years before they had sent men and ships and leaders to help America win her independence, and that America, in turn, should help France. American ships on the high seas were captured by vessels of both nations, and their cargoes were taken without thought of justice or payment. American seamen were seized by British men-of-war and made to serve in the British navy, because "Once an Englishman, always an Englishman," Great Britain claimed. Many Americans were angered by such treatment, but still President Washington avoided war.

Chief Justice, to England to make a treaty. Jay soon found that Great Britain would concede very little to the new country. He was also hampered by the need to stay within the bounds of an earlier treaty of friendship and commerce with France. To add to his troubles, while Jay was in Britain, Hamilton promised an English delegate in the United States that this country would never engage in a war with Great Britain. Thus, Jay could neither make useful concessions or meaningful threats. But as any terms would bring improvement to the existing conditions, Jay accepted the best terms he could get and carried the new treaty back to America.

All that Britain agreed to do was to give up the forts which she was holding in the western part of the American lands. No mention at all was made of the freedom of the seas or the seizing of American seamen. Unsatisfactory as the terms were, President Washington urged that the treaty be accepted, for he realized that it was the best that could be had at the time.

The American people, however, were sorely disappointed. At the close of the Revolutionary War, Great Britain had promised to give up their forts in the West, but had not done so. It was felt that all Jay had accomplished was to get the British to promise to do something that should have been done long before. Jay became extremely unpopular, and even such great leaders as Washington and Hamilton were greeted with jeers and catcalls when they spoke in behalf of the treaty. Hamilton on one occasion was even stoned, and Washington was led to remark that at such a time he would rather be in his grave than be President of the United States. The Jay Treaty served only to increase bitterness toward the British.

Washington's Farewell Address

In 1797, George Washington retired from the Presidency, having refused to

George Washington's beloved home at Mount Vernon, Virginia, where he retired.

run for a third term. Shortly before he left office, he wrote his famous farewell address to the people of the United States. In it he gave the country advice that was to prove valuable in the years to come, pointing out the dangers of foreign entanglements and alliances with European powers. He also warned of a danger nearer home, that of too-heated political division.

Looking Back

1. Who were the chief advisers whom Washington chose to help him?
2. By what measures did Hamilton propose to raise money for the new government?
3. What were the basic differences between the two major political parties?
4. Why did Washington wish to keep the United States neutral in regard to the European conflicts?
5. For what reasons was the Jay Treaty so unpopular in the United States?

2. Adams Serves in Troubled Times

It would have been difficult for any president to follow a man of the stature of Washington. No one else in the country appealed so much to the public. Adams realized this. He also knew that he had not been elected by a great majority, and that the anti-Federalists were numerically very strong.

However, the difficulties of the Adams administration should in no way lessen our respect for John Adams. He was a man of great influence during the trying days of the Revolution. His record as a diplomat sent by the United States to Holland and Great Britain was a brilliant one. Even his enemies spoke of him as "Honest John Adams," recognizing that he was a sincere patriot.

Adams had served well through two terms as Vice-President under Washington. Since he was a strong Federalist, the rising tide of the Democratic-Republican party made his administration a difficult one. John Adams was the first President to serve as Chief Executive in the new capital at Washington, D.C. As the first occupant of the White House, he wrote a special prayer for those who at future times would live within its walls. The prayer now appears engraved on a mantel in the State Dining Room of the White House.

"I pray Heaven to bestow the best of blessings on This House and all that shall hereafter inhabit it. May none but honest and wise men ever rule under this roof."
—John Adams, Nov. 2, 1800

The X Y Z Affair

The Citizen Genêt episode increased French bitterness toward the United States. French warships on the high seas captured American vessels and sold them in French ports. Insults were hurled at the United States in every French town.

Hoping to avoid war, President Adams sent three representatives to

171

The famous White House mantel, engraved with a prayer written by John Adams in 1800. His hopes for America were not much different from the ones we hold today.

France in 1797. They were met by three Frenchmen representing the French government. The Frenchmen said that war could only be avoided by the payment of large sums of money to help France carry on her war with Great Britain. To this disgraceful proposal, Charles Pinckney, one of the American representatives, exclaimed, "No! No! Not a sixpence!" The story later became widespread that he had cried, "Millions for defense! Not one cent for tribute!"

Soon a report of the affair was made to Congress. To avoid complications, the names of the three French representatives were removed from the report, and the letters X, Y, and Z were put in their places. For this reason, the conference in France became known as the *X Y Z Affair*.

Throughout America swept a wave of indignation, and the motto "Millions for defense! Not one cent for tribute!" became a patriotic slogan. American warships put out to sea and captured two French frigates so easily that the French began to feel that a war with the United States might not be desirable after all. Accordingly, Napoleon Bonaparte, who had just come into power in France, made peace with the United States.

People in the United States held varying opinions regarding what was happening in Europe. Some wanted to side with England against France; some wanted to take up arms with France against England. Few supported the Federalist policy of neutrality. Thus began the crumbling of Federalist power. This crumbling was aided by the ever-increasing group of immigrants entering the country. Most of the immigrants supported Jefferson, the great champion of the common people, and his party, the Democratic-Republican.

The Alien and Sedition Laws

The Federalists wished to stop the criticism of their policies and to check

Jefferson's growing army of followers. To do this, Congress, with the approval of President John Adams, passed in 1798 a series of laws known as the Alien and Sedition Laws. The first of these, the *Alien Law*, gave the President the power to send from the country any foreigner whose influence he felt was dangerous. It also increased the length of time which had to pass before a foreign immigrant could become an American citizen and could vote. The *Sedition Law* provided heavy fines and prison sentences for those who published false or unfriendly criticisms of the government.

The Kentucky and Virginia Resolutions

At Jefferson's suggestion, Virginia and the new state of Kentucky at once declared that the Alien and Sedition Laws should not be enforced within their borders. These declarations became known as the *Kentucky and Virginia Resolutions*. This action raised the burning question of whether the national government had the power to enforce its laws against the opposition of a state, or whether the states had the right to disregard national laws.

Before any move was made, the offending laws were repealed; the question was left undecided to trouble following generations. The main result of the affair was to widen the breach between the Federalists and the Democratic-Republicans and to discredit further the Federalist party.

The Death of Washington

In 1799, in the height of the excitement caused by the Virginia and Kentucky Resolutions, George Washington died on his estate at Mount Vernon. The whole country mourned for its great leader. Even the French and British, who still had little regard for the United States, showed how highly they esteemed the man, George Washington, by lowering their flags in token of respect.

While these events were taking place in America, the war in Europe was still going on. Napoleon Bonaparte, a brilliant young army officer who had seized control of the French government, was leading the French armies with great success against Britain, Prussia, Spain, Austria, and other allied countries. Desire was still strong on both sides to bring America into the war, and the maintaining of her peace became the most important problem facing the United States.

A New Capital

During Adams' administration, the capital of the United States was moved

Thomas Jefferson memorial statue located in Washington, D.C.

173

from Philadelphia to its present location. George Washington had taken the oath of office in New York City and soon after that, the seat of government was moved to Philadelphia, then the largest city of the country. This aroused jealousy, for each state wanted the capital within its borders. So bitter did the rivalry become that it was decided that no state should have the honor. A separate region, the District of Columbia, lying between Maryland and Virginia, was set aside, and a new national capital was built in it. The new capital was named for President Washington, and from that day to this the city of Washington has been the capital of the United States.

The Winds of Change

The Federalists guided the country through a dangerous period at home and abroad. However, in the presidential election of 1800 the Federalists were decisively defeated by the Democratic-Republicans, who polled thousands of new immigrant votes. So distressed was Adams at the turn of affairs that when he left office he refused to shake hands with his successor, Thomas Jefferson, the first Democratic-Republican President of the United States.

Looking Back

1. What was the "X Y Z Affair"?
2. How did the Alien and Sedition Laws affect life in America?
3. How did the new concept in the Kentucky and Virginia Resolutions create a problem?
4. For what reasons was the District of Columbia created?
5. How can you account for the defeat of the Federalists in 1800?

3. Jefferson and a New Party Steer the Nation

The Election of 1800

The election of 1800 brought into power a new political party and two famous men: Thomas Jefferson, the new President; and Aaron Burr, the new Vice-President. It also brought about a needed reform in the machinery of electing the President. Before this time the electors, chosen by the people, each voted for two candidates, without stating which should be President and which Vice-President. The candidate receiving the highest number of votes became President and the one receiving the next highest became Vice-President. It happened that Jefferson and Burr received the same number of electoral votes, and it was left to the House of Representatives to decide which should hold the office of President and which should be Vice-President. Alexander Hamilton disliked Burr even more than he disliked Jefferson, and he used his influence to secure Jefferson's election. To avoid any more tie votes for the Presidency, Congress and the states passed the Twelfth Amendment to the Constitution. This amendment provides that the electors should vote separately for the President and Vice-President, and that no one could be a candidate for both offices. Our voting today is done according to the Twelfth Amendment.

Future events were to prove that the choice of Jefferson for the Presidency was a good one. Burr later quarreled with Alexander Hamilton and killed that great Federalist statesman in a duel. Later still, he traveled to the Southwest with a group of armed companions. No one knows exactly what he was trying to do, but it was widely believed that he was trying to establish an empire of his own in the neighboring Spanish lands. He was arrested and accused of treason. Though he was not convicted, there has ever since been a shadow on the name of Aaron Burr.

A Man of the People Takes Action

Jefferson was very different from the two Federalist Presidents who had preceded him. He affected none of the pomp and grandeur of Washington and Adams, both of whom believed that the President should hold himself aloof from the people. The new President was interested in seeing the country run by and for the ordinary man. An aristocracy was about to give way to a truly democratic republic. Instead of elaborate costumes, Jefferson wore only the simple clothes of the man on the street. Often he could be seen riding his saddle horse, the magnificent Wildair, through the countryside or the streets of the capital. All who wished to see him in his office could do so without formality. He was a true representative of the people, and he soon became a great favorite with them.

Jefferson rode in Washington streets often. Could he today? Explain why not.

The Barbary Pirates. One of the first acts of Jefferson's administration was the suppression of the Barbary pirates of North Africa, who had long been preying on American shipping. The pirates demanded large sums of money as the price of not molesting American ships. Instead of the money, Jefferson sent a fleet of warships which defeated the pirates. For a time this ended the practice of seizing ships and forcing peaceful nations to pay bribes.

The Louisiana Purchase. Jefferson had not been long in office when he had an opportunity to prove his ability as President. France, under Napoleon, persuaded Spain, through a treaty, to cede back to the French the great

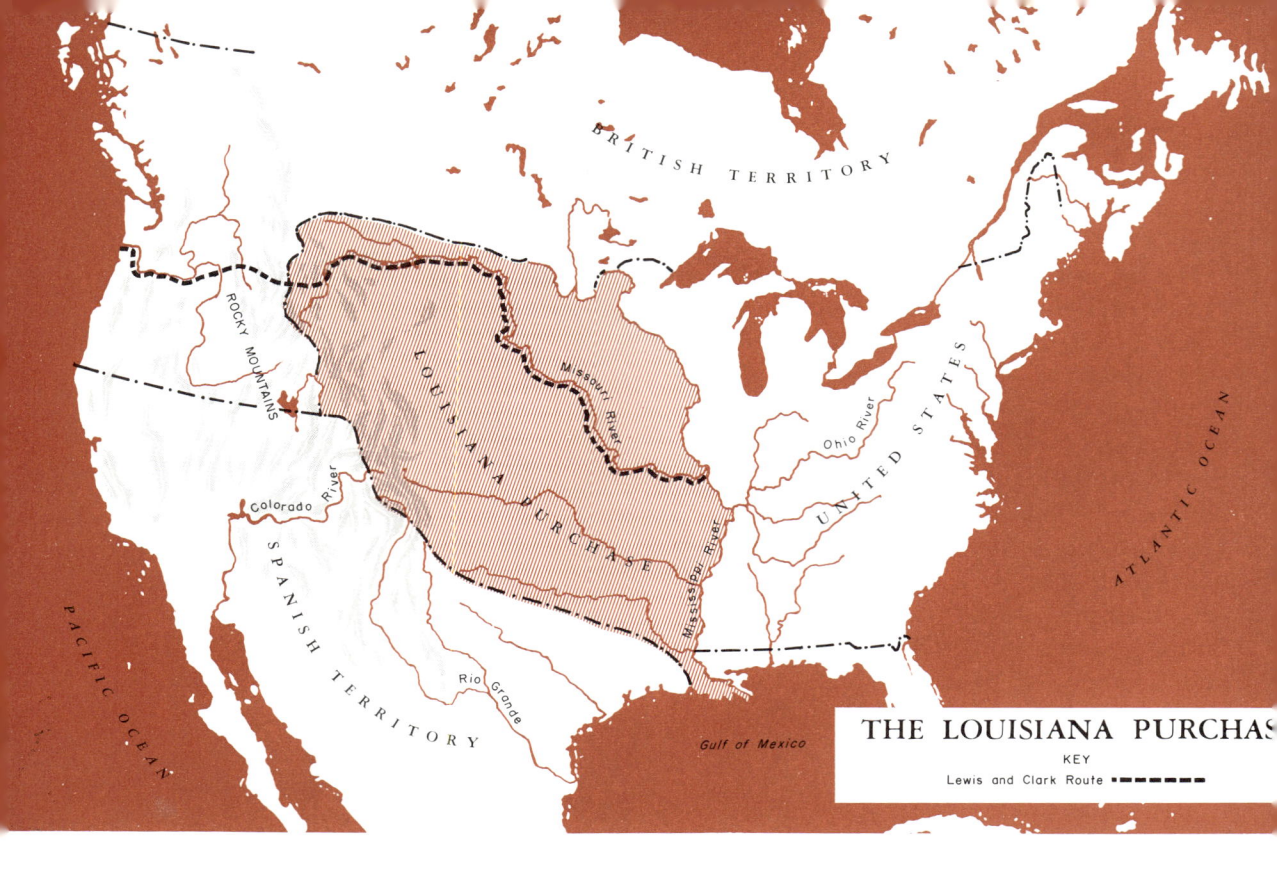

THE LOUISIANA PURCHASE
KEY
Lewis and Clark Route ▪▪▪▪▪▪▪

territory of Louisiana which controlled the mouth of the Mississippi River. Napoleon's purpose was to build up a French empire, with broad and valuable lands in the New World.

The many Americans who had pushed on into the land to the east of the Mississippi were much alarmed when they heard of this move of Napoleon. Instead of weak Spain, they were to have powerful France for a neighbor. If Napoleon succeeded in his wars, it seemed likely that before very long the United States would be threatened with French armies from the west. On the other hand, if Napoleon failed and the British won, it was entirely possible that Louisiana would be ceded to Great Britain, and that strong and dangerous nation would then menace the United States. What should Jefferson do?

The American minister to France was Robert R. Livingston. Jefferson sent James Monroe to join Livingston, and the two were to try to buy from France the city of New Orleans and some of the French land near the city. The American envoys found Napoleon ready to sell. The war had lately been going against him, and his dream of a French empire in America now seemed very faint. The one thing which he needed more than anything else was money, and he showed a great willingness to sell all of France's possessions in the New World for a small amount of ready cash. Monroe and Livingston had come to buy only a small tract of land near New Orleans, but when they reported the situation to Jefferson in 1803, he decided that the United States ought to purchase the entire province of Louisiana.

The trouble was that the Constitution did not give the President or Congress the right to make such a purchase, and Jefferson was the great champion of the strict construction of the Constitution! He was deeply troubled, but at last he decided that this was too great a bargain to be missed. For the sum of about $15,000,000 he bought from France an area larger than the entire United States of that day. The United States had suddenly more than doubled in size.

The New Land. The purchase of Louisiana opened up new lands into which the country's growing population could expand. The valley of the Mississippi had rich soil and could easily be made into a great agricultural region which would supply food for the cities along the eastern coast. Since roads were few, and railroads were unknown, the mighty Mississippi River would provide a highway. Boats could navigate the broad river, carrying the products of the West to the Gulf of Mexico, and thence out to sea. Finally, there was no longer a possibility of a strong neighbor in the West which might at any time overwhelm and conquer the young United States.

Sacajawea (above), was translator, guide and contact with the Indians for Lewis and Clark. Without her, it is said the expedition would not have gone beyond Idaho.

The Lewis and Clark Expedition

In 1804 Jefferson sent out an expedition under Meriwether Lewis and William Clark to explore the new territory. In their canoes they started from

---

America Should Be a Refuge For the Oppressed

Let us consecrate a sanctuary for those whom the misrule of Europe may compel to seek happiness in other climes. This refuge once known will produce reaction on the happiness of those who remain there, by warning their task-masters that when the evils of ... oppression become heavier than those of the abandonment of country, another ... is open where their subjects will be received as brothers, and secured against ... oppressions by a participation in the right of self-government.

—Thomas Jefferson to George Flower (1817)

St. Louis, on the Mississippi, and followed the course of the Missouri River northwest. Guided by Sacajawea (SACK'-uh-juh-WEE'uh), a Shoshoni (show-SHOW'nee) Indian squaw with a papoose on her back, they entered one of the Missouri's branches, up which they traveled for many days. Then, leaving this stream, they went overland until they reached the Snake River. Downstream they paddled to the point where it joins the Columbia. Floating down the broad waters of the Columbia, Lewis and Clark at last came to the Pacific Ocean. Having traveled as far to the west as they could go, the hardy explorers turned about and set out for St. Louis, returning to that city after an absence of nearly two and a half years. It was partly due to their explorations that America later laid claim to the great Pacific Northwest.

Lewis and Clark told of the many rich furs to be had in the far Northwest, furs which the English were already collecting. Before long an ambitious American named John Jacob Astor had founded the Pacific Fur Company and was establishing a line of trading posts from the Missouri almost to the Pacific coast. This proved to be a very successful venture and led to further penetration of the area by other Americans.

Continuing Problems in Foreign Relations

Effect of Blockades. Still the war in Europe continued with all its bitterness. Both France and Great Britain, hoping to starve each other into submission, declared each other's ports blockaded and forbade the United States to carry on commerce with them. In trying to pass through these blockades, American ships were seized and their goods taken by warships of both nations. The British, moreover,

Indians used many materials in canoe building. Among the most popular was birchbark, shown in the drawing below. Lewis and Clark built and used these canoes on their journey.

continued their policy of stopping American ships and seizing American sailors to serve in the British Navy.

The climax came when a British man-of-war, the *Leopard,* stopped an American ship, the *Chesapeake.* Though the *Chesapeake* was a warship, she was not then equipped for fighting. Because the *Chesapeake's* captain would not permit his ship to be boarded, the British opened fire, killing more than twenty Americans. They then came aboard and took four sailors, one of whom was promptly hanged from the yardarm as a deserter. When news of this reached the United States, public indignation knew no bounds.

The Embargo Act. Congress at once passed the *Embargo Act,* which forbade any American ship to leave port for any foreign port. It was hoped that this would starve the warring nations into respecting American rights, but it came much nearer to destroying American trade. Discontent was felt everywhere, and some of the states, especially those whose fishing trade had been ruined by the law, threatened to withdraw from the Union.

The Nonintercourse Act. Faced with this danger, Congress withdrew the Embargo Act in 1809 and passed in its place the *Nonintercourse Act.* The new law stated that American ships should not trade with either France or Great Britain, but gave them the right to deal with any other country. Trade was once more resumed, and so were the unfriendly actions of British and French ships upon the high seas.

Looking Back

1. In what ways was the election of 1800 unusual?
2. How did Jefferson meet the problem of the Barbary pirates?
3. Why did the United States prefer having Spain rather than France control Louisiana?
4. What factors prompted Jefferson to favor the Louisiana Purchase?
5. For what reasons was the Embargo Act disliked by most Americans?

The Chapter in Perspective

Who Are These People?

Jefferson	Jay
Knox	Livingston
Randolph	Burr
Napoleon Bonaparte	Monroe
Hamilton	Lewis
Citizen Genêt	Clark
Adams	Astor

Where Are These Places?

District of Columbia	New Orleans
Columbia River	

What Do These Dates and Terms Mean?

cabinet	Jay Treaty
1794	1797
1791	Farewell Address

Tonnage Act
Embargo Act
Sedition Law
X Y Z Affair
Barbary pirates
Louisiana Purchase
Nonintercourse Act
Whiskey Rebellion
strict construction
broad construction
Bank of the United States
Proclamation of Neutrality
Democratic-Republicans
Kentucky and Virginia Resolutions

1798
Alien Law
tariff
1803

Questions for Study

1. What were the major accomplishments of the Federalists from 1789 to 1800?
2. Discuss the causes and results of the Whiskey Rebellion.
3. How did Hamilton's financial program meet the needs of the nation?
4. Would you have joined those who favored a strict or a broad construction of the Constitution? Why?
5. Explain the arguments of those favoring American intervention in the European war on the side of France (or England).
6. Why may it be said that Washington both preached and practiced a policy of isolationism in foreign affairs?
7. How did the Louisiana Purchase force Jefferson to switch positions on the matter of strict and broad interpretation of the Constitution?
8. Of what importance to the United States was the Lewis and Clark expedition?
9. List the states and parts of states that were included in the land acquired by the Louisiana Purchase.
10. Why did the geographic area included in the Louisana Purchase give it such great economic importance?

Place Yourself in History

Today is Feb. 16, 1801—and despite the fact that the election was held in November, we have no President to take office about two weeks from now. This was caused by Jefferson and Burr both receiving the same number of electoral votes, thus sending the election to the House of Representatives as provided for in the Constitution. Here, voting by states, we have already cast thirty-five ballots without having made a choice. Alexander Hamilton, Jefferson's arch foe, spoke to me today in favor of Jefferson! We vote again tomorrow.

What would you have done? Would you have supported Jefferson or Burr? What political moves had caused the tie? Who was really the choice of the Democratic-Republicans? Why did Hamilton move to defeat Burr? What were the immediate and long-range results for Hamilton?

The United States Gains the Respect of Other Nations

Immediately after winning independence, the United States did not appear to be very strong. Most Europeans felt that democracy would not work and that, eventually, the new nation would be forced to join some European nation that still owned land on the American continent.

However, under the first three presidents, Washington, Adams, and Jefferson, the nation gained in prestige by doubling in size and potential wealth. Thus, the fourth President, James Madison, entered office heading a nation which was envied by many European nations. The strong and effective union under the Constitution made it possible for the United States to demand respect and to back up its demands with military force if necessary.

1. The Nation Fights Once More For Independence

Trouble on the High Seas

The United States was trying to remain neutral in the continuing disagreements between France and Britain when James Madison, fourth President, was elected in 1808. Madison believed that peaceful trade could be continued with both Great Britain and France. Consequently, he was delighted when in 1809 the British minister to America, David Erskine, stated that Great Britain would no longer molest American commerce if America would promise to trade with her and not with France. Madison happily agreed to this.

Many American ships promptly set sail for the British Isles but soon returned. The King and Parliament said that they knew nothing of Mr. Erskine's proposal, and that they would not promise to respect American ships and American commerce on the seas. So trade with Great Britain was again discontinued.

Next, Napoleon, now Emperor of France, came forward with the proposal that if America would trade with France and not with Great Britain, he would no longer seize American ships. The French Emperor, however, did not keep his word and continued to attack American shipping. His sole purpose was to create ill feeling between Great Britain and the United States by tempting American ships into trying to run the British blockade.

A Declaration of War

A desire for war was now growing in some of the states. A group in Congress, headed by Henry Clay of Kentucky and John C. Calhoun of South Carolina, was anxious for an excuse to have the United States invade and conquer Canada, and, if possible, Florida. These "War Hawks" did much to stir up the country. The war fever increased when Tecumseh (teh-KUM′-seh), a powerful Indian leader, led attacks on some of the frontier towns. His men were defeated by General William Henry Harrison in the battle of Tippecanoe. Many believed that the British in Canada had urged Tecumseh to make this attack, and American indignation burned hotly.

Because of the widespread feeling of resentment in the United States toward Great Britain, it was inevitable that the British seizure of American ships at sea would sooner or later lead to war. "Free trade and sailors' rights" was the war cry. The United States was taking up arms to defend her right to trade

Navigational equipment, 1812 warship. Speed was figured by dragging "log" (2) in water. As line (1) ran out, hourglass (3) timed it. Octant (4) for fixing position. Wheel and pulley lines for operating rudder (5). Anchor (6).

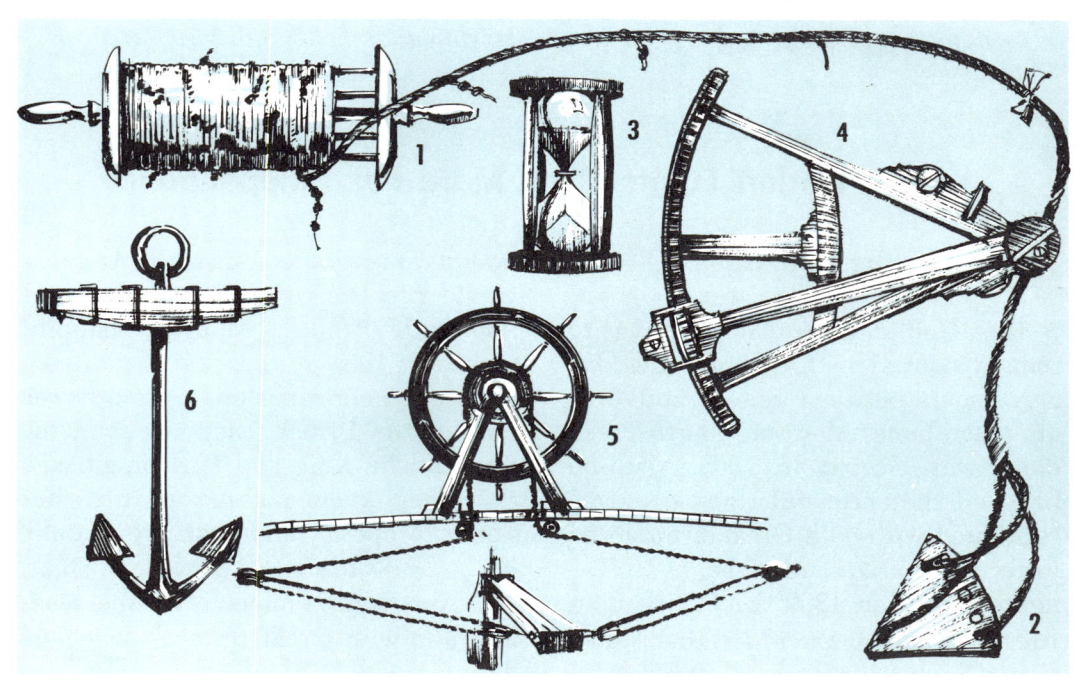

with whatever country she wished and to ensure her sailors freedom from seizure by foreign navies.

The War on the Sea

No sooner had war been declared than the little American navy set out to meet its enemy. Again it was like David setting out to meet Goliath. Against Britain's thousand mighty warships, the United States had but sixteen, and, although they were well built, well armed, and manned by expert sailors, their task seemed hopeless.

The first important sea fight occurred when the United States frigate *Constitution* met the British frigate *Guerriere* (gary-AIR') in the Gulf of St. Lawrence. The two ships were about equal in size and armament, but Captain Isaac Hull of the *Constitution* managed his ship well. So skillful were his gunners that in twenty minutes the *Guerriere* was a hopeless wreck—her masts gone, most of her crew dead, her guns out of action. In less than half an hour she surrendered. The *Constitution* later treated the British frigate *Java* to the same fate. After these two battles, the *Constitution* was so little damaged that she became known as "*Old Ironsides*."

Astonishing American Successes. Other American successes upon the sea soon astonished the world. The American sloop *Wasp* captured the British *Frolic*, the *United States* defeated the *Macedonian*, and the *Hornet* destroyed the *Peacock*.

The *Chesapeake* had earlier lost a skirmish to the British *Leopard*. At that time the *Chesapeake* was unarmed and trying to sail through the British blockade. Now, fully armed,

The *U.S.S. Constitution*, or "Old Ironsides," pride of the American fleet, under full sail.

she was again defeated, this time by the British warship *Shannon*. Captain James Lawrence of the *Chesapeake* was killed in the battle, but as he lay dying he cried, "Don't give up the ship." These words become the motto of the American Navy throughout the war.

The sixteen American warships were soon reinforced by five hundred privateers—privately owned merchant vessels which were armed with cannon and sent out to destroy British shipping. Before the end of the war, the British merchant vessels destroyed or captured by these privateers almost equalled in number the American merchant vessels destroyed or captured by the entire British Navy. The valor of the American sailors was a constant source of inspiration to the people of the United States.

The British Blockade. Great consternation was caused in Great Britain by the American naval victories. One British naval man wrote, "I don't like Americans. I have no wish to eat with them, drink with them, or, let me tell the whole truth, fight with them." And the London *Times*, the leading newspaper of England, said, "If the Americans fight, they are sure to conquer. If they fly, they are sure to escape." But in spite of the American victories, the odds were too great, and Britain's mighty navy was able to blockade the American coast and sweep practically all American shipping from the seas.

The War in the West

The Loss of Detroit. The war went poorly for the United States on the land. Even before the formal declaration of war, an American army under General William Hull started to march to Detroit, which was to serve as the base for a possible invasion of Canada. Hull led his army successfully through forests and swamps and at last reached Detroit. War had now been declared, but Hull had not yet learned this, although his Canadian enemies had.

It must have come as a great surprise to Hull to find himself faced by an army made up of British and Indians. A much larger force, they seized his supplies, and confronted him with a choice of surrender or massacre. If Hull surrendered, Detroit, a key military post, would be lost, perhaps for the rest of the war. But the threat of massacre was too great. Hull hesitated, then surrendered without firing a shot.

Later in the year another American army, under General Harrison, tried to retake Detroit. Though they fought bravely, the attack was in vain, for they were unable to drive the British from their stronghold.

Victory on Lake Erie. One great obstacle in the path of American victory was the fleet of warships which the British had launched upon Lake Erie. A young American naval commander named Oliver Hazard Perry was sent to capture or destroy this fleet. Gathering his men on the banks of Lake Erie, Perry at once set about building an American fleet of warships. They were hastily put together and were made of green timber, but they carried heavy guns and were manned by skillful sailors. As soon as the little fleet was completed, Perry set out to find the British. The British, meanwhile, were looking for Perry.

On September 10, 1813, the two fleets met, and at once a furious battle began. The British concentrated the fire of all their guns on the first ship of the American line, the *Lawrence*. Solid shot smashed the deck, knocked the guns from their carriages, and toppled the masts into the water. Soon victory was important because it gave control of Lake Erie to American forces. Before they controlled the lake, supplies had to be sent through treacherous swampland to General Harrison, camped near Detroit. Supplied by ships which could now cross Lake Erie, and encouraged by the good news of Perry's victory, Harrison was able to storm Detroit and recapture it from the British.

The British Plan of Attack

The war in Europe continued, but by the next year, 1814, Napoleon's French troops had been defeated. Great Britain now felt free to send larger armies and more warships to fight against America. The British were ready to carry out a master plan to divide the new nation into three sections, each of which would be easier to deal with than a united, proud country. To do this, Great Britain had to take advantage of the disunity that was already there.

New England disagreed greatly with many of the policies of the other states and the federal government during the War of 1812. Great Britain felt that with strong encouragement New England might secede from the other states and rejoin the mother country. Therefore, one British plan was to send an army down from the North by way of the Champlain Valley. This army was to isolate New England from the rest of the nation.

The British also hoped to attack the Southern and Middle States. A large British force was to be sent to New Orleans. This force was eventually to capture the city and gain control of the Mississippi, which would allow the

Perry's Monument, at Put-in-Bay in Lake Erie, commemorates Perry's victory over the British.

the *Lawrence* was put completely out of action, and only Commander Perry and a few of his sailors were left uninjured. Taking his remaining sailors and his little twelve-year-old brother, Perry set out in a small boat for the next American ship. Bullets and shells plowed up the water around him, but he and his men reached the *Niagara* in safety, and soon he was again directing the battle. It was not long before the British fleet was so hopelessly shattered that it was forced to surrender.

On the back of an old envelope, Perry wrote to William Henry Harrison, "We have met the enemy and they are ours: two ships, two brigs, one schooner, and one sloop." Perry's

British to split off another section of the United States, the newly purchased Louisiana Territory. Since the British never recognized the validity of Napoleon's sale of the Louisiana Territory to the United States, they planned to claim this area for their own after they had captured it.

Still another British army was to proceed into the Chesapeake Bay area. This force was supposed to attempt only a diversionary feint. In other words it was sent only to confuse the American forces and to draw troops needed in the North and the South away from those critical areas. Oddly, this third attack, the least important of the three, was the only one that was successful for the British.

American Success on Lake Champlain. The British commander in the Champlain Valley had not counted upon the fleet of warships which the Americans now built and launched on Lake Champlain in the hope of keeping the invaders out of New York State. This fleet was commanded by Commodore Thomas MacDonough, and to it was entrusted the task of defeating a British fleet which had also been launched on Lake Champlain. If the American fleet were defeated, the British vessels would be able to land fourteen thousand British soldiers at the southern end of the lake, and the enemy would have a firm foothold in the state of New York.

The British found the American ships anchored off Plattsburg and opened fire. The battle was much like that of Lake Erie. For nearly three hours cannon roared and solid shot smashed through the sides of wooden vessels. Then the British, out-maneuvered and out-gunned, broke their formation, and, while some of the ships surrendered, others sought places of safety near the northern end of the lake.

The British attack from the north had been foiled, and the British troops, waiting at Plattsburg, retreated to Canada. With the lake under American control, they dared not advance farther to the south, for their supply lines would be cut. They would face the fate Burgoyne had experienced in the Revolutionary War thirty-seven years earlier, when he was forced to surrender his entire starving army. New England was not cut off from the rest of the country.

A Coastal Attack. The second British attack, along the Atlantic coast, was more successful. A British fleet sailed up Chesapeake Bay and landed some soldiers on the Maryland coast. At Bladensburg, this invading force met an American group which had been hastily gathered together for the defense of the city of Washington. After a short but spirited stand, the Americans were driven back. The British entered the capital in triumph and burned the government buildings, as the Americans had previously done at York (now Toronto).

The city of Baltimore was then attacked by the same British force which had captured Washington. Here the British fleet met with unexpected resistance, for Fort McHenry in Baltimore harbor matched them shot for shot and kept the British warships at a distance. All night the ships bombarded the fort, but they could not capture it and Baltimore was saved.

An American, Francis Scott Key, was on one of the British ships during the attack on Baltimore. With great pride he saw the American flag fly over Fort McHenry. All through that night of continued firing, Key was anxious to know whether or not the flag still floated over the fort. When the morning sun showed the Stars and Stripes still flying, Key, in his joy, wrote a poem in commemoration of the event. This poem, *The Star Spangled Banner*, has since been adopted as the American national anthem.

The Battle of New Orleans. The third British attack led to the bloodiest battle of the war. Sir Edward Pakenham, in command of the British troops, planned to make a vigorous attack on the city of New Orleans. He landed his army of ten thousand veteran soldiers, expecting an easy victory and a quick conquest of the town.

But New Orleans was defended by a very able officer, General Andrew Jackson. Expecting the attack, he had dug entrenchments and built breastworks about the city, and behind these he placed his five thousand soldiers. Jackson's army was an oddly assorted one. It contained some regular soldiers, but it also had many woodsmen from Virginia and Kentucky, some citizens who had volunteered, some Negroes, and even a few pirates! All, however, knew how to handle a rifle and how to shoot straight.

On January 8, 1815, the British forces swept forward in a great charge, and were met by volley after volley of shots. "Stand by your guns," "See that every shot tells," were Jackson's orders. In less than half an hour, over two thousand of the British soldiers had fallen to the ground, dead or wounded, while the American casualties totaled only seventy-one. Pakenham himself was killed, and his army withdrew, beaten.

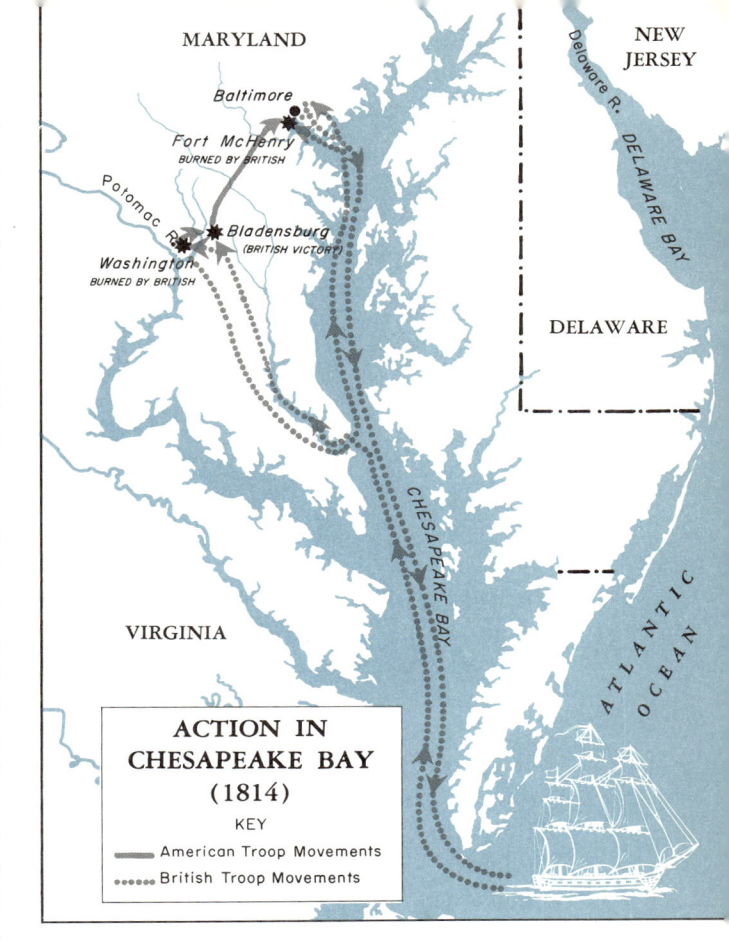

The Treaty of Ghent

Before the Battle of New Orleans was fought, a treaty of peace had already been signed at Ghent, Belgium. Strange to relate, the treaty settled none of the questions which had caused the war. Neither side had won, and peace was made only because both nations wanted peace. The treaty provided that fighting should stop at once, that all conquered territory should be returned, and that any questions arising from the war should be settled by a commission which was to meet at a later date.

Although Great Britain had given no promise to leave American shipping

This street scene in New Orleans shows the heritage left by the French and their descendants.

alone, the war was not without favorable results for the young republic. It showed the nations of Europe that the Americans would fight for their rights. Documents released long after the battle have shown that had the British won at New Orleans, they would have ignored the peace treaty signed at Ghent. Therefore, even though a treaty had been signed, it was necessary that Jackson fight and win at New Orleans. If he had not, America might have lost the Louisiana Territory and the respect of the world.

After the war European respect for the United States increased so greatly that American ships were no longer troubled on the high seas. The War of 1812 has been called the second war for independence. The Revolution won for the United States political independence of Great Britain, and the War of 1812 won commercial independence of the nations of Europe.

The Hartford Convention. Throughout the War of 1812, groups in New England were opposed to the war for a variety of reasons. The policies of the Federalist party were strong there. Many New Englanders wished to set up their own stronghold where there would be no Southern planters or rough backwoodsmen to dispute Federalist policies. Some New Englanders also felt that sensible agreements with the British could be worked out if New England could separate itself from the rest of the nation. This opposition to the war was what the British had hoped to exploit if they could have isolated New England. As we have seen, the British were not successful in this venture.

The failure of the British, however, did not stop New England's discontent about the war. On December 15, 1814, representatives of each New England state met in Hartford to discuss their grievances against the government in Washington and against the war. Their main purpose was to protect themselves against the influence of the South and the West in Congress and the government. Luckily the news of the Treaty of Ghent and the victory at New Orleans united all Americans in celebration. The Hartford Convention, formed out of discontent with war policies, died when the war ended.

Looking Back

1. Who were the "War Hawks" and what were their aims?
2. Explain why "Old Ironsides" remains an American shrine to this day.
3. Explain the strategic importance of Detroit and discuss the part it played in the war.
4. Why was Perry's victory of great importance?
5. What was the significance of the Hartford Convention?

2. The United States Moves Ahead Under Madison

Madison's term of office was concerned chiefly with the war with England, the situations which led to the war, and the actual fighting of it. However, Madison's eight years as President cannot be viewed strictly in terms of the war. There were significant developments in national growth, in judicial interpretation of the Constitution, and in foreign relations.

A Growing Sense of Nationalism

Article I of the Constitution provides that a census be taken every ten years, chiefly for the purpose of apportioning representation in the House of Representatives. In 1800, the U.S. Bureau of the Census reported that the population had reached well over five million. Ten years later, during Madison's first administration, the figure was over seven million. By 1820, the United States could boast of having almost ten million inhabitants.

The experience of coming to a new country united many of the four and a half million people who came to America between 1800 and 1820. Combined with the pride brought about by the legendary Revolution and the War of 1812, the American experience gave rise to a great surge of truly national pride, pride in the country as a whole. This new *"nationalism"* thrived on American accomplishments in war, diplomacy, commerce, and population growth.

The Madison administrations created a fertile field for such national pride. Two new states had been added to the Union, Louisiana and Indiana. People were moving into the West in large numbers. Prospects for additional states to be added to the Union were good. Following the war, the country seemed to be literally bursting at the seams. America was expanding in all areas.

A New Role for the Supreme Court

One of the most important changes which came about during Madison's administration had to do with the role of the Supreme Court. John Marshall, who had been appointed Chief Justice at the very end of the Adams administration, was responsible for this change.

John Marshall's Role. Marshall declared that the function of the Supreme Court was to examine the laws passed by the legislative branch to see if they were in agreement with the United States Constitution. If the laws were not in agreement, they could be declared *unconstitutional* by the court. Thus the court became the interpreter of the Constitution, and the right to interpret laws that Congress had passed became known as the right of *judicial review*. This new right gave the Supreme Court power and prestige it had not enjoyed before and made it a truly important part of the government.

Freedom of the Seas

But other changes, every bit as important as the one brought about by John Marshall, came about in the early years of the nineteenth century. When the War of 1812 was over, President Madison had to face the threats of

Algerian pirates raiding American ships in the Mediterranean. The Dey (DAY), or ruler, of Algiers seized American ships, imprisoned American citizens, and demanded that a tribute be paid to his country. At Madison's request, Congress authorized war with Algiers. Madison immediately sent Captain Stephen Decatur to the Mediterranean with a fleet of ten ships. Decatur captured several of the pirate ships, entered the harbor of Algiers, and forced the Dey to sign a treaty releasing American prisoners and ending Algerian demands for tribute. Similar treaties were soon arranged with Tunis and Tripoli. The Americans had won an important victory.

But the most important result of the victory was not merely that American ships were free to roam the seas. The young nation had shown the world, by her actions in Algiers, that she was strong and vigorous, and that no one could take advantage of her. When Madison left office in 1817, his country was at peace, and the Constitution was a solidly respected document. Madison's administration laid the groundwork for years of growth and peace.

Looking Back

1. What signs of nationalism were evident in Madison's administrations?
2. Explain the principle of judicial review established by Marshall.
3. How did Madison continue Jefferson's policy regarding Mediterranean pirates?

3. The Nation Enters An "Era of Good Feeling"

Following the War of 1812, an era of national progress and unity lasted through several decades until the country was again divided over the slavery question. This period of development began with Monroe's term of office, which is sometimes referred to as the "era of good feeling."

James Monroe entered the Presidency after an excellent record of long service to his country. He saw action during the Revolution, served in the Continental Congress and the United States Senate. He then served as Minister to France. Upon returning home, he was elected Governor of Virginia. President Jefferson again sent him to France to assist in the negotiations for the purchase of New Orleans. Partially through his efforts, the United States purchased not only New Orleans but the entire Louisiana Territory. When Madison became President, he asked Monroe to join the cabinet as Secretary of State. Few men have entered the Presidency with more experience than James Monroe.

National Prosperity

Monroe's first inauguration address, March 4, 1817, set the tone for the following years. Although a Democratic-Republican, he proposed to follow many of the Federalist economic and political policies. The Federalists had supported a strong federal government rather than unwieldy and powerful state governments. The Federalists also had financial policies which encouraged industrial development. These Monroe pledged his administration to continue. Another feature of Federalist policy was the establishment of an adequate army and navy to discourage a repetition of foreign invasion like the one during the War of 1812. All this tended to develop a feeling of national pride in contrast to mere party or local pride.

Such feeling was very much in evidence when Monroe made a tour of the country, traveling as far west as Detroit. Everywhere he was given an enthusiastic reception. Everyone seemed to be benefiting by governmental policies: farmers could buy land more cheaply; manufacturers enjoyed a protective tariff; and financiers could depend on the National Bank and sound currency. All profited by the system of roads and canals which made decided improvements in the nation's transportation.

Sectional Differences

During Monroe's first administration, a Boston newspaper wrote of the period as an "era of good feeling." We still use this phrase to describe the period. However, it is not accurate in all respects. On the surface, party battles had been subdued and no serious complaints were expressed by any particular group, but, in reality, Monroe's administration was a calm before the storm. Many differences existed below the calm surface of good feeling. National tariffs helped some sections and penalized others. New England manufacturers prospered while rural southerners grew poorer. The slave question had begun to smoulder. Some states had no need for, or were revolted by, slavery. Others could overlook the immorality of slavery by seeing the institution only in terms of profit and loss. Various sections of the nation developed different and conflicting interests.

International Agreements

The Canadian Border. Considerable uneasiness existed along the Canadian border in the years immediately after the War of 1812. This area had seen a great deal of fighting both on land and on the Great Lakes. Great Britain and the United States felt the need to protect their borders. The arming of vessels in the Great Lakes proved to be very expensive to both countries. Ensuing correspondence between the British minister to the United States Charles Bagot and the United States Acting Secretary of State Richard Rush resulted in an agreement (the Rush-Bagot Agreement) to limit armaments on the Lakes. Great Britain and the United States agreed to limit their naval forces to four small armed ships each on the Great Lakes. This agreement looked forward to the time when the two countries could establish complete disarmament along the border. Gradually over the next fifty years such disarmament was accomplished.

Another agreement with Great Britain in the same year as the Rush-Bagot Agreement was called the Convention of 1818. It established the northwest boundary between the two countries at the 49th parallel from the Lake of the Woods, in what is now Minnesota, west to the Rocky Mountains. A further provision of the Convention stated that there would be a joint occupation of the Oregon Territory for the next

This monument to 150 years of good Canadian-American border relations stands near Blaine, Washington. The American side of the monument is inscribed "Children of a Common Mother," and on the Canadian side is written "Brothers Dwelling Together in Unity."

ten years. Settlement would be open to both British and Americans.

Missouri Compromise

Balance in the Senate. When the territory of Missouri applied for admission to the Union as a slaveholding state in 1818, the question of slavery in the United States became one of national importance. There were at that time eleven slave states and eleven free states, and the addition of Missouri would give those favoring slavery a majority in the Senate. Moreover, Missouri would be the first state lying entirely west of the Mississippi River. If slavery were permitted there, little precedent would exist for keeping it out of any part of the West.

When, therefore, the bill providing for the admission of Missouri came before the House of Representatives, James Tallmadge of New York introduced an amendment. This provided that "the further introduction of slavery be prohibited, and that all children born within the said state, after admission thereof into the Union, shall be free at the age of twenty-five years." Though the House of Representatives passed both the bill and the amendment, the Senate did not, and Missouri was forced to wait.

Maine and Missouri. The solution to Missouri's problem came in 1820. Maine, which had been part of Massachusetts since 1677, drew up a constitution and petitioned for admission to the Union. Here was a free state to counterbalance slaveholding Missouri. A new bill, called the Missouri Compromise, championed in Congress by Henry Clay of Kentucky, provided for the admission of Missouri as a slave state and Maine as a free state. The bill also stated that slavery should be prohibited in any other state formed out of the Louisiana Purchase territory north of the line of 36° 30′ north latitude, the Virginia-North Carolina, Kentucky-Tennessee borders. This bill was passed by Congress, and the two states were admitted, Maine in 1820 and Missouri, due to a delay in ratifying her constitution, one year later.

The Monroe Doctrine

The Concert of Europe. At the Congress of Vienna, which met to draw up the peace treaties after the defeat of Napoleon, four European nations banded together in a league known as the *Quadruple Alliance*. Each member country promised to send soldiers to help any of the others whose government should be threatened by popular revolts. Also all promised to help suppress revolutions wherever they occurred, even in nations which were not members of the alliance. Soon most of the other European countries joined the Quadruple Alliance, which then became known as the *Concert of Europe.*

The Concert of Europe was very effective in putting down revolutions. In 1820 it sent an Austrian army into Italy which suppressed an uprising there, and soon afterwards it sent a French army into Spain to put down a revolt against King Ferdinand VII. During the Spanish revolution, the Spanish colonies in South America had stood by their king, but when he was restored to power, he did not show gratitude. Instead, he taxed the colonies unmercifully and tried to make Spain rich at their expense. The colonies would not stand for this, and they revolted under the leadership of Simón Bolívar and José de San Martín. To put down the revolt in South America, Spain once more called upon the Concert of Europe.

British-American Concern. The move filled the American people with alarm. If European governments were going to band together to help Spain hold her colonies, might they not also help Great Britain or France to reconquer their North American possessions? Such a procedure must be stopped, and must be stopped quickly.

Great Britain, for her part, was as much opposed to the Concert of Europe as the United States was, for she feared that the powerful nations might attack her. The British government even went so far as to suggest that Great Britain and America combine to oppose all moves of the Concert.

U.S. Action. Remembering Washington's and Jefferson's opposition to foreign treaties and alliances with foreign governments, Congress refused the British offer of alliance, announcing that the United States would act alone. Monroe was at first inclined to accept the British invitation, but later changed his mind and took the advice of his able Secretary of State, John Quincy Adams. At Adams' suggestion, President Monroe appeared before Congress in 1823 and stated that the United States would maintain the following principles:

(1) That no more colonies should be planted in North America or South America by any European nation.

(2) That if any nation should interfere with any of the American nations, the United States would regard it as "an unfriendly act."

(3) That if the Americans were left alone, the United States would not interfere with the internal affairs of any European nation.

This statement was known as the *Monroe Doctrine,* and it has had a great effect upon the history of the United States. Until recent times no European power has persisted in trying to colonize or conquer any part of either American continent.

Effect of the Monroe Doctrine. The nations of the Concert of Europe had not planned to intervene seriously in Latin America, so it would be a mistake to say that the Monroe Doctrine kept South America from being invaded by European armies. Generally, in fact, the European nations were not concerned about the Monroe Doctrine, especially since America was still a young nation, not able or willing to wage a war in defense of republics to the south.

However, although the Monroe Doctrine is not based on international law, it has had a strong effect on world diplomacy, especially in the last eighty years. Many Americans view the Monroe Doctrine as a patriotic principle which must be defended. European nations have become aware of this, and in the recent past few nations have tried to extend their influence into the Western Hemisphere.

Looking Back

1. Why do many historians consider Monroe to have been one of the best prepared men for the Presidency?
2. Discuss the reasons why this period is known as the "era of good feeling."
3. What steps were taken to ensure peaceful relations along the Canadian-American border?
4. For what reasons was the admission of Missouri to the Union of great importance?
5. Summarize the three basic principles of the Monroe Doctrine.

The Chapter in Perspective

Where Are These Places?

Tippecanoe	Algiers	Plattsburg	Oregon
Detroit	Great Lakes	Fort McHenry	Missouri
Lake Erie	49th parallel	New Orleans	36° 30'

What Do These Dates and Terms Mean?

1808	Era of Good Feeling	joint occupation	1817
blockade	*Star Spangled Banner*	*Constitution*	1813
Treaty of Ghent	Convention of 1818	Missouri Compromise	1818
nationalism	Tallmadge amendment	Concert of Europe	1820
judicial review	"Old Ironsides"	Quadruple Alliance	1823
Jan. 8, 1815	privateers	Hartford Convention	
War Hawks	blockade	Monroe Doctrine	

Who Are These People?

Madison	Jackson
Erskine	Pakenham
Tecumseh	John Marshall
Harrison	Decatur
Isaac Hull	Monroe
William Hull	Rush
Perry	Bagot
J. Q. Adams	Clay
F. S. Key	Bolivar

Questions for Study

1. Why did most Federalists and some Democratic-Republicans object to the War of 1812?
2. How did the terms of the Treaty of Ghent indicate that the war was a victory for neither side?
3. Account for the sectional support or non-support of the American war effort.
4. Why, despite brilliant individual naval victories, was American shipping driven off the high seas during the war?
5. In what ways did Napoleon's defeat in 1814 affect British war policies against America?
6. Explain why Jackson's victory at New Orleans was a brilliant military and strategic victory.
7. What signs of growing sectionalism were beginning to be evident during Monroe's terms?
8. How did the Missouri Compromise solve the slavery problem temporarily?
9. Referring to a map of the area, which side, in your opinion, gained the most in the Missouri Compromise? Why?
10. Which nations today occupy the areas once known as the Barbary States?

Place Yourself in History

You are representing your country at a crucial meeting of the Concert of Europe. With you are representatives of most of the major nations of Europe. The purpose of the meeting is to decide what action, if any, is to be taken to help Spain win back her colonies in Latin America. Suddenly a messenger enters and presents a just-arrived copy of Monroe's message to Congress of December 2, 1823—the Monroe Doctrine.

What are your thoughts? What do you say as a diplomat? How do your fellow delegates view the announcement from America?

10 Industrial and Social Developments

From the period of colonization to the period called the "era of good feeling," Americans had made tremendous progress in the military, political, economic and social fields. The founding fathers never dreamed that by 1825 the country would develop into the growing giant that it was, bold enough to try telling the countries of Europe to stay out of the Western Hemisphere. They never imagined that the young United States would fight two wars with England and in one be able to gain her independence and in the other to maintain it against almost overwhelming odds.

1. American Know-How Goes Into Operation

By 1830, no country in the world had experimented so boldly and developed political theories so successfully as had the United States. Americans added many new political ideas to the ones inherited from England. The natural resources of the country made it possible for the new nation to become wealthy. But the wealth would have remained undeveloped had not the dedicated, industrious settlers labored to harvest it. The many favorable harbors on the Atlantic coast, where the colonies were located, made trade possible. And Americans soon mastered the art of shipbuilding to the extent that American ships were the fastest and most seaworthy on the oceans.

Social progress means progress in education, culture, religious freedom, leisure, and the distribution of knowledge. Americans have always been conscious of their rights and their freedoms to choose those who govern, to worship as they wish, and to develop a vigorous culture. The development of culture was a part of their effort to improve on the manner of life that they had in the Old World—to make social progress. By 1830 the ordinary American lived a completely different life than his European counterpart.

Western Migration

Horace Greeley, a famous newspaper man, once advised a young man asking advice to "Go West, young man, go West." But the idea of seeking opportunity in the West did not start with him. In the last days of the Roman Empire, barbarians from eastern Europe and Asia swept west into Italy and across the borders of France and Spain. In later years explorers and colonists from the Old World sailed west across the Atlantic to settle on the shores of North America. Yet another wave of western migration was to take place, for the inhabitants of the eastern states of America began journeying to the West into the lands which lay between the Appalachian Mountains and the Mississippi.

Two great obstacles stood in the way of this western migration. One was the Indians. They naturally resented the large numbers of white settlers who were pouring into and across their lands. These newcomers killed or frightened away the game on which the Indians lived, and built settlements in their hunting grounds. Worse, they brought always the promise of more white people to follow. Soon there would be no room left for the Indians.

The suppression of the great Indian chief Tecumseh broke the spirit of the Indians. The decisive defeat of the Indians at Tippecanoe robbed them of their leading warriors. Never again were they a massive threat to white colonization.

The other obstacle in the path of migration was harder to surmount. This was the great unbroken forest which shut off the coast from the interior plains. Men could travel along the forest trails on foot or on horseback, and pack horses loaded with provisions could be led along. But wagons could make no headway in the forests,

Perhaps the greatest obstacle in the path of Western immigration was the Indians. In this painting, *An Old-Time Plains Fight*, artist Frederic Remington captured the spirit of Indian fighting. Forced to dismount, a group of mountain men defend themselves.

The Remington Art Memorial

and thus it was no easy matter to transport goods and supplies and families.

Roads to the West

Roads were needed, and the early years of the western migration were years of intense road building. Along the Hudson River a highway, or turnpike, ran from New York to Albany. Another was built to the West, from Albany into the thinly settled lands of western New York State, at last reaching the shores of Lake Erie. The roads connecting such important cities as Boston, New York, and Philadelphia were constantly improved, as more and heavier traffic flowed over them.

The westward movement led to many improvements in roadbuilding. A layer of heavy crushed stone (2) was laid on top of graded subsoil (1). Then another layer of smaller stones (3) was added. Finally a heavy layer of stone dust (4) was placed on top of it all.

The highway which most affected western migration, however, was the *Cumberland Road*, also known as the *National Road*. At the insistence of Thomas Jefferson, Congress authorized the building of this road at national expense to help in the settling of the West. Starting at Cumberland, Maryland, the road ran northwest to Wheeling, West Virginia, and from there west through Ohio and Indiana, ending in the town of Vandalia, Illinois. The Cumberland Road was paved with heavy stones covered with gravel, and was about eight hundred miles long. Though the work was started in 1811, it was 1838 before the road was completed as far as Vandalia. Though Congress spent $7,000,000 between 1811 and 1838 in building and repairing the National Road, it was a wise investment, for it greatly aided in the settlement of the West.

Flatboats and Packets

Not all the people traveling into the West made their entire journey by land. Where the Cumberland Road crossed the Ohio River at Wheeling, many flatboats were launched on the stream, and in them whole families with their goods traveled to the southwest toward the mighty Mississippi.

Traveling in flatboats offered many disadvantages. Though the boats were broad and steady and would carry great loads, they were so bulky that they were hard to manage. Quite frequently a flatboat ran aground or was dashed against rocks where the current was swift. Since they depended for their motive power on the current of the river, they could be used only in traveling downstream.

Travel to the west on the National Road was slow and tiring. Inns such as this one were a welcome sight to travelers who had bumped along all day in a stagecoach. The Headley Inn, shown here on route 40 near Zanesville, Ohio, is one of the few inns to continue to operate in the 1960's. In its own time, it was famous throughout the Northwest Territory.

It was not long before the flatboats were replaced on the main rivers by packet boats, driven by sail, and carrying passengers and freight. The packets, too, had their disadvantages, for they were very slow when traveling upstream, and they were entirely dependent upon the wind and current to drive them.

Moving Against the Current

During the time of the flatboats and packet boats, there lived in New York City a young man by the name of Robert Fulton. He was an artist, and he also enjoyed inventing things. When only a boy he made a pair of paddle wheels with which he was able to drive a small boat much faster than his friends could send one along by means of poles. On a trip to France, Fulton became interested in making a ship which would move regardless of wind or tide. He made several experiments while he was in Europe. When he returned to the United States, he set to work to build a steamboat.

It is a lucky thing that Robert Fulton was not easily discouraged, for thousands of people flocked to the shipyard to watch him work, and to tell him how ridiculous it was to try to build a vessel driven by steam power. Everywhere he met with laughter and ridicule, and there were few indeed who believed that his boat would ever succeed. True, James Rumsey and John Fitch had earlier built steamboats, but most people failed to consider them practical means of travel.

The "Clermont." At last his little steamboat, the *Clermont*, was launched at New York City, and great crowds came down to the dock to see what would happen, ready to scoff and jeer at the inventor if his invention failed. Even the guests whom Fulton had invited on board were inclined to think that the young man was far too hopeful when he believed that the boat would move at all. When all was ready, Fulton started the machinery, and slowly the paddle wheels began to turn. To the amazement of everybody, the *Clermont* moved steadily away from the dock and out into the stream. But there it stopped.

Hastily assuring his passengers that all was well, Fulton went to the en-

Fulton's *Clermont* pulls away from shore. The crowd, which had come to see Fulton fail, saw him succeed. Their jeers turned to cheers as he steamed away.

gine and quickly found the trouble. Little more than a minute was needed to fix it, and once more the paddle wheels turned and the *Clermont* moved on its way, never stopping until it had traveled all the way to Albany, 150 miles, in 32 hours. This was in 1807, during Jefferson's last term of office. The steamboat was important to the growth of the nation.

Steamboats on the Mississippi. Robert Fulton's steamboat was a great success on the quiet, slow-flowing rivers of the East, but on the swifter, shallower waters of the Mississippi and Ohio it was not so practical. The first boat of this type to be launched on the western waters made the trip downstream without much difficulty, but was unable to force its way back upstream against the current. It remained for another inventor, Henry M. Shreve, to build a steamboat suitable for use on the Mississippi. Instead of having a narrow, deep-floating hull, as Fulton's boat had, Shreve's steamboat had a broad, shallow hull that would, as the inventor expressed it, "float on a heavy dew." Instead of narrow, deep-dipping paddle wheels on the sides, the Shreve boat had a single, broad, shallow paddle wheel at the stern. Shreve's steamboats passed easily up and down the Ohio and Mississippi, floating safely over shoals and sandbars and carrying passengers and freight throughout the whole wide Mississippi River system. Boats of this type are still in use along the Mississippi, Missouri, and Ohio Rivers.

In 1836 came another important improvement in the steamboat, for in that year John Ericsson invented the screw propeller. This was a revolving hub with blades like those of an electric fan. It was smaller and less cumbersome than the heavy paddle wheels, but was no less effective in driving a boat forward. Today all of the largest ships have screw propellers.

Man-Made Waterways

With travel by water improving so steadily, a desire arose for more and better waterways. If only there were some way for boats to travel from Lake Erie to the Hudson River, how cheaply goods could be transported to the seaport of New York! This idea occurred to the farmers of the West, and also to Governor DeWitt Clinton of New York. Governor Clinton did more than dream of such a waterway; he built one.

The Erie Canal. The difficulties to be overcome in building a canal across New York State were so great that many thought the venture to be impossible. The waters of Lake Erie are nearly six hundred feet higher than the waters of the Hudson. Hills and valleys lie between. Few people imagined that such a thing could be accomplished.

Clinton, however, was fired by his dream and was determined to make it come true. In 1817 bands of workmen started to dig "Clinton's big ditch," as people called it. For eight years they toiled away, cutting a channel through the hills and across the valleys. At last the work was complete. The use of locks, by which vessels could be raised and lowered, overcame the disadvantage of the varying water levels. The Erie Canal was formally opened in

The remains of an Ohio River towboat, near Clarington, Ohio, a relic of another era.

The Erie Canal at Lockport, New York, as it appeared 120 years ago.

October, 1825, the year John Quincy Adams became President.

The building of the Erie Canal had many important results. The cost of carrying farm products from the West to the East was brought down to a small fraction of what it had been. Comfortable boats carried passengers across the state. New towns, such as Buffalo, Rochester, Syracuse, and Utica, grew up along this great waterway. Because the canal made it easy to obtain materials and to ship finished goods, these towns flourished and became important trade centers. A great volume of goods, which before the building of the canal would have been sent down the Mississippi to the ocean was now sent through the canal and down the Hudson to New York City, which soon became the greatest seaport of North America. Thus did "Clinton's big ditch" far exceed even his fondest hopes.

Era of Canal Building. An era of canal building followed Clinton's successful venture. Encouraged, other

AMERICAN ROADS, RAILROADS, AND CANALS (1860)

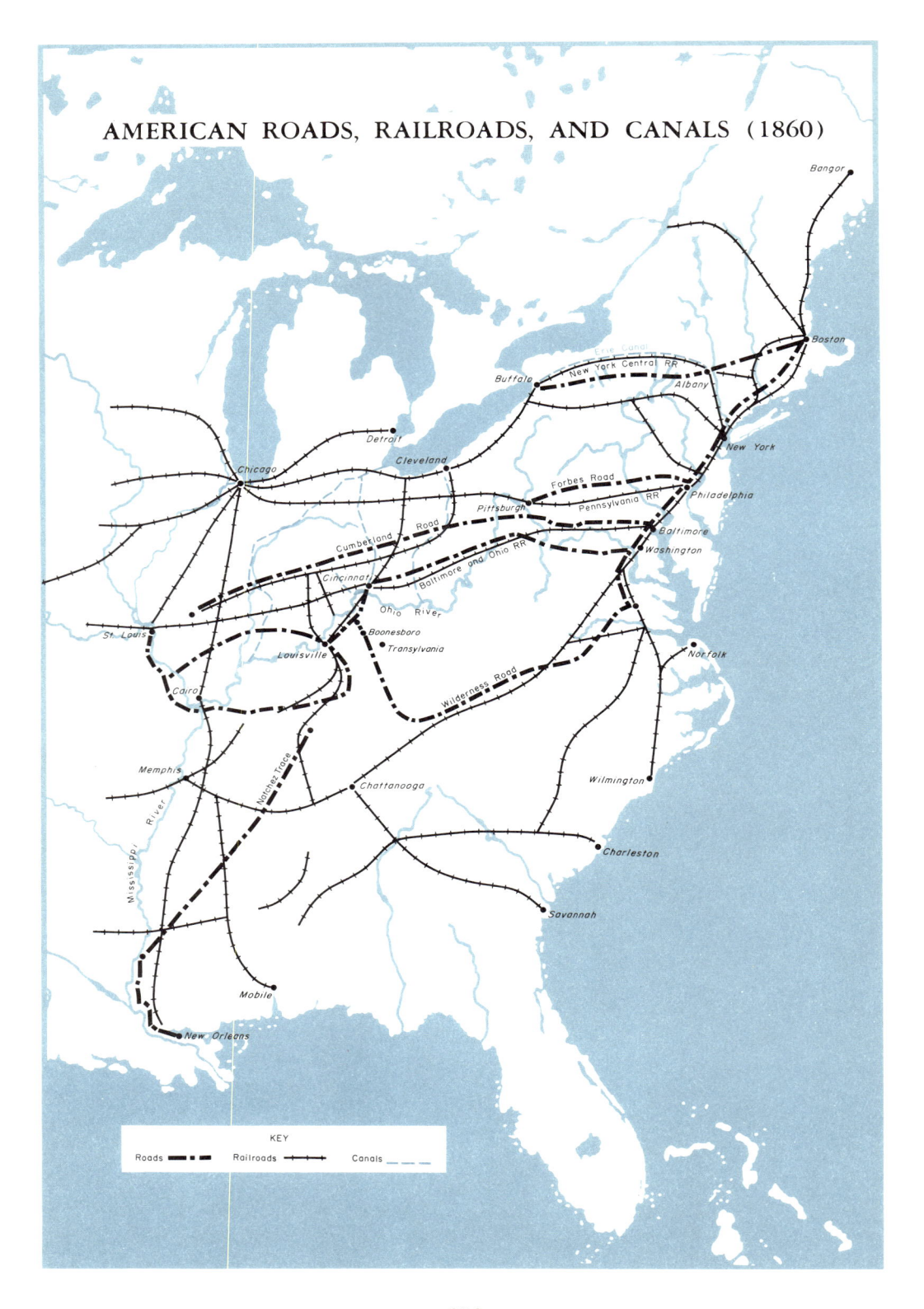

states dug canals of their own to connect bodies of water and to make transportation easier and cheaper. Pennsylvania undertook the most interesting project. That state constructed a canal from Philadelphia to Pittsburgh, but the boats traveled part of the way by rail. This was necessary since the route of the canal crossed the Allegheny Mountains. By using a series of cables and rails, engineers managed to haul the boats from part of the canal up one mountain and down another into the continuation of the canal. Other canals were started in Maryland, Ohio, Indiana, and Virginia, but not all of them were finished. John Quincy Adams, sixth President of the United States, turned the first spadeful of earth for the Chesapeake and Ohio Canal, which was supposed to connect Chesapeake Bay with the Ohio River. This ambitious project was never completed.

Baltimore and Ohio Railroad

In 1828, on the same day that President John Quincy Adams was digging up the first spadeful of earth to begin the construction of the Chesapeake and Ohio Canal, another man was performing a similar ceremony to begin what was to become a much more important project. He was Charles Carroll of Carrollton, the last surviving signer of the Declaration in Independence. The spadeful of earth which he dug up marked the beginning of America's first railroad line, the Baltimore and Ohio. Carroll at that moment represented a link between the past and the future of the United States.

At first, the Baltimore and Ohio Railroad did not amount to much. Over a stone roadway were laid rails of wood covered on top with flat strips of iron. On these rails traveled small, four-wheeled carts drawn by horses. It was merely a smoother type of highway, nothing more. In Great Britain, however, a Scottish inventor named George Stephenson had invented a steam locomotive which was successfully used to haul cars on the straight, level railroads which were being built there. One of Stephenson's locomotives was brought to Baltimore, but it did not prove successful on the curving, steeply-graded rails of the Baltimore and Ohio. In 1830, however, Peter Cooper, an American, built a locomotive which could successfully navigate the winding route of the Baltimore and Ohio, and until recently, steam-driven locomotives have pulled American trains. Now they have been replaced by diesel-powered engines.

Railroads vs. Canals

Once they had their start, the railroads of America developed and improved rapidly. Wooden rails gave way to iron, and iron gave way to steel. Locomotives increased in size, in speed, and in pulling power. Dozens of short lines were built, some to succeed, some to fail, and others to combine into huge railroad systems. Cars increased in size and in comfort from mere carts or stagecoaches on rails to longer, heavier railway cars with eight or more wheels each. It was not long before the railroads of America were competing so successfully with the canals that the canals began to lose business, and intense rivalry soon developed between these two leading means of transportation.

The famous early American train, the DeWitt Clinton, named after the man who promoted the Erie Canal. Note the similarity of the cars to stagecoaches. The engine burned wood.

Soon the railroads made various improvements in engines and track conditions. As a result, they could offer faster, more efficient service than they could in the early days of railroading when the trip from New York to Philadelphia was a daring venture. The canals were destined always to be slow and leisurely means of transportation. Soon the railroads had taken most of the business from the canals. Although inland water transportation is still with us, it is not as important as it was in the colorful early 1800's. Today, the high-powered tractor-trailers that travel our nation's highways challenge the railroads, much as the railroads at one time challenged the canals.

Looking Back

1. What barriers stood in the way of westward migration?
2. Discuss the advantages and disadvantages of water transportation prior to the development of the steamboat.
3. How did the completion of the Erie Canal affect the city of New York?
4. In what way did Stephenson and Cooper help revolutionize transportation on land?
5. Why did the railroads replace the canals as the major transportation facility?

2. The Industrial Revolution Reaches America

Even before the United States became a nation, people in America and Europe began to improve on the early ways of making things. In the last half of the eighteenth century and the first half of the nineteenth, great progress was made. This changing of the methods of production and distribution of manufactured articles was known as the Industrial Revolution.

Developments in Cloth-making

Spinning and Weaving. From the very beginning of civilization, thread had been spun by hand with the aid of spinning wheels or other simple devices. This was slow and difficult work. Then, toward the end of the eighteenth century, an Englishman invented a machine that could spin eight threads at once. Others adopted the principle of the invention and improved its methods until someone invented a machine which could spin many hundreds of wool or cotton threads at one time. With thread being spun at this rate, the hand looms for weaving the thread into cloth were far from equal to their task. So, in 1785, a loom run by water power was made. With the power loom one person could weave more woolen or cotton cloth in a given time than a hundred could weave on hand looms.

An early American sewing machine, around 1850. By 1870, 500,000 were manufactured per year.

Whitney's Cotton Gin. In 1793, Eli Whitney, a young Connecticut school teacher, invented a device known as the cotton gin. Before Whitney's day all cotton fiber had to be separated from its seeds by hand, and this took a long time. At best, one man could separate but a very few pounds of cotton in a day, and it was this fact, more than anything else, that kept the cotton crop from being a great source of wealth to the southerners. Whitney's cotton gin quickly and efficiently separated cotton fiber from its seeds and did the work about fifty times as fast as a man could do it by hand. Cotton soon became king of all southern products.

Howe's Sewing Machine. It was fortunate that the invention of the power loom and the cotton gin came so close together, for the two worked hand in hand. The cotton gin supplied cotton fiber for manufacturing many times faster than it had ever been supplied before. Then, after the fibers were spun into threads, the power loom wove them quickly into cloth. Naturally, this greatly increased the use of cotton and wool.

Later, in 1846, the sewing machine was invented by a New England mechanic named Elias Howe, and textile manufacturing took another great step forward. It was these three machines that formed much of the basis of early American manufacturing.

The Growth of Manufacturing

Textile Industry. New England soon became the leading manufacturing area of the country. As early as 1790, a spinning mill was built in

Slater's Mill, like most early factories, was built of wood and lighted by kerosene lamps. Many mills of this type burned down, killing employees. Few improvements were made until about 1890.

Pawtucket, Rhode Island, by Samuel Slater. The laws of Great Britain forbade mill workers to leave the country and prohibited export of any plans or drawings of machines. Slater memorized the plans of a number of machines, came to America disguised as a farm worker, and built his first mill from memory. Slater's mill, which contained many spinning and weaving machines, was the first real factory in the United States. It gave New England its start as a manufacturer of textiles. The region had ample water power for the running of manufacturing machinery of all kinds, and factories grew up along the many rivers of the New England states. Towns in which the factory workers lived were built around the factories. New England still has many such manufacturing towns. Today, however, textile manufacturing is not as important as it once was in New England. Large empty mills stand as testimony to the fact that many companies have moved from New England to the southern states. North Carolina and Georgia are now among the leading states in the manufacture of textiles.

Standardized Parts. Eli Whitney, of Connecticut, who had invented the cotton gin in 1793, made another notable contribution to American industry and to manufacturing in general. About 1800, Whitney was part-owner of a gun factory near New Haven, Connecticut. Before that time, each gun had been made as a separate unit, resembling, but not exactly matching, other guns of the same design. The parts of one gun could not be used in any other gun, as they were sure to differ slightly in their measurements.

Receiving a large order for guns from the United States government, Whitney decided that it would be better if every part of every gun could be made exactly the same as the corresponding parts of all other guns of the same type. Then, if the hammer or trigger or some other part of a gun became broken, another could be substituted at once and would be sure to fit. Standardizing the parts would also make manufacturing a faster and more efficient process. The use of standardized, interchangeable parts, built to exact specifications, began in Whitney's factory and has been an important factor in manufacturing ever since.

Steam Power. Another great step forward in manufacturing came when it was found that steam could be used to drive machinery and could take the place of water power. Factories could now be built anywhere regardless of nearness to flowing streams.

Since wood burned quickly and gave too little heat, coal now came into favor as a fuel for generating the steam to drive the engines. Coal was found in Pennsylvania. Miners swarmed into that state and went to work digging the valuable black mineral from the earth.

Early in the nineteenth century a Pennsylvania blacksmith named Joseph Smith invented a grate for holding coal. Smith's grate held the coal above the floor of the furnace. This allowed air to enter below the coal, creating a draft and causing the fire to burn much better.

Iron and Steel. The growth of the iron and steel industry occurred at the same time as the increase in coal mining. Coal is very important in the process of making iron and steel since a great deal of heat is needed to separate, or smelt, the pure iron from the ore which is found in the ground. Charcoal was used in the smelting process for a while, but since it was made from wood, it was quite expensive. Furthermore, it gave out comparatively little heat.

Ironworkers found that coal gave out much more heat than charcoal, but even coal was not efficient. Soon they found that by "cooking" coal, they could make a product called *coke* which would burn at a very high heat and which was perfect for smelting iron ore quickly and easily. After the invention of coke, the iron and steel industry grew into what is today America's largest basic industry.

Vulcanized Rubber. The work of Charles Goodyear greatly helped the development of the rubber industry. In the early years of the nineteenth century, rubber was of little use. Hot summer weather made the rubber soft and sticky, while in the cold of winter it would harden and crack. After years of experimenting, Goodyear discovered around 1840 that rubber mixed with sulphur and then heated to the melting point was usable for many purposes and was not affected by changes in temperature. He patented his process, called vulcanizing, in 1844.

Results of the Industrial Revolution

Increased Cultivation. Inevitably, the Industrial Revolution brought great changes to various parts of the country. Just as it increased the wealth of New England by building up the manufacturing trade there, so did it increase the wealth of the South by providing a ready market for her cotton. As the cotton market grew, the cotton belt extended out through the southern states until at last it reached the Mississippi.

The reaping of crops had always been a long and difficult process, performed for centuries with crude implements like the scythe and cradle. When, in 1834, Cyrus McCormick invented a mechanical reaper, the time and labor of harvesting crops were greatly lessened. The invention was a great aid in the development of the West. Crops from large fields could be harvested in much less time than ever before, and settlers moved west to cultivate the many square miles of fertile prairie lands. The Industrial Revolution was all that was needed to complete the settlement of the land west of the Appalachian Mountains.

Growth of Cities. But the Industrial Revolution brought results other than the settling of the land. Manufacing companies built their factories where they would be likely to find or attract a large work force, and where they had access to good harbors, and water power. Naturally, cities that were already established were likely places for factories. At the same time, the presence of a factory in a town tended to attract more people because a factory meant more jobs. Immigrants sought out these factory jobs and flocked to the cities to find them. The result was that cities grew larger and larger.

Working Conditions. As the cities grew, the population took on new characteristics. Before 1830 in the United States, the average man owned his own home and land. People were dependent upon themselves for the food they ate, and the clothes they wore. Any money they got was through selling what they could raise or make. As the factory system grew, however,

When did the urban population begin to overtake the rural population? Why did the total population grow relatively slowly at first? When did it begin to rise rapidly? Can you give reason for the large increase in the American population after 1840?

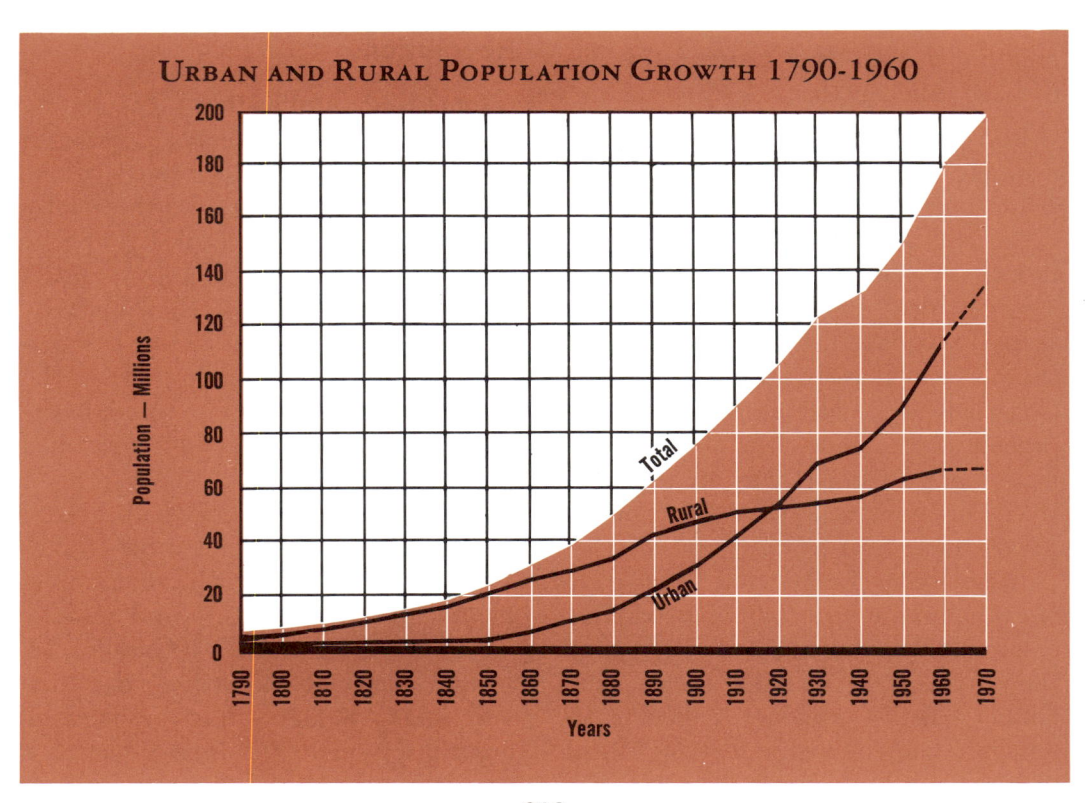

URBAN AND RURAL POPULATION GROWTH 1790-1960

working men and women became dependent upon their employers, who paid them wages. With the money they received, they were able to buy the things that they had once been able to raise. Factory workers needed to be close to their work, and they no longer needed land to raise crops since they obtained money by selling their labor and time.

City Life. Employers made full use of the labor and time of their employees. Often, in fact, they took advantage of the situation to underpay the workers and take great profits for themselves. Once an average worker was committed to city life, there was little escape for him. If his wages were cut off, he would starve. He generally had no savings he could use to buy land in the country, so this method of escape was closed to him. In many cases the factory owner also owned a "company store" to which the laborer could go to buy what he needed in the way of food and clothing. Often the laborer became extremely indebted to the company store, having pledged the paychecks that he had not yet received. In these cases, the worker became almost a slave of his employer. Naturally this caused a great deal of discontent among the working classes, and poverty combined with crowded living conditions to give rise to crime and violence.

The evils of city life, crime and discontent, were serious ones. The problems brought about by the Industrial Revolution, the exploitation of one man by another, were things Thomas Jefferson had been concerned about in many of his writings. He had favored rural development as opposed to city expansion. "Life, liberty, and the pursuit of happiness" were more possible in the country than they were in the city, he said. Though Jefferson may have been correct in his predictions, the city has become an important part of our national culture, and through community planning we have found ways to solve many of the problems brought on by city growth.

Formation of Labor Unions

Conditions in Factories. Although the Industrial Revolution changed working conditions greatly throughout the country, it changed conditions in the home even more. Before the 1800's, the women of each household manufactured by hand most of the goods needed. Those they could not make were made by craftsmen. With the coming of the factory system, however, thousands of men and women left their homes and spent many hours of each day working to help make some useful product. As time went on and the demand for factory workers increased, many children, too, worked in the factories. Child labor came about partly because the heads of families were not paid living wages.

Conditions were very bad for the workers. Most of them toiled over their machines or tools fourteen to sixteen hours a day. When work was over, they had only the strength to go home and sleep in preparation for the next day's work. Especially alarming was that great numbers of women and children worked long hours. Deaths from overwork were not unusual. To improve these horrible conditions, workers formed labor unions early in the nineteenth century.

Union Gains. As the years went by, the unions became better organized, and gradually they gained better working conditions. The long deadly hours were cut down, and safety devices, better lighting, more ventilation, and more pleasant surroundings were demanded and attained in some factories. Laws were passed limiting the number of hours each week which women and children might work, and also forbidding the employment of children below a minimum age.

As the hours of daily labor came down from fourteen to twelve, to ten, and even less, the lot of the workman improved. He now had time for some small pleasures in addition to his daily work. Since wages had risen, he had money enough to pay for more than just food and clothing. He was able to support his family and allow his children to go to school. The labor unions have done much to improve the lot of American workers although they fought a long difficult battle.

Looking Back

1. How did the invention of the power loom create a need for the invention of other machines?
2. Why did the textile industry first flourish and then decline in New England?
3. In what ways did Whitney's standardized, interchangeable parts change manufacturing procedures?
4. What effect did the development of steam to drive machinery have on later locations of factories?
5. Describe early factory conditions that led to the growth of labor unions.

3. The Government Encourages Industrial Growth

First American Tariffs

It is generally recognized that no country can progress very far if its people are employed in only one type of work. The greatest countries are those in which many industries thrive. The leaders of the American government saw quickly that something must be done to avoid any danger of the United States becoming a purely agricultural country. Consequently, manufacturing, trade, and industry were encouraged.

Hamilton's Measures. The first move toward encouraging industrial growth was made by Alexander Hamilton in 1789, when the first American tariff act was passed. The tariff had a double purpose. Its main object was to bring badly needed money to the nation's treasury by putting a tax on certain imported goods. (In other words, it was a *revenue tariff*, unlike the later tariff of 1816, which was primarily intended to protect growing manufacturers.) Since it raised the selling price of these imported goods, it helped to protect manufacturers from foreign competition. But this was not its main purpose. The levying of a tonnage tax on all foreign ships entering American harbors gave American vessels an advantage which it was felt would lead to an increase in the shipping trade. Helped by such protection, the United States soon began to develop as a trading nation.

Declining Trade. The Embargo and Nonintercourse Acts stifled American trade, as did the British blockade during the War of 1812. During these periods, few goods were imported from Europe. With the importation of European goods nearly cut off, American manufacturing got its first real start. By the close of the war, factories were springing up throughout the country, but mostly in the New England states.

Protecting "Infant Industries." Congress sought to protect the *infant industries*, as they were called, by a new tariff bill slightly different from the original 1789 tariff. The Tariff Bill of 1816 placed a tax on all imported goods which were also being made in America or could be made profitably in America. Such a tariff is known as a *protective tariff*. It differs in its purpose from a tariff levied only for the raising of money, or revenue. A revenue tariff is intentionally placed low enough so that the taxed goods will continue to be imported and the tariff on them paid. A protective tariff is usually high enough to prevent the importation of the taxed products.

Opposition to the Tariff

It is interesting that although ninety-five per cent of the factories in America were in the northern states, both the North and South were at first in favor of protective tariffs. There were two reasons for this. First, the manufacturing North was in favor of tariff protection, and the southern states, too, favored it because the market for their raw materials was in the North. The South also hoped to develop their own manufacturing until it equaled that of New England. Second, both sections of the country realized that the government needed money, and favored the tariff for that reason.

Sectional Differences. Unfortunately, however, the South was not really fitted to become a manufacturing section in the nineteenth century. Most of her workmen were slaves who had not been trained to run factory machinery. There was less water power, too, in the southern states than in New England. Men had not yet learned how to make the best use of such slowly flowing streams as are found in the South. In addition, the hot climate of the South made work in southern factories far more uncomfortable than in northern factories. The South's dream of becoming a great manufacturing center was not to come true for a century, and the southerners devoted themselves to producing the important crops of cotton, tobacco, rice, and sugar.

Even after the Tariff of 1816, the manufacturers in the North were hurt by European competition. While it no longer threatened to destroy their business, it did lessen their profits. For that reason the New England states demanded in 1824 that a still higher tax be laid on foreign goods. This demand caused violent opposition. The Treasury was full, and the government did not need increased revenue from import duties.

The Tariff of 1824. The people of the South had now come to feel that a tariff levied for protection favored only one part of the country, while it merely served to increase prices in

American manufactured goods: (1) a Hitchcock chair, very common and popular around 1810. They were shipped to all parts of the country and were priced at $1.50 each. (2) A tin lamp of the early 19th century. It burned a tallow candle. (3) A pewter teapot. "Pewter" was made from an alloy of copper and tin, and many household utensils were made from it. (4) Some of the world's finest clocks were turned out in Colonial New England. This one was manufactured by the Willard family of Massachusetts. Glassmaking (5) and pottery (6) were important American industries also. (7) After Eli Whitney invented the cotton gin in 1783, cotton cloth like his print fabric became important trade goods.

other sections. Southerners felt the tariff was unfair. If they had to buy manufactured goods they wanted to pay as little as possible. They wanted all taxes taken off imported goods and free trade between the United States and other countries. Nevertheless, despite their opposition, the Tariff Bill of 1824 was passed by a narrow margin in both the House of Representatives and the Senate. By its terms the average duty on foreign products was raised from twenty to thirty-six per cent.

Needless to say, the people of the South were very indignant at the passage of the Tariff Bill of 1824. And when, in 1827, the northern manufacturers asked for still more protection, the attitude in the southern states became threatening indeed. One of the southern leaders, Charles Pinckney (PINK'nee), arose at a southern banquet and proposed a toast, "Let *New England beware how she imitates Old England.*" The feeling began to spread that if the tariff went any further it would be well for the South to withdraw from the Union.

The Tariff of Abominations. Knowing that direct opposition to the tax was of little use because the North had many more members than the South in both houses of Congress, the southerners planned a most ingenious trick to defeat the proposed new tariff bill. The New England states wanted a very high protective tariff on all manufactured goods, but they also insisted on a very low tariff, or none at all, on the raw materials which they used in their factories. Many of these raw materials were now raised in the western lands of the United States. The southerners argued that it would be very much to the advantage of the westerners if high tariffs were also put on raw materials imported from Europe. If this were done, the westerners could charge the northern manufacturers much higher prices for the raw materials supplied them. The westerners thought this a fine idea and joined with the South in framing a tariff bill which granted to the northern manufacturers the protection they wished on manufactured goods. However, the bill also boosted the tariff on raw materials so high as to completely destroy the good effects of the protection. Naturally, the North was expected to oppose the new tariff bill bitterly.

To the great surprise and chagrin of everyone, the *Tariff of Abominations*, as it was called, was passed in 1828. New England did not profit from it, because it increased the price of the raw materials which she needed. The western states did not profit, because the bill raised the prices they would have to pay for manufactured goods, and this offset the increased high price which they would get for their raw materials. The South fared worst of all, since the new tariff increased the cost of living. However, John C. Calhoun, Vice-President of the United States, and a native of South Carolina, advised the southerners to do nothing rash, but to wait and see if the election of 1828 would bring some relief.

Party Split Over Tariff. As it turned out, the passing of the Tariff of Abominations served to make John Quincy Adams' administration very unpopular. While he was in office, the old Democratic-Republican party had been divided into two new parties. One of these, the National Republicans, favored what was known as the *American System*, a favorite idea of Henry Clay's. The American System provided for a high tariff and the extensive use of money from the United States Treasury to improve the country by building roads and canals and making other improvements. The other party, the Democrats, denied that the government had the right to levy any tax except for revenue and opposed the spending of money from the United States Treasury for internal improvements. In 1828, Adams, the National Republican candidate, was decisively defeated by Andrew Jackson, a Democrat. John C. Calhoun, staunch enemy of the protective tariff, was elected Vice-President for a second term.

The tariff reform which the South had confidently expected would follow Jackson's inauguration did not come about. Although the new President let it be known that he believed the tariff was a little too high, he made no positive move to reduce it, and the South continued to complain.

Doctrine of States' Rights

In 1832 a new tariff law was passed, and though it decreased the rates somewhat, it did not decrease the indignation of the South. The state of South Carolina promptly declared that: (1) the tariff laws of 1828 and 1832 were unconstitutional; (2) the new law would not be enforced in the state of South Carolina; (3) if the government made any move to enforce it, South Carolina would at once withdraw from the Union.

The belief that each state had a right to decide for itself whether or not a law was constitutional and should be obeyed was known as the doctrine of States' Rights, although this term has come to mean many different things since that time. In this particular case, the conflict revolved around the concept called "nullification" originated by John C. Calhoun to describe the right of a state to nullify or ignore a federal law.

President Jackson's reply to South Carolina concerning nullification was that no state could withdraw from the Union, and that he was ready to send 40,000 soldiers to South Carolina to see that the law was enforced. Serious trouble seemed imminent, and the Union was in great danger.

Clay's Compromise. At this point Senator Henry Clay came to the rescue. Clay proposed a new tariff bill by which the rates would be gradually reduced until, in 1842, they would be as low as they had been in 1816. This compromise tariff became a law in March, 1833. At the same time a law was passed giving the President the right to use the army and navy to collect duties in a rebellious state. An intelligent and peace-loving statesman had averted, for the time being at least, serious civil strife within the United States.

Looking Back

1. Explain the difference between a revenue tariff and a protective tariff. How does a protective tariff protect?
2. How did the Embargo and the War of 1812 encourage American manufacturing?

3. What disadvantages did the South face when it wished to become a manufacturing section?
4. Why did the Tariff of 1824 arouse strong sectional feelings?
5. In what way did Clay again prove his ability as a compromise maker in the tariff controversy?
6. Why was the tariff passed in 1828 called the "Tariff of Abominations?"
7. What position has the Republican Party usually taken on tariffs in its platforms?
8. Explain the doctrine of states' rights. Does it mean the same thing today that it did in 1832?

4. The Social Revolution Brings Enlightenment

It is very difficult to imagine an America in which there were no libraries, newspapers, nor magazines. Today, we see books everywhere. This was not always so. In the period of history we are studying, few public schools existed. Only the wealthy and some of the people who lived in towns where schools happened to be located were able to acquire an education. In fact, for most of the people there was not much time to read or to improve the mind. Most people spent so much time working for the necessities of life, such as food and clothing, that they could not be concerned at all about books, art, or learning.

Today we hear a great deal about the responsibility of voting when election day comes. In the early nineteenth century only the men who owned property could vote. Democracy had not really been extended to the entire population. Before 1800 this was not a problem since almost everyone owned his own land, mainly because it was free for the asking. However, when large numbers of factory workers moved to the cities, they had to rent dwellings. If these people could not vote just because they owned no land, then citizens were not enjoying the privileges for which the Revolution was fought. A different kind of a revolution would be needed before this would become a reality. The struggle to weave these reforms into the life of the country was not a simple undertaking. There was a great deal of strife and bitterness, a great deal of discussion from pulpit and lecture platform, and an upsurge of demands from the underprivileged for new social changes.

The concern for change and social reform led to progress in these areas. More and better education was made available to all people. Real religious freedom and universal voting privileges no longer seemed like mere dreams framed in words of promise. Newspapers began to report the real truth behind the news and literature began to flower.

Educational Advances

Education is another field which the country has developed greatly since early times. For over one hundred years before the Revolution there were schools in New England, and during that time a number of universities were

Charles Bulfinch, American architect, designed this building at Andover Academy in 1818.

established. But, during the Revolution people were too busy fighting for independence to think much about learning, and little educational progress was made.

Public and Private Schools. A reawakening of interest in education, however, began even before the war was over and led to the founding of several private academies. Between 1763 and 1790, Governor Dummer Academy, Phillips Academy at Andover, and Phillips Exeter Academy were established in New England to prepare boys for the universities. All of these academies have prospered and are still numbered among the leading American schools.

Public school systems, paid for by taxation, lagged far behind the private schools. Although DeWitt Clinton, then a member of the New York State legislature, persuaded that body to pass a bill establishing in 1812 free public schools, little progress was made in New York, and still less in other states. Until well into the nineteenth century, even the largest cities had few schools staffed by trained teachers. The pupils were given a smattering of reading, writing, spelling, and arithmetic. It was felt that any other training was unnecessary.

Horace Mann. Improvement in education was badly needed, and it was supplied by a group of able and ardent educational reformers. In Pennsylvania, the legislature took a long forward step by passing a law in 1834 providing that schooling must be available for all children, regardless of their parents' ability to pay. Horace Mann, the Secretary of the Massachusetts Board of Education from 1837 to 1848, was responsible for many reforms. In 1839, he persuaded the Massachusetts

An early 19th century schoolroom. Note hornbooks and stern schoolmaster.

legislature to establish the first state-supported normal school for the training of teachers. He also managed to put through a provision for the grading of pupils according to age and another calling for compulsory school attendance through the early grades. Other states followed Mann's lead in establishing forward-looking policies.

Many boys who wished to go to college could not afford to attend the private academies. Consequently, state and local governments soon saw the need for public high schools which would further the work of the grade schools. The first of these was established in 1821 in Boston, and a few years later New York and Philadelphia followed suit. From this beginning the idea spread rapidly throughout the country, and it was not long before every city of any size had its high school. As these schools progressed, they extended their field so that they not only prepared boys for college, but also gave training in various lines of business.

With the greatly increased number of academies and high schools in the country, the few American colleges were unable to care for all who wanted a higher education. The Northwest Ordinance set aside public lands to aid education. Gradually other colleges were founded, and many of the states established state colleges to provide free education. North Carolina, South Carolina, Virginia, Ohio, Indiana, and Michigan all had such state colleges before 1841, and other states followed in rapid order. Skilled educators became members of their faculties, and in time their students were given as fine an education as could be had anywhere.

Cutler Hall is the oldest building at Ohio University, first college in the Northwest territory. It was established in 1803.

Schools for Girls. The schools established before the Revolution were exclusively for boys. In those days it was thought that all the training a girl needed was in cooking, sewing, and housekeeping. This idea lasted long after the colonies had become the United States of America. There were some people, however, who believed that girls were entitled to the same educational advantages granted to boys. One of these was Emma Willard, who founded a young ladies' seminary in the year 1814 at Middlebury, Vermont. This school was moved in 1821 to Troy, New York, where it still exists under the name of the Emma Willard School.

Another famous woman educator was Mary Lyon. She was distressed at the small number of colleges which women could attend and at the idea that women were believed incapable of learning college subjects. In 1836 she established a seminary at South

Hadley, Massachusetts, for the purpose of giving women a college education. This seminary, called Mt. Holyoke Seminary, later become known as Mt. Holyoke College.

Religious Freedom

In the meantime, America was developing in other ways, not less important. Many of the English colonies were founded by people who crossed the ocean to gain religious freedom. As a result, these colonies were owned and governed by members of a particular religion. In some colonies, people with other beliefs were not welcome. Massachusetts drove out a band of Quakers who moved there, and when some of them returned they were beaten, imprisoned, and a few were even put to death. Other colonies permitted those of all religions to live there, but would allow only people of their own religion to hold office. In general, the members of one colony looked with suspicion and jealousy upon those of other colonies with different religions.

Soon after the colonies became states, these religious differences became less important, and early in the nineteenth century they were of only slight consequence. People of all religions were soon welcomed in all states, and few were badly treated because of their beliefs. This freedom has grown increasingly marked in our country's history, and today there is no country more liberal in its religious toleration than the United States.

The Extension of Suffrage

Hand in hand with the question of religious toleration went the question of suffrage, or the right to vote. In the original colonies there were many re-

Frontier families invented the husking bee to make fun out of work. Pioneers gathered to remove the husks from corn as quickly as possible, talking or singing while they worked.

strictions as to who could vote. There was often an age limit; usually only those over 21 had the right to vote. There was a limitation of sex, for only men were allowed to vote, and it was felt that women had no place in public life. Sometimes, as we have seen, voting rights were given only to those of the same faith as the people who had founded or who governed the colony. Finally there were restrictions of property holding, for in many colonies only those who owned a certain amount of land had the right to vote or run for office.

With the exception of the restriction on age, each of these restrictions was in time removed. Certain of them, however, lasted for some time in the various states, and it was not until after 1860 that all male citizens, except slaves and Negroes, over twenty-one years of age were allowed to vote. In 1870, the Fifteenth Amendment declared that males of all racial groups should have the right to vote. Fifty years later, women over twenty-one years of age were granted the voting privilege.

Beginnings of American Literature

Along with the other cultural and social developments came the flowering of American literature in the first fifty years of the 1800's. More Americans were learning to read than ever before, and they were eager to read the literature of the new country of which they were so proud. Such writers as James Fenimore Cooper and Washington Irving, both from New York State, wrote about subjects that were distinctly American: Indians, the

An early American newspaper, *The Essex Gazette,* published in 1774.

Revolution, exploration, and the people in an American city like New York City. New England also was a center of literature. Some of our best-known poets, Emerson, Longfellow, Whittier, lived and wrote in New England in the early nineteenth century. By 1850, it could be truly said that American literature occupied an important place in the world of literature. In fact, such a writer as Edgar Allan Poe influenced many French writers later in the century. American writers were making themselves known to a skeptical world.

The Newspapers

Along with the country's literature, her newspapers developed. Although the first printing press was brought to Massachusetts as early as 1639, newspapers were very rare for nearly a century. It was not until Washington's administration that daily newspapers put in their appearance, and then only

The center of the frontier family's domestic life was the kitchen, and the most important feature of the kitchen was the fireplace. It contained pothooks and andirons and was flanked by ovens and dishwarmers. It vanished when modern stoves replaced it.

four of the forty American papers were dailies. Most of the others came out only once a week. The papers of the early days contained very little news, and what there was might be two weeks old, or, if it came from Europe, at least a month old. Articles and advertisements filled the pages for the most part.

By the late 1840's newspaper printing became more efficient thanks to Richard Hoe's invention of the fast rotary printing press. In 1850 there were more than three hundred daily newspapers in the country, and well over two thousand weeklies. The papers of that day were beginning to make themselves felt as a strong political force, for they were gaining great influence over public thought in America.

The power and influence of the press has steadily increased ever since the invention of the rotary press, and, with the help of modern linotype machines, high-speed printing presses, telegraph cables, wireless dispatches, and other rapid means of communication, the newspaper has come to fill an important place in American life. News of the world is almost at once received throughout the country, and many millions of people are better informed as a result. Thus has the tiny seed planted in 1639 grown into a mighty oak—the American press.

Looking Back

1. How did voting requirements and the movement of laborers to the cities tend to limit the number of citizens eligible to vote?
2. What were the contributions of Horace Mann to the cause of education?
3. Show how changes were made in the education of girls.
4. Which was the last official restriction on suffrage to be removed?
5. What factors have helped newspapers acquire their present influence in America?
6. When did the first truly American literature begin to develop? Name two writers who achieved fame at that time.

The Chapter in Perspective

What Do These Dates and Terms Mean?

Cumberland Road	National Road	vulcanized rubber
standardized parts	1807	Compromise Tariff
coke	flatboats	shallow paddle wheel
automatic reaper	packets	Tariff of 1824
American System	*Clermont*	1789
Democrats	infant industries	Tariff of Abominations
Tariff of 1832	1846	1833
states' rights	screw propeller	1837
nullification	Erie Canal	suffrage
National Republicans	1844	rotary printing press
Baltimore and Ohio Railroad	1834	sewing machine
1817–1825	revenue tariff	1793
locomotive	Tariff of 1816	company store
power loom	protective tariff	
cotton gin	1828	

Who Are These People?

Fulton	Cooper	McCormick	Jackson	Goodyear
Shreve	Whitney	Calhoun	Horace Mann	Emma Willard
Ericsson	Howe	Clay	Hoe	DeWitt Clinton
Stephenson	Slater	J. Q. Adams	Mary Lyon	

Where Are These Places?

Cumberland	Albany
Wheeling	Pawtucket
Vandalia	South Carolina

Questions for Study

1. More progress in transportation was made in the 150 years after Fulton's *Clermont* than in all pre-

vious recorded history. Tell why you agree or disagree with the statement.

2. Can you justify the use of federal funds raised in all the states to build the National Road through a few chosen states? Give reasons.

3. Why are the events covered in this chapter often referred to as the Industrial Revolution?

4. Discuss new problems that were caused by the growth of factories and cities.

5. Summarize the main points in the history of the tariff in the United States from 1789 to 1833.

6. How did Jackson meet the threat of South Carolina in 1833?

7. How did the availability of iron ore, coal, and transportation help determine the location of our steel centers?

8. You wish to move your family and possessions from Boston, Massachusetts, to Columbus, Ohio. What were the possible routes and methods in 1837?

Place Yourself in History

In November, 1832, South Carolina adopted an Ordinance of Nullification declaring the tariff Acts of 1828 and 1832 "null, void and no law." The federal government was warned that attempts to enforce the law after February 1, 1833, would cause South Carolina to secede from the Union. Jackson was reported to have said—". . . if one drop of blood be shed there in defiance of the laws of the United States, I will hang the first of them I can get my hands on to the first tree I can find." To the public, he presented a more moderate, but firm policy. Trouble threatened.

You rise from your seat in the United States Senate to present your views on the situation. What will you say?

Expanding Your Outlook

Doing It Yourself

1. Prepare a biography of either Hamilton, Burr, Gallatin, or Horace Mann for presentation to the class.
2. Make a map of the United States in 1820 showing the areas affected by the Rush-Bagot Treaty, the Convention of 1818, and the Missouri Compromise.
3. Imagine you accompanied Lewis and Clark on their expedition. Prepare entries in your diary for reading to the class.
4. Make a series of cartoons attacking either the Federalists or the anti-Federalists.
5. Draw a series of posters to urge either a. enlistment during the War of 1812, b. investment in the Erie Canal Company.
6. Make a chart of the inventions mentioned in this unit. Head your columns: name of invention, date, inventor, effect of invention.

7. Write an editorial for a newspaper—or a newspaper article—covering Washington's "Farewell Address."
8. Prepare a talk to the class supporting or attacking the Virginia and Kentucky Resolutions.
9. Write a report showing how the Monroe Doctrine might have been viewed in an English or a Spanish newspaper in 1823.

Working with the Class

1. Organize a committee to represent Washington and the members of his Cabinet. Under discussion is Hamilton's proposed financial program. Allow the class to hear the discussion.
2. A round-table discussion of the tariff problem and the sectional views is to be presented to the class with speakers representing the South, the West, and the East. Be a participant.
3. Organize a committee to review American foreign problems from 1789 through 1823. Let each member represent a specific nation.
4. Form a group to represent delegates sent to the Hartford Convention. Have the group give its views in a session before the class.
5. For an all-class discussion: "The War of 1812 Was Needless and Useless."
6. You are an American reporter at a meeting of the Quadruple Alliance. Conduct a public interview of member representatives to determine their purposes and goals.

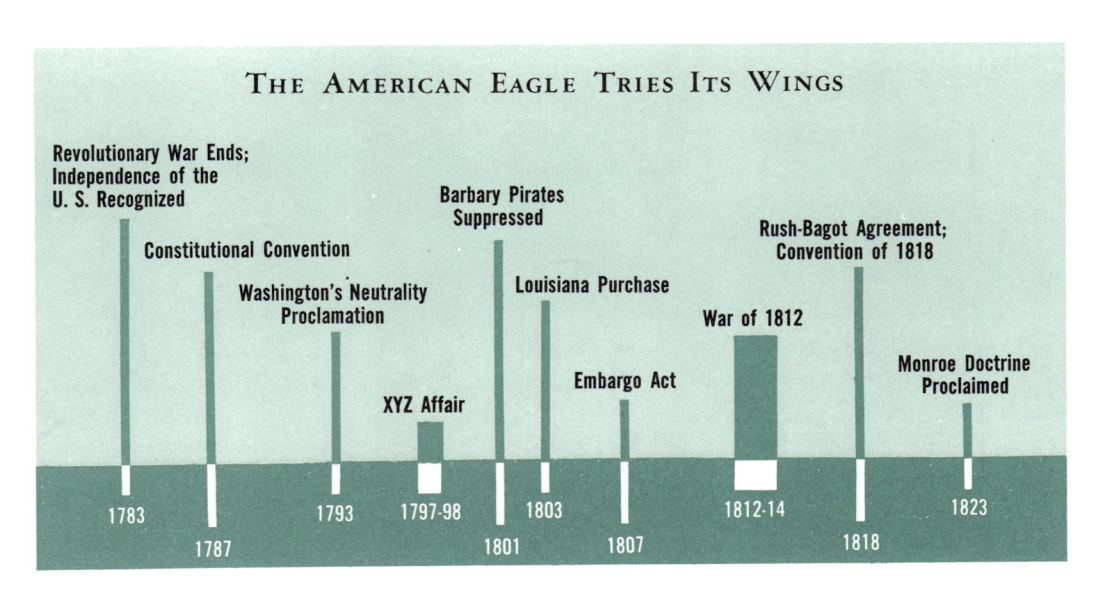

THE AMERICAN EAGLE TRIES ITS WINGS

- 1783 — Revolutionary War Ends; Independence of the U. S. Recognized
- 1787 — Constitutional Convention
- 1793 — Washington's Neutrality Proclamation
- 1797-98 — XYZ Affair
- 1801 — Barbary Pirates Suppressed
- 1803 — Louisiana Purchase
- 1807 — Embargo Act
- 1812-14 — War of 1812
- 1818 — Rush-Bagot Agreement; Convention of 1818
- 1823 — Monroe Doctrine Proclaimed

This painting by George Caleb Bingham is called Stump Speaking. *In it the artist has included all the vigor and spirit of 19th century American democracy. The Jacksonian Era was an age of territorial expansion and an age when representatives to the Congress maintained close contact with their electorate. In Jackson's day, stump speeches, like the one being given below, kept the voters informed in much the same way that television does today. Bingham's painting represents a rich era in our country's history.*

The State Historical Society of Miss

ONE NATION INDIVISIBLE

UNIT 4

American Horizons Extend and Widen

11. Jackson and the New West

1. Western Settlement Poses New Problems • **2.** The Western Movement Affects the Nation • **3.** Democracy Gains Strength under Andrew Jackson

12. How the United States Gained More Territory

1. The United States Grows through Treaties • **2.** Territory Acquired through War • **3.** Land Purchases Complete Continental Borders

11

Jackson and the New West

Against the backdrop of an ever-moving frontier that divided the known from the unknown, the American West has played a profound role on the stage of the nation's history. It was the West, with its abundance of cheap land, that attracted thousands of Europeans to American shores. And it was that very fact of settlement that confirmed American control of the Western lands. With the passing of the years, the West has had a continuing effect on the economic, the political, and the social growth of the new nation.

1. Western Settlement Poses New Problems

Reasons for Western advance were varied. Many of the men who went to the West did so for adventure. Some were motivated by the lure of owning their own land. Others sought the new life in the West because of the freedom from restraint it offered. Still others looked upon the broad lands beyond the Mississippi as an ideal place to get rich through land speculation or trade.

In 1763, at the close of the French and Indian War, the British king announced that no settlements should be made west of the Allegheny Mountains. That land was to be reserved for the Indians. One reason for this reservation was to prevent any interference with the valuable fur trade with the Indians. An important cause of the French and Indian War was the desire of the British colonists to do away with French control of this land which they claimed and coveted for themselves. With the land won they were much distressed that the British king wanted to hem them in on the eastern side of the mountains. There was always danger, moreover, of bands of Indians sweeping out of the West

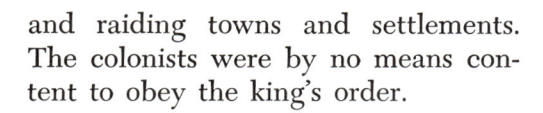

Daniel Boone's rifle and powderhorn. His name is carved on both.

and raiding towns and settlements. The colonists were by no means content to obey the king's order.

Pathways into the Wilderness

Boone of Boonesboro. In 1769, a North Carolina woodsman named Daniel Boone, with five companions, went into the region called Kentucky. Kentucky was a stretch of country lying between the lands of the northern and the southern tribes of Indians, who used it for a hunting ground. They fiercely resented the coming of the white man.

For over a year Boone and his men hunted in Kentucky, always in danger of attack. After they returned to North Carolina, a treaty was made which allowed the white men to settle in the Indian hunting ground. Again Boone set out for Kentucky, this time at the head of a band of pioneers. Through the Cumberland Pass they went, opening a pathway which led to the Kentucky River. This first pathway into the wilderness was called "The Wilderness Road." Reaching the Kentucky River, Boone's party built a fort and named it Boonesboro. Boonesboro soon grew into a settlement. Other settlements followed. The settlers called their new lands Transylvania, but soon they discovered that the lands lay

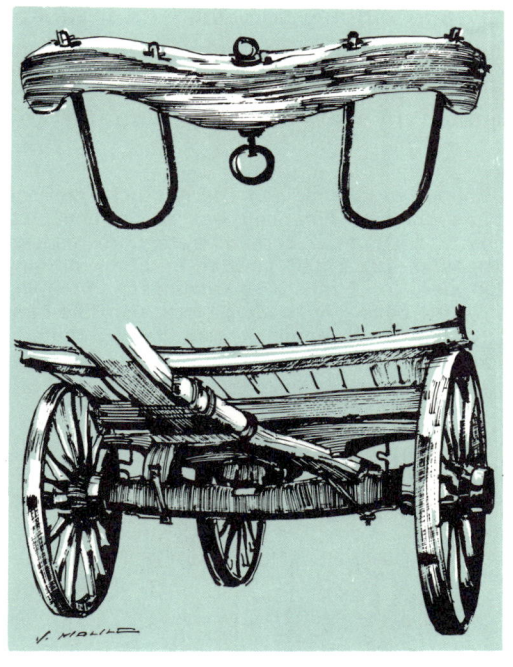

Oxen yoke and wagon wheels of 1800's. Wheels are a prairie schooner's, a modified Conestoga wagon usually pulled by oxen.

George Caleb Bingham painted many scenes of American life. In this one, called The Emigration of Daniel Boone," he captures the determination and anticipation of settlers moving west. His depiction of frontier dress is probably inaccurate and drawn from hearsay rather than actual examination. The picture hangs at Washington University, St. Louis, Missouri.

within the borders of Virginia, whose state government organized them into the county of Kentucky.

Robertson and Sevier. In the meantime another band of settlers, led by James Robertson, crossed the mountains and settled in what is now Tennessee. Two years later they were joined by yet another group, led by John Sevier (sa-VER'). All these settlers of the West carried on war with the Indians. So successful were they that by the time of the Revolutionary War, a great section west of the Allegheny Mountains was held and settled by pioneers from the colonies along the Atlantic.

Peace and Statehood. Towards the end of the Revolution, George Rogers Clark concluded his famous expedition against Kaskaskia, Cahokia, and Vincennes. What the woodsmen started, Clark finished. Clark's army routed the British and frightened the Indians. After this, peace in the area was more secure.

In later years the road through the Cumberland pass brought many inhabitants to Kentucky and the lands now called Tennessee. This led to the settlement of other districts farther to the west. In 1790, the Tennessee region and some land farther to the south were organized as the Southwest Territory. Kentucky became a state and was admitted to the Union in 1792. Tennessee followed four years later.

Frontier equipment. (1) The Kentucky flintlock rifle, uniquely American, was accurate at 300 yards. (2) Powder horn with staghorn measuring cup. (3) Small powder horn for priming powder. (4) Flints. (5) Patches for wrapping (6) rifle balls. (7) Loading block. (8) Rifle ramrod end. (9) Maple-handled hunting knife.

The Settling of the Southwest

The invention of the cotton gin by Eli Whitney led to the settlement of another part of the West. Much more cotton could now profitably be gathered than in the past, and it was desirable to add to the cotton-growing section of the country. So, bit by bit, the fields and plantations of the South were extended westward toward the Mississippi. Jefferson's purchase of Louisiana in 1803 greatly added to the territory into which the cotton-growing settlers could move. Before very long the cotton belt extended from the

Steamboating spans a fascinating era of American history. The first steamboats were quite slow, taking as long as 25 days for the upstream voyage from New Orleans to Louisville, Ky. By 1853, however, the time had been reduced to four days. Steamboat races grew popular in the 1850's and reached a peak in the 1870's. People all over the country followed these races, much in the same way we follow football or basketball. Boats like the one shown were perfected to run at 20 miles an hour, a fantastic speed in the 1870's.

Encyclopaedia Britannica Films, Inc.

Atlantic Ocean to the southwestern border of the Louisiana Purchase.

As more and more people moved into the southwestern land, it was divided into territories—lands not lying in any established state, but owned and governed by the national government. Later, constitutions were drawn up for these territories, and they were admitted to the United States as new states. In this way Louisiana entered the Union in 1812, Mississippi in 1817, Alabama in 1819, and Missouri in 1821. The addition of these southern states helped to keep the representation of the South in the Senate equal to that of the North, for Vermont was added in 1791, Ohio in 1803, Indiana in 1816, Illinois in 1818, and Maine in 1820.

Role of the Steamboat. A most important factor in the development of the Southwest was the steamboat. Following Shreve's successful invention of a practical river steamboat, many such boats were built and launched in the Mississippi and Ohio Rivers. Soon the Mississippi became an important trade route, and along its banks flourishing towns sprang up.

The Opening of the Northwest

The first settlers in the land north of the Ohio River, known then as the Northwest Territory, were fur traders who hunted and trapped, and who opened woodland trails through the wilderness from one trading post to another. All during the period when France owned this region, it was populated by only a scattered handful of these "woods runners," as they were called.

The Northwest Ordinance. The Ordinance of 1785 provided for the sale of the public lands of the Northwest Territory to bring revenue to the government. It even provided for the education and religious instruction of the settlers by insisting that land—a "school lot" and a "gospel lot"—be set aside in each settlement for a school building and a church. Nevertheless, for many years settlers did not enter the territory in large numbers, principally due to the danger from hostile Indians.

General Harrison's defeat of the Indians at Tippecanoe opened the Northwest to settlers. After the surrender of

A Conestoga wagon and oxen team stand in front of a reconstructed frontier farm in New Salem, Illinois. Originating in the Conestoga region of Pennsylvania in 1750, wagons of this type carried settlers into the Northwest Territory for many years. Its western counterpart, the prairie schooner, was larger, lighter, and more suited to flatland travel.

the British garrisons at Detroit and other important points, increasing numbers of people began to cross the mountains and establish little pioneer settlements in the Northwest Territory.

Steamboats and Canals. The use of steamboats on the Ohio and Mississippi Rivers led to their appearance on the Great Lakes. In 1818, the steamboat *Walk-in-the-Water* was launched on Lake Erie. Many others followed, and trade on the Great Lakes began to grow. The western farmers profited by this because they could now more easily send their crops to the East.

The opening of the Erie Canal in 1825 increased the value of the Great Lakes as a trade route and brought added prosperity to the West by providing a new water route to the great port of New York. Clinton's "big ditch" helped not only the state through which it ran but also many regions hundreds of miles to the west.

Migration Routes

The much-traveled Cumberland Road, or Old National Road, was most effective in opening up the Northwest Territory. More settlers traveled this route than any other, although other routes were frequently used. Over these routes on regular schedules ran great, heavy stagecoaches and freight wagons. Travel was slow and uncomfortable, and both freight and passenger rates were high. It took about twenty days for the stage coaches and the Conestoga wagons, as the freight carriers were called, to make the journey from Philadelphia to Pittsburgh. A modern automobile can cover the same distance easily in half a day.

Looking Back

1. Who led the Americans into the Kentucky and Tennessee areas?
2. How did the invention of the cotton gin hasten the settlement of the Southwest?
3. What factors made settlement in the Northwest Territory attractive?
4. In what way do present-day students benefit from the Northwest Ordinance?
5. Describe the methods of transportation used during this period.

2. The Western Movement Affects the Nation

More than any other single factor, the frontier has shaped the character of the American people and the destiny of the American nation. The first people to occupy many western areas were hunters or trappers, as we have seen. Following them, families came to settle pioneer homesteads. Their ways of life were rough and primitive, but all this began to change when large groups of settlers came to lands which had only before been occupied by isolated pioneer families. For one thing, these new settlers carried eastern ideas, eastern customs, and eastern manners of living into the West. Houses became more livable; clothes brought from the East were bought in stores, not woven on primitive looms. On the other hand, the men who left the East had to accept the more democratic ways of the West.

One of the finest features of frontier life was the spirit of good will and helpfulness that prevailed among most settlers. A family without friends might arrive at a piece of land only to find that within a matter of hours other settlers were helping to clear land or build their home. Below is shown a houseraising. Often groups of frontier farmers built houses in two days.

Politics on the Frontier

Western Equality. Most of those who went west had to depend upon their own strength and cleverness and could not count on favors because of their social positions. In the West all differences of rank were forgotten and every man had an equal say in the government. The democratic ideas of the western territories and states gradually came to influence the East and South. To a large extent they were responsible for the removal of limitations on voting and for the eventual extension of citizenship to all men over twenty-one years of age in those parts of the country.

The "War Hawks." In the halls of Congress, the vigorous westerners made themselves felt through their representatives. Their constant sacrifices and struggles to extend the borders of the country had made the pioneers and settlers intensely patriotic, and they were much quicker to resent any real or fancied insult to the country than were the easterners. The people of the West had no real concern with Britain's seizing of ships and the impressment of American seamen into British service. Still, they so loudly urged the War of 1812 that their representatives gained for themselves the name of "War Hawks."

Demands of the Westerners. Westerners, naturally enough, hoped that the federal government would help the West. Most westerners wished that some day their region could be as financially well-developed as the East. They asked financial support from the government for the building of railroads and canals. They clamored for the sale of government lands which would bring more settlers, more wealth, and greater prosperity to the West. Their demands were heeded, and Congress appropriated large sums of money to grant some of their wishes.

A Great Leader. Perhaps the greatest leader that the West produced was Henry Clay, of Kentucky. While still a very young man, he became so convincing a speaker and so inspiring a leader that he was elected to the United States Senate before he had reached the required age of thirty years. He was well fitted to represent Kentucky, for he had gained the trust and confidence of the ablest statesmen as well as the humblest backwoodsmen. In 1811, he changed from the Senate to the House of Representatives, and later became the Speaker of that body. Clay was a peacemaker. It was largely through his efforts that the United States was saved from the horrors of a civil war during the early years when it could not have survived such a conflict. America owes much to this soft-spoken, but persuasive, statesman.

Henry Clay, famous Kentucky congressman.

As settlers moved west, they needed goods from the East. As a result, freight companies were formed. Their caravans of Conestoga wagons like these traveled wilderness roads.

Effects on the Economy

As the population grew and more acreage was put under cultivation, the West had tremendous effects upon our economy. Food products and minerals were shipped to the East. In turn, the West, with its vast natural resources of lumber and minerals, needed tools and utensils and a greater variety of other products manufactured in the East. A healthy internal trade began in which the needs of each section were met. Eastern manufacturers stepped up production to meet the demands of the new West and found they could ship any surplus to European markets. This, in turn, fostered European interest in American lands, and European investors began to buy up acreage in the American West. Needless to say, complicated economic problems were arising which demanded government supervision.

Under every presidential administration of this period attempts were made to control economic growth. It was essential that all citizens in the West be protected from unfair practices that might restrain trade or hinder rights guaranteed by the Constitution. President Jackson and his successor President Van Buren were especially interested in these problems. Their interest stemmed from the generous support the West gave them in the elections.

Looking Back

1. What have been the effects of the frontier on American life?
2. Why did the "War Hawks" favor war with England in 1812?
3. List and discuss the demands made by westerners to the federal government.
4. How did Henry Clay contribute to the life of his nation?
5. In what ways did a prosperous West help bring prosperity to the East?

3. Democracy Gains Strength Under Andrew Jackson

Probably no other administration strengthened democracy in the United States more than did Andrew Jackson's. During his term of office, which lasted from 1829 to 1837, every effort was made to wrest control of the government from the hands of the privileged few and put it under control of all the people. The voting privilege was extended to include most Americans. Under Jackson, the small landowners, the working classes, the dirt farmers and backwoodsmen could all make their voices heard in government. Political reforms characterized the reign of Jackson; a new role was played by labor in the affairs of American government.

Dawn of a New Era

The enemies of Jackson were sure that some dreadful catastrophe faced the nation with the election of the frontier general. They feared that Washington would be under mob control with riots similar to those of the French Revolution. The inauguration proceedings did not change their concern.

Jackson's Inauguration

Since Jackson considered himself a champion of the people, the inauguration was their celebration as much as his, he thought. Classes of people never before seen at the solemn ceremonies of a new President taking office appeared in the capital. They came from the remote frontier, from the factories, and from isolated rural areas in the East and South. Washington had never entertained such a motley group of people. To the surprise of all, the President-elect invited everyone who attended the ceremonies to the White House. Here the frontiersmen and members of the working class mingled with Washington society and foreign diplomats. They were so enthusiastic for their hero, General Jackson, that if his friends had not helped him escape through a side door he might have been injured by the press of the crowd.

This did not really disturb Jackson for he felt that the White House belonged to the people. They had elected him, and so a visit to the Executive Mansion was their right. However, servants at the White House were highly annoyed by the lack of respect the unruly mob showed toward the mansion's furnishings. They came into

Andrew Jackson as President.

the President's house with muddy shoes and stood on top of the furniture. They pulled down curtains, and collected a great variety of souvenirs by cutting parts of bedspreads and drapes and taking anything which could be carried off. The mob finally moved out of the mansion when White House attendants announced that punch was being served on the lawn!

Orderly Government

Many people feared that unruly mobs of unqualified individuals might get control of the government. Fortunately, things settled down and orderly procedures were the rule after the inauguration ceremonies. Jackson did not begin his administration with drastic changes. Yet, it is correct to speak of the Jackson period as a new era, but not in the sense that his enemies thought it would be. Democracy based on law and order was not overthrown by an undisciplined mob. In fact, the reverse was true. Jackson's administration, noted for its order and its emphasis on strong executive power, was opposed to all kinds of undemocratic action from the states or from individuals. His administration brought about an extension of democracy so that it touched more people and allowed them to participate in the operation of the government. This participation made more people feel that it was their own government in a very particular way.

The Spoils System

Jackson valued the ability of the common man highly. Therefore he felt that many of the common people who voted for him deserved all the offices available in the new administration. Jackson, like Jefferson before him, felt that the average man was the backbone of the American system, and that any man of average intelligence could perform the duties of government office. Therefore, over the eight-year span of his two administrations, he dismissed about one-fifth of the old government employees and replaced them with his own men. Jackson was severely criticized for this action. In fact, his political opponents labeled him "King Andrew" because they felt he was behaving in a way not befitting an American Chief of State.

Jackson had many sound defenses for his actions, however. For one thing, Jefferson had done the same thing, although not on as large a scale. Moreover, Jackson felt that rotation in office would make for more honest service on the part of those he appointed. He further explained that he needed to have people working in the government who were wholeheartedly supporting the principles on which the election had been won. All these arguments are realistic ones, and since Jackson's election, the custom of making political appointments according to the party in power has prevailed in many local, state, and national elections. We call this the *spoils system*.

The Webster-Hayne Debates

Western Land Sales. The Webster-Hayne debates raised a number of important issues, some of which are not settled to this day. These famous debates in the halls of Congress came about through a Connecticut senator's resolution which suggested that the Federal government limit the sale of western land. Two factors in the political thinking of New Englanders caused the congressmen from that area to support the resolution. First, population was being drawn into the West because of the liberal land policy of the government. Loss of population affected the labor supply for New England manufacturing. Secondly, the Eastern states knew that the new western senators would vote along with southerners on matters like the tariff. New Englanders didn't want this to happen.

The Nature of the Union. To the resolution of Senator Foot of Connecticut, Thomas Hart Benton, the Senator from Missouri, replied that the eastern interests were trying to interfere with the growth of the West. Senator Hayne from South Carolina stated that to prohibit the sale of land is an attempt to weaken "the independence of the states" and to grant undue power to the federal government. Hayne was answered by the eloquent orator and Senator from Massachusetts, Daniel Webster. He not only defended the original resolution to change the land policy in the West, but criticized the South for having only a weak interest in the defense of the Union.

The debates finally centered around a discussion of the Constitution: Was it a compact made between sovereign states which could dissolve it at will, or was it a contract made by the people to create a lasting Union? No permanent decision was made on exactly what the Constitution was intended to be. However, antagonism continued between the Western and Southern interests against the industrial Northeast.

The Webster-Hayne debates were among the most significant ever to take place in the halls of Congress. In them the issues of states' rights and sectionalism were placed in opposition to the growth of a unified nation. Many of these same issues are still alive today.

Jackson and the Bank

Jackson's Veto. President Andrew Jackson from the beginning had been opposed to the United States Bank. The charter of the first national bank had expired in 1811, and a second bank had been established in 1816, which was enormously prosperous. Besides the great central bank in Philadelphia, there were by 1831 twenty-five branch banks in the leading cities of the country. Jackson felt that the institution was growing too strong, and gaining too firm a hold throughout the United States. He doubted, moreover, whether it was constitutional to establish such a bank in the first place. When a bill for the renewal of the charter of the United States Bank was passed by Congress, in 1832, President Jackson vetoed it.

End of the National Bank. Jackson's destruction of the Bank provided the issue for the election of 1832. Jackson, seeking re-election with the support of the Democratic Party, stood by his action in destroying the Bank. His opponent, Henry Clay, was the candidate of the National Republicans. Clay favored the Bank as an important part of his American System. As a result of the election, Jackson was re-elected, and the Bank was doomed. Early in 1833 the President instructed his Secretary of the Treasury to start withdrawing the government's funds from the Bank. When the government withdrew its large amounts of money, the banks could no longer function.

Paper Money From Private Banks. The destruction of the United States Bank as a government institution led to the creation of hundreds of private banks throughout the country. Many of these had little capital behind them, but most of them proceeded to issue great quantities of paper money also known as bank notes. This led to much the same situation as had existed before the first national bank was chartered. People did not trust the private bank money, and the farther from home a man traveled, the less his paper money was worth.

The Specie Circular. Thousands of people used paper money in large quantities to pay the government for the western lands that they were buying. Consequently, the Treasury soon was overloaded with bank notes of doubtful value. Fearing many of the banks would fail, and that the money would lose most or all of its value, President Jackson in 1836 issued what was known as the *Specie Circular*. This forbade the officers of the United States Treasury to accept any money except gold or silver in payment for public lands.

The result was sudden and disastrous. People carried their paper money to the banks and demanded gold and silver for it. But the banks lacked the gold and silver to supply the demand, and bank after bank failed, leaving its depositors ruined, with their purses full of worthless paper money.

Land buying fell off enormously. Land values fell. Half-completed canals and railroads were abandoned, and the entire West was thrown into great distress.

A Backward Glance at Jackson

Disappointed Supporters. The events of Jackson's administration proved a great disappointment to the people of the West and the South. When he was elected, the people of those sections rejoiced and felt that they had gained a great triumph. The new President was a Westerner and a representative of the common people. He was replacing the aristocratic John Quincy Adams of New England, who favored high tariffs and other things distasteful to those in distant parts of the country. The feeling of triumph, however, was short-lived, for Jackson refused to oppose the tariff, vigorously opposed the doctrine of nullification dear to the hearts of Southerners and Westerners, and ruined the great Western land boom by his Specie Circular. In doing these things he was merely doing what he thought best for the nation as a whole.

Jackson's spoils system and his sometimes ruthless manner of using the power of his office led to the creation of a new political party—the *Whigs*. Taking the name of the British party which had opposed the tyrannical rule of King George III, the Whigs declared that Jackson should be "cast from the throne" and that less power should be allowed the President and the central government. In spite of their opposition, Jackson was succeeded by another Democratic President, Martin Van Buren, who defeated William Henry Harrison and three other Whigs in the election of 1836.

Looking Back

1. How did Jackson's inauguration prove that a new era had come to Washington?
2. In what way did Jackson defend the spoils system?
3. Why did many easterners dislike to see the rapid growth of the West?
4. What was the chief significance of the Webster-Hayne debate?
5. For what reasons did Jackson oppose the United States Bank?

The Chapter in Perspective

Who Are These People?

Boone	Webster
Robertson	Hayne
Sevier	Benton
Clay	Van Buren
Jackson	Harrison

Where Are These Places?

Cumberland Pass	Tennessee
Wilderness Road	Kentucky

What Do These Dates and Terms Mean?

1792	1836
Conestoga wagon	1829
United States Bank	spoils system
Specie Circular	Whigs

Questions for Study

1. How did the location of the Wilderness Road and the work of Boone help Kentucky become the first western state to enter the Union?
2. Why was the South almost enabled to maintain a balance of power in the Senate while it lost power in the House?
3. What were the contributions of the steamboats and canals to the development of the West?
4. Discuss the democratic influences that moved from the West to the East. Why was this so?
5. Tell how a debate about the sale of western lands became a debate about the nature of the Union.
6. By what steps did Jackson destroy the United States Bank?
7. What effect did the destruction of the Bank have on the American money system?
8. What was the purpose of the Specie Circular? What were its results?

Place Yourself in History

When John Q. Adams became President, you were appointed to a federal position. You fulfilled your duties with distinction and received several promotions. In April of 1829, a month after Jackson came into the White House, you were replaced by a Democrat who had supported the new administration in the recent election.

What can you do about being "fired"? Was it fair for Jackson to dismiss you solely because of your political allegiance? Will government work and government workers benefit from such a policy? Why?

How the United States Gained More Territory

12

Immediately after the Declaration of Independence was signed, the United States consisted of only a few small colonies stretched from Maine to Florida along the Atlantic coast. The land beyond the Appalachian Mountains was barely explored, and its ownership was still very much in doubt. In this chapter is told the exciting story of how the fledgling American government made the broad lands from the Appalachians to the Pacific its own. Beginning with the acquisition of Louisiana and ending with the Gadsden Purchase, it is a story of the development of American diplomacy, war, and territorial growth.

1. The United States Grows Through Treaties

The peace treaties at the close of the Revolution and the War of 1812 did not settle the disputed boundary claims along the Canadian border in the area of Maine and the Northwest Territory. Several attempts had been made to reach satisfactory agreements, but none had been successful. It appears that Great Britain had hoped to stop the expansion of the United States and therefore refused to give official recognition to our claims to the Louisiana territory even as late as 1814.

Furthermore, Great Britain was not eager to fix the boundary line between Canada and the United States from the Great Lakes west to the Pacific. Great Britain hoped that more British settlers would move into the disputed areas, thus insuring that they would be British. Other European nations also were slow to consider seriously our Monroe Doctrine, especially the section of it that claimed that the Americas were closed to any future colonization. Most European countries were reluctant to give up any old claims to areas within the present United States. This reluctance made it rather difficult for the new, pioneer Americans to move into some western lands which were still nominally claimed by European countries. Only through skillful diplomatic negotiations were boundaries settled or new lands added to the United States.

American-British Convention of 1818

Northern Boundary. In 1818, a treaty was signed in London by representatives of the British government, the American Minister to Great Britain and our Minister to France. By the terms of this agreement, the northern boundary of the Louisiana Purchase was finally settled. It gave the United States clear title to the land south of the 49th parallel from the Lake of the Woods, in the present state of Minnesota, to the eastern edge of the Rocky Mountains. No boundary was agreed upon for the region west of the mountains. England was still reluctant to admit United States claims to any of the Far West, partially because of her desire to keep America "contained." In other words, Great Britain wished to make it difficult for her daughter nation to challenge her influence in the Western Hemisphere.

However, the two nations did agree under the Convention of 1818 that the citizens of either nation could feel that the territory was free and open to them for settlement or for trade. It was, in a sense, a joint occupation, one which was to last for ten years, but which in reality lasted longer. At the end of ten years the claims of each nation would again be subjected to arbitration. Thus the possession of the Northwest remained an unsettled question until 1846.

Log houses, introduced to America by Swedes and Finns in Delaware, 1630, were common by 1750. Top: round logs, notched at corners, left chinks in walls. Bottom: squared logs gave tighter fit.

240

Fishing Rights. Negotiations during the Convention of 1818 also provided a solution to the problem of fishing rights of American fishermen along the eastern coast. Areas were designated where United States fishing privileges could be exercised off the coasts of Labrador and Newfoundland. Specifications were made as to shores on which American fishermen might dry and cure their catch. To some New England states this was of tremendous importance since they made their living from the sea.

Webster-Ashburton Treaty

For many years after the War of 1812, it appeared to leaders of both Great Britain and the United States that the two countries might again engage in a war. The Convention of 1818 did not settle the far western boundary or the boundary in Maine, but it did tend to reduce the tension between Britain and America.

In 1841, shortly after assuming the office of Secretary of State under President Harrison, Daniel Webster made a suggestion to the British minister in Washington. Webster's suggestion was that the United States and Great Britain resume negotiations concerning the northeast boundary between the two countries. The London authorities agreed to send a special minister to Washington for consultations with Webster. The choice was a fortunate one. Lord Ashburton, the English representative, had married an American and was eager to see peaceful relationships maintained.

Since the representatives of both nations were eager for settlement of a boundary dispute which had existed almost sixty years, it did not prove too difficult to divide the territory. The United States received 7000 of the 12,000 square miles in question. Although Great Britain received less land, she kept a military road that had previously been built between Montreal and St. John along the coast. The northern boundaries of New York State and Vermont were settled at the 45th parallel. The boundary between Lake Superior and the Lake of the Woods was also agreed upon. Other articles of the treaty dealt with the navigation rights of the two countries on the St. John River and a joint effort to suppress the slave trade along the coast of Africa.

(1) Rochester brassbowl "coal oil" lamp. (2) wooden matches 1830. (3) foot warmer—filled with live coals. (4) hot coal carrier for transporting fire from place to place.

> *A Letter From the Alamo*
>
> "Commandancy of the Alamo, Bexar, February 24, 1836.—
>
> To the people of Texas and all Americans in the World.
>
> Fellow citizens and compatriots: I am besieged by a thousand or more of the Mexicans under Santa Anna. I have sustained a continual bombardment and cannonade for twenty-four hours and have not lost a man. The enemy has demanded a surrender at discretion; otherwise the garrison are to be put to the sword if the fort is taken. I have answered the demand with a cannon shot, and our flag still waves proudly from the walls. I shall never surrender nor retreat. Then, I call on you in the name of liberty, of patriotism, and everything dear to the American character, to come to our aid with all dispatch. The enemy is receiving reinforcements daily and will no doubt increase to three or four thousand in four or five days. If this call is neglected, I am determined to sustain myself as long as possible and die like a soldier who never forgets what is due to his own honor and that of his country. VICTORY OR DEATH."
>
> —William Barret Travis
> Lieutenant Colonel Commandant

Just prior to the negotiations, a map had been discovered in the archives of the French government which showed the boundary line as suggested in the Treaty of Paris of 1783. The line was exactly the same as that claimed by the British. At the same time, the British government had in their possession a map (not known to Lord Ashburton and not shown to the Americans until after the Webster-Ashburton Treaty was signed) which corresponded exactly with the American claims. Other maps discovered since prove that the original American claim was the one agreed to in 1783. This being the case, no territory would have had to be surrendered if the American representatives had had these additional maps in their possession.

The Annexation of Texas

Americans in Texas. In 1821 Mexico revolted and secured her independence from Spain. At this time, she gained control over what is now southwestern United States, including Texas and California territory which had previously been under Spanish rule. Mexi-

Six thousand Mexican troops besieged 187 Texans in this old Mission. It is now a historic shrine. Those who died there are the heroes of Texan independence.

co invited settlers from the United States into the territories, offering them a liberal land policy. Later, a new government attempted to check the migration from the United States, but it was practically impossible to stop the flow of settlers. Naturally, since slavery was forbidden in Mexico, conflicts between the Mexican government and the settlers in Texas, who were mostly southerners, soon erupted.

When the Mexican dictator, Santa Anna, asserted his rule by marching into land Texans had claimed, civil war broke out. The United States settlers in Texas had long before this sent several petitions to the Mexican government for a change of policy toward immigration from the United States. In 1833, the Texans held a convention which passed a resolution to separate from Mexico. Stephen Austin went to Mexico City to present these resolutions, but the Mexican government would not consider the desires of the Texans. In fact, Austin was imprisoned for eight months. Conditions worsened until armed clashes occurred in 1835.

The Alamo. In February, 1836, Santa Anna again entered the Texas territory, this time with three thousand Mexicans, and besieged the Alamo (AL'uh-moh), an old Spanish mission in San Antonio which had been converted into a garrison. One hundred and eighty-seven men, commanded by Lieutenant Colonel William Travis, held out against the Mexicans for eleven days. Included with the heroic defenders were the famed Davy Crockett and James Bowie, whose family originated the "Bowie knife."

Despite the heroic defense by the Texans, overwhelming odds in favor of the Mexicans brought defeat to the garrison. Santa Anna massacred the entire group of defenders. The slaughter at the Alamo aroused all Texans to fight the invaders. "Remember the Alamo" became the cry throughout Texas.

Texan Independence. While the Alamo was being besieged, a convention, held in the Texan town of Washington-on-the-Brazos, adopted a declaration of independence and

Rugged Texas frontiersmen were independent and self-reliant and guarded fiercely their families and homes.

formed a constitution very similar to that of the United States. But the Mexicans, still on Texan soil, had to be defeated before the "Lone Star Republic" could become a reality. The Texan victory finally occurred at the battle of San Jacinto (san ha-SIN'toh) where the Texan forces under Sam Houston defeated 1200 Mexicans and captured Santa Anna. A treaty was never agreed upon by Mexico and Texas although Santa Anna had pledged to ensure the independence of Texas from Mexico. With or without their independence, the Texans installed Sam Houston as the first president. Rather reluctantly, the United States recognized the new republic. The next year, 1837, Texas formally applied for annexation to the United States. The application, however, was refused.

Move Toward Annexation. For several decades, many in the United States had favored adding Texas to our country. In 1827, President John Quincy Adams had tried to buy the territory for a million dollars, and in 1829 and 1835 Andrew Jackson had offered Mexico five times as much. In every case the offer had been refused. But now that Texas had won its independence and had asked to be admitted to the United States, the government hesitated to annex it because this might bring trouble with Mexico.

There was strong opposition for another reason, too. The new Texas Republic permitted slavery, and its addition to the Union would mean many more members in Congress who favored the holding of slaves. Northerners who opposed slavery did not want Texas to join the United States, so the question dragged on from year to year. It was scarcely discussed at all during the entire administration of Martin Van Buren (1837-41), the

Marcus Whitman and his wife traveled to the Oregon country in a small caravan of prairie schooners.

> *Washington Irving Describes the Oregon Territory*
>
> " . . . The surrounding country was in all the freshness of spring; the trees were in the young leaf, the weather was superb, and everything looked delightful to men just emancipated from a long confinement on shipboard. . . . All hands now set to work cutting down trees, clearing away thickets, and marking out the place for the residence, storehouse, and powder magazine, which were to be built of logs and covered with bark. Others landed the timbers intended for the frame of the coasting vessel, and proceeded to put them together, while others prepared a garden spot, and sowed the seeds of various vegetables."
>
> —Washington Irving, in "Astoria"

Democratic President from New York who had succeeded Andrew Jackson.

Many Texans, however, were former citizens of the United States, and they were very anxious to see their new lands added to their native land. When President Harrison, who opposed annexation, died in office and was succeeded by his Vice-President, John Tyler, sentiment was revived for the annexation of Texas.

Polk and Annexation. The election of 1844 settled the question of annexing Texas. Henry Clay, the candidate who was supported by the Whig party, first declared that he was opposed to annexation and then made a statement in favor of it. As a result, nobody was sure just what he would do if he were elected. On the other hand, James K. Polk, the Democratic candidate, came out boldly in favor of taking in both Texas and Oregon. His slogan was "the reannexation of Texas and reoccupation of Oregon." This was misleading since the United States had never occupied Oregon, except jointly with Great Britain, and had never annexed Texas at all. Polk won the election by a narrow margin. His victory was regarded by the retiring President, John Tyler, as evidence that a majority of the American people favored annexing Texas, and Tyler pushed through the annexation of this big, new territory on March 1, 1845, only three days before retiring from office.

It soon became evident that trouble would result. Texas had claimed as her boundary the Rio Grande (rio GRAAN'-day) River, but Mexico claimed that the boundary lay far to the north. The border remained an unsettled question, and one which could certainly lead to war.

The Oregon Territory

The Whitmans. In 1836, Doctor Marcus Whitman of New York organized a group to explore the Oregon territory, and to be missionaries to the Indians. He took his young wife with him in a covered wagon on what was then an almost unbelievable journey. Their way was studded with obstacles: Indians, scorching heat, bitter cold, and, finally, the Rocky Mountains. But in spite of all this, and in spite of wreck-

Breathtaking sights like this waterfall in Yellowstone greeted the westward pioneers.

ing their wagon on the rough mountain trails, the little band persisted. Whitman's young wife Narcissa, and Eliza Spalding, wife of Henry Spalding the other missionary in the party, were the first white women to cross the continental divide.

Although by treaty the area was open to Americans and British, the English were opposed to American colonization, since it would mean interference with the flourishing British fur trade. However, when the Whitmans arrived at Vancouver, in what is now British Columbia, they were welcomed by an Englishman named John McLoughlin, known as the "Father of Oregon." He had been appointed by the British to head the west coast division of the Hudson's Bay Company and to be governor of the new territory. In the true pioneer spirit, he helped the Whitmans to settle there, in spite of the fact that such help was contrary to the interests he represented.

Six years after his arrival in Oregon, Doctor Whitman made the long trip to the East to persuade other people to settle in the Oregon region. In five months he traveled over three thousand miles to Boston. There he gathered some followers, and in 1843 they started west. Crossing into Oregon, they built homes and were soon joined by other settlers, who founded several towns.

"54° 40′ or Fight." Now that Oregon was settled by Americans, the idea spread, especially among expansionists in the Democratic party, that the British had no right to the territory at all, and that they should abandon it. "Fifty-four forty, or fight!" said the Democratic party platform in 1844. This meant that the United States must be granted the whole Oregon territory, and the boundary line must be established at 54° 40′ north latitude, or war would be declared against Great Britain. The issue was exciting and the slogan helped Polk to win the election in 1844.

Peaceful Settlement. But there are other ways than fighting to settle most disputes, and both the United States and Great Britain had had enough of war. So, in 1846 representatives of the two countries met and made a treaty by which Oregon was divided. It was agreed that the northern boundary of the United States should continue to follow the 49th parallel through to the Pacific Ocean, and that the part of Oregon south of the line should belong to the United States while the northern part should be added to the British possessions in Canada.

The settlement of the Oregon question marked a great step forward in the international affairs of the United States. Before 1846 America had twice gone to war with Great Britain to settle their differences. When it was seen how much better peaceful arbitration was than bloody warfare, both nations were indeed glad that they had not gone to war. Since the War of 1812, America has had several disputes with her former mother country across the sea, but in every case the questions have been peacefully settled.

Utah's Settlement

The Mormons. Another area settled in the 1840's was Utah. A religious group, the Church of Jesus Christ of Latter-Day Saints, or Mormons, left Illinois in 1846, going west to escape unfriendly neighbors and religious persecution. Led by Brigham Young, the Mormons entered Mexican Territory, the area near present-day Utah's Great Salt Lake, in 1847. After the territory had passed into the hands of the United States, the Mormons, in 1849, asked for statehood, but were granted only territorial rights in 1850.

Looking Back

1. How did the Convention of 1818 solve some American-British problems?
2. Why were Americans in Texas first welcomed and then made unwelcome by the Mexicans?
3. What was the final solution to the Oregon problem?
4. On what were American claims to Oregon based?

2. Territory Acquired Through War

The acquisition of territory by our country through war dates back to the Revolution, when the patriots fought for the land they were living upon: the thirteen colonies. However, the patriots in that war knew that independence could not be maintained if the infant nation was confined to the area of the original thirteen colonies. Had England maintained her hold on the land to the north and to the west, the newly gained independence would have been of short duration. Since many settlers had moved west of the Appalachian Mountains prior to the war, it seemed only logical for our representatives at the Treaty of Paris in 1783 to demand the territory west of the mountains to the Mississippi River.

Florida Gained From Spain

Disputed Territory. On the Southern frontier, another great addition to the United States was the Spanish territory of Florida. This addition came about in a peculiar way. West Florida, a strip of land lying along the northern coast of the Gulf of Mexico (lower parts of Mississippi and Alabama), was claimed by Spain and was also claimed by the United States as a part of Louisiana. In the year 1810, President Madison sent an army into West Florida. This army occupied the area and then went on into East Florida (the present state of Florida), a region to which the United States had no claim at all. So strong was the opposition, not only from Spain but also from Great Britain and other European

The Castle of San Marcos, built by the Spanish in 1672, had flown the flags of Spain, France and England when it passed into American hands with the cession of Florida in 1819.

nations, that Madison was forced to withdraw the army from Florida and cease pressing claims to either region.

Border Raids. Still, the United States wanted Florida badly. Valuable harbors in West Florida would be worth much to the United States as outlets for her cotton exports. Then, too, as long as it was Spanish property it served as a refuge for Indians and runaway slaves. Once safely in Florida, these people formed bands and made dangerous raids across the border into the United States. Though Spain had promised to see that such raids were stopped, she proved unequal to the task.

Jackson's Campaign. Residents of lower Alabama, Georgia, and Mississippi complained loud and long about losing their former slaves over the border. Their complaints grew more intense when these slaves joined with renegade Indians and white criminals in raids on their farms and homes. Finally, President Monroe ordered Andrew Jackson (who later became President) to move into Florida to wipe out these groups, even if it meant violating Spanish territory. Jackson, who enjoyed a fight, was only too glad to comply. He charged into West Florida, severely punishing any and all bands of border raiders he found there.

Spain was, of course, indignant at the invasion of her territory. The United States government, however, maintained that the Spaniards had not lived up to their promise to keep the raiding parties under control, and that Jackson's campaign had the backing of the government. It was further stated that unless Spain really exerted herself to keep peace along the border, she must surrender Florida to the United States.

This statue of Andrew Jackson at the Battle of New Orleans stands across the street from the White House in Washington.

Cession of Florida. At home the Spanish king was faced with problems resulting from the period of French rule. He had already lost most of his American colonies through national wars for independence. Accordingly, in 1819, he ceded Florida to the United States, on condition that the United States would pay $5,000,000 in claims held by citizens of Florida against the Spanish government.

The Seminoles

One big problem which arose after the purchase of the Florida territory was what to do with the Indians there. The original Indian inhabitants of Florida had developed a high civilization much like that of the Aztecs in Mexico, but they had been entirely wiped out by the more warlike Creek and Seminole (SEM'i-nol) Indians from the north. These tribes were dangerous to the white men, and many wanted them driven away from the territory.

In 1832 and 1833, treaties were made with the chiefs of the two tribes, by which they agreed to leave Florida if they might have in exchange an equal area of land in the western part of the United States. When all was ready for the transfer, the Indians objected and decided not to move. Armies were sent into Florida, and occasional fighting was carried on from 1836 to 1842 before the Indians were subdued. With the exception of a few Seminoles, all of the Florida Indians were at last pushed out of Florida, and settled in the Southwest on unoccupied land which is now the state of Oklahoma. A few years later, in 1845, Florida was admitted to the Union as a new state.

The Mexican War

Texas Border Disputes. When annexation of Texas to the United States was announced, Mexico immediately took steps to resist it. Both Mexico and the United States ordered troops to the Texan border. The United States forces were known as the "Army of Observation" and were under the command of General Zachary Taylor. At the same time, James Buchanan, President Polk's Secretary of State, suggested a secret mission to Mexico as a last effort to avoid war. The government sent John Slidell to Mexico to attempt to purchase the area of California and New Mexico where numerous Americans had settled. Mexico refused to receive him.

A Reason for War. General Zachary Taylor then led his American army to the Rio Grande and dug in on its northern bank in the territory which both sides claimed as their own. The Mexican general ordered him to leave, but Taylor refused. Soon afterwards an army of Mexicans crossed the river and attacked a small scouting party of Americans, killing or wounding sixteen.

The American government now had an excuse to go to war. Polk's message

After the Seminole Wars of 1836–1842, only a few Seminole Indians stayed in Florida. Among their most colorful descendents was an old chief, Billy Bowlegs (seated, right) who, when he died in 1964, was reported to have been 104 years old. Although only 3,000 Seminoles live in Florida today, their population is increasing.

to Congress pointed out that every effort had been made to bring about a peaceful settlement on American terms, but that Mexico had now crossed the border and had "shed American blood on American soil." General Taylor, eager for battle, was even then driving the Mexicans across the Rio Grande. A state of war existed between the two countries, and President Polk insisted that Mexico had brought it on.

Taylor's Victories. In spite of strong opposition from the North, Congress now formally declared war. Taylor quickly struck at the Mexican army. Winning two battles north of the Rio Grande, he drove the Mexicans across it, and followed close upon their heels. Next he marched to the west, and then south, capturing the cities of Monterrey (mahn-teh-RAY'), Buena Vista (BWAY'nah VEES'tah), and Tampico (tahm-PEE'ko).

War in California. Another American army, under Colonel Stephen W. Kearney, left Fort Leavenworth in Kansas and marched into what is now New Mexico. Capturing the town of Santa Fe, Kearney then led his men west to San Diego, California, and then north to Los Angeles. He found little opposition, for California had already been subdued by an American naval expedition under Commodore Sloat and a volunteer army under Captain John Frémont. When Sloat's fleet appeared off Monterrey, that city surrendered, and the Mexicans in the other parts of California also wisely offered no resistance.

The rapid victories of Taylor, Sloat, Frémont, and Kearny had shown that the American forces were much more efficient than were the Mexican. Nonetheless, when peace was offered in 1846 it was scornfully refused by the Mexicans, and President Polk decided to strike at the heart of Mexico and end the war quickly.

The Invasion of Mexico. An army of 12,000 men commanded by General Winfield Scott sailed across the Gulf of Mexico and landed at Vera Cruz, on the east coast of Mexico. A larger army, which had been sent by the Mexicans to repulse or destroy him, was met by Taylor's men and driven back. Scott then began his advance on Mexico City.

From March to August, 1847, Scott worked his way inland, winning bat-

California "sourdoughs" or "forty-niners" panning for gold.

Gold nuggets were usually washed out of gravel. 1. A pan was the simplest method for doing this. Full of wet gravel, it was shaken until heavy gold was left at the bottom. 2. A faster means was the cradle. One man poured wet gravel into the box while another rocked it to make gold fall into the trough. 3. The "long tom" placed in a stream and tended by several miners was even faster. 4. The best method was the sluice box, often fifty feet long. As wet gravel and water ran through it, the gold stayed on ripple bars running across the box. 5. A pick, shovel and bucket were all-important.

tles against a larger Mexican army with apparent ease. Snipers picked off his men from behind rocks. Hostile Indians attacked him. But there was no single force which seemed able to stop his advance.

As he approached Mexico City, Scott hesitated in order to give the Mexicans one last chance to make peace. When they refused, he attacked with vigor. The fortress of Chapultepec (chah-POOL′teh-PECK′), which guarded the city and was supposed to be too strong to capture, was stormed by American soldiers. Poorly aimed bullets and cannon balls flew by Scott's men, and the Americans took the fortress, with small loss of life. On the 13th of September, 1847, Mexico City fell, and the fighting was over.

Treaty of Guadalupe-Hidalgo

The treaty ending the Mexican War was signed in January, 1848, in the village of Guadalupe-Hidalgo (gwah-dah-LOO′pay ih-DAHL′go), just outside Mexico City. It provided for the following terms:

(1) Mexico no longer claimed any Texan territory above the Rio Grande;

(2) Mexico ceded to the United States the present area of California, New Mexico, and parts of Utah, Nevada, Arizona, Wyoming, and Colorado;

(3) The United States agreed to pay Mexico $15,000,000 for the new territory;

(4) Claims of U.S. citizens against the Mexican government totaling more than $3,000,000 were to be paid by the United States;

(5) The Mexican-U.S. boundary was settled along the Rio Grande and Gila

American clipper ship *Flying Cloud* sailed in 89 days from New York to San Francisco. At the time (1851) this was a record.

(HEE′lah) rivers to the Colorado River and thence directly west to the Pacific.

Results of the Mexican War

The Mexican War added valuable territory to the southwestern part of the United States, including beautiful California where gold was discovered in 1848. But the gain in wealth and land was made at the expense of suspicion and ill will between the United States and its neighbors to the south. Mexicans in particular have always felt that Americans took advantage of them. Nor were the territorial gains all favorable for the United States. Now that all this new land had been added to the country, men were asking one another whether the territory should be slave or free. Out of that great question was destined to arise one of the most terrible events in American history—the Civil War.

The Gold Rush

The Discovery. Not long before the signing of the Treaty of Guadalupe-Hidalgo, gold was discovered in California at the mill of Johann Sutter, a settler near the present site of Sacramento. The news of this discovery spread rapidly through the settled areas of the United States and then south to the countries of South America. Since California was becoming a part of the United States, settlers were already flocking there. The discovery of gold in California turned this migration into an authentic "rush."

Gold Fever. Actually the settlement of California was unlike that of any other area in this country's history. It is frequently spoken of as "California's Gold Rush," and correctly so, but gold was not the only attraction.

Daniel Webster opposed the admission of California as a state. There seemed to him to be no reason for the concern of the North over western development. This is what he said:

"What do we want with this vast, worthless area, this region of savages and wild beasts, of shifting sands and whirlpools of dust, of cactus and prairie dogs?

"To what use could we ever hope to put these great deserts or these great mountain ranges, impenetrable and covered to their base with eternal snow?

"Mr. President, I will never vote one cent from the public treasury to place the Pacific Coast one inch nearer Boston than it is now."

Many were attracted to California by the lure of land speculation. Adventurers came from the East, from the South, from the Northwest, and from places as far away as Australia. In one year (1849) it is estimated that 100,000 people moved into California.

The news of the gold discovery came at an opportune time. It spread like a fever over the country. In the East, times were not the most prosperous. Many veterans, just returned from the Mexican War, looked upon the Far West as the place affording the greatest opportunities. Often large segments of a particular town or county would make up a wagon train for California, leaving behind empty houses and abandoned farms.

Routes of the Gold-Seekers. The average gold-seeker had little or no experience in mining. He was lured to California by the fantastic reports which came back to the East about the wealth that could be had for the taking. Some gold-seekers were able to dig several hundred dollars worth of gold each day for weeks. Three years after the discovery, California was producing gold at an annual rate of $55,000,000. The gold rush increased the production of gold in the United States seventy-three times over what it had been in the mid-1840's.

The settlers traveled to California over several routes. The cheapest routes were overland across the Great Plains or over the northern part of Mexico along the Gila and Colorado rivers. The route by sea to the Isthmus and then the fifty mile trek across Panama was probably the shortest in terms of time. Although much traveled, it had many dangers and became a death-trap to less hardened adventurers. The all-sea route by way of Cape Horn at the southern tip of South America also involved many risks. The fastest clipper ship needed practically three months to reach California by this route. Foreigners from Europe and the Far East also arrived by ship in the excellent harbor at San Francisco. During the height of the gold rush, hundreds of ships could be seen anchored in the bay.

Clayton-Bulwer Treaty, 1850

By the mid-nineteenth century both England and the United States were interested in building a canal across the Isthmus of Panama, especially since California was rapidly being settled and trade with that area would increase proportionately. The interest of the two countries soon developed into rivalry.

The American Secretary of State under Zachary Taylor, John M. Clay-

Pioneers wandering through the West were often discoverers by accident of great natural wonders—like Arizona's Petrified Forest.

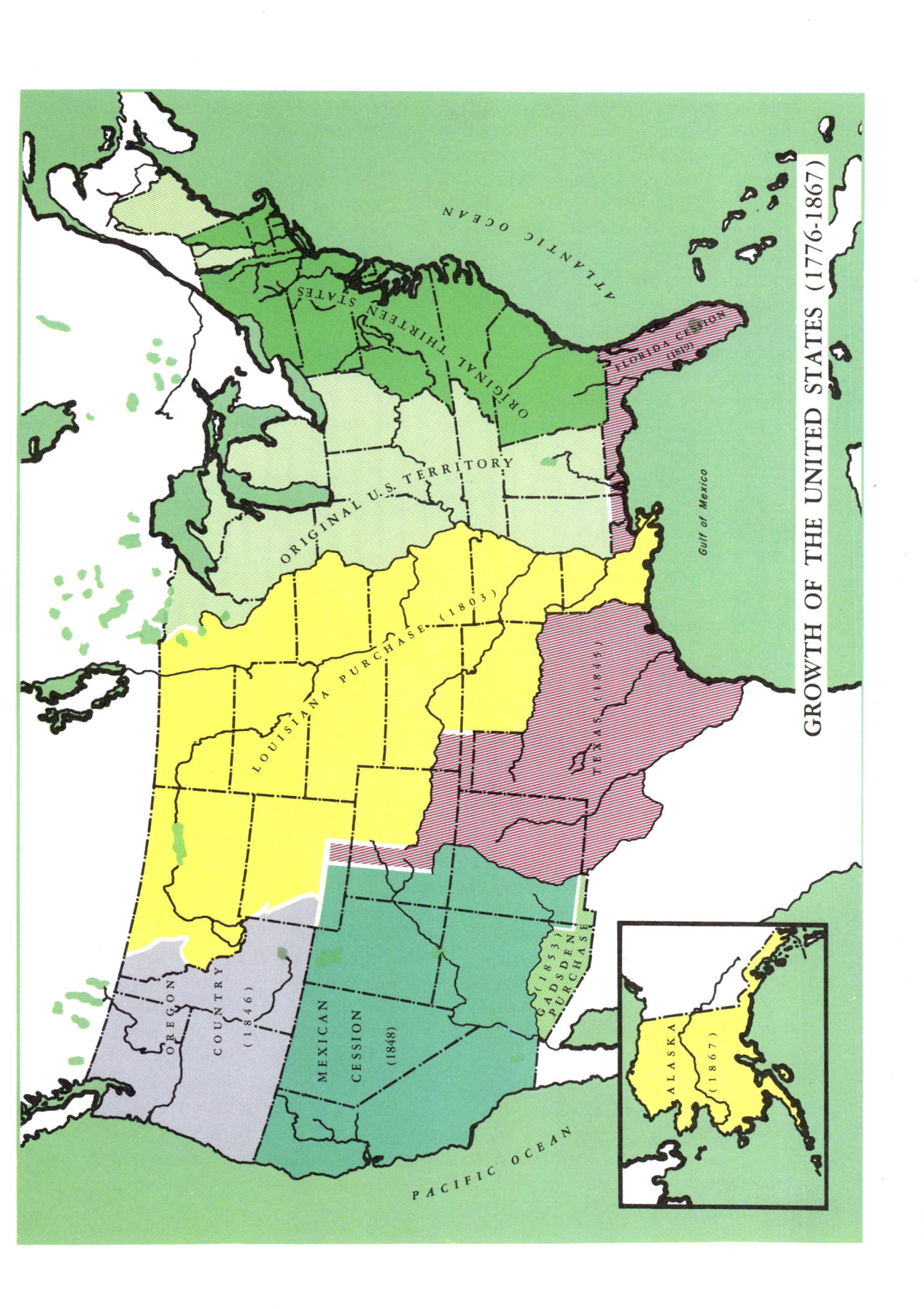

GROWTH OF THE UNITED STATES (1776-1867)

ton, suggested to the British Minister to the United States, Sir Henry Bulwer, the possibility of the two countries' negotiating a treaty. The result was the Clayton-Bulwer Treaty of 1850. England and the United States agreed never to establish exclusive control over a future canal that either country might build. A future canal was to be a neutral zone, open equally to ships and nationals of either nation. The two countries furthermore pledged that they would not colonize at any future time the area of Central America. This treaty was a direct outcome of the Mexican War and the expansion of the United States to the Pacific coast. It did not add new territory, but it widened our sphere of influence.

Looking Back

1. What were the conflicting claims to West Florida?
2. How did border raids from Florida lead to an invasion by Jackson?
3. By what means did the Seminole Indians create a problem for the United States?
4. What were the main events of the Mexican War?
5. Give the terms of the Treaty of Guadalupe-Hidalgo.

3. Land Purchases Complete Continental Borders

The Louisiana Purchase

The third method of acquiring territory was by purchase. The first area to be added to the United States through this means was the Louisiana Territory, purchased from France in 1803. It will be remembered that at that time the American commissioners were sent to Europe to purchase some land on the lower Mississippi for a port. Later they were instructed to attempt to purchase New Orleans and West Florida. James Monroe and Robert Livingston, the American representatives, were amazed that Napoleon offered all the Louisiana territory for sale.

The American representatives exceeded their orders when they bought Louisiana for $15,000,000. Although it was an excellent bargain, President Jefferson was much disturbed over the purchase. He followed a strict interpretation of the Constitution and felt that the purchase might not be proper without a special clause granting such permission. However, Jefferson could not ignore such a bargain, and he decided to agree to the purchase.

Since Jefferson's administration set such a precedent, the United States government has often purchased land for various purposes. Many examples can be found in the period of American history after the Civil War and before World War I.

The $5,000,000 purchase of Florida after American troops had, in effect, captured it, settled the American dispute with Spain over the Florida boundary and the boundary between the western Spanish lands and Louisiana. By the terms of the treaty of 1819, a zigzag boundary line between the United States and the Spanish possessions was set up. The setting up of this boundary line entitled the United States to Spain's former claim to Oregon.

The Gadsden Purchase

The Mexican War had a sequel five years after its close. The southern boundary of New Mexico had first been settled at the Gila River. But in 1853 the section between this boundary and the present one was bought from Mexico for $10,000,000 in order to avoid high mountain ranges in laying out the route of the proposed Southern Pacific Railroad. As the purchase was brought about by Mr. James Gadsden, the area was referred to as the Gadsden Purchase. Many felt that in paying Mexico so high a price for so small a territory, the United States was giving more than the land was worth and amply paying Mexico for her losses in the war. The Gadsden Purchase completed the boundaries of the United States, giving our country the same shape and size that it has today except for the addition of Alaska and Hawaii as new states in 1959.

California became a state in 1850. The remaining land won from Mexico became the territory of New Mexico. In addition to Florida, Texas, and California, the states of Arkansas, Michigan, Iowa, Wisconsin, Minnesota, and Oregon were added to the Union between 1830 and 1860. The original thirteen states had now been joined by twenty others.

Looking Back

1. What was the strategic importance of New Orleans that prompted the Louisiana Purchase?
2. How did the treaty line of 1819 affect later American land claims?
3. For what reasons did the United States make the Gadsden Purchase?
4. What did many people believe were the reasons for paying such a large sum for the Gadsden Purchase?

The Chapter in Perspective

Who Are These People?

Webster	Clay	
Ashburton	Polk	
Santa Anna	Whitman	
Austin	Gadsden	
Travis	Taylor	
Crockett	Slidell	

Where Are These Places?

49th parallel	San Jacinto
Lake of the Woods	Rio Grande
Maine	Oregon
45th parallel	54° 40′
Texas	West Florida
Florida	

What Do These Dates and Terms Mean?

American-British Convention	"Remember the Alamo"	Texan Revolt
Webster-Ashburton Treaty	Clayton-Bulwer Treaty	1835
"reannexation of Texas and reoccupation of Oregon"		1844

1819
1850
Seminoles
1818
"54° 40' or Fight"
Gadsden Purchase
"Lone Star Republic"
Treaty of Guadalupe-Hidalgo

1803
gold rush
1842
1853

Questions for Study

1. Give the reasons why Texas was refused admission to the Union in 1837 but admitted in 1845.
2. How did the Whitmans aid American claims to Oregon?
3. Trace the steps by which the United States acquired Florida.
4. Would you consider the Mexican War an unnecessary war? Why?
5. Under what flags have the people of Florida lived? Under what flags have Texans lived?
6. Why was California's status as a territory so brief?
7. Which acquisition of territory was, in your opinion, the most important to the United States? Why?
8. Show how the United States rounded out its boundaries by treaties, war, and purchase.
9. What states and portions of states were carved from the land acquired from Mexico in 1848?

Place Yourself in History

His name is James W. Marshall. He is employed at a sawmill construction site near Sacramento. On January 24, 1848, he reports a discovery to his employers. The discovery has no bearing on his regular work. His employer asks to keep the discovery a secret, but word leaks out. As a result, a fever which rapidly affects thousands all over the United States and Europe spreads.

The employer is John A. Sutter. The discovery is gold. The fever is gold fever.

How would you have reacted to the discovery of gold in California? What methods were used to get to California? What were the immediate and long-range results of the discovery?

Expanding Your Outlook

Doing It Yourself

1. Prepare for class presentation a biography of one of the heroic leaders of the westward movement.
2. Make a scale model of a typical westward settlement such as the one at Boonesboro.
3. Make a map of the United States in 1853 showing the land acquisitions starting with the original boundaries in 1783.
4. On a map of the United States, indicate the chief routes that were used in the westward movement.
5. Make some posters to display in the United States Bank attacking Jackson's policies toward the Bank.

6. By a series of cartoons, show how Jackson's enemies pictured him and attacked his policies.
7. Write an editorial for an Eastern newspaper that did not favor the Mexican War. (Or for a Western newspaper viewing the slaughter at the Alamo).

Working with the Class

1. Form two committees to prepare campaign literature, signs, slogans, and cartoons which might have been used in the campaign for the Presidency in 1828.
2. Let the classroom be the United States Senate, while students read the key parts in the great debate between Webster and Hayne. Then let the class debate the issues.
3. A group of four students may present a formal debate to the class on the issue: Resolved: The United States was not justified in declaring war on Mexico in 1848.
4. A group interested in dramatics may prepare a brief presentation showing how a family prepared to leave its Ohio home for Oregon in 1847.
5. A round-table discussion on the rights of a state to declare null and void an act of the United States Congress should be interesting. The views of Calhoun, Webster, Jackson, and others should be presented.
6. Imagine you are an "on the spot" interviewer talking with gold miners in Sacramento in 1850. Interview three "prepared" miners who can tell the classroom audience of their varied experiences.

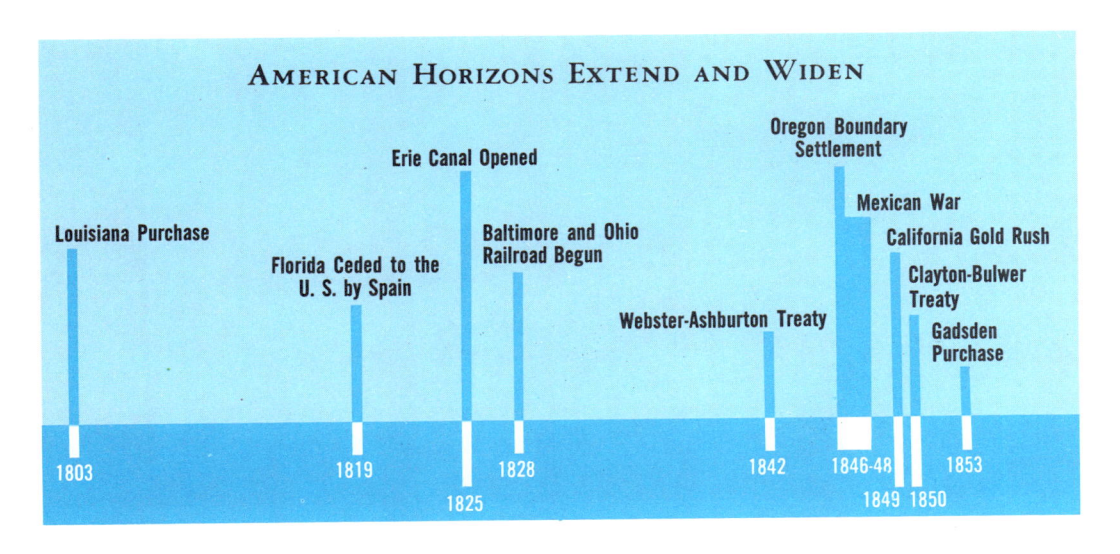

American Horizons Extend and Widen

1803	Louisiana Purchase
1819	Florida Ceded to the U. S. by Spain
1825	Erie Canal Opened
1828	Baltimore and Ohio Railroad Begun
1842	Webster-Ashburton Treaty
1846-48	Mexican War
1846-48	Oregon Boundary Settlement
1849	California Gold Rush
1850	Clayton-Bulwer Treaty
1853	Gadsden Purchase

This painting by George P. Healy, is called The Peacemakers. *Healy has depicted Generals Sherman and Grant, President Lincoln, and Admiral Porter discussing the possibilities of peace. They sit in a cabin on the Mississippi River steamer, the* River Queen, *near the end of the Civil War. In the hands of these men, Lincoln's cabinet, and a few senators and congressmen was the future of the South and the entire United States.*

The White Ho

ONE NATION INDIVISIBLE

UNIT 5

The Union Breaks Apart and Mends More Strongly

13. The Underlying Causes of Secession

1. The Slavery Issue Draws Sharp Sectional Lines • **2.** Land Additions Heighten North-South Controversy • **3.** States' Rights Become a Continuing Issue

14. A Nation at War with Itself: Civil War

1. The First Year Brings Confederate Victories • **2.** The Second Year is Indecisive • **3.** The Union Forges Ahead in the Third Year • **4.** Grant Leads Union Forces in Fourth Year • **5.** The Fifth Year of War Brings Union Victory

15. The Nation Rebuilds

1. The South's Condition in 1865 is Desperate • **2.** Congress and the President Wage Their Own War • **3.** Congressional Reconstruction Brings Bitterness

13 The Underlying Causes of Secession

"A house divided against itself cannot stand," said Abraham Lincoln, one of our greatest Presidents. The United States had gradually become such a house. A bitter quarrel flared between the North and South. Despite the earnest work of the nation's great peacemakers, the rift between the rival sections grew wider and wider, and at last war threatened. The end of the Union seemed very near.

1. The Slavery Issue Draws Sharp Sectional Lines

It is very difficult to determine exactly what led to secession of the Southern states for the causes were numerous and varied. The causes for the resulting Civil War had many years to develop before they led to armed conflict. At the time, the secession of the Southern states, which proved to be the final step toward the Civil War, seemed inevitable in the South, at least. Historians today sometimes speak of the chain of events as "The Irrepressible Conflict."

It is safe to say that three of the most outstanding causes of the division of the country were slavery, expansion, and states' rights. Undoubtedly, the single issue of slavery had great influence on the other two causes as well.

Today, it seems scarcely possible that slavery in its simplest form could exist in the United States. From our earliest times, we Americans were aware of the necessity for individual freedom, sensitive to the basic human needs, and conscious of the basic dignity of each human being. Many settlers came to this country because they had come from countries that did not offer the promise of real freedom that America did. Our Declaration of Independence stated in bold

262

language: ". . . all men are created equal; that they are endowed by their Creator with certain unalienable rights; that among these are life, liberty, and the pursuit of happiness."

Today we readily agree that slavery in any form is a mockery of the principles of the Declaration. A similar view was held by many citizens a hundred, even two hundred years ago. How then can we explain the existence of this totally undemocratic institution?

The Background of Slavery

At one time or another nearly every country in the world has had some type of slavery. In fact, a careful study of slavery reveals that at some time members of practically every race and every creed have been enslaved. The Greeks, Romans, and Persians all enslaved enemies they had conquered. In the middle ages, the lord of a manor held his serfs in a mild kind of slavery. Since then various types of bondage have existed. These have been sometimes economic, sometimes political, sometimes religious.

Even in ancient Greece and Rome, philosophers and most thinking people deplored the institution of slavery, although many of the same philosophers owned slaves themselves. The first laws regulating slavery in Europe were passed in 1685, when Louis XIV, King of France, issued what was known as the "Black Code," which protected slaves from cruel treatment. England and Spain issued a similar code some years later. Even though these codes did not specifically abolish slavery, they were steps in the right direction. They did at least acknowledge that slaves were in fact human beings.

Freedom for Slaves. At last in 1789, France, again the leader in this field, freed all her slaves. Great Britain soon followed suit, passing a law in 1807 stating that after 1808 the infamous slave trade would be ended throughout the British Empire. The United States also stopped import-

Boone Hall, a plantation house built in 1750, was rebuilt in 1935 from its original stones. It stands today near Charleston, South Carolina. The slave cabins are original; they stood to the right of the house in a grove of trees.

RESULT OF MISSOURI COMPROMISE OF 1820

RESULT OF COMPROMISE OF 1850

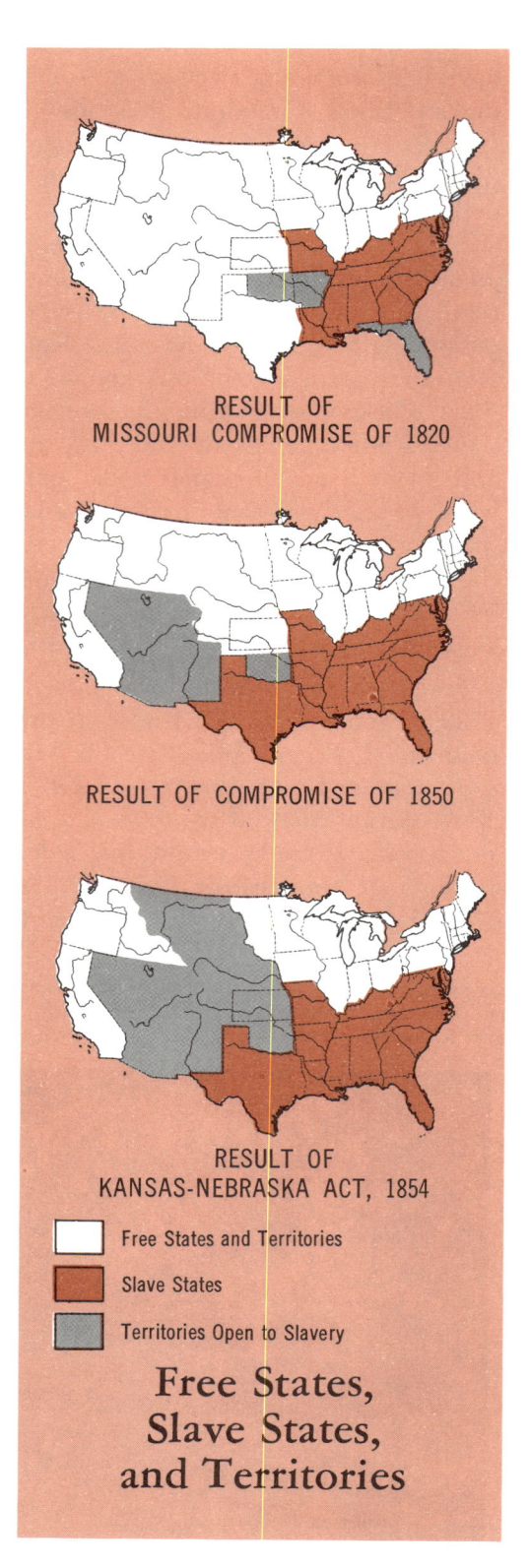

RESULT OF KANSAS-NEBRASKA ACT, 1854

- Free States and Territories
- Slave States
- Territories Open to Slavery

Free States, Slave States, and Territories

ing slaves in 1808, but by then there was a large slave population rooted in this country. Children born to slaves became slaves and thus the number of slaves grew.

Our country retained the slave system, although many individuals in all parts of the nation opposed it. It was retained largely because Southern planters had invested heavily in slaves to work the large plantations, and the planters were not eager to give up what they considered to be their property. The fact that human beings are much more than mere property had been conveniently forgotten by some and overlooked by others.

It is not proper to fix all the blame for slavery upon the Southern planters, however. In a certain sense, those who objected to it but failed to protest or to make known their feelings were just as guilty as those who owned slaves.

Slavery and the Constitution

Early Disagreements. Slavery first became a political issue when the Articles of Confederation was being written. It remained a national problem until the Reconstruction period following the Civil War. One of the provisions of the Northwest Ordinance of 1787 was the exclusion of slavery from the Northwest Territory. The southern boundary of that huge area was the Ohio River; this in time became the northern boundary of the slave states.

If the theories so brilliantly stated in the Declaration of Independence had been put into practice immediately, slavery would not have existed after 1788, when the nation was finally constituted. In fact, many Northern states did free their slaves immediately after the Revolution. But some states did not free their slaves, and the disagreement between those who did and those who did not was to flare up finally into the American Civil War.

The Compromise. The first disagreements sprang up at the Constitutional Convention in 1787. Southern states, naturally enough, wished to have as much power as possible in the legislative department of the government. To gain more power, they wanted to count their slaves in the population, which would ensure them a larger number of representatives in the lower house. The North did not seem to object to the Southern proposal, provided that the slaves could be taxed at the same rate as the farmers and planters in the South.

To the North it seemed as though the Southerners wanted to have their cake and eat it too. The Southerners wanted to count the slaves as voters, although it was obvious slaves would never get to vote, and yet they did not want to pay taxes based on the number of slaves. Finally, North and South compromised. They decided that each slave would count, for purposes of taxation *and* representation, as three-fifths of a free person. Although such a compromise ignored the human dignity of the slaves, it was effective politically, and it allowed the Constitution to be completed.

Slave Trade. The Constitution also refers specifically to the slave trade. Some Southern states, especially South Carolina where slavery seemed to be the most profitable, feared that the national government might hinder further importation of slaves. The result of the Southern concern was Article I, Section 9, Clause 1. of the Constitution. This clause prohibited any congressional interference with the slave trade in the twenty year period between 1788 and 1808, and no import tax exceeding ten dollars could be imposed on any slave.

African Negroes arrived in America packed like this into slave ships. Chained cruelly, many died on the trip from Africa.

Slavery in the South

The vast majority of white men in the South owned no slaves. In fact, three-fourths of them were yeomen (independent) farmers who worked their own relatively small plots of land. Of the remainder, about twenty-three per cent were small plantation owners who owned anywhere from 1 to 20 slaves. The owners of the large plantations which employed 20 to 200 slaves constituted

Slaveowners "educated" their slaves in the Christian religion, which Negroes made their own. Slaves were encouraged to preach and attend church.

only about one per cent of the population. But even though the slaves were owned by a relatively small percentage of the population, most white men in the South were fierce defenders of the system.

Southern Logic. There are various reasons for the defense of slavery by men who had little to gain directly from it. Many of the white owners of very small farms in the South feared that the Negro, if freed, would compete with him for land and for markets for produce. Like the white city workers, the farmers believed in preserving the opportunities they had. Since some white workers were afraid that the Negroes would work for lower wages than they themselves were willing to accept, they also fought the abolition movement.

Small planters also opposed abolition, mainly because they hoped to become big planters, and they felt that they could not do this without their slaves. All the reasons were not self-interested ones however. Some people in the South actually felt that the Negro would be harmed by gaining his freedom. Planters who had owned slaves felt that Negroes would not be able to take care of themselves in the free world. This genuine but misguided feeling led to a defense of slavery on moral grounds by some who might have opposed it had they lived in the North.

Plantation Life. Although the owners of large plantations made up only a small percentage of the population of the South, the plantations were the focal points for Southern life and culture. The owners of the biggest, most prosperous plantations were usually the descendants of families that had settled in the South in colonial times. These early settlers had claimed large tracts of land that stayed in the same family for generations. This rigid control of land by relatively few families led to a sort of aristocracy in the South. Plantation owners who controlled the land and most of the money established the social patterns for the farmers and small planters to follow. It was the great ambition of most small planters to become rich and influential like the large owners. The small farmers also gazed wistfully at the rich plantation life, hoping that they might someday share in it. Finally, the majority of slaves lived on plantations.

A Negro Culture. Out of necessity, the slaves established a culture of their own. Excluded from the activities of their masters, which often took the form of lavish balls and hunts, they created their own pastimes. Dances, games, singing and religion occupied what little free time the average Negro slave was allowed. Some of the songs, especially the deeply religious Negro spirituals, survive as a vital part of our culture. Modern day "jazz" and "the blues" are both outgrowths of the Negro slave's need for a means of expression. Negroes adapted Christianity and music to fit their particular needs. Negroes, however, made other uses of their time. As is natural with all mankind, many Negroes wished more than anything else to be free. Although there is some evidence that a few were satisfied with life on the plantations, many devoted great efforts to plans for escape. These plans, and the eventual success of many of them, upset Southern plantation owners greatly.

The Fugitive Slave Law

A law was passed in 1793 to aid the Southern slave owners in recovering slaves who had escaped to the North. This law had, however, proved ineffective, partially due to the fact that in the Northern states there were many antislavery people who were assisting the slaves to escape. While the Southern states were threatening to secede in the late 1840's, both Northern and Southern leaders recognized the need to write a new Fugitive Slave Law.

The new law was passed in 1850. Cases of escaped slaves were now placed exclusively under federal control, with United States commissioners authorized to issue warrants of arrest and certificates for the return of slaves to their owners. The fugitives were not permitted the right of trial by jury nor were they permitted to enter testimony in any proceedings of the law. Any attempt to evade the law was punishable by heavy fines. The law was certainly one which favored the South. From 1850–1860, much ill will between the slave and free states can be traced to this attempt by the government to legislate against runaway slaves.

Most household items on a plantation were homemade. Soap, being made below, consisted of grease and lye boiled together. Salt was added to make it hard.

Negro slaves in most cases were deprived of education and entertainment, so they fashioned their own. Their entertainment was a mixture of their African cultural heritage and American music. The mixture was a rich one indeed, resulting in songs and dances like the one above.

The Underground Railroad

It is estimated that by 1860, the South was losing about a thousand slaves a year by escape to the North, despite the Fugitive Slave Law. What angered the Southerners more than the loss of the so-called "property" was the fact that many Northerners assisted the slaves to escape and in their assistance felt that they were acting righteously. The South was quick to remind the North that slavery was indeed protected by the Constitution and the laws of the land. Nevertheless, some Northern states passed laws making it illegal to obey the federal law for the return of slaves.

The Underground Railroad was not a real railroad at all. It was an organized attempt by antislavery people in the free states to serve as "conductors" to runaway slaves in their attempt to escape to Canada. Once in Canada, the slaves were assured of freedom. Most important, they were beyond the reach of the Fugitive Slave Law. Most of the "stations" on the Underground Railroad were in private homes where the slaves would stay in hiding during the day before traveling to the next station at night.

Some homes built in the decade before the Civil War had special secret rooms designed especially to hide slaves. Sometimes these rooms were beneath the household kitchen, built with a secret trap door from the kitchen floor and a secret tunnel which connected this room with an adjacent field. The conductor of one station would direct the slave to the next station, providing food and clothing for travel if necessary.

More than three thousand active workers have been identified with the Underground Railroad. Among its leaders were escaped slaves such as Harriet Tubman, affectionately known as "Moses." To the slave, any route to the North would bring freedom, so various routes were used. Most escaping slaves were guided by the North Star, which led them northward at night. Probably more slaves escaped to Ohio than to any other state. Its geographical position and the antislavery sentiment of its people accounted for this.

The Abolitionists

Ben Lundy. In 1821, Benjamin Lundy, an Ohio printer, published a paper known as *The Genius of Universal Emancipation*, which contained articles urging the abolition of slavery. Lundy favored freeing the slaves and sending them to distant colonies where they could live by themselves in freedom and happiness. So convinced did he become that this was the solution that he traveled throughout the country to spread his doctrine and form antislavery societies.

W. L. Garrison. Before long, Lundy's ardor won him an ally in Boston. He was William Lloyd Garrison, a young printer. From the first, Garrison adopted with vigor the cause of freedom for the slaves. In 1831 he founded a paper, *The Liberator*, which opposed slavery even more forcefully than did Lundy's publication. Garrison and Lundy soon had many followers who wrote scathing editorials for newspapers, made speeches whenever they could gather an audience, and flooded Congress with thousands of petitions pressing for the complete and immediate liberation of all slaves.

Note prices on poster. Is it important that foreign language editions existed?

The "underground railroad" helped slaves escape in many ways. This tunnel, near Cleveland, Ohio, led from a basement way station.

STATUS OF UNITED STATES (AUGUST, 1861)

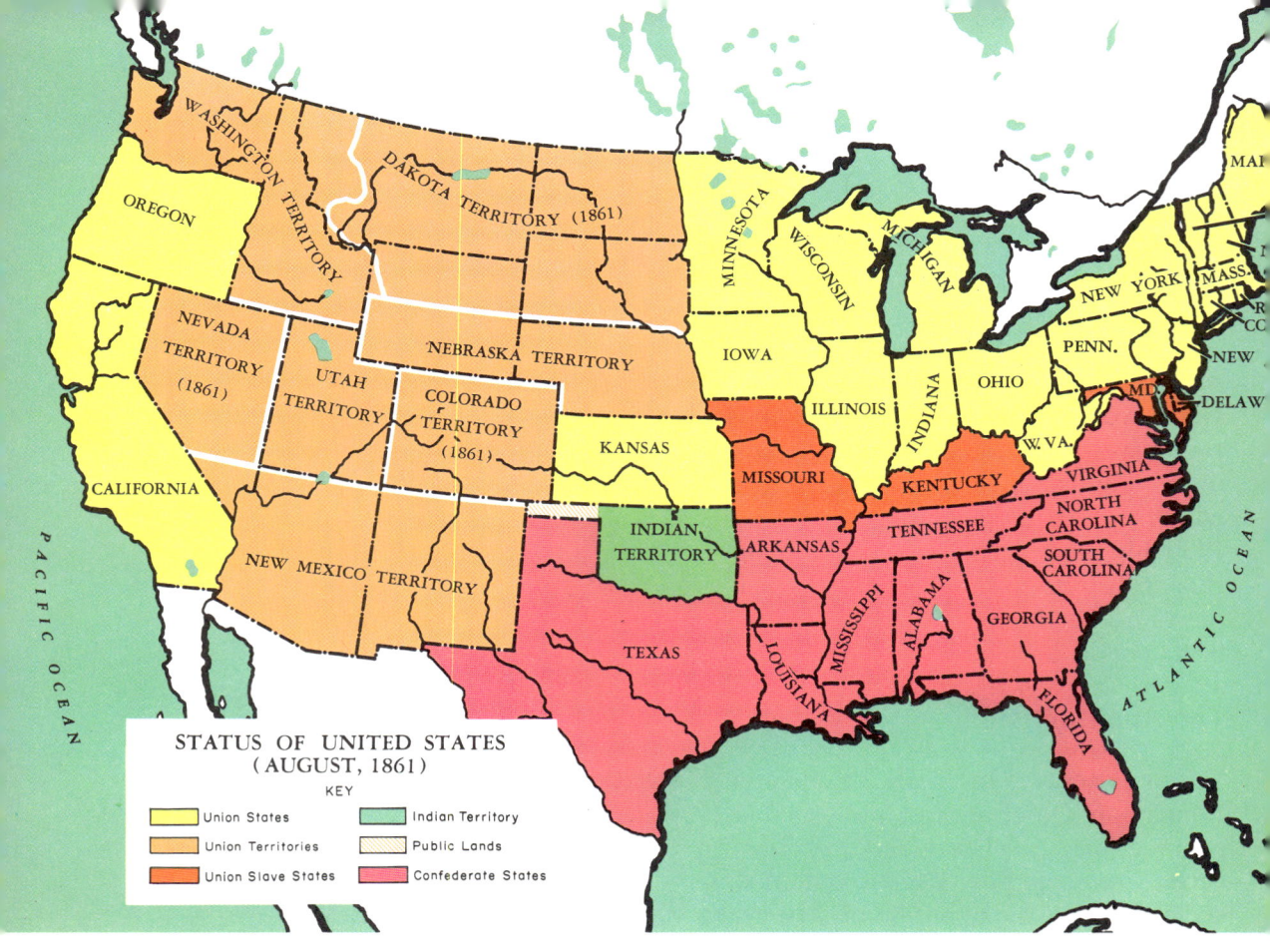

KEY
- Union States
- Union Territories
- Union Slave States
- Indian Territory
- Public Lands
- Confederate States

At the outbreak of the Civil War, the United States looked like this. Name the slave states; then name the Confederate States. Which number is larger? Why? Which territories were open to slavery? Read ahead until you can answer these questions; then look again at this map.

Uncle Tom's Cabin. Undoubtedly the most influential single item of abolitionist literature was a sentimental, rambling novel called *Uncle Tom's Cabin* written by Harriet Beecher Stowe. Mrs. Stowe, the sister of an ardent abolitionist, Henry Ward Beecher, painted an inaccurate but sincere picture of life in the South. The book stirred up great abolitionist sentiment in the North and bitter feeling in the South. Generally *Uncle Tom's Cabin* was a great help to those who wanted to free the slaves, but it did the escaped slaves great injustice. It described them as simpleminded, helpless people, kindhearted but unable to take care of themselves. This, of course, was not generally true.

The Dred Scott Case

In 1857 an event took place which had a great influence on the slavery question. The Supreme Court handed down a decision, *Dred Scott vs. Sanford*, which shook the nation. Dred Scott was a slave owned by a resident of the state of Missouri. The owner of Scott took him to Illinois and then into Minnesota territory. In both of these areas slavery was forbidden. When Scott was taken back to Missouri, a slave state, he was persuaded by some abolitionists to bring suit for his freedom. The argument offered was that residence in free territory would automatically set a slave free.

Presiding over the Supreme Court was the aged Chief Justice Taney, who came from the slave state of Maryland. Taney had been appointed many years earlier by President Jackson. In his decision he implied agreement with the extremists of the South who demanded that slavery be made legal in all the territories. He held to the theory that the states, not the Congress, had the right to decide upon the legality of slavery. The opinion of the Court was that slaves were property, and that their owners were protected by the Constitution. The case intensified bitterness between North and South.

The case of Dred Scott had first been tried in the courts of Missouri where he had been declared a slave regardless of his residence outside the state. While the case was being tried, he was sold to a Mr. Sanford in New York state. Sanford was an abolitionist who eventually freed Scott. One year after his freedom was granted, however, Scott died of tuberculosis.

Looking Back

1. How did the framers of the Constitution deal with the problem of slavery and slave trading?
2. On what grounds did Southerners defend slavery?
3. What was the purpose of the Fugitive Slave Law of 1850?
4. Describe the functioning of the Underground Railroad.
5. Why was the Dred Scott Case of such great importance?

2. Land Additions Heighten North-South Controversy

The Balance of Power

Following the Mexican War of 1846-1848, the extension of slavery again became a vital issue. Should slavery be legal or illegal in new land gained from Mexico? In Congress, David Wilmot of Pennsylvania presented a bill providing that "neither slavery nor involuntary servitude shall ever exist in any part of the territory acquired from Mexico." Although the Wilmot Proviso, as it was called, was passed by the Senate, the House did not pass it.

The question of slavery also came up in connection with the new Oregon territory. In 1846, Jefferson Davis of Mississippi offered an amendment to a bill relating to Oregon. This amendment provided that slavery should not be prohibited in Oregon so long as it was a territory of the United States. As in the case of the Wilmot Proviso, this amendment was not passed.

As the disagreements over the slavery question continued, it became very clear that whoever had the more votes in the Congress, North or South, would be able to decide the issue. In 1846, the South held the majority in the Senate, while the North held the majority in the House of Representatives. Given this arrangement, the Senate could veto any bill brought to it through the Northern-dominated House, and the House could veto any bill coming to it from the Southern-controlled Senate. Thus the balance of power between the two major sections of the country enabled them to cancel each other out. The main reason Southerners fought to keep new, free states out of the Union was that they wished that this balance might not be upset to their disadvantage. Southerners knew that the only way they could gain great influence in the halls of Congress would be to ensure that the new states clamoring to be admitted to the Union were states which accepted slavery as legal.

The Compromise of 1850

Northern Demands. In 1850, Congress was faced with a thorny situation. The antislavery citizens of the North demanded that California be admitted immediately as a free state. They urged the passing of the Wilmot Proviso prohibiting slavery in the territory of New Mexico and that the state of Texas be reduced in size. Furthermore, they suggested that slavery be abolished in the nationally-owned District of Columbia and that every Negro who was accused of being a fugitive should be given a jury trial.

Southern Demands. The Southerners, on the other hand, demanded that the territory of California should permit slavery. They also wanted slavery allowed in the territory of New Mexico. Southerners asserted that the state of Texas should have the same boundaries as before admission to the Union. They also wished that slavery be continued in the District of Columbia and that a new law be passed requiring the return of runaway slaves without trial by jury. How was it possible to satisfy both sides?

Clay's Compromise. To the rescue came Henry Clay, the peacemaker. Thirty years before, he had settled existing difficulties with the Missouri Compromise. Now he had another, more elaborate, compromise to bring peace to both North and South. The bill which he proposed had five major provisions:

(1) California should enter the Union as a free state.

(2) All other land gained from Mexico should be divided into two territories at the 37° of north latitude, the northern territory to be known as Utah and the southern as New Mexico. The people of each territory should have the right to declare whether or not slavery should be permitted within their lands. This decision by the people was known as "squatter sovereignty."

(3) The boundaries of Texas should be cut down to reduce the state from 379,000 square miles to 264,000. The land thus taken was to be added to the New Mexico territory, and Texas was to be paid $10,000,000 in return to help pay the debts of her war with Mexico.

(4) The slave trade should be prohibited in the District of Columbia, though slavery was to be permitted.

(5) A new fugitive law should be passed to make it easier for slaveholders to recover their runaway slaves.

Clay's bill was known as the Compromise of 1850, but was popularly called the "Omnibus Bill" because it carried so many provisions.

Debate in Congress. Opinions differed on the wisdom of adopting Clay's compromise bill. Clay himself, now an old man, came out of his retirement and spoke with great feeling in behalf of the measure without which he felt that the Union could not be preserved. Daniel Webster, too, gave a powerful oration in favor of the bill. On the other hand, John C. Calhoun, old, feeble, and dying of tuberculosis, prepared a powerful speech opposing the bill as being unfair to the South. So weakened was Calhoun that he could not deliver the speech himself, but sat in the Senate chamber while it was read for him. William H. Seward, a senator from New York, also spoke against the bill, maintaining that it should not be adopted because it allowed the extension of slavery, which was morally wrong.

It soon became evident that the bill stood little chance of becoming a law. Though Congress passed it, the vote was close. President Zachary Taylor, an antislavery Whig, was very much opposed to it because it gave slavery a chance to extend. Should he veto the bill, it would be impossible to get the two-thirds vote in both houses of Congress needed to pass it over his veto.

Passage of Omnibus Bill. President Taylor, however, never had a chance to veto the Omnibus Bill. On July 5, 1850, he suddenly became ill, and four days later he died. The Vice-President, Millard Fillmore, succeeded him in the White House and signed the bill, making it a law.

Just as the North had profited by the Missouri Compromise of 1820, so did the South profit by the Omnibus Bill. While, on the one hand, California entered the Union as a free state, the rest of the entire territory gained from Mexico was now open to slavery, although territorial citizens could vote slavery down if they chose. The slave-owning state of Texas was made prosperous by the payment of $10,000,000. The new fugitive slave law offered such inducements for the return of slaves, and assigned such punishment for aiding them to escape, that the property of the slave owners was protected as never before. The prohibition of the slave trade in the tiny District of Columbia mattered little to either side.

The Kansas-Nebraska Bill

Now that California had become a state, a new problem arose. Between California and the three territories of Oregon, Utah, and New Mexico in the West and the remaining states of the Union in the East lay a vast expanse of land, jutting into the country like a great wedge and cutting it nearly in two.

"Popular Sovereignty." In 1852 Franklin Pierce, a Democrat, was elected President. When he took office in the following year, one of his first acts was to appoint a committee to work out some solution to the problems of this territory. Stephen A. Douglas, senator from Illinois, was chairman of the committee, and it was largely due to his individual work that a bill, known as the Nebraska Bill, was prepared. This provided that the great region in question should become a territory under the name of Nebraska, and that the question of slavery should be left to the decision of the people occupying the land. Douglas called this policy *popular sovereignty*.

Repeal of Missouri Compromise. It is easy to see that the Nebraska Bill was in direct contradiction to the Missouri Compromise, which forbade slavery in the land north of 36° 30′, except in the state of Missouri. Since the Nebraska Bill said nothing at all about the Missouri Compromise, many of the Southern leaders felt that the Compromise should be repealed if its principles were to be violated. Consequently, Douglas drafted a new bill, the Kansas-Nebraska Bill, repealing the Missouri Compromise, and dividing the unorganized land into two territories, separated by the line of 40° north latitude. The territory to the south was to be known as Kansas and that to the north as Nebraska. The question of slavery in each territory was to be settled by popular sovereignty.

The North was extremely indignant at the possibility that some of the new states could become slave states, and meetings were held throughout the various free states. However, the Kansas-Nebraska Bill passed Congress and became a law when President Pierce signed it. The passage of the bill was largely due to Douglas' brilliant speeches in its behalf. The Missouri Compromise was now dead, and a great new area was opened to the extension of slavery.

"Bleeding Kansas." When the Kansas-Nebraska Bill was passed, everyone expected that the southern territory, Kansas, would be occupied by slaveholders and that slavery would be permitted there, and that Northerners would enter Nebraska, which would

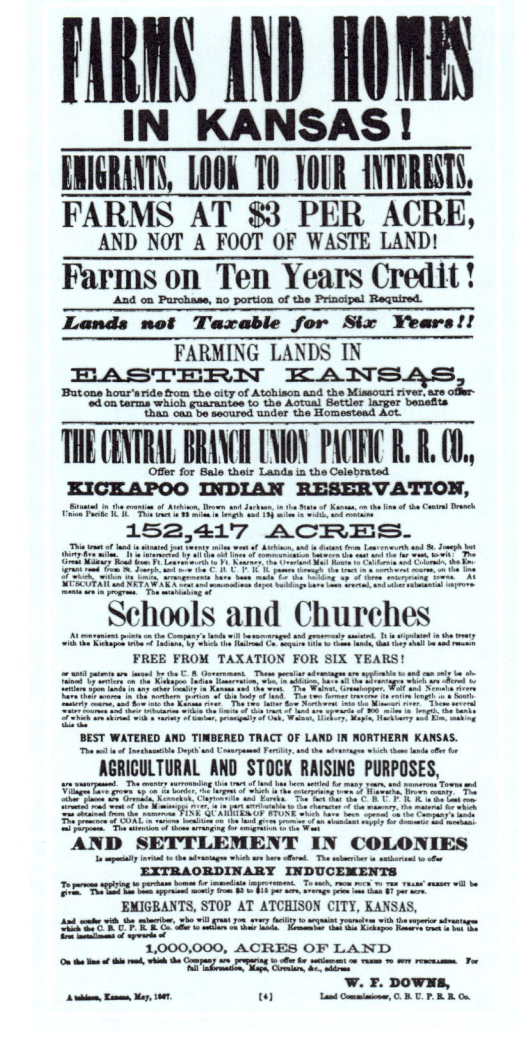

This poster illustrates why America was a "land of opportunity."

become free. Such, however, was not the case. Northerners founded a society known as "The Emigrant Aid Society" for the purpose of sending settlers opposed to slavery to Kansas, with the intention of making that territory free. The first group of these settlers started in 1854. By 1855 several hundred had entered the territory, establishing the little town of Lawrence. It began to look as though Kansas would not be a slave territory after all.

A Power Struggle. The slaveholders of the South soon realized what was going on and became very indignant. People in the neighboring state of Missouri were especially distressed. All along the border, bands of armed men were organized to see to it that Kansas should never become a free territory. Whenever an election was held, thousands of desperate characters swarmed across the border, masquerading as citizens, and cast enough votes to keep the free-soil people from gaining a majority.

Violence. It was inevitable that sooner or later bloodshed would result. A slaveholding sheriff was shot by an unknown assassin in the town of Lawrence. At once an army of slaveholders gathered to attack the town. A furious battle followed; the town was taken, burned, and many of its inhabitants were killed.

The attack on Lawrence was the signal for wholesale trouble. Whenever members of the rival parties met, shooting was sure to occur. Many people gave up their lives in the struggle in Kansas between those who favored slavery and those who did not, so many in fact that the territory became known as "Bleeding Kansas." The situation at last grew so serious that President Pierce was forced to send United States troops to drive the Missouri "border ruffians" back into their own state.

The Lecompton Constitution. To bring order out of confusion, President Pierce appointed a reliable and fair man, Robert J. Walker, to serve as governor of Kansas. Walker called a meeting at Lecompton, Kansas, in 1857, to draw up a constitution. Only those favoring slavery attended, for the champions of freedom, remembering the violence and bloodshed of earlier elections, were suspicious of the move.

The constitution drawn up at Lecompton showed that those who attended favored slavery, for it provided, among other things, that all slaves already held in the territory should be retained. When this constitution was placed before the people, they were asked to vote for it either "with slavery" or "without slavery." This was widely regarded as a trick, for if the people voted "with slavery," the territory would be wide open to slaveholders and the slave trade. Even if they voted "without slavery," those slaves already held within the territory might still continue to be held. Either way Kansas would be a slaveholding territory. The antislavery people, however, saw through the deception and insisted on voting merely on whether they should adopt the constitution or not. It was decisively defeated.

Looking Back

1. To what did "the balance of power between the two main sections of the country" refer?
2. Give the terms of the Compromise of 1850.
3. Why, in your opinion, did some Northerners support the Compromise of 1850?
4. Give the arguments used by those who favored and opposed the Kansas-Nebraska Bill.
5. How did the term "Bleeding Kansas" come into being?

3. States' Rights Become a Continuing Issue

A third area of disagreement between the North and the South which led directly to secession of the South was states' rights. Do the states have the right to judge for themselves whether a law passed by Congress is constitutional or not? Can they refuse to obey a law which they decide is unconstitutional? Has the central government the right to enforce obedience? These questions led to bitter quarrels in the early years of American history and continued to do so through and even after the Civil War.

Early Controversies

Virginia and Kentucky Resolutions. From the earliest days of our separation from Britain, debate raged in the state legislative halls as to how much power should be granted to the state governments. Many felt that the best guarantee for the preservation of our liberties was to be found in a weakened federal government. The Jeffersonians or Democratic-Republicans felt especially that the states should have the larger share of authority. The Federalists led by Hamilton, on the other hand, were determined to maintain a strong federal government. The Federalists' interpretation led to the passage of the Alien and the Sedition laws in the Adams administration. When Kentucky and Virginia attempted to disregard these national laws within their borders, the question of states' rights nearly became a national crisis. The repeal of the offending laws only left the question unsettled to vex coming generations.

Hartford Convention. The Hartford Convention in 1814 again raised the problem of states' rights. At that time the Federalists of New England proposed that the money raised by national taxes in the richer New England states should go to defend these states, and not to finance the War of 1812. The representatives at Hartford spoke for only a small proportion of the people so the convention did not command national attention. Since then ideas concerning states' rights have been debated with each generation.

Georgia vs. the Indians. After the Hartford Convention, Georgia was the next state to try to undermine the power of the Union. Within the borders of Georgia lived the Cherokee and Creek Indian tribes. Members of both tribes were among the most highly developed of their race. Many possessed courage, beauty, adaptability, and a quickness to grasp and maintain the ways of the colonists. By 1820, their property, which had been a gigantic tract of land stretching from the Ohio River to the Gulf of Mexico, had been reduced by a series of questionable treaties to a small tract in Georgia. The Cherokees, with the aid of missionaries from New England, early adapted themselves to the economy and government of the United States. In fact, in 1827 the Cherokee people drew up a written constitution, published a newspaper, and invented an Indian alphabet.

The Georgians resented this progress and prosperity of the Cherokee people. Steps were taken to remove them from what was left of their lands. The governor of Georgia took the first step when he decided to take over the Cherokee lands. Even though President John Quincy Adams warned him that he was violating a sacred treaty with the Indians, Georgia's governor continued his surveying and parceling of the Indian land. He had successfully defied the United States government.

Supreme Court Rulings

The victory of the state of Georgia against the federal government was counterbalanced, however, by the case of *McCulloch* vs. *Maryland*, which was tried in the United States Supreme Court. Maryland attempted to levy a tax on the business done by a branch of the United States Bank which was operating in the state, claiming that the Constitution gave Congress no power to establish such a bank. John Marshall, the Chief Justice of the Court, handed down a decision stating that Congress had the right to establish the bank in order to help carry out the laws for raising revenue and regulating currency. Maryland was forbidden to tax the business of the bank.

Other Supreme Court cases tried under Chief Justice Marshall had the important effect of strengthening the federal power as opposed to the power of the states. Chief Justice Marshall and the Court had already decided, in the case of *Marbury* vs. *Madison*, that the Supreme Court of the United States had the right to declare that laws passed by Congress were unconstitutional. Now, in the case of *Fletcher* vs. *Peck*, the Court decided that it could also declare state laws unconstitutional.

In two other cases, Chief Justice Marshall and the Court decided that the Supreme Court of the United States had the right to overrule and reverse decisions made by the supreme courts of the different states. In the *Dartmouth College Case*, Chief Justice Marshall and his Court ruled that a state could not change the terms of a charter which it had once issued. Finally, in the case of *Gibbons* vs. *Ogden*, Chief Justice Marshall and the Court forbade a state to grant to a company the exclusive right to use a trade route which crossed state boundaries, since Congress had the power to regulate all interstate trade.

These important decisions by the Supreme Court had the effect of reducing the privileges of the states, and were therefore victories for the federal government in the states' rights question.

Cherokees, like other Indians, were craftsmen. They made papoose carriers, moccasins, and tobacco pouches from skins and beads.

DEVELOPMENT OF POLITICAL PARTIES

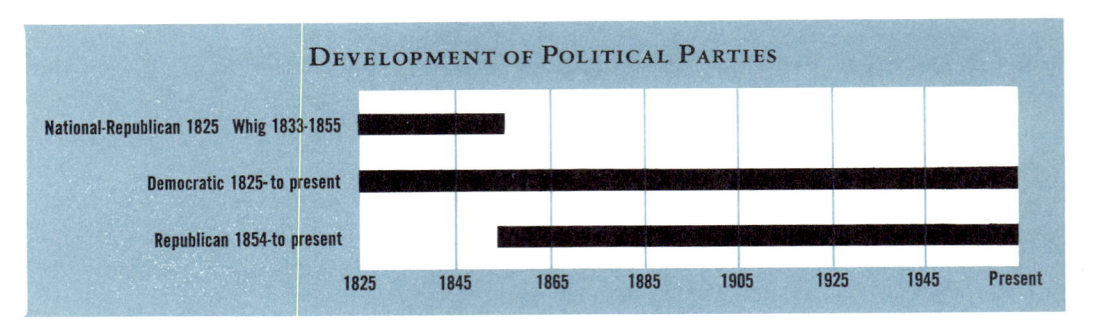

National-Republican 1825   Whig 1833-1855
Democratic 1825-to present
Republican 1854-to present

1825   1845   1865   1885   1905   1925   1945   Present

Political parties cannot exist without leaders and issues to make them grow. The Republican Party as we know it today had its beginning in what year according to this graph? What were the major issues surrounding its founding? Who were its leaders?

Tariff Controversy

Again in 1828 and 1832 this perplexing question of states' rights came up. In 1828 South Carolina protested against the Tariff of Abominations, and Calhoun declared in the South Carolina legislature that the tariff was unconstitutional, that it favored only one part of the country, and that it could not be enforced in any state. The states, he said, had existed first and had given the national government what power it had. The government, therefore, could not have more power than the states.

When the tariff law of 1832 was passed, South Carolina went so far as to declare the law would not be obeyed within her borders. President Jackson announced his determination to use force, if necessary, to see that the tariff was collected. Serious trouble seemed imminent, and it looked as though the question, would be settled one way or another, once and for all. Henry Clay's compromise tariff, however, again postponed the issue.

Lincoln-Douglas Debates

The Republican Party. The Republican party, as it is called today, had its beginning when forces in other political parties united in opposition to the extension of slavery. The early Republicans included in their ranks antislavery people of all sorts. Their party was made up of most of the former members of the now-dead Whig party as well as Northern Democrats who could no longer agree with their Southern colleagues on the slavery issue. In 1854 the growing party went on record as being opposed to the Fugitive Slave Law and the Kansas-Nebraska Act. Even though their candidate for President, John C. Frémont, was defeated in 1856, by James Buchanan, a Democrat, the strong showing made by the Republicans foreshadowed supremacy in years to come. The next election (1860) saw the Republican candidate, Abraham Lincoln, elected President of the United States. With two exceptions, Grover Cleveland and Woodrow Wilson, Republicans were to occupy the White House for the next seventy-two years.

The Opposing Candidates. In the presidential election of 1860, Lincoln ran against the man who had defeated him for a United States Senate seat in Illinois only two years before, Stephen

A. Douglas, a Democrat. During the 1858 senatorial contest between these two men, seven debates were held. The debates between Lincoln and Douglas proved to be turning points in the history of our nation. Douglas was very short in stature, a crafty, forceful speaker, and a smart politician. Lincoln was tall and awkward, a powerful man who spoke slowly and argued cleverly. Any confrontation between two men so different in looks and manner was bound to be interesting. The subjects these two debated were the crucial ones of slavery and expansion, the Dred Scott case, and states' rights.

The Freeport Debate. Undoubtedly, the most important of the seven debates was the one held at Freeport, Illinois. Douglas had, before the debate, coined a new term, "popular sovereignty," to describe the right of a newly formed state to decide for itself key issues such as that of slavery. However, the Dred Scott decision contradicted this new policy of Douglas', and Douglas had said that he believed in accepting all the decisions of the Supreme Court. Clearly Douglas could not effectively maintain allegiance to both stands. The Dred Scott decision had taken away from Congress and the territories the right to prohibit slavery. Popular sovereignty would allow the territories to decide.

Lincoln saw a chance to score an important point against Douglas by asking him to define his position more clearly. Douglas escaped from his dilemma by saying that although the Supreme Court could decide the validity of laws, it was up to the local law enforcement officials to enforce them. If state and local officials did not enforce the Dred Scott decision, very little could be done about it. Douglas' answer was temporarily satisfactory, and he won a narrow victory in the contest for the Senate seat. However, in the presidential election two years later, Douglas lost the support of his Southern fellow-Democrats, and he was beaten by Abraham Lincoln. Douglas' stand at Freeport cost him his Southern support because he had said, in effect, that each territory could decide for itself whether or not it was to be slave or free.

Election of Lincoln and Secession

Immediately after Lincoln's election in 1860, the legislature of South Carolina called delegates to a state conven-

This photograph shows Lincoln as he looked around 1850.

tion. The purpose of this was no secret to the delegates or to the nation as a whole. Within a few days they voted to take their state out of the Union, a step they had threatened to take during the campaign if Lincoln should be elected. The state leaders, relying upon the economic strength of their state, would not tolerate subjecting themselves to the continued "rule" of the North.

The Confederate States of America. Increasingly the South came to look upon their section of the country as a very distinct section, literally a separate nation. They preferred to rule themselves. While seeking such independence, they explained that their chief motive was to secure Southern rights. Such a term had different meanings to different people. Basically, the South opposed the tariff regulations of the North and the industrialization which caused them to be enacted. The South simply felt that, as a section maintaining its own way of life, it could do better economically if a new nation were to be formed.

After South Carolina declared her secession from the Union, she was joined by Mississippi, Florida, Alabama, Louisiana, Georgia, and Texas within a few weeks. Delegates from each of the seceding states met at Montgomery, Alabama, in February, 1861. A new and separate government was organized. They drew up their own constitution and adopted a new flag, the Stars and Bars. The new nation, the Confederate States of America, elected Jefferson Davis, a former United States Senator, as their new president. President-elect Lincoln, and President Buchanan, as we will discover in the next chapter, never recognized such secession as legally possible. The Southern states were considered as being in rebellion but not as a new nation.

Secession by Default. In vain did the Northern leaders assure the seceding states that if they stayed in the Union, they need have no fear of being deprived of their slaves. President Buchanan, fearful that a war would break out in his last weeks in

---

Stars And Bars

The Confederate flag of 1861 had the same color and the same general arrangement as the Federal flag, the Stars and Stripes. It had seven (later eleven) stars placed in a circle and only three stripes (bars), a white between two red ones. The similarity of the Confederate and Federal flags caused confusion and so the Confederate Battle Flag was designed. Placed upon a square red flag was a blue diagonal cross with thirteen white stars on it. In 1863 a "Second Confederate Flag" was adopted by the Confederate Congress. On it the Battle Flag replaced the circle of stars and a plain white field replaced the stripes. One year later, an upright red band was placed on the flying edge for visibility.

This photograph of Harper's Ferry shows the town much as it looked when John Brown's raid took place. Colonel Robert E. Lee was the officer who captured Brown.

office, submitted meekly to secession. Even when the Southerners began to seize forts, supplies, and money belonging to the United States, he took no action.

In vain did Senator Crittenden of Kentucky propose amendments to the Constitution which would guarantee slavery throughout the territory south of the Missouri Compromise line of 36° 30', and would provide Southern slave owners with full payment by the government for their escaped slaves. The Southern states were determined on a government of their own, free from antislavery feeling, and no coaxing or persuasion could bring them back into the Union.

Lincoln Enters Office

With North and South tottering on the brink of war, Lincoln succeeded Buchanan as President of the United States. In his inaugural address he showed nothing but kindness toward the seceded Southern states. He pleaded with them to consider calmly and carefully before doing any rash act. He appealed to the patriotism of the South which had fought so bravely in the Revolution, the War of 1812, and the Mexican War asking that the Union for which they had fought be not now destroyed.

Lincoln's main purpose in his inaugural address was to reassure the Southern states, to coax them back into the Union. He calmly argued against secession. More significantly perhaps, he told the South that they could return peacefully and be welcomed back, or they could fight to stay out. The South refused to heed Lincoln's pleas.

After he entered office, Lincoln set about the choosing of his Cabinet, and in making his choice he paid little heed to the customs of the spoils system. The ablest statesmen of the country were appointed although most of them were his political enemies. William H. Seward, Secretary of State, and Salmon P. Chase, Secretary of the Treasury, had even been his rivals for the Republican nomination. Many of the others were Democrats. Some of his appointees gave him their full support, while others were motivated by selfish political ambitions and failed to help the administration or the country as much as they might have.

The Threat of War

Few men were ever faced with a more appalling situation than was Abraham Lincoln when he accepted the Presidency of the United States. His very election was sure to bring trouble between the North and South, for he was a Republican, and the South opposed all the principles for which he and his party stood. The Republican platform in 1860 stated:

(1) that it was the right and duty of Congress to prohibit the further spread of slavery in the territories;

(2) that the recent Democratic administration had handled the Kansas situation poorly;

(3) that Kansas should immediately be admitted as a free state;

(4) that Justice Taney's decision in the Dred Scott Case was unjustified.

It was certain that the election of a Republican President would arouse bitter resentment in the South.

Nor was much of a spark needed to kindle the smouldering feelings of the North and South into an active flame. Already blood had been shed in Kansas. Already John Brown, an extreme abolitionist, had led an attack on Harper's Ferry in Virginia. Brown hoped to free slaves to join his forces. He was finally suppressed by a force of United States Marines in a bloody and pointless battle. It required but little excuse to send the North and South at each other's throats. War between the two parts of the country was at hand.

Looking Back

1. Review the states' rights issues developed by the Virginia and Kentucky Resolutions and the Hartford Convention.
2. How did Georgia defy the United States in the Cherokee Indian dispute?
3. Show how the Supreme Court, under Marshall's leadership, assumed strong powers.
4. Why did the tariff issue again raise the states' rights issue in 1832?
5. From what sources did the Republicans draw their strength in the 1854-1860 period?

The Chapter in Perspective

What Do These Dates and Terms Mean?

yeoman	Lincoln-Douglas debates	*Uncle Tom's Cabin*
1793	Lecompton Constitution	Underground Railroad
Omnibus Bill	*McCulloch* vs. *Maryland*	Kansas-Nebraska Bill
1831	*Marbury* vs. *Madison*	Compromise of 1850
Wilmot Proviso	Dartmouth College Case	Fugitive Slave Law
The Liberator	"Bleeding Kansas"	Dred Scott Case

Who Are These People?

Tubman
Lundy
Garrison
Stowe
Wilmot
Calhoun
Taylor
Fillmore
Pierce
Douglas
Walker
Seward

Where Are These Places?

New Mexico Territory
37th parallel
Utah Territory
Freeport, Illinois.
Harper's Ferry, Virginia
Lawrence, Kansas

Questions for Study

1. Explain the factors that caused slavery to flourish in the South and to win little acceptance in the North.
2. To what groups in present society may the early abolitionists be compared?
3. How did the Dred Scott decision upset previous congressional attempts to handle the slavery problem?
4. Why did most Southerners regard the Compromise of 1850 and the Kansas-Nebraska Bill as victories for their section? Do you agree? Why?
5. Would it have been possible to avert "Bleeding Kansas"? Support your answer.
6. Discuss issues other than slavery that tended to increase sectional feelings between the North and South from 1830 to 1860.
7. What were the major planks of the Republican party platform in 1860? How did the South view these planks?
8. Evaluate the part played by Buchanan from the time of Lincoln's election to his inaugural.
9. An historian once wrote, "Geography determined which states would secede from the Union." What did he mean?
10. Which was the first state to secede? Which states were in the Confederacy when delegates met in Montgomery? Of the remaining southern states, which did not eventually join the Confederacy?

Place Yourself in History

You are Stephen A. Douglas, United States Senator from Illinois. In 1854, you sponsored the Kansas-Nebraska Bill which had the effect of repealing the Missouri Compromise line of 36° 30'. This won you many friends in the South. Your aspirations to the Presidency are recognized. In 1858, Abraham Lincoln is your opponent as you seek re-election to the Senate. At a debate in Freeport, he asks you "Can a territory, in any lawful way, against the wish of any citizen of the United States, exclude slavery from its limits prior to the formation of a state constitution?"

How would you have answered? What was the background for this question? How were you forced to choose between the Dred Scott decision and popular sovereignty? What answer did Douglas give? What were the results of his answer?

14 A Nation at War with Itself: Civil War

War is a terrible thing, and a war of brother against brother, neighbor against neighbor, and friend against friend is doubly terrible. For four years the United States was shaken by a war that threatened to undo the work of nearly a century of patriotic effort.

1. The First Year Brings Confederate Victories

Comparison of North and South

Northern Advantages. The economy of the Southern states was based to some extent upon cotton and other agricultural products like tobacco and rice while their manufacturing economy was only beginning to develop slowly. The Northern states raised a number of crops and they were also blessed with a booming industrial economy. The result was that the North had a tremendous advantage at the outset of the Civil War because the North already had a store of weapons and the factories to manufacture more.

But other things were as important as the Northern superiority in weapons. The North embodied the federal government, and as such, was equipped with a ready-made army and the government to administer it. Also, many Northern cities were trading as well as manufacturing centers, and with the Federal Navy to protect Northern shipping and to blockade Southern shipping, the North could go about business as usual, while the South could be forced into economic chaos.

The North was also fortunate enough to have most of the railway lines of the United States running through her territory. Possession of the key railroad lines gave the North a tremendous advantage in troop movements and transportation in general. In land area and population also, the North had numerous advantages. It was easier for the North to muster an army out of the large cities than it was for the South to ask a yeoman farmer to leave his land in the care of his wife and children. The North also had the advantage of what was felt to be a moral and worthwhile cause, although the Southern states seemed to believe just as strongly in slavery and their own rigid social system. The Southern way of life embodied the very things the North was fighting against and that the South was seeking to preserve.

Southern Advantages. Aside from the devotion they felt to their "cause," the South had only a few advantages. Many of the United States Army officers who had fought in the Mexican War were Southerners, and at the beginning of the war, they threw in their lot with the South. Also, the South would have the distinct advantages of fighting a defensive war, mainly on its own soil. In fact, many Southern soldiers fought on the same land on which they had grown up. This made the war for many of them a very personal thing. Northern soldiers were fighting away from home, in unfamiliar territory. Southern soldiers were directly involved in protection of their families, farms and livestock.

However, even though the Southern army included experienced officers and spirited men, the shortage of weapons, faulty communications, poor transportation, and later the lack of enough food, were to cause terrible destruction to its forces and eventual defeat.

The Bombardment of Fort Sumter

Lincoln did not wish to allow the seceding Southern states to seize property which belonged to the Union. So he informed the governor of South Carolina that he intended to hold Fort Sumter, which stood on an island in Charleston harbor. He also said that he would send a ship to land food and

Bustling factory towns like Pittsburgh gave the North superiority in manufacturing. Note river traffic and bridges. What rivers come together here?

ADVANTAGES OF EACH SIDE OF THE CIVIL WAR

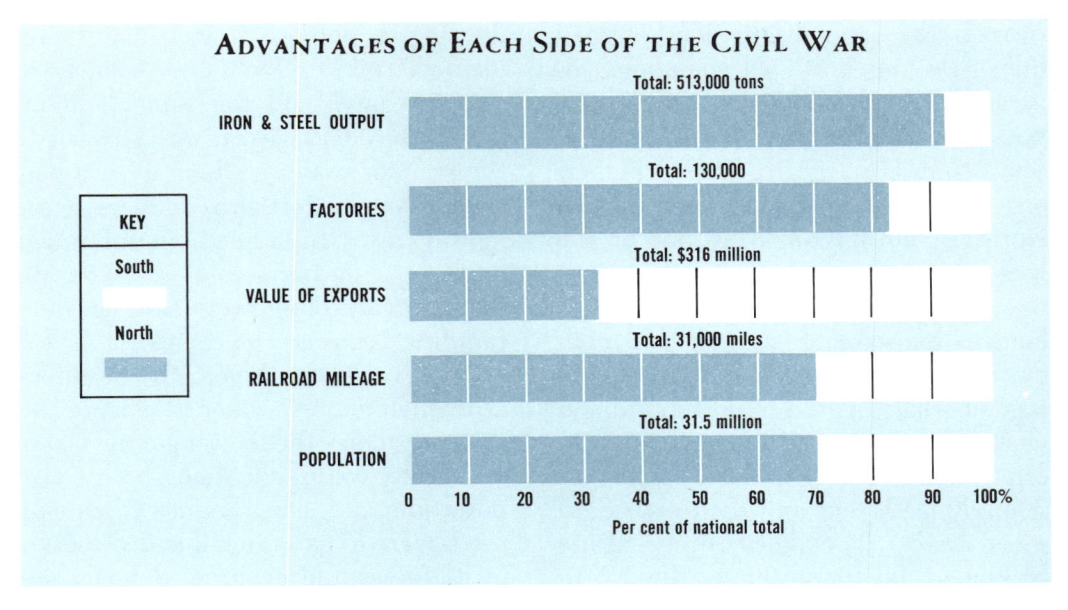

Category	Total
IRON & STEEL OUTPUT	513,000 tons
FACTORIES	130,000
VALUE OF EXPORTS	$316 million
RAILROAD MILEAGE	31,000 miles
POPULATION	31.5 million

Per cent of national total

As you can see, the South led the North in only one department. Was it an important one to the war? Which department was *most* important. Where did the North possess its greatest advantage? What effect would this advantage have?

provisions at the fort, though no guns or soldiers would be landed unless the Southern batteries opened fire. The presence of Union-held Fort Sumter in a Southern harbor was too bitter a pill for the government of the Confederate States to swallow. As a result General Beauregard (bow'ree-gard), the Confederate commander at Charleston, was instructed to capture the fort.

Early in the morning of April 12, 1861, Confederate cannon in Charleston harbor belched flame and smoke, and shells began to break around the fort. From the first, the little garrison had no chance. Firing an occasional shot in response, to show that they were still defiant, the eighty-three defenders sought what protection they could find behind the walls, which were rapidly being battered to pieces about them. For two days the bombardment continued. Shells burst in the fort, knocking the masonry to pieces and setting the woodwork on fire. At the end of the second day the garrison was forced to surrender.

The Call to Arms

There was now no longer any hope of bringing the seceded states peacefully back into the Union. On April 15, 1861, President Lincoln announced that the seven states which had seceded had violated the laws of the nation. He then called for 75,000 troops to preserve the Union. The war had begun.

Further Secessions. The fall of Fort Sumter and Lincoln's call to arms caused great waves of patriotism to sweep through both the North and the South. The Confederate government at Montgomery felt that the call for troops foretold the invasion of the South, and at once set out to raise an army of 100,000 men, and to borrow

$50,000,000, with which to fight the Union soldiers. Furthermore, four states which had not already seceded now joined the ranks of the Confederates. These four states were Virginia, North Carolina, Arkansas, and Tennessee. They brought the number of seceded states to eleven.

Support of Lincoln. In the North, even Lincoln's bitterest enemies flocked to the support of his government. Douglas, once champion of the South, pledged to do his best to uphold the Union. Pierce and Buchanan, ex-Presidents who had sympathized strongly with the slaveholding Southerners, now declared their undivided allegiance to the Northern cause. All felt that the Union must be preserved.

Loyal Border States. Abraham Lincoln early showed his great tact and statesmanship in his dealings with the few states which had neither seceded nor declared their allegiance to the Union. He spoke to them not of slavery, but of patriotism, and of the preservation of the Union for which the heroes of the past had fought. Under his persuasion, Kentucky, Maryland, and Delaware swore to remain loyal. Missouri, after a bitter and bloody conflict within the state, at last stayed in the Union.

During the war, two new states were added to the Union. In spite of their state's secession, the mountaineers of the western part of Virginia declared that they would favor the Union cause. In 1863, their land became a separate state under the name of West Virginia. The next year, Nevada was admitted to the Union as a free state.

Threat to Washington. The secession of Virginia was a sad blow to the Union cause. It meant that the capital city of Washington was but a stone's throw from the lands of the Confederacy. Northern forces feared that at any minute Southern armies might sweep in and take the capital, or Southern gunboats might sail up the Potomac and attack the city. As a result the citizens of Washington fled by thousands to safer grounds, and the President himself paced back and forth in his office in an agony of anxiety lest the city be attacked before Union troops could come to protect it.

Meanwhile, help was on the way. Troops from New York and Massachusetts moved into the state of Maryland where they expected to find friendship. Instead, they found violent opposition. Many of the citizens of Maryland were in favor of secession and it angered

Confederate shore battery scores a direct hit on Fort Sumter. Note ramrod left of cannon, and cannonballs, right.

CONFEDERATE STATES OF AMERICA

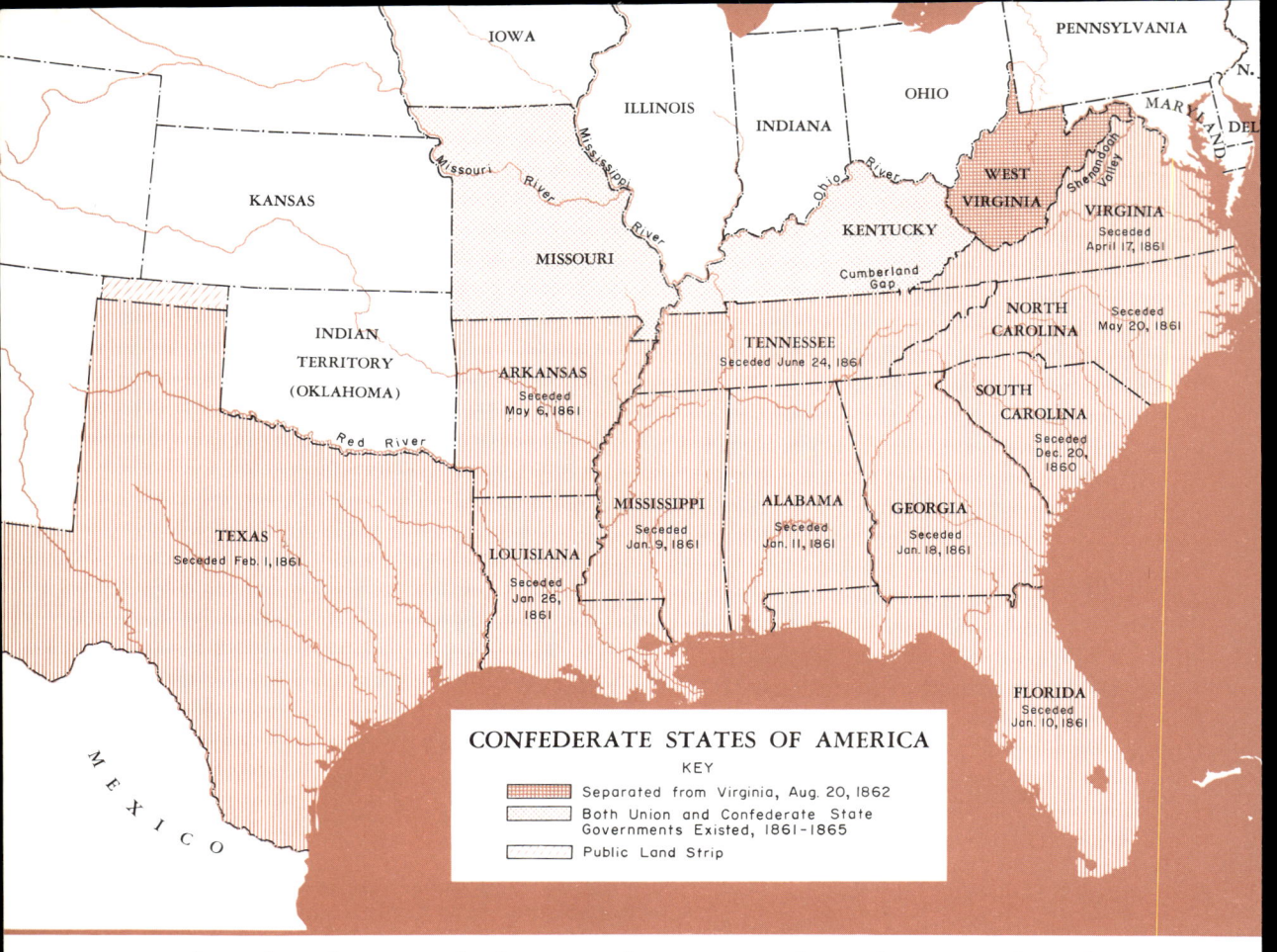

KEY
- Separated from Virginia, Aug. 20, 1862
- Both Union and Confederate State Governments Existed, 1861-1865
- Public Land Strip

them that their state had remained in the Union. Railroads were torn up before the advancing Union armies, and bridges were destroyed. In Baltimore a column of troops was mobbed in the street and had to fight its way through. At last, however, the soldiers reached Washington, and as they marched through the city, confidence was restored. The Confederates were not now so likely to capture the city.

First Battle of Bull Run

A New Southern Capital. Soon after the beginning of the war, the Confederates moved their capital from Montgomery, Alabama, to Richmond, Virginia. The Confederate reasons for moving the capital from Montgomery to Richmond are not altogether clear. However, the presence of the Tredegar Iron Works, the main supplier of Confederate cannon, certainly had something to do with the strategic importance of Richmond. Since the Tredegar Works was located in Richmond, the South used it as a center for experimentation in naval and land warfare.

Northern Confidence. If Richmond could be taken and the Southern leaders captured, Northern military men felt that the Confederacy and the war might both end at once. Consequently, two Union armies started out from Washington toward Richmond. One army, under General Patterson, was to march down the Shenandoah Valley and attack a Confederate army under General J. E. Johnston. The other Northern army, under General McDowell, was to attack the Confederate commander, Beauregard, at Manassus (mah-NAS'us) Junction on a stream called Bull Run, about thirty-five miles southwest of Washington. So confident were the Northerners of winning this battle that many Washington civilians went with the army to watch its victory.

"Stonewall" Jackson. McDowell's forces attacked the Confederates, and at once the Union troops began to force the enemy to retreat. More and more it looked like a victory for the North. Only one Southern division held its ground, that under General T. J. Jackson. "Look, there is Jackson standing like a stone wall." cried one of the Southern officers, and from that time on the name "Stonewall" Jackson stuck to this great Confederate leader.

Southern Victory. Suddenly, Johnston's army appeared, having eluded Patterson's forces. The unexpected reinforcements put new life into the Southern soldiers, and back they swept in a heroic charge, completely overcoming the Union soldiers and driving them toward Washington. Into the capital city straggled McDowell's forces, which had marched out so confidently but a day before.

Although they were beaten at Bull Run, the Northern armies profited more from the battle than the Southerners did. The defeat broke down their overconfidence and showed them that they had a strong and crafty enemy to fight.

The Peninsular Campaign

George B. McClellan, an ambitious young general skilled in the drilling and organizing of troops, was now appointed as commander of the Union army. McClellan fitted out a splendid force of 180,000 men for the purpose of taking Richmond and of ending the war.

Unfortunately, the young leader was too cautious. He delayed his attack until the Confederates were strongly fortified. At last, however, he led his army forward. Up the peninsula lying between the James and York Rivers, the troops advanced on Richmond. Without meeting serious resistance, the Union soldiers came so near the Con-

Union soldier (left) and Confederate (right) carried much the same kind of equipment: blanket roll, haversack, rifle.

federate capital that the buildings of the city could be seen in the distance. And then, with victory seemingly in his grasp, McClellan again hesitated. He had to send back to Washington 40,000 of his men to defend the city against "Stonewall" Jackson, for that shrewd Confederate commander had evaded the Union forces and was menacing the capital. Although he still greatly outnumbered his enemies, McClellan decided that without the 40,000 men he had sent back to Washington his forces were too weak to attack Richmond, and he withdrew. Successfully beating off Southern attacks as he retreated, the Union leader returned again to the vicinity of Washington without having accomplished anything.

The Blockade

Effect on the South. But if the Northern armies were accomplishing little, the United States Navy was doing valuable work. Soon after the declaration of war, Union warships appeared off all the principal Southern ports and by blockading these ports bottled up Southern commerce. Only very fast ships, called blockade runners, could hope to evade the Union warships, and few of these were successful. Cotton could not be exported, and money ceased to flow into the Southern states. The manufactured articles which the South had formerly purchased from European nations and from the North could now no longer be obtained. Even if the armies on land did nothing but hold the Southerners in check, sooner or later the South would be starved into surrender.

The "Trent" Affair. But this same Union blockade came near winning valuable allies for the Confederates. Great Britain and France, though they did not favor slavery, were very friendly to the Southern states. Both of these nations would have been gratified to see the United States of America broken up into two small and feeble countries, neither of which would be strong enough to be dangerous. A critical incident occurred when a Union

To evade the Northern blockade of their seaports, Southerners fashioned fast ships called blockade runners from clipper hulls and steamboat engines.

war vessel stopped the British mail steamer *Trent* as it was leaving Havana harbor. The captain of the warship seized two Southern representatives on their way to Great Britain and France. After this incident, most Southerners felt that now the British might enter the war on their side.

Lincoln and the other Northern leaders quickly realized the danger of their position. The stopping of the *Trent* was little different from the British outrages that had started the War of 1812, and Great Britain was provided with a good and valid excuse to go to war. As a result, these captured Southern representatives, Mason and Slidell, were at once released and were allowed to continue their interrupted journey in peace. War feeling in Great Britain died down, and trouble was averted, although the blockade continued.

Looking Back

1. Compare the advantages held by the North and the South at the outbreak of war.
2. Can you think of any reasons why the Confederate capital was moved to Richmond?
3. What steps did Lincoln take to keep the border states in the Union?
4. Could a more aggressive McClellan have possibly shortened the war during the Peninsular Campaign?
5. Describe the effect of the blockade on the South.

2. The Second Year Is Indecisive

First Battle of the Ironclads

The Confederates were not content to sit idly by and let Union warships blockade their harbors. Off Hampton Roads, Virginia, lay five Union men-of-war, and the Confederates set about building a vessel that would be more than a match for all of them.

The "Virginia." From the bottom of Norfolk harbor they raised the half-burned hulk of the Union warship *Merrimac*, which had been sunk to prevent its falling into Confederate hands. The steam engines of the *Merrimac* were in working order, and around them the clever Confederate shipwrights built a hull of iron, strong enough to resist the shells of any cannon. This strange craft they renamed the *Virginia*.

Early on the morning of March 8, 1862, watchers on the Union warships saw what looked like the roof of a barn coming out from shore towards them. It was the long, low *Virginia*, her sloping iron sides bristling with cannon. From the Union warship *Cumberland* came a roar and a great puff of smoke as she fired a broadside at her oncoming foe. The great shells glanced harmlessly off the armored deck, and the *Virginia* continued her relentless course. Another frantic volley from the *Cumberland* did little harm. Then the *Virginia*'s iron beak rammed deep into the ribs of her wooden opponent, and the *Cumberland* rolled over on her side and slowly sank, carrying down many of her crew.

Backing away from her stricken enemy, the *Virginia* next attacked the

Congress, whose gunfire did no more damage than had that of the *Cumberland*. Red hot cannonballs set the *Congress* on fire, and the *Virginia* withdrew to wait until high tide next day to destroy the remaining Union vessels.

Ericsson's "Monitor." That night, the most curious warship the world had ever seen came steaming into Hampton Roads. It was the Union ironclad *Monitor*, invented by John Ericsson, who nearly thirty years before had invented the screw propeller. Much smaller than the *Virginia,* the *Monitor* carried only two guns. But these were set in a revolving iron turret and could be fired in any direction. Like her ironclad opponent, she was protected with iron armor which no shell could penetrate. Near the remaining Union ships the little *Monitor* dropped anchor.

Importance of the Battle. The next morning, when the *Virginia* came out to finish her work, the *Monitor* went bravely forward to meet her. For hours the two ships blasted away at each other with their heavy guns, but neither could harm the other. At last, with her ammunition nearly gone and her men weary of battle, the *Virginia* turned back to her harbor and left the Union fleet in peace. For the first time, ironclad warships had engaged in battle, and it was plain to all the world that the day of the wooden warship had passed.

This battle between the Monitor and Virginia (or Merrimac) changed the course of naval history. These ships were the direct ancestors of the steel vessels of today.

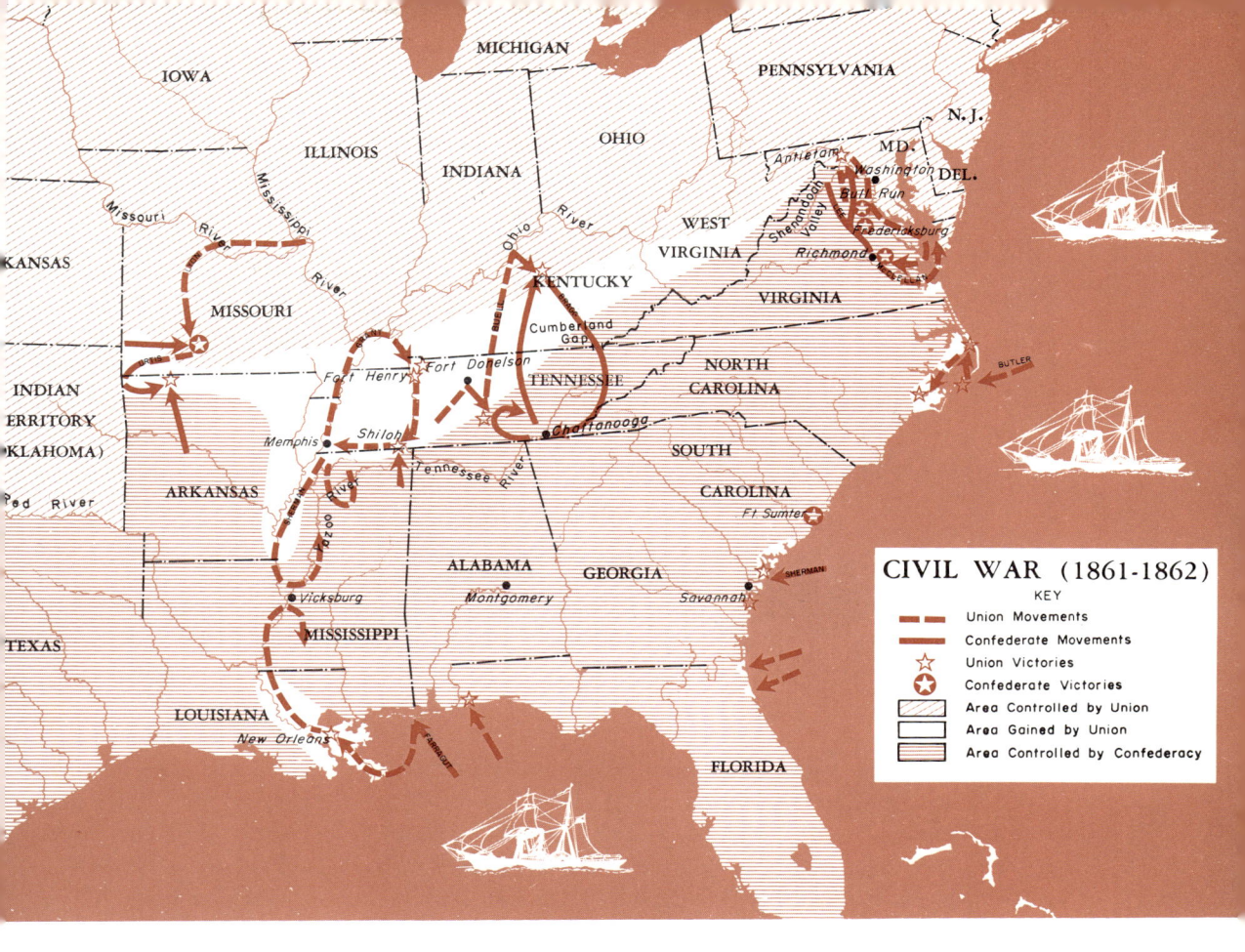

Union Capture of New Orleans

Fortification. Another brilliant naval exploit in the spring of 1862 was the attack on New Orleans. Because they held New Orleans, the Confederates controlled the mouth of the Mississippi. The North was most anxious to gain this control for herself. However, the great Southern port was well defended. Seventy-five miles below it, on both sides of the river, were powerful forts which swept the river with their heavy guns. Below the forts, stretching from one side of the river to the other, were giant chains to stop vessels from using the river. Between the forts and the city was a fleet of Confederate war vessels. The city certainly seemed safe.

The Union fleet, under Captain David G. Farragut, consisted of more than forty vessels, but they all were wooden ships. Besides his regular warships, Farragut had a number of smaller vessels carrying guns so mounted that they could send shells high in the air to drop on the forts.

Up the River. Farragut steamed nearly up to the forts, and at once a terrific battle took place between the guns upon the shore and the guns upon the ships. For nearly a week the tremendous cannon duel continued, and then Farragut determined to break through the chains and run his

Union Army Battery at Ft. Brady, on the James River in Virginia. Northern superiority in weapons and armaments helped win the war.

ships past the forts. Two gunboats were sent ahead to cut the chains, and behind them came Farragut and his warships, sailing along in spite of the rain of shells from the two forts.

Successfully past the forts, Farragut's fleet opened fire on the Confederate ships. At last the Union commander sank or captured them all, and had the city of New Orleans at his mercy. All valuable Confederate stores were ablaze when the Northern soldiers landed, but the important city was taken. Soon after, Farragut was promoted to Rear-Admiral.

Fort Henry and Fort Donelson

While Farragut was capturing New Orleans and opening up the lower Mississippi, a Union general, Ulysses S. Grant, was forcing his way down from the north. Two strong Confederate forts, Fort Henry and Fort Donelson, controlled the Tennessee and Cumberland Rivers. These Grant and his Union soldiers seized with the help of Commodore Foote's river gunboats. Fort Henry fell quickly, but for three days the forces in Fort Donelson held out and returned shot for shot. Then the Confederate commander sent word to Grant that he was ready to give up, and asked for Grant's terms of surrender. Grant replied, "No terms except an unconditional and immediate surrender can be accepted." Fort Donelson fell, and from that time on General U.S. Grant was referred to as "Unconditional Surrender" Grant.

Battle of Shiloh

After capturing the two forts, Grant and his army marched up the Tennessee River Valley in search of the Confederates under General Albert Sidney Johnston. The Confederates retreated before them, abandoning important cities in Tennessee and leaving that state in Union hands. Finally, at Pittsburg Landing, or Shiloh, the armies clashed.

During the first day of fighting at Shiloh, Grant and his Northerners were driven back by Johnston's fighting troops. But during that night Northern reinforcements arrived under General Buell, and the next morning Grant went forward to a great victory. It was one of the bloodiest battles of the war, for 25,000 men fell dead or wounded on the field, and Johnston, the great Southern leader, was among those killed. The Confederates now lost hope of holding the upper Mississippi and abandoned it as far south as Vicksburg.

Second Battle of Bull Run

Although the Confederates had lost ground in the Mississippi Valley, they experienced numerous successes in the East. General "Stonewall" Jackson was advancing through Virginia, toward the North. General Robert E. Lee was carefully planning to invade Maryland and then advance toward Washington, D.C. It appeared to many, both in the North and the South as well as in Europe, that the North could never subdue the South.

In the meantime, Major General Henry W. Halleck was appointed by President Lincoln as General-in-chief of the Northern armies. He consolidated the Union forces in Virginia, placing them under the direct command of General John Pope assisted by Generals Burnside and McClellan. These forces met the Confederates at the second Battle of Bull Run. Here the Confederates under Generals Lee, Jackson, and Longstreet decisively defeated the Union forces, leaving Washington open to attack.

Battle of Antietam

Lee followed up his victory by an invasion of Maryland, hoping to persuade that state to join the Confederacy. His plans were to move on Washington. However, General McClellan checked Lee's invasion at Antietam (an-TEE'tum) and the Confederates were forced to retreat to Virginia. Antietam was a costly battle to both sides, for approximately 20,000 soldiers lost their lives. It was also one of the most important battles because it proved a turning point in European reaction to the Confederacy. The South thought that a victory at this time might cause France and Great Britain to recognize the Confederacy. Such recognition would give to the South very valuable help, but the Confederate setback stifled all hopes of gaining European support.

By the time the Union forces recovered sufficiently to pursue Lee, he had entrenched his army in Fredericksburg. The Northern forces tried in vain to dislodge him from this position.

Looking Back

1. What were the immediate and long-range results of the battle between the *Virginia* and the *Monitor*?
2. Why was the capture of New Orleans a great military and strategic victory?
3. Of what military significance was the fall of Fort Henry and Fort Donelson?
4. Discuss the significance of the battles at Shiloh, Bull Run, and Antietam. Which was most important? Why?

3. The Union Forges Ahead in the Third Year

The Emancipation Proclamation

Announcement of the Proclamation. Immediately after the battle of Antietam, Abraham Lincoln issued his famous *Emancipation Proclamation*. It freed slaves in all territories still in rebellion. It did not apply to Kentucky, Missouri, Maryland or Delaware, slave states which had remained in the union, or to Tennessee or parts of states such as Louisiana which had been occupied by Northern forces and were no longer part of the Confederacy. Lincoln felt slavery was wrong, but he also felt that it would not be right to use his presidential powers against American citizens who owned slaves. He could, however, free slaves in states still in rebellion.

Historians disagree about Lincoln's reasoning in issuing the Emancipation Proclamation. Some say he did it because he was pressured into it by Congress. Others feel that he did it to cripple the South by taking away its farm laborers. In any case, the effects it had were many.

Effects of the Proclamation. In the first place, the Emancipation Proclamation made the Civil War seem like one being fought for the freedom of an enslaved people. Lincoln wanted to free the slaves, it is true, but he had always wanted to free them gradually, allowing the states themselves to make the final decisions. Another effect of the proclamation was that European nations, especially Great Britain and

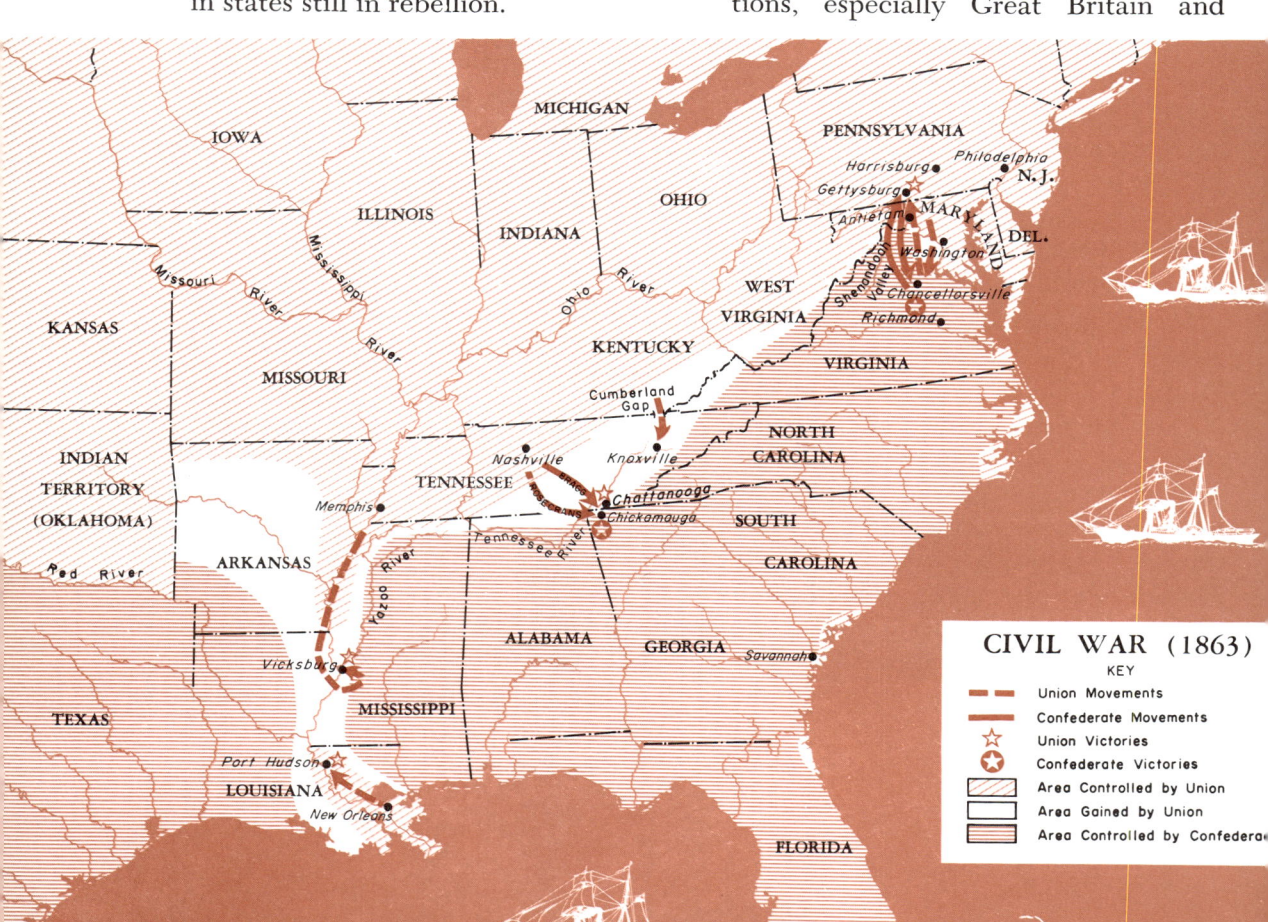

Cemetery and cannon at the Gettysburg battlefield. Today it is a national historical park. Lincoln dedicated this ground with the "Gettysburg Address."

France, supported the South much less strongly after its issue. Influential groups in many European nations believed very strongly in the abolition of slavery, and when the North became more firmly identified with abolition, Europe withdrew support from the South.

However, the Emancipation Proclamation did not have every effect it was supposed to have. Primarily, it was meant to free the slaves, but it only freed some of them. Slavery still remained in those border states which allowed it, and in the deep South, in states like Alabama and Mississippi, there was no way to enforce the proclamation. Also, long before the issuing of the Emancipation Proclamation, Congress had offered freedom to any slaves who would serve in the Union Army. Therefore, any male slaves who had known of Congress' offer could have obtained freedom long before the proclamation by enlisting in the Army.

Chancellorsville

It was the spring of 1863 before the Union army of the East again saw action. Then it was once more led toward Richmond. Hooker met the Confederates under Lee and "Stonewall" Jackson at Chancellorsville. Before either side was able to gain a victory, Hooker was wounded, and without its leader the Union army went to pieces. Back they were driven, and again Richmond was saved. Unfortunately for the South, the battle cost the life of General "Stonewall" Jackson, who was accidentally wounded by one of his own men and died four days later of pneumonia.

The Siege of Vicksburg

Early the next spring Grant moved against the Southern stronghold of Vicksburg. Two Southern armies hastened to the defense of the city. One reached it, but Grant intercepted the other army and defeated it. Then, with 70,000 men, he laid siege to Vicksburg, which was defended by the Confederate commander, Pemberton, and 30,000 soldiers.

Those within the city, both soldiers and civilians, suffered terribly. The constant shelling by Union cannon and Union gunboats knocked houses and buildings into hopeless ruins. Hunger added to the distress. The unfortunate Confederates were reduced to eating a single cracker and a small piece of meat each day. Mules and horses were killed and eaten, and when these were consumed, dogs, cats, and rats served to keep the defenders alive. At last, on July 4, 1863, the citizens of Vicksburg could hold out no longer, and the city was surrendered. Five days later Port Hudson, to the south, surrendered, and the Mississippi was open to Union vessels from its source to its mouth.

The Union's "Anaconda Policy"

After the fall of Vicksburg the Union commanders worked out, for the first time, a definite plan for the war. The eastern army, called the Army of the Potomac, was to sweep down into Virginia and attack the Confederacy from the north. Part of the western army in the meantime was to cross into Georgia, conquering as it went, and attack the Confederacy from the south. The

---

President Lincoln's address at the dedication of the National Cemetery, Gettysburg, Pennsylvania, November 19, 1863

"Fourscore and seven years ago our fathers brought forth on this continent a new nation, conceived in liberty, and dedicated to the proposition that all men are created equal. Now we are engaged in a great civil war, testing whether that nation, or any nation so conceived and so dedicated, can long endure. We are met on a great battlefield of that war. We have come to dedicate a portion of that field as a final resting-place for those who here gave their lives that that nation might live. It is altogether fitting and proper that we should do this.

"But in a larger sense, we cannot dedicate—we cannot consecrate—we cannot hallow—this ground. The brave men, living and dead, who struggled here have consecrated it far above our poor power to add or detract. The world will little note nor long remember what we say here, but it can never forget what they did here. It is for us, the living, rather, to be dedicated here to the unfinished work which they who fought here have thus far so nobly advanced. It is rather for us to be here dedicated to the great task remaining before us—that from these honored dead we take increased devotion to that cause for which they gave the last full measure of devotion; that we here highly resolve that these dead shall not have died in vain; that this nation, under God, shall have a new birth of freedom; and that government of the people, by the people, for the people shall not perish from the earth."

Officers of the 8th Kansas Volunteer Infantry Regiment in Alabama, one month before they participated in the action at Chickamauga. The picture is posed, as were almost all pictures in the Civil War. Since cameras were not yet perfected and would not "stop" motion, photographer's subjects had to remain rigid for ½ minute or more.

rest of the western troops were to hold the West. Surrounded by Union forces, the Confederate armies would be attacked from all sides. This was called the Anaconda (An-a-ᴋᴏɴ′dah) Policy, after a huge snake which squeezes its prey to death.

Gettysburg

In the summer of 1863, Lee decided to make a daring move. If he could bring the war home to the Northerners and could win a victory on Northern soil, he felt that many would cease to support the Union cause and that the war might soon be won for the South. Crossing into Pennsylvania, he set the capital, Harrisburg, as his goal, planning to attack the city of Philadelphia if he were successful at Harrisburg.

Pickett's Charge. But before Lee reached Harrisburg, he had to fight a Union army under General Meade at Gettysburg. For two days the two armies jockeyed for position, with no great advantage to either side. Then, on the third day, Lee made a fatal move. Placing all his hopes on a single blow, he ordered General Pickett with 15,000 chosen men to storm the strongest Union position on Cemetery Ridge. The Confederates swept forward shouting their inspiring war cry. Though withering volleys of shot and shell tore great holes in their ranks, they marched on. The Union marksmanship was deadly. When Pickett's men reached the foot of Cemetery Ridge, less than half of the heroic 15,000 were still alive. A gallant handful swept over the top of the ridge, some to die gloriously but uselessly, and the pitiful remnant to be driven back to the Confederate lines. On the following day Lee led his beaten forces toward the South.

The battle of Gettysburg was a Union victory, but not so great a victory as it might have been. General Meade, like McClellan, failed to strike the enemy when he had them at his mercy, and Lee's army, still nearly 60,000 strong, once more escaped into Virginia.

Gettysburg Address. At Gettysburg a great national cemetery was established in memory of the men on both sides who fell there. At its dedi-

> ### General Grant Writes of His Quartermaster Corps
>
> "There never was a corps better organized than was the quartermaster's corps with the Army of the Potomac in 1864. With a wagon-train that would have extended from the Rapidan to Richmond, stretched along in single file and separated as the teams necessarily would be when moving, we could still carry only three days' forage and about ten to twelve days' rations, besides a supply of ammunition. To overcome all difficulties, the chief quartermaster, General Rufus Ingalls, had marked on each wagon the corps badge with the division color and the number of the brigade. At a glance, the particular brigade to which any wagon belonged could be told. The wagons were also marked to note the contents: if ammunition, whether for artillery or infantry; if forage, whether grain or hay; if rations, whether bread, pork, beans, rice, sugar, coffee or whatever it might be. Empty wagons were never allowed to follow the army or stay in camp. As soon as a wagon was empty it would return to the base of supply for a load of precisely the same article that had been taken from it. Empty trains were obliged to leave the road for loaded ones."

cation in November, 1863, President Lincoln spoke. His Gettysburg Address, though very brief, was so sincere and heartfelt that it has been given a place among the greatest speeches of our language.

The Rock of Chickamauga

During the summer of 1863, a part of the western Union army under General Rosecrans started through Tennessee. The town of Chattanooga was occupied by the Confederates under General Braxton Bragg, but at the approach of the Union army he retired into the mountains. Thoroughly confident of victory, Rosecrans pursued the Confederates to Chickamauga where, because of an unwise order, his army became divided.

Quick to see his opportunity, Bragg turned upon the Union forces, sending his men in between the two divisions and driving the men with Rosecrans from the field in great confusion. The part of the army which had been separated from Rosecrans, however, proved to be a better fighting unit. Their leader, General Thomas, ordered his 25,000 men into a good defensive position at Chickamauga. For four hours he withstood the attack of more than twice as many Confederates, earning for himself the nickname "The Rock of Chickamauga." When darkness fell, Thomas retired to Chattanooga. Not long afterwards, he succeeded Rosecrans in command of the Union Army of the Cumberland.

Chattanooga

When the Southern forces laid siege to Chattanooga, Grant withdrew his army from Vicksburg and hastened to relieve Rosecrans and Thomas. In three days of fighting, the Union army was everywhere successful. Troops brought from Virginia, under General Hooker, were given the task of capturing the Confederate positions on steep Lookout Mountain. The Union soldiers swarmed up the steep slopes, losing many men as Confederate bullets and cannon balls thinned their ranks, but always pushing on. At last they drove the Confederates from their position, and the "battle above the clouds," as it was called, became a Union victory. The next day, the troops under General Thomas attacked and captured the main Confederate positions on Missionary Ridge. By nightfall, the Confederate army was retreating, and Chattanooga remained in the possession of the Union armies.

Grant was now recalled to Washington, where he was given the title of Lieutenant-General and placed in charge of all the Union forces. The western army he left in charge of General Sherman, who had fought brilliantly in the campaigns around Vicksburg and Chattanooga. The plan of attack arranged for following Vicksburg was now to be carried out. Grant was to hammer the Confederates from the north, while Sherman entered Georgia and harassed them from the south.

Looking Back

1. Why did Lincoln issue the Emancipation Proclamation?
2. How did the fall of Vicksburg almost complete a North-South split of the Confederacy?
3. Describe the "Anaconda Policy" adopted by the North.
4. Why may Gettysburg be considered the "high water mark" of the Confederacy?
5. What western victories speeded the shifting of Grant to the eastern front?

4. Grant Leads Union Forces in Fourth Year

Wilderness Campaign

It was after a long and discouraging series of campaigns against Richmond that Grant was at last put in charge of the Union armies. He had fought well in opening up the Ohio and the Mississippi and in the battle of Chattanooga. Lincoln felt that at last the right general had been placed in charge of the Northern forces.

Advance Toward Richmond. Like his predecessors, Grant, in the spring of 1864, began an advance on Richmond. His route led through a region of small trees, tangled underbrush, and bushes, known as "the Wilderness." Here the Confederates put up a strong resistance, but Grant, despite the loss of nearly 18,000 men, kept pushing on, and at last succeeded in driving the Confederates out of the region. So heavy had been Grant's losses that his soldiers expected a retreat, but to their satisfaction the General announced that they would continue on to the south. "I will fight it out along this line if it takes all summer," said Grant.

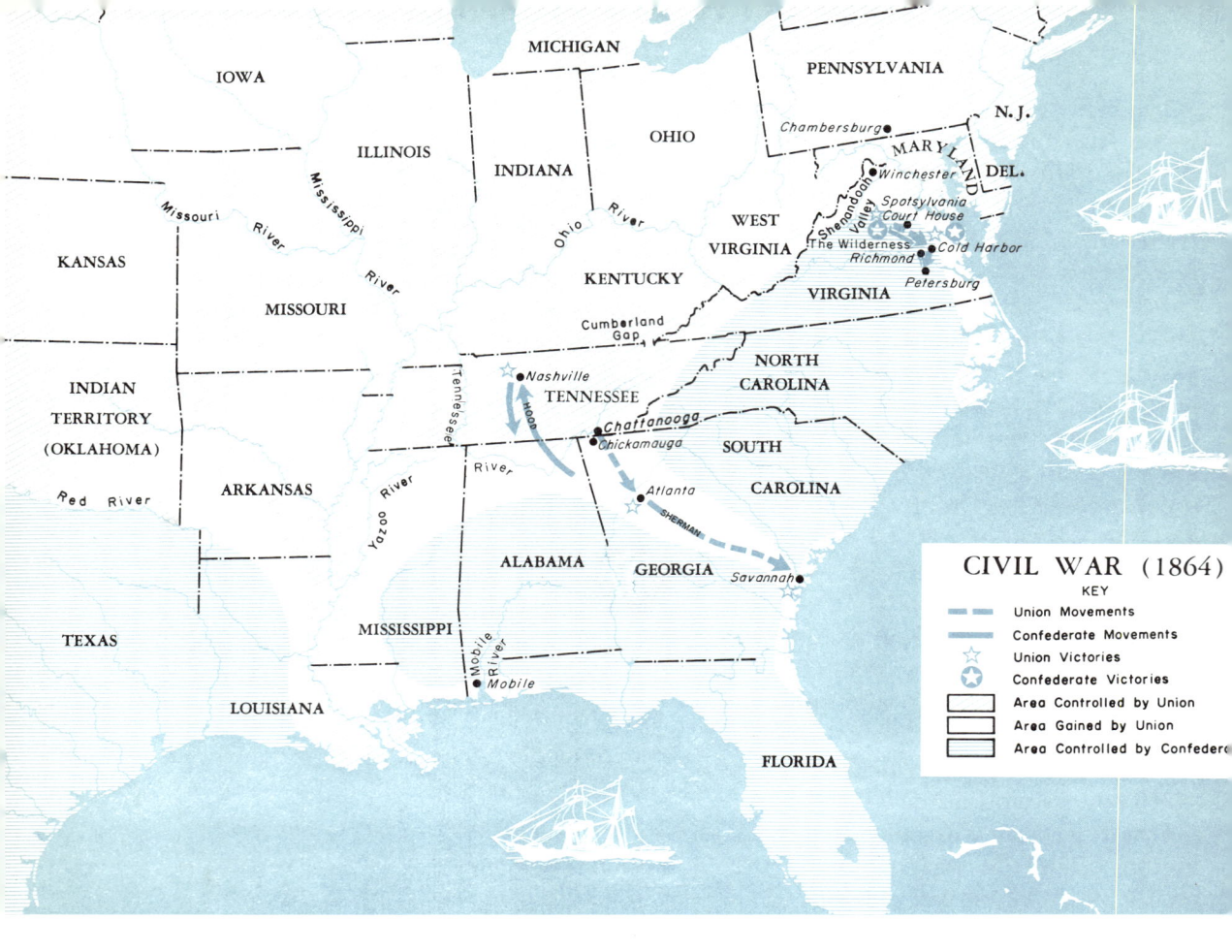

Grant struck at the enemy at Spotsylvania Court House, and again he suffered heavy losses, but kept on advancing. Then he attacked Lee, who held a strongly fortified position at Cold Harbor. Here the gallant Union forces were repulsed with a loss of 10,000 soldiers. Still Grant would not give up. The Confederates marveled at this general, so unlike those who had gone before him, who kept right on attacking even though he lost.

Siege of Petersburg. After the attack on Cold Harbor, Grant decided to swing around and attack Richmond from the south. He marched down to Petersburg. There again he found Lee facing him. This Confederate town was too strongly fortified to be taken by assault, so the Union artillery opened fire, and the siege of Petersburg began.

The Shenandoah Valley Campaign

While Grant was besieging Petersburg, Lee sent General Early with a strong cavalry detachment to attack Washington. When Early found that the city was too strongly fortified to be taken, he went up the Shenandoah Valley, reaching at last the town of Chambersburg, Pennsylvania, which he burned.

A month later Grant, who was still laying siege to Petersburg, sent General Sheridan with a detachment of cavalry to lay waste the Shenandoah Valley, so that no more Confederate raiders would travel through it. Everything of value was destroyed or removed, and Sheridan made certain that there was not enough food left in the entire valley to support an army.

Early's and Sheridan's forces met in September, 1864, and the brilliant Union leader, Sheridan, succeeded in driving back his enemy. Early, however, was not beaten, and some time later, when he learned that Sheridan was absent from his army, made a surprise attack on the Union forces. Twenty miles from the scene of the battle, in Winchester, Virginia, Sheridan heard the sound of guns. Springing on his horse, he sped to the help of his men. As he drew near he met panic-stricken Union soldiers fleeing from the Confederates. "Turn about," cried Sheridan, and inspired by the command his soldiers returned to the battle and won the day. Early was once more driven back.

Sherman's March Through Georgia

In the spring of 1864 Sherman started his campaign. Slowly but irresistibly his armies moved to the southeast. During the summer he reached Atlanta, Georgia, and here the Confederates put up a determined resistance. But Sherman was not to be beaten, and on September 3, Atlanta fell.

The Confederate army in the South was now commanded by General Hood, who made a desperate attempt to stop Sherman's relentless march. Moving his army at high speed, Hood started toward Tennessee, hoping to tempt the Union soldiers to hurry back to the defense of Chattanooga and the territory they had so dearly won. Sherman remembered Thomas' determined stand at Chickamauga and decided to let that general take care of Hood while he continued on toward the sea.

Fall of Savannah. During the rest of his march Sherman found no opposition. His soldiers pushed on through a rich and fertile country, leaving nothing but desolation in their path. Everything that could serve an army was taken—horses, mules, supplies. Railroads were torn up. Houses and buildings were burned. Great stores of cotton were destroyed. It was Sherman's plan to make the state of Georgia an example to the South, and he succeeded well. Late in December the city of Savannah was taken from a weak force of Confederates, and Sherman's great march across the South was completed.

Defeat of Hood. But what, meanwhile, had General Hood been doing to the part of the Union army under Thomas? Hood's lightning-like stroke to take Tennessee had ended at Nashville, where Thomas' men not only defeated him but cut his army to pieces and drove out of the state those Confederate soldiers who were not killed. The Union troops of the western army had carried out their part of the double attack on the Confederacy admirably well.

Naval Battles

The "Alabama." During the fourth year of the war, important events were taking place on the sea. A warship named the *Alabama* had been built in Britain and sold to the Confederacy. For months she roamed the sea, eluding all Union warships and sinking or capturing scores of Union merchant

The Alabama, *a Confederate raider, slides beneath the waves after having been battered by the* Kearsarge.

ships. At last, on June 19, 1864, the *Alabama* was overtaken by the United States warship *Kearsarge* off the northern coast of France. A furious battle followed which ended when the *Alabama*, badly battered by the heavy guns of the *Kearsarge*, turned her bow to the sky and slid stern first beneath the waves.

Mobile Bay. In 1864, Admiral Farragut turned his attention to Mobile Bay on the Gulf of Mexico. This was a Confederate stronghold from which warships and blockade runners had occasionally gone out to harass Union shipping. Farragut determined that Mobile must be captured from the Confederates.

Into Mobile Bay steamed his fleet of warships, past two forts which opened fire. At the head of the line was the ironclad ram *Tecumseh,* and she was closely followed by three other ironclads. Behind them came the wooden ships, headed by the *Brooklyn* and Farragut's flagship, the *Hartford.*

As the *Tecumseh* steamed into the bay with Confederate shells breaking around her, a great explosion occurred. She suddenly stopped, quivered, and plunged bow first to the bottom. She had been sunk by a submarine mine, or torpedo. At once the wooden ship *Brooklyn* began to turn back, and the dreaded cry of "Torpedoes!" rang throughout the fleet.

Farragut decided to ignore the torpedoes, and at his orders the flagship *Hartford* went into the lead. Confederate mines could be heard scraping against the ship's bottom, but none exploded, and one after another the Union ships passed into the harbor and on

---

Excerpt from Abraham Lincoln's Second Inaugural Address

" . . . With malice toward none; with charity for all; with firmness in the right as God gives us to see the right let us strive on to finish the work we are in; to bind up the nation's wounds; to care for him who shall have borne the battle, and for his widow, and his orphan—to do all which may achieve and cherish a just and lasting peace among ourselves, and with all nations."

to victory. The Confederate fleet was destroyed, and the battle, for all practical purposes, was over. Soon afterward, the forts surrendered, and Mobile Bay was in possession of Farragut and his men.

The Election of 1864

In the election of 1864 Lincoln won a great victory, defeating his Democratic opponent, General McClellan, by an electoral vote of 212 to 21. In his second inaugural speech, in March, 1865, the President declared his intention of continuing the great work of preserving the Union, "with malice toward none, with charity for all." His reelection meant that the war would be carried on until victory was achieved.

Looking Back

1. Compare Grant's tactics in the Wilderness Campaign with those of McClellan in the Peninsula Campaign.
2. How did victories by Sheridan and Sherman aid the Union cause?
3. Why was the sinking of the *Alabama* a blow to the Confederacy?
4. By what daring step did Farragut again blunt Confederate power?
5. Who were the opposing candidates in the election of 1864?

5. The Fifth Year of War Brings Union Victory

Lee's Surrender to Grant

When the spring of 1865 came, Grant was still laying siege to Petersburg. At last, on April 3, 1865, that stronghold fell, and the Union forces took the city. Later in the same day they entered Richmond. Lee, with a small remnant of his army, retreated to the south.

Southern resistance was now useless, and both Lee and Grant knew it. Before long the Confederate commander found that he was trapped between Grant's army on the north and Sheridan's cavalry on the south, for Sheridan had made a brilliant circling move for this very purpose. There was nothing left for Lee to do but surrender, and on April 9, 1865, he and Grant met at Appomattox Court House, about seventy-five miles from Richmond. The terms of surrender were generous. All that Grant required was that the Southern soldiers lay down their arms and

Robert E. Lee may have been the finest military strategist in American history.

return to their homes. No prisoners were taken. The half-starved Southern men were fed from the Union supplies and were released. The war was over, and the United States was once more a single, undivided nation.

Results of the War

What were the results of these four years of bloodshed? The most horrible result was that huge numbers of soldiers on both sides had been killed or wounded. Families had been disrupted, and hatred remained in the hearts of many. Lincoln's Emancipation Proclamation had eventually freed most of the slaves. The Thirteenth Amendment to the Constitution, adopted in 1865, confirmed their freedom and also freed those in the slaveholding states not covered by the Proclamation, with the words,

"Neither slavery nor involuntary servitude, except as a punishment for crime whereof the party shall have been duly convicted, shall exist within the United States or any place subject to their jurisdiction. Congress shall have power to enforce this article by appropriate legislation."

Finally, the troublesome question of whether the states or the central government was supreme had been answered forever.

Lincoln's Assassination

Amid the general rejoicing at the end of the war there came a terrible blow which struck sadness to the heart

---

General Grant Recalls Lee's Surrender

"When news of the surrender first reached our lines our men commenced firing a salute of a hundred guns in honor of the victory. I at once sent word, however, to have it stopped. The Confederates were now our prisoners, and we did not want to exult over their downfall.

I determined to return to Washington at once, with a view to putting a stop to the purchase of supplies, and what I now deemed other useless outlay of money. Before leaving, however, I thought I would like to see General Lee again; so next morning I rode out beyond our lines towards his headquarters, preceded by a bugler and a staff-officer carrying a white flag.

Lee soon mounted his horse, seeing who it was, and met me. We had there between the lines, sitting on horseback, a very pleasant conversation of over half an hour....

I was accompanied by my staff and other officers, some of whom seemed to have a great desire to go inside the Confederate lines. They finally asked permission of Lee to do so for the purpose of seeing some of their old army friends, and the permission was granted. They went over, had a very pleasant time with their old friends, and brought some of them back with them when they returned."

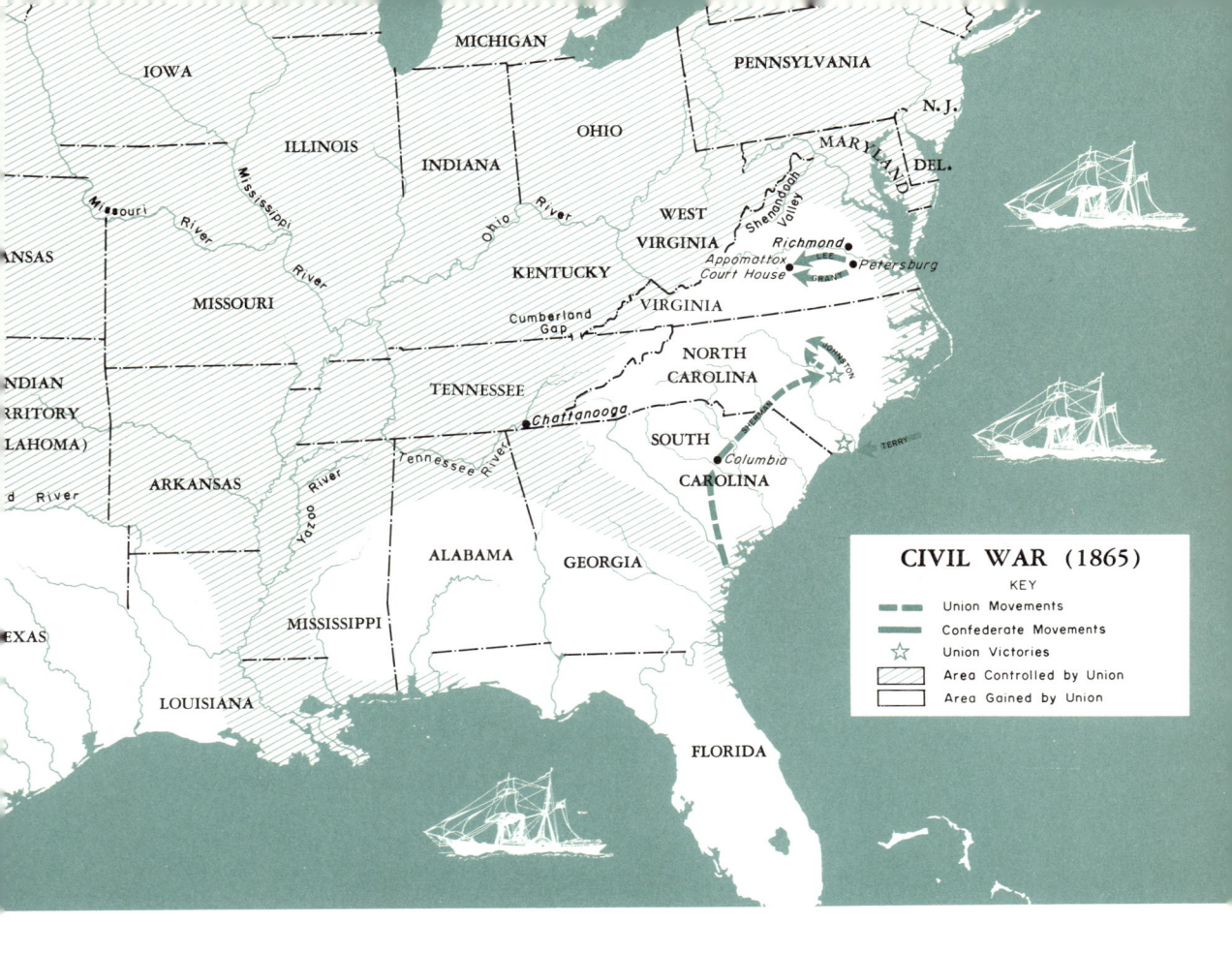

of every American. President Lincoln, the beloved preserver of the Union, at last free from the horrible responsibilities of the war, claimed an evening of relaxation at Ford's Theater in Washington. As he entered the presidential box everyone rose to greet the nation's deliverer. The play went on. It was a humorous play, and Lincoln laughed heartily. While his attention was thus engaged, a crazed actor, John Wilkes Booth, slipped silently into the presidential box from the rear. Pressing a pistol against the back of Lincoln's head, he fired, then leaped to the stage and cried, "*Sic semper tyrannis!*" ("So may it ever be with tyrants!") and escaped. Lincoln died early the next morning in a house across from the theater. As the great heart ceased to beat, Secretary of War Stanton cried out in a voice choked with emotion, "Now he belongs to the ages."

Maximilian in Mexico

Between 1861 and 1865, while the war was at its height, the people of America had been too much concerned with the great problems within their borders to pay much attention to anything else. An event of importance, however, had occurred which vitally affected their interests. Napoleon III, Emperor of France between 1856 and 1870, thought that the American Civil War afforded his country a fine chance to gain a colony in the New World.

Lincoln and his cabinet in a formal pose.

Accordingly he sent to Mexico an army of 50,000 Frenchmen, who conquered the country and placed the Archduke Maximilian of Austria on the throne, with the title of Emperor. This new little empire under French control prospered as long as the Confederates kept the Union Army too busy to disturb it.

When the war was finally over, Secretary of State Seward promptly informed Napoleon III that the Monroe Doctrine would be enforced and that the United States would not tolerate European conquest of any part of the New World. At the same time an army under General Sheridan was sent to the Mexican border ready to take any steps which seemed necessary. Napoleon realized that the Americans were very much in earnest, and withdrew his French army, leaving the unfortunate Maximilian defenseless. The Mexicans at once captured their ruler, tried him, and shot him.

The "Alabama" Claims

Trouble also followed with Great Britain. During the war, at least until the Emancipation Proclamation, British sympathy had been strongly with the South, and British shipyards had been used to supply the Confederates with warships. Besides the famous *Alabama*, the *Florida* and *Shenandoah* were also launched from British yards and did great damage to Union shipping until the close of the war. Even more serious, two ironclad rams were built. As these were about to sail to attack Union vessels, Charles Francis Adams, the American minister to Great Britain, informed the British foreign secretary, "It would be superfluous in me to point out to your lordship that this is war." The ironclads were not used.

The *Alabama, Florida,* and *Shenandoah* did millions of dollars' worth of damage, and for this the United States held Great Britain responsible. War might have resulted between the two countries, but Great Britain and America had learned of a better way to settle their differences. As in the case of the Oregon boundary dispute, the "*Alabama* claims," as they were called, were submitted to a court of arbitration which met at Geneva, in Switzerland. Besides one American and one British representative, there were statesmen from Switzerland, Italy, and Brazil. After calm deliberation, this group decided that Great Britain had violated the laws of neutrality, and awarded the United States $15,500,000.

Epilogue

The United States had passed through a civil war, the worst of all kinds of war. North and South had both suffered terribly. Half a million men had lost their lives, and many thousand families were saddened. But in spite of all the misery, the country came through with the strength to repair her losses, to demand justice from foreign countries, and to face the future with renewed purpose. Greatest of all, the United States had established itself as one nation, indivisible.

Fort Sumter—1861 and 1865

1861

Major Robert Anderson writes concerning his surrender to the Confederates:

"Having defended Fort Sumter for thirty-four hours, until the quarters were entirely burned, the main gates destroyed by fire, the gorge walls seriously impaired, the magazine surrounded by flames and its door closed from the effects of the heat, four barrels and three cartridges of powder only being available and no provisions remaining but pork, I accepted terms of evacuation offered by General Beauregard (being the same offered by him on the 11th instant, prior to the commencement of hostilities) and marched out of the fort on Sunday afternoon, the 14th instant, with flying colors and drums beating, bringing away company and private property, and saluting my flag with fifty guns."

1865

Secretary of War Edwin M. Stanton writes to Major General Robert Anderson:

"I have the pleasure of communicating to you the inclosed order of the President, directing the flag of the United States to be raised and planted upon the ruins of Fort Sumter by your hands, on the 14th day of April next, the fourth anniversary of the evacuation of that post by the United States forces under your command."

Excerpts from *The Heritage of America* edited by Commager and Nevins, 1951. Published by Little, Brown.

Looking Back

1. How did the end of the war solve some problems, leave some unsolved, and present new ones?
2. By what actions had Napoleon III taken advantage of the American conflict?
3. What steps did the United States take against the reign of Maximilian in Mexico? What were the results?
4. Why was Britain subject to claims against her for damages done by Confederate raiders?
5. In what way were our claims against Britain settled?

The Chapter in Perspective

Who Are These People?

"Stonewall" Jackson
Maximilian
McClellan
Ericsson
Farragut
Grant
Napoleon III
Pickett
Meade
Thomas
Sherman
Sheridan
Lee

Where Are These Places?

Ft. Sumter
Richmond
Bull Run
Ft. Henry
Appomattox
Shiloh
Antietam
Vicksburg
Gettysburg
Chickamauga
Chattanooga
Mobile Bay

What Do These Dates and Terms Mean?

border states
Jan. 1, 1863
Alabama claims
"Anaconda Policy"
Gettysburg Address
Wilderness Campaign
Peninsular Campaign
Emancipation Proclamation
the *Alabama*
Trent affair
blockade
Monitor
1864
1863

Questions for Study

1. Evaluate the effect of the Union blockade on the South.
2. Why did France and England sympathize with the Confederacy but fail to give substantial aid?
3. For what reasons did Lincoln fail to abolish slavery at the beginning of the war and then issue the Emancipation Proclamation?
4. Compare the aims and military strategy of the South with that of the North.
5. Who, in your opinion, was the outstanding military man of the war? Give reasons for your choice.
6. How would you view Sherman's march through Georgia as a Southerner? as a Northerner?
7. By what means did Lincoln help to contribute to the Union victory?
8. What reasons can you give for the ultimate surrender of the South?
9. On a map, show how the "Anaconda Policy" slowly but surely gained its objectives.

Place Yourself in History

You are an honor graduate of West Point. Your wife is the great-granddaughter of Martha Washington. For almost thirty years, you have distinguished yourself in the service of the United States Army. When John Brown threatened the peace at Harper's Ferry, you commanded the detachment that captured him.

Now the nation you have served so well and so long is faced with war. The President of the United States sends for you and offers you command of the army. Your name is Robert E. Lee.

What were the circumstances under which Lincoln made his offer to Lee? What would you have done? Why? What factors influenced Lee to make his decision? What were the effects of his decision?

15

The Nation Rebuilds

The terrible struggle of the Civil War raised many perplexing questions. Should the defeated Southern states be treated as though there had been no war and they had never left the Union? Or should the South be treated as a conquered country? Should the leaders of the Confederacy be forgiven? Or should they be punished as traitors? Should the debts of the Confederacy be paid? If so, who should pay them, the North or the South? What should be done with the freed Negroes? All of these questions challenged the country's greatest statesmen. How would you have answered them?

1. The South's Condition in 1865 Is Desperate

The Civil War proved disastrous for the South. Crops and property were seized or destroyed by the soldiers of both armies. After the slaves were freed, there was practically no one to work the fields of the great plantations or of the smaller farms. With the defeat of the Southern armies, the Confederacy came to an end. The paper money which the Confederate government had issued became worthless, and hundreds of families were left penniless. The Confederate states lost their influence in the federal government, and the South was left without resources, and with thousands upon thousands of her men dead.

Effects of War on the Economy

It is difficult to describe the condition of the South after the Civil War. Destruction was everywhere in evidence.

The cities of Columbia and Charleston, South Carolina, and Atlanta, Georgia, were almost completely destroyed. A Northern author who saw the city of Columbia called it a "wilderness of ruins." No stores or large buildings were left standing; every public building was destroyed. Charred chimneys were the only reminders of what had once been a flourishing business section.

Most of the war had been fought in the Southern states with both armies constantly crossing and recrossing the land. Some twenty-two hundred battles were fought in the Civil War, an overwhelming majority of them occurring on Southern soil: approximately three hundred in Tennessee and over five hundred in Virginia. A number of these battles were skirmishes rather than full-scale engagements, but even so they brought extensive destruction. Wherever the armies moved, they left barren lands.

Farms and Crops. Most evident was the effect of the war on the crops and the farms. Agriculture suffered from the soldiers' destroying the crops after they had been planted or from lack of labor to do the seeding, cultivating, and harvesting. Many of the farm owners enlisted in the army, leaving the land idle except for small portions which were worked by the women and the children. On most of the large plantations, the master and the overseer had gone off to war. The slaves, without the threat of punishment, naturally did not want to work someone else's land without being paid like other farm workers. In many cases, slaves simply left the plantation when they were informed of the Emancipation Proclamation which became effective January 1, 1863. All of these conditions decreased farm pro-

Two of General Sherman's soldiers bend a red-hot rail around a tree. After these rails were bent almost double, they were called "Sherman's hairpins." Can you guess why?

duction to such an extent that in many parts of the South the population existed on a near starvation diet.

Railroads. In every war, railroads are targets for military destruction. The Southern railroad system was almost completely demolished by the end of the war. Often Northern army units heated and then twisted the rails into grotesque patterns. Sometimes they piled up great heaps of railroad ties and burned them. Bridges were blown up, freight stations destroyed; all in all everything possible was done to interfere with transportation in the Southern states. So complete was the destruction of the railroad lines that in some cases the entire road had to be rebuilt.

Homes and Cities. Those people who traveled extensively through the South in the years after 1865, whether they came from Europe or from the North, expressed surprise at the destruction of the railroads. However, they could scarcely believe their eyes when they saw the almost innumerable number of private homes destroyed seemingly for no good reason. Cities which were not military objectives had also been destroyed. Most of the important cities in the South felt the scourge of the fighting armies.

Industry. The entire economic life of the South was brought to a standstill as a result of the ravages of war. The labor force, agricultural production, transportation, manufacturing, and banking were affected. Confederate money became completely worthless after Lee's surrender. To soldiers returning home, the country appeared as though it could never recover. Decades were required for the South to reach full economic recovery.

Problems in Politics and Voting

Ex-Confederate Leaders. One of the greatest political difficulties brought about by the Civil War was the problem of deciding which Southerners should be permitted to vote and which should not. Many leaders in the North felt that anyone who had been associated with the Confederacy, whether in a military or a civil capacity, should not have the voting privilege. Certain Northerners felt that the

The remains of the railroad station at Richmond, Virginia, after the war. Little could be done to repair damage like this. It took years for southern railroads to recover.

former leaders of the Confederacy were no more than traitors from whom all rights of citizenship should be taken. Some Northern congressmen wished to eliminate completely any Confederate leaders from the federal government and from the new state governments. Others thought they should seek pardon and then pledge allegiance to the Constitution and to the federal government before their rights were restored.

Carpetbaggers and Scalawags. Another political problem concerned both the North and the South. What was to be done with the former slaves? Negroes had been taught by their former owners that the right to vote was a right only to be enjoyed by white people. Therefore, when former slaves were given this right, they often were not familiar with the procedures and the issues involved. For many of them, politics was a complete mystery. Therefore, they looked to white people to tell them what to do, and there were many Northerners and Southerners ready and willing to do this for their own purposes. Some of those people were sincere and capable men who earnestly tried to help the former slaves. Others proved to be neither sincere nor capable; these were men solely interested in promoting their own personal interests, either financially or politically. Fortune-seekers who traveled from the North into the South were called *carpetbaggers,* because they carried their possessions in a carpetbag. Men who lived in the South and had not taken any part in the Confederacy, were, sometimes unjustly, called *scalawags* by their fellow Southerners.

Carpetbaggers and scalawags were looked upon as troublemakers by most Southerners. These two groups proceeded to use the freed Negroes to set up governments in the Southern states.

A typical carpet bag, like the one above, actually was made from carpet.

Although the Negroes participated with high motives for the most part, the total inexperience of many of them with governmental processes created a situation that was unfortunate for all concerned. The poor among the white population demonstrated an inability, similar to the freed Negroes, to take an active part in the political scene. A large number from these two groups (freed slaves and poor whites) could neither read nor write. Prior to 1865 they had never voted nor had they ever paid taxes.

Corrupt Government. High salaries were voted for the new officeholders. Great sums of money were squandered, stolen, or wasted in many foolish ways. To pay for all this, the taxes on property were sharply increased. The entire social system of the South was overturned. The former leaders were shorn of their power, and the carpetbaggers,

> *March 31, 1876, An Early Plea For Civil Rights. A Negro Senator, Blanche K. Bruce, speaks in the Senate.*
>
> "It will not accord with the laws of nature or history to brand colored people a race of cowards. On more than one historic field, beginning in 1776 and coming down to this centennial year of the Republic, they have attested in blood their courage as well as a love of liberty. I ask Senators to believe that no consideration of fear or personal danger has kept us quiet and forbearing under the provocations and wrongs that have so sorely tried our souls. But feeling kindly toward our white fellow-citizens . . . and, above all, abhoring a war of races, we appeal to the good sense and justice of the American people. . . ."

scalawags, and former slaves were now in positions of influence. To the unhappy Southern minority of wealthy planters, the situation appeared desperate. It seemed that they could do very little to check the power of the carpetbag governments, for their rule was backed by the army of the United States.

The period following the Civil War is one of the most wasteful and tragic periods in American history. Southerners who had served many years in both the Federal and the Confederate governments were barred from any participation at a time when the South could ill afford to be without their wisdom and experience. More objectionable than the inexperience of the new officials, was the inefficiency and extravagance of some "carpetbag" governments. Yet, these governments did write new constitutions, established many reforms, and widened the franchise or voting privilege.

A New Way of Life

With the close of the war, drastic social changes came to the South creating an entirely different pattern from that of the prewar years. The Southern "way of life" became a totally different one. Slavery was, fortunately, gone forever. With it went the rigid social system which had existed in the South since the early days of settlement. The change affected in an equally drastic manner both the planter and the slave. For the planter, everything to which he had previously clung desperately was altered. For the freed slave, the future appeared as the dawning of better days—days in which he could finally enjoy some of the privileges of the great country of which he was a part.

The Freed Negroes. The fall of the Confederacy gave freedom to about three and a half million slaves. Virtually all of them had been tied to their plantations for their entire lives. When this way of life ended for them and they were no longer slaves, they had some problems adjusting to their newfound freedom. Also, since they were used to believing what white people told them, they often believed fantastic rumors. One of these rumors was that each of the slaves would be awarded forty acres of land and a mule with which to work it. Some freed slaves even felt that the government would award them sums of money. Often, immediately after the war, the Negroes were exploited almost as much by those who did not own them as they had been by those who had owned them. Many, Negroes and whites alike, felt that gradual emancipation and education would have solved many social problems which plague the South even today.

The Emancipated Whites. Another group affected by the changed social conditions after the war was the poor whites who before the war owned neither slaves nor property. This group, by allying itself with Northern Republicans, acquired positions in the new governments set up by the Union forces. For the first time, many of them were able to become land owners. The future held for this group improved status and greater economic opportunity. However, relationships with the Negroes brought tension and jealousy. The poor whites considered themselves emancipated too, not from slavery as were the colored people, but from the dominance of the aristocracy. Before the war, they had little opportunity to improve their lot as laborers or tenant farmers. They were very much afraid of competing with Negroes for their new social status, so they became the bitterest enemies of the colored people. The planters had always claimed that they were the best friends of the Negroes. It was no doubt true that after the Civil War white planters treated the Negroes better than did other groups in the South.

Looking Back

1. Why was most of the war damage found in the South?
2. For what reasons are agricultural and transportation facilities major military targets?
3. Describe the extensive war damage suffered by the South.
4. What problems arose concerning the right of Southerners to vote?
5. In what ways did the "carpetbaggers" and "scalawags" participate in Southern life?

2. Congress and the President Wage Their Own War

The period of American history from 1865 to 1877 is frequently called *Reconstruction*. It is also called the Tragic Era, especially because of the troublesome economic, political, and social conditions connected with Reconstruction in the South. In the same period, the relationship between Congress and the Chief Executive also had elements of tragedy. Both the Congress and President Johnson tried desperately to gain the upper hand over each other. Neither won, but the battle left the government exhausted. The legislative functions of the Congress were disrupted by one powerful group, the radical faction of the Republican party. President Andrew Johnson was impeached by the House of Representatives. Corruption infiltrated the government. Many of the radical congressmen wished to take revenge on the South, and thus passed laws which were quite unfair to that section of the country. Sectional politics was accentuated. The government showed itself to be both weak and unfair; undoubtedly American history was darkened by the events of Reconstruction.

Lincoln's Reconstruction Policy

Abraham Lincoln, always farsighted and kind-hearted, had his own plan for mending the Union and restoring the Southern states to their former place. From the beginning of the war he had declared that the seceded states had never left the Union because no state could leave the Union. Lincoln felt that neither the states nor the people of the states were at fault, but merely certain groups within the states which had caused the trouble. The President had the power of pardon, and this he intended to use freely so that the Southerners would not be punished. As early as December, 1863, he issued a declaration that any Southern state could be accepted in the Union as soon as ten per cent of the people who had voted in 1860 should form a loyal government and agree to comply with the rulings of Congress on the subject of slavery. Had Lincoln lived and been able to put this plan into operation, much of the bitterness of the Reconstruction period might have been avoided. Unfortunately he was assassinated in April, 1865.

Andrew Johnson and Reconstruction

Johnson's Plan. When Lincoln died, his Vice-President, Andrew Johnson, at once took his place. Johnson was honest and patriotic, but had few other qualities to recommend him for so high an office. He was blunt and tactless, a harsh man who cared little for the opinions of others. Since the situation in the country required great tact and thorough cooperation between Congress and the President, Johnson was not the best man to assume the high office of the Presidency at such a critical time. Johnson's theories were not so bad. He simply was not the man to carry them out. He wanted each Southern state to hold a constitutional convention, repeal its act of secession, disown its war debt, ratify the Thirteenth Amendment (which abolished slavery), and provide for the election of congressmen and senators. These wishes were much the same as Presi-

Many felt that Andrew Johnson never fully understood the relationship between Congress and the Presidency.

Thaddeus Stevens was President Johnson's bitterest foe. He hated the South and was determined to punish it.

dent Lincoln's. Johnson's real mistake was in making his plans without consulting Congress, which was not in session when he announced them. Some of the Southern states did follow Johnson's recommendations and sent their legislators to Washington to sit in the upcoming session of Congress.

Opposition by Congress. When Congress assembled in December of 1865, Johnson's mistake became apparent. Many congressmen and senators were furious that they had not been consulted in regard to the readmission of the Southern states to the Union. Thus, when the hopeful, newly appointed Southern senators and congressmen asked to be admitted to the United States Congress, they were curtly refused by hostile Northerners. This was a sad blow to the hopes for national reunion and harmony.

Furthermore, the plan which Johnson was trying to put into effect afforded little protection for the Negroes who had been so recently freed. Already certain of the Southern states had passed laws known as Vagrancy Laws and Apprentice Laws. The Vagrancy Laws provided that any Negro caught wandering about without a home should be fined, and that any white man who paid the fine could make the Negro work for him until the debt was paid. The Apprentice Laws assigned young Negroes to "guardians" for whom they should work without pay until they reached a certain age. These laws practically reduced the Negroes to slavery again, and this would have cancelled all the progress that had been made in the last ten years. Another reason that Congress opposed Johnson's plan was that some members wished to punish the Southern white men who had fought against the Union.

Angered by Congress's attitude, Johnson immediately became hostile. In a public speech he declared that Congress was unfairly attempting to deprive the Southern states of their legal rights, and to rob the President of the United States of the powers which he should exercise. He even went so far as to say that his own assassination by order of Congress did not seem improbable. The President and Congress were now involved in a bitter contest.

Stevens and Sumner. When we consider the leaders in the Congress of 1867, we can readily see why its members were not willing to follow the President's plan. The two acknowledged leaders were Thaddeus Stevens and

Charles Sumner. Stevens was a representative from Pennsylvania. He was also the Chairman of the Committee on Ways and Means, one of the most important committees in Congress. Feeling bitter resentment towards the South, he strongly favored severe punishment for Confederates. The influence which Stevens exercised over the other members of Congress has seldom been equaled by that of any American political leader.

Charles Sumner, famous Senator from Massachusetts, felt bitterness towards many Southerners. However, he took a great interest in the free Negroes, and he felt that they should be granted all the rights promised them in the Constitution. Sumner was an intense, moralistic, partially unbalanced man who had little patience for those who disagreed with him. Led by two such men, Congress was not satisfied with Johnson's plan of reconstruction.

Impeachment of President Johnson

Congress respected neither the political ideas nor the person of President Johnson. Although he did not possess tact, he did have sincere convictions. As he carefully stated at the beginning of his administration, he was determined to follow a plan of reconstruction similar to that proposed earlier by President Lincoln. Lincoln's plan was for the gradual emancipation and education of the freed slaves. Generally it was kind and generous to the destroyed South. Johnson's continuance of Lincoln's plan brought him into perpetual opposition to Congress and its efforts to punish the South and the leaders of the Confederacy.

Annoyed at his constant opposition, Congress passed over Johnson's veto a series of laws which greatly reduced his power. One of these, the Tenure of Office Act, forbade the President to discharge members of his own Cabinet without the consent of the Senate, a right which had been enjoyed by every President before this time. Disregarding this law, Johnson dismissed Secretary of War Edwin Stanton, and the House of Representatives decided to impeach him before the Senate for "high crimes and misdemeanors" and to attempt to remove him from office. When the impeach-

Congressman Ben Butler of Massachusetts, one of Johnson's harshest critics, speaks for his impeachment on the House floor.

ment was presented to the Senate, it was defeated by a single vote. The President therefore remained in office.

Looking Back

1. What was Lincoln's reconstruction policy?
2. Why did Johnson's plans arouse the opposition of Congress?
3. How did treatment of the liberated slaves arouse feelings in the North?
4. Who were the leaders in Congress who opposed Johnson's plans?
5. What drastic step did Congress take to show its displeasure with President Johnson? What were the results of this action?

3. Congressional Reconstruction Brings Bitterness

In spite of President Johnson's resistance, Congress quickly took control of Reconstruction. Since the Republican majority in the legislative branch of the government had threatened to treat the South as a conquered country, any plans of reconstruction would be designed to deal severely with it. The leaders in Congress wanted to establish a military occupation in the South, supposedly to protect the freed Negroes and to establish the kind of government in which Negroes could participate. More accurately, the Republicans wanted to keep their party in power by hindering a rise in the strength of the old Democratic party of the South. If military occupation should be removed, Southern Democrats would send men to the Senate who would fight against Republican control.

Constitutional Amendments

Thirteenth Amendment. Three amendments to the Constitution were passed by the Congress and ratified by the states during the years of Reconstruction. Early in 1865, Congress passed the Thirteenth Amendment, which prohibited slavery in the United States or "any place subject to their jurisdiction." This amendment was aimed particularly at the border states and those areas of the Confederacy not covered by the Emancipation Proclamation, namely, the portions conquered by the Union armies.

Fourteenth Amendment. Congress next passed the Fourteenth Amendment to the Constitution. This provided that all persons born or naturalized in the United States and subject to its jurisdiction were citizens. Furthermore, this amendment stated that no citizen, white or colored, could be deprived of his rights except as punishment for crime, and that each citizen was to be granted due process and equal protection of the laws. The amendment provided further that any state which should deprive any of its inhabitants of their rights should have its representation in the House of Representatives decreased. Men who had formerly been United States or state officials and had sided with the Confederacy were excluded by the amendment from holding any national or state office, though Congress reserved the right to remove this restriction, which it did partially in 1872 and fully in 1896. Finally, the amendment forbade any of the states, or the United States, from paying the war debts which the Confederacy had contracted during the war. The Southerners felt that these terms were very harsh, and the only Southern state to ratify the amendment immediately was Tennessee, which was at once readmitted to the Union.

Fifteenth Amendment. In 1868 the Fifteenth Amendment was passed. This provided that "the right of citizens of the United States to vote shall not be denied or abridged by the United States or any state on account of race, color, or previous condition of servitude." This amendment raised the Negro to full political power equal to that of any white man. The Thirteenth Amendment had declared his freedom, the Fourteenth Amendment had made him a citizen, and now the Fifteenth Amendment insured him the right of voting.

Civil Rights Act

Congress had taken Reconstruction into its own hands. A bill was passed extending the life of the Freedmen's Bureau, an organization which had been created in March, 1865, to insure the rights of the freed Negroes. With this bill the Civil Rights Act was also passed, protecting the privileges, property, and freedom of the Negroes. Although the President promptly vetoed both bills, Congress passed the Civil Rights Act over his veto by the necessary two-thirds majority, and it became a law without the President's signature. The bill extending the Freedman's Bureau did not pass, but it was the last bill which President Johnson successfully vetoed.

Military Reconstruction

Reconstruction Acts. The Reconstruction Acts were next passed by Congress, in March, 1867. These provided that all of the states which had seceded, except Tennessee, were to be divided into five military districts, each under an officer of the United States Army. Under the military rule, all male citizens over twenty-one years of age, Negro or white, except former Confederate soldiers or legislators, were allowed to vote, and sufficient Union soldiers were sent into the South to make sure that this provision was carried out. The governments of the Southern states had no powers but were subject to the federal government through its representatives, the military governors.

Military Occupation of the South. Strictly speaking, military occupation of the South may have been unconstitutional. Congress assumed powers which before had belonged to the President. As Commander-in-chief, only he had the authority to direct the military. Furthermore, the Supreme Court had ruled in 1866 that civilians could not be tried in military courts when civil courts were functioning, as they were in the South. The whole system of military reconstruction violated the guarantees of rights and liberties of the Constitution.

In time, the people throughout the North showed their disapproval of the laws on military occupation passed by the radical Congress. Less radical men were elected to the House and Senate. The Supreme Court also played a role in condemning the acts of Congress by declaring them to be unconstitutional.

Southern Resistance

"Solid South." Naturally Southerners, defeated in the war, their social system uprooted, tended to feel antagonistic to the North, and with some justification. The radical Republican-dominated Congress was enacting unfair measures which crippled the already wounded South even more. White men in the South, in resistance to the federal government, banded together to use their votes, and in some cases weapons and whips, to oppose the Northerners. Their votes, taken all together, at first made little impression in National elections. Soon, however, the *"solid South"* began to play an important role in the Democratic Party and National politics.

The Southerners also used illegal powers, feeling at the time that desperate steps were justified. Forming groups such as the Ku Klux Klan, they dressed up in weird costumes and roamed from house to house at night, torturing Negroes and intimidating whites into voting as the Klan said they should. Often, the Klan took matters into its own hands and assumed the roles of judge and jury over a person's life. Many so-called scalawags were hanged, as were many carpetbaggers. The Negroes were afraid to use their new-found and long-awaited powers, granted under the Constitution. Once again a white minority controlled the South, mainly by means of intimidation and physical violence.

The Recovery of the South

In spite of the power and persuasiveness of Stevens, Sumner, and their followers, popular opinion in the North

Ku Klux Klansmen used weapons, torture and "scare" tactics to force people to accept their point of view.

slowly but steadily swung against the abuses which the Southerners were enduring from their carpetbag governments. Southern leaders made stirring appeals for understanding before audiences of Northern people, who were gradually coming to see the plight of the South in a more sympathetic light.

End of Reconstruction. It was due to the increased understanding on the part of the Northerners that the intolerable conditions in the South were gradually improved. In 1872, Congress passed the General Amnesty Act, restoring the political rights of all but a handful of the Southerners. One by one the carpetbag governments were eliminated, until by 1877 there were only three left. These three disappeared when Rutherford B. Hayes withdrew the last of the Union troops from the South in 1877. The period of Reconstruction had ended.

Agriculture. The Southern states were slow to regain their economic stability. The struggles of the Reconstruction period left a feeling of uncertainty as to the future which discouraged ambition. Many of the freed Negroes could find no jobs but their old ones on the plantations, which they did not want. Without many laborers the plantations could not be worked, and for several years production in the South was at a low ebb.

Only gradually, and at first very slowly, did the Southern states recover from the war. Many former slaves eventually returned to work, although they no longer worked without pay. The plantations were divided into smaller farms which needed fewer men to work them. Cotton continued to be grown on these smaller farms, but considerable acreage was devoted to food crops.

Manufacturing. Before the Civil War, the South had made a modest beginning in manufacturing. For example, the Tredegar Iron Works in Richmond, Virginia, was the third largest manufacturer of iron and iron products in the United States as early as the mid-1850's. In fact, this particular ironworks had made most of the cannon used by both sides in the Civil War. But after the war, the manufacturing industries in the South grew rapidly, especially the textile and cloth industries.

In pre-Civil War days, raw cotton was shipped to New England or to Europe and there was spun into cloth. But in time some of the larger Southern cities developed their own factories for the manufacture of cotton cloth. These have continued to prosper until, today, the Southern states have displaced New England in the position of leadership in cloth manufacture.

Recovery: Slow, but Complete. One of the strongest arguments for the system of slavery in the South had always been that without it the economic system would collapse. The recovery of the South after the war illustrated perfectly the fallacy of such an argument. After the slaves were freed, the Southerners, with the aid of various types of farm machinery, greatly increased their production of cotton, and also added to their wealth by many other lines of farming. The amount of cotton exported each year from 1880 to 1890 was many times that of the most prosperous year during the period of slavery. Though the South recovered slowly from the war, her economic recovery was complete.

Looking Back

1. Summarize the contents of the Thirteenth, Fourteenth, and Fifteenth Amendments.
2. What were the purposes of the Freedmen's Bureau and the Civil Rights Bill?
3. How was the South to be governed under the Reconstruction Acts of 1867?
4. For what reasons did the "solid South" come into being?
5. By what means was the end of Reconstruction accomplished?
6. How were Negroes in the South denied their voting privileges after the Civil War and the passage of the Fifteenth Amendment?
7. What changes in agriculture had to be made immediately in the South after the war?
8. For what reasons did many members of Congress seek to impose harsh controls over the defeated South?

The Chapter in Perspective

Who Are These People?

Johnson Sumner
Stevens Stanton

What Do These Dates and Terms Mean?

Reconstruction 1865
carpetbagger 1872
scalawag 1868
Vagrancy Laws 1867
Apprentice Laws
"Solid South"
Civil Rights Bill
Freedmen's Bureau
Reconstruction Acts
Thirteenth Amendment
Tragic Era
Fifteenth Amendment
Fourteenth Amendment

Questions for Study

1. What problems did the freed Negroes present to the North? to the South?
2. Do you think that Lincoln's plan for restoring the Union would have worked had he lived? Why?
3. Discuss the factors that led to the sharp break between Johnson and Congress. Who was more to blame? Why?
4. Why was it necessary to set up military governments to carry out the congressional plan for Reconstruction?
5. What legal and illegal steps did the South take in opposing the wrongs of Reconstruction?
6. Give reasons why the period of Reconstruction is often referred to as "The Tragic Era."
7. For what reasons did many Northerners begin to favor the withdrawal of federal troops from the South?
8. How did the destruction caused by the war set the stage for the development of a "New South"?
9. On a map of the South, indicate where new industries and new crops flourish in place of "King Cotton."

Place Yourself in History

May 26, 1868, is the day of decision. For almost two months the trial has dragged on in the Senate. Chief Justice Salmon P. Chase presided in the first and only such case in American history. Sharp, bitter charges and countercharges have been made. The President of the United States, Andrew Johnson, is on trial.

You are a member of the United States Senate. You have listened carefully to the evidence. How most other Senators will vote is known. You are one of the few Senators who alone knows how you will vote. Then, you cast your ballot.

When the vote is announced, it stands at 35 guilty to 19 not guilty—one vote short of the necessary two-thirds majority required for removal from office!

How did you vote? Why? Why did those who voted the other way do so?

Expanding Your Outlook

Doing It Yourself

1. Prepare a script for a radio program dramatizing an event in a "station" of the Underground Railroad.
2. Write an editorial concerning William Lloyd Garrison and his activities for a Boston newspaper. Then write on the same topic for a Richmond paper.
3. A runaway slave has been captured by federal marshals in Columbus, Ohio. Write a newspaper account of the incident. Try to catch the feeling of public opinion.
4. You are now a Northern sympathizer in "Bleeding Kansas." Write a letter describing your experiences to your cousins in Illinois. (A Southern sympathizer may write to relatives in Alabama.)
5. Write a participant's view (Northern or Southern) of the battle of Gettysburg. (Similarly: Vicksburg, Bull Run, the *Monitor* vs. the *Merrimac*, or the surrender at Appomattox).
6. Prepare a report to the class on civilian life in the North (or the South) as the war drew to a close.
7. Write a Southern view of Lincoln at his death or a Northern view of Jefferson Davis at his capture.
8. Imagine that you were on a Southern blockade runner. Recount your experiences to the class.
9. As a foreign military analyst, explain how the South was able to hold off the North for four years.
10. Some historians believe that the Civil War could have been avoided. Make a list of facts which you think support this argument.

Working with the Class

1. Let the classroom be the Senate of the United States as the various issues of the Compromise of 1850 are debated and settled.
2. Assign a committee to prepare a dramatization of the actions of Confederate and Union soldiers as they mingled together after the surrender.
3. Imagine that you and a group of friends are members of a secret abolitionist group. Allow the members of your class to "listen in" to one of your meetings.
4. A class collection of pictures, drawings, or models of items connected with the Civil War may be made by a group of volunteers.
5. Immediately after the Civil War, a committee of two Northerners and two Southerners meet to discuss the methods to restore the Union. Let your classmates hear your ideas.
6. An investigating committee of northern industrialists returned from visiting the South late in 1865. Allow the committee to report its findings to the class.

The Union Breaks Apart and Mends More Strongly

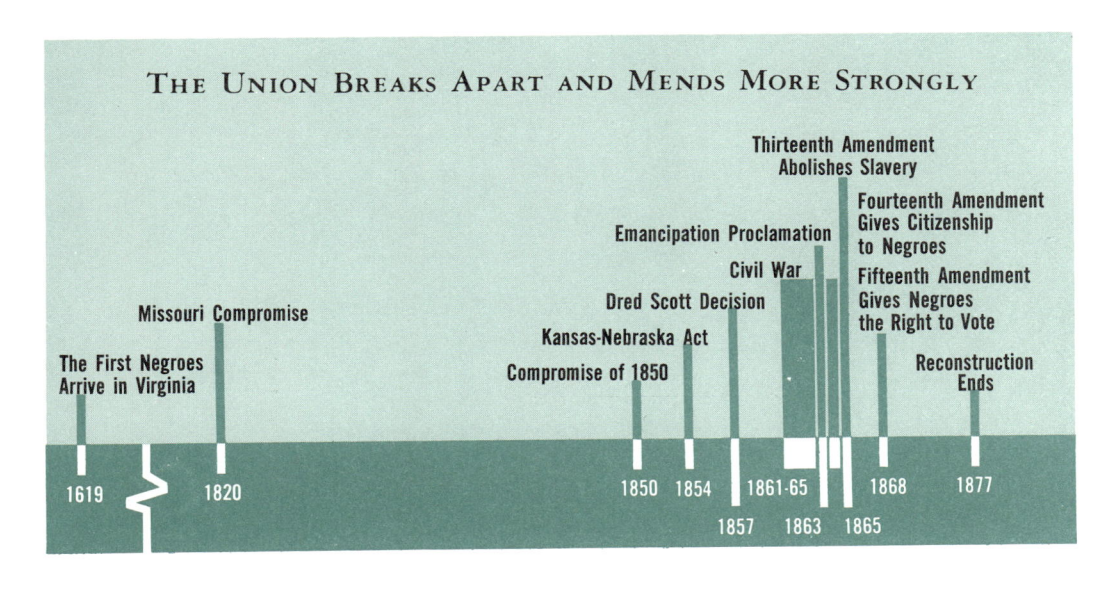

- 1619 — The First Negroes Arrive in Virginia
- 1820 — Missouri Compromise
- 1850 — Compromise of 1850
- 1854 — Kansas-Nebraska Act
- 1857 — Dred Scott Decision
- 1861-65 — Civil War
- 1863 — Emancipation Proclamation
- 1865 — Thirteenth Amendment Abolishes Slavery
- 1868 — Fourteenth Amendment Gives Citizenship to Negroes; Fifteenth Amendment Gives Negroes the Right to Vote
- 1877 — Reconstruction Ends

Henry Farney's painting, Song of the Talking Wire, depicts a lonely Indian listening to the sound of the telegraph wires as it reverberated through the pole. The telegraph lines were the first tentacles of the American population. Settlers followed them, until finally, where once only Indians and wild animals roamed the plains, farms and homesteads dotted them. The lonely Indian, his land taken from him and his game scared away, watched with wonder from his reservations as the American miracle took place.

The Taft Museum—Cincinnati,

ONE NATION INDIVISIBLE

UNIT 6

The Wide Open Spaces Are Filled

16. The Awakening Industrial Giant
1. America Invents Ways to Use Her Natural Resources • **2.** Enterprising Inventors Develop America's Wealth • **3.** Large Companies Manage Men, Money, and Markets

17. The Vanishing Frontier
1. The Iron Horse Spans a Continent • **2.** Cattle Kings Have Their Day • **3.** Natural Wealth Helps to Populate the West • **4.** The Indians Make a Last Stand

18. The Farmer and the Land
1. Expansion of Agriculture Brings Problems • **2.** Farmers Organize for Self-Improvement • **3.** Western Farmers Demand Cheap Money • **4.** The Country Deals with the Silver Question

19. Immigration and the Advance of Labor
1. Workers Band Together to Improve Labor Conditions • **2.** Immigrants Swell the Labor Force

16 The Awakening Industrial Giant

The American who lived in the years between the end of the Civil War and the beginning of the twentieth century must have been amazed by the changes that took place in his country. America was transformed from a land of farms and villages into a complex country of cities and factories. New inventions, new sources of light and power, machinery of mammoth proportions, all were parts of the emergence of America's industrial development. The American population jumped in only 35 years from 31,000,000 to 76,000,000. It was truly an age of change.

1. America Invents Ways to Use Her Natural Resources

"Oh beautiful for spacious skies,
For amber waves of grain;
For purple mountain majesties
Beyond the fruited plain."

Americans sing these words every day, probably not always realizing what they mean. Today we tend to think of the United States as a land of great industrial development, her steel mills pouring fire into the skies, her heavy industries turning out everything from pins to airplanes. But it has not always been this way. Indeed, none of America's industrial development could have taken place without the great storehouses of natural resources available in this country, and the men who knew how to make use of them.

The Story of Steel

One of America's most important natural resources is iron. From the time of the first Virginia colonists, it was known that iron ore could be found along the eastern coast of the continent. By 1775, the colonies were producing one-seventh of the world's iron. However, the Age of Steel did not begin until after the Civil War, when men learned how to make steel by blowing air through molten iron in order to burn out the carbon and other impurities. This operation, known as the Bessemer process, produced a metal that was much harder and more useful than iron.

At first the steel industry was concentrated in western Pennsylvania and Ohio, where there was plenty of iron ore and coal. Then new sources of iron were found in northern Michigan. In the 1890's the steelmen were digging ore in the famous Mesabi range in Minnesota, which became the greatest ore-producing area in the world. Since the Mesabi ore could be transported easily to Lake Superior, the Great Lakes became the most frequently used route for shipping. Large steamships loaded with ore stopped at Cleveland, Chicago, Detroit, and Lorain, where the ore was refined into steel. Ore deposits near Birmingham, Alabama, and Pittsburgh, Pennsylvania, led to the prominence of those cities in the steel industry.

Andrew Carnegie. Many men deserve credit for the tremendous expansion of American industry in the post-Civil War period, but a few of them stand out like giants above the others. One of these is Andrew Carnegie, a Scotsman who came to the United States in 1848. He rose from poverty to become master of the steel industry.

Carnegie, who had started as a cotton mill worker at $1.20 for a 72-hour week and had later grown prosperous as a railroader and ironmaker, now turned his energies to steel. Using methods of finance which were similar to those used by other great industrialists of the day, he quickly achieved spectacular success. Since Carnegie shipped so much steel, he could usually persuade the railroads, who depended on his business, to charge him less than they did other shippers. The railroads granted him what were called rebates. These were refunds on shipping costs,

Ore pit near Virginia, Minnesota. The great pits of the Mesabi Range in Minnesota, first worked in 1890, still supply the steel industry with iron ore today.

not granted to his competitors. Because Carnegie saved on shipping costs, he could afford to sell his steel for less than competing companies and forced many of them out of business.

Carnegie tried to maintain good relations with his workers, although he resented their organizing to try to force him to do anything. Consequently he was very much against unions and fought against their demands for higher wages and fewer hours. Carnegie improved the production of steel by using the latest scientific methods. But above all, he was successful in forming what is called a "vertical combination"—that is, he became owner of everything that goes into the making of steel from start to finish. His companies controlled the raw materials of iron ore and coal, the ships and railroads to bring them to his mills, and the blast furnaces to turn them into steel.

Carnegie's Last Years. In 1892 Carnegie decided to retire from active management of his great companies and placed them in the hands of one of his most efficient associates. Eight years later he sold his holdings to the banking house of J. Pierpont Morgan. Now he was free to spend the last years of his life in devoting his wealth to the public good. He made available about $350,000,000 to build libraries, promote international peace, establish funds for scholars and teachers, and support many charities.

Demand for Steel. A tremendous demand for steel meant riches for Carnegie's and other steel companies. Steel was the metal used for rails and coaches, for huge beams for buildings and bridges, and for ships. In 1887 the American Navy began to use steel armor plates to strengthen ships against enemy gunfire. The metallurgists (scientists who study the structure of metals and the means for testing them) developed new alloys for making high speed tools and stainless steels. The tough, heat-resistant steel that they developed went into electric motors, dynamos, and specialized machine tools.

The Oil Story

Strangely enough, men knew about the existence of oil many years before they knew what to do with it. The Indians found it oozing out of springs and used it for medicine. Later it was discovered that mineral oil, after it had been filtered or distilled, gave a better

Andrew Carnegie, a ruthless tycoon in middle age, later became a philanthropist, founding libraries and research funds.

Drake's first oil well. It was sunk at a depth of only 69½ feet on August 27, 1859. At first it produced only 25 barrels of oil a day, a mere trickle compared with present day wells. During the rest of the year, the well produced 2000 barrels of oil.

light than whale oil. For lubrication, it was better than animal fat which had a tendency to burn up at much lower temperatures than did mineral oil.

Drake's Folly. In 1855 a Yale professor named Benjamin Silliman analyzed a sample of oil and reported that it could be used commercially for lighting purposes, for lubrication of machinery, and as a source for other chemicals. Encouraged by this report, George H. Bissell raised money to drill the first oil well in the United States. It was put down in 1859 at Titusville, Pennsylvania, by one of Bissell's employees, Edwin Drake. At first, the skeptical neighbors called it "Drake's Folly," but when it began to produce hundreds of gallons a month, other promoters became interested and started to drill wells. A great "Oil Rush" began, especially in Ohio, West Virginia, and Pennsylvania.

John D. Rockefeller. In Cleveland, Ohio, a young businessman named John D. Rockefeller followed the early development of the oil industry with great interest. His keen mind quickly perceived that there was a fortune to be made in petroleum, and he gathered what funds he could and used them to finance an oil distillery. Profits began to pour in almost at once.

Rockefeller's oil business grew not only from the sale of oil but also from the ruthless methods used to destroy his competitors. Within a very few years twenty of the twenty-six competing oil companies in Cleveland had been forced to sell out to Rockefeller at whatever price he wished to offer. The addition of these companies increased his strength and resources and permitted him to carry his campaign of swallowing his competitors far beyond Cleveland and throughout the country as a whole.

Rockefeller used the same method of controlling the railroads that Carnegie did. Since he was a big shipper, he could demand reduced rates and get them. The railroads, dependent on his patronage, paid him rebates on large shipments.

Like Carnegie and other great business magnates of the time, Rockefeller used some of his millions to set up funds and foundations. These provided money to further scholarly research and education.

Further Revolutions in Industry

Side by side with the basic steel and oil industries, other great enterprises sprang up before the end of the last century.

Meat Packing. In Chicago, meat packing flourished, led by such firms as Armour, Swift, and Wilson. Originally meat was preserved by pickling, salting, or smoking. Later it was canned or refrigerated, transported in special cars, and stored in great warehouses.

Linotype machines, such as this 1886 model, can set up an entire line of type at one time.

Those later processes were quite expensive, which meant that the industry was gradually monopolized by a few wealthy companies.

Textiles. The textile industry also grew prosperous. Before the Civil War, cotton was shipped in great quantities from the South to New England, where there was plenty of cheap water power to run the mills. Later, however, mills sprang up in the South, a region which attracted mill owners by offering cheap labor, low taxes, and a supply of coal for steam power. The invention of carding machines to separate wool fibers led to a growth in the manufacture of woolen cloth. Raw silk imported from Japan and China was woven into rich silk cloth, at first in New England but later in the South and West as well.

Leather. The manufacture of shoes, belts, suitcases, and other leather goods became a very important American industry. Old-fashioned cobblers were true craftsmen. They made each shoe by hand. But under the new system of mass production, the cobbler became a mere machine operator who had little connection with the finished product. Devices such as stitching and cutting machines saved time and labor, and, on the whole American shoes became cheaper to buy and better to wear.

Printing. Other laborsaving inventions revolutionized the printing industry. The linotype machine, the rotary press, and new and more effective ink made large-scale printing possible. The modern newspaper, the colorful textbook you are now reading, and today's interesting magazines, have all been made possible by advances in the printing industry.

Looking Back

1. How did the Bessemer process help develop the Age of Steel?
2. By what means did Carnegie rise to a strong position in the steel industry?
3. Why do some people feel that Carnegie's greatest accomplishments came after his retirement?
4. Trace the growth of the oil industry from Drake through Rockefeller.
5. What improvements and developments took place in the meat-packing, textile, and leather industries.

2. Enterprising Inventors Develop America's Wealth

The discovery of great supplies of iron ore and oil would have meant very little had not men devised ways in which such supplies could be used. The nineteenth century in the United States was an age of invention. In that period, many of the products that we use today were first used in their earliest, crudest forms.

Improvements in Farming

John Deere. The first significant early improvement in farming procedures came when John Deere began to manufacture steel plows. These plows could rip through the rockiest soil without danger of breaking or becoming so dull that they were useless. Deere set up his plant at Moline, Illinois, in 1847.

Cyrus McCormick. While the steel plow made the cultivation of grain easier, the harvesting process was quite unmechanized until 1850. In this year, Cyrus McCormick, who had invented a reaper in 1834, began mass-producing his reaper in Chicago. In that year alone he turned out about three thousand reapers. McCormick's reaper enabled a few men to gather as much wheat in a day as had formerly been gathered by many men using tools such as the scythe, sickle, and cradle.

The Threshing Machine. As a result of better plowing and harvesting methods, the grain grower's crops were greatly increased. He could now grow and harvest large amounts of wheat, oats, or barley with relatively little help. However, he still needed a more efficient way to separate the grain from the stalk. The threshing machine was the best answer to this problem.

The threshing machine had been developed in Scotland in the late 1700's, but it did not come into wide use until about 1840. By the time of the Civil War, threshing machines were commonplace. They turned seven days of hard work by many men into a day's work by a single machine operated by only ten men.

Early threshing machines were powered by hand or by horses. With the application of the steam engine to the thresher in the 1870's, the reaper and the threshing machine were united to form a combine.

Improvements in Communications

By the Civil War, the country had expanded so much and people lived in

> ### A New Weapon For the Troops
>
> While the Civil War was going on, a certain Dr. Richard Gatling was granted a patent for the first practical machine gun to be used in warfare. This early weapon had six revolving barrels turned by a hand crank. Despite its death-dealing capability, the new gun was not accepted by the Army Ordnance Department, and it saw little service in the Civil War. After the great conflict was over, however, it became an official Army weapon and was produced in quantity by Colt Patent Fire Arms Company.
>
> In the 1870's and 1880's the gun found favor with various European and South American governments. Its light weight and rapid rate of fire made it a deadly weapon in many little colonial wars. Improved models were used effectively by American troops in the Spanish American War.
>
> Other Americans—Hotchkiss, Maxim, and Browning—share with Gatling the credit for developing rapid fire guns. The slang word "gat", meaning a repeating hand gun, is derived from the name of the early inventor.

so many different places that ways had to be found to communicate more efficiently and quickly. The telegraph, which had been in use since the 1840's, was extended over much of the nation by 1860. By 1866, Cyrus W. Field, a retired paper merchant, finally succeeded in completing his pet project, the laying of a cable across the Atlantic Ocean. Direct communication with Europe was now possible.

Within the next ten years, Alexander Graham Bell had successfully communicated the human voice over a wire. The telephone became a reality soon afterward, and by 1890, the American Telephone and Telegraph Company, to which Bell had sold his rights, had installed telephones in half a million homes.

The communications revolution brought about great changes in national life. Like the railroads, the telegraph and telephone made large national organizations possible and changed the regional and sectional nature of the United States. Improvements in printing and the invention of the typewriter by Christopher Sholes in 1868 also improved the methods of written communications. The processes of business became less tedious and more efficient.

Electricity

The harnessing of electricity in the 1870's was, undoubtedly, the greatest single achievement in the United States in the nineteenth century. Charles F. Brush of Cleveland, Ohio, developed a commercial means of converting electricity to usable power. Brush also later invented the arc-light street lamp.

Thomas A. Edison, however, was probably the greatest single developer

Wright plane over Ft. Myers, Va., 1908. Orville Wright is the pilot.

of electrical equipment. His only real invention was the mechanical phonograph, but he developed the incandescent lamp and other electrical apparatus which brought cheap and effective light to homes and offices for the first time.

It did not take long for someone to find a way to use electric power in the transportation industry. F. J. Sprague, an associate of Thomas A. Edison, organized the Sprague Electric Railway and Motor Co. about 1886. After adapting an electric motor which would run a street railway in Richmond, Virginia, he moved on to harness electric power in elevators and other conveyances. Motor driven elevated trains of his design flourished in a number of large cities beginning about 1895.

Automobiles and Airplanes

The first gasoline-driven ground vehicle in the United States was developed by the Duryea brothers, Charles and Frank, in 1893. Other famous men, such as Henry Ford and Ransom Olds, followed soon in the Duryeas' footsteps. Automobile races were held in the country as early as 1895.

A type of wall telephone used around 1895 in the United States and Canada.

Following the development of the automobile, two Dayton, Ohio, brothers, who were originally bicycle manufacturers, began experimenting with machines which might be able to fly. First Wilbur and Orville Wright tried various tests with gliders. Then, after trying out a gasoline motor, they set up a flight strip on the beach at Kitty Hawk, North Carolina. In 1903 their first airplane stayed in the air for a short while under its own power. It was a small beginning, but it signified the start of the air age.

Looking Back

1. Discuss the improvements in agriculture that made mass production of crops possible.
2. How did new inventions and improvements bring about a communication revolution?
3. The harnessing of electricity in the 1870's was the greatest single achievement in the United States in the nineteenth century. Tell why you agree or disagree with this statement.
4. What were the effects of the invention of the automobile on American life?
5. The boundaries of the world began to "shrink" after the event at Kitty Hawk. Why?

3. Large Companies Manage Men, Money, and Markets

In order to understand how industrial companies grew so big and produced such great quantities of goods, it is necessary to observe how they handled their men, money, and markets.

Organization of Big Business

Corporation. The earliest American factories were owned and equipped by individual people who bought the machinery and buildings with their own personal money or entered partnerships with friends. As factories grew, however, they became too expensive to be built by one person's money and some new method had to be adopted. Companies known as *corporations* were formed. Several men would form such a company, and would announce that they were going to establish a business and offer to sell stock in it. People who bought this stock were entitled to a share of the profits of the company when business was good. Aided by the money paid for the stock, the owners built huge factories and carried on their business on a large scale.

Eliminating Competition. Very often the large corporations, in order to reduce competition, would try to control the policies of other corporations in the same business. In this way they could keep prices up and make a larger profit. Various means were used to accomplish this. The simplest was the agreement, by which each competitor agreed to charge standard prices and carry on business in the same way as the other competitors. Another was the pool, by which corporations divided up marketing areas and shared the profits. Another device was the interlocking directorate; that is, the directors of one corporation also sat on the board of directors of a similar corporation. In this way, they could work to coordinate the policies of the two corporations and thus avoid wasteful competition. Sometimes competition was eliminated by means of a merger. This meant that one company simply bought out the entire assets of another.

Trusts and Monopoly. One of the most important devices for gaining control of a whole industry was the *trust*. To form a trust, one large company received the shares of stock owned by the stockholders of other allied companies. In return the stockholders were given "trust certificates" which entitled them to share in the profits of the trust itself. However, the stockholders surrendered their voting rights and could no longer dictate the policies of their respective companies. That power now passed to a group in charge of the trust, known as the board of trustees.

The first trust, and one of the greatest, was the Standard Oil Trust formed by John D. Rockefeller in 1882. The owners of stock in seventy allied companies turned their stock and voting rights over to nine "trustees" including Rockefeller and eight partners. The profits of the seventy-seven companies were pooled and distributed equally to all. Even though one of the companies might operate at a loss temporarily, the profits for the whole great combination made it almost certain that dividends (the amount of money received by investors) would remain high.

It can be easily seen that a trust could soon become a monopoly; that is, it could control everything in its

Henry Ford's first car, his tools, and his equipment in the Detroit shed where he built this automobile.

field and raise prices without fear of competition. As other industries imitated Standard Oil, protests began to arise from the public. By 1890 about fifteen states, mostly in the West and South, had passed laws against trusts and other combinations that prevented free competition.

Regulation of Corporations

The Holding Company. In 1892 the Supreme Court of the State of Ohio forced the Standard Oil Trust to cease its operation in Ohio. Rockefeller evaded the ruling, however, by organizing a *holding company* in New Jersey, where state laws were more favorable to corporations. A holding company buys just enough of the stock of other companies to win control over them. Thus the Standard Oil Company of New Jersey "held" or controlled the other companies in the Standard group.

Sherman Antitrust Act. It soon became apparent that state laws were not effective in controlling monopolies. The national government would have to act. In July, 1890, Congress passed the Sherman Antitrust Act. This act, based upon the power of Congress to regulate interstate commerce, prohibited any combination, trust, or conspiracy which restrained trade or which promoted a monopoly.

Actually, there was little attempt by the courts to enforce the law. In the first eleven years after the passage of the act, only fourteen suits against offending companies were started by the Justice Department, and there were almost no convictions. It was not until the administrations of Presidents Theodore Roosevelt and William Taft that effective action was taken under the Sherman Antitrust Act.

Looking Back

1. Explain how corporations function.
2. What steps were often taken to limit or eliminate competition?
3. How did the formation of giant trusts often create monopolies?
4. By what means is a holding company different from a trust?
5. Discuss the terms of the Sherman Antitrust Act.

The Chapter in Perspective

What Do These Dates and Terms Mean?

typewriter	Bessemer process	automobile	1876
electricity	transatlantic cable	1890	1868
1903	interlocking directorate	airplane	"Drake's Folly"
1834	holding company	corporations	"oil rush"
1866	Sherman Antitrust Act	pool	steel plows
vertical	Age of Steel	merger trust	reaper
combination	telephone	monopoly	

340

Who Are These People?

Carnegie	Sholes
Silliman	Brush
Drake	Edison
Deere	Duryea
McCormick	Ford
Field	Olds
Bell	Wright

Where Are These Places?

Mesabi range	Titusville
Kitty Hawk	

Questions for Study

1. Why was steel an improvement over iron?
2. What are the advantages of a "vertical combination" in business? Can you name one functioning today?
3. How did the early basic uses of oil differ from its use today?
4. For what reasons did Chicago become the center of the meat-packing industry?
5. Account for the shift of many textile plants from New England to the South.
6. Show how one improvement in farming created a need for another which called for further improvement.
7. Which improvement in communication do you consider the most important? Why?
8. List and discuss five changes in the American way of life that came about because of the automobile.
9. How did the location of iron ore and coal deposits and transportation facilities help determine the location of steel centers in America?
10. Where were the early oil fields in the United States located?

Place Yourself in History

Your great-grandfather started the family business in the small New England town that has been home to his descendants for almost one hundred years. Time has brought many changes to the textile factory that you have inherited. Now you are faced with a decision to either rebuild the factory or move it elsewhere. In the outer office are representatives from your native town and from a Southern town. Each seeks your new factory.

What arguments might be given by your fellow townsmen? by the southerners? What will your decision be? Why?

17

The Vanishing Frontier

When the war between North and South ended, the energies of the American people could be directed toward a new task—the settling of the vast area extending from the western borders of the Mississippi Valley across the Great Plains to the far western highlands. The drama of the West is a magnificent one, full of color and adventure, with the parts being played by railroad construction gangs, rugged miners, hard-riding cattlemen and Indians, and shrewd financiers and politicians. Let us raise the curtain on this drama.

1. The Iron Horse Spans a Continent

In 1865 the nation had about 40,000 miles of railroad track, but by 1900 the railroads had laid almost 200,000 miles of track, more than that of all the European countries put together. The railroad was truly significant in the opening up of the North American continent. The new settlers of the plains states depended on the railroad for shipping their crops and cattle and for bringing them necessary manufactured goods. Factories no longer had to be located so near the natural resources that they used. Railroads made it possible to ship large quantities of materials and manufactured goods great distances. All of these things made the country less regional in nature and more truly national in scope.

The "Wedding of the Rails"

The Union Pacific. In 1862, even while the Civil War was being fought, Congress made plans for starting a transcontinental railroad. It authorized

> *An eyewitness to the driving of the "golden Spike" described it this way:*
>
> "When they came to drive the last spike, Governor Stanford, president of the Central Pacific, took the sledge, and the first time he struck he missed the spike and hit the rail.
>
> "What a howl went up! Irish, Chinese, Mexicans, and everybody yelled with delight. 'He missed it. Yee.' The engineers blew the whistles and rang their bells. Then Stanford tried it again and tapped the spike and the telegraph operators had fixed their instruments so that the tap was reported in all the offices east and west, and set bells to tapping in hundreds of towns and cities.... Then Vice President T. C. Durant of the Union Pacific took up the sledge and he missed the spike the first time. Then everybody slapped everybody else and yelled, 'He missed it too, yow!!' "
> —"Reminiscences of Alexander Toponce, Pioneer"

a new company, the Union Pacific, to begin building a line westward from Omaha, Nebraska. Since it was a costly and dangerous project, the government encouraged the builders by granting them twenty square miles of land for each mile of track constructed. The railroad company also got 30-year loans ranging from $16,000 to $48,000 per mile depending on whether the rails were laid on the flat prairie or through difficult mountainous territory. Work started slowly, but when the war ended in 1865, the rails were laid down at a furious pace by Irish, German, and Chinese immigrant workers.

The Central Pacific. By the 1860's the population of California had increased greatly, and the people were demanding better connections with the East. Men such as Leland Stanford and Collis Huntington promoted the Central Pacific Railway and secured government subsidies to start their line eastward. This road began construction even before the Union Pacific, setting out from Sacramento and heading across the Sierra Nevada mountains.

When the completion of the first transcontinental railway linked the oceans, a photographer made this picture of the ceremony. East-bound and West-bound locomotives touched cow-catchers and the golden spike was driven. Of the occasion, Robert Louis Stevenson, British author, wrote: "It seems to me as if this railroad were the one typical achievement of the age in which we live, as if it brought together into one plot all the ends of the world and all degrees of social rank...."

An 1870 freight train pulled by the "American" 4-4-0 engine, which had four small front wheels, four large driving wheels, and no wheels beneath the cab. The "balloon" smokestack was wide enough to catch sparks thrown off by burning wood.

The company imported thousands of Chinese to make the roadbed and lay the rails.

Linking the Oceans. Railroads were built under tremendous handicaps. The men had to lay track through mountain ranges, cross the scorching desert, and fight off hostile Indians. The job required great physical endurance and engineering skills. Little by little the two lines drew closer; the Union Pacific under the direction of Grenville Dodge, the Central Pacific under Theodore Judah. At last, in May, 1869, the "wedding of the rails" took place at Promontory Point in Utah

One of the first Pullman sleeping cars. It contained a stove and washroom at each end. A berth cost $2.00 per night.

Territory. The railroads held a lively ceremony which included toasts with champagne and the driving of a golden spike by Leland Stanford. They sent the news eastward by telegraph and the whole country rejoiced. The Union Pacific had laid 1086 miles of track, the Central Pacific, 689. Now a railroad linked the Atlantic with the Pacific!

An Expanding Network

Within a generation other transcontinental lines were built with the help of the national or state governments. The Southern Pacific ran from San Francisco to San Antonio and New Orleans. The Northern Pacific went from St. Paul and Minneapolis to Portland, Oregon, and Tacoma, Washington. The Atchison, Topeka and Santa Fe linked Atchison, Kansas, and San Diego, California. The Great Northern, founded by James J. Hill without the help of the government, extended from St. Paul, Minnesota, to Portland, Oregon.

The older Eastern railroad networks were also expanded. Beginning in 1862,

"Commodore" Cornelius Vanderbilt, who had already made a fortune in steamboating, built railroads between New York and Chicago and created the New York Central. The Pennsylvania Railroad and the Baltimore and Ohio built other roads extending their control to the Middle West. The development of these railroads helped the country by speeding up industrialization, stimulating mining and agriculture, opening new markets, and spurring the growth of cities and towns.

Advances in Railroading

Travel by rail became safer and more convenient as new devices came into use. One improvement was the steel rail, which replaced the softer iron tracks. At first the tracks were laid in various widths, but later a standard width (4 feet, 8 1/2 inches) was adopted. It was thus easier to switch cars from one line to another. Cars were made heavier and locomotives more powerful. In 1865 George Pullman built the first sleeping car. George Westinghouse patented the compressed air brake in 1869 and soon most companies were using his braking equipment. The many terrible train wrecks of the early days were later reduced by automatic signal systems, stronger coupling devices, and the use of a second set of tracks where railroad traffic was heavy.

Corrupt Practices

Crédit Mobilier. Some of the practices of corrupt promoters turned the public against the railroads. One of the most famous examples of dishonesty was uncovered by an investigation of the Crédit Mobilier (Mo-BEEL'yer) in 1872. This was a construction company formed by men who were also directors of the Union Pacific. As directors of the railroad, they awarded very profit-

When were the first and second great upsurges in railroad mileage? Can you offer any explanation for these increases? Why was railroad growth relatively slow during 1860–1870?

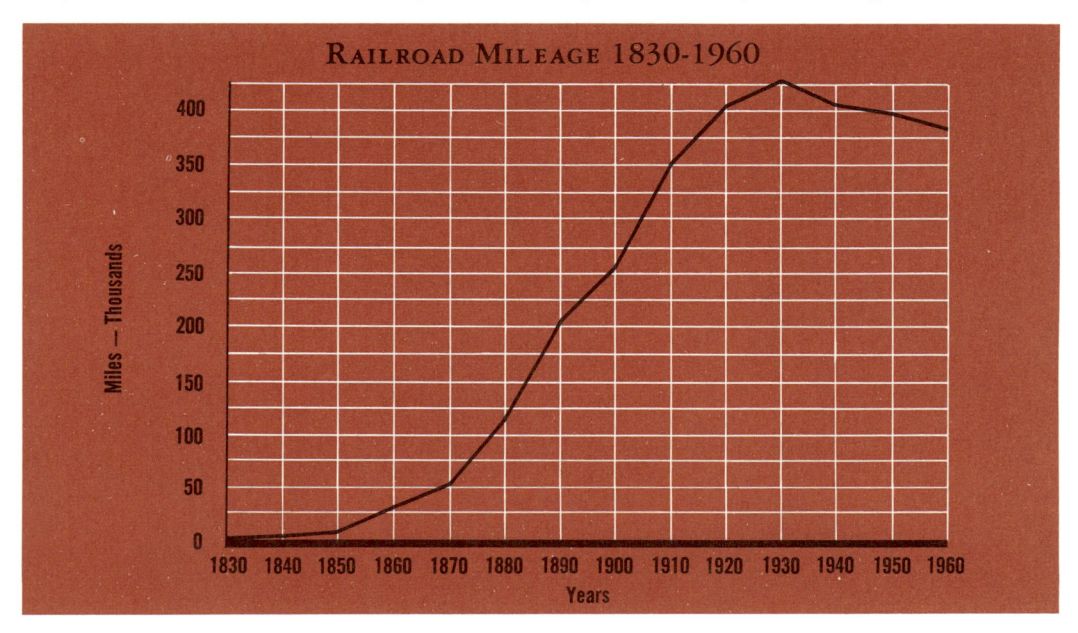

RAILROAD MILEAGE 1830-1960

able contracts to the Crédit Mobilier. The construction company then drained away the money which the railroad had received from the government and from private investors. In order to protect themselves from investigation, the promoters gave shares in the company to such high government officials as Vice-President Schuyler Colfax.

Need for Government Control. Some railroads used the land they had been given for questionable purposes. For example, sometimes railroads sold for large profits land which they had received free or at small cost from the government. The money which they received for this was used not for sound construction of lines, but to buy more land which they then could resell. Needless to say, this practice benefited no one but the railroad owners. Others ran into debt because of wasteful competition and inefficient

Why could the Union Pacific lay so much more track than the Central Pacific? Can you think of any geographical reasons? How much track was laid by each railroad?

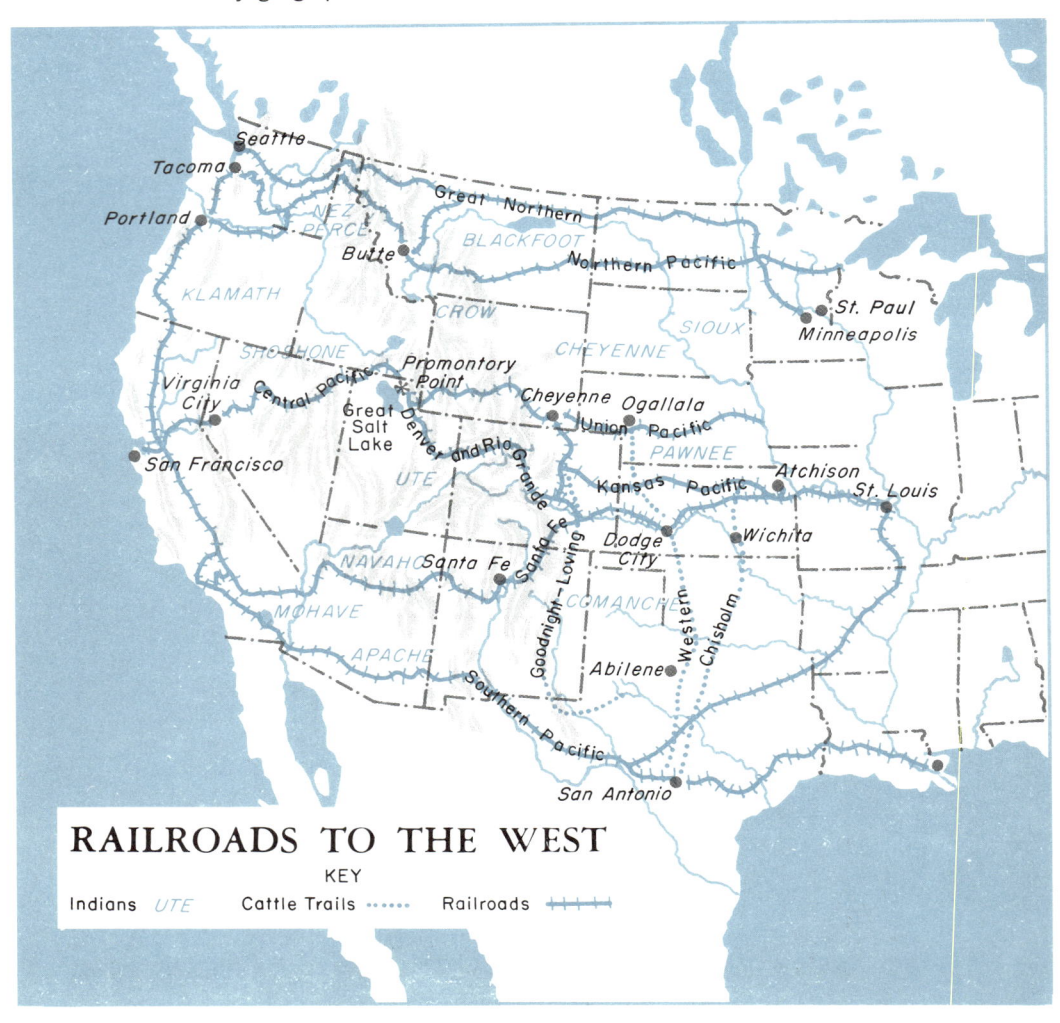

RAILROADS TO THE WEST

KEY

Indians *UTE*   Cattle Trails ······   Railroads ┤┤┤┤┤

management. Others angered farmers by overcharging them. Sometimes they offered to return a part of the rate to big shippers. This was known as a rebate. Stock speculators like Jay Gould, James Fisk, and Daniel Drew became rich at the expense of smaller stockholders. Some lines made secret agreements to raise their rates and then "pooled" their profits. Others cut their rates in areas where they had to meet competition and made up losses by overcharging on non-competing branches. Issuing free passes and offering bribes to legislators and judges was a fairly common practice.

Such dishonest practices led to organized protest, especially by the farmers. Through the Grange, to which most of the farmers belonged, they fought for controls to protect themselves and all small shippers from excessive freight rates. Through state legislatures, which the Grange controlled in most of the Midwest, they were able to pass laws limiting unfair practices. Finally, in 1887 the Congress passed the Interstate Commerce Act which exercised federal control over all interstate shipments.

Looking Back

1. How did the growth of the railroads affect the expansion of America and its economy?

2. For what reasons did the government decide to make loans and grants of land to private railroad builders?

3. Name several of the leading railroads constructed during this period. Are they in operation today? Why?

4. What early improvements were made to make the railroads safer and faster?

5. List and explain the complaints made against the railroads.

2. Cattle Kings Have Their Day

The Long Drive

The open range—that is, the vast unclaimed grasslands of the Great Plains—was the home of the Cattle Kingdom. The cattle industry began in Texas, where several million hardy, longhorned cattle, descended from stock brought in by the Spaniards, roamed freely. From the Mexicans, the Americans learned the techniques of cattle raising, branding, roping, and roundups. After the Civil War, ranchers began to organize huge herds for the "Long Drive" to various railheads in Missouri and Kansas. From there they were shipped to the great stockyards at Kansas City and Chicago. The story of the "Long Drive" is one of the most fascinating chapters in the history of the West.

In the spring of 1866 a group of Texas cattle raisers experimented in driving a large herd to a distant market at Sedalia, Missouri. There they were to be loaded on the Missouri Pacific Railroad for shipment to the Chicago slaughter houses. Although many of the animals were lost to Indians, outlaws, and cattle fever, enough survived to prove that the long journey could

A grizzled cowboy herds longhorn cattle across the Great Plains. "Longhorns," brought by the Spanish, were lean and mean. They have been replaced by shorter, heavier stock.

yield profits. Abilene, Kansas, became a favorite terminal point for herds which started from San Antonio and followed the Chisholm Trail. Dodge City and Wichita became flourishing market outlets in Kansas, as did Ogallala in Nebraska and Cheyenne in Wyoming.

From Range to Ranch

The drives brought rich profits. This caused Eastern and foreign businessmen to invest in the cattle industry,

---

A cowboy describes his experiences on the "long trail."

"On the trail we were each allowed to take a pair of bed blankets and a sack containing a little extra clothing. No more load than was considered actually necessary was to be allowed on the wagon, for there would be no wagon road over most of the country which we were to traverse, and there was plenty of rough country, with creeks and steep-banked rivers to be crossed. We had no tents or shelter of any sort other than our blankets. Our food and cooking utensils were the same as those used in cow camps of the brush country. No provision was made for the care of men in case of accident. Should anyone become injured, wounded, or sick, he would be strictly 'out of luck.' A quick recovery and a sudden death were the only desirable alternatives in such cases, for much of the time the outfit would be far from the settlements and from medical or surgical aid."

—James H. Cook, *Fifty Years on the Old Frontier* (University of Oklahoma Press) 1923, 39–40.

and the result was overproduction and a fall in prices. Already pressed by farmers and sheepherders who were demanding their share of the public domain, the cattlemen slowly abandoned the long drives. The famous trails—Chisholm, Western, Sedalia, and Goodnight-Loving—were no longer used. Between 1885 and 1887 the Great Plains suffered from terrible droughts and blizzards which brought ruin to many cattlemen.

The golden age of the cowboy came to an end. Cattlemen began to fence in their holdings, raise hay for winter feed, and develop fatter breeds which could be kept in one place until prices were high. The open range gave way to huge ranches, some of which are still in existence. The largest is the King Ranch in southern Texas, which covers an area larger than the entire state of Rhode Island. Another famous ranch, founded on an island which was not then a part of the United States, is the Parker Ranch in Hawaii.

By 1890 the open-range period was finished. According to the federal census of that year, there was no longer a Western frontier. The Great Plains had been conquered!

Looking Back

1. What was meant by the "long drive"?
2. To what perils were the cattle exposed on the "long drive"?
3. Why did the cattle raisers fight to maintain the open range?
4. For what reasons might the cowboys have sung "Don't Fence Me In"?

3. Natural Wealth Helps to Populate the West

Gold, Silver, and Copper Strikes

The discovery of precious metals played an important part in the opening of the West, especially in the years between 1858 and 1880. Gold was still being mined in California when the news came of gold and silver strikes in Colorado and Nevada. Californians and Easterners rushed into the Pikes Peak district and then into the area of the fabulous Comstock Lode at Virginia City, Nevada. Other strikes were made in Montana and Idaho. Soon the mining frontier became dotted with boomtowns, where life was boisterous and exciting, and very often short.

In 1864 rich veins of copper were found near Butte, Montana. Ten years later a great gold strike was made in the Black Hills of southwestern Dakota Territory. Thousands of prospectors flocked into this area by stagecoach and horseback, since it was then beyond reach of the railroads. West of the Great Lakes, in Minnesota, huge deposits of iron ore were uncovered, attracting more thousands of eager adventurers.

When the first gold prospectors arrived at the scene of a strike, they would skim off the surface metal by washing the ore in pans. Then they would move on to other likely spots. After the surface deposits were worked out, big corporations would bring in expensive machinery to dig out and smash the gold-bearing quartz. Finally, the area would be abandoned, the population would decline, and only ghost towns would remain. Some of the mining towns lived on, however, and became flourishing cities.

The Wild West

Many of the boomtowns had very picturesque names, such as Spearfish, Deadwood, and Tombstone. Life in the towns was hard and dangerous. In gambling places and saloons there gathered the desperadoes, gunmen, sheriffs, and murderers whose names are familiar to most Americans—Wild Bill Hickok, Wyatt Earp, Calamity Jane, Buffalo Bill Cody, "Billy the Kid" Bonney, and many others. It was a colorful life that now lives on only in the literature of the day—books like Mark Twain's *Roughing It*—or in the somewhat inaccurate portrayals on television.

Although the miner was soon replaced by the farmer, he played an important role in the history of the West. His discoveries attracted thousands of men who remained as settlers. The gold and silver from the mines helped to put the currency of the country on a sound basis. Mining stimulated the building of railroads. The adventures of the miners furnished materials which became part of American literature and folklore.

Lumbering

Still another source of wealth tempted settlers into the West. Already the Eastern forests had begun to thin out, and lumber and pulp for making paper were becoming scarce. North of the great prairies spread extensive forests, and there Western lumber camps were established. Strong, hardy men occupied the camps for years at a time, felling the timber with axes and with saws, dragging it to streams and rivers down which it would float to the paper pulp mills and the sawmills. Lumbering was carried on in winter as well as summer, for the snow made an easy surface over which to drag heavy logs on great sleighs.

As time went on the lumbering industry began to thin out the Western forests, as it had those in the East. At last it became evident that if something were not done, most of the valuable trees would be gone, and the United States would suffer from a great

The pony express lasted only 18 months, but it is one of the most romantic stories in American history. Young, courageous riders, changing horses every 15 miles, sped the mail across the central U.S.

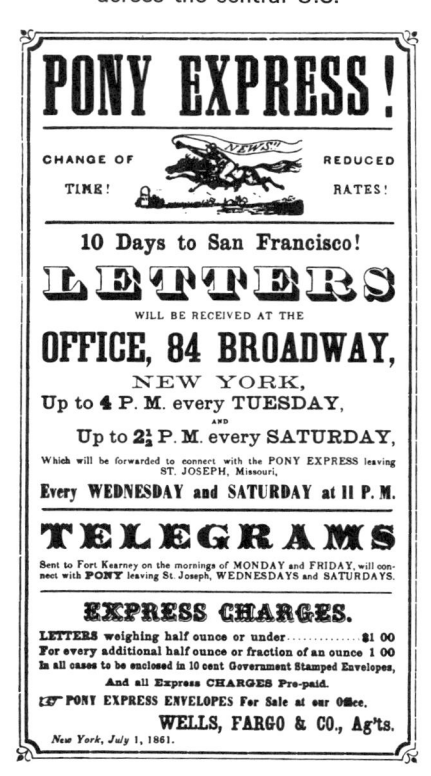

PONY EXPRESS!

CHANGE OF TIME! REDUCED RATES!

10 Days to San Francisco!

LETTERS

WILL BE RECEIVED AT THE

OFFICE, 84 BROADWAY,

NEW YORK,

Up to 4 P. M. every TUESDAY,

AND

Up to 2½ P. M. every SATURDAY,

Which will be forwarded to connect with the PONY EXPRESS leaving ST. JOSEPH, Missouri,

Every WEDNESDAY and SATURDAY at 11 P. M.

TELEGRAMS

Sent to Fort Kearney on the mornings of MONDAY and FRIDAY, will connect with PONY leaving St. Joseph, WEDNESDAYS and SATURDAYS.

EXPRESS CHARGES.

LETTERS weighing half ounce or under.............. $1 00
For every additional half ounce or fraction of an ounce 1 00
In all cases to be enclosed in 10 cent Government Stamped Envelopes,
And all Express CHARGES Pre-paid.

☞ PONY EXPRESS Envelopes For Sale at our Office.

WELLS, FARGO & CO., Ag'ts.

New York, July 1, 1861.

As railroads made it possible for lumber to be transported, the lumber business grew. It was also one of the important suppliers of railroad materials. Ties and trestles, such as those in the picture, were made of wood.

lumber shortage. Even worse, the removal of the protecting forest cover permitted the rain water to run off the land too quickly, washing away fertile topsoil and causing disastrous floods. A movement, called reforestation, was started and is still developing to replace those trees that have been cut so that there will always be a supply. Such a farsighted policy means continued prosperity to the lumbering industry, plentiful lumber for the country in the years to come, the conservation of soil, and protection against floods.

Looking Back

1. What valuable metal deposits played an important part in the opening of the West?

2. Why did many locations quickly change from "boomtowns" to "ghost towns"?

3. How did these mining discoveries affect the economy of the nation?

4. Explain why reforestation and conservation became necessary in the lumbering industry.

4. The Indians Make a Last Stand

When the miners and cattlemen pushed into the last frontier, they met resistance from the Plains Indians, who were fiercer and more warlike than the Woods Indians in the East. Superb horsemen and good shots, this "light cavalry" of the plains was able to fight off the United States Army for almost twenty years after the Civil War.

Subduing the Red Man

To tell the full story of the Sioux, Cheyenne, Arapaho, Comanche, Blackfoot, Crow, Pawnee, and Nez Percé would take another book. Their leaders' names live in our country's history —Geronimo, Cochise, Little Crow, Black Kettle, Red Cloud, Sitting Bull, Rain-in-the-Face, Crazy Horse, Wovoka, and Chief Joseph. Eventually they were all subdued, partly by the slaughter of the great buffalo herds which supplied them with food, partly by the diseases of the white man, and partly by the superior weapons of the army and the white settlers.

The fierce Plains Indian warrior of 1870 stands in sharp contrast to the peaceful Navajo shepherds in Monument Valley, Arizona, today.

For years the Indians had been driven farther and farther to the west by the frontier of the white man's civilization. Promises of permanent rights to large tracts of land were given to many Indian tribes, which the government treated as separate nations. However, the promises were not kept, and as the Indian lands were gradually used for other purposes, the Indians themselves were forced into smaller and smaller reservations.

Finally the government forced or persuaded the Indians to live on reservations in the Indian Territory, Dakota Territory, and other places. Here they were supposed to give up hunting and take up farming, while the government helped them with supplies of food and clothing. In 1871 Congress abolished the practice of treating the tribes as separate nations, hoping to break the ties of tribal loyalty which bound Indians of the same group together.

The Great Sioux Uprising. Some of the Indians refused to stay on the res-

Washakie, Chief of the Shoshone tribe, stands with his warriors in front of their teepees. When the Buffalo were killed, the Shoshones were forced into reservation life.

ervations and continued to attack white settlements and army detachments. One of the most famous battles took place in Montana, where the Sioux Indians under Sitting Bull and Crazy Horse led a great uprising in 1876. Three army columns were sent to round them up. Colonel George A. Custer, commanding the Seventh Cavalry, was ordered to cut off the Sioux retreat toward the Big Horn Mountains. His plan failed, however, and he and his force of over 200 men were trapped by 2500 warriors under Sitting Bull. Custer and all of his men were killed.

A New Way of Life. In 1887 Congress made another attempt to force the Indians to follow the way of the white man by passing the Dawes Severalty Act. This act authorized the President to divide the tribal lands, giving 160 acres to each head of a family and smaller pieces to others. The holdings were to be held in trust by the government for twenty-five years to prevent their being sold before the family could adopt white customs. Each landholder could become a citizen of the United States.

The plan met with varying success, although it was difficult for most of the Indians to adopt new ways. It was not until 1924 that full rights of citizenship were given to all Indians.

Looking Back

1. Why did the Indians fight against the coming of the white man?
2. Do you feel that the Plains Indians received a fair deal from the government? Why?
3. How did the government attempt to aid the Indians by the Davies Act?
4. When did the Indians get full rights of American citizenship?

The Chapter in Perspective

Who Are These People?
Stanford
Huntington
Hill
Vanderbilt
Pullman
Custer
Westinghouse
Gould
Fisk
Sitting Bull
Crazy Horse

Where Are These Places?
Sacramento
Black Hills
Butte
Promontory Point
Virginia City

What Do These Dates and Terms Mean?
Union Pacific
Central Pacific
1869
1887
Great Northern
sleeping car
air brake
New York Central
Dawes Severalty Act
Interstate Commerce Commission
1876
Crédit Mobilier
long drive
open range
Comstock Lode
reforestation

Questions for Study

1. Did the farmers need the railroads more than the railroads needed the farmers? Why?
2. How did the building of the transcontinental railroads affect the flow of immigrants to America?
3. What reasons can you give for all railroads using the same track width?
4. Discuss the purposes and effects of the Crédit Mobilier.
5. Why did "pooling" by the railroads anger shippers?
6. Tell why the rapidly growing area was often called the "Wild West."
7. What effects did a careless program of lumbering have on our natural resources?
8. As an Indian, would you have accepted life on a reservation? Why?
9. Why was it natural for certain locations mentioned in this chapter to become transportation centers?
10. What western state or territory would you have selected to migrate to in 1890? Why?

Place Yourself in History

The year is 1876. As chieftain of your tribe, you are attending an important war council. Gathered together with you are the chiefs of the leading tribes. You have heard Sitting Bull and Crazy Horse call for war against the white man. Other chiefs have been unwilling to agree for one reason or another.

Now it is your turn to speak. All eyes are on you, for you are a chief whose opinion is respected.

What would you have said? Why?

18

The Farmer and the Land

One of the most important economic events in the nineteenth century was the revolution that took place in agriculture. At the time of the Civil War farmers began to use machinery on their farms, partly because so many of their laborers were called away to fight. This mechanization made it possible for the farmer to harvest great crops to feed the growing population of the cities. Soon over-production, both in America and abroad, drove prices down, and the farmers began to suffer. They complained of unjust treatment by the banks, the railroads, and the middlemen who stored and sold their crops. Finally they joined in forming pressure groups to persuade Congress to pass laws which would favor their interests.

1. Expansion of Agriculture Brings Problems

At first the farmers were reluctant to spend their hard-earned dollars for the new machines that appeared on the market. They soon realized, however, that machinery would help them to supply not only their own needs but also to supply a profitable market in the growing cities. Between 1860 and 1900 farmers put millions of new acres under cultivation. Prices for farm products were so high that growers began to specialize in a single crop such as cotton, corn, or wheat. By raising large volumes of a high-priced crop, the farmer felt he could make more money.

Over-Production and the One-Crop System

As the farmer turned to a one-crop system, concentrating on oats, wheat, corn, or hogs in the Middle West, cotton or tobacco in the South, and wool in the Mountain states, he found him-

FARMING BECOMES EFFICIENT

[Bar chart showing Hours Per Acre for various crops, comparing Hand vs Machine methods:
- Wheat: 1830 (hand) ~60, 1890 (machine) ~3
- Oats: 1830 (hand) ~65, 1890 (machine) ~7
- Cotton: 1841 (hand) ~175, 1890 (machine) ~78
- Corn: 1855 (hand) ~40, 1890 (machine) ~20
- Potatoes: 1866 (hand) ~105, 1890 (machine) ~40
- Rice: 1870 (hand) ~62, 1890 (machine) ~18]

Machines made a revolutionary difference in the harvesting of crops. Which crop benefited most? Why? Which crop still took a relatively long time to harvest? Why? Which of the crops were most important in 1890? Which today?

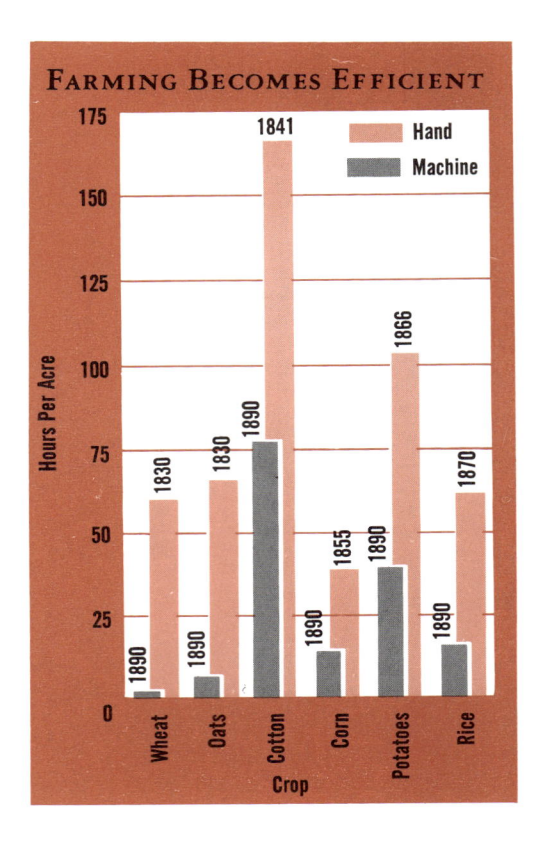

self in the same position as that of the manufacturer who sold only one specialty. When prices were high, he was confident and happy. But the American farmer began to produce more than the home market could use, so he had to depend upon export sales to foreign countries. However, other countries—especially Brazil, Argentina, Canada, Australia, New Zealand, and Russia—were also learning how to produce more abundant crops. When sharp competition, both at home and abroad, brought down prices, the American farmer found himself in trouble, since he depended completely on one crop.

Wasted Resources. When the one-crop system had exhausted his land, the farmer abandoned it and moved to fresh soil. He did this because it was easier than fertilizing the old soil or raising a different crop in each field each year so as to preserve the richness of the ground. If all trees in an area are cut down and if the soil is not plowed properly, the open lands become eroded—that is, rains and overflowing streams cut deep gullies into them. Because of careless and wasteful methods of farming, and because of the one-crop system, great areas of America became barren and useless.

A Lesson from Industry. In his struggle to find a profitable market for his crops, the farmer did not have the same advantages as the manufacturer. So that he could ensure a ready market for his goods, the manufacturer successfully attempted to persuade Congress to pass high tariff (tax on imported materials) laws to keep foreign goods from entering the country. Furthermore, manufacturers had learned how to combine their efforts by means of trusts and holding companies so as to control prices. The farmer, on the other hand, was slow to engage in cooperative measures to regulate production and prices. Manufacturers held a third advantage since they could predict fairly accurately how much they would be able to produce in a given year and how much the demand would be. The farmer was at the mercy of Mother Nature. Very often his crops would be ruined by floods, droughts, or the ravages of grasshoppers and other insects.

A problem that has plagued farmers continually is that of soil erosion. This eroded gulley in Missouri was caused by rainwater runoff and wind. In 1880 very little could be done about the problem. Today scientists and agricultural experts like the men in the picture are finding answers.

Financial Plight of the Farmers

Farm Mortgages. In addition to his other troubles, the farmer found it difficult to borrow money to tide him over a bad season. As he fell deeper into debt, he was forced to mortgage his property. Loan companies and banks based in Eastern states were ready to lend, but they charged high rates of interest, ranging from eight to twenty-five per cent and occasionally as high as forty per cent per year. This interest went back to the already prosperous East. If the unlucky farmer could not meet his mortgage, he had to stand by while his property was auctioned off by the sheriff. Many farmers became rent-paying tenants instead of landowners. By 1880 one-fourth of the country's farms were operated by tenants, and by the 1890's slightly more than one-fourth of the privately owned farms were weighted

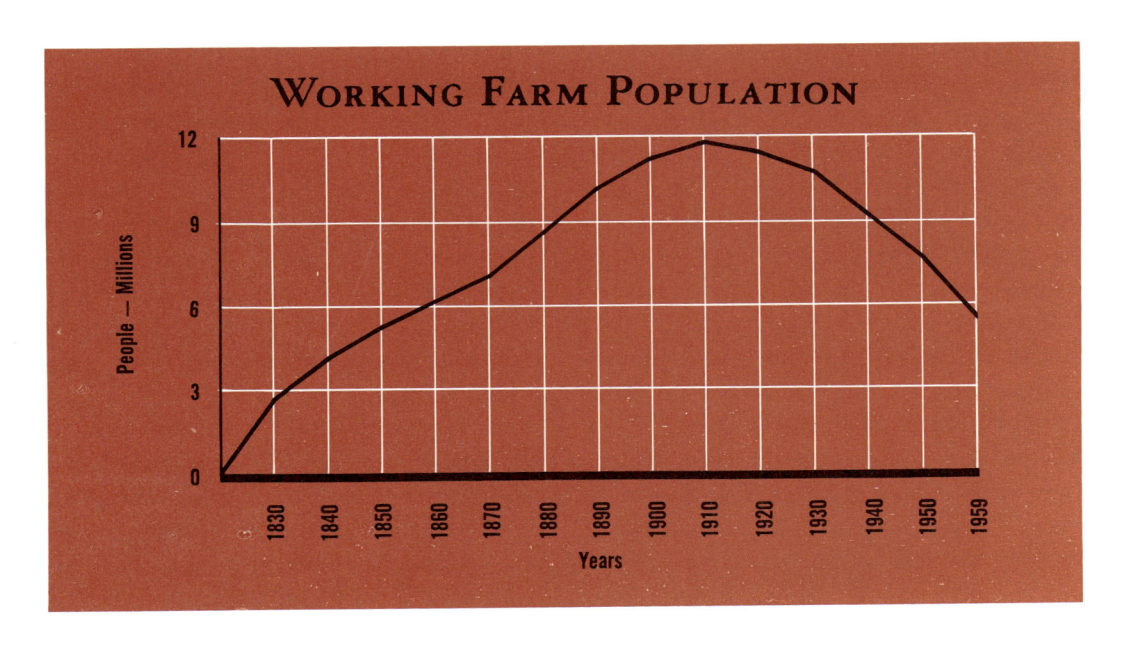

WORKING FARM POPULATION

A sod house might use up an acre of heavy prairie sod, cut from the ground by a turning plow into pieces of 2' by 3'. Inside walls were "plastered" with clay and ashes.

down by mortgages held by Easterners. It was no wonder that farmers grew to hate the Eastern loan sharks and bankers who grew richer while they grew poorer.

The Railroads. Another grievance of the farmer was that against the railroads, on which he depended absolutely for the transportation of his crops to the great marketing and storage centers like Chicago. Often the railroads charged higher rates for grain shipments than for others, and freight rates were higher in the West and South than in the Northeast. Sometimes the rates were so high that farmers found it cheaper to let crops rot or use them for fuel. The farmers also rebelled against excessive storage rates in the grain elevators and warehouses owned by the railroads or by middlemen.

A Hard and Lonely Life

The farmers' resentment against the railroads and the "moneymasters" of the East was made sharper by the fact that his daily life was often bare and comfortless. In the early days, at least, the Western dirt farmer lived in a small house built of sod dug from the prairie, or of logs from the trees that he had cleared away. He had few schools, churches, or libraries. Weather conditions and poor roads often prevented him from visiting neighbors or journeying to the country store to buy supplies. It was a lonely life, particularly hard on women and children. As time went on these conditions improved, but still the farmer felt that he should be better rewarded for his efforts to feed the nation. He believed that his situation was not understood by the public.

Looking Back

1. How did the one-crop system bring both wealth and trouble to farmers?
2. What were the advantages held by the manufacturers over the farmers in their respective activities?
3. Explain what a mortgage is.
4. Why did the farmers often complain about the railroads?
5. Show how the life of the early western farmer was a hard and lonely one.
6. How did foreign agriculture affect the position of the American farmer?

2. Farmers Organize for Self-Improvement

The Grange

As a means of bettering their hard lot, the farmers at last decided to organize themselves into a group that could force the state and national government to pass laws that would help them. The leading spirit in this movement was Oliver H. Kelley, a government clerk in the Department of Agriculture in Washington. Since he had been a farmer himself, he understood the problems of rural life. In 1867 he started the National Grange of the Patrons of Husbandry—more widely known as the Grange.

Growth of Movement. Not only farmers but anyone interested in agriculture, including small-town storekeepers and professional men, could belong to the Grange. It was a secret fraternal order for both men and women, founded originally for social and educational purposes. The movement grew rapidly, especially during the hard times of the mid-1870's. At the height of its growth it had nearly a million members who met in 21,000 local lodges, or "granges," scattered throughout the country. At these lodge meetings the members were entertained by speeches and theatrical performances, and enjoyed the opportunity of discussing problems that concerned all of them.

Political Activity. It was natural that a group like this would turn to politics. Soon they were busily working to influence elections and get laws passed for the regulation of railroads. They also wanted lower rates for grain storage, better educational facilities for rural areas, and many other useful reforms. In order to reduce farmers' costs, they tried to organize cooperative stores and warehouses and to manufacture their own harvesting machin-

This Grange meeting hall, located in Hardin County, Ohio, is typical of others across the nation's farmbelt. The Grange is still an active force on the American rural scene.

ery. The movement was popular with farmers, and the Granges continue to be active today, although their interests are mainly social rather than political.

The National Farmers' Alliance

Granger Laws. In 1887, twenty years after the founding of the Grange, a similar organization was established. This was the National Farmers' Alliance. Its aims, purposes, and methods were much like those of the Grange, and the two organizations worked hand in hand. In effect they were much like labor unions. The various state branches, backed by the great body of farmers, succeeded in passing Granger laws in many of the states to control the railroads and ensure fair prices and no discrimination. This improved conditions greatly for a time, but in 1886 the Supreme Court decided that no state had the right to regulate a railroad whose lines extended beyond that state's boundaries. Since practically all important railroads crossed state borders, this decision effectively killed the Granger laws, and the farmers continued to suffer.

The Interstate Commerce Act. In 1887, due largely to the influence of the Grangers, Congress passed the Interstate Commerce Act which provided that the railroads must not charge unreasonable rates; that they must not charge one person more than another; and that a group of five men was to be appointed, called the Interstate Commerce Commission, to hear complaints against the railroads and to make sure that the railroads obeyed the laws.

The Interstate Commerce Commission also benefited the railroads because it eliminated disastrous price wars.

In addition to these great changes, the Grange and the Farmers' Alliance have also been active in supplying the farmers with literature on the best ways to carry on the farming industry and to maintain health in farming communities. They have done much to improve the life of the farmer throughout the country.

Looking Back

1. For what reasons was the Grange founded? Why did it grow?
2. What steps were taken by the Grange to achieve its goals?
3. How did the Supreme Court nullify much of the progress made by the Granger laws?
4. By what means did the Interstate Commerce Act curb the power of the railroads?

3. Western Farmers Demand Cheap Money

The Greenback Party

The Western farmers, also made themselves felt in another way. "Greenbacks," the paper dollars which the United States government had been issuing since 1862, were worth less than gold during the 1870's. This was because the people of the country did not have confidence that the government would stand back of them to their full value. For their few dollars in gold, the farmers felt that they could get a great many more paper dollars and would thus be able to pay their debts more easily.

For this reason they founded the Greenback party, whose platform, in 1876, provided for the issuing of more paper money. Their candidate, however, was not successful. Three years after the election, in 1879, paper money returned to the same value as gold when the government announced that all paper dollars would be exchanged at the Treasury for their face value in gold.

The Populist Party

By 1890 the farmers' protests about the money question had reached a fever pitch, especially in Kansas, Nebraska, and the Dakotas. Farmers listened eagerly as reformers and orators blasted the Eastern financiers, the railroads and trusts, the gold standard, and the conservative Republicans and Democrats who refused to do anything about the farm problem. The crusade took definite form when the discontented farmers resolved to form a national political party as a challenge to the two older parties.

National Convention. This party, which adopted the name of People's (Populist) party, sprang from the "grass roots" and was one of the most important third parties in American history. It held its first convention in Omaha, Nebraska, in 1892, and nominated General James B. Weaver of Iowa as its candidate for President and James G. Field of Virginia as its

Front and back of "Greenback" dollar, Aug. 1, 1862. These dollars are among the first ever issued.

candidate for Vice-President. Present at the convention were delegates from the Grange, the Farmers' Alliance, and labor unions.

Importance of Platform. The platform (principles on which the party stood) adopted at the convention is a very interesting one because it called for a number of reforms which have been adopted since. Among these were (1) a graduated income tax that would force the wealthy to contribute more heavily to the cost of government, (2) the direct election of United States Senators by popular vote rather than by state legislatures, (3) a postal savings system that citizens could use instead of privately owned banks, (4) a secret ballot to protect voters from outside pressures, (5) proposals that would give voters a chance to tell their elected officials which laws should be passed and which should be abolished

—that is, the "initiative" and the "referendum."

Other demands in the Populist platform clearly reflected the influence of the farmers: (1) putting more money into circulation by means of silver and paper money issued by the Federal Treasury, (2) government ownership of all transportation and communication facilities, (3) the forbidding of aliens to own land. In an effort to win the support of organized labor, the Populists inserted planks into the platform calling for a shorter working day, the abolition of strikebreaking agencies, and the restriction of immigration. The Populist party, like most third-party movements in American history, performed a valuable service in publicizing necessary reforms many of which the major parties later adopted.

The Populists in Politics. In the election of 1892 the Democratic candidate, Grover Cleveland, defeated the Republican candidate, Benjamin Harrison, by an electoral count of 277 to 145. The Populist candidate, James Weaver, received 22 electoral votes and a popular vote of 1,041,028—a very respectable showing for a third party. All twenty-two of Weaver's electoral votes came from states located west of the Mississippi River.

In the campaign of 1896, the Populists supported William Jennings Bryan for President. He was also the candidate of the Democrat and Free Silver parties, but he was defeated by William McKinley, a Republican.

Looking Back

1. What were the greenbacks? Why did they present a problem?
2. Name the groups who joined together under the banner of the Populist party.
3. List and explain the planks of the Omaha platform that have since become law.
4. List and explain the planks of the Omaha platform that never became national law.
5. Who were the opposing candidates in the elections of 1892 and 1896?

4. The Country Deals with the Silver Question

Free Coinage of Silver

The argument over the coining of silver was not new. Beginning in 1792, the Treasury Department of the government had accepted raw silver and gold and had exchanged for them an equal weight of coined silver and gold dollars. The process was called "free-coinage." It had the effect of making silver and gold dollars equal in value in America. The gold dollar at this time contained only one-fifteenth as much gold as a silver dollar contained silver. This was known as "the ratio of 15 to 1."

The 16:1 Ratio. It was soon seen that the ratio of 15 to 1 was not correct. Because gold was worth more than fifteen times as much as silver on the world market, many Americans were shipping gold to foreign countries. In exchange, they received a little more than fifteen times the weight of their gold in silver. To stop this, Congress passed a law in 1834 providing for a ratio of 16 to 1. This meant that the gold dollar would now contain only one-sixteenth as much gold as the silver dollar contained silver.

The law of 1834 made too great a change, for gold was not worth sixteen times as much as silver. Many Americans, therefore, started shipping silver abroad, and received in exchange slightly more than one-sixteenth as much gold.

To put a stop to this making of profits at government expense, Congress passed a law in 1853 reducing the amount of silver in the fifty-cent piece, the quarter, and the dime, though the silver dollar itself remained unchanged. As a result, these lesser coins remained in circulation instead of being shipped abroad.

Adoption of the Gold Standard

In 1873 Congress passed a law providing that the free coining of silver should stop and that the gold dollar alone should, from this time on, be the only standard of money value in the United States. Such acts had already been passed by the leading European nations, and the United States was merely following their example in adopting a gold standard. At the time, no one cared very much, for jewelers and silversmiths were paying more for silver than the government had been paying.

New Discoveries in the West. Soon after 1870, great deposits of silver were found in the West, and so much of this metal was produced that its value began to drop. The silver dollars which had once been worth as much as gold dollars now fell off in value until the silver in them was worth only about sixty cents.

Both sides of an early American ten dollar gold piece—1795, about two years after they were first issued.

The Bland-Allison Act. During the 1870's when the new sources of silver were discovered in Nevada and other Western states, the jewelers and silversmiths could no longer use all of the silver that was mined, and the price dropped far below that which the government had been paying. The owners of silver mines and the many farmers of the West loudly demanded a continued free coinage. At last, in 1878, the sentiment for silver grew so strong that Congress passed the Bland-Allison Act providing that the United States should buy silver at the rate of "not less than $2,000,000 worth per month, nor more than $4,000,000 worth," and should coin it into silver dollars at the ratio of 16 to 1.

The Sherman Silver Act. In spite of the great amounts of silver bought by the government under the Bland-

Allison Act, those who favored a silver standard were not satisfied. Accordingly, in 1890, Congress passed the Sherman Silver Act, providing that the Treasury Department should buy each month, at the market price, not less than 4,500,000 ounces of silver and should pay for it by issuing paper money redeemable in either gold or silver coin, whichever the Secretary of the Treasury preferred.

Panic of 1893. The country was soon deluged with paper money, and so many people promptly turned it in for its value in gold that the gold supply of the Treasury grew dangerously low. The fear then spread that when the gold was gone the notes would be redeemed in silver, which might fall in value. This loss of confidence caused a decline in prices and in business, and many banks and business houses failed. Large numbers of people were thrown out of work, and the country suffered greatly from the panic of 1893.

Cleveland's Solution. The cause of the panic of 1893 was very apparent to President Grover Cleveland. He was a man of wisdom and of sound business principles, and he saw that silver was not only threatening business but was also threatening to drain all of the gold from the country. The foreign nations and foreign business houses were demanding gold in payment for their goods. Also, many American citizens were cashing in their paper money for gold and were hoarding the gold out of circulation. Little by little the gold coin was being drawn from the Treasury, leaving only the less valuable silver. In accordance with Cleveland's desire, Congress therefore repealed the Sherman Act during the year of the panic. Later, President Cleveland also had to borrow large stocks of gold from the banking house headed by J. P. Morgan in order to build up the Treasury's gold supply.

Politics and the Single Standard

The silver question was raised once more in 1896. William J. Bryan, supported by the Democrat, Populist, and Free Silver parties, ran on a platform which provided for the free and unlimited coining of silver (at a ratio of 16 to 1), a proposal which would have placed the United States back on the double standard of silver and gold. His Republican opponent was William McKinley, who stood for the single gold standard. Popular opinion was very evenly divided, but McKinley was elected President, and his victory meant defeat for the double money standard. In 1900, the Gold Standard Act was passed, officially making gold the only basis for American money. Until 1933, the United States was on a gold standard. Then President Franklin D. Roosevelt proclaimed that banks should not redeem paper money with gold. This practically took the country off the gold standard.

Looking Back

1. What is meant by "free coinage" of silver?
2. Why did the relative values of gold and silver create problems?
3. How did the discovery of large amounts of silver affect our money system?
4. By what means did the Bland-Allison Act and the Sherman Silver Act try to meet the coinage problem?

The Chapter in Perspective

Who Are These People?
Kelley
Weaver
Cleveland
Morgan
Harrison
McKinley
Bryan

What Do These Dates and Terms Mean?
1867
mortgage
1887
greenbacks
1892
income tax
direct election
1896
postal savings
Granger Laws
Interstate Commerce Act
National Farmers Alliance
Gold Standard Act
National Grange
Greenback party
Populist party
Bland-Allison Act
Sherman Silver Act
one-crop system
1876
referendum
1878
1890
free-coinage
1900
secret ballot
initiative
Panic of 1893

Questions for Study

1. Describe the practices of the one-crop system that led to a great waste of our natural resources.
2. Are farmers as much at the mercy of the railroads today as they were in the 1890's? Why?
3. Compare the life and work of a modern farmer with that of his counterpart in the 1890's.
4. Why might the Granger movement be compared with the labor union movement?
5. As an eastern laborer would you have joined the Populist party? Why?
6. Summarize in your own words the history of the gold-silver ratio in American history.
7. Why was there little objection at the time to the law passed in 1873 and then much protest against it within a few years?
8. The election of 1896 is considered to have been a key election in American history. Explain why.
9. Name the areas of the United States where the one-crop system flourished and identify the crop of each area.
10. Where were the centers of Populist party support? Can you account for their location?

Place Yourself in History

The time is 1896. You have just turned twenty-one and are going to vote for President of the United States for the first time. The choice of a party is yours to make for you live in a democracy.

One of the most intense political campaigns in the history of the United States is being waged. Each party predicts disaster if it is defeated. Both Bryan and McKinley offer salvation and each seeks support and your vote. You alone can make the decision for yourself.

How would you have voted in 1896? Why?

19 Immigration and the Advance of Labor

The Civil War signaled a real break in the pattern of American life. Before it, the country had been predominantly a land of farms and villages. After it, the country began turning into a land of cities and manufacturing. This shift from one kind of life to the other carried along with it numerous problems regarding labor and immigration. How much should the great numbers of workers be paid? What working conditions could the labor force expect from their employers? Where would city-dwelling laborers live in comfort and cleanliness? What would be done to bring the great numbers of immigrants who came to work in the factories into traditional American life? People began to ask these burning questions after the Civil War.

1. Workers Band Together to Improve Labor Conditions

Early Obstacles

Individual laborers could not fight singlehandedly for their rights against large corporations, so they had to band together. At first, for a number of reasons, the odds were against them. The employers could use the new railroads to pour unemployed men, including newly arrived immigrants, into factory towns where wages were high. The immigrants, accustomed to low wages in Europe, would accept wages much lower than the standard. So, often, big industries imported large groups of immigrants and hired them at low wages. They displaced the union men who had held jobs before and had fought for their higher standard of living.

Naturally, the union men resented the loss of their jobs to immigrant laborers who would accept less pay.

When they tried to take their grievances to court, the employers were able to hire experienced lawyers to fight the lawsuits. The employers also often controlled the newspapers and could put pressure on lawmakers not to act against them. Often the only power left to the unions was the power to strike, but once a strike started, the corporations could usually persuade federal judges to issue an *injunction* to stop the strike. An injunction is a court order which must be obeyed under penalty of law. If the workers disobeyed the order and created unrest, the corporations could request state and federal authorities to send police or troops to suppress the strike. This was done on a number of occasions.

Lockouts and Yellow Dogs. Other weapons of the employers were the "lockout," the "yellow dog contract," and the "blacklist." A lockout meant simply that the owner locked his gates and kept the worker away from his job. The yellow dog contract was an agreement signed by the worker that he would not join a union. Its picturesque name was derived from the term which union members used in ridiculing a man who would work when a union was striking. The blacklist was a list of active unionists that was sent from one employer to another; a man whose name appeared on this list could not get a job.

Union Beginnings

Despite all obstacles the unions increased in number. Prior to the business collapse known as the Panic of 1873 many local unions and about thirty national unions had been formed. Such short-lived organizations as the Workingmen's Benevolent Association and the Knights of St. Crispin came into being immediately after the Civil War. The most important of the new unions was the National Labor Union, organized in 1866. It lasted six years and had about 600,000 members.

Strikes and Violence. The depression that followed the Panic of 1873 led to unemployment, hunger, and violence among the workers. Radicals and terrorists began to stir up the unions. Among these were the "Molly Maguires" in the Pennsylvania coal fields. This group advocated direct and lawless action such as the assassination of employers.

Another example of destructive action was the great railroad strike of 1877. This strike started when four Eastern railroads cut wages by ten per

Pennsylvania coal miner, 1870. He carries pick and lunch bucket and wears a candle on his hat in order to see in the mine.

cent, but at the same time continued to pay large dividends to stockholders. The public sympathized with the strike and it quickly spread to the Western railroads. Rioting and property damage occurred in many cities. In Baltimore rioters fought the state militia and forced them to retreat. In Pittsburgh some of the militia joined the strikers. Finally President Hayes ordered federal troops to Pittsburgh and other cities to restore order.

The failure of the strike of 1877 and the country's horror at the extent of mob violence weakened the labor movement. Its best leaders now realized that radicals and thugs must be kept out, and that workers must have better training and discipline.

The Knights of Labor. Another national labor organization now began to attract members. This was the Noble Order of the Knights of Labor, founded as a secret society in 1869 by Uriah Stephens. Instead of trying to join entire unions together as the National Labor Union had done, the Knights aimed to include individual workmen in "one big union." Their definition of workmen was very broad—it included men and women of all races, skilled and unskilled, and excluded only gamblers, liquor dealers, lawyers, and bankers.

In 1879 the hard-working Terence V. Powderly, who had been elected mayor of Scranton, Pennsylvania, the year before, became head of the Knights. Under his leadership the union began to win strikes, including one against Jay Gould's Erie railroad system. Powderly was a reasonable man who opposed strikes and preferred to settle disputes by *arbitration*, that is, the act of trying to arrive at an agreement between two opposing parties with the help of an impartial third party.

A number of things contributed to the downfall of the Knights of Labor. For example, some of Powderly's followers engaged in useless strikes without his consent. The union also wasted money trying to set up consumers' cooperatives like those that the Grangers had attempted. The skilled workers began to drop out, complaining that their dues were higher than those of the unskilled.

The Haymarket Riot. Another reason for the decline of the Knights of Labor was their alleged part in the bloody Haymarket Riot in Chicago. For some time there had been great unrest in the city, some of it caused by *anarchists*. (An anarchist is one who believes in the overthrow of all government, by force.) On May 4, 1886, the Chicago

John P. Altgeld, governor of Illinois, was a courageous leader, freeing two unpopular anarchists whom he felt had been tried unfairly.

police were ordered to stand guard at a peaceful meeting of three thousand workers who had gathered to protest against police brutalities. When the police, for no apparent reason, tried to force the meeting to break up, an unknown terrorist threw a dynamite bomb which killed seven policemen and injured others. The police opened fire on the crowd and killed four.

Although the identity of the bomb thrower was never proved, a storm of anger broke out in the city, and eight known anarchists were rounded up and charged with murder. Seven were sentenced to death and one to prison. Of the seven, four were executed, one committed suicide, and two had their sentences changed to life imprisonment. In 1893 Governor John P. Altgeld, after studying the case carefully, freed the two remaining prisoners on the ground that the trial had been a miscarriage of justice.

The Knights had little to do with the meeting, and they condemned the vicious bomb thrower; nevertheless, the public connected them with the anarchists, and they quickly lost the support of workers.

The Rise of the American Federation of Labor

Samuel Gompers. As the Knights of Labor declined, the American Federation of Labor (A. F. of L.) took the lead in the labor movement. Founded in 1886 in Columbus, Ohio, as an outgrowth of an earlier organization, the union elected Samuel Gompers as its first president. Gompers was born in a poor district in London and came to America at the age of thirteen. He rose rapidly in the ranks of labor and became head of the Cigar Makers Union. His later career as president of the A. F. of L. was a remarkable one. Except for the year 1895, he held the office until his death in 1924, when he was succeeded by William Green.

More than anything else, Samuel Gompers was a practical labor leader. At all times a patriotic American, he was the father of unionism.

Gompers was not a socialist or radical, and he did not believe that one class of people should struggle against another. His chief aim was simply to use practical methods to get better jobs for workers so that they could become respected Americans. He believed that unions should be composed only of skilled workers. Each craft would have its own union, and each union would belong to the A. F. of L. When one union was having trouble, the other unions in the federation would come to its aid.

Accomplishments. On the whole, the policies of the A. F. of L. were quite conservative. It avoided strikes except as a last resort. Its dues were high in order to build up a fund to provide for members in case of sickness or unemployment. It strove for higher wages, shorter work days, and uniform regulations throughout any one particular industry. For example, the union wanted workers in the shoemaking industry to have the same hours and privileges, no matter whether they worked in Minneapolis or Atlanta. The A. F. of L. was so well organized that it survived the hard times after the Panic of 1893, and by 1900 it had increased its membership to 550,000.

Labor and the Public. In the years between 1880 and 1900 there was much labor unrest in America, and thousands of strikes caused losses of millions of dollars to both employers and employees. But slowly the public began to realize that labor had the right to organize and to fight for its rights. In 1894 Labor Day was made a legal holiday by an act of Congress. This act indicated that the government, as well as the people, was becoming more sympathetic with the aims of the working man. And it also indicated that the American industrial system was supporting more and more working men. They were becoming a potent political force.

Most of the states passed laws regulating working conditions, and the average work day was reduced from twelve to ten hours, and in some cases to eight hours. Some of the more progressive employers began to offer old-age pensions, profit-sharing plans, and compensation in case of injury suffered on the job. Most of the employers remained hostile to unions, however, and it was not until the 1930's that labor approached equality with industry.

Looking Back

1. Why did labor unions oppose large-scale immigration?
2. Discuss the weapons used by employers against organized labor.
3. What were the reasons for the early successes and then failure of the Knights of Labor?
4. How did the A. F. of L. differ from previous attempts to organize unions?
5. In what ways have labor unions benefited workers?

2. Immigrants Swell the Labor Force

The Surge of Immigration

Many complex reasons exist for the great surge of immigration in the years between 1815 and 1900. For one thing, the French Revolution and the many other European wars had for all intents and purposes, ended in 1815, freeing great numbers of men from military service. Many of these men and their families turned their eyes westward toward the vast, unoccupied American wilderness. Another reason for the tide of immigration was that the American pioneer experience was a proven one. Stories began to filter back to Europe of the success enjoyed by many who had taken the desperate gamble of emi-

Between 1892 and 1943, Ellis Island, in New York Bay, was the nation's chief immigration station. When the great wave of immigrants swept over the country in the 1890's, scenes like the one above were typical at Ellis Island.

grating to America. Encouraged by these stories, many who might not have gone at first bought passage on the ever-increasing fleet of ships taking Europeans to the United States.

Reasons for Increase. Although the tide of immigrants moved slowly at first, between 1840 and 1850 immigration from Europe suddenly increased. This came about partly because of hard times and poor crops, partly because of unsettled political conditions. Most of the new arrivals were from England, Ireland, Germany, and the Scandinavian countries. Generally they settled in the North, since their sympathies lay with the free North rather than with the slaveholding South. In the Civil War they were a source of fresh manpower for the North and added to its wealth by working in the factories and fields.

Employment of Immigrants. Unlike Europe in 1815, the United States did not find itself flooded with unemployed men when the great armies were disbanded at the close of the Civil War. There was plenty of work for everyone. The thousands of square miles of prairie land in the West need-

The Statue of Liberty, actually called "Liberty Enlightening the World" by the sculptor Frederic Auguste Bartholdi, was built in Paris in the 1870's and early 1880's. It was shipped to the United States in sections in 1885. Unveiled in 1886, it stood during the great age of American immigration as a symbol of hope for hundreds of immigrants. It is still symbolic of our nation's dedication to liberty and freedom.

ed to be occupied and made productive. There were railroads and telegraph lines to be built. Hundreds of thousands of workmen were needed to work in the coal mines, the steel mills, the manufacturing plants, and the many other industries that were rapidly becoming important throughout the land. In the South, the rundown plantations had to be repaired and again put into operation, or else divided up into smaller farms. America was a land of real opportunity for most men.

The "New" Immigration. In the years between 1870 and 1900 the population of the United States rose from about 40 million to almost 76 million. A considerable portion of this startling increase was made up of immigrants. The stream of aliens grew to a river in the 1880's, when about 5,000,000 knocked at America's gates. In the single year of 1882, almost 800,000 poured in.

Until the 1880's the immigrants could learn American ways fairly easily. Like the original American stock, they came from the British Isles and Western Europe. They were similar to the Americans in appearance, customs, and manners. In the 1880's, however, the stream began to flow from another area—the Southern and Eastern parts of Europe. This "new" immigration was made up of Italians, Hungarians, Bohemians, Austrians, Slovaks, Greeks, and Jews from Poland and Russia. This colorful new stock came for the same reasons that had attracted the "old" Anglo-Saxon immigrants—to escape poverty and oppression and to better their lives in a land of opportunity. The newcomers were hard to digest, however, because their language and habits were strange to the "native" Americans.

Immigrants in Industry

At first the immigrants were welcomed with open arms, for they were willing to work in the factories for very small wages. As their numbers increased, however, various anti-foreign organizations raised a cry of protest. They pointed out that foreign groups tended to live by themselves in "Little Polands" or "Little Italies." Since they had only small amounts of money, they were forced to live in slums that were breeding places for crime. Many of them were illiterate even in their own language. They could be easily influenced by anarchists, radicals, and unscrupulous politicians.

Laws to Control Immigration

Early Restrictions. Congress finally voted to restrict immigration. In 1882 the gates were closed to all convicts, criminals, and paupers. In 1885, under pressure from the labor unions, Congress abolished the contract labor system. Under this system employers had paid for the passage of immigrants into the country, provided they signed contracts to work, usually for very low wages. This was similar to the system of indentured servitude prevalent in this country before the Revolutionary War. Later laws prohibited the entry of other undesirables such as the insane, alcoholics, people with contagious diseases, and anarchists and other radicals.

Chinese Laborers. In 1882 the government passed a law aimed at a particular racial group, the Chinese. In the 1870's these quiet, hard-working people had come in large numbers to California, where there was a great demand for them as workers on the railroads and in the mines. The people in the Western states disliked and ridiculed them. In 1877 they supported a bill to keep all Chinese out of the country. President Hayes vetoed the bill because it violated an earlier treaty with China. The law which finally got through Congress in 1882 stated that all Chinese laborers, but not students or businessmen, were forbidden to enter the United States.

The "Gentlemen's Agreement." After the Russo-Japanese War of 1904-

It is quite likely that most of the men in this railroad crew in 1891 spoke little or no English. Irish, Germans, Poles, Italians or Swedes might make up a great part of this group in Greenville, Pennsylvania. The railroads employed great numbers of immigrants.

1905, large numbers of Japanese workmen began coming to our shores to seek work. Again the people on the West Coast objected. San Francisco's school board barred Japanese children from schools attended by American children. The Japanese government regarded this as an insult that violated a treaty between the United States and Japan. There was even some talk of war. President Theodore Roosevelt, however, managed to restore good feeling in 1907 by promoting what was known as the *Gentlemen's Agreement*. By the terms of this agreement, Japanese children in the United States would be admitted to the public schools on equal terms with other children, and Japanese workmen would not be expelled or excluded from our country, provided Japan would agree to permit no more of them to come here. This odd-sounding arrangement permitted the Japanese to "save face" in what would otherwise have been an embarrassing situation. It solved a knotty international problem.

Later Immigration Laws. In 1917 Congress added to the rather mild restrictions of the law of 1882 by passing legislation excluding from the United States all persons who could not pass a "literacy test"—that is, a test proving that they could read. Although President Wilson vetoed this law, Congress passed it over his veto by obtaining the necessary two-thirds vote. In 1921 another law was passed to prevent a great

Around 1910, immigrants arriving at Ellis Island underwent physical examinations. Immigrants are now processed in their own countries and speedily admitted to the U.S.

Many immigrants never did leave the city to which they first came, New York. They crowded together in tenements like these on New York's lower East side, 1902.

tide of immigration like the one which had followed the Civil War. This law provided that no one country could send to the United States within one year more than three per cent as many foreign-born people of that nationality as had been living here in 1910. This new law meant that in 1917, for example, only three hundred Italians could enter the country per ten thousand who had lived here in 1910. In 1924 this law was amended, and placed an even greater restriction by reducing the percentage to two per cent of the number living here in 1890. This law also excluded from the United States Japanese workmen, whose admittance was opposed by the same kind of people who had opposed the Chinese in 1882. Japan protested this violation of the "Gentlemen's Agreement," but the bill was passed.

The immigration amendment of 1924 further provided that after July 1, 1927, all nations should be allowed to send at least 100 immigrants apiece each year, the total from all nations not to exceed 150,000. Each nation was to be allowed a definite percentage of the 150,000 yearly total. It was 1929, however, before this went into effect. Though these restrictions have resulted in a great reduction in recorded immigration, they have led to the smuggling in of thousands of illegal immigrants.

Recent Immigration

In 1933, when the German government under Adolf Hitler began to persecute Jews and others who did not support the government's activities, our country began to receive political refugees fleeing from Germany. Among these were some of the great men of this century such as Albert Einstein, a famous scientist; Thomas Mann, a leading writer; Heinrich Bruening, a statesman and teacher. During and after the war in Europe, thousands of new immigrants arrived. They had been driven from their homes, or were released from prisons and concentration camps where they had been held because of their beliefs. In many cases they had lost their citizenship because of changes of government or boundaries. They did not dare to go home. Like other countries in the Western world, our country offered a home and a new start to these people.

Many different opinions are held by Americans concerning immigration. Some approve of our present laws but feel that all aliens who intend to make their homes here should become American citizens. Others believe that America should be saved for Americans and that no immigrants at all should be allowed to land. Some think that too many immigrants are incapable of understanding and adopting the American way of life. Others maintain however, that no people are better fitted to appreciate and use our freedom wisely than those who have experienced the loss of their own freedom.

In normal times, most fair-minded Americans favor the admission of as many immigrants each year as American schools and American living conditions can educate and support.

Looking Back

1. What factors caused the tide of immigration to the United States from Europe?
2. Why was there more opposition to the "new" immigration than to the "old"?
3. At whom were the earliest immigration controls directed?
4. How did the Gentlemen's Agreement solve an awkward problem?
5. Summarize the laws passed to control immigration from 1917 to the present.

The Chapter in Perspective

Who Are These People?

Hayes	Altgeld
Stephens	Gompers
Powderly	Green

Where Are These Places?

| Chicago | Columbus |
| Scranton | Minneapolis |

What Do These Dates and Terms Mean?

strike	Knights of Labor	1886	quota system
1866	"yellow dog" contract	1921	literacy test
injunction	Gentlemen's Agreement	arbitration	railroad strike
1907	1877	anarchists	Haymarket Riot
lockout	National Labor Union	A. F. of L.	"new" immigration
1869	Molly Maguires	1917	blacklist

Questions for Study

1. How did destructive strikes, terror, and violence hurt the early cause of unionism?

2. Would you support or oppose the use of federal troops when a strike is in progress? Why?

3. Can you see why the Haymarket Riot set back labor unions in the public opinion? Explain.

4. What were the contributions of Gompers to the cause of trade unionism?

5. Select five imaginary Americans living in different parts of the country in 1900 and tell what views they might have held on immigration.

6. What contributions to the American way of life have been made by the immigrants?

7. How did the shift of population to the industrial cities and the arrival of large numbers of immigrants create new problems for Americans to solve?

8. Do you favor restrictions on immigration today? Why?

9. In what parts of the country did labor unions first start? Would these places show large union memberships today? Why?

10. In what areas of the country did the post-1890 immigrants tend to settle? Why? What evidences are there of their settlement?

Place Yourself in History

As far back as available records show, your family has lived within thirty miles of the European village in which you reside. Your ancestors tilled the same soil that you and your father now till. The same royal house has ruled your land for many years.

Today a letter arrived from your mother's brother—your uncle—who left for America two years ago. He writes a glowing report of the opportunities in America. As his favorite, you are offered the chance to join him in the United States.

What would be the possible advantages of such a trip? What would be the disadvantages? What advice might you receive from relatives and friends? What would be your decision? Why? Do you know anyone who faced that decision? What reasons prompted their action?

Expanding Your Outlook

Doing It Yourself

1. Report to the class on the struggle between those who wanted the "open range" and those who wanted to fence in the "wide open spaces." Indicate what was at stake.
2. Make a chart listing the new inventions and discoveries covered in this unit. Column headings: invention, inventor, date, effects.
3. On an outline map of the United States, indicate the locations of our major natural resources. Use pictorial designations or a key for quick identification.
4. Draw a cartoon representing the farmers' plight as it might have appeared in a Grange publication or in an Eastern newspaper.
5. For those mechanically inclined, report to the class how one of the new inventions of the period functioned. Pictures or a model will help your presentation.
6. Write a biography of one of the "captains of industry" mentioned in the unit.
7. List the planks in the Populist platform of 1892 and discuss the conditions that brought about their entry into national politics.
8. Write an editorial on the passage of the Sherman Antitrust Act as it might have appeared in a Western newspaper (or an Eastern newspaper).
9. As a silver miner, give your views on the adoption of the gold standard in 1900.
10. Present a report to the class summarizing how the American Indian was treated officially and unofficially from the end of the Civil War to 1924.

Working with the Class

1. Organize committees within the class to report on major changes and contributions to the American way of life in the following industries: railroads, cattle raising, steel, oil, mining, and communication.
2. Form a group to report on the first arrivals, problems, and contributions of various immigrant groups in your section of the country.
3. Organize a panel discussion on the problems, goals, and accomplishments of the A. F. of L. from its formation to the early 1900's.
4. Dramatize a farmers' meeting as they discussed the problems they faced in the 1890's.

5. Have two committees prepare campaign literature, posters, banners, and slogans for the vital election of 1896.
6. Organize a committee to report on the effect of the automobile on American life. Include reports on changes in mobility, speed of transportation, industries adversely affected, new industries created or old one benefited, and the living habits of our citizens.

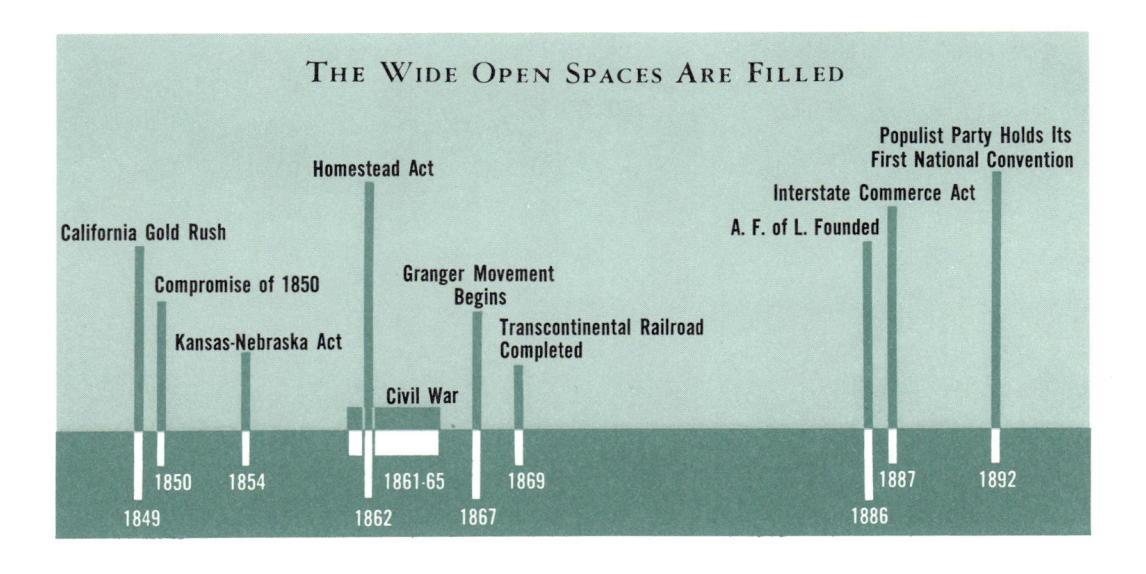

THE WIDE OPEN SPACES ARE FILLED

- 1849 — California Gold Rush
- 1850 — Compromise of 1850
- 1854 — Kansas-Nebraska Act
- 1862 — Homestead Act
- 1861-65 — Civil War
- 1867 — Granger Movement Begins
- 1869 — Transcontinental Railroad Completed
- 1886 — A. F. of L. Founded
- 1887 — Interstate Commerce Act
- 1892 — Populist Party Holds Its First National Convention

The painting below, called Six O'clock, *by the artist Charles Burchfield, depicts the grim reality of urban existence. These row houses, all alike, are symbolic of the monotony of life in the city. Yet, even in the midst of the greyness, the warmth of 19th century America can be seen through the kitchen window. Unit Seven is about the great changes that took place in American life and culture between Reconstruction and the entry of the United States into world affairs. Perhaps the great movement from farm to city typifies those changes better than any other event.*

From the Permanent Collection of the Everson Museum of

ONE NATION INDIVISIBLE
UNIT 7

Americans Build for a Complex Future

20. Cultural and Social Change

1. More Students Attend More Schools • **2.** Education Booms in the Twentieth Century • **3.** The Written Word Spreads and Gains in Influence • **4.** Americans Experiment in Art and Architecture

21. Life in City and Country

1. Corruption and Injustice Accompany Urban Growth • **2.** Spirit of Reform Grows in the Twentieth Century • **3.** Americans Find Time to Enjoy Life

22. A New Role on the World Stage

1. The Spirit of Imperialism Leads to Territorial Expansion • **2.** The United States Wages and Wins a Foreign War • **3.** U. S. Imperialists Look to Asia • **4.** The Nation Governs Its New Empire

20

Cultural and Social Change

We have seen how the American people conquered the frontier, tilled the rich earth, dug treasure from the mines, threaded the country with railroads, and built great factories. But such material progress must be accompanied by advances in education, art, and literature. How has the United States progressed in these important fields?

1. More Students Attend More Schools

The last three decades in the nineteenth century and the first two in the twentieth saw many changes in American life. This was especially true in public education. People were beginning to accept the principle of free public education for all, realizing that without such education a free democracy cannot exist. Even so, there was still much room for improvement in the educational system as the new century opened.

The American Educational System

Elementary Education. In 1900 most Americans had attended school for less than six years, and a considerable number of adults were unable to read or write. Students attended elementary school an average of 68 days out of a school year of only 143 days. Most of the elementary school teachers were poorly prepared. In fact, very few states required them to have even a high school diploma. Women teachers were paid, on an average, only $38.00 a month and the salary for men was not much higher. By 1914, however, the elementary system was much improved—the school year was lengthened to 158 days, attendance was better, and teachers' salaries were higher.

The improvement in school facilities was most noticeable in the Northeast, less so in the West, and least in the

Part of Stanford University, Palo Alto, California. Leland Stanford, railroad builder, governor and senator of California, founded the University as a memorial to his son in 1891.

South. The chief reason for the lag in the South was that the Civil War and Reconstruction had overturned its economy and its social system. Nevertheless, the Southern states, led by North Carolina, raised taxes for school purposes and made good use of money donated by private philanthropists like John D. Rockefeller.

In the late 1800's the kindergarten, a type of school common in Germany, began to appear in American communities. By 1900 several thousand kindergartens were in operation. Another type of school that showed rapid growth was the parochial school. The "new" immigrants who came to the United States in the 1880's and 1890's were mostly Roman Catholics, and this situation resulted in the building of many private Catholic parochial schools, which lessened the burden on the public school system.

High School Education. Before the Civil War most education at the high school level was supplied by private academies. In 1860 there were only about one hundred public high schools in the country, but by 1900 the number had risen to six thousand. By 1914 this number had almost doubled. High school enrollment rose from about 500,000 in 1900 to 1,200,000 in 1914, and to about 2,500,000 in 1920.

By the time of World War I most of the younger high school teachers were college graduates. Many of the leading universities were busily setting up schools or departments of education designed to improve classroom methods and teaching skills. A leader in this field was Teachers College of Colum-

These ivy covered buildings built around 1900 are the oldest at Mt. Holyoke College. It was the first college for women, founded in 1836.

bia University, where the ideas of the philosopher John Dewey exercised great influence. Dewey believed that schools should not only provide knowledge but should teach the student to become a useful member of a democratic society. He taught that learning facts was not enough, but that the child should "learn by doing"—that is, he should relate what he learned to the actual life going on around him in order that he might become a better citizen. Dewey believed that the old curriculum, which had been confined to the "three R's" and a few other subjects, should be enlarged to give better preparation for earning a living.

Colleges and Universities. The Morrill Land Grant Act of 1862 aided greatly in the establishment of new colleges after the Civil War. The act gave tracts of land to the states for the support of colleges that would teach "agriculture and the mechanic arts," as well as other subjects. Sixty-nine "land grant" colleges, many of which are now great centers of learning, were established, built by funds derived from the sale of thirteen million acres of land.

Wealthy individuals also contributed to the cause of higher education. Rockefeller and Carnegie gave millions of dollars to Columbia, Yale, Harvard, and many other institutions. Other benefactors, like Johns Hopkins, Paul Tulane, and Leland Stanford, Jr., endowed universities which were named after them. As the universities acquired more financial support, they improved their buildings, enlarged their library and research facilities, and founded graduate schools offering advanced degrees. The universities were also enabled to attract great college presidents like Charles Eliot of Harvard, Frederick Barnard of Columbia, and James Angell of the University of Chicago and later of Yale.

The Education of Women

For many generations the education of women lagged behind that of men. Girls were not allowed to attend the early colonial schools, as it was felt that their place was in the home sewing and cooking, rather than in school learning mathematics and spelling. In some parts of the country until after the Civil War, girls were not permitted to enter public high schools, for it was thought that if they wanted higher education they should attend one of the private girls' schools which were then putting in an appearance. As the rural schools developed, however, this ban was removed and girls were given the same instruction as boys.

College education was opened to women in 1833, when Oberlin College in Ohio opened its doors to both men and women. In 1836, Mount Holyoke Seminary for women was founded in Massachusetts by Miss Mary Lyon. Wesleyan College in Macon, Georgia, was established also in the same year. In 1865 Vassar College was opened at Poughkeepsie (po-KIP′si) to be for women "what Harvard and Yale are for men." Educational opportunities for women were most widespread in the Middle West. Here the state universities began to open their doors to both men and women. Today, throughout the whole field of education, women enjoy the same advantages as men.

The Education of Negroes

Improved educational facilities were not shared equally by all groups in American society. In the South and in many parts of the North, Negroes attended elementary and secondary schools that were generally much more poorly equipped than the schools for white students. Most Negroes wishing a higher education were not allowed to attend American colleges, which only white students had attended. Therefore, colleges were established for Negroes only. Among these were Fisk University in Nashville, Howard University in Washington, and the Tuskegee Institute in Alabama.

Negro Leaders. Tuskegee was headed by Booker T. Washington, a noted Negro educator who was invited to conduct the new institute in 1881. At the beginning, it was a very humble institution, with only forty students. Professor Washington kept at his task, however, and set up a program of practical studies that he hoped would equip young Negroes to improve their economic standing. He believed that the first goal of the Negroes should be economic improvement rather than social or political equality.

Another Negro leader in the first fight for better facilities and equality was W. E. B. DuBois, a brilliant writer and a graduate of Harvard. In 1905 he called a conference of Negro leaders at Niagara Falls and launched a drive to end discrimination in the schools and elsewhere. Aided by many white reformers, he founded the National Association for the Advancement of Colored People (NAACP) in 1909.

Founders Library, Howard University, Washington, D.C. Howard is the largest university founded primarily for Negroes. However, it now accepts students of all races and is fully integrated.

Booker T. Washington, American educator. As a Negro leader, some felt that his goals were too limited.

The NAACP has since taken a leading part in the struggle for equal rights for the colored races.

Two Court Decisions. The problem of Negro segregation finally reached the Supreme Court. In a series of important decisions, the Court gave new interpretations of an earlier Supreme Court ruling (*Plessy* vs. *Ferguson*, 1896). In that case, the Court decided that the Fourteenth Amendment's requirement that states guarantee "equal protection of the laws" meant "separate but equal" schools could be set aside for Negroes. In 1954 the Court ruled that Negroes, especially in graduate schools, were not receiving equal treatment when they were forced to attend out-of-state schools, even though their own state paid the tuition. The Court also ruled that the problem could not be solved within the state by setting up separate graduate schools for Negroes, or by allowing Negroes to attend white schools provided that they sat apart in classrooms, libraries, and eating places.

Finally, in May, 1954, the Court rendered a key decision in the case of *Brown* vs. *Board of Education of Topeka*. Chief Justice Earl Warren delivered the unanimous opinion of the Court that in the field of public education the doctrine of "separate but equal" has no place, and that it violates the Fourteenth Amendment by denying to persons "the equal protection of the laws."

Move toward Integration. The Court realized that such an important definition of policy would meet with a mixed reaction, and that in some areas the process of desegregation would be difficult. Consequently, it stated that the policy should be carried out by local school authorities with "all deliberate speed." In some of the states, public opinion favored immediate acceptance. Others preferred to proceed gradually, and still others tried to prevent integration by legal obstacles and

Roy Wilkins, a prominent leader in the Negro's drive for civil rights and director of the NAACP.

mob action. By the early 1960's, however, it was recognized by forward-looking leaders in both the North and South that eventually Americans of all races will share equally in the benefits of American education.

Looking Back

1. How did elementary school education improve during the latter 1800's?

2. How did Dewey's ideas on education help bring many changes?

3. From what main sources did the early growth of American colleges find financial support?

4. Trace the steps by which the Negro has gained better educational opportunities.

5. Why has integration in the field of public education been a difficult problem?

2. Education Booms in the Twentieth Century

Higher Education

In the first two decades of the twentieth century American colleges and universities witnessed a tremendous growth in enrollments. The ever-increasing number of junior colleges opened new opportunities for higher education, as did the extension courses which many universities began to offer. New professional schools appeared on university campuses, offering excellent training in medicine, law, journalism, education, business administration, and engineering. More and more students sought advanced degrees, and by 1920

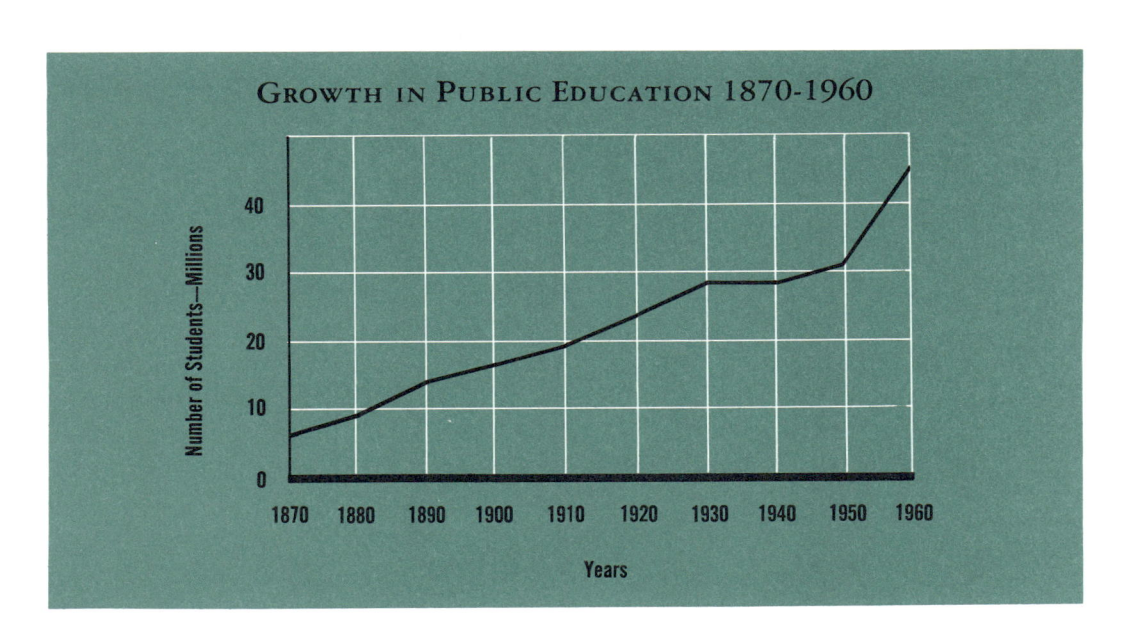

GROWTH IN PUBLIC EDUCATION 1870-1960

GROWTH IN HIGHER EDUCATION 1870-1960

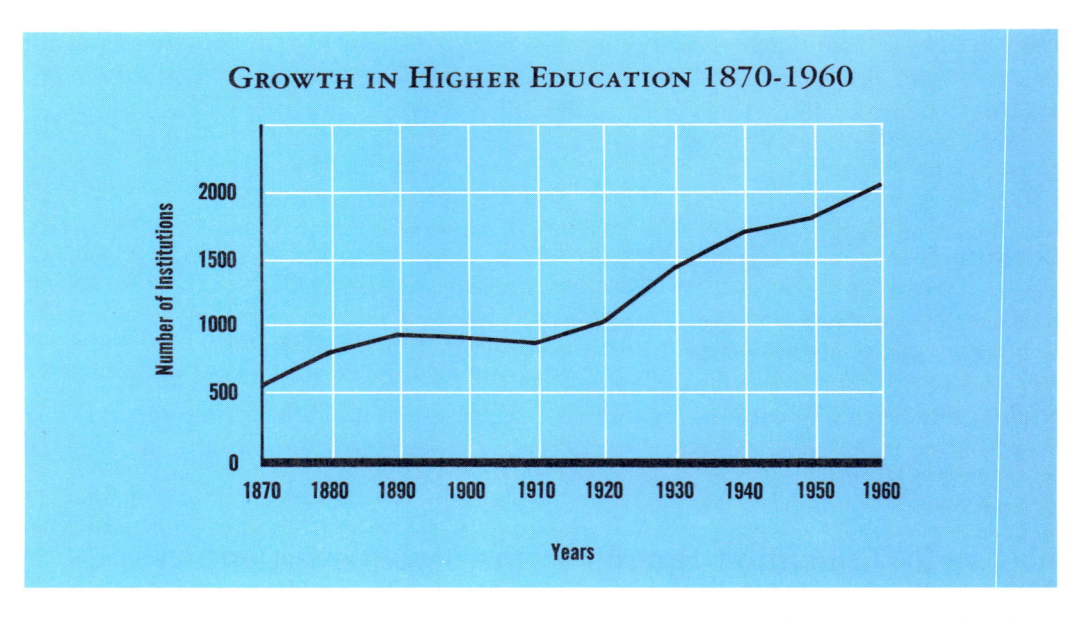

Remember that this graph only shows the increase in the number of colleges and universities. Would the same growth appear in the college population? Why not?

American universities were offering graduate instruction and research facilities that were the equal of those in the great European universities.

Growth of New Schools

As the population of the country increased during the 1920's, the enrollment in the public schools jumped correspondingly. The number of high school students increased from about 2,500,000 in 1920 to double that number in 1930. Better roads and automobiles brought about changes in rural education. The one-room elementary school was replaced by the consolidated, graded school. The high schools began to enlarge their curricula by supplying vocational courses to help students who were not inclined toward the usual academic programs.

Schools in the Depression. The Great Depression of the early 1930's had a serious effect on the nation's schools. Lack of funds caused many towns and cities to close some of their schools, to cut teachers' salaries, and to shorten the school year. This reduction in the school program was temporary, however, and by 1935 more and more students were crowding into the nation's high schools and colleges. The Depression had taught them that when jobs were available, they would usually be given to those young people who were best educated—and not to the "drop-outs." By 1940 the boom in education was again in full swing.

War and Education. During World War II many thousands of young Americans became convinced that higher education was valuable and necessary, since they observed that the most interesting assignments in the armed services were usually given to those who had graduated from high school or attended college. The government also aroused interest in higher education by selecting many promising servicemen for short-term courses in college, where they received training in engineering, medicine, government, and other subjects. After the war thousands of veterans, aided by a government bill which provided for their education, swarmed onto the nation's campuses.

College enrollment slackened somewhat during the Korean War, but expansion was resumed soon after the cease-fire. Throughout the 1950's and early 1960's this educational trend continued. By the mid 1960's college enrollments had reached the amazing total of 4,500,000. According to some educators, this figure may be doubled by 1980.

Looking Back

1. What factors helped bring about the great increase in the number of those seeking education?
2. How did the Great Depression affect education in the United States?
3. By what means did World War II and government actions spur the demand for expanded educational facilities and opportunities.

3. The Written Word Spreads and Gains in Influence

Libraries

An important aid to education is the public library, which has been called "the poor man's university." Andrew Carnegie gave huge sums of money to build such libraries, with the provision that those communities which accepted his donations should pay for the maintenance of the libraries.

The famous Library of Congress, a tremendous storehouse of the world's knowledge, was founded in 1800 "to purchase such books as may be necessary for the use of Congress." In 1897, when it possessed almost a million books, it was moved into its own building. It is the largest library in the United States, used freely by scholars and teachers as well as government officials. Great public libraries like those in New York and Boston were used by eager readers from all over the

Interior of the Library of Congress. In 1870, an act was passed declaring that all books copyrighted in the United States must go into the Library of Congress. It is now open to the public as a reference library supported by Congressional appropriations.

country. It is estimated that by 1900 there were about nine thousand free circulating libraries in the country. Besides the public libraries, thousands of readers had access to rapidly growing libraries on university campuses.

New Interest in Books. One result of the hard times of the late 1920's and early 1930's was that people began to turn in large numbers to the public libraries as a form of entertainment they could afford. They also economized in book buying by joining book clubs. The wide membership in such organizations enabled publishers to offer bargain prices for selected volumes. When publishers began to market paperbound books at newsstands and in department stores, knowledge was spread even more widely. At first these inexpensive editions concentrated on romances and mystery stories, but later there was a booming market for reprints of classical literature and for books on all sorts of academic subjects. Today the paperbacks are an important part of the stock in commercial and college bookshops.

The Expanding Power of the Press

As more people began to read widely, newspaper circulation increased vastly. The papers became more attractive in appearance and printed more pictures. Unfortunately some newspapers began to appeal to thrill-seeking readers by headlining crime, scandal, and other sensational stories. This sort of reporting became known as "yellow journalism."

Pioneers in Journalism. The pioneer in modern American journalism was Joseph Pulitzer, an enterprising newsman who began his career in St. Louis in the 1870's. In 1883 he moved to New York and bought the *New York World* from the famous financier and railroad magnate, Jay Gould. Under his management the *World* became America's foremost newspaper. It covered the news efficiently, supported many reforms in government and labor, and pleased its many readers with cartoons, comics, and feature stories.

A more sensational journalist was William Randolph Hearst, who bought the *New York Journal* in 1895. In an effort to sell more newspapers than the *World*, he used all sorts of devices to increase the circulation of his paper. Hearst's newspaper has often been accused of starting the Spanish-American War of 1898. The *New York Journal* published vivid accounts, biased and

The New York Journal devoted its entire front page to the explosion of the Maine. Its headlines excited popular imagination.

often untrue, of conditions in Spanish Cuba. These accounts, and others like them, inflamed public opinion. Stories of crimes and scandals, violent editorials, and flaming headlines also characterized the "yellow journalism" of Hearst and his imitators.

Growth of Newspapers. More efficient presses and the increased demand for paid advertising space made it possible to sell newspapers for a few pennies. The wide appeal of newspapers is shown by the fact that the number of daily newspapers rose from 544 in 1870 to 1611 in 1900. By the time World War I broke out newspapers had expanded their circulation tremendously by introducing syndicated articles, puzzles, bedtime stories, recipes, and special pages for sports, business, and social activities. News gathering agencies like the Associated Press and the United Press supplied editors with reliable, unbiased news from around the world. In spite of the "yellow press," journalism became a respected profession, and some universities began to offer courses in newspaper writing and management.

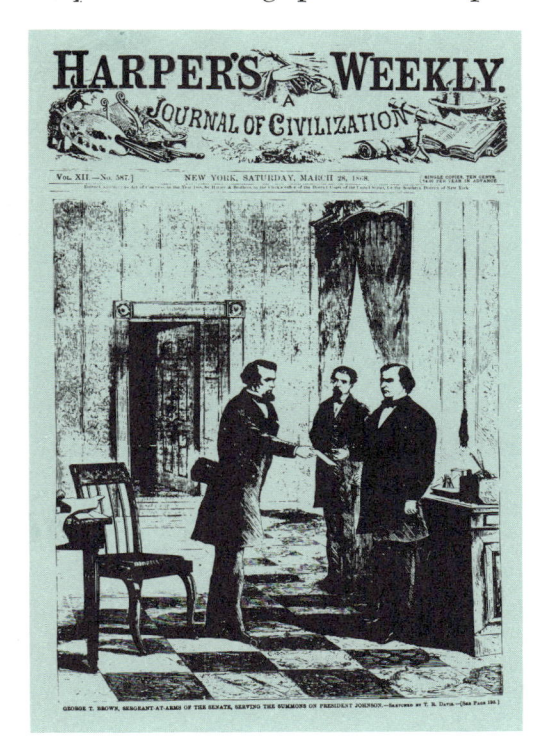

Periodical Magazines. Magazines became popular after the Civil War, when increasing numbers of reading Americans had more leisure time. Enterprising editors hired artists and storywriters to feed the increasing demands of the public. Although some magazines were expensive, like *Harper's* and the *Atlantic Monthly*, many people bought and read them. The famous *Saturday Evening Post* began to be popular also in this era.

In the 1920's and 1930's a number of new magazines appeared on the stands, while some of the older ones, unable to stand the competition, retired from the scene. *The New Yorker* became a favorite of those who liked witty, sophisticated writing. The *Reader's Digest* offered a wide bill of fare by condensing articles from other sources. Henry Luce, one of the leading publishers of the period after World War I, scored a success when he began to publish a weekly news magazine in 1925. Five years later he added a monthly devoted to business and finance, and in 1936 he put out the first issues of a popular pictorial weekly. Since the end of World War II, many new, specialized magazines have made their appearance on the American scene, some only to disappear later. Many magazines devoted to sports now have wide circulations, as do gardening magazines, travel magazines, and political weeklies.

The Remington Art Memorial

Courtesy of
The Art Institute
of Chicago

1

2 National Gallery of Art—Washington, D.C.
Gift of Mrs. Huttleston Rogers

3

4

Oil on Canvas, 36¼"x48¼"
The Cleveland Museum of Art,

National Gallery of Art—Washington, D.C.— Harris Whittemore Collection

National Gallery of Art—Washington, D.C.— W.L. and May T. Mellon Foundation

5

Courtesy of The Art Institute of Chicago Harriott A. Fox fund

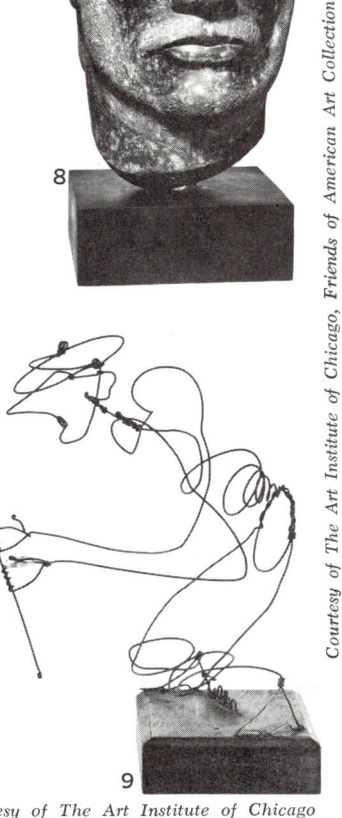

6

These few samples of American painting and sculpture only begin to convey the variety of subject and style in American art. William Greenough's (1805–52) bust *Abdiel, The Faithful Angel,* (1) is styled after Greek and Roman classic sculpture. George Inness' (1825–94) picture *The Lackawanna Valley* (2) depicts early railroading. Frederic Remington's (1861–1909) painting called *Riding the Snow Trail* (3) shows a scouting party of Indians. George Bellows (1882–1925) painted scenes of stark realism such as *Stag at Sharkey's* (4). James M. Whistler (1834–1903) painted *The White Girl* (5). Winslow Homer (1836–1910) created *Breezing Up.* (6). Grant Wood (1892–1942) painted *American Gothic* (7). William Zorach's (1887–   ) *Head of a Prophet* (8) and Alexander Calder's (1898–   ) *John D. Rockefeller* (9) are good examples of new trends in 20th century sculpture.

7

8

Courtesy of The Art Institute of Chicago, Friends of American Art Collection

9

Courtesy of The Art Institute of Chicago Gift of Mrs. Daniel Huger

Looking Back

1. How has the Library of Congress changed its functions over the years?
2. By what means do libraries earn the title "the poor man's university"?
3. What have been the effects of the paperback book "boom"?
4. In what ways do newspapers help form public opinion?
5. How can you account for the great increase in magazine circulation during the past fifty years?

4. Americans Experiment in Art and Architecture

After the Civil War, as Americans acquired more wealth and leisure, they became more interested in art and architecture. Although most American painters in the last two decades of the century are not now well known, they had admirers both at home and abroad.

The Art of Painting

The American Scene. One of the favorite artists of the time was Frederick Remington, who died in 1909 at the age of forty-eight. While wandering on the Great Plains, he made many drawings which later appeared in magazines. His paintings are a colorful record of the Indian fights, the cowboys, and the life of the Wild West.

Many American artists, for example James MacNeill Whistler, John Singer Sargent, and Mary Cassatt, appealed to popular taste with their portraits, family scenes, and sentimental depictions of children or landscapes. Like many artistic Americans of the late nineteenth century, Whistler, Sargent, and Cassatt learned a great deal of their craft in Europe. Winslow Homer, the famous Boston artist, developed his own special style here in the United States. Homer loved the sea and the outdoors, and painted memorable, lively pictures of both.

At the beginning of the twentieth century a small group of painters from Philadelphia and New York led by Robert Henri introduced new themes in painting. They became known as the Ash Can School because they chose as their subjects the slums, city streets, and ordinary people. One of the best of them was George Bellows, who produced many strong paintings of boxing and other sports, as well as landscapes and cityscapes.

"Modern Art." The "modern" period in American art is sometimes said to date from 1913, when a group of artists organized a spectacular exhibition of European art in an armory in New York. The Armory Show, as their exhibition is called, introduced Americans to the new experimental techniques of famous Europeans, mostly French. Most viewers were startled and bewildered by the creations of these "cubists" and "expressionists," but their new methods were destined to exert a great influence on American artists during the next two decades. It also stimulated public interest in art. Not only did private collectors increase their investments in the work of the artists, but also a great number of American cities, both large and small, organized and supported their own local museums.

Amateur Artists. Not all painters who became well known were trained professionals. In recent years the work of these unschooled painters has gained considerable popularity because of its freshness and sincerity. The best known are John Kane, Horace Pippin, and "Grandma" (Anna Mary) Moses.

Kane, an ex-miner, railroad worker, and boxer, began his art work by coloring photographs and painting houses. Then he began to draw pictures on pieces of beaverboard which he was able to sell to workmen for small sums. Pippin was a Pennsylvania Negro whose right arm had been partly crippled by a sniper's bullet in World War I. Despite this handicap, he produced a number of powerful paintings, the best known being "John Brown Goes to his Hanging" and "End of the War: Starting Home." Grandma Moses, born on a farm in upper New York State, did not attract notice until she was nearly eighty years old. In 1938 a druggist put some of her simple pictures in the window for sale. A New York art expert saw them, was impressed by their gaiety and charm, and called people's attention to them. She continued to paint until her death in 1961, at the age of 101.

Experiments in Building

The Skyscraper. The most distinctive form of American architecture in the first two decades of this century was the skyscraper. Guided by Louis Sullivan and other Chicago architects, builders thrust steel skeletons high into the air. In New York City the limited space and the hard granite base of Manhattan made the skyscraper a practical construction form. The first real skyscraper in New York was the Flatiron Building, finished in 1902. In the years since then a succession of gigantic buildings has made the New York skyline the thrilling sight it is today.

Originality in Architecture. In the 1920's the boom in building encouraged architects to strive for beauty and originality in their designs. Some preferred to emphasize the familiar Greek qualities of simplicity and clean lines, an example of which is Henry Bacon's Lincoln Memorial in Washington, D.C. Others used the more elaborate Gothic style, which can be observed in designs for the Cathedral of St. John the Divine in New York City and for many university buildings in the East.

One of the most original American architects was Frank Lloyd Wright, whose functional designs and bold use of new materials gave a new look to residential and commercial construction. Today, as the country's communities grow in size and population, one sees on every hand a willingness to experiment with new styles and materials, both in public buildings and in private homes.

Men of Letters

Now let us turn from art and architecture, and observe what was being produced by America's men of letters in the years that bridge the nineteenth and twentieth centuries. As in many other aspects of living, it was a period of change and experimentation.

American architecture, like American art, has taken many different forms. The first great buildings, like the (1) Wren Building (1695) at William and Mary College in Williamsburg were designed by English architects. (2) Westover, the William Byrd Mansion, in Virginia was designed by William Byrd, a colonist, in 1730. (3) Monticello, completed in 1809 was designed by Thomas Jefferson, who made use of European styles. (4) a house in Jerome, Arizona, a ghost town. (5) Duke University Chapel, a good example of Gothic architecture. (6, 7, 8) all designed by America's greatest original architect, Frank Lloyd Wright. (6) Johnson's Wax Building, Racine, Wisconsin (7) The Guggenheim Museum, New York City. (8) Library, Florida Southern College (9) Marina Towers, Chicago, Illinois.

5

8

7

6

9

> *Samuel Clemens (Mark Twain) describes his Uncle John's farm as it was in 1845.*
>
> It was a heavenly place for a boy, that farm of my Uncle John's. The house was a double log one, with a spacious floor (roofed in) connecting it with the kitchen. In the summer the table was set in the middle of that spacious and breezy floor, and the sumptuous meals—well, it makes me cry to think of them. Fried chicken, roast pig; wild and tame turkeys, ducks and geese; venison just killed; squirrels, rabbits, pheasants, partridges, prairie-chickens; biscuits, hot batter cakes, hot buckwheat cakes, hot "wheat bread", hot rolls, hot corn pone; fresh corn boiled on the ear, succotash, butter-beans, stringbeans, tomatoes, peas, Irish potatoes, sweet potatoes; buttermilk, sweet milk, "clabber" [cottage cheese]; watermelons, muskmelons, cantaloupes—all fresh from the garden; apple pie, peach pie, pumpkin pie, apple dumplings, peach cobbler—I can't remember the rest.

After the Civil War, book publishing became a flourishing business. At first most publishing firms sold books on a subscription basis, but later they began to advertise their publications and reached their public through the bookstores. A ready market awaited books of all sorts, ranging from those of real literary merit to "dime novels" and juvenile yarns like those of Horatio Alger, Jr.

Local Color. Many of the novelists in the post-Civil War period belonged to the "local color" school—that is, they attempted to give realistic pictures of particular parts of the country with which they were most familiar. One of the best of these was Mark Twain, whose real name was Samuel Clemens. (He took his name from "mark twain," a river boatman's cry that means "two fathoms.") In his *Life on the Mississippi*, *The Adventures of Tom Sawyer*, and *Huckleberry Finn*, he told stories based on his own experiences.

Generally, after the Civil War, American novelists changed their modes of writing. Earlier authors, such as Nathaniel Hawthorne and James Fenimore Cooper, had written romantic, idealized stories of American life. Such authors as William Dean

John Steinbeck, 1962 Nobel Prize winner.

Howells, Stephen Crane, and Jack London all tried, although in different ways, to present life "as it really is." Crane depicted the agonies of a Civil War soldier in *The Red Badge of Courage;* Howells illustrated the private thoughts and activities of a young man rising in the business world in *The Rise of Silas Lapham.* Jack London wrote a number of novels dealing with raw, sometimes shocking and brutal, adventure.

Social Protest. Later novelists used the same realistic method to write novels protesting certain aspects of American life. This was known as "social protest." Upton Sinclair's novel *The Jungle* about the unsanitary meat-packing industry helped bring about reforms in food handling and manufacturing. In the same sense, Frank Norris's novel *The Pit* made people aware of the evils of speculation at the grain exchange in Chicago. After World War I, such authors as Sinclair Lewis, who wrote *Main Street,* and John Steinbeck, who wrote novels about the poor and downtrodden in America, made Americans aware that there were serious defects in our national way of life. William Faulkner, John Dos Passos, and Thomas Wolfe continued this spirit of "social protest" throughout the thirties and forties.

In a very broad sense, playwrights, poets, essayists, and artists all contributed to the "social protest" movement. The plays of Eugene O'Neill were often bitter and disillusioned. He depicted the fate of the common laborer and the aristocratic young man alike. Poets such as T. S. Eliot wrote gloomy and pessimistic verses about city life and the problems of a single man in a growing nation. H. L. Mencken, a great essayist and linguist, wrote scathing denunciations of everything from automobiles to hairpins. Finally the artists of the thirties and forties painted the poor and the starving of the American depression. All these people were writing and painting in the hope of bringing about some change in what they saw around them.

William Faulkner, 1949 Nobel Prize winner.

Looking Back

1. What does the term "painters of the American scene" mean to you?

2. Do you find "modern art" attractive? Why?

3. What have been the American contributions to the field of architecture?

4. How did the pre-Civil War romantic writers differ from the later life "as it really is" group?

5. By what means did the "social protest" writers help change life in America?

The Chapter in Perspective

Who Are These People?

Dewey	Pulitzer
B. T. Washington	Hearst
Steinbeck	Sullivan
Du Bois	Wright
Carnegie	Clemens

What Do These Dates and Terms Mean?

kindergarten	Morrill Land Act
1862	Tuskegee Institute
1896	*Plessey* vs. *Ferguson*
NAACP	*Brown* vs. *Board of Education*
1905	
1954	"separate but equal"
"yellow press"	"all deliberate speed"

Questions for Study

1. Why is the education of women given greater emphasis today than it was fifty years ago?

2. Show how the Supreme Court decision in *Brown* vs. *Board of Education* set a social revolution into motion.

3. Is a college education more necessary for you than it was for your grandfather? Why?

4. Write several sample headlines once as they might appear in the "yellow press" and a second time as they might appear in a conservative newspaper.

5. Are newspapers as important today as they were fifty years ago in influencing public opinion? Why?

6. Why is a "free" press an important factor in democratic life?

7. How may the art and literature of a period create an impression of life during that period?

8. Do you feel that the "new" pictorial magazines have aided the spread of American education and culture? Why?

9. What city in the United States most clearly demonstrates an American contribution to architecture? Why?

10. Where were most of the targets of the "social protest" writers located? Why?

Place Yourself in History

You are attending a town meeting in 1877. Under discussion has been a motion to build a tax-supported public high school. The town's leading citizen and wealthiest man has just attacked the idea as being socialistic. His children, who graduated from private academies, are not of public school age. "Education, like food, clothing, medical care, music lessons, and religion, is the responsibility of the individual parents and not of the community," he argued. "To force a person to pay taxes for the education of the children of others may well be unconstitutional," he concluded.

What would you have said at the town meeting? Why?

21

Life in City and Country

The growth of American industry, with its heavy dependence on skilled and unskilled manpower, led to a concentration of population in towns and cities. This population shift, which is known as "urbanization," brought many serious problems in its wake. Life in the new industrial age was often hard and monotonous, but gradually the use of machinery shortened the time necessary for producing goods. Although the working day was still quite long, people were beginning to find time to enjoy themselves.

1. Corruption and Injustice Accompany Urban Growth

A spectacular movement of people into the urban centers took place in America as the country became industrialized. In 1860 only about one-sixth of the American population lived in towns of 8000 or more, but fifty years later the proportion of city-dwellers had doubled. By 1900 New York, with about three million inhabitants, was one of the largest cities in the world, rivaling London and Paris.

The magnets that drew people to the large towns and cities were (1) the jobs that were available in the factories, (2) higher wages than could be made on farms, (3) the excitement of city life. Although some of the newly arrived immigrants pushed on to the West and worked on farms, most of them preferred to stay in the cities where they could more easily get jobs and find the companionship of people who spoke their native language. In the 1890's, according to one writer, Greater New York had as many Italians as Naples, as many Germans as Hamburg, and twice as many Irish as Dublin.

Problems of Urbanization

Housing. Urbanization brought many problems which had to be solved by usually inexperienced city governments. One of the most serious of these problems was housing. City slums were ugly and unsanitary but, unfortunately, profitable to those who owned them. Thousands of low-paid workers were forced to crowd into dark, poorly ventilated tenements. The urban water supply was often inadequate and polluted by sewage that caused disease. The factories gave off smoke that fouled the air. Fire and police protection were inadequate. Park and recreational facilities were pitifully limited as a result of the failure of city authorities to effect proper zoning. Although these conditions were probably not as bad as the conditions in some European cities, they helped to breed discontent and crime.

Wages and Working Conditions. Other problems of the city laborer were those of poor wages and dangerous working conditions. The scanty incomes of heads of families often forced them to allow their wives and children to work. One estimate states that in 1900 about 1,170,000 children between the ages of ten and fifteen worked in America's factories, in addition to those who worked on farms. The working days were long; sometimes they lasted sixteen hours. Conditions were particularly bad in the garment-making fac-

Why are 1890 and 1920 key dates on this graph. Examine both curves carefully at these two dates. What happened around each date? What reasons can you give for the great upswing in urban population? When did your own ancestors come to America?

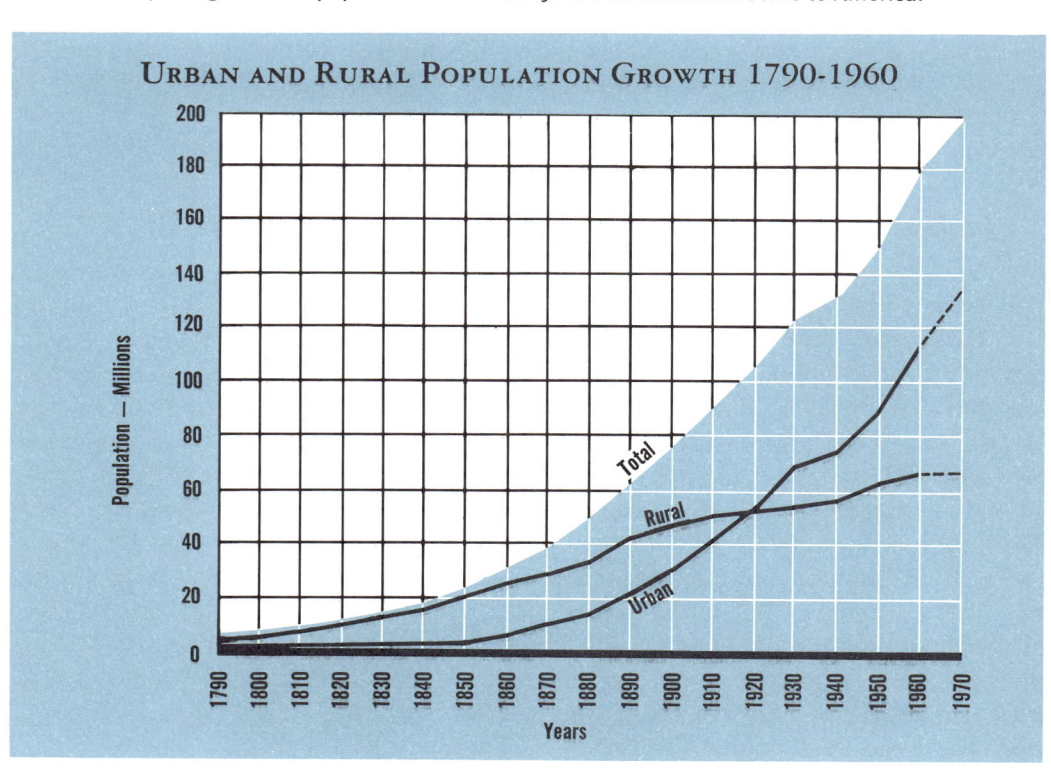

URBAN AND RURAL POPULATION GROWTH 1790-1960

tories in New York City. Most of these were firetraps, badly ventilated and lighted, with inadequate fire escapes. It was not until 1911, when a disastrous fire in the Triangle Shirtwaist Factory cost the lives of 148 women, that New York began a determined effort to improve factory conditions.

Industrial Accidents. Industrial accidents of all kinds were very common and workers were often injured or even killed by unsafe machinery. Coal miners had special problems. Mines were often little more than tunnels in the ground, and cave-ins in the years prior to 1935 killed hundreds of miners. In 1907, a mine in Monongah, West Virginia, collapsed killing 361 miners in one accident alone. Another problem was explosive gas within the mines which killed many miners by suffocation and explosion. Few of the safety devices that are used today had been developed and many factory and mine operators were indifferent to the hazards that existed for the workers.

Laws for the Laborer. Not until the state and federal governments began to answer organized labor's demand for improved working conditions in industry and mining was the safety of the laborer improved. At long last the number of unnecessary deaths moved the lawmakers to take action. Workmen's compensation laws, passed by some states, guaranteed the injured worker some payment until he could once again work. Private campaigns led by medical associations helped curtail occupational diseases like lead or phosphorous poisoning suffered by workers in paint or match factories. Safety campaigns organized by the state and federal governments alerted workers and owners to the dangers in factories and mines and resulted in the development of new safety devices as well as improved and safer methods of operation.

Finally, in 1935 the Wagner Act (National Labor Relations Act) was passed by Congress, permitting the miners as well as other laborers to organize in labor unions which could bargain for better working conditions as well as higher pay, using representatives of their own choosing. Today, after a long battle, most American workers enjoy safe, pleasant working conditions and enough pay to provide an adequate standard of living.

Tenement housing in New York. Note how clothes were hung to dry. Would they be clean when they had dried?

Disaster Strikes Chicago

The growth of great cities makes an interesting chapter in the history of our country. But sometimes it is a story of panic and disaster, as was the case of Chicago in October, 1871. This city then had a population of 300,000, most of whom lived in wooden houses. The autumn season had been very dry, and the city's fire department was concerned lest some careless person start a fire which could not be controlled.

On Sunday night, October 8, their fears were realized. According to reports, a cow belonging to Mrs. Patrick O'Leary kicked over a lantern which set fire to a shed. A strong wind fanned the flames. Neighboring buildings, dry as tinder, caught fire. In the next twenty-four hours about 18,000 buildings in the heart of the city were consumed by the flames, and 100,000 were rendered homeless. About 300 lost their lives.

But Chicago, then as now a vigorous and enterprising city, was not defeated. Within a year gleaming new buildings were rising from the ashes of the old.

Corruption in City Government

Party Machines. Municipal governments, especially in the period from 1870 to 1900, often fell into the hands of dishonest groups of men who gained control of a local political party. These groups, known as *machines* practiced graft in order to enrich themselves and their friends. By controlling the city councils and various commissions and boards, machine politicians were able to award contracts for constructing

A "machine" politician, with derby and cigar, made sure the voters backed his man. Today such practices are illegal.

buildings and paving roads to favored contractors who would give them a part of the profits. They made regulations and gave licenses for the benefit of those who were willing to pay for the service. Sometimes they could influence judges to render court decisions in their favor.

"Boss" Tweed. The most notorious, although by no means the worst, of these machines was Tammany Hall, a group led by "Boss" William Tweed that controlled the local Democratic party in New York City in 1868. The power of Tweed and his lieutenants lay in their influence with the large numbers of newly-arrived immigrants in the city. To win votes, the machine helped the immigrants to gain citizenship by illegal means. Sometimes the machine filled the ballot boxes with votes of nonexistent persons, falsified the count of votes, and bribed voters to cast their ballots as instructed. The old method of voting made it easy for the hirelings of the machine to ensure that instructions were carried out. The secret ballot did not come into use until the late 1880's, and the parties provided their own ballots, sometimes printed on brightly colored paper. A watchful agent, stationed near the ballot box, could quickly tell if the right color were used.

The machine was able to win the support of the foreign-born because they were generally poorly educated and unfamiliar with the American process of government. The machine's district leaders could retain the loyalty of the newly-arrived immigrants by giving them Christmas gifts and free groceries, by finding jobs for them, and by persuading judges to be lenient when they broke the laws. To the immigrant, the political worker was a friend in need and often the only one to pay him any attention. As much to blame for the success of the machine in graft and corruption, however, was the "respected" businessman who often worked hand in glove with the crooked politicians in order to secure favors that would help him to make money.

Can you see any significance in the size of Boss Tweed's stomach? Why did cartoonist Thomas Nast draw him thus?

Graft in New York. It is estimated that in the three years he was in power, Tweed and his gang cheated the city out of $100 million. For example, they induced the city to build a courthouse, the actual cost of which was $3 million. The bill to the taxpayers, however, came to $11 million after the books had been falsified and the graft paid out.

By 1871 public opinion was thoroughly aroused. The editors of *The New York Times*, cartoonist Thomas Nast, and others carried on unceasing warfare against the Tweed Ring. Property owners and honest citizens regained control of the government, and Tweed was sent to prison.

Corruption in State Governments. Boss Tweed and his gang were only one example of many corrupt city government machines existing throughout the country. These city governments, moreover, were only symptoms of a deeperbased disease rampant in several state legislatures. In some states, Pennsylvania and Ohio are examples, the legislatures were controlled by big business. Pennsylvania legislators sometimes acted as agents of the Pennsylvania Railroad. In the same sense, the Standard Oil Company held undue influence in enacting Ohio state laws. In New York, certain state congressmen could be "bought," or bribed to vote in a certain way. Such shocking behavior was a part of political life of the times. However, it resulted in a mockery of the democratic process.

The city machine politician often owed his political life to services he performed for those who needed it—the immigrants and the poor. Some immoral state politicians, however, listened only to the jingling of money in the pockets of the Vanderbilts, the Morgans, and the Rockefellers of the era. In the Midwest, certain states were run at the beck and call of the railroads. Business was well represented, but the people—the dirt farmers, the small town merchants, the workers—were not represented fairly in their state and local governments. When corruption began to creep into the national government, these people began to protest more vigorously.

Looking Back

1. What caused the migration to the cities when America became industrialized?

2. List and discuss the many problems caused by rapid urbanization.

3. Explain how political machines obtained and maintained control of city politics.

4. How was it possible for "Boss" Tweed to cheat New York City out of so much money?

5. By what means did corruption begin to spread to state governments?

2. Spirit of Reform Grows in the Twentieth Century

The reform movement in America came about for various reasons other than the ones just cited—corruption in government and poor living conditions. Generally, however, it can be said that social advances had failed to keep up with technical advances. Men were making great strides in the fields of invention and experimentation, but nothing had been done to improve the way the average man earned a living or went about the pursuit of happiness. Foolishly, most people expected that the old ways of life would be sufficient to deal with the advances in technology. But the new inventions, the large cities, and the huge, sometimes impersonal corporations, posed new social problems for Americans. The reform movement went about trying to solve these new problems.

"Muckrakers"

As the twentieth century opened, the spirit of reform gathered momentum. A talented group of writers used their literary skill to attack the evils in American society. Their magazine articles, books, and poems were widely read and discussed by concerned citizens. It was not long before they became known as the *Muckrakers,* so called because their purpose was to rake and uncover the wrongdoings of the day. The Muckrakers managed to bring about considerable improvements in the targets of their protest. Ida M. Tarbell unveiled the evils of the oil industry. Lincoln Steffens, a famous journalist, wrote angry articles attacking corruption in the cities. Their main function was to alert the public to the things that were going on around them. The public in turn reacted by electing more honest and efficient officials. They also vehemently demanded reform legislation.

Reforms in Government

City Government. In the field of city government, too, there was evidence of reform. In Toledo, Ohio, the Republican machine secured the election in 1897 of Samuel M. Jones as mayor of the city. Jones was a progressive and forward looking businessman who had come to this country from Wales when he was only an infant.

In his oil-drilling equipment business, Jones had instituted various labor reforms such as an eight-hour day, a minimum wage, and vacations with pay for the workers. When he was elected mayor of Toledo, he advocated the same benefits for city employees.

One of the great reformers of his time was "Battling Bob" LaFollette, a senator from Wisconsin. He was nominated for President in 1924 by the Progressive Party and received 5,000,000 votes in the election, finishing third.

He was also exceedingly honest. Contrary to the expectations of the Republican party bosses, he refused to use his position to grant favors. His honesty and zeal in promoting good causes earned him the nickname of "Golden Rule" Jones, and the grateful people kept him in office until his death in 1904.

State Government. On the state level, the battle against the bosses continued. Among the leaders in this battle was the colorful Robert M. La Follette of Wisconsin, who served as governor in his state from 1900 to 1906 and then as U.S. Senator until he died

Salvation Army bands helped raise funds.

in 1925. He carried out many progressive programs leading to laws providing for workmen's compensation, fairer taxation of corporations, regulation of the railroads, and conservation of natural resources. He also instituted direct primary elections which allowed all the members of a party to help in choosing their candidates. The direct primary cut off the power of the political bosses to name party candidates in a small meeting of party insiders who picked the men they wanted to run for office.

Workers for Social Justice

Others besides public officials tried to improve living conditions in towns and cities. The movement to help the poor, the sick, and the unemployed was started by private individuals. Jane Addams, an experienced social worker, founded the famous Hull House in Chicago in 1889. This was a "settlement" house where people of all nationalities could come for assistance and companionship. Four years later Lillian Wald founded the Henry Street Settlement in a slum section of New York. Similar organizations were started by public-spirited groups or individuals in other cities.

Clergymen aided the reform movement by preaching what came to be known as "the social gospel"—that is, the belief that the church should be concerned with the economic problems of their people as well as the spiritual. Protestant ministers, Catholic priests, and Jewish rabbis worked in the slums to better the lives of the less fortunate. The Salvation Army, which had been organized in England by William Booth, set up an American branch in 1880 to give aid to neglected slum-dwellers. As conditions among the poor and unemployed worsened, religious and private groups combined with civic welfare groups in programs of relief and aid.

Ending the "Spoils System"

Politicians in all ages and countries have followed the practice of rewarding their supporters by getting jobs for them. Once in office, the politician enjoys a certain amount of *patronage,* which means that he has the opportunity to place people on the public payroll. This is known as the *spoils system,* (see page 235) based on the principle that "to the victor belongs the spoils." Although the system is not entirely bad, it can easily lead to dishonesty and inefficiency in government. Very often a person was given a job even though he might be entirely unqualified for it. This waste of public funds disgusted many able men who might otherwise have run for office, especially in the generation following the Civil War.

Hayes and Civil Service. Although many had seen the evils of the "spoils system," no one did much about it until Rutherford B. Hayes of Ohio became President in 1877. He appointed the noted civil service reformer, Carl Schurz, to his cabinet as Secretary of the Interior and forbade federal officeholders to contribute money for political purposes. This act was violently resisted by some of his fellow Republicans, who applied the term "snivel service reform" to the President's program.

Assassination of Garfield. In the election of 1880 the Republican candidate, James A. Garfield of Ohio, a former Union brigadier general, won the Presidency. After a few months in office Garfield was shot down by a Chicago lawyer who had become mentally unbalanced after he had been refused a government position.

The Pendleton Act. This murder so shocked the country that Congress passed the Pendleton Act in 1883. This act, which has been called "the Magna Carta of civil service reform," provided that:

(1) the President could place on a "classified list" those federal jobs which could be filled only according to rules laid down by a Civil Service Commission,

(2) government employees were to be chosen on the basis of their grades in examinations,

What the well dressed woman of (left to right) 1880, 1900, 1910, and 1925 would wear. Which clothes resemble today's most closely?

In the 1890's fancy carriages and teams of horses were symbols of wealth and status. Here the "fashionable set" drives through New York's Central Park.

(3) no government employee could be required to contribute money for political campaigns.

The act aimed at replacing the "spoils system" with the "merit system."

Extending Civil Service. Those who favored the spoils system, however, felt that their cause would be advanced by the death of Garfield, for his Vice-President was Chester A. Arthur, who had been a friend of powerful political bosses in New York. Arthur proved a surprise to friends and foes alike, for he vigorously supported the Pendleton Act, which placed about 16,000 government positions on the civil service list. The next President, Grover Cleveland, carried on the good work, as did President Harrison, whose term of office came between the two terms of Cleveland. In succeeding administrations, the classified list gradually lengthened and today it covers more than eighty-five per cent of our federal employees.

New Roles for Women

After the Civil War most men enjoyed the right to vote, but all women were denied a share in the government. In other ways, too, women did not have equal rights with men. Often if they had property when they married, this property passed into the hands of their husbands, who also held custody of the children. If women wished to enter a profession, they found most doors closed to them. The only professions open to them were teaching and nursing, both of which paid them next to nothing.

Dorothea Dix. It was no wonder, then, that from mid-century on, women should try to take an active part in national affairs and to demand full equality with men. One of the most aggressive of these women was Dorothea Dix, a Massachusetts school teacher who led reforms in the treatment of the mentally unbalanced. Prior to Dorothea Dix' efforts, those with mental problems were treated like criminals and locked in jails. Miss Dix conducted investigations of this shocking procedure and persuaded legislators to pass laws establishing asylums where the mentally ill could be treated properly. This reform spread to other states and even to other countries.

The Right to Vote. Women realized very clearly that the key to equality was the right to vote. As early as 1848 they held a convention at Seneca Falls, New York, and drew up a long list of grievances, maintaining stoutly that "all men and women are created equal."

At first the women's rights movement was quite ineffective, but slowly it gained headway. In 1869 the legislature of Wyoming gave women the right to vote. In the same year the National Woman Suffrage Association was organized by Susan B. Anthony. By 1914 women could vote in twelve states, all west of the Mississippi. In 1916 Montana elected the first woman to the U. S. House of Representatives. Finally Congress gave in to the demands of women and passed the Nineteenth Amendment which guaranteed women's voting rights. In 1920 it was ratified by the necessary three-fourths of the states—and at last American women had the right to vote.

Looking Back

1. How did the "muckrakers" contribute to the reform movement?
2. By what means did Wisconsin under La Follette pioneer in reforms?
3. Who were the leaders in the struggle for social justice? Tell how each contributed to the cause.
4. Show how the terms of the Pendleton Act helped replace the "spoils system."
5. How did the Nineteenth Amendment crown a long struggle by women?

For those who "couldn't afford a carriage" a bicycle built for two was cheap and romantic transportation. It was also a means of conveyance in which women gained some equality with men. Notice in this picture that the young lady is steering.

3. Americans Find Time to Enjoy Life

In the 1880's and 1890's people worked longer hours in factories and offices than they do now, but they could still take time for recreation. Most of them, like Americans today, found their greatest pleasure in outdoor living and in sports. There was other entertainment in considerable abundance—so much of it in fact, that part of this period of American history is known as "the Gay Nineties."

Theatrical Entertainment

Drama. Improved rail transportation made possible the traveling theatrical road company, made up of actors and often headed by a well-known star. These companies presented many Shakespearean plays, as well as sentimental dramas depicting American life. The public appetite for such dramatic fare was very strong. The popular dramas of the period dealt with family life and domestic problems. They were not great plays, but they enjoyed wide popularity.

The Circus. Vaudeville acts performed by comedians, singers, and acrobats were enjoyed by all. Phineas T. Barnum, later joined by James A. Bailey, created "The Greatest Show on Earth"—the circus. The "Wild West" shows of Buffalo Bill Cody delighted children of those days as much as the television "westerns" do today.

The Movies. The first movie theaters were small halls equipped with uncomfortable seats and sometimes a tinkling piano on which an enthusiastic player would render an accompani-

The circus was a flourishing spectacle in the 1880's and 1890's. The invention of the electric light bulb made night performances possible. This circus troupe was photographed around 1890. Can you identify any of the attractions or sideshow characters?

Left: Football game played between Rochester University (in white) and Cornell University in 1889. Right: An 1889 football player. How have uniforms changed today?

ment to the picture. These theaters were known as *nickelodeons* because the usual price of admission was five cents. The first movies had no plots. In fact they usually consisted of representations of everyday life. Nevertheless the audiences were delighted with a series of pictures that "moved." "The Great Train Robbery," produced in 1903, was the first to have a plot. However, twelve years later, when D. W. Griffith produced "The Birth of a Nation," a movie presenting a view of Southern life after the Civil War, audiences could view a real feature show with camera effects somewhat like those in a modern film. In 1927 the first "talkie" movie, "The Jazz Singer," with Al Jolson as the star performer, created a sensational new demand for movies.

Chautauqua. For rural communities an important means of entertainment and education was the Chautauqua. This movement began as a summer study group of Sunday School teachers at Lake Chautauqua, New York. So much interest was aroused that the summer sessions were lengthened and lectures on various subjects were given. Often the performances were given in a large tent that held hundreds of spectators. Other communities adopted the idea. Chautauqua companies were formed to bring good plays, music, and lectures to people who could not easily travel to the cities.

Music

In the 1880's a craze for popular music swept the country. Thomas Edison's phonograph was being improved by this time, and by the turn of the century music-lovers were rushing to buy records and phonographs. Serious music also gained wide public support. Symphony orchestras were formed in Boston, New York, and Chicago. The famous Metropolitan Opera House of New York, which opened in 1883, played host to many great foreign singers. American composers began to earn European recognition, as well as the applause of Americans. The best known of the American composers was Edward A. McDowell, whose concertos were performed in Europe as well as in the United States.

Organized Sports

Baseball. The game of baseball, forms of which had been played long before the Civil War, became so popular that professionals organized teams to play for money. The first professional team was the Cincinnati Red Stockings, which appeared in 1869. Seven years later the present National League was organized. A rival league called the American Association appeared soon after. It eventually passed out of existence and was replaced by the American League, organized in 1900 by Ban Johnson.

Football. Football, derived from the English game of rugby, was played at first by rival groups in the same college. The first inter-collegiate game was played in 1869 between Princeton and Rutgers, with twenty-five men on each side!

As more colleges adopted the sport, they formed an association to standardize the rules. Walter Camp, a great Yale athlete who has been called "the father of American football," devised a set of rules that were accepted by the colleges. College football was a major sport by 1893, when the Yale-Princeton game attracted a crowd of fifty thousand excited fans.

Prizefighting. Prizefighting was illegal in most states before the 1880's. Boxers fought without gloves, and the fight lasted until one of the contestants was knocked down. When the *Marquis-of-Queensberry Rules* were introduced from England about 1885, the sport became legal. John L. Sullivan was the first heavyweight cham-

John L. Sullivan fought the last bare knuckle championship fight in 1889 with Jake Kilrain. The fight lasted 75 rounds, about 3 hours.

pion to win under the new rules, which called for padded gloves and three-minute rounds. Other great fighters in this period were "Gentleman Jim" Corbett, Bob Fitzsimmons, and Jim Jeffries.

Basketball. Basketball, destined to become one of the greatest indoor sports in America, was invented in 1891 by Dr. James Naismith of Springfield College, Springfield, Massachusetts. This fast, exciting game grew rapidly in popularity as a winter sport which could be played in gymnasiums.

Summary

On the whole, life in our country as the twentieth century dawned was full of interest and hopeful expectation. In many ways living was simpler than it is today and lacked many of the comforts we now enjoy. Nevertheless, thousands of older Americans looked back upon the period with nostalgia, and think of it as "the good old days."

Like most people, Americans tended to remember the best things and forget the worst. To the person who had lived through the years from the Civil War to the Gay Nineties, the gaiety, the industrial progress, and the growing pains of the United States were things that could be remembered with pleasure and pride. However, the squalor and filth of city tenements, the indecently low wages on which men had to live, and the corruption in government were things most people wished to forget. In reality, the "good old days" are usually products of people's memories, which are not always accurate.

Looking Back

1. What were the chief forms of entertainment in the 1890's?
2. What sports are popular today that were not so popular in the 1890's and early 1900's?
3. How good were the "good old days"?

The Chapter in Perspective

Who Are These People?

Tweed	Garfield	La Follette	Booth
Tarbell	Arthur	Addams	Susan B. Anthony
Steffens	Dorothea Dix	Wald	Barnum and Bailey

What Do These Dates and Terms Mean?

urbanization
Wagner Act
party machine
Tammany Hall
naturalization
muckrakers
direct primaries
Hull House
Salvation Army
Pendleton Act
workmen's compensation
Nineteenth Amendment
Seneca Falls Convention
Henry Street Settlement

1848
1883
patronage
spoils system
1920
1935
Civil Service
merit system
Chautauqua

Questions for Study

1. Has the migration from farms to the city continued, been halted, or reversed itself? Prove your answer.
2. What problems of urbanization remain with us today?
3. List five gains made by labor since the beginning of the twentieth century.
4. Have graft and corruption been removed from our present governments? Can you support your answer?
5. If you were a "muckraker" today what evils would you attack? Why?
6. How does the merit system function?
7. Do you feel that we will have a woman as President some day? Why?
8. Why does the average American have more leisure time today than his counterpart at the beginning of the century?
9. What cities were represented in the original professional sport leagues? Why was the area west of the Mississippi poorly represented?
10. Why is it easier for political machines to be organized in urban areas than in rural areas?

Place Yourself in History

On March 1, 1877, the man to be inaugurated as President on the following Monday had not yet been selected. The November election and the December meeting of the Electoral College had failed to make a clear cut choice because of special circumstances. The country was uneasy and federal troops were on the alert for possible trouble.

The fate of the Presidency and perhaps of the nation, is in the hands of eight Republicans and seven Democrats who are members of the special Electoral Commission.

What were the special circumstances that led to the need for the Electoral Commission? What were the immediate and long-range results of its decisions? How would you have voted as a member of the Commission? Why?

22
A New Role on the World Stage

By the 1890's, Americans had become justifiably proud of the growing wealth and power of their country. The frontier had dissolved under the impact of thousands of settlers, and immigrants had swelled and varied the population enormously. Factories and farms were producing goods to clothe, feed, and supply the needs of millions of new Americans, and the country was regarded in Europe as an industrial miracle. Now that the population of the United States was spread from the Atlantic to the Pacific, many Americans looked to the rest of the world for places to expend their pioneering energy. Manufacturers sought foreign markets, and statesmen looked to the day when American power would be felt in other parts of the world. For better or for worse, the United States embarked upon a world course.

1. The Spirit of Imperialism Leads to Territorial Expansion

Since 1867, when Secretary of State William Seward had arranged the purchase of Alaska from Russia for $7,200,000, the United States had acquired no territory outside her continental boundaries. Many European nations, especially Germany, France, and England, however, had won vast colonial possessions in Africa and Asia during the closing years of the nineteenth century.

The spirit of imperialism—that is, the desire to extend a nation's power and possessions—infiltrated the United States late in the 1800's. Some Americans in the 1890's, like Senators Albert J. Beveridge and Henry Cabot Lodge, urged the government to acquire holdings in the Pacific and Atlantic.

The concept of imperialism was refined in books written by a brilliant naval historian, Captain Alfred T. Mahan. In 1890 he published a widely read book, *The Influence of Sea Power Upon History, 1660–1783*, and followed it in 1897 with *The Interest of America in Sea Power*. Mahan argued that American greatness depended upon a powerful navy and merchant marine, colonies to provide raw materials and markets, a canal across the isthmus of Central America, and defensive island naval bases in the Caribbean and the Pacific.

The Annexation of Hawaii

Long before Mahan wrote his books, Americans had shown a keen interest in the beautiful Hawaiian Islands, lying in the Pacific about 2400 miles southwest of San Francisco. Here American traders and whalers as well as those of other nations had provisioned their ships in the early 1800's. In 1820 New England missionaries arrived to convert the natives to Christianity. They were followed by Yankee merchants and sugar planters who rapidly gained economic control of the islands and dominated the policies of the native kings.

Sugar and the Islands. At various times the Russians, French, and British had shown interest in the Hawaiian Islands, but gradually American influence prevailed. The bonds were strengthened in 1875 when a reciprocity treaty was signed allowing Hawaiian sugar to enter the United States duty-free on condition that Hawaii give no territorial rights to other powers. In 1887 the United States was given the exclusive use of Pearl Harbor as a naval station.

In 1890 the prosperous sugar growers and refiners were alarmed when the McKinley Tariff removed the duty on *all* foreign raw sugar and gave American growers a bounty. This new tariff would mean that sugar refined in Hawaii could not be imported cheaply into the United States. Since the United States was Hawaii's main mar-

The annexation of Hawaii added its beauty to the land area of the U.S. and contributed cultural influences from Korea, Japan, China, and Polynesia to American Society.

ket for sugar, the economy of the islands would be seriously injured. The planters were further distressed by the policies of a new ruler, Queen Liliuokalani (LIH′lee-oo-oh-kah-lah′nee), who seemed determined to reduce American influence and restore Hawaii to the Hawaiians.

The Republic of Hawaii. Although they were only a small minority, the Europeans and Americans started a revolution in 1893, hoping that the United States would use the revolution as an excuse to annex the islands. It took only a few hours for the plot to succeed, partly because the pro-annexationist American minister, John L. Stevens, ordered marines from a warship in the harbor to go ashore to protect Americans and their property. The rebels sent a committee to Washington to negotiate a treaty of annexation. President Cleveland, a Democrat who had just succeeded President Harrison, refused to sign the treaty. However, he did agree to recognize the new Republic of Hawaii which had been set up with Sanford B. Dole as president.

The 50th State. After five years as a republic and after Cleveland was out of office, Hawaii was annexed as a territory of the United States in 1898, by authority of a joint resolution of both houses of Congress. In 1959, after years of agitation by journalists, educators, and businessmen, Hawaii was admitted to the Union as the 50th state. Alaska had won statehood earlier in the same year.

The Protectorate of Samoa

Far to the south of Hawaii lay the Samoan Islands. As American trade with Asia, Australia, and New Zealand increased, these islands became valuable as a place to stop for fuel and fresh water. The navy was especially interested in the harbor of Pago Pago on the island of Tutuila (Too-too-ee′-lah), so they tried to obtain rights to it. In 1878 a treaty with a Samoan chief secured for the United States a naval station in this fine anchorage.

Germany and Great Britain also saw the value of Samoa and hastened to make treaties with various native chiefs. For ten years the three nations struggled and plotted for control, often coming dangerously close to war. In 1889 German and American warships in the harbor seemed ready to clash. Before a shot was fired, however, a tropical hurricane arose and wrecked the ships. This event sobered the contestants, and they worked out a solution at the conference table. A three-way protectorate of Samoa was agreed upon for ten years. In 1899 Great Britain withdrew, leaving the islands under the control of Germany and the United States. New Zealand acquired the German interests in the islands at the end of World War I.

Looking Back

1. What were Captain Mahan's views on what America needed to become a great power?
2. How were Hawaiian-American relations strengthened?
3. Why did President Cleveland refuse to take steps to annex Hawaii?
4. By what steps did the Samoan Islands come under the protection of the United States?

2. The United States Wages and Wins a Foreign War

In 1896 the Republicans, now known as the party of Big Business, nominated William McKinley of Ohio for President. The Republican platform favored high tariffs and the gold standard. McKinley's campaign, heavily financed by Eastern conservatives, was managed by Ohio businessman Mark Hanna.

The Democrats were divided but finally chose William Jennings Bryan of Nebraska as their candidate. At the Democratic convention in Chicago, Bryan delivered a dramatic oration attacking the gold standard. (See Chapter XVII.) His "Cross of Gold" speech thrilled the Democrats and won him the nomination. Bryan conducted a vigorous campaign through twenty-seven states, making hundreds of eloquent speeches advocating "Free Silver." Intensely interested in the issues and excited by the personalities of the two candidates, the voters went to the polls in great numbers. The popular vote was quite close—7,104,779 for McKinley and 6,502,925 for Bryan—but McKinley won decisively in the electoral college with 271 votes to Bryan's 176.

Little more than one short year after his election, McKinley was faced with a serious decision. He had to decide whether or not to involve the United States in their first foreign war in fifty years. His final choice and how he made it were to have a profound effect on American history.

Spanish Rule in Cuba

The people of Cuba had long resented the corrupt rule of Spain. Between 1868 and 1878 they had fought an unsuccessful rebellion (the Ten Years War) against their mother country. Americans were sympathetic to the Cuban cause, but maintained official neutrality. In 1895 another revolution broke out, partly because of continued Spanish mismanagement and partly because a high American tariff (passed

Between 1894–1896, the Chatauqua circuit listed William Jennings Bryan among its outstanding attractions.

Two explosions destroyed the *Maine*. The first, a small one, set off the second one of the ship's powder supply in the forward half of the ship. The *Maine's* stern then slowly sank. Since the explosion occurred at 9:40 P.M., the whole harbor was illuminated.

in 1894) on raw sugar reduced sales and hurt the Cuban economy.

The Madrid government, determined to suppress the rebellion, sent General Valeriano Weyler to Cuba in 1896. "Butcher" Weyler, as he was known in the American press, attempted to crush the revolution by herding civilians into concentration camps where they would be powerless to help their armed countrymen. These camps lacked proper sanitation and many civilians died of disease.

Pro-Cuban Sympathies of Americans

The "Yellow Press." Americans were shocked by the cruelty of the Spanish military, which was reported in a sensational way by the "yellow press." The *New York World* of Joseph Pulitzer and the *New York Journal* of William Randolph Hearst printed exaggerated accounts of the Spanish atrocities, and other papers followed their lead. A sympathetic Congress passed a resolution favoring the Cuban side, but President Cleveland ignored it, for he believed that both sides were at fault in Cuba.

The "Maine." When McKinley took over the Presidency early in 1897, he did not want war. Nevertheless, he sent a protest to Spain against the bloodshed in Cuba. The Spanish government, fearing American intervention, recalled General Weyler, reduced the evils of the concentration camps, and promised to allow some measure of self-government to the Cubans. The tension decreased, and it looked as if war might be averted. Then, early in 1898, two events occurred that threw the country into an uproar.

In February a Cuban agent in Havana stole a private letter written by Dupuy de Lôme, the Spanish minister to the United States. The letter described McKinley as a weak politician who followed the crowds. The

The demolished *Maine* lay on the harbor bottom in Havana. The wreck was mute evidence in the unsolved mystery of the vessel's explosion.

letter was acquired by Hearst's *New York Journal*. When it was published, an angry American public condemned it as an insult. De Lôme promptly resigned, but the damage was done.

On February 15, the battleship *Maine*, which had been sent to Havana to protect American interests, blew up while anchored in the harbor, with a loss of 260 lives. To this day it is not known what caused the explosion. It may have been an internal explosion of the ship's magazines. Cuban rebels may have exploded a mine near the ship, hoping to force American intervention on their side. It may have been the work of Spanish agents under orders from Madrid. In any case the press assumed that the fault lay with the Spanish government, and the headlines screamed, "Remember the *Maine*."

Declaration of War. Although McKinley continued to try for a peaceful solution, he was forced at last to give way to public opinion. On April 11, he sent a message to Congress asking for permission to use the armed forces to end the fighting in Cuba and to establish a stable government in the island. Congress consented and added the Teller Amendment. This stated that the United States would not annex Cuba and would ensure the independence of its people. War was formally declared on April 25, 1898.

The Spanish-American War

Manila Bay. At the outbreak of the war the American Asiatic Squadron, under Commodore George Dewey, was anchored near Hong Kong. Theodore Roosevelt, then Assistant Secretary of the Navy, had sent secret orders to Dewey on February 25 to be ready to attack the Spanish fleet in the Philippines in case of war. On May 1, Dewey carried out his orders and entered Manila Bay, where the Spanish fleet was anchored. When the firing was over, the Spanish ships were completely destroyed and 381 Spaniards were killed. One American sailor died from a heat stroke, and a handful were wounded.

The country rejoiced at Dewey's brilliant feat, and the government quickly sent a force of soldiers to follow up the victory. The Filipinos, led by Emilio Aguinaldo, joined the Americans and forced the Spanish garrison in Manila to surrender on August 13, 1898.

Naval Blockade of Santiago. Another Spanish fleet under Admiral Cervera lay at the Cape Verde Islands off Africa's west coast in the Atlantic Ocean, and at the outbreak of the war these vessels set sail westward into American waters. Cervera's fleet threatened the entire Atlantic coast of the United States. To combat this threat, the navy sent two American fleets, one under Admiral Sampson and one under Commodore Schley, to intercept the Spanish fleet before it could do any damage.

Eluding the two American fleets, the Spaniards slipped unobserved into the harbor of Santiago, Cuba. Here they remained in hiding for several weeks, while the inhabitants of coast towns in the United States expected daily to see them appear and to hear the bursting of Spanish shells. Then, towards the end of May, Admiral Sampson discovered the whereabouts of the Spanish fleet and promptly bottled it up in Santiago harbor.

At the time when the Spanish fleet was discovered at Santiago, the United States battleship *Oregon* was in San Francisco harbor. At once she put to sea to join the blockading squadron. Down the Pacific coasts of North and South America she dashed at her fastest speed, through the Straits of Magellan, and north to Santiago. Her voyage took seventy-one days, but she arrived in time to take an active part in the blockade.

"The Rough Riders." An American army of nearly 17,000 men had meanwhile been sent to Cuba. Among the

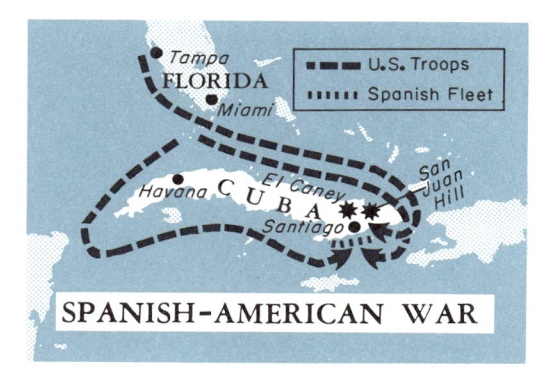

This "Rough Rider" was lucky enough to get a horse. The horses, and half the men, had been left in Tampa, Florida, in the confusion of leaving for Cuba.

SPANISH-AMERICAN WAR

Teddy Roosevelt (standing, with glasses, in the center) and his "Rough Riders" at San Juan Hill, Cuba, 1898. Since the Rough Riders had very few horses, their name didn't really describe them. They fought bravely and heroically and have become a legend.

regiments was one known as *the Rough Riders* led by Colonel Leonard Wood and later by Colonel Theodore Roosevelt. This famous regiment was made up of hard-riding Western plainsmen and young college graduates from the East. Although commissioned as a cavalry outfit, the Rough Riders fought on foot during most of the war.

The American army landed near Santiago and at once made a vigorous attack on the Spanish fortifications at San Juan Hill and El Caney. In spite of the hot fire of the defenders, these two strongholds were soon forced to surrender to the Americans, who promptly entrenched themselves near the city of Santiago.

Richard Harding Davis, an observer in the Spanish-American War in Cuba, recorded these impressions of the Battle of San Juan Hill and its heroes, Teddy Roosevelt and General Hawkins.

General Hawkins, with hair as white as snow . . . was so noble a sight that you felt inclined to pray for his safety; on the other hand, Roosevelt, mounted high on horseback, and charging the rifle-pits at a gallop and quite alone, made you feel that you would like to cheer. He wore on his sombrero a blue polka-dot handkerchief . . ., which, as he advanced, floated out straight behind his head. . . . Afterward, the men of his regiment who followed this flag adopted a polka-dot handkerchief as the badge of the Rough Riders.

Battle of Santiago. Had the Spaniards but known it, the city was safe from immediate capture. The Americans did not have sufficient men to storm the fortifications from the land side, and what troops they did have were poorly equipped, with insufficient food and with uniforms far too heavy for the hot climate of Cuba. The big guns of the Spanish ships, moreover, could easily have wreaked great havoc in the American lines and driven the American forces from their position.

The Spanish leaders, however, overestimated American strength and believed the city to be in danger of immediate capture. In terror lest their fleet of four cruisers and two destroyers be taken when the city fell, they determined on a bold attempt to run the blockade of Sampson's fleet and try to escape to the open sea. On Sunday morning, July 3, the attempt was made. Past the sunken hull of a coaling steamer with which the Americans had tried unsuccessfully to block the harbor entrance, sailed the Spanish warships, one by one. Then they were discovered, and the American ships were after them with smoke pouring from their funnels and flame belching from their guns.

The battle was much like that of Manila Bay. The Spaniards fired rapidly but inaccurately. The American gunners, taking careful aim, did frightful damage to the fleeing vessels. One by one the Spanish ships were disabled. Burning and sinking, they turned towards the coast in an attempt to save their crews. Only the *Cristóbal Colón*, named after Christopher Columbus, had a chance. That vessel, with her brave crew, kept up a running fight with the American cruiser *Brooklyn* and the great battleship *Oregon* for more than forty-five miles before she was beached, a hopeless wreck.

As at Manila the American loss was slight—one man killed and only one badly wounded. The Spaniards, however, had lost more than five hundred brave men, and their entire fleet had

The Spanish-American War captured the imaginations of many Americans. Relics of the war, such as this steel rifle from a Spanish ship, were hauled from small town to small town all over the nation. This picture was taken in Williamsburg, Ohio.

been destroyed. Never have there been two such decisive naval battles with so little cost to the victors.

End of Hostilities. After the destruction of Cervera's fleet, the Spanish surrendered Santiago. To fight longer would have been hopeless. Although the American troops suffered terribly from heat and from fever, they showed no sign of giving up their siege, and the guns of Sampson's fleet were a constant menace from the sea. Sooner or later the city must fall, and the Spanish were wise in surrendering when they did.

To the astonishment of the world, the American forces had quickly overcome the Spaniards. By August the war was over and the Spanish were asking for terms. Only 460 Americans were killed in battle or died of wounds, but about 5200 succumbed to various tropical diseases.

Results of the War. In October, 1898, representatives of Spain and the United States met in Paris to conduct peace negotiations. A treaty was signed on December 10. Spain agreed to withdraw from Cuba, and to turn over the islands of Puerto Rico, Guam, and the entire Philippine group to the United States. In return, Spain was to receive a payment of twenty million dollars.

Looking Back

1. List the candidates, issues, and results of the election of 1896.
2. Discuss the complaints against the Spanish rule in Cuba.
3. For what reasons did the United States declare war on Spain in 1898?
4. What were the results of the Spanish-American War?

3. U. S. Imperialists Look to Asia

Acquisition of the Philippines

When the treaty was submitted to the Senate, it met with much opposition. The chief objection was the acquisition of the Philippines. Most Democrats and a number of Republicans argued that it was not fair for the United States to occupy the Philippines for the purpose of helping American trade, especially since the Filipinos wanted to be independent. Others argued that possession of the islands would add to American naval and economic strength in the Far East, and that if the United States did not take the islands, they would fall into the hands of some other major power.

After weeks of vigorous debate the Senate ratified the treaty in February, 1899, by a very narrow margin. In the presidential election of 1900, the principal issue was the question of "imperialism." William Jennings Bryan, the Democratic nominee, advocated freeing the Philippines from United States control if the Democrats and Bryan won. McKinley, the champion of imperialism, whom the Republicans had again nominated as their standard-bearer, defeated Bryan soundly. The colorful Colonel "Teddy" Roosevelt was elected Vice-President.

The Open Door in China

Spheres of Influence. The acquisition of the Philippines stimulated American interest in the other parts of the Far East as well. Businessmen hoped that Manila would become a great trading center like Hong Kong, and that Americans would capture a much larger share of the trade with China. This ancient country had become feeble and helpless, and was in danger of being carved up, like Africa, by the stronger powers. Already, in 1895, the Japanese had attacked China and had annexed Formosa and the Pescadores. While the Spanish-American War was being fought, European imperialistic nations—Great Britain, France, Russia, and Germany—had forced the Chinese government to grant concessions and "leases" whereby they could exercise special privileges and enjoy *"spheres of influence."*

Open Door Principles. In 1898 the British, who along with the other large European powers, controlled most of the China trade, proposed that the United States issue a declaration favoring an *Open Door* in China in which the British would later join. The Open Door policy contained three principles: (1) each major power, Great Britain, Russia, Germany, France, and the United States, would respect the rights and privileges of other nations in its own sphere of influence. (That is, if the United States enjoyed trading rights in a certain area, or if they were the only nation to be welcome in a certain area, Southern China for example, they would not hinder other nations from attempting to establish trading rights there.); (2) Chinese officials would continue to collect tariff duties in all spheres; (3) no nation would discriminate against another in charging railroad rates and port dues.

John Hay, American Secretary of State, collaborating with the British, formulated these principles and in 1899 addressed a circular letter to the other powers (Germany, Russia, France, Japan and Italy) asking that they agree to the Open Door policy. Although the other powers made no firm promises, they politely agreed in principle, and the Open Door became an important objective in American foreign policy.

The Boxer Rebellion

In 1900 a secret Chinese patriotic society called "Fists of Universal Harmony"—or Boxers—started an uprising against foreigners in China. They killed

John Hay started his career as secretary to President Lincoln. He was Secretary of State from 1898 until he died in 1905.

over two hundred foreigners and besieged the foreign diplomats in the British embassy in Peking. The "foreign devils" held out until they were rescued by an international expeditionary force, which included 2500 American troops.

In an effort to prevent the powers from using the uprising as an excuse for seizing Chinese territory, McKinley and Hay again asked support for the Open Door policy. With the cooperation of Great Britain and Germany, they succeeded in persuading the powers to accept money for the losses and inconveniences in China instead of territorial gains. The Chinese government was assessed $332,000,000 for damages, of which the United States received about $25,000,000, a figure far in excess of American damages. The United States later gave back about $12,000,000, which the Chinese government used to educate Chinese students in America.

Looking Back

1. What arguments were made for and against the annexation of the Philippines?
2. How did the acquisition of the Philippines stimulate American interest in the Far East?
3. What was the "Open Door" policy?
4. Discuss the causes and results of the Boxer Rebellion.

4. The Nation Governs Its New Empire

The new American empire now stretched from the Caribbean to the western Pacific. It included the Philippines, Hawaii, Samoa, Guam, Alaska, Puerto Rico, and a string of small Pacific Islands including Wake and Midway. How were these dependencies to be governed? Would their inhabitants automatically become American citizens? Could they send goods into the mainland United States without paying a duty? Each of the new dependencies presented a problem.

The Philippine Insurrection

Little did the United States realize what administrative troubles lay ahead in the Philippines. Bitterly disappointed at not receiving independence, Aguinaldo and his followers prepared to resist the Americans. The insurrection began in February, 1899, and continued for two weary years. The Filipinos used vicious guerrilla warfare, fighting fiercely in the swamps and forests. The United States sent 60,000 troops to break the backbone of this revolt. America won the war, but at a cost of 4300 American lives.

Civil government took over from the army in 1901. Even while the fighting was going on, President McKinley had sent a commission to the islands to make preparations for the transfer from military to civilian rule. William Howard Taft, later to become President, headed the commission. He genuinely liked the Filipinos and did much to prepare their country for independence. The American program called

in 1946. Today the Filipinos are among our firmest friends in Southeast Asia.

The Platt Amendment for Cuba

At the beginning of the Spanish-American War the United States had promised in the Teller Amendment to allow the Cubans to govern themselves when order was restored. However, for nearly four years after the war it was necessary for American troops to remain in the country.

Under the able administration of General Leonard Wood, the Cuban government was modernized, finances were organized, and schools and roads were built. An army medical officer, Major William C. Gorgas, conquered the dreaded yellow fever by cleaning up the breeding places of the mosquito that carried the disease.

In 1901 the Cubans adopted a constitution modeled on that of the United States, and the following year the military occupation came to an end. The Cubans agreed to the terms of the

Emilio Aguinaldo led the revolt against Spain which helped the U.S. win the Phillipines. Against all foreign domination, he fought the U.S. later.

for the distribution of land to the peasants, promotion of education, and the popular election of local officials. In 1907 the Filipinos were allowed to elect their own legislature, although the United States continued to appoint the territorial governor. In 1916 the Filipinos were promised their independence, and this was finally granted

Major Gorgas gives instructions for swamp drainage in Cuba. He rid that island, and later Panama, of yellow fever.

Platt Amendment, which provided that:
(1) Cuba should not make treaties with other nations that would weaken its independence,
(2) it would keep its finances in order,
(3) the United States could intervene to preserve order,
(4) Cuba should lease to the United States lands for naval stations. The last provision resulted in the establishment of an American naval base at Guantanamo Bay.

Puerto Rico

The people of Puerto Rico willingly accepted American rule, and military occupation of the island was ended in 1900. A congressional act passed in 1900 provided for a governor and upper house to be appointed from Washington, and a lower house to be elected by the Puerto Ricans. In 1917 Puerto Ricans were made citizens of the United States by passage of the Jones Act. Since then thousands of them have migrated to New York and other cities where job opportunities are somewhat better than those in Puerto Rico. In 1947 the Puerto Ricans were given the right to elect their own governor, and in 1952 the island became a self-governing commonwealth.

The Dawn of a New Century

The nineteenth century was good to the United States. From a tiny nation with a weak and experimental government, and with military and naval forces which were derided by the great powers of the world, the country grew into an important powerful nation. The many troubles and questions which had threatened to split the Union were settled. The states were bound inseparably together as a single, united country.

The Spanish-American War and the trouble with Germany in the Samoan Islands showed the American people the need for a strong navy. Money was freely expended on ships, and although this greatly increased government expenses, it served to make the United States a strong naval power. The inadequacy and unpreparedness of the American army, which became evident at the time of the war with Spain, also

Ancient El Morro Fortress, San Juan, Puerto Rico. The Caribbean island of Puerto Rico is one of the most beautiful U.S. possessions. Its people and its culture both have influenced life in the United States, especially in New York, where there is a large Puerto Rican population.

brought about a thorough reorganization of that department and led to the building up of a stronger land force.

The policy of *isolation,* so necessary for the early development of the new little country, was beginning to be questioned, and the United States reluctantly acknowledged that she now had great and world-wide responsibilities. The dawn of the twentieth century found the United States becoming a world power.

Looking Back

1. What is the present status of the Philippine Islands?
2. How did Wood and Gorgas contribute to the development of Cuba?
3. List the provisions of the Platt Amendment.
4. Show how Puerto Rico has gained increasing self-rule from 1898 to the present.

The Chapter in Perspective

Who Are These People?

Mahan	Aguinaldo
Cleveland	Sampson
McKinley	Wood
Bryan	Roosevelt
Dewey	Hay

Where Are These Places?

Hawaii	Santiago
Samoan Islands	Philippines
Cuba	Guam
Hong Kong	Puerto Rico
Manila	China

What Do These Dates and Terms Mean?

imperialism	de Lôme letter
1896	1946
1898	1959
annexation	*Oregon*
statehood	Rough Riders
1899	Boxer Rebellion
yellow press	
"Remember the *Maine*"	
Teller Amendment	

Philippine insurrection
Platt Amendment
spheres of influence
"Open Door" policy

Questions for Study

1. Discuss the effect on Spanish-American relations of the de Lôme letter, the sinking of the *Maine,* and the "yellow press."
2. In your opinion, could the Spanish-American War have been averted? Support your position.
3. In what ways did the Spanish-American War change the status of the United States as a world power?
4. How did the United States earn international respect by honoring the Teller Amendment?
5. Critics of American policy claim the Platt Amendment made Cuba an American protectorate. Do you agree? Why?

6. Account for the growing interest of the United States and major European powers in the Pacific region after the 1850's.

7. Why were the world powers greatly interested in China?

8. What were the main raw materials and natural resources of each of the American possessions?

Place Yourself in History

On April 11, 1898, President McKinley reported to the Congress of the United States as follows:

"Forcible intervention in Cuba is justifiable. First. In the cause of humanity and to put an end to the barbarities, starvation, and horrible miseries now existing there. It is no answer to say that all this is in another country, belonging to another nation and is therefore none of our business. It is specially our duty for it is right at our door.

"Second. We owe it to our citizens in Cuba to afford them that protection for life and property . . . . .

"Third. The right to intervene may be justified by the very serious injury to the commerce, trade and business of our people . . . . . .

"Fourth. The present condition of affairs in Cuba is a constant menace to our peace."

As a member of the Senate Foreign Relations Committee, you have been kept aware of all developments in the worsening relations between the United States and Spain. In the debate that follows the above message, what would you say? Why?

Expanding Your Outlook

Doing It Yourself

1. Prepare a talk to the class on the increase of the number of people acquiring of high school education from 1865 to the present. Use attendance statistics to make your presentation graphic.
2. Report on the effect of *Brown* vs. *Board of Education of Topeka* on your school system.
3. Prepare a biography of one of the following: Booker T. Washington, George W. Carver, Lillian Wald, Jane Addams, Joseph Pulitzer. If you wish, you may choose any person mentioned in the unit about whom you and your class may wish to learn more.
4. Make a list of the problems that were caused by the rapid growth of urbanization. Show how you would solve these problems.
5. Report to the class on the status of women from 1865 to the present.
6. For those with artistic ability, draw a series of pictures showing the major sports of the period and the uniforms worn by the participants.
7. Make a chart indicating the territorial acquisitions of the United States from 1867 to 1917. Include name, from whom acquired, how acquired, date, special significance.

8. Report on the causes, and results of the Philippine Insurrection.
9. Prepare a report on the Spanish-American War as it might have appeared in a British newspaper.

Working with the Class

1. Divide the class into committees representing the territorial acquisitions since 1867. Let each committee report on the geography, history, natural resources, chief occupations, and products of each.
2. Prepare a mock trial for "Boss" Tweed by assigning specific roles for some of the class with the others to serve as the jury.
3. Form a bulletin board committee to display the art, sculpture, architecture, and literature of the people mentioned in the unit.
4. Present a panel discussion to the class on the topic: "Could the United States have avoided participation in the Spanish-American War?"
5. Prepare a formal debate before the class on the subject: Resolved: American foreign policy in China during the Boxer Rebellion and the Open-Door negotiations were in the best interests of China."

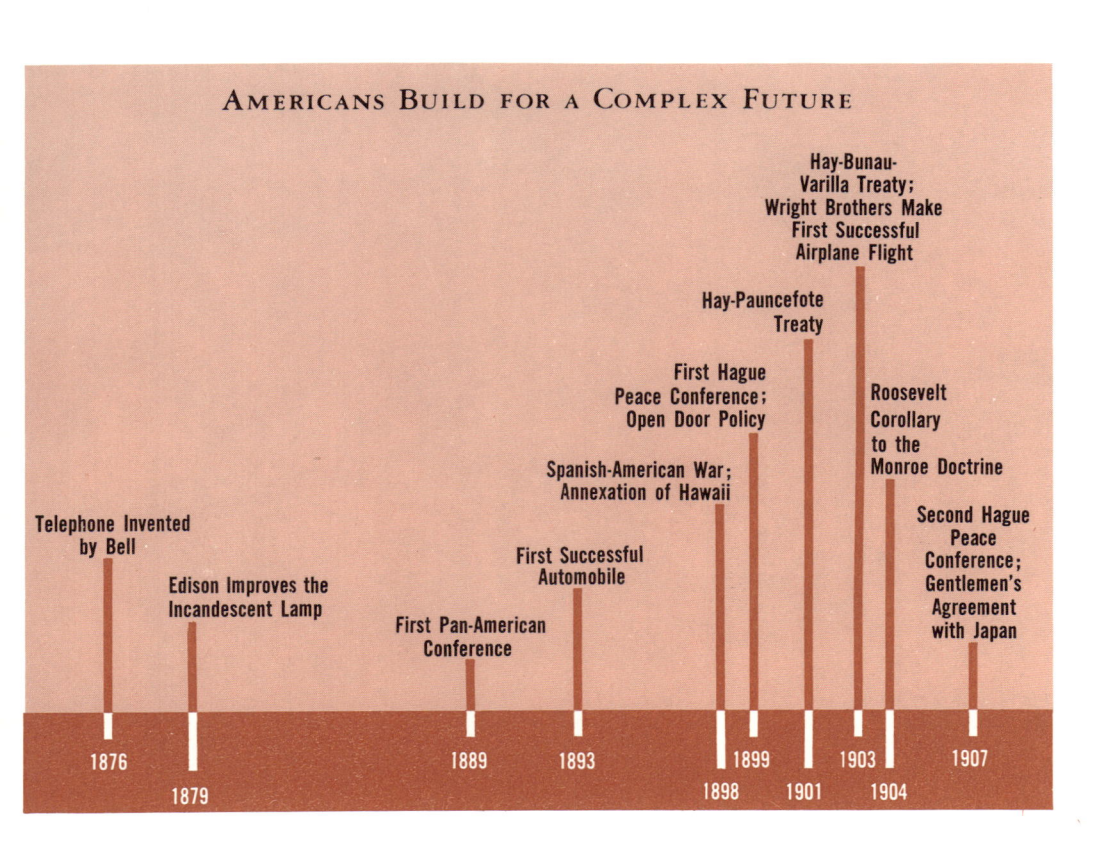

AMERICANS BUILD FOR A COMPLEX FUTURE

1876	Telephone Invented by Bell
1879	Edison Improves the Incandescent Lamp
1889	First Pan-American Conference
1893	First Successful Automobile
1898	Spanish-American War; Annexation of Hawaii
1899	First Hague Peace Conference; Open Door Policy
1901	Hay-Pauncefote Treaty
1903	Hay-Bunau-Varilla Treaty; Wright Brothers Make First Successful Airplane Flight
1904	Roosevelt Corollary to the Monroe Doctrine
1907	Second Hague Peace Conference; Gentlemen's Agreement with Japan

The bustling gaiety of New York City, the "El" or elevated train, neon lights, and working girls lent new perspectives of sound and sight to American life. John Sloan's painting called Sixth Avenue Elevated at 3rd Street, *captures this new "modern" vitality. Unit Eight tells the story of how America became a modern country, at ease in world diplomacy, complacent in its richness at home.*

1928. Oil.—Collection of Whitney Museum of American Art, New

ONE NATION INDIVISIBLE
UNIT 8

Americans Find Ways to Solve New Problems

23. The Progressives and the "Square Deal"
1. A Progressive President Faces Domestic Issues • **2.** Roosevelt Wields the "Big Stick" in Foreign Affairs • **3.** Taft Attempts to Follow Roosevelt's Policies

24. A Challenge to the "New Freedom"
1. A Democratic Administration Moves on the Home Front • **2.** Smouldering European Rivalries Burst into Flames • **3.** The United States is Drawn into the Conflict

25. Peacetime Problems
1. A War-Weary World Disarms for Peace • **2.** The "Good Old Days" Vanish Forever • **3.** The Great Depression Strikes America and the World

23 The Progressives and the "Square Deal"

The first two decades of the twentieth century were marked by many reforms that made our government more democratic and efficient. Progressive statesmen, businessmen, writers, and educators promoted laws to help workers, protect consumers, and reduce corruption in politics. In the field of foreign relations, the United States made new interpretations of the Monroe Doctrine and secured domination of the Caribbean. The government tried to maintain a balance of power among foreign nations. The armed forces were strengthened, and the foreign service in the State Department was improved. America became a powerful force in international affairs.

1. A Progressive President Faces Domestic Issues

Roosevelt, the Man and the Leader

In September, 1901, only six months after his second inauguration President McKinley was fatally wounded by a mentally disturbed anarchist (a person who desires no government at all) in Buffalo, New York. Vice-President Roosevelt was hastily summoned to Buffalo. When he arrived, he felt Mr. McKinley would recover and returned home. Eight days later, September 14, 1901, Mr. McKinley died of his wounds. Theodore Roosevelt became America's youngest Chief Executive that day.

Theodore Roosevelt was a vigorous and likable person who had varied interests and many talents. Coming from a wealthy, socially prominent family, he had exceptional opportunities in education and travel. His fortunate background, combined with the gift of understanding all sorts of people, made him a natural politician. Many, even those who disagreed with him, could not help being swept along by his enthusiasm and drive.

He was not a radical reformer, ready to turn the whole American system over, but he was genuinely eager to remedy the defects in it. Furthermore, he was quite ready to use the great powers of his office to force through many badly needed changes. He was a leader of the so-called "progressive movement" of the day—a movement that fought for social justice and political reform.

Roosevelt realized that to achieve his goals he had to win the support of the Republicans in Congress, many of whom distrusted his new ideas. He also had to surround himself with able and loyal assistants who were devoted to him. He was able to accomplish both of these objectives. In the election of 1904 he won the Republican nomination and went on to win the Presidency easily.

The "Square Deal"

In his first inaugural message to Congress, Roosevelt made it plain that he believed in the regulation of the big trusts and combines, groups which controlled whole individual industries like oil or steel. These trusts could fix prices to their liking, often at the expense of the customer and the laborer. He realized that there were economic advantages in consolidation within an industry, but he also believed that the government should have the power to regulate corporations and protect the consumer against unfair treatment. He called his policy a *Square Deal* for both management and labor.

"Trust-busting." Part of the Square Deal program was the strengthening of the Sherman Antitrust Act which had been the first step in the regulation of large combinations and trusts. Before Roosevelt came into office this act had been almost useless, except when aimed at labor unions. Large corporations, fortified by armies of lawyers, could find numerous ways to escape the Sherman Antitrust law. Although nowadays labor unions have real power and influence, they did not early in this century. Therefore, when the Sherman law was aimed at them, they had neither the money nor the influence to fight it.

In 1902 Roosevelt ordered the Attorney General to file a suit against the Northern Securities Company, a holding company formed to monopolize the railroad systems in the Northwest. The

Teddy Roosevelt is a heroic historical figure, largely because he used most of his constitutional powers as President.

In the turmoil of the Pennsylvania coal mines, clashes between miners and soldiers or police were common.

Supreme Court decided in March, 1904, that the company had violated the Sherman Act and ordered it to dissolve. This and other examples of *"trust-busting"* made Roosevelt very popular with the progressives in the country.

Trouble in the Coal Fields. Another test of the Square Deal was a serious coal strike in 1902, when 140,000 underpaid mining workers in the dangerous anthracite coal mines of Pennsylvania left their jobs. As winter came on and coal supplies dwindled, Roosevelt angrily summoned union leaders and mine owners to the White House. The union was willing to let a neutral third party settle the dispute, but the owners stubbornly refused until Roosevelt threatened to seize the mines and operate them with federal troops. Although he probably could not have done this legally, the owners reluctantly accepted a compromise. They gave the miners a small raise and reduced the working day from ten hours to nine. They refused, however, to recognize the union as bargaining agent for the miners, and they did not make great improvements in mine safety.

This strike was interesting because it was the first time a President had used the powers of his office to settle a strike by negotiation rather than by the use of force against strikers.

The Railroads. Another achievement of Theodore Roosevelt was his success in persuading Congress to pass laws regulating the railroads. These acts forbade free passes for politicians and other friends of the railroads, and prohibited rebates to favored customers. The railroad regulation laws also set maximum rates which railroads could charge, and forced railroad management to give up their interests in other businesses, such as mining. In effect these laws struck a heavy blow at the vertical trusts.

Conserving the Nation's Resources

American Presidents, especially since the time of Rutherford B. Hayes, have tried to preserve our natural resources. They had made it easy at one time for a settler to buy up to 640 acres of arid public land at $1.25 an acre, on the condition that the buyer would put it under irrigation and raise crops on it. Public timberlands had been closed

Theodore Roosevelt gave impetus to the formation of the U.S. Forest Service. In this picture, taken in 1919, two foresters get ready for a forest inspection tour.

to settlement in order to preserve our magnificent forests. The government had set aside arid Western lands for states that would agree to irrigate the land to make it useful for settlement.

Roosevelt, who loved the outdoors and the West, vigorously continued this policy of conservation. Aided by Gifford Pinchot, a government official who was an expert forester, he set aside in federal reserves great areas of forest and mineral land, as well as water power sources. He also supported regulations which provided that the proceeds from the sale of Western lands would be used for irrigation

Why did National Park acreage begin to increase in 1900?

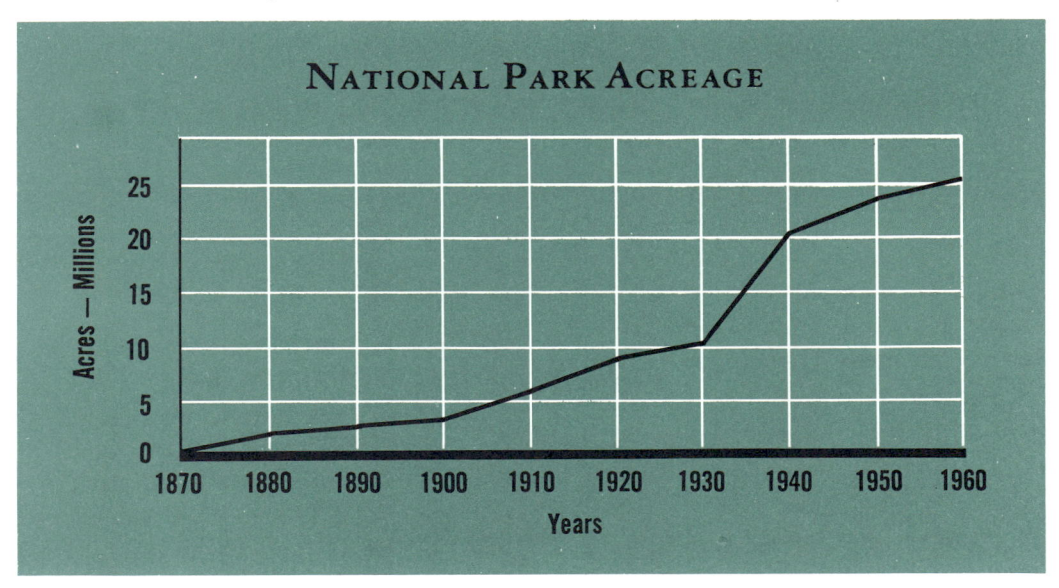

NATIONAL PARK ACREAGE

projects like the Columbia Basin Project in Washington. Those who used the water would pay for it, and this money would go back into a fund to pay for further irrigation. These regulations were meant to help small landholders, since only those who owned 160 acres or less and actually lived on the land were eligible to buy the water rights.

Conservation of natural resources was one of Theodore Roosevelt's greatest achievements.

Pure Foods and Drugs

Another of Roosevelt's valuable reforms concerned the sale of unclean and poisonous foods. Upton Sinclair, a novelist, had made people aware of this danger by writing a book called *The Jungle,* dealing with the unsanitary handling of meat in the stockyards. But it was not only meat and meat products that were unsanitary. Dairy products frequently reached the market in a contaminated condition. Sawdust and food coloring, often poisonous, were added to ground meat and sausage. Packages were often mislabeled, leading the customer to believe he was getting something he was not. Patent medicines, medicines which are not prescribed by a doctor, were often poisonous or otherwise harmful. In 1906 Congress passed regulations which helped to prevent the manufacture and sale of unclean or misbranded food and medicines.

Looking Back

1. What did Theodore Roosevelt mean by his "Square Deal"?
2. How did Roosevelt put his Square Deal into action?
3. Why was the settlement of the coal strike an important move by a new method?
4. By what steps did Roosevelt act to conserve the natural resources of the nation?
5. Show how the ordinary consumer benefited from Roosevelt's program concerning pure food and drugs.

2. Roosevelt Wields the "Big Stick" in Foreign Affairs

President Theodore Roosevelt was very active in foreign affairs and did much to increase the prestige of the United States among the nations of the world. He had traveled widely in Europe, he spoke French and German, and he had a good knowledge of history. Although Roosevelt worked for peace among nations, he also insisted that the United States have a strong army and navy. One of his favorite expressions was, "*Speak softly and carry a big stick.*" On occasions he was quite ready to use the "Big Stick."

A Canal to Link the Oceans

The Need for the Canal. For years American statesmen and military experts had seen the need of a canal across the isthmus of Central America. Such a canal would make it easier for the navy to defend both the East and West coasts, as well as the Philippines, Hawaii, and the Caribbean possessions.

It would also shorten the journey of merchant ships carrying goods to and from Europe and the Far East, and shipping between the west coast of the United States and South America to European and eastern American ports would be made easier.

The first step was to get a new treaty with Great Britain to replace the Clayton-Bulwer Treaty of 1850, in which the United States had promised not to secure exclusive rights in the isthmus. The British obligingly agreed to a new treaty in 1901 which gave United States the exclusive right not only to build and own a canal, but to fortify the area surrounding it. Soon afterwards the British withdrew their naval forces from the area near Panama to the West Indies. The United States now controlled both sides of the isthmus.

The Canal Route Chosen. The next problem was the choice of a route for the canal. In 1890 a private French company had given up its attempt to dig a canal at Panama. The successor to this company was anxious to salvage something from the venture and offered its rights and equipment to the United States. American engineering experts, however, recommended a route through Nicaragua. But the opportunity to buy the route across the isthmus seemed too good to ignore when the asking price was drastically cut, and Congress finally accepted the Panama route. By 1902 it had authorized Roosevelt to negotiate with Colombia for a right of way across the isthmus which Colombia had acquired when she gained her independence from Spain. If negotiation failed, Roosevelt was to turn to Nicaragua.

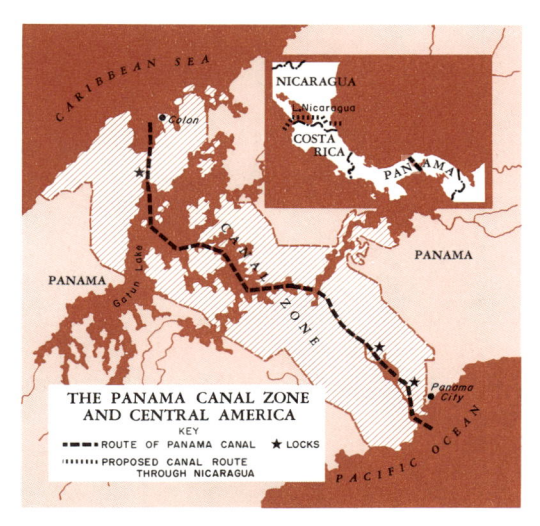

Can you see any advantage in the proposed canal route across Nicaragua?

Secretary of State Hay then succeeded in arranging a treaty with Colombia for a canal through the isthmus of Panama. The treaty provided that the United States would pay $10,000,000 and an annual rental for a lease on a strip of land six miles wide. The legislature of Colombia refused to ratify the treaty, saying that the price was too low. The refusal angered Roosevelt, who charged that the Colombians were trying to extort money from the United States.

Revolt in Panama. On November 3, 1901, the Panamanian people, who had long wished to be independent of Colombia, arose in revolt. Colombian troops attempted to crush the rebellion but were prevented from landing by an American cruiser which had arrived at the scene the day before. Three days after the uprising the American government recognized the new nation of Panama, as did some European governments. Two weeks later, a treaty with Panama was signed in Washington. The price for the canal right of way

The Panama Canal was the first canal built with "modern machinery." Steam dredges scooped mud from the bottom which was hauled away by "donkey" engines like the one in the picture.

remained the same, but the zone was widened from six to ten miles. The Panamanian revolution had proved a very great convenience for Roosevelt's policies.

Construction of the Canal. Roosevelt now resolved to "make the dirt fly." The first move in building the canal was to make Panama a fit place in which to live. Colonel William C. Gorgas, who had halted the spread of yellow fever in Cuba, was assigned to do this work. Swamps were drained; pools of water were covered with oil, which destroyed the larvae and eggs of mosquitoes that landed on the water to breed; sanitary hospitals were built. Soon mosquitoes became scarce, and the danger of a terrible epidemic, such as had wrecked the hopes of the French engineers, was removed.

A West Point engineer, Colonel George Goethals, was put in charge of construction. Great steam shovels bit into the soil, and foot by foot the mighty slot of the canal began to cut across the isthmus. Despite great landslides and other difficulties, the work went ahead. The canal was finally completed in 1914, just as World War I was starting. This mighty project was a great tribute to American engineering skill.

Protecting the Canal. In continuing her policy of gaining control of the Caribbean Sea for the protection of the Panama Canal, the United States purchased three of the Virgin Islands, St. Thomas, St. Croix, and St. John, from Denmark in 1917. The islands are small and the price, $25,000,000, was large, but one more valuable naval base was obtained for the United States in southern waters.

Importance of the Canal. The building of the canal had many important effects. The seaports on the Pacific coast of both North and South America were at once brought thousands of miles nearer to the ports of Europe and of eastern North America, and a great and booming trade sprang up.

The ports that benefited most from the building of the canal were those on the Gulf coast. New Orleans was now thousands of miles closer to the Pacific coast than it had been, and both their exports and imports were greatly increased. Accordingly, trade down the Mississippi to New Orleans increased, and the products of the upper valley, which had formerly gone west overland, now went down the river and were reshipped at New Orleans on steamships bound for Pacific ports by way of the canal.

Roosevelt's tactics in gaining control of the Panama Canal Zone placed the United States in a difficult diplomatic position at the time. Colombia especially felt cheated and with some justification. When Panama revolted against Colombia, American warships prevented Colombian troops from subduing the revolution. Thus the people of Colombia held the Americans directly responsible for Colombia's loss of valuable territory.

Other South American nations agreed with Colombia, and a distrust of the motives of the United States spread throughout the continent. Many citizens of the United States also felt that Colombia had been treated badly. In 1922 that nation was paid $25,000,000 in settlement.

Today the canal is still an important communication asset, but the modern age of air power has made it less vital than formerly, both for trade and for national defense.

This picture illustrates the change in water level in the Panama Canal today. Ships are transiting both North and South in the Gatun Locks (see map, pg. 441).

Roosevelt Corollary to the Monroe Doctrine

In 1904, President Theodore Roosevelt took a step which had very important effects upon our relations with the other New World nations. The little Dominican Republic on the island of Hispaniola was in trouble, for she owed large sums of money to various European nations and seemed to have no prospect of paying them. France, Italy, and Belgium were openly threatening to use force in collecting what was owed them. This seemed to President Roosevelt to be a violation of the Monroe Doctrine. In a message to Congress, he declared that the United States might have to act as an international policeman in this hemisphere in order to keep situations from arising that might give foreign nations an excuse to interfere by force. This policy of interfering in the affairs of our hemisphere neighbors, whether they wanted us to or not, became known as the *Roosevelt Corollary to the Monroe Doctrine.*

U. S. Intervention. Acting in accord with the Roosevelt Corollary, the United States forced the Dominican Republic to sign a treaty in 1905. This treaty granted to the United States the right to take over the administration of the little country's finances. Her debts were enormous, and dishonest officials were stealing so much of her money that she was deeper in debt each year. President Theodore Roosevelt put the country's finances under the control of an efficient American overseer. At once the Dominican Republic began to grow more prosperous and to pay off her debts. Later, in 1916, a revolution seemed imminent, and President Wilson was forced to send soldiers, who restored peace.

Nicaragua experienced similar difficulties in 1912. United States troops were sent to the country to maintain order and to supervise elections. An American overseer was placed in charge of finances. When troops were at last withdrawn the Nicaraguans had a sound financial system and a well-trained army and were better prepared to conduct their own affairs than ever before.

In 1915, the republic of Haiti experienced a bloody uprising, and United States troops were sent to restore order. This they did. A treaty was then made with the Haitians, allowing the United States to control the finances of the country, to train a native police force, and to bring about other improvements.

Arguments Pro and Con. Many people, both in our country and abroad, feel that the United States had no right to meddle in the affairs of these little independent countries. Others favor such activity, and point to the great improvements which have come about under United States guidance.

Hemispheric Organizations

During the administration of President Harrison (1889), an organization was established that was known as the International Bureau of the American Republics, later called the Pan American Union. The purpose behind its founding was the encouragement of better understanding among the nations of the Western Hemisphere and the peaceful settlement of disputes.

The meeting of 1889 was the first of many for this group, and much good has come from their meetings over the years.

The Organization of American States (OAS), the present hemispheric administrative body, was founded as a result of one of the meetings of the old International Bureau of American Republics. Since its founding, this organization has done a great deal to ensure peace in the Western Hemisphere. It is now understood that all of the countries represented will submit their troubles to arbitration rather than attempt to use force. However, since certain Latin American governments are in a perpetual state of change, this is not always possible.

Trade treaties have been made between most member countries of the OAS, giving mutual advantages to all concerned in the carrying on of certain lines of commerce. There has been an exchange of students so that citizens of one country who have been educated in another will be able to promote a better understanding through their knowledge of the manners and customs of both countries.

In this contemporary cartoon by W. A. Rogers, Teddy Roosevelt is shown with a "big stick" leading a line of "war elephants" away from Morocco. How does the cartoon reflect the American public's idea of America's importance in the world in 1906? Was Roosevelt's effort to settle the problem finally successful?

Roosevelt's Contributions to World Peace

Algeciras Conference. Although Roosevelt was willing to use the "Big Stick" to defend American interests, he was sincere in supporting arbitration as a means of preventing war between other nations. An example of this is the part he played in the Algeciras Conference in Spain in 1906.

This conference settled a dispute regarding Morocco. Both France and Germany wished to control this North African nation, and the two European powers were on the brink of war. At the last moment the German Kaiser asked Roosevelt to try to settle things between the opposing powers. For the time being he was successful, but in only nine short years, a European war broke out between these same countries.

Court of Arbitration. Another American contribution to the peace effort was our participation in the Second Hague Conference in 1907. At this conference, a permanent arbitration court was set up for the peaceful settlement of disputes. In 1908 Roosevelt and Secretary of State Elihu Root negotiated treaties with numerous other nations providing for arbitration. Although these treaties were not always effective, they were a step in the right direction.

Roosevelt's appointment of Elihu Root to the cabinet was one of his wisest decisions. Root became Roosevelt's right hand man and instituted many improvements in government. Elihu Root deserves much credit for his efforts to improve our foreign service—a campaign which others are carrying on today.

The Nobel Award. Perhaps Theodore Roosevelt's greatest contribution to world peace was the treaty he promoted and negotiated to end the Russo-Japanese War. He brought representatives of the two nations together at Portsmouth, New Hampshire, to settle their dispute. The next year, (1906) he received the Nobel Peace Prize for his efforts.

Looking Back

1. How has the Panama Canal helped the United States? the world?
2. Why is the Panama Canal less important now than fifty years ago?
3. Define the Roosevelt Corollary to the Monroe Doctrine.
4. How was the Roosevelt Corollary used in the Dominican Republic? in Nicaragua? in Haiti?
5. What have been the accomplishments of the O. A. S.?
6. Why was the Nobel Peace Prize awarded to Roosevelt in 1906?

3. Taft Attempts to Follow Roosevelt's Policies

In 1908 Roosevelt was so popular that he probably could have won another term as President. He had promised in 1904, however, that he would not run for a third term. At the Republican convention in Chicago he had enough influence to pick his successor—William Howard Taft, a moderate progressive. At their convention in Denver, the Democrats again nominated William Jennings Bryan.

The election of 1908 was an overwhelming victory for the Republicans and Taft. The new President won with 321 electoral votes to Bryan's 162. Roosevelt, confident that his policies would be carried on by Taft, left soon after the election to hunt lions in Africa.

Taft's Progressivism

Although he was not so skillful as Roosevelt in making policies and influencing Congress, the big, kindly Taft was a good administrator and did his best to hold to the principles of the Square Deal. During his administration Congress passed an act which gave the Interstate Commerce Commission authority to control the rates of telephone, telegraph, and cable companies. Another measure established a postal savings system and provided that post offices could receive money on deposit and pay two per cent interest. This measure forced the private savings banks to offer better service and security for their customers. Taft's "trustbusting" exceeded that of Roosevelt. He brought suit against ninety trusts in four years, whereas Roosevelt brought only forty-four in seven and a half years.

During Taft's term of office, Congress proposed two important amendments to the Constitution. These were the Sixteenth Amendment, which gives Congress the power "to lay and collect taxes on incomes, from whatever source derived," and the Seventeenth Amendment, which provides for the direct election of Senators by the people rather than by the state legislatures.

The Election of 1912

In spite of Taft's good intentions, he began to lose support. Many felt his efforts to pass a lower tariff bill, which the farmers in the Midwest wanted, were ineffective and weak. In contrast to Roosevelt he failed to push conservation measures. He also depended increasingly on conservative, "Old Guard" Republicans. The reformist wing of the Republican party, led by Senator La Follette of Wisconsin, turned against the President. "Teddy" Roosevelt, back from Africa, criticized Taft's weakness and an-

What years did the smallest percentage of voters go to the polls? Did radio and television influence the percentage of voters? If so, how much? Can you think of any reason for the high interest in the election of 1896?

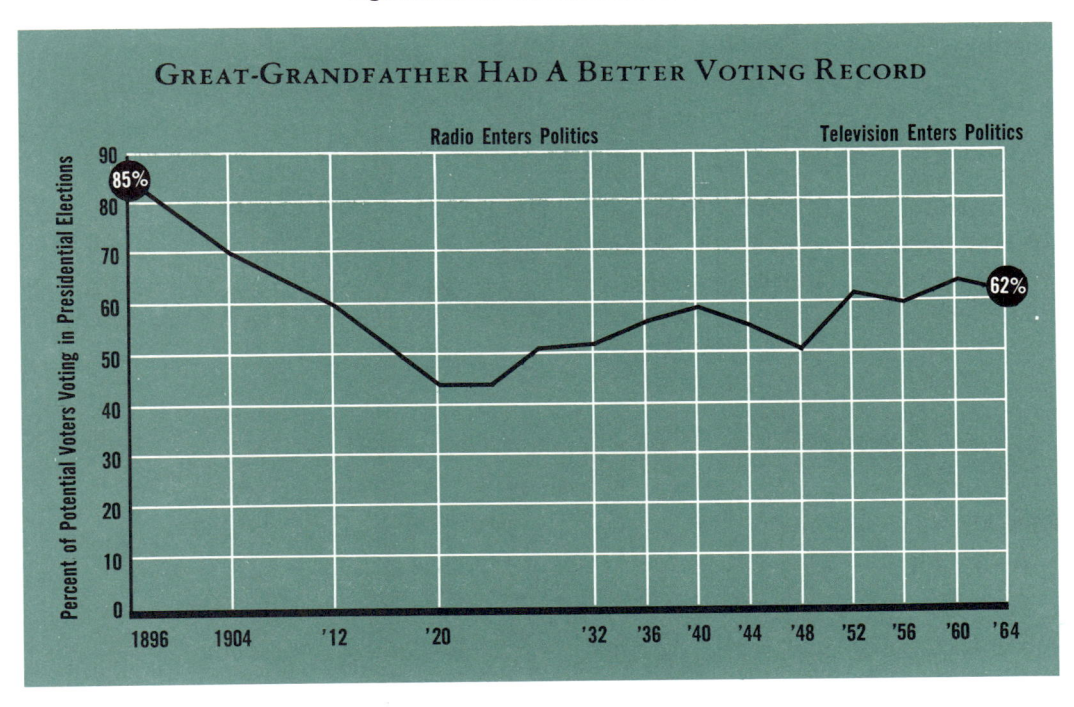

GREAT-GRANDFATHER HAD A BETTER VOTING RECORD

nounced that his "hat was in the ring" for the coming election.

"Bull Moose Campaign." At the Republican convention of 1912 Roosevelt had many enthusiastic supporters, but Taft won the nomination. Roosevelt then announced that he would run as the candidate of a new third party. His supporters gathered in Chicago and organized the Progressive party. Saying that he felt "fit as a bull moose," Roosevelt prepared to conduct an exciting "Bull Moose" campaign.

At the Democratic convention there was much rejoicing at the split in the Republican party since it practically ensured the election of a Democrat. After considerable debate the delegates nominated Woodrow Wilson, former president of Princeton University who had later made a fine record as a reform governor of New Jersey.

Defeat of "Old Guard." The election was a triumph for the forces favoring reform and change, and a defeat for the "Old Guard" conservatives. Although he failed to win a majority of the popular vote (Wilson had approximately 6,000,000, Taft 3,000,000, Roosevelt 4,000,000), Wilson won the greatest victory in the electoral college since Monroe's election in 1820. So many Republican sections of the country split their votes between Taft and Roosevelt that Wilson received 435 electoral votes to Roosevelt's 88 and Taft's 8. Actually, Wilson was a minority president, since he did not receive as many votes as the other two candidates combined.

Because two "progressives," Wilson and Roosevelt, received the great majority of votes, it was quite evident from this election that the people of America were eager to speed up the progressive movement and to modernize the machinery of government. All eyes were now turned on the new President, the first Democrat to enter the White House since Cleveland won his second victory in 1892.

Looking Back

1. What are the provisions of the Sixteenth Amendment? the Seventeenth Amendment?
2. For what reasons did Taft lose the support of some of his fellow Republicans?
3. Why did the entry of the "Bull Moose" party in the election of 1912 please the Democrats?
4. Who were the candidates for the Presidency in 1912? Who won?
5. For what reasons did the results of the election indicate that an era of change was to begin?

The Chapter in Perspective

Who Are These People?

Roosevelt	Goethals
Pinchot	Gorgas
Root	Taft
Hay	Wilson

Where Are These Places?

Nicaragua	Morocco
Haiti	Panama
Virgin Islands	Colombia
Dominican Republic	

What Do These Dates and Terms Mean?

progressive
1850
Square Deal
1889
trustbusting
1901
coal strike
conservation
1902
"Big Stick"
Roosevelt Corollary
Pan-American Union
Algeciras Conference
Second Hague Conference
arbitration treaties
Clayton-Bulwer Treaty
Sixteenth Amendment
Northern Securities Company
Seventeenth Amendment

1904
OAS
1906
1908
1912
yellow fever
"Bull Moose"
1917
"Old Guard"
1915

Questions for Study

1. Why was the settlement of the coal strike in 1902 of much greater national significance than it might be today?
2. Do you feel that the laws governing the food and drugs you buy today are adequate? Why?
3. Would you have supported Roosevelt's view that the United States should be an international policeman in Latin American affairs? Why?
4. As a citizen of the Dominican Republic (Haiti or Nicaragua) would you have approved the Roosevelt Corollary? Why?
5. Summarize the steps taken by Roosevelt to eliminate the possibilities of war in different parts of the world.
6. How did the Spanish-American War affect American interest in a transoceanic canal?
7. Tell why you would or would not have approved the treaty with Colombia in 1922.
8. How has the ratification of the Sixteenth Amendment changed the economic policies of the United States?
9. By what distance is an ocean trip from San Francisco to New York shortened by use of the Panama Canal?
10. What parts of the United States benefited from Roosevelt's conservation policies? Prove your answer.

Place Yourself in History

You have always been a staunch Republican. Theodore Roosevelt brought success and achievement for your party. Taft was Roosevelt's choice for the Presidency. On record is a statement by Roosevelt that he would not seek the Presidency again. Now you see your party split. Claiming a "theft of the delegates," Roosevelt has started the Progressive ("Bull Moose") party.

As election night approaches, you must make a decision. Wilson and Debs do not receive any consideration from you for you feel loyal to your party.

For whom would you have voted in 1912 under the above circumstances? Why?

24

A Challenge to the "New Freedom"

After 1912 the United States continued to strengthen and improve its government so that more of its citizens could enjoy security and prosperity. In 1914, however, a terrible war broke out in Europe, and Americans began to realize that their lives could be affected by events abroad, as well as by conditions at home. Why did the United States abandon its ancient policy of neutrality in 1917 and send soldiers across the sea to take part in Europe's war? What caused this war, and how did it end?

1. A Democratic Administration Moves on the Home Front

President Wilson, who was to be America's leader in the First World War, was born into a religious Virginia family. He was a sincere and devout man who held a strong desire to help his fellow men. Wilson combined some of the best traits of former presidents. Like Jefferson he was a noted scholar. Like Lincoln he was an inspiring orator. But both these fine attributes were at times set off by the fact that he was not an easy person to know or to like. Often stubborn and unbending, he sometimes made enemies of his friends. A vigorous reformer, he initiated much progressive activity both as president of Princeton University and later as governor of New Jersey. He believed that the President of the United States should be a strong leader, and it quickly became evident that he intended to be one.

In a short, eloquent inaugural address before a great crowd on March 4, 1913, Wilson clearly described his program, which he called the New

Freedom. He wanted to do away with the evils of industrialism and big business, to stop the waste of natural resources, and to protect the consumer. In many ways his program sounded like the Square Deal of Theodore Roosevelt.

Wilson's Financial Program

The Underwood-Simmons Tariff. On the day he took office, Wilson set out to do some of the things promised in his inaugural address. He called for a special session of Congress to take up the question of tariff reform. At this session, he delivered his message in person, instead of having it read to Congress. No American President had done this since Jefferson in 1801.

With Wilson's support, Representative Oscar W. Underwood of Alabama introduced a bill in the House calling for the first real tariff reduction since the Civil War. A swarm of lobbyists representing manufacturers tried to persuade the legislators to weaken the bill (which was later called the *Underwood-Simmons Act*), as they had weakened similar bills on previous occasions. Despite the efforts of the lobbyists, the bill passed the House easily. However, this was not the case in the Senate. Many senators had personal investments in their own states or were obligated to industrial interests and so voted against the tariff because it would be a personal disadvantage. Investigations were made into "personal voting" in the Senate, and many senators were embarrassed by the outcome. After Wilson had appealed to the people, and as a result of the investigations, the Senate passed the bill.

A friend of Woodrow Wilson describes Wilson's inauguration.

"A presidential inauguration is a picturesque affair even when the weather is stormy, as it frequently is on the fourth of March in Washington. It is a brilliant affair when the sun shines bright and the air is balmy, as happened on March 4, 1913, when Woodrow Wilson took the oath of office at noon, delivered his inaugural address a few minutes later, reviewed the parade immediately after luncheon, and before nightfall was at his desk in the White House transacting the business of the Government. To the popular imagination Inauguration Day represents crowds and hurrahs, brass bands and processions. The hotels, restaurants, and boarding houses of Washington overflow with people from all parts of the country who have come to 'see the show.' The pavements, windows, and housetops along Pennsylvania Avenue from the east front of the Capitol to the western gate of the White House are crowded with folk eager to see the procession with its military column and marching clubs. From an improvised stand in front of the White House, surrounded by his friends, the new President reviews the parade...."

—*Woodrow Wilson As I Know Him,* Joseph P. Tumulty (Garden City, 1921) 139–43.

The Underwood-Simmons Act reduced the tariff rates on about nine hundred products. This meant that foreign firms that made these products could compete more easily with American firms. The American firms, which had previously enjoyed a monopoly, now had to meet this foreign competition by reducing their prices—which was what the people wanted. The act raised the tariff on certain items, mostly luxuries. The purpose here was to make money for the government. It should be noted that a tariff has two purposes: (1) to protect American firms against foreign competition *when they need protection,* (2) to raise money for the expenses of running the government.

The Income Tax. An interesting supplementary feature of the Underwood-Simmons Act was that it provided for a graduated income tax. This tax, which had been authorized earlier by the Sixteenth Amendment, partly made up for the income which was lost by the lowering of the tariff rates. The income tax was very low compared to that of today. Individuals and corporations had to pay a basic tax of 1% on all income over $4,000 and an additional surtax of 1% on income over $20,000, ranging up to a maximum of 6% on incomes over $500,000.

Ever since the passage of the Underwood-Simmons Act, the income tax has been an important part of the federal revenue. Since 1913 the rates have steadily climbed until now the paying of the income tax has become a major expense for millions of Americans. Not only individuals but also corporations must now pay taxes on their earnings. To aid in this process, the government in 1943 changed the method of collecting income taxes. Instead of collecting once a year, on March 15, as had been done, it now required all employers to hold out and pay regularly to the government a percentage of each employee's paycheck. The total is tabulated on April 15 of each year.

The Federal Reserve System. Another important reform in the Wilson administration was accomplished by the Federal Reserve Act of 1913. This act set up a banking system designed to make our currency secure and to provide enough money for carrying on the country's business.

The Federal Reserve Act of 1913 divided the country into twelve districts and set up a central Federal Reserve Bank in each district. All national banks are now required to belong to the system, and any other bank may belong. A Federal Reserve Bank does business only with member banks, not with individuals. In the

Woodrow Wilson was quiet and reserved, but he learned to be an enthusiastic campaigner and a forceful speaker.

> *Here a famous writer, William Allen White, describes his meeting—and his impression of Woodrow Wilson.*
>
> "I had no great personal liking for Wilson. When I met him, he seemed to be a cold fish. I remember I came home from the meeting at Madison, Wisconsin, and told Mrs. White that the hand he gave me to shake felt like a ten-cent pickled mackerel in brown paper—irresponsive and lifeless. He had a highty-tighty way that repulsed me. When he tried to be pleasant, he creaked. But he had done a fine liberal job in New Jersey. I liked the way he gathered the Irish politicians about him and let them teach him the game in his gubernatorial fights. In every contest he rang true."
> —From *The Autobiography of William Allen White.* Copyright 1946 and used with permission of The Macmillan Company.

central banks in each district are kept supplies of money which can be lent to member banks to meet the demands of increased business or to help in cases of unusual financial conditions such as a panic.

In order to get help from the Federal Reserve Bank of any district, one of the smaller member banks has only to deposit with the central bank promissory notes (promises to pay), United States bonds, or other forms of security. In exchange it receives federal reserve notes (paper money issued by the Federal Reserve Bank). The member bank may then lend these notes to its customers. When the loan is repaid, the member bank turns back the notes to the district Federal Reserve Bank and receives back the promise-to-pay or other security for which the exchange was made. A Federal Reserve Board in Washington supervises and manages the entire system. Certain defects which were revealed by the stock market crash of 1929 and the depression of the early 1930's were remedied by later legislation. The Federal Reserve system has worked very successfully to prevent any rapid change in the value of money.

Reforms in Government and Industry

Federal Trade Commission. In 1914 government control over trusts was strengthened by the creation of the Federal Trade Commission. This was a body empowered to investigate corporations doing business in more than one state, for the purpose of discovering whether they were obeying antitrust laws. False advertising, mislabeling, unfair monopoly are all matters investigated by the Federal Trade Commission. The commission makes recommendations to prevent unfair competition and aids the Attorney General in enforcing the antitrust laws.

The Clayton Act. A few weeks after the creation of the Federal Trade Commission, a new antitrust act was passed, known as the Clayton Act. This was a much stronger law than the Sherman Antitrust Law passed in 1890. It specifically forbade companies to gain sole control of any kind of business or to carry on any other form of unfair competition. Under the Clayton Act many great companies were broken up and their fields opened to small competitors.

Election of Senators. In 1913 an important change was made in the national government which gave the people much more direct participation in it. Before this time, members of the Senate, two from each state, were elected by the state legislatures. The men who wrote the Constitution in 1787 were not sure how wise the people would be in casting their ballots, and they did not want to place the selection of both houses of Congress in the hands of the people. Time proved that the representatives elected by the people were just as good as those selected by the legislatures. The Seventeenth Amendment to the Constitution, which became effective in May, 1913, provided for the direct election of senators by the people of the different states.

The Neighbor to the South

One of Wilson's most difficult problems in the field of foreign policy concerned Mexico. In the years after the Mexican War of 1848, Americans and other foreigners had gained extensive economic holdings in Mexico. By 1910 American interests in Mexico were worth about one billion dollars, most of it invested in railroads, mines, and oil. About 30,000 American citizens, residents of Mexico, were taking care of this business.

The Díaz Era. Maximilian's empire collapsed in 1867 after the end of the American Civil War. Early in 1877, a republic was proclaimed and Porfirio Díaz became President. The administration of Díaz was not a very good one, but it lasted a long time. For thirty-five years he held office, successfully subduing all who opposed him. He had the support of most of the foreigners within the country, including some Americans, mainly because he granted them many trade

Pancho Villa leading his troops. Villa was a guerrilla fighter whose ragged band was pitted against both the Mexican and the American government. He was assassinated in 1923.

General Pershing leads his troops across a river in pursuit of Pancho Villa in 1916.

rights and certain valuable oil lands. He put the finances of the country on a firm basis, and this was a great help to business. But a large portion of the population suffered, for the foreigners and the wealthy Mexicans gained possession of their lands, and they were forced to bear the brunt of taxation and to work very hard for a living.

"Watchful Waiting." In 1911, only a year before Wilson's election, the common people revolted. There was unrest and violence as various leaders strove to seize power. The United States, as well as European powers, watched this struggle uneasily, fearing for the safety of their citizens in Mexico. After his inauguration, President Wilson adopted a policy known as "watchful waiting"—ready to interfere if necessary but doing nothing until action was unavoidable.

Villa and Pershing. Finally General Venustiano Carranza gained control, and his government was recognized by the United States. But Carranza had a strong rival in Mexico named "Pancho" Villa (VEE'yah), who refused to join in the new government. At a meeting of the Pan American Union the situation was discussed, and it was at last decided that Carranza should be recognized as president. This decision in no way pleased Villa, and in 1916, he attempted to start a war between the United States and Mexico. Villa and his band of followers crossed the border and raided the town of Columbus, New Mexico. At once President Wilson ordered General Pershing to lead an army into Mexico to capture Villa. The bandit leader proved difficult to find, but at last the pursuit became so close that he disbanded his army and fled to the mountains.

President Carranza, in the meantime, was much distressed by this invasion of Mexico by American troops. He ordered his army to resist Pershing's force, and a few skirmishes took place which strained relations between the two countries and made war seem likely. When it seemed that nothing could preserve peace, Wilson recalled Pershing and his army back to the United States. Thus trouble was averted.

Looking Back

1. What forces favored and opposed the Underwood-Simmons Tariff?
2. How did the Sixteenth Amendment make a permanent change in American life?
3. Describe the functions of the Federal Reserve System.
4. In what ways did the Federal Trade Commission Act and Clayton Act strengthen the role of the government in business?
5. Why is the Seventeenth Amendment considered a forward step in democracy?

2. Smouldering European Rivalries Burst into Flames

While the United States was busily tending to its own domestic and hemispheric affairs, the industrial nations of Europe were engaged in a smouldering rivalry which suddenly burst into the flames of war. The immediate cause of the First World War was the assassination of the Archduke Francis Ferdinand of Austria by a young Serbian student. Why should the murder of one man and his wife plunge the greatest nations of the world into armed conflict?

The Power Struggle in Europe

To answer that question we have to look back into the previous century. In 1870 the Kingdom of Prussia and France went to war. Prussia won a swift and smashing victory and forced France to cede to her the valuable provinces of Alsace and Lorraine. France also had to pay Prussia large sums of money.

The Triple Alliance. From that time the rise of Prussia was rapid. Under her leadership, the other German states banded together into the German Empire, and the king of Prussia became the emperor of Germany. In 1879, the German Empire, already one of the most powerful nations in Europe, further strengthened its position by forming a military alliance with Austria. Three years later, Italy joined, thus completing a three-sided military agreement which became known as the Triple Alliance.

The Triple Entente. The other nations of Europe were startled and afraid. The French, who had so recently felt Prussia's might, saw in the Triple Alliance a combination of powers which might conquer still more French territory. The British viewed with alarm the rise of German industries, the building of a German merchant marine able to compete with their own, and the development of German colonies in Africa and eastern Asia. Great Britain's supremacy was being threatened in three of her most cherished fields! The Russians heard with dismay of plans to build a German railroad from Berlin to Bagdad, by way of Constantinople. Would not such a line increase Germany's influence in the Balkan peninsula and seriously interfere with Russia's own plans to gain Constantinople as a great southern seaport for the shipping of Russian goods? Something must be done to check the growth of German power!

France, Russia, and Great Britain now formed a loose alliance—called the Triple Entente—ready to dispute the mastery of Europe with the Triple Alliance. It was a dangerous situation, for a quarrel between any opposing members of these alliances was almost certain to involve all six and to lead to a general European war.

Rivalries on Land and Sea. Desperately, each of the great European nations built up its armed forces. Fear and suspicion mounted as the armies grew larger and weapons became more deadly. Fear was driving the European nations toward the very thing they feared—war with each other!

On the sea, too, there was rivalry in armaments. Great Britain was determined not to lose her mastery of the sea. With another nation disputing her sea power, her great ocean commerce and her far-flung colonies would not be safe. So the British naval experts studied the new German ships, and hastily designed ships of their own which would be even more powerful.

Outbreak of Hostilities

Spark at Sarajevo. On June 28, 1914, Francis Ferdinand, heir to the Austrian throne, made a visit to the town of Sarajevo in the province of Bosnia. This province, inhabited largely by Serbs, was one of two which Austria had taken from Turkey in 1908. (The area where the Serbs lived is now included in the modern country of Yugoslavia.) The Serbs, encouraged by the Russians, were plotting to gain independence from Austria and to unite all Serbs in this southeastern area of Europe. Austria, with the consent of Germany, was determined to suppress Serbian ambitions. On the occasion of the Archduke's visit to Sarajevo, he and his

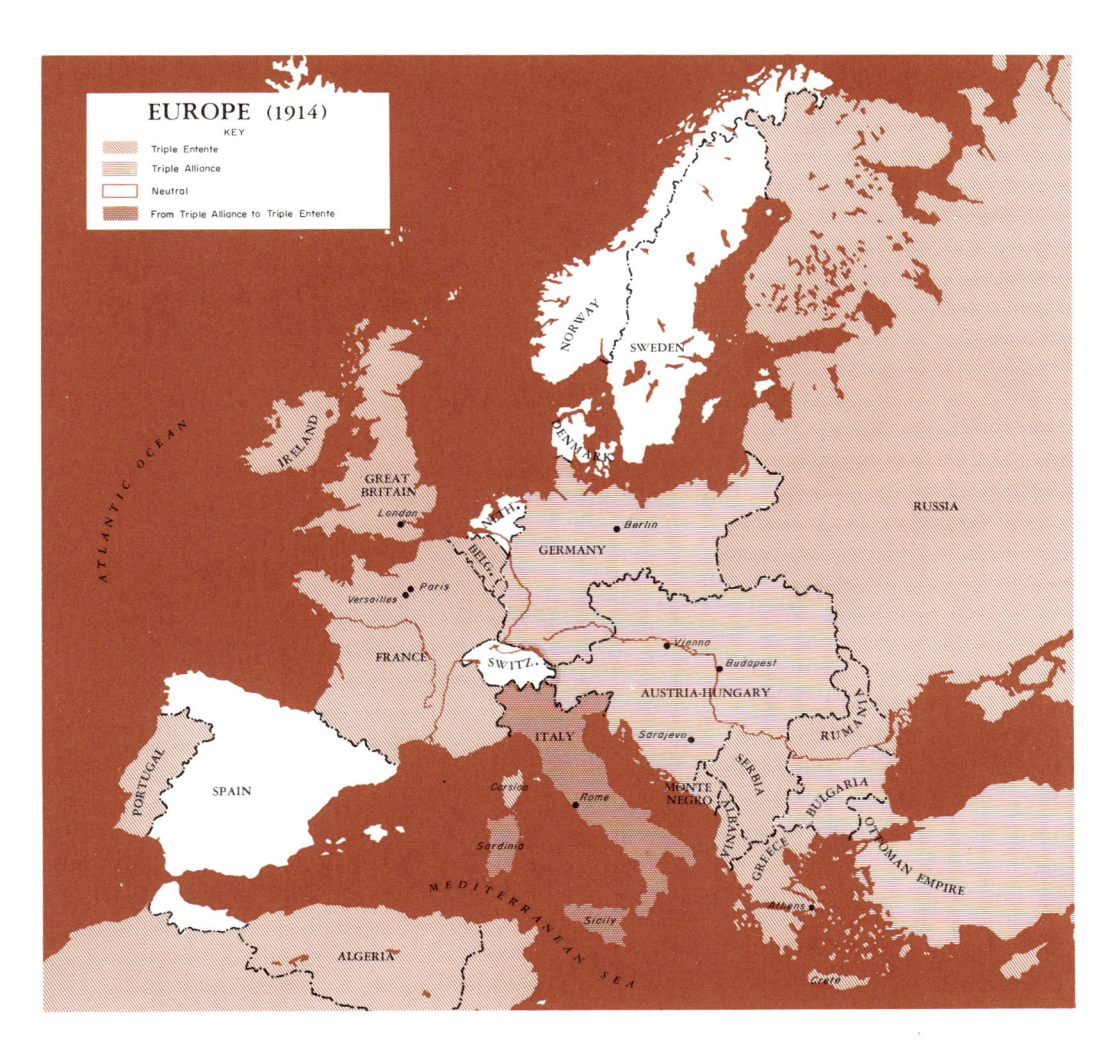

A Serbian anarchist rushed to the car in which Archduke Ferdinand and his wife were riding and shot them point-blank.

wife were fatally shot by a young Serbian. The assassin was caught, and it was learned that he belonged to a society whose purpose was the joining of Bosnia to Serbia. This was a motive attributed to the Russians. Now the spark was struck which would light the fuse of war.

War Declarations. On July 28, 1914, Austria-Hungary declared war on Serbia, and began to mobilize her forces. Russia threatened to defend the little country, and started to gather her troops. When Russia mobilized, Germany once more stood by her ally, Austria-Hungary. Germany gave Russia twelve hours in which to stop her preparations for war, and France was given eighteen hours in which to declare whether or not she would remain neutral in case of war between Germany and Russia. The Russians disregarded the threat and continued to mass their armies, and the French refused point-blank to promise neutrality. On August 1, Germany officially declared war on Russia; on August 3, Germany declared war on France.

First Years of War

A "Scrap of Paper." The German generals decided that the easiest way to smash the French was to plunge through Belgium and cross the undefended boundary line between Belgium and France. This strategy was in direct violation of a treaty which the Germans had made with France and England to respect the neutrality of Belgium. As the flood of Germans poured over the Belgian frontier, it became obvious that the Germans regarded the treaty as "a scrap of paper," as it was named by a German official.

Although the little Belgian army fought bravely against the invaders, they were destroyed by the hordes of well drilled Germans. By this time the British had agreed to aid their French allies in the defense of Paris against the onrushing Germans. By September 6 the Germans were only forty miles away from the city. The officers of the French government fled to Bordeaux, and it seemed that Paris was doomed.

The Western Front. A gallant French general, Joffre, had been organizing strong defenses along the Marne River. Reinforced by troops which had been transported from Paris by an immense caravan of taxicabs, the French and British not only held the Marne but drove the Germans back to the Aisne River in northern France. Near the Aisne, both sides dug trenches and erected barbed wire entanglements. These made it difficult for either side to advance, and the line where the armies entrenched themselves remained little changed for about three years.

The Eastern Front. While the armies of both sides were held in check on the western front, important things were happening in Eastern Europe. Russia mobilized more quickly than Germany had thought she possibly could, so the Germans and Austrians were forced to send many of their strongest troops to the east. This greatly weakened their western front, and lessened the danger of another great attack on Paris.

New Allies. In the closing months of 1914 each side gained a new ally. Since 1902, Great Britain and Japan had had a treaty by which each promised to help the other in case of war with more than one other country. So the Japanese entered the war on the side of the Allies—France, Great Britain, Russia, Serbia, and Belgium.

Some time later, Turkey joined the side of the Central Powers, as Germany and Austria-Hungary were

A German machine gun crew faces the Russians on the Eastern front in 1915, early in World War I.

called. Turkey's action was important, for the Turks controlled the narrow straits of the Dardanelles and the Bosporus, through which ships would have to pass in traveling between the Black Sea and the Mediterranean. The Russian Black Sea fleet was now bottled up and was made useless to the Allies.

Bulgaria, later, in 1915, joined the Central Powers. The Bulgarians had long hated the Serbians, and now

One of the most spectacular troop movements in modern history occurred when Paris taxi drivers volunteered to drive French troops to the front. Soldiers piled into cabs as drivers shuttled back and forth between Paris and the front for long hours.

Blindfolded, so as to be completely impartial, Secretary of War Newton D. Baker draws the first number in the second military draft, June 27, 1918. When the United States entered the war, soldiers were chosen in this way.

they saw their chance to join Austria-Hungary in crushing that little country. Before the end of the year the Bulgarians from the east and the Austrians from the north had completely conquered Serbia.

In May, 1915, Italy entered the war on the side of the Allies. Though she had been a member of the Triple Alliance, she refused to join Germany and Austria-Hungary when the fighting began. Immediately after joining the Allies, she began to attack Austria-Hungary from the south. Another ally joined the forces fighting Germany in 1916. This was Rumania, another of the Balkan countries of Eastern Europe. Bulgarian and Austrian troops swarmed across her borders, however, and she was soon knocked out of the war, while her oil wells and wheat land fell into the enemies' hands.

Submarine Warfare. It was during 1916 that the German navy came out to fight. Off Jutland on the Danish coast the British and German fleets met in the greatest naval battle of the war. The superior British fleet forced the German ships to seek the shelter of their harbors. For the remainder of the war the British controlled the North Sea, and the German battleships never again came out to offer battle.

With her army and navy deadlocked on sea and land, Germany now resorted to submarine warfare. Her fleet of submarines, at that time the most powerful in the world, had succeeded in sinking several British warships. Germany now undertook to starve Great Britain by cutting off her commerce on the sea. Many British ships were sunk by German submarines. It was this submarine warfare that first aroused a general feeling of hostility toward Germany in the United States.

Looking Back

1. How did rivalries and fears divide Europe into an armed camp?

2. By what steps did the "spark" at Sarajevo grow to a blaze that involved most of Europe?

3. Name the countries that made up the Allied Powers and those that were known as the Central Powers.

4. What reasons prompted the Germans to resort to submarine warfare?

3. The United States Is Drawn into the Conflict

Attempts at Neutrality

From the very beginning, the United States had tried to remain neutral, but this did not prove an easy task. A large part of the American population had immigrated from Europe, and most of these people were intensely sympathetic with the countries from which they had come. Many crossed the ocean to fight in the European armies, and many others did all in their power to arouse war feeling in the United States.

British Blockade. The nations at war themselves made it difficult for the United States to remain neutral. The warships of the British blockade stopped and searched American vessels, and often illegally seized them and confiscated their cargoes. This was much like Great Britain's treatment of American ships in the years preceding the War of 1812, and it aroused bitter resentment in many Americans.

German Submarines. But the acts of the British were greatly overshadowed by those of the Germans. German submarines lurked below the surface of the Atlantic and torpedoed merchant vessels containing sometimes hundreds of passengers. More than one hundred American citizens were included in the 1100 persons who lost their lives on the *Lusitania*, and other ships were sunk in the same manner. Many vessels flying the American flag were torpedoed, and the number of American lives lost continued to increase.

President Woodrow Wilson sent note after note to the authorities in Germany to find out just what their aims were, and whether they intended to continue their submarine warfare. Time after time the Germans promised to restrict the activities of their submarines, but always some new horror soon showed that they had forgotten their pledge. At last, after the great liner *Sussex* had been sunk with an appalling loss of life, the Germans pledged not to sink merchant vessels without warning and without ensuring the safety of the people on them, provided that such ships did not resist or try to escape. Like the others, this pledge was not kept for long.

Part of Woodrow Wilson's War Message to Congress, 1917

"We have no quarrel with the German people. We have no feeling toward them but one of sympathy and friendship. It was not upon their impulse that their government acted in entering the war. It was not with their previous knowledge or approval. It was a war determined upon as wars used to be determined upon in the old, unhappy days when peoples were nowhere consulted by their rulers and wars were provoked and waged in the interest of dynasties or of little groups of ambitious men who were accustomed to use their fellow men as pawns and tools . . ."

The Zimmermann Note. As the war in Europe went on, German subversive agents were active in the United States. They attempted to slow down the manufacture of war materials intended for the allied powers by encouraging strikes and by sabotage. It was generally believed that these activities were carried out with the help of the German and Austrian embassies.

German plotting and undercover work in America reached a climax when the government authorities learned of the famous Zimmermann note to Mexico. This was a letter from Herr Zimmermann, the German foreign minister, to the German representative in Mexico. It spoke of a campaign of unrestricted submarine warfare to be started February 1, 1917, to starve Great Britain into submission. It instructed the German minister to Mexico to stir up feeling against the United States, and to lead Mexico to try to reconquer her lost territory in New Mexico, California, Texas, and Arizona. The German minister was further instructed to suggest to the president of Mexico that he open negotiations with Japan to attack the United States from the west.

Fortunately, the Zimmermann plan fell through. The Mexicans realized that a war between their country and the United States would be suicide for them, and the plan never was carried out. The Zimmermann note, however, spread such indignation throughout the United States that it became evident that the United States could not stay out of the war.

U. S. Declaration of War

On April 2, 1917, President Wilson asked Congress to declare war. Although Wilson had been re-elected in 1916 partly because of the people's belief that "he kept us out of war," it was apparent that the actions of Germany would make war unavoidable. "It is a fearful thing to lead this great peaceful people into war," said the President, "but the right is more

American pilot with maintenance crew standing by a World War I aircraft at Issodun, France, 1918. The airplane is a French-made Nieuport 27. The first air battles in the history of the world took place in World War I.

precious than peace, and we shall fight for the things which we have always carried nearest our hearts. . . . The world must be made safe for democracy."

On April 4, the Senate by a vote of 86 to 6 declared that a state of war existed, and on April 6 the House agreed by a vote of 373 to 50. War against Austria was not declared, however, until December 7, 1917, and no declaration of war was made against Bulgaria or Turkey.

Wartime Measures

The Armed Forces. In 1915, when the *Lusitania* was sunk, the American army was small and poorly equipped. There were few factories for manufacturing ammunition and supplies. The new financial system of the country, the Federal Reserve System, was relatively untried. By 1917 the country was still unprepared, but conditions were better. For one thing, the minor operations against Villa in Mexico had given the army valuable experience. Also, factories had been enlarged and new weapons had been studied. America's new Federal Reserve System was proving itself day by day.

It was no easy task to raise a large army in the United States. Congress quickly passed a bill to call the state militia to active duty, and to draft a national army. Although there had been compulsory drafts of men in the Civil War, conscription was contrary to American tradition. Nevertheless, the Selective Service Act was passed on May 18, 1917, compelling all male citizens between 21 and 30 years to enroll for military service. From the names of the enrolled men, 500,000

An American "doughboy" 1918. An American army was drafted, trained, and outfitted for the war in one year.

were selected by lot to be trained. In the meantime volunteers had increased the regular army from about 80,000 to 287,000 men. The government established camps all over the country for the training of these officers and men.

Originally the War Department planned to begin sending the American army to France in the spring of 1918, but the hard-pressed armies of the Allies needed American support earlier than that. The Germans were digging in behind strong defensive positions known as "the Hindenburg Line," and their submarines were mercilessly sinking Allied ships. Accordingly, General Pershing and his staff went to Europe in June, 1917, and American troops followed them at the rate of 10,000 a day. Neither the Germans nor the Allies had expected reinforcements so quickly or in such large numbers.

Financing the War. In the meantime, the work of financing the war was ably carried on. About one-third of the money needed to support the war effort was raised by taxation, the rest from the sale of government bonds. Income, inheritance, and excise taxes were raised sharply. Excess profits taxes on corporations rose as high as sixty per cent. Taxes were placed on luxuries and amusements.

The sale of government bonds—in other words, borrowing from the people—was achieved by four "Liberty Loan" campaigns and one "Victory Loan." The value of the bonds was placed as low as $50, which made them attractive to millions of people who had never before purchased a government bond. The American people bought all the bonds offered for sale, with the result that the government had enough funds to carry on the war.

Food and Fuel. One of the most immediate problems of the country was to supply food for the armed forces. Care had to be taken that profiteers did not buy up grain, sugar, and other foods in order to sell them at a profit. A Food Control Act gave the government power to control foods, fuel, and all the tools and machinery needed for the production and distribution of food. Food administration was placed under the direction of Herbert Hoover, who did a splendid job in encouraging Americans to plant "war gardens" and to conserve food. People managed to get along with limited supplies of coal.

Service Groups. To France went many other Americans besides the fighters. The American Red Cross sent ambulances, nurses, interns, and doctors who carried on the heroic work of saving lives, often under fire. The Young Men's Christian Association, the Young Women's Christian Association, the Young Men's Hebrew Association, the Salvation Army, and the Knights of Columbus sent hundreds of workers across to establish rest houses, furnish refreshments and amusements, and support the morale of the fighters.

Progress of the War

The Russian Revolution. It was well that America had entered the war when she did. Russia, whose army was one of the key forces in the war, was beset by domestic difficulties. The Russian army fought well from 1914

American Red Cross nurse, 1918. The Red Cross poured millions of dollars for relief into Europe during and after the war.

to 1917, but in 1917, unrest with the despotic, cruel government of the Czar led to a great revolution. After a second revolution, the new leaders of the Russian government called themselves Communists and claimed to represent the peasants and common people. After fighting three years of war on its own western border and fighting a revolution at home, the Russian army was exhausted, demoralized and disorganized. Russia was forced to pull out of the war and signed a treaty with the Germans.

The treaty was negotiated at Brest Litovsk, in Russia, and it was known by the name of the town. Under the terms of the treaty of Brest Litovsk, Russia agreed to give up a part of her land claims in Eastern Europe, which included the countries formerly called Latvia and Estonia, part of Poland, and part of Turkey. She was also forced to pay a large war reparation, and to recognize the independence of some of her own territory.

Germany's Final Drives. Hundreds of thousands of German troops who had been fighting on the eastern front were now rushed to join the battle against the rest of the Allies. The German strategy was to throw four sledgehammer blows at various points along the Allied line of defense. They hoped to break through, divide the Allied forces, and win the war. The first German drive was launched against Amiens, where the French and British armies overlapped. The Germans attacked at this point because they hoped that the French and British might not work well together. A terrific German onslaught cracked the Allied line and it looked as though

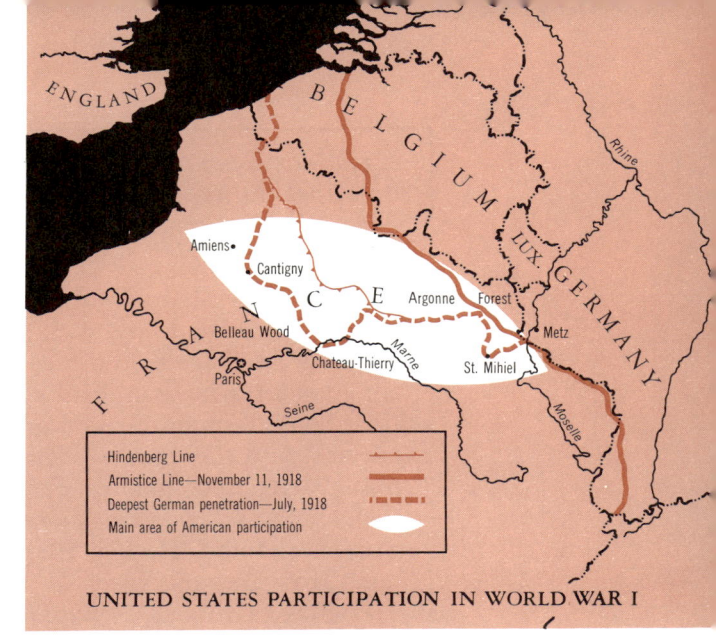

UNITED STATES PARTICIPATION IN WORLD WAR I

the Germans might pour to the very heart of France. But though the Allies were pushed aside, they were not beaten, and reserves rushed to fill the gap. French, British, and a regiment of the newly arrived Americans fought stubbornly, and at last this German drive was stopped.

From the near disaster at Amiens, the Allies learned the lesson that all of their forces should be under the command of one man. Accordingly, General Foch, one of the most brilliant of the French generals, was put in supreme command. From this time onward the Allied armies worked as a single unit.

In April the Germans struck their second great blow. This time the attack came on the northern end of the line, defended by the British, and the object was to gain possession of the French ports which might serve as submarine bases for the Germans. Should the Germans capture these ports, England would be cut off from France. In this battle the British made a gallant stand against a superior German army. When strong French re-

> *A war correspondent for the* Chicago Tribune, *Floyd Gibbons, describes the reception received by General Pershing and the American troops when they arrived in France to participate in World War I.*
>
> "Old grey-haired fathers of French fighting men bared their heads and with tears streaming down their cheeks shouted greetings to the tall, thin, grey-moustached American commander who was leading new armies to the support of their sons. Women heaped armfuls of roses into the General's car and into the cars of other American officers that followed him. Paris street gamins climbed the lamp-posts and waved their caps and wooden shoes and shouted shrilly. . . . Some women shouted 'Hello,' 'Heep, Heep, hourrah,' 'Good Morning,' 'How are you, keed?'"
> —Floyd Gibbons, And They Thought We Wouldn't Fight (New York, 1918), 52–60

inforcements and a few regiments of Americans were thrown into the line, the German attack bogged down completely. The channel ports were saved.

Arrival of Americans. It was in the defense against the third German drive in May that American troops first played an important and decisive part. From the city of Rheims, the kaiser's troops swept straight for Paris. The combined Allied forces were successful in stopping this drive, and soon after, the American troops proved their mettle by recapturing the town of Cantigny from the Germans.

Only thirty miles from Paris, another part of the advancing German line met United States Marines at Belleau Wood. This was the Germans' first real contact with the "devil dogs," as they soon came to call the marines. Not only did the marines stop the foe, but they launched a counterattack which cleared the entire wood of German forces.

The last drive on Paris began in July. A massive German thrust reached the Marne, but here the French and Americans staged a counterattack. They struck the Germans at Château-Thierry and at last succeeded in driving them from the town. The Germans had staked everything and had failed to take Paris. Now the shoe was to be on the other foot, for General Foch had planned a tremendous offensive to break the Germans' line and drive them back.

The St. Mihiel Salient. General Foch assigned important work to the American troops in this great advance. Southeast of Rheims there was a long, thin slice of territory which the Germans had captured, the St. Mihiel Salient, pointing straight towards Paris. This the Americans were given the task of capturing with the aid of French troops. One morning in September the attack commenced with a tremendous artillery bombardment. When the shells stopped bursting in

Troops had to hold back the happy crowds when Armistice was announced in New York City.

the German lines, Americans and French swept forward, and so great was their victory that the St. Mihiel Salient no longer pointed towards Paris, but now extended out in the other direction toward the German city of Metz.

The Argonne. Just north of St. Mihiel lay the great Argonne Forest. Here the Germans had fortified themselves strongly. On the day after the Germans had been driven from the St. Mihiel Salient, the Allied forces started forward against the German

---

An American combat officer describes the feeling of the troops at the end of the fighting of World War I.

"All over the world on November 11, 1918, people were celebrating, dancing in the streets, drinking champagne, hailing the armistice that meant the end of the war. But at the front there was no celebration. Many soldiers believed the Armistice only a temporary measure and that the war would soon go on. As night came, the quietness, unearthly in its penetration, began to eat into their souls. The men sat around log fires, the first they had ever had at the front. They were trying to reassure themselves that there were no enemy batteries spying on them from the next hill and no German bombing planes approaching to blast them out of existence."

—From *Soldiers of Darkness* by Thomas R. Gowenlock with Guy Murchie. Copyright 1936, 1937 by Doubleday & Co., Inc. Reprinted by permission of the publisher.

position in the Argonne. Before the Frenchmen and Americans stopped advancing, the Germans had been driven completely out of the Argonne Forest. The victorious Allies crossed a part of the far-famed Hindenburg Line in their advance, and the Germans awoke to a realization that their position was not so secure as they had thought.

The Armistice

In the meantime British, French, and Americans farther north had punctured the Hindenburg Line at other points. Everywhere the German forces were giving way. Still the Allied push continued, and the orderly retreat became a rout. The city of Sedan fell to the American troops on November 6, and five days later, on November 11, 1918, Germany surrendered when a group of German representatives signed an armistice, or agreement to cease fighting. The war was over. Already the Kaiser had abdicated and fled into Holland, and Germany was no longer an autocratic monarchy, but a republic.

By the terms of the armistice which ended the war, Germany was compelled (1) to remove her troops from Allied territory and from the part of Germany west of the Rhine River, (2) to cancel the peace treaties she had signed with Russia and Rumania, and (3) to surrender enormous amounts of fighting equipment, including most of her navy.

Allied armies advanced and occupied Alsace and Lorraine, which Germany had conquered in 1870. Across the boundary line into Germany went English, French, and American troops to occupy peacefully the three important cities of Cologne, Coblenz, and Mainz on the Rhine River. Peace had at last come to Europe.

Looking Back

1. What actions by England and Germany made it difficult for the United States to remain neutral?
2. How did the contents of the Zimmermann note affect German-American relations?
3. Show how the United States took steps to provide men, money, food, and fuel for the war effort.
4. Why was the Russian Revolution a severe blow to the Allies?
5. In which battles and campaigns did the Americans participate actively in bringing the Germans to surrender?

The Chapter in Perspective

Who Are These People?

Wilson	Francis Ferdinand
Diaz	Joffre
Carranza	Hoover
Villa	Foch
Pershing	

Where Are These Places?

Mexico	Estonia
Columbus	Cantigny
Serbia	Belleau Wood
Marne River	St. Mihiel
Latvia	Argonne

What Do These Dates and Terms Mean?

New Freedom
1913
1914
Clayton Act
Apr. 6, 1917
Triple Alliance
Triple Entente
Central Powers
Underwood-Simmons Tariff
Zimmermann Note
Selective Service Act
"watchful waiting"
Food Control Act
Russian Revolution
Federal Reserve Act
Federal Trade Commission
submarine warfare
Allies
Lusitania
Nov. 11, 1918
Liberty bonds
Communists
Brest Litovsk
Armistice

Questions for Study

1. Cite the far-reaching reforms and changes introduced by Wilson's domestic program.

2. Which new legislation sponsored by Wilson do you feel was the most important? Support your choice.

3. How did the United States again find itself involved in Mexican affairs?

4. Many claim that the assassination of Francis Ferdinand sparked the flames of nationalism, imperialism, militarism, and commercialism to cause the war. Comment.

5. What were the reasons for the entry of the United States into World War I?

6. Why did Germany return to a policy of unrestricted submarine warfare despite promises to the United States?

7. In what ways did the United States Navy contribute to the Allied victory?

8. What were the terms of the Armistice?

9. What countries found on a map of Europe in 1914 are no longer in existence? Which nations appear on a current map of Europe that did not appear in 1914?

10. How did the location of Belgium and the geography of the area favor the invasion of Belgium by the Germans?

Place Yourself in History

With the aid of American supplies and manpower, the Allies put increasing pressure on the weakening Central Powers so that the latter began to crumble. Turkey and Bulgaria stopped fighting. In early November, Austria accepted truce terms. Mutiny broke out in the German fleet. On November 8 Foch gave the Germans armistice terms and seventy-two hours in which to accept them. The next day the Kaiser abdicated and then fled to Holland. On November 11, 1918, at 11:00 A.M. the war was over!

How would you have reacted if you had been a German soldier in the trenches? a German civilian at home? a United States Marine in the front line? a French resident of Paris? a British soldier? a United States Senator?

25

Peacetime Problems

When World War I had ended, and the casualty lists were totaled, the leaders of the nations of the world were profoundly shocked. They had just survived the most terrible war in the history of the world. The young men of Europe were greatly reduced in number, and in the United States, many families mourned the death or disability of a son or a brother. The American President, Woodrow Wilson, was deeply moved by the suffering the war had caused, and he tried to think of a way which would guarantee that war would not happen again. He proposed a League of Nations in which nations could settle their differences peacefully. The appeal of such an idea was great, but when the United States did not join the League, it was doomed to failure. War was to break out again only twenty years later.

1. A War-Weary World Disarms for Peace

As early as January, 1918, President Wilson had formulated a program which he hoped would ensure a "peace without victory"—a peace that would be enduring. His program was summed up in the famous *Fourteen Points*. What was the nature of these points, and to what extent were they followed at the Treaty of Versailles which ended the war?

The Treaty of Versailles

Of Wilson's Fourteen Points, the first five were aimed at the prevention of war. They urged that all treaties and conferences should be open and above board, that all nations should enjoy freedom of the seas and equality in trading opportunities, that there should be a reduction of armaments, and that the claims of various nations to colonial possessions should be fairly considered. It was hoped that these provisions would reduce international jealousy and suspicion, and lessen the danger of war. Points 6-13 dealt with "self-determination" for the people of Europe—that is, their right to choose their own governments and to regain territory that had been taken from them.

A League of Nations. The fourteenth point provided for a League of Nations to secure peace, independence, and territorial security to all countries, large and small. This was President Wilson's favorite point. Although he was forced, against his will and against his better judgment, to give in on many of the other points, he steadfastly defended his League of Nations until the provision for the League was accepted. Wilson well knew that some grave defects were being written into the treaty, but he was confident that his League, once created, would succeed in righting all such wrongs.

The "Big Four." A few weeks after the Germans laid down their arms in 1918, Wilson and the delegates from twenty-six other countries met at Versailles, a suburb of Paris. This was the first time that a President of the United States had left the country while still in office. The British delegation was headed by Prime Minister Lloyd George, the French by Premier Georges Clemenceau, the Italian by Premier Vittorio Orlando. These four leaders were the "Big Four" in the peace negotiations, and they dominated the conference, which began on January 12, 1919.

Several problems existed from the very beginning of the conference. For example, the Russian people were engaged in a revolution. Since there was no stable Russian government, Russia, one of the major powers and a

President Wilson (right) and other members of the "Big Four." Left to right: Lloyd George of England, Orlando of Italy, and Clemenceau of France.

large force in the war was not represented at Versailles. Furthermore, Germany, defeated in the war, was not even represented at the Conference. This later proved to be a great mistake.

Also to President Wilson's great distress, he found that the statesmen who had gathered at Paris to draw up the peace treaty were much less interested in building a lasting peace than in seeing what they could do to strengthen their own countries and keep them supreme. He was surprised to learn that there were secret treaties among the Allies which conflicted with some of his Fourteen Points. In general, he succeeded in saving only those points which favored the victorious nations.

A Victors' Treaty. After much wrangling and bitter debate, the delegates finally produced a treaty in June, 1919. It was a "victors' treaty" which contained a number of harsh clauses which may have contributed to the outbreak of another war twenty years later. Germany was forced to give up much of her territory and to pay a great sum of money as reparations. It was also necessary for her to agree to a "war guilt" clause whereby she acknowledged responsibility for starting the war. She gave up Alsace-Lorraine, which she had taken from France in 1871, and her colonial possessions were divided among the victors, who were to administer them under the supervision of the League of Nations. The French won temporary control over the Saar and its rich coal deposits, even though the area was inhabited by Germans. To the east, Germany lost much territory to Poland, which was now restored as an independent nation. A Polish "corridor" gave that country access to the Baltic Sea and separated East Prussia from Germany.

Woodrow Wilson's fight for American acceptance of the League of Nations left him ill and weary. His fatigue shows in this 1921 picture, taken on his 65th birthday.

Germany's allies also paid heavily for their part in the war. Austria was separated from Hungary, and parts of the old Austrian Empire were given to Rumania and to the new states of Czechoslovakia and Yugoslavia. Bulgaria lost certain areas to Greece and Yugoslavia, while Turkey gave up most of her non-Turkish land. Italy received strategic areas inhabited by Austrians. The map of Europe had indeed changed!

American Response to the League

Defeat in the Senate. There is little doubt that President Wilson worked so hard on the treaty because he felt that the entire United States was behind the principles it stood for. When he returned to this country, he was greeted by cheering crowds. However, Wilson's plan for a League of Nations was not well received. When it went to the Senate for ratification, the opposition to it was formidable. After vigorous debate, the Senate finally refused to ratify the entire treaty, largely because of the clause regarding the League. The nation and the world were shocked that the President of a nation which had originated many of the points of the treaty could have so little support at home. The United States never did join the League of Nations, and because of this, the organization never was as effective as it might have been.

The technical point upon which the treaty was defeated in the Senate hinged around Article X, which called upon the various nations involved to go to war if necessary to enforce justice. This was deemed to conflict with the provision of the Constitution which gives to Congress the sole right to declare war. Later, in 1921, the United States signed separate peace treaties with Germany, Austria, and Hungary.

Wilson and the League. Wilson continued his battle to get the United States to join the League even after the Senate refused to cooperate. He made a tour throughout the country, making speeches everywhere in its defense, and incidentally wearing himself out to such an extent that he suffered a stroke after the trip. Wilson lay completely unable to function as President for some months. His devoted wife and his doctor decided what business he could and could not do. In effect, Mrs. Wilson was acting President of the United States during her husband's illness.

The presidential election of 1920 was largely fought over the issue of the League: most Democrats favored it and many Republicans opposed it. Since Wilson's illness had left the Democratic party leaderless for a vital period of time, the Republicans won easily. Warren G. Harding, the Republican candidate, was victorious over James Cox, the Democrat, and the United States did not join the League of Nations.

The World Court

Although President Harding opposed America's entry into the League,

The Peace Palace at the Hague, capital of South Holland, was completed in 1913. It houses the International Court of Justice, of which the U.S. is now a member.

he favored our becoming a member of the World Court, as did his successors —Calvin Coolidge, Herbert Hoover, and Franklin Roosevelt. The Permanent Court of International Justice, or World Court, located at the Hague in the Netherlands, was a relatively powerless agency of the League. Its purpose was to settle international disputes. Although a group in the Senate always succeeded in keeping the United States out of the Court, individual Americans served as "observers" of the Court's activities, and two former American Secretaries of State became judges of the Court.

The Washington Disarmament Conference

Deeply concerned by developments in the Far East and disturbed by a growing friction between the United States and Japan, President Harding proposed in August, 1921, that nations having an interest in the Pacific meet in Washington to discuss disarmament. Belgium, China, France, Great Britain, Italy, Japan, Holland, and Portugal responded and sent delegates to take part in this important meeting. From November, 1921, to February, 1922, the delegates conferred and finally drew up a series of three treaties—the Five-Power Treaty, the Four-Power Treaty, and the Nine-Power Treaty. These treaties concerned: (1) limitation of naval and land armaments and rules for the use of new weapons of war, (2) the disposal of the Pacific islands which Germany had formerly controlled, and (3) the treatment of China.

The 5-5-3 Ratio. No sooner had the conference started than Charles E. Hughes, United States Secretary of State, arose and challenged Great Britain, Japan, France, and Italy to a sweeping reduction of sea power. After much discussion, these nations reached an agreement and signed a treaty. By the terms of the treaty, the United States, Great Britain, and Japan were to scrap a number of old battleships and a few new ones which were not yet completed. No more battleships were to be built by any of the five nations for a period of ten

Battleships like this one were the pride of the American fleet in World War I.

years. The treaty limited the battleship fleets of the United States and Great Britain to a total of 525,000 tons each and Japan's battleship fleet to 315,000 tons, a provision which became known as "the 5-5-3 ratio." The battleship fleets of France and Italy were limited to 175,000 tons each.

Importance of the Treaty. The Washington Naval Treaty was important for it tended to prevent naval competition like that which Great Britain and Germany had carried on before the First World War. It should be pointed out, however, that the large, cumbersome battleships used in World War I had been proved somewhat impractical. Light cruisers, submarines, and aircraft carriers were the ships of the future. The countries were not giving up a great deal when they gave up their battleships. The treaty was important in other ways, however, because it began a discussion of arms control, one of the serious problems of our time. The powers at the conference agreed to prohibit the use of poison gas, which had been responsible for a huge number of horrible deaths in World War I. They also decided not to allow submarine attacks on merchant vessels. When it came to the limitation of armies, however, no agreement could be reached.

Other Agreements. The Four-Power Treaty was a pact between the United States, Great Britain, Japan, and France. These powers agreed to respect each other's holdings in the Pacific and to settle disputes by arbitration rather than by war. The pact also ended the alliance between Great Britain and Japan which had been formed in 1902 and had brought Japan into the war against Germany in 1914. This earlier alliance had caused uneasiness in the United States, and it was unpopular in Australia, New Zealand, and Canada, mainly because Asia and North America were both within reach of Japanese power. If Britain were not permitted to oppose Japan, Japan might be tempted to take over American holdings in the Pacific.

The Nine-Power Treaty provided that all of the signatories would preserve equal commercial rights in China and that none would try to obtain special rights in that country. The province of Shantung, which Japan had previously taken from China, was to be returned to China.

The Kellogg-Briand Treaty

French Foreign Minister Aristide Briand was encouraged by a growing desire for peace among the nations of Europe. Consequently he announced in 1927 that his country was willing to sign a treaty with the United States outlawing war as a means of settling disputes between the two nations. The American Secretary of State, Frank Kellogg, agreed to this, but proposed that other nations should also be invited to sign the treaty. By July, 1929, more than sixty nations had signed and had thus renounced war as a means of settling disputes. Unfortunately, the mere outlawing of declarations of war does not automatically prevent the use of force. Within a very few years the European nations would learn to their dismay that conflict could occur even without any declaration of war!

The London Disarmament Conferences

Although the Kellogg-Briand Treaty could not prevent war, it did have some good effects. Most important, perhaps, it created an atmosphere of good will among nations which had been extremely nervous about their future. France, for example, felt much more secure about her safety after other nations had spoken against war. England and the United States were much more disposed to discuss disarmament. President Hoover, a few months after he was elected in 1928, invited the newly-elected British Prime Minister, Ramsay Macdonald, to the United States.

Three-Power Pact. Preliminary negotiations were held at President Hoover's Virginia fishing camp between President Hoover and Mr. Macdonald. As a result, a disarmament conference among the nations which had signed the Five-Power Treaty was convened in London in January, 1930. Great Britain, the United States, and Japan agreed to a further limitation of naval armament. France and Italy, however, refused to sign the treaty because they could not agree on a fixed formula for reducing their naval strength.

Early in 1936 a second London Naval Conference was held. Japan, unwilling to accept the 10-10-7 ratio, left the conference, but the United States, Great Britain, and France, after many disagreements, at last signed a new treaty. This treaty forbade the building of large cruisers and limited the sizes and armaments of any battleships, aircraft carriers, submarines, or other warships which any of the three signing nations should build before 1942.

The "Escalator Clause." A strange provision called *"the escalator clause"* was written into this treaty, permitting the signing nations to increase their navies if they felt endangered by some outside power. Long before 1942, it became evident that Japan was building a tremendous navy, so both the United States and Great Britain were forced to make use of the escalator clause and build up their fleets of battleships, cruisers, and other warships. The days of peaceful disarmament were at an end.

Looking Back

1. How did Wilson hope to avert future wars by the adoption of his Fourteen Points?
2. Give the main clauses of the Treaty of Versailles.
3. Why did the Senate reject the treaty?
4. List the major accomplishments of the Washington Disarmament Conference.
5. Was the Kellog-Briand Treaty a success? Why?

2. The "Good Old Days" Vanish Forever

When World War I ended in 1918, Americans wanted nothing more than to return to "the good old days" and to withdraw from international politics. This was impossible, however, because the war had produced many permanent changes in American society.

From Prosperity to Depression

As soon as hostilities were over, vast numbers of men were released from military service and found their way back to peacetime jobs. The railroads, which had been controlled by the government during the war, were

476

Automobiles, trucks, and buses first made their appearance around 1900. Foreground: a Simplex "speed car" (1910) could go 80 MPH. Right: A 1907 truck. Left: an early (1900) bus called the "Electric Tally Ho." It was powered by electricity and had tiller steering. All were chain driven like a bicycle.

turned back to private operators. Factory workers, who had become accustomed to high wartime wages, had created a strong labor movement, and in 1919 many strikes broke out. Farmers, who had enjoyed high prices for their crops, now faced hard times as the market dropped. By 1921 the country was in the midst of a depression.

Two New Amendments

In January, 1919, the Eighteenth Amendment was ratified, prohibiting the sale of liquor. In October Congress passed the Volstead Act, which enforced this amendment by forbidding the sale of all liquor containing more than one-half of one per cent alcohol. Many sections of the country already had local "dry" laws, but now prohibition was enforced on a national scale. This was a great victory for the Anti-Saloon League, the Women's Christian Temperance Union (W.C.T.U.) and other organizations which had fought for many years for this reform. However, prohibition brought with it a great crime wave as bootleggers (men who sold illegal whiskey) tried to evade the law and many thousands of Americans refused to obey it.

In June, 1919, Congress approved the Nineteenth Amendment which would give women the right to vote. Ratified in October, 1920, it gave women the opportunity to vote in the presidential election that year. This amendment was long overdue and represented a great advance in American democracy.

The "Red Scare"

The end of the war also witnessed a great crusade against Communists, Socialists, and radicals of all sorts. Those who were active in strikes by

Carry Nation was the scourge of American saloonkeepers and the heroine of prohibition. She destroyed her first saloon in Medicine Lodge, Kansas, moving on to chop up countless others over the country.

labor unions were especially subject to attack. As a result, public opinion turned against unions, even when their efforts to win higher wages were clearly justified. United States Attorney General A. Mitchell Palmer conducted relentless raids against Communists and succeeded in having many of them deported. Palmer's actions encouraged a wave of violence, and intolerance and fear swept the country. Prejudice was aroused not only against Communists but also against aliens, Jews, Negroes, Catholics, and other minority groups. The "Red Scare" soon passed away, how-

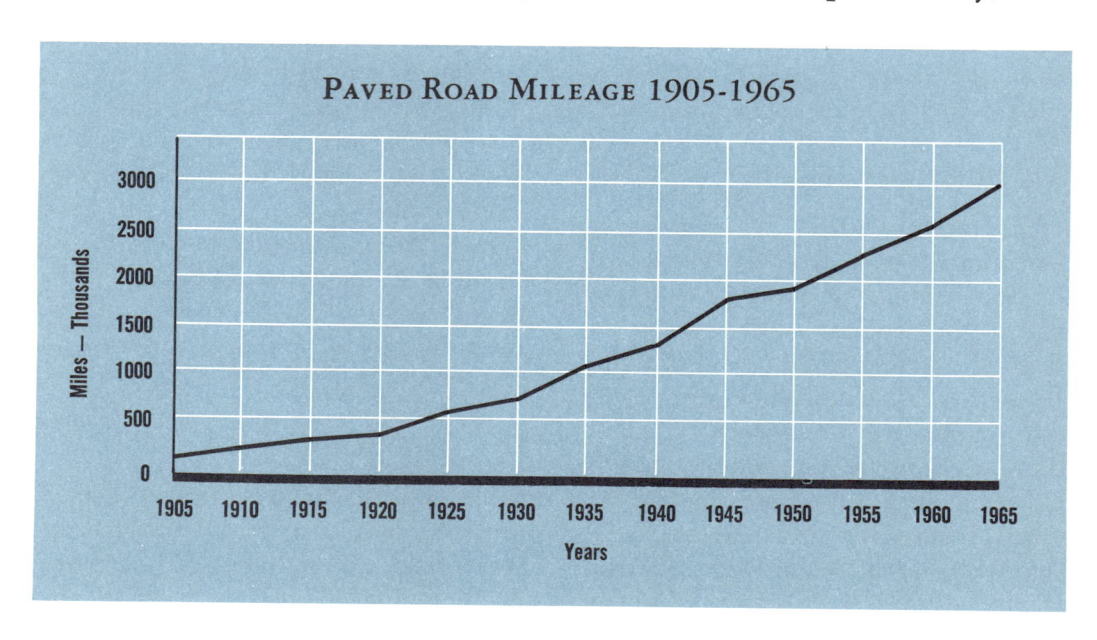

PAVED ROAD MILEAGE 1905-1965

ever, as many Americans began to realize that it was unfair to persecute people for their beliefs and that such persecution threatened our traditional democratic liberties.

The depression of 1921 soon ended, and the country rapidly expanded its industrial output. Automobile production increased tremendously during the 1920's. Other industries which supplied automobile manufacturers, such as steel, rubber, and glass, also prospered. The building of roads, public utilities, textile mills, and countless new products brought about a remarkable rise in the national income. However, in the midst of what seemed to be plenty there were ominous signs. Workers during the war had been paid high wages, mainly because their services were absolutely necessary to the war effort. But after the war, when many large corporations began producing more goods and raising prices on them, laborers were given less pay. Labor unions were given a bad name by the "Palmer raids" as they were known, and business in many cases managed to destroy the gains laborers had made in the 1880's and 1890's.

Since the labor force of the nation was becoming a major population group, they also made up a large group of consumers. In other words, they were the ones who bought much of what the manufacturers manufactured. With lower wages and facing higher prices, the average worker could buy little, and the country slid unsuspectingly toward another, far worse depression. In one way at least, the period known as the "Golden Twenties" was not, in reality, very golden. Underneath the glittering surface was a great deal of unrest and economic disorder.

Betrayal of a Trust

At their convention in 1920 the Republicans had nominated Senator Warren G. Harding of Ohio, with Governor Calvin Coolidge of Massachusetts as his running mate. The Democrats had chosen James M. Cox of Ohio as their candidate for the Presidency. Their Vice-Presidential candidate was Franklin D. Roosevelt, then

Automobile production. The great increase in the number of cars signalled the end of the "good old days." Large factories, noise, air pollution, were all by-products.

> *In his memoirs, Senator James E. Watson of Indiana characterized his good friend Warren G. Harding, twenty-eighth President of the United States.*
>
> "I had a great affection for Warren G. Harding. We were born on the same day and had been personal and political friends for many years. He was about as handsome a man as I ever saw, and he had one of those affidavit faces whose very appearance carries conviction, and withal he was a magnificent figure. He just loved fellowship. He wanted to have a crowd around and have a good time. He could smoke a cigarette, or a cigar, or a pipe, he could take a nip of liquor without ever using it to excess, he liked to indulge in a game of poker whenever an idle hour permitted, and he was exceedingly fond of golf. The truth about it is that he was altogether too urbane, too good-natured, too generous-hearted, and too fond of having a good time for his own good.
>
> "The simple fact is that my dear old friend just did not like to work...."
>
> —From *As I Knew Them: Memoirs of James E. Watson*, copyright 1936, by The Bobbs-Merrill Co., Inc., reprinted by permission of the publishers.

Assistant Secretary of the Navy. Harding won a landslide victory, with 404 electoral votes to 127 for Cox.

Harding's Appointments. Harding was a genial, handsome man who did his best in a position for which he was not particularly well fitted. He lacked political skill and was inclined to place too much faith in those whom he regarded as friends. Some of his cabinet appointments were excellent—such men as Secretary of State Charles Evans Hughes and Secretary of Commerce Herbert Hoover—but others proved to be incompetent or dishonest.

Corruption in High Places. Some of Harding's friends began to use their positions to make money for themselves. This corruption reached a climax when certain private oil companies were permitted to gain control of some of our naval oil reserves and to sell the oil for their own profit. News of the transaction leaked out, and, in the investigation which followed, it became evident that the dishonesty was widespread and that many prominent people were concerned in it. It is possible that President Harding never knew how his dishonest friends had betrayed his trust in them, for he died shortly before the oil deals were uncovered.

Coolidge Prosperity

President Harding was followed in office by his Vice-President, Calvin Coolidge. At the moment Harding died, Coolidge was visiting his father in the old family home in Vermont. There, in the light of a kerosene lamp, he took the oath of office, administered by his father, a justice-of-the-peace. This scene, which took place in simple, rustic surroundings, pleased the American public. Here was a Chief Executive, they thought, who had virtues that all could admire. He was simple, folksy, frugal, and conservative.

Victory at the Polls. After serving out Harding's term, Coolidge entered the campaign of 1924 as the Republican standard bearer. The Democratic candidate was John W. Davis, a New York lawyer who was the compromise choice of his badly disorganized party. A third party appeared in this campaign when groups of farmers and workingmen, led by Senator Robert La Follette of Wisconsin, organized a new Progressive party. La Follette was the presidential nominee of this party.

Although Coolidge was not a dynamic or inspiring leader, the country was enjoying what appeared on the surface to be great prosperity, and the voters were content with the conservative policies of their President. His victory at the polls was decisive—he won 382 electoral votes, against 136 for Davis and 16 for La Follette.

Coolidge's father administered his oath of office. When a President dies, his Vice-President may be sworn in by almost any convenient public official so that the country will not be without a President for any length of time.

Business and the Country. In his inaugural address, Coolidge spoke about the great prosperity of the country and promised to keep things as they were. The government, in his

---

Thomas L. Stokes, a Washington newspaper man, describes his impression of Calvin Coolidge.

"The impression I had of Coolidge the person, and still have, is of a country fellow who had just come to town, a shrewd fellow, with a crude kind of rural humor that smacked of casual, cryptic barnyard chatter. This impression, as far as physical appearance contributed, was heightened by the fact that he always wore his hat gingerly on his head, not comfortably. It always seemed just a shade too small. It sat too far up on his head. He looked as I've seen the farmer look on Sunday. He was overly neat, stiff of manner, as if not quite accustomed to his position...."

—Excerpts from *Chip Off My Shoulder* by T. L. Stokes. Published by Princeton University Press, copyright 1940.

Parades, especially Fourth of July parades, were popular entertainments that whole towns turned out to see in the 1920's. Above is a typical "Main Street Spectacular."

opinion, should keep out of business because, he said, what was good for business was good for the country. And, indeed, his principles of government seemed to be working effectively. Except for weak spots here and there, the economy of the country appeared to be extremely sound. Dozens of new industries sprang up, production increased, and payrolls were generally high. Mass production of automobiles and new developments in radio and motion pictures added to the comfort and pleasure of millions of Americans. It seemed that Americans had indeed found the secret of wealth and happiness.

The Election of 1928

The Candidates. President Coolidge announced that he did not wish to run for re-election in 1928, and the Republicans selected Herbert Hoover as their candidate. Hoover's platform promised " two chickens in every pot and a car in every garage"—in other words, continued prosperity in alliance with business. The Republican nominee's record made him an attractive candidate. Starting as an orphaned

Iowa farm boy, he made his way to Stanford University, where he studied mining engineering. Later he made a fortune in this profession. He successfully managed war relief programs in Europe, acted as wartime food administrator in the United States, and served as Secretary of Commerce under Harding and Coolidge.

The Democrats also chose an able man as their candidate—the colorful Alfred E. Smith, who, in his four terms as governor of New York, had proved himself to be a brilliant politician and administrator. "Al" Smith's great political disadvantage was that he was a Catholic. Catholics were a minority group in the United States, and the American public had rarely permitted a representative of a minority group to hold high public office. Hate groups, like the Ku Klux Klan, had stirred up much bad feeling about minorities all during the twenties. No one knows how greatly prejudice affected the election of 1928.

The Prohibition Issue. Although the campaign was a heated one, with a considerable amount of mudslinging, there were no significant differences between the platforms of the two parties. Both favored government cooperation with business and the maintenance of prosperity. The chief concrete issue was prohibition. Hoover supported it, but Smith was willing to see the Volstead Act amended so that individual states could sell light wines and beer. In the election, Hoover won a decisive victory. It is likely that religious prejudice as well as public disfavor of Smith's position concerning the sale of beer and wine were the chief reasons for Smith's defeat.

A New Administration. When Hoover took office in March, 1929, the most pressing problems were: (1) prohibition and the gangsterism which accompanied it, (2) relief for the farmers, and (3) aid for business and industry.

To get the facts about enforcement of prohibition, Hoover appointed a distinguished commission headed by George Wickersham. This commission reported that the Eighteenth Amendment was practically unenforceable largely because many ordinarily law-abiding citizens took pleasure in violating it. Although Hoover himself referred to prohibition as "the noble experiment," millions of Americans began to doubt that it was worth the crime and corruption that resulted from it. Early in 1933 Congress approved the Twenty-first Amendment, which repealed prohibition and the states ratified the amendment in December of that year.

Herbert Hoover, 1874–1964, great American public servant, held many government positions, including that of President.

> *Rugged Individualism*
>
> In a key speech delivered in October, 1928, Herbert Hoover stated the principles of government to which he and the Republican Party were committed, as follows:
>
> ".... Nor do I wish to be misinterpreted as believing that the United States is free-for-all and devil-take-the-hindmost. The very essence of equality of opportunity and of American individualism is that there shall be no domination by any group or combinations in this Republic, whether it be business or political. On the contrary, it demands economic justice as well as political and social justice. It is no system of laissez-faire ... By adherence to the principles of decentralized government, ordered liberty, equal opportunity, and freedom to the individual, our American experiment in human welfare has yielded a degree of well-being unparalled in all the world ..."

Looking Back

1. What changes came into being with the ratification of the Eighteenth and Nineteenth Amendments?
2. How can you explain the "Red Scare" in democratic America?
3. Who were the candidates and victors in the election of 1920, 1924, and 1928?
4. Compare Harding and Coolidge as Presidents.
5. Why was prohibition an important issue during this period? How was the matter eventually settled?

3. The Great Depression Strikes America and the World

For two years before Hoover's election the prices of stocks had risen steadily as greater numbers of people speculated in the stock market. Despite indications here and there that the prosperity "boom" had passed its peak and that many corporations were not earning enough to justify the high prices of their stock, the fever of speculation gripped the unwary investors.

The Tumbling Stock Market

In September, 1929, the market began to weaken. Some investors sold their stocks and took their profits, but most kept their stocks, hoping for higher prices. Suddenly, late in October, the market dropped sharply. Worried speculators rushed to sell their stocks for any price they could get. The avalanche of selling drove prices down even further, and by mid-November the average value of stocks had dropped almost fifty per cent. Many of the speculators in the stock market were people of modest means who risked their life's savings by buying stocks on margin. Under the margin plan, as little as $100 could be used by the speculator to buy stock valued at $1000. The balance was put

Jobless men stand in line for food in the depression. Men who had been wealthy as well as men who had been poor were forced to beg for food in this tragic period.

up as a loan. When stock prices fell, these people were forced to sell out at a loss to repay their loans.

Causes of the Depression

No one knows exactly what caused the Great Depression, but after it was over, economists suggested various reasons. Some felt that the great industrial growth that the country was experiencing had happened too fast, and that the workers and farmers were not sharing in the progress made by big business. Also, automation (the use of machines to do men's work) had begun to throw some of the labor force out of work, just as it does today. Plain human fear certainly had a great deal to do with causing the depression. Hundreds of investors, sensing the trouble the country was getting into, compounded it by panicking and hoarding. At any rate, millions were

---

Frederick Lewis Allen, well-known American author, describes the conditions during the depression.

First, the breadlines in the poorer districts. Second, those bleak settlements ironically known as "Hoovervilles" in the outskirts of cities and on vacant lots—groups of makeshift shacks constructed out of packing boxes, scrap iron, anything that could be picked up free in a diligent combing of the city dumps: shacks in which men and sometimes whole families of evicted people were sleeping on automobile seats carried from auto-graveyards, warming themselves before fires of rubbish in grease drums. Third, the homeless people sleeping in doorways or on park benches, and going the rounds of the restaurants for leftover half-eaten biscuits, piecrusts, anything to keep the fires of life burning. Fourth, a huge army of drifters ever on the move, searching half-aimlessly for a place where there might be a job. . . .

—*Since Yesterday* by Frederick Lewis Allen (Harper & Brothers, 1939, 1940), pp. 59–64.

put out of work, and men who had never known real hunger or discomfort were suddenly faced with poverty.

Hoover's Relief Measures

President Hoover tried to restore confidence by holding meetings of business and labor leaders who pledged themselves not to discharge workers or make new wage demands. He spoke about a cut in taxes and arranged for increased federal credit for business. He also persuaded Congress to establish Federal Home Loan Banks to provide credit for builders and to prevent foreclosure of home mortgages.

One of his most important measures was the Reconstruction Finance Corporation (RFC), which he pressed Congress to establish in January, 1932. During that year this government agency lent huge sums of money to business concerns, railroads, banks, and local governments. The money was to be used for projects that would become self-supporting so that the government could be repaid sometime in the future. It was argued that lending money to important businesses would in reality help all the people, for much of the money would find its way into the pay envelopes of employees, who would spend it and thus increase the demand for goods.

President Hoover had hoped that the Reconstruction Finance Corporation would aid the entire country. In theory, money it lent to various businesses would find its way down to the laborers and other average Americans. Although the methods of the Reconstruction Finance Corporation did not work quickly enough to end the depression immediately, it did lay the groundwork for eventual recovery.

The Election of 1932

The efforts made by President Hoover and the Republicans in power did not seem to satisfy the American people. As often happens in periods of distress, they turned against the party in power. In the congressional election of 1930, the Republicans lost control of the House of Representatives and were reduced to even terms with the Democrats in the Senate, where each party had 48 members. In the election of 1932, President Hoover was decisively defeated by Franklin D. Roosevelt, and the Democrats took over control of the government. As the new administration came into office, the American people were promised a "New Deal," and help was pledged

Franklin D. Roosevelt won the 1932 election by over 7,000,000 votes, a sure indication that the country wished a change in government policies.

for "the forgotten man"—meaning the ordinary American working man, who had been receiving little direct help.

The new President attacked the problems of the depression with great energy. During the campaign, Roosevelt had realized that the problems plaguing the country were mainly economic ones. He recruited a group of expert economists, mainly college professors, to advise him and help form the economic policies with which he would put the nation back on its feet.

Looking Back

1. What part did the stock market play in causing the Great Depression?
2. Explain other factors that are also considered to be causes of the collapse.
3. How did Hoover try to remedy the situation?
4. Discuss the purposes and effects of the R. F. C.
5. What did the American people do to get a "New Deal" in 1932?

The Chapter in Perspective

Who Are These People?

Lloyd George	Coolidge
Clemenceau	Davis
Orlando	La Follette
Harding	Hoover
Cox	Smith
Hughes	Roosevelt

Where Are These Places?

Versailles	Polish "corridor"
Alsace-Lorraine	Hague
Yugoslavia	Czechoslovakia

What Do These Dates and Terms Mean?

1919	5-5-3 ratio
"Red Scare"	1930
1932	R. F. C.
1936	"New Deal"
margin	1921–22

1920
"Big Four"
World Court
Progressive party
Four Power Treaty
Five Power Treaty
Nine Power Treaty
Kellogg-Briand Treaty
"Golden Twenties"
Washington Disarmament Conference
Twenty-first Amendment
Great Depression
London Disarmament Conference
League of Nations
"escalator clause"
Eighteenth Amendment
Nineteenth Amendment
Fourteen Points
"self-determination"

1924
1928
1929

487

Questions for Study

1. What postwar conditions in America brought about the "Red Scare"?

2. Why was the term "Golden Twenties" applied to this period?

3. Summarize the arguments used by Americans to support and oppose the League of Nations.

4. Some people feel that the Treaty of Versailles was too hard on the Germans; others feel it was too mild. What do you think? Why?

5. Are disarmament agreements a path to peace? Why?

6. How can you explain American sentiment toward the League of Nations and the United Nations?

7. Why, in your opinion, was there so much opposition to and violation of the Eighteenth Amendment?

8. Locate the nations that participated in the Washington Disarmament Conference. What did they have in common? What areas of the world were affected by the treaties signed here?

Place Yourself in History

You are a representative of your nation at the Washington Disarmament Conference. The startling proposal made by Hughes to scrap both old and new battleships has caught you by surprise. Frantically you send coded diplomatic messages to your government for instructions. The 5-5-3-1.7-1.7 ratio for the major nations is a new approach in the search for peace, but you note that it applies to battleships only.

The next day you rise to address the Conference. What do you say as a representative of Great Britain? Japan? France? Italy?

Expanding Your Outlook

Doing It Yourself

1. Report to the class on how the Pure Food and Drug Administration acts to protect the interests of Americans.
2. Prepare a board talk explaining how the locks of the Panama Canal function to lift or lower ships.
3. Imagine that you lived in Latin America when the "Roosevelt Corollary" was in effect. Write a letter to a friend in the United States giving your views on American policy.
4. Prepare a report to the class on the accomplishments and failures of the O.A.S.
5. Make a series of drawings that illustrate the weapons, uniforms, and types of warfare used in World War I. If you cannot draw, a bulletin board display of pictures will interest the class. Some talented class members may make models.
6. Write an editorial that would have favored (or opposed) ratification of the Treaty of Versailles.
7. Make a list of the accomplishments of the various attempts to obtain

international disarmament and peace in the fifteen years after World War I.
8. Report to the class the arguments used favoring passage of the Eighteenth and Twenty-first Amendments.
9. Assume that you were a newspaper reporter assigned to Wall Street on October 29, 1929. Write an account of what you witnessed.

Working with the Class

1. Assign roles to members of the class who are to be members of the group charged with settling the coal strike of 1902. Allow the class to "listen-in" on one of your meetings.
2. Let the class become the United States Senate as it debates ratification of the Treaty of Versailles.
3. Organize a committee to make a series of posters for the home front during World War I.
4. We see ourselves as others see us by having reports from various world capitals with observers giving their views of post-World War I America.
5. A group of students may make a graphic presentation comparing the various wars fought by the United States. Costs, number of men involved, casualties, methods of raising fighting forces, results, and other factors may be considered.

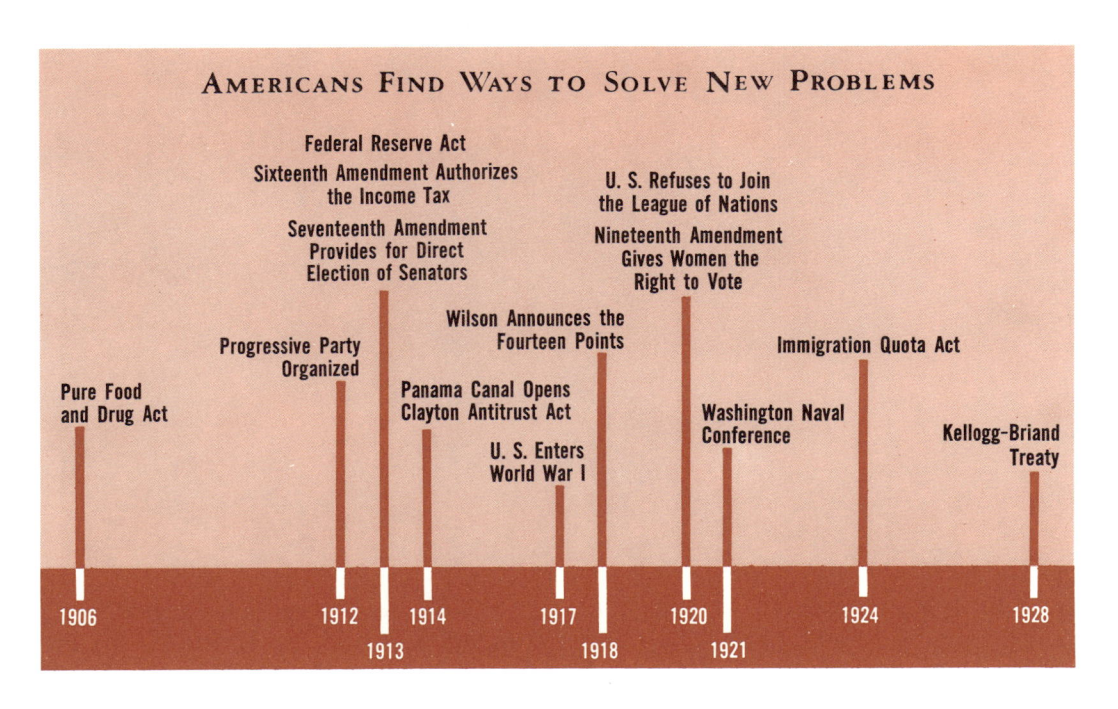

AMERICANS FIND WAYS TO SOLVE NEW PROBLEMS

- 1906 — Pure Food and Drug Act
- 1912 — Progressive Party Organized
- 1913 — Federal Reserve Act; Sixteenth Amendment Authorizes the Income Tax; Seventeenth Amendment Provides for Direct Election of Senators
- 1914 — Panama Canal Opens; Clayton Antitrust Act
- 1917 — U. S. Enters World War I
- 1918 — Wilson Announces the Fourteen Points
- 1920 — U. S. Refuses to Join the League of Nations; Nineteenth Amendment Gives Women the Right to Vote
- 1921 — Washington Naval Conference
- 1924 — Immigration Quota Act
- 1928 — Kellogg-Briand Treaty

United States Air Force Photo

This painting of air action in the Pacific depicts an American P-38 pouring shells into a Japanese bomber. World War II, the first war in which aircraft played an all-important part, signaled the entry of modern technology into warfare.

ONE NATION INDIVISIBLE

UNIT 9

America Participates in the Problems of the World

26. Recovery and the Road to War

1. Roosevelt Gives the Nation a Domestic New Deal • 2. Roosevelt Steers a Middle Course in Foreign Policy • 3. Aggressive Militarism Leads World Again into War

27. The World in Flames

1. Most of Europe Falls to the Aggressors • 2. America Increases Aid to Allies • 3. War Spreads to Other Lands and Continents

28. Days of Infamy and Victory

1. America Wages a Struggle for Life in the Pacific • 2. Allies Move toward Victory in Europe • 3. A Terrible Force is Loosed to End a Terrible War

26

Recovery and the Road to War

A confident and vibrant personality entered the White House on March 4, 1933, in the midst of an economic crisis at home and brewing political crises abroad. His domestic program, which he called the New Deal, has also been described as the "Three R's"—relief, recovery, and reform. President Roosevelt's first problem was to get people back to work and to relieve them from hunger and want. Then he had to take measures to stimulate business and production. Finally, it was necessary to pass laws to prevent future breakdowns in the American economy. Even as Roosevelt labored to rejuvenate America, aggressive nations around the globe were planning what became the most terrible war in the history of the world.

1. Roosevelt Gives the Nation a Domestic New Deal

Many of the New Deal reforms were merely developments of programs that had been started in the earlier administrations of Theodore Roosevelt, Woodrow Wilson, and Herbert Hoover. Others were so new that the New Deal period may properly be described as revolutionary. It is not necessary to follow all of the reforms in detail, but we should know something about the more important ones.

Meeting the Financial Crisis

By the end of Hoover's term of office, a serious banking crisis faced the nation. Since 1929, thousands of banks had failed. By the time of Roosevelt's inauguration on March 4, 1933, most of the states had closed their banks in order to prevent depositors from causing disastrous "runs" on the banks by withdrawing all their money. On March 6, Roosevelt ordered a country-wide *bank holiday,* closing all banks for an indefinite period.

Banks Reopened. On March 9, Congress swiftly authorized large loans to the stronger banks and arranged for the investigation of others. If their accounts were in sound condition, the banks were given licenses to reopen. On March 12 the President addressed the nation over the radio in the first of his famous *fireside chats.* In ringing tones he declared, "I can assure you that it is safer to keep your money in a reopened bank than under your mattress."

These measures were successful. Within a few days most of the banks in the Federal Reserve System reopened. Depositors who had hoarded their money now hastened to put it back in the banks. Most of the unsafe banks went out of business, and thereafter there were very few bank failures in the country.

End of Gold Standard. During these uncertain times, many people hoarded gold coins because they felt that gold would retain its value better than paper money. Because so much gold went into hiding, or was exported abroad, the gold reserves in the Federal Treasury had sunk far below their normal level. In April, 1933, the administration issued an order forbidding the private hoarding of gold. The order required that all gold should be surrendered to Federal Reserve banks in exchange for ordinary paper money. Later a law was passed stating that paper money, bonds, and other securities which contained a promise that they could be redeemed in gold would be redeemed instead in paper money or silver. The practical effect of these moves was to take United States currency off the gold standard, for the government's paper was now no longer redeemable in gold.

Insured Bank Deposits. In later months the President signed other acts designed to increase the financial security of American citizens. One of these established a government corpo-

---

Not all members of the Roosevelt family were sympathetic with Franklin Delano Roosevelt's plans to revitalize the American economy, and one at least, Nicholas Roosevelt, was quite sympathetic with the plight of President Hoover.

"It was Hoover's misfortune to have come to power only a few months before the world plunged into the worst depression of modern times. . . . No man in the White House—or elsewhere—could have checked the ensuing economic paralysis. Because Mr. Hoover was no wiser than anyone else in foreseeing the depression or in anticipating its intensity, and yet was head of the nation, people began to blame him for their troubles. By 1932, his name had become synonymous in the public mind with hunger, unemployment, and financial disaster."

—*A Front Row Seat.* Nicholas Roosevelt (U. of Oklahoma Press, 1953) 236–37

Franklin Delano Roosevelt addresses a joint session of Congress in Washington. Roosevelt worked closely with Congress to solve the problems of the depression.

ration which insured bank deposits so that people would be protected against bank failure. Another strengthened the management of the Federal Reserve system. Another, the so-called "Truth in Securities" Act of 1933, required companies to register all new issues of stocks and bonds and to provide accurate information so that the government could investigate their soundness. Another act, passed in 1934, established a Securities and Exchange Commission (SEC) to regulate stock exchanges for the purpose of reducing speculation and stock gambling. All of these measures helped to protect investors from losing their money.

Relief for the Jobless

One of the first problems of the New Deal was to feed the millions of unemployed. This was done partly by the Federal Emergency Relief Administration (FERA) which granted federal money directly to the states for the care of their needy unemployed.

Civilian Conservation Corps. Congress also created the Civilian Conservation Corps (CCC), a large body of unemployed young men between the ages of seventeen and twenty-eight who were to do useful work in preserving the forests and in flood control. The men lived in CCC camps under the command of army officers. They were paid thirty dollars a month, of which they were required to send twenty-five dollars home to help support their families. This scheme was one of the most successful measures of the New Deal, since it improved the health and morale of the young men and taught them how to do many useful jobs.

Alphabetical Work Agencies. In order to care for the unemployed during the winter of 1933-34, a Civil Works Administration (CWA) put four million people to work on emergency projects. A Public Works Administration (PWA) was created to build useful and lasting works such as dams, hospitals, and other big structures. The Works Progress Administration (WPA), on the other hand, was created to employ as many people as possible in work which did not require the purchase of large amounts of material. This included building roads, preventing soil erosion, and other manual labor. An important division of the WPA was the National Youth Administration (NYA), created in 1935. The purpose of this organization was to help young people between the ages of sixteen and twenty-five, so that they might continue their studies instead of being forced to leave school and join the ranks of the unemployed.

Aid for the Farmers

The government also came to the assistance of the farmers, who had continued to suffer from falling prices for their products in spite of the efforts of the Federal Farm Board.

The AAA. The Agricultural Adjustment Act of 1933 provided that farmers should be paid for raising smaller crops of certain products, so that the scarcity of these products would keep the prices up and give farmers greater returns for their labor. For each acre of land which the farmer did not use for raising specified crops, the government paid him a "rent" of from three to eleven dollars. In this way, the nation's cotton, wheat, tobacco, corn, peanut, and other crops were limited, and the high price level was maintained. The price of meat was also raised by the slaughter of millions of young pigs and by restrictions which were placed on the number of hogs and cattle which could be raised.

To make up for part of the money which the government paid the farmers, taxes called processing taxes were placed on products manufactured from cotton and other farm crops regulated by the terms of the Agricultural Adjustment Act. To carry out the Agricultural Adjustment Act of 1933, the Agricultural Adjustment Administration (AAA) was set up.

Early in 1936 the Supreme Court decided that the powers granted the

The CCC created projects for young men in the depression. The chance to work outdoors and to do good, solid, man's work appealed to many regardless of the low pay offered.

The NRA Blue Eagle was the symbol of recovery from the depression. Cooperating businesses displayed the sign, which read "We do our part."

Agricultural Adjustment Administration were unconstitutional. A few days later, the same court declared that several million dollars in processing taxes which the government was holding should be returned to the manufacturers who had paid them. These two decisions meant the end of the AAA of 1933.

Later Measures. Not long after the AAA had been declared unconstitutional, the Soil Conservation and Domestic Allotment Act was passed. This law provided that farmers should be paid for raising grass or other soil-protecting or soil-enriching crops instead of vegetables and other paying crops.

Many other acts were passed to aid the farmer—acts to insure his crops against flood and drought, to provide loans, to offer training programs so that he could manage his farm more efficiently, and to help him pay off mortgages on his property.

Regulating Private Industry

In June, 1933, a governing body called the National Recovery Administration (NRA) was formed to exercise control over private industries. Manufacturers, storekeepers, and all other businessmen were urged to sign an agreement to live up to certain provisions, or "codes." These codes forbade the employment of children under a certain age, limited the working hours of employees, and set minimum wages. To enforce the codes, Roose-

John L. Lewis, American labor leader, influenced many with his great oratorical ability and his expressive face. These three studies of him were done in 1940.

GROWTH OF LABOR UNIONS 1900-1965

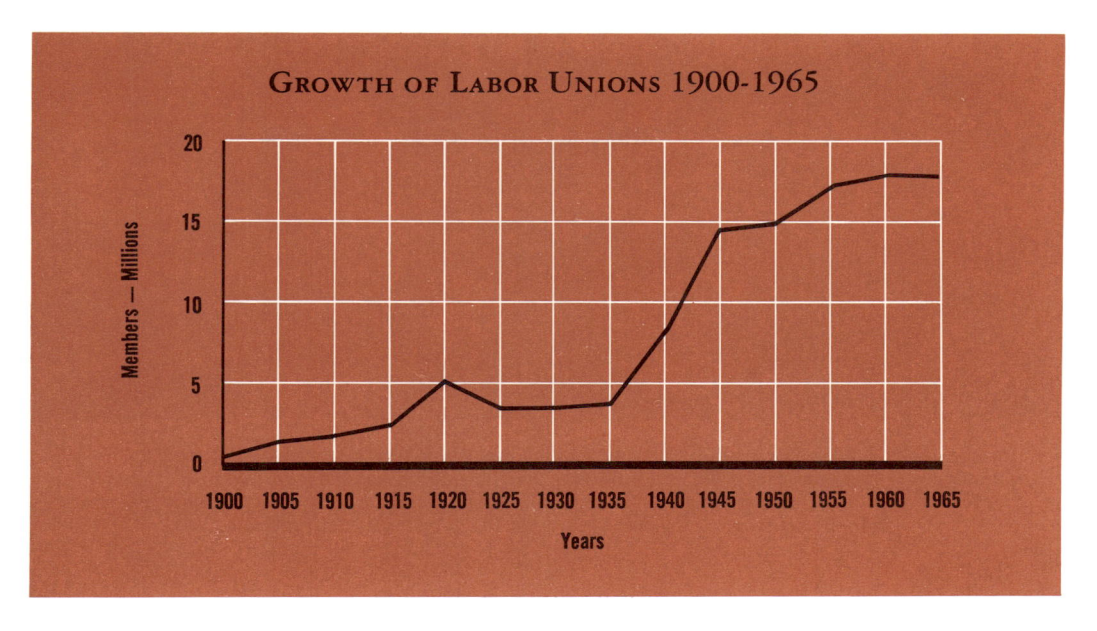

Can you think of any reasons for the sudden decline in Labor Union membership in 1920? Why did it rise suddenly in 1935? Why has growth been relatively small since 1945?

velt appointed a vigorous, hard-working, ex-army officer, General Hugh S. Johnson. Business firms which signed code agreements displayed the NRA Blue Eagle sign with the words "We Do Our Part."

For two years, business in the United States was regulated by the NRA, but in June, 1935, the entire program was upset when the Supreme Court decided that it was unconstitutional for Congress to delegate to the President its lawmaking power, or for the federal government to control industries not engaged in interstate commerce.

New Labor Legislation

In an effort to salvage some of the advantages of the NRA, Congress passed a number of laws protecting labor. The Wages and Hours Act, passed in 1938, was intended to prohibit starvation wages and excessively long working hours in industry by placing "a floor under wages and a roof over hours." The act provided for an eventual minimum wage of 40 cents an hour and a 40-hour working week. Child labor was also prohibited in industry.

One of the most important examples of labor legislation was the National Labor Relations Act (the so-called Wagner Act) passed by Congress in 1935. This act created the National Labor Relations Board (NLRB) to study and eliminate the causes of labor disputes. It asserted that employees should have the right to join unions and that employers should stop anti-union activities and agree to bargain with representatives of organized labor.

The Rise of the C.I.O.

The union movement received a great stimulus from Section 7-a of the

Franklin Roosevelt, shown here campaigning in the West Virginia coal fields, was an able campaigner. In spite of the fact that he was born to wealth and social position, he never lost touch with the "common man." He understood the problems of men like this coal miner and tried to do something for them and other Americans.

National Recovery Act. This section guaranteed the workers' right to form unions and bargain collectively with employers. As a result, membership in the American Federation of Labor increased rapidly in 1933.

Vertical vs. Horizontal Organization. Within the A.F. of L. a group led by John L. Lewis, president of the United Mine Workers, began to campaign for

These electric power generators are at the Watts Bar Dam on the Tennessee River. This dam was built in 1939–42.

a new way of organizing workers in the great mass production industries such as automobiles, steel, and textiles. Instead of uniting workers according to their craft (such as carpenter, machinist, or electrician), Lewis proposed that all workers in an industry, whether skilled or unskilled, should be organized in one big union for that industry. In other words, they would join an "industrial" or "vertical" union instead of the "craft" or "horizontal" union which the A.F. of L. favored. Lewis and his associates called themselves the Committee For Industrial Organization (C.I.O.).

A New Labor Union. The conservative A.F. of L. leaders objected bitterly to this plan, and eventually the C.I.O. broke away from the A.F. of L. and formed its own national organization, which was named the Congress of Industrial Organizations.

In 1936 the C.I.O. succeeded in getting recognition from the United States Steel Corporation, which granted increased wages and a 40-hour week. The next year, after a series of "sit-

498

down" strikes, the United Auto Workers Union, chartered by the C.I.O., won a contract from General Motors. By 1941, the C.I.O. had organized the entire steel and automobile industries. Since that time it has become a very powerful force in American labor.

In 1955, in a joint conference in New York City, the A.F. of L. and the C.I.O. decided that it would be to their mutual interest to merge, which they did. Soon after, the state unions within the two groups merged also. Ohio's A.F. of L. merged with the Ohio C.I.O. in 1958, for example.

Public Utilities

Public utilities are services which play an important part in the lives of the people as a whole. A few of these, such as the postal service, are carried on by the government. Others, such as the railroads, the telephones and telegraph lines, the streetcar and bus systems, and the gas and electric services, are ordinarily run by private companies for profit.

There are those who feel that all utilities should be owned and operated by the government, so that the public would receive the services at cost and would not have to pay higher rates than necessary to provide a profit for the owners. Others feel that the only utilities which the government should run are those which do not yield a profit, and that there should be no government competition in any profitable field of business.

Usually public utilities are privately owned and subject to some control by the government. The main reason for this control is that public utilities are rarely competitive. In other words, the gas company in a city is usually the only gas company, and if a customer is displeased with its service, he has no other place to go for it. Thus, there is a "legal monopoly" subject to government control.

Putting Water to Work. Early in 1933, Congress, at the request of President Roosevelt, passed the Tennessee Valley Authority Act. Under the provisions of the act, a three-man board was set up called the Tennessee Valley Authority (TVA). This board had responsibility for developing the Tennessee Valley region so that living and working conditions would be improved for those who lived there. The board accomplished much more than the modest purposes it began with.

There have been no important "third parties" since 1917, although there still are some unimportant ones. In an almanac, look up their names and the votes they have received in recent elections.

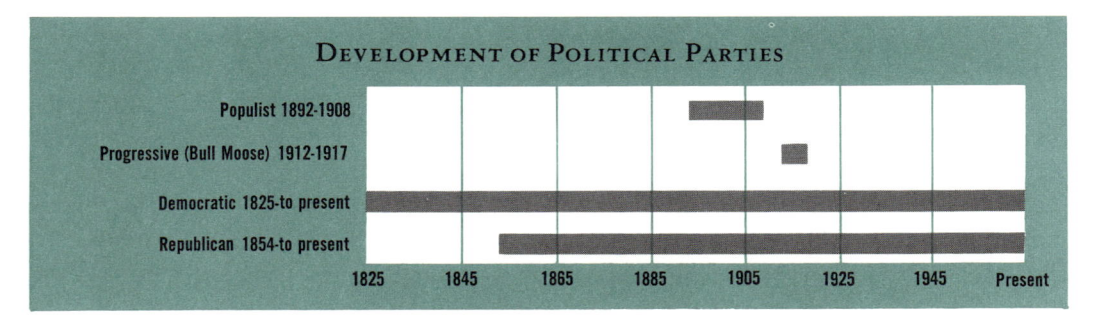

DEVELOPMENT OF POLITICAL PARTIES

Populist 1892-1908	
Progressive (Bull Moose) 1912-1917	
Democratic 1825-to present	
Republican 1854-to present	

1825   1845   1865   1885   1905   1925   1945   Present

Using the long-neglected Wilson Dam, built during the First World War, as a starting place, the TVA built other dams and power stations, lakes and recreational areas. When the project was completed, it supplied cheap electric power to almost 5,000,000 people in seven states. It also permitted greater navigation on rivers which had previously been impossible to use. Floods were at last controlled in the area as a result of the TVA Act, and since half of the TVA land was forested, it provided a steady, cheap source of wood and wood products.

Since the creation of the TVA, other power plants have been established at the Grand Coulee and Bonneville Dams in the Columbia River, at Hoover Dam in the Colorado River, and at a number of places in the Missouri Valley. These government-operated power plants supply needed electricity to large sections of the country, although there are those who oppose such government activity.

Helping the Railroads. Another form of public utility in which our government has been much interested is the railroads. Even before the depression began in 1929, some railroads had been losing money because of the increasing competition of buses, automobiles, trucks, planes, and canal barges. After the financial crash their plight was even worse since the closed-down industries were making no shipments, and people had no money with which to travel.

To help the railroads, Congress passed the Emergency Railroad Transportation Act of 1933 which reorganized the railroads in such a way that their expenses were lower and many unnecessary duplications of service were eliminated. Early in 1936 the Interstate Commerce Commission (ICC) ordered the railroads to reduce their passenger rates. This helped the railroads by greatly increasing the number of people traveling by train.

A "slum" is a city area in which owners or tenants cannot keep their buildings clean and in good repair. Many slums that were aggravated by the depression remain today.

Housing and Slum Clearance

One of the serious effects of the depression was a decrease in the building and repairing of houses throughout the country. Many home owners were unable to meet their mortgage payments and were in danger of losing their homes. Congress therefore established the Home Owners Loan Corporation (HOLC), which lent money at low interest rates to those who wished to build or repair homes. The HOLC was also given power to take over the mortgages of those who could not keep up their payments, and to reduce the interest rates which these people had been paying.

In many cities there were large slum areas that were breeding places for crime and disease. Very often the cities did not have enough funds to tear down buildings and replace them with clean, modern structures. The administration therefore set up a Housing Authority which used federal funds to help the cities in slum clearance.

Social Security

The care of the unemployed and of people too old to work was a tremendous national problem which our government had long neglected. The Social Security Act of 1935 undertook to solve these problems, which Great Britain and other leading European countries had attacked long before.

The Social Security Act provided grants of money to the states to help care for disabled persons and dependent children. It also created a nationwide system of unemployment insurance. The money to pay for the insurance came from a payroll tax on employers. The act also provided old-age pensions ranging from $15 to $80 per month for those who retired at age 65. Part of this money came from pay deductions, part from contributions by the employer.

At first social security did not apply to all occupations. In 1949 benefits were extended to new groups, including teachers and the self-employed. Today social security protects most jobholders, and changes in the system are constantly being proposed in order to make it more efficient.

Economic Recovery

It is difficult to determine just how effective the measures of Franklin D. Roosevelt's administrations were in ending the great depression. Certainly they were effective in relieving unemployment, at least in part, and in accomplishing much desirable building and many worthwhile reforms. Just as certainly, they added enormously to the expense of our government and to our national debt.

We will never know how much President Roosevelt's economic policies contributed to the future economic health of the United States. When World War II broke out in 1940, the nation went on the same type of wartime economy as it did in 1916. The unemployed found jobs in the hundreds of new defense factories. Wages increased, and, much as it had in 1917, business recovered strongly.

Looking Back

1. What steps were taken by Roosevelt to meet and to solve the banking crisis?
2. In what ways did the New Deal act to bring relief and jobs to the unemployed?
3. How did the New Deal act to aid the farmers?
4. Discuss the gains made by organized labor under New Deal legislation.
5. Why was the creation of the T. V. A. a precedent-breaking move?
6. What were the aims of the Social Security Act?

2. Roosevelt Steers a Middle Course in Foreign Policy

During the late 1920's, the American Congress, in the hope of protecting American industry from European competition, passed a series of high tariffs. These tariffs had the effect of keeping European products almost completely out of American stores. Naturally enough, European nations were extremely indignant. A large part of their market had been cut off by the high American tariffs. In retaliation, many European nations raised their tariffs, thus protecting their own markets and keeping American goods out of Europe. The effect of all this was disastrous. World commerce ground to a halt.

Reciprocal Trade Agreements

By the time Roosevelt was inaugurated, Congress saw that international trade had to be restored to help the economy move forward once again. American factories needed the markets of Europe, and American consumers had a definite need for some European goods. Congress acted to reduce tariffs on foreign goods by as much as fifty per cent, provided that European nations would reduce their own import tariffs by a like amount. This act was named the Reciprocal Trade Agreements Act, and it signaled the return of the United States to the world market. The act had immediate good economic effects.

Recognition of Soviet Russia

The Reciprocal Trade Agreements Act of 1934 indicated a lessening of the basic distrust which the American people had held of the European nations. Combined with American recognition of Soviet Russia, which had occurred in 1933, it meant increased American participation in world affairs.

Ever since they had seized power in 1917, the Bolsheviks (those who had overthrown the Russian government in 1917) had refused to pay their country's debts to the United States and had engaged in plots to undermine capitalism everywhere. By 1933, however, most other countries had recognized Russia, and she was admitted to the League of Nations. In return for promises to pay her debts and to refrain from subversive activities in the United States (promises which were not kept), we resumed diplomatic relations with the Soviets.

Neutrality Acts

By 1935, as it became evident that Japan, Germany, and Italy were preparing for war, though American foreign policy was directed toward maintaining neutrality, people remembered how the country had slipped into World War I, and they were determined not to let it happen again.

In 1935, 1936, 1937, and 1939, Congress passed Neutrality Acts which forbade the sale of arms and the lending of money to nations at war. American citizens were warned that they might travel on ships belonging to countries at war only at their own risk. Raw materials could be sold to warring nations only if the purchasers paid cash and transported the materials on their own ships.

The "Good Neighbor"

President Roosevelt and Secretary of State Cordell Hull made constructive efforts to maintain good relations with our Western Hemisphere neighbors. They promoted a Pan-American Conference in Lima, Peru, in 1938. At this conference the member nations agreed to unite against any threat from non-American countries. This "Declaration of Lima" was aimed particularly at Germany and Italy, since these countries had begun to spread their influence in various parts of Latin America.

The declaration was followed by increased economic and military aid from the United States to Latin American countries. Canada was also brought under the protection of this enlarged Monroe Doctrine when Roosevelt promised in 1938 that the United States would not stand idly by and permit a foreign invasion of Canada.

Looking Back

1. How did the Reciprocal Trade Agreements seek to spur international trade?
2. Why did the United States resume diplomatic relations with the Soviet Union in 1933?
3. What steps did the United States take to avoid involvement in any foreign wars?
4. In what ways did the United States seek to promote hemispheric solidarity at Lima and elsewhere?

3. Aggressive Militarism Leads World Again into War

Japan on the March

When the First World War broke out in 1914, Japan had joined the Allies and quickly captured the German-held city of Kiaochow, on the Chinese coast. She also took possession of a large number of Pacific islands which had been held by the Germans. Kiaochow was later assigned to China, but the islands were entrusted to Japan as mandates by the League of Nations, with the understanding that they were never to be fortified. This promise was not kept, for the Japanese began almost at once to equip the islands as bases for planes and submarines.

Invasion of Manchuria. In September, 1931, Japan made another aggressive move. Her armed forces launched a sudden, well-prepared attack on Chinese positions in South Manchuria. This attack was a brutal violation of the Nine-Power Pact, the Kellogg-Briand Pact, and the charter of the League of Nations. Neither the League nor the United States took effective action to punish Japan for her broken promises, so the Japanese proceeded to make plans for further expansion. In 1932, after overrunning Manchuria, they set up a puppet government in the area and renamed it Manchukuo. When the League of Nations adopted an anti-Japanese resolution condemning this obvious subterfuge, Japan announced that she would give up her membership in the League.

The United States' gunboat *Panay* sits on the bottom of the Yangtze River in China. The incident marked the first real sign of American-Japanese conflict.

Undeclared War on China. Japan's next move came in 1935 and 1936 when she marched into China's northern provinces. In August, 1937, heavy fighting took place at Shanghai, during which thousands of Chinese civilians were slaughtered. Since this invasion of China was conducted without a formal declaration of war, President Roosevelt did not put our Neutrality Act into effect. The United States continued to sell war supplies to both China and Japan. The latter, however, had the advantage of a large merchant marine which enabled her to buy and transport materials on a cash-and-carry basis while the Chinese could not.

The "Panay" Incident. As the Japanese soldiers advanced, they began to mistreat American citizens in the Chinese cities. American schools and hospitals were bombed, even though they were plainly marked by American flags. In December, 1937, Japanese planes bombed and sank the *Panay*, an American gunboat stationed on the Yangtze River to protect American interests. Two of the crew were killed and thirty wounded. Three oil tankers flying the American flag were also destroyed.

This irresponsible attack on the *Panay* and the American tankers apparently was not authorized by Japanese headquarters. Tokyo hastily offered profuse apologies and paid over $2,000,000 in reparation. Although the *Panay* Incident caused considerable excitement in the United States, Americans were in no mood to go to war in the Far East. The United States government accepted the apologies, and the crisis blew over. Nevertheless, it was obvious that dangerous pressures were being built up in Japanese-American relations.

The New Italian Empire

By 1935 the Fascist party, founded after World War I by Benito Mussolini, was in firm control of the government of Italy. The tough-minded Fascists had imposed upon the country a warlike dictatorship which had robbed the people of their liberties.

Mussolini's Promises. In speech after speech, Mussolini declared that Italy must arm to regain its rightful place in the world. He shouted that Italy had been robbed by the Treaty of Versailles, for she had been given only a few little pieces of land instead of the many rich territories which he said should have been her share. He would lead the Italians on to victory, and would regain for them the glory they had had in the days of the mighty Roman Empire!

Invasion of Ethiopia. Mussolini delivered his first blow for the "glory" of Italy in 1935. Between Italian Eritrea and Italian Somaliland, in East Africa, lay the independent kingdom of Ethiopia. Many years before, in 1896, an Italian army had attempted to conquer Ethiopia and had been badly beaten by the fierce Ethiopian tribesmen. Here was Mussolini's chance to erase a stain from the Italian record and at the same time gain a valuable piece of territory for the Italian Empire. It was easy to stir up a dispute about the boundary between the Italian possessions and Ethiopia, and in 1935 Italian armies invaded Ethiopia.

The "Rome-Berlin Axis." Haile Selassie, Emperor of Ethiopia, promptly appealed to the League of Nations for help. Although the League branded Italy as an aggressor, it took no action to stop the flow of oil and other supplies which the Italian armed forces needed. In this case, as in the case of Japan, the United States declined to join with the League in boycotting an aggressor. As a result, Ethiopia was quickly crushed, and in May, 1935, the country was formally proclaimed to be a part of the Italian Empire. Then Italy withdrew from

Two of the most brutal and ruthless national leaders in modern history, Benito Mussolini and Adolph Hitler, were mainly responsible for starting World War II. Their regimes were characterized by a complete disregard of human rights. They stifled all opinion which did not agree with them; they burned books; worst of all, Hitler and his henchmen were responsible for the murder of 6,000,000 Jews and others.

the League and joined with Hitler to form a "Rome-Berlin Axis," or alliance.

Three years later, in 1939, Italy attacked and conquered another weak and inoffensive country, Albania. The conquest of this country gave the Italians control of the Adriatic Sea and supplied them with a foothold for later campaigns in the Balkans.

Ernest Hemingway, American novelist, journeyed to Spain to report on the Spanish Civil War. It aroused much interest in the United States.

Civil War in Spain

In 1931, a revolution had broken out in Spain. King Alfonso XIII was driven from the country, and a socialistic republic was established. The lands of wealthy nobles were taken over by the government and were divided among the poor peasants, most of whom had never had any land of their own.

All this activity—the war in Spain, Italian invasions in Africa, Japan's militaristic activity in the Far East—provoked widespread reaction in the United States. Many Americans, including novelist Ernest Hemingway, volunteered for duty in the war in Spain. Many others were intensely disturbed by events in Italy and Japan, although fewer went to these areas than to Spain. On the other hand, a large body of Americans felt that the United States should have nothing whatsoever to do with the troubles in Europe. However, the menace of Germany was rising on the horizon. It would prove to be hard to ignore.

The Rise of Hitler

Mein Kampf. Germany came out of World War I enfeebled and bitter. Her people were frustrated by the heavy penalties imposed on them by the Treaty of Versailles. The republic which had replaced the Kaiser's government was weak and inexperienced in the ways of democracy. In 1923 a small group of politicians attempted to seize control of the government. The uprising failed and the leaders were thrown into prison. While confined there, one of them, Adolf Hitler, wrote a book in which he described his ideas for reviving Germany and bringing Europe under German domination. This book, *Mein Kampf* ("My Struggle"), was later to have a tremendous effect on the German nation and the rest of the world.

The Nazis. Before he was sent to prison, Hitler had been the leader of a political group of followers like Mussolini's Fascists. These German Fascists called themselves National Socialists, or Nazis. After his release, Hitler devoted himself to building up the power of the Nazis, who were supported by many of the wealthiest German manufacturers.

Der Fuehrer. By 1933, the Nazis had gained so much powerful support that von Hindenburg, President of the German Republic, was forced to appoint Hitler to the office of chancellor. This was all the political help the Nazi leader needed. When von Hindenburg died in 1934, Hitler seized the office of president, while still keeping that of chancellor. Combining the powers of the two offices, he made himself absolute leader of the German state, with the title of fuehrer, or leader. The road was now clear for him to build up his armed forces and carry out the ideas which he had expressed in *Mein Kampf*.

The Road to War

Austria. By 1938 Hitler was ready to tread the dangerous road to war. In March he proclaimed that Austria was now a part of Germany. Although

How many nations, or parts of nations, did Germany control by 1941?

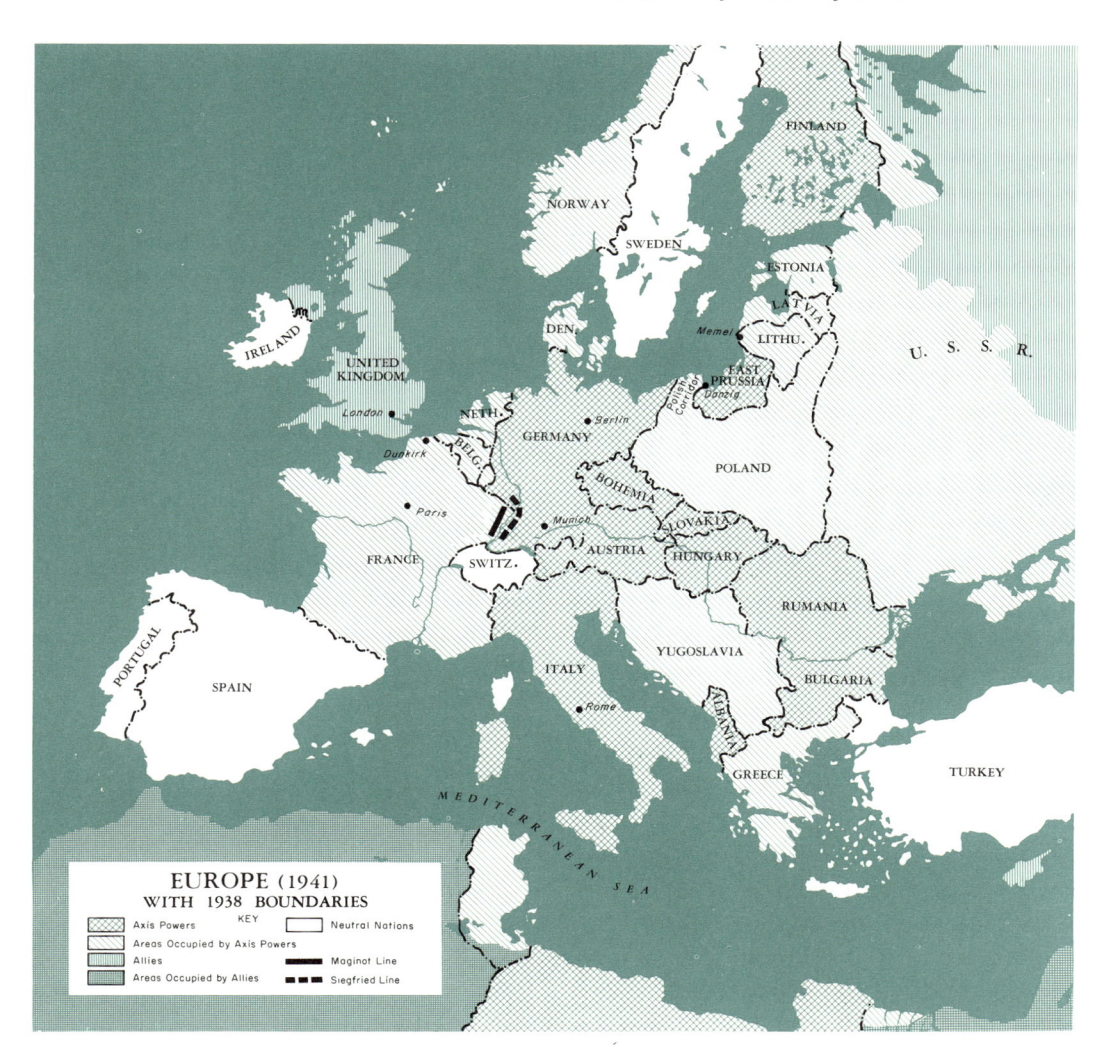

EUROPE (1941) WITH 1938 BOUNDARIES

KEY
- Axis Powers
- Areas Occupied by Axis Powers
- Allies
- Areas Occupied by Allies
- Neutral Nations
- Maginot Line
- Siegfried Line

Mussolini had previously supported the independence of Austria, he made no objection when German troops crossed the Austrian frontier. On the contrary, he sent a message of approval to Hitler. The Rome-Berlin Axis was beginning to produce results!

Czechoslovakia. Hitler now began to make demands on Czechoslovakia, claiming that the Sudeten area near the border, where many German-speaking people lived, should be ceded to Germany. The Czechs were willing to fight to defend their territory, but they received no support from other European countries. At Munich on September 29 the British and French signed a pact with Hitler granting Germany's demands. Said Hitler, "We have no further demands to make in Europe. We want no Czechs."

Adolf Hitler's promise to take no more Czech territory soon proved to be entirely worthless. In March, 1939, German troops crossed into the remainder of the country and took possession of it. Czechoslovakia was divided among Germany, Hungary, and Poland. This brazen step by Hitler shocked the statesmen of France and Great Britain. Military preparations in both countries were greatly increased, but no definite step was taken to check Germany's expansion.

Memel. Within a few days of the final division of Czechoslovakia, Hitler made another conquest. This was the Lithuanian seaport of Memel, a city which had once belonged to Germany but had been granted to the Lithuanians when that country was created at the end of the First World War. Into Memel harbor sailed a German battle fleet, bearing Hitler himself. Threatened by the big guns of the warships, the Lithuanians offered no resistance. Memel became a German seaport.

Demands on Poland. Now that he had Austria, Czechoslovakia, and Memel firmly in his grasp, Hitler turned his attention eastward to the country of Poland. He was interested in Poland for several reasons: because much of Poland had belonged to Germany before the First World War; because a long, thin neck of Polish land, the Polish Corridor, extended to the sea through Germany and separated East Prussia from the other German lands; and because the Free City of Danzig, which had once been an important German seaport, lay at the northern end of the Polish Corridor. Early in 1939, Hitler demanded Danzig and the Polish Corridor.

The Poles were willing to discuss the situation and perhaps even to give up some of the lands that Hitler demanded, but they were unwilling to give in completely to the German demands. Probably they did not believe that the Germans would really attack them, for France and Great Britain were now aroused and were warning Hitler to leave the Poles alone. Even more important to the people of Poland was the presence of powerful Russia, lying just to the east. Surely, Russia would never permit the Germans to invade Polish soil and seize lands so near the Russian borders!

Russo-German Nonaggression Pact. In August, 1939, the situation suddenly changed. The people of Poland were horrified to learn that Premier Joseph Stalin of Russia and Adolf Hitler of Germany had signed a nonaggression pact—a treaty in which they guaranteed not to go to war with one another for at least ten years. No longer were the Poles protected by their Russian neighbors! Their only protectors now were Great Britain and France, still largely unprepared for war and too far away to be of much immediate help.

Declarations of War. No sooner had the pact been signed, than Hitler increased his demands for Polish territory. Poland was not even given a chance to agree. Almost at once, German troops poured across the Polish frontiers and engaged in battle with the surprised Poles. This was September 1, 1939. Great Britain and France at once sent messages asking the Germans to withdraw their forces. The ultimatum was ignored, and on September 3 both Great Britain and France declared war on Germany. The Second World War had begun.

Looking Back

1. What aggressive steps were taken by Japan against China?
2. Trace the military steps taken by Mussolini to increase his empire.
3. How did conditions in Germany favor the rise of Hitler?
4. Why do many people consider the Munich Conference to be a turning point in Hitler's career?
5. How did Hitler's series of land grabs change the terms of the Treaty of Versailles?

The Chapter in Perspective

Who Are These People?

Lewis	Hitler
Hull	Haile Selassie
Mussolini	

What Do These Dates and Terms Mean?

bank holiday	craft union
S. E. C.	C. I. O.
C. C. C.	T. V. A.
P. W. A.	H. O. L. C.
W. P. A.	Social Security
N. Y. A.	neutrality acts
A. A. A.	vertical union
processing tax	1931

N. R. A.
1935
Wagner Act
N. L. R. B.
industrial union
Sept. 1, 1939
Rome-Berlin Axis
Wages and Hours Act
Manchurian invasion
Russo-German Pact
Reciprocal Trade Agreements
horizontal union
Pan-American Conference
Panay incident

Mein Kampf
Nazis
World War II
1937
1938
Fascists

Where Are These Places?

Grand Coulee Dam	Ethiopia
Bonneville Dam	Albania
Hoover Dam	Austria
Lima	Munich
Manchukuo	Memel
Danzig	

Questions for Study

1. What were the chief problems facing Roosevelt when he entered office in 1933?
2. How were the youth of the nation aided by the C. C. C. and the N. Y. A.?
3. Why did those who supported the New Deal feel that the creation of jobs would solve some of the problems of the depression? Do you agree with this policy? Why?
4. By what actions did the Supreme Court affect New Deal legislation?
5. As a union member would you favor an "industrial" or a "craft" union? Why?
6. In what ways did the League of Nations prove itself unable to handle growing international tensions?
7. Why, in your opinion, did France and England yield to Hitler at Munich?
8. Summarize the events that led to the outbreak of World War II.
9. On a map of the world locate the areas affected by the prewar expansion by Japan, Italy, and Germany.
10. Why would a study of the map of Europe reveal that the Russo-German Nonaggression Pact of 1939 was a strategic victory for Hitler?

Place Yourself in History

In the early months of 1933, financial paralysis swept over the nation. Banks were unable to meet the demands of depositors and thus were forced to close their doors. As the news spread, panic followed. Frightened depositors lined up by the hundreds to withdraw their deposits. Banks called upon other banks which in turn made demands on those who owed them money. These people and firms tried to raise funds and a vicious cycle was in progress. Several governors closed all the banks in their states and fear spread rapidly.

What would you have done if you had money deposited in banks? **Why?** For what reasons were the banks unable to meet the legitimate demands made by depositors? What steps were taken to prevent the repetition of such a panic?

27

The World in Flames

After a series of lightning moves by the aggressors, World War II seemed to grind to an uneasy halt. But it was only the calm before the storm. Renewed warfare soon brought most of Western Europe to its knees. As the war spread and increased in intensity, American attempts to remain free from the conflict became ever more difficult. The sympathetic neutrality of the United States changed to active assistance for the Allies as the country drew closer to the brink of war.

1. Most of Europe Falls to the Aggressors

Russian Advances

Two weeks after the Germans struck the reeling Poles from the west, the Russians attacked from the east. After a brave but hopeless resistance, the Poles were forced to surrender, and their country was divided between the invaders. Next, the Russians occupied the small nations of Estonia, Lithuania, and Latvia on the Baltic Sea. When Finland refused to give in to Russian demands, she was attacked by strong Russian forces late in November. The heroic Finns resisted for three months before they were overwhelmed. The Russians now occupied strategic positions along the Baltic.

The Western Front

Prelude to Action. During the early months of the war, the western front, along the French-German border, was very quiet. All along the German border, the French had erected a series of tremendous underground fortifications called the *Maginot Line,* and upon these forts they depended for protection against any German attack. The Germans, for their part, had built a similar, though somewhat shorter, line of defensive positions which they referred to as the Westwall, or the *Siegfried Line*. So strong were these two lines of defense that neither side launched any strong attacks. For a long time, the only activity on the western front consisted of raids, small scouting expeditions, and occasional artillery duels.

Denmark and Norway. Early in 1940, Hitler's armies surprised the world by striking simultaneously at the neutral countries of Denmark and Norway. In Denmark, there was almost no resistance. The country was quickly overrun and was promptly put to use as a base for invading Norway. The Norwegians fought bravely to defend their country, and British forces were rushed to their assistance. For a time, Norway was the scene of fierce battles on land and sea and in the air. The German attack, however, proved too strong; the British forces were driven out and Norway was conquered. A Norwegian traitor named Quisling, who was willing to obey the wishes of the Germans, was placed in charge of the Norwegian government. From his name we get the term "quisling," now used throughout the world for any traitor who will permit himself to be placed in power over his own people for the purpose of governing them as an invader wishes.

Collapse of the Low Countries. After securing their northern front, the German armies suddenly struck at the western front. Now the quiet war of waiting—nicknamed "the phony war"—became one of frantic activity. The blow was not directed at the Maginot Line, which was too strong to be taken by direct assault, but at the Netherlands and Belgium which extended like a wedge between Germany and the northern boundaries of France.

With paralyzing swiftness, German troops (aided by a few Belgian and Dutch traitors) seized key positions and overran the Netherlands. Queen Wilhelmina and her government were forced to flee to Great Britain. The story of Belgium was much the same. Overcome by the speed of the attack (known as "blitzkrieg" or "lightning war") the Belgians were forced steadily back, even though British and French troops rushed to their assistance. As the situation grew desperate, King Leopold suddenly announced that his na-

The German army struck surprisingly and quickly. Here soldiers are shown advancing into the streets of Warsaw, Poland.

tion would resist no more, and the Belgian troops threw down their arms.

Rescue at Dunkirk. After the Belgians surrendered in May, 1940, German armored divisions raced to the sea in order to split British and French forces. They formed a semicircle around a British army of 300,000 men and forced them back toward the port of Dunkirk on the French side of the English Channel. Pinned against the Channel, and with German planes sweeping the skies above them, the British seemed doomed.

The British rose magnificently to meet the peril. Every plane that could be spared flew across the Channel to engage the German air force. Boats of every sort put out from British ports—warships, excursion steamers, ferry boats, and even private yachts and motorboats piloted by civilians. Straight to Dunkirk they went, there to pick up desperate soldiers who were wading out into the Channel but who still kept firing grimly at an enemy which had literally driven them into the sea. The British managed to save most of their trapped army.

Paris Abandoned. The French armies farther to the south did not fare so well. Into France across the Belgian border poured the German forces, led by the dreaded Panzer divisions—fast columns of tanks and other armored combat vehicles. Now the Germans were behind the Maginot Line, and the soldiers manning the great forts had to abandon them quickly to avoid being surrounded and captured. Back towards Paris fell the French. A series of air raids on the great capital city caused the French to abandon it and to declare it an "open city"—that is, an undefended city harboring no military activities—in order to prevent its complete destruction. The government was moved to Tours and then to Bordeaux. France seemed to be at the very end of her resources.

Fall of France. Now it was Italy's turn to move. Up to this point, Mussolini's government had remained neutral, though the leader himself had made many warlike speeches demanding that France cede to him Corsica, Tunisia, and the seaport of Jibuti in East Africa. Now that France seemed definitely beaten, Mussolini saw his chance for a cheap and easy victory. Italian armies poured into France from the south, attacking the already-beaten French armies from behind. On June 22, 1940, France gave up and signed an armistice with the victorious Germans and Italians.

By the terms of the armistice, France was divided into two parts: Occupied France, ruled by the Germans and garrisoned by German troops; and Unoccupied France, ruled by Marshal Henri Petain and his assistants with their headquarters in the town of Vichy. To Mussolini's distress, Hitler did not grant him any French territory at all, in spite of his belated help in overthrowing France.

The Free French. Though France was beaten, not all Frenchmen were willing to give in and admit defeat. In England, there were many French soldiers who had been rescued with their English comrades at Dunkirk. These were joined by other brave and patriotic Frenchmen who escaped from the Germans as French resistance went to pieces. These Free French, as they called themselves,

This photograph of Charles DeGaulle was taken in 1943 when he was leader of the Free French in England. Later he became President of his nation.

soon found a leader in General Charles de Gaulle, one of the few ranking French officers who still thought that France should fight on against her enemies. Under his leadership, the Free French—later known as the Fighting French—continued to give valiant service.

Axis Attack on Greece and Yugoslavia

The Axis (the name for the alliance between Germany and Italy) Powers, especially Germany, had tried for a long time to persuade Yugoslavia and Greece to sign treaties with them. Finally in October, 1940, tired of trying to bargain, Mussolini sent his legions into Greece. Greatly outnumbered, but better mountain fighters, the Greeks drove Mussolini all the way back into Albania. Later the Germans, who were then masters of most of Western Europe, sent help to their embarrassed ally.

Help for Mussolini. In April, 1941, the Germans struck at both Greece and Yugoslavia. Yugoslav resistance collapsed within a few days, and the Germans poured across that country into Greece. Back fell the gallant Greeks and the small British and Australian forces which had landed to assist them. Finally they withdrew to the island of Crete, far out in the Mediterranean.

An Air-Borne Invasion. Then the Germans did an amazing thing. They undertook the first completely airborne invasion in history. Over Crete flew huge flights of German planes, dropping swarms of parachute troops who seized the airfields, thus making it possible for troop-carrying planes and gliders to land still more soldiers. After several days of desperate fighting, Crete was in German hands.

The Battle for Britain

With the fall of France, Great Britain had become the only great power which still resisted Germany. In the autumn of 1940, the Germans prepared to smash Britain as they had smashed all their other opponents. Heavy guns were installed along the French coast of the English Channel, blocking any counter-invasion from the English coast. Great airfields were built in Occupied France. Powerful armies, equipped with sea-going barges and other transport vessels, gathered at many of the Channel ports. Huge fleets of bombers took off in an attempt to destroy the British cities and to "soften up" the British people through fear and suffering. To many people throughout the world, it looked as though Great Britain was about to be conquered.

The Britons themselves showed remarkable courage. When the German bombing squadrons came over, dropping high explosive and fire bombs on London and other cities, the people worked with quiet desperation to put out the fires, to care for the wounded, to bury the dead, and to repair the damage. Aided by a new secret weapon, radar, British antiaircraft guns and fighter planes brought down great numbers of the German bombers. At the height of the raids, almost two hundred German planes a day were being destroyed. It became a question of which could take its punishment longer, the British people or the German air force. The British people won. The German raids diminished in number and intensity. Daylight raids became scarce. The British people had not been "softened up," but the German air force had.

The German high command felt that they could never launch a massive ground invasion of England unless the German air force controlled the skies. When the German air force failed, Britain was safe from invasion. The British could breathe a sigh of relief and concentrate their forces for a return to the continent.

The second World War was the first war in which aerial bombing played an important role. Cities such as London (shown below), Dresden, Rotterdam, and finally, Berlin, were left in rubble.

Looking Back

1. What caused the term "phony war" to be originated?
2. By what means did the Nazis bypass the Maginot Line?
3. Why was the British action at Dunkirk remarkable?
4. How did the Italian entry into the fighting help and hurt the Nazis?
5. Describe the "Battle for Britain."

2. America Increases Aid to Allies

Defensive Measures

During the period from 1935 to 1939, Congress had passed various acts, called the Neutrality Acts, which were aimed at keeping the United States out of any foreign war. The passage of these acts indicated that many Americans wished to avoid and ignore European problems altogether. However, the fall of France and Germany's massive attack on England had a sobering effect in the United States. Congress swiftly reversed itself and voted billions of dollars to strengthen the armed forces. Included in the defense build-up were plans to construct a two-ocean navy. This decision was made when Japan announced in the fall of 1940 that she had joined the Rome-Berlin Axis.

Selective Service. In September, 1940, the Selective Training and Service Act was passed. Passage of this act meant that all male citizens between the ages of 21 and 36 had to register for the draft, and were liable for a year's military training. A year later the act was extended to include men from 20 to 44, and it gave the President the power to lengthen the term of service. Congress had never before arranged for a draft of manpower in peacetime. Their doing so indicated that the threat of war was very real.

Destroyers for Bases. By the summer of 1940, German submarines were taking a terrible toll of British ships. The best defense against the long-range, powerful submarines was the destroyer. The British needed destroyers badly, so in September, Winston Churchill and President Roosevelt completed a transaction which Churchill later admitted was "a decidedly unneutral act." In return for a ninety-nine year lease on eight naval and air bases extending from Newfoundland to British Guiana, Roosevelt agreed to turn over fifty old destroyers to the British. In addition, Roosevelt boldly stated that America should "scrape the bottom of the barrel" to make it possible for Britain to buy arms and supplies.

America's Role Debated

There was much disagreement in the United States about America's role in dealing with the war in Europe.

An America First rally. For a brief period, the "America Firsters" stirred up all the emotion of a political campaign.

Some people felt the United States could not survive a war, and thus should stay out of it. These people, who believed that they had America's best interests at heart, were known as "America Firsters" because they represented the views of the "America First Committee." Such public figures as Charles Lindbergh, Senators Norris, Nye, and Wheeler, and various wealthy businessmen lent distinguished support to this point of view. Unfortunately, the America First Committee also attracted some less honorable support.

Representing the point of view that America should give economic and military aid to the European nations being attacked by the Germans was a "Committee to Defend America by Aiding the Allies." This committee, headed by the famous Kansas editor, William Allen White, wished to aid enemies of Hitler in any way it could. Eventually their position was adopted by both presidential candidates in the 1940 campaign.

A Third Term for Roosevelt

When the Democrats met for their national convention in the summer of 1940, they abandoned the two-term tradition and nominated Roosevelt. Roosevelt accepted, saying that although he wished to return to private life, the crisis that faced the country demanded an experienced leader in the White House. The Republicans nominated Wendell L. Willkie, an attractive and intelligent businessman who was a newcomer to politics. The platforms of the two parties were very much alike. Both promised aid to nations in danger of aggression, to build

Wendell Wilkie opposed President Roosevelt in the 1940 campaign, but he later agreed with many Roosevelt war policies.

up the national defenses, and to keep American boys out of foreign wars.

In November the people went to the polls and elected Roosevelt by a vote of 449 to 82 in the electoral college, although the approximate popular vote was 27,000,000 to 22,000,000. The vote was a clear approval of Roosevelt's foreign policy.

Lend-Lease—The End of Neutrality

The results of the election convinced Roosevelt that most Americans agreed with his policy of extending all possible aid to the Allies short of actual war. Mere dollars were not enough—our European allies needed an unlimited supply of heavy military equipment. In January, 1941, the so-

> *In his annual message to Congress in January, 1941, President Roosevelt recommended the passage of the Lend-Lease Act, which permitted the transfer of arms and supplies in order to support nations friendly to the United States. In this address he described the "four freedoms" which we should seek.*
>
> "In the future days, which we seek to make secure, we look forward to a world founded upon four essential human freedoms.
>
> The first is freedom of speech and expression—everywhere in the world.
>
> The second is freedom of every person to worship God in his own way—everywhere in the world.
>
> The third is freedom from want—which, translated into world terms, means economic understandings which will secure to every nation a healthy peacetime life for its inhabitants—everywhere in the world.
>
> The fourth is freedom from fear—which, translated into world terms, means a world-wide reduction of armaments to such a point and in such a thorough fashion that no nation will be in a position to commit an act of physical aggression against any neighbor—everywhere in the world."

called Lend-Lease Bill was introduced into Congress. After furious debate, the bill was passed by a margin of 60 to 31 in the Senate and 317 to 71 in the House. The passage of this bill was very important because it marked the end of neutrality—in fact, it was almost a declaration of war since the United States was eventually to lend fifty billion dollars worth of goods and services to the European allies.

In April, 1941, a month after Roosevelt signed the Lend-Lease Bill, the United States took another step in the undeclared war by occupying Greenland, which belonged to Denmark. The Danish government, now dominated by Hitler, protested to no avail. The possibility of German troops in Greenland could not be tolerated, since they would be a threat to the defense of the hemisphere.

The Atlantic Charter

In August, 1941, a statement of American aims was given to the world. Prime Minister Winston Churchill met secretly with Roosevelt in a warship off the Newfoundland coast. They discussed lend-lease, Japanese aggression in the Far East, defense measures, and other problems. They also issued an eight-point peace program for the two countries.

When summarized, this "Atlantic Charter" sounds much like Wilson's Fourteen Points. Its aims were the following: no seizure of other nations' territory, the right of a nation to choose its own government, the sharing on equal terms of raw materials and trade, the improvement of labor standards and living conditions, peace and disarmament, and a permanent organization for the general security of nations.

Looking Back

1. What steps were taken at home to strengthen American military power?
2. Why did Churchill later state that the destroyers for bases swap was an unneutral act? Do you agree? Why?
3. Would you have joined the "America First Committee"? Why?
4. How did the election of 1940 abandon an old American tradition?
5. What steps were taken in 1941 to indicate that the United States was no longer neutral?

3. War Spreads to Other Lands and Continents

The War in Africa

Meanwhile, as European developments gradually involved the United States, the war effort of the Allies shifted to Africa. Not long after Italy entered the war, a powerful Italian army moved eastward from Libya against British forces in Egypt. After some successes the Italian drive bogged down, and a British force under Sir Archibald Wavell counterattacked and penetrated to the Libyan seaport of Bengasi.

In the meantime, other British Empire forces had been engaged in the conquest of Italian East Africa. Eritrea, Italian Somaliland, and Ethiopia were quickly occupied by Great Britain. As a result, in May, 1941, Haile Selassie resumed the throne from which the Italians had driven him five years before.

Soon after the British captured Bengasi, German reinforcements began to arrive in Libya under the command of General Rommel. Back and forth the

One of Germany's most brilliant generals was Erwin Rommel, the "Desert Fox." He was a German wartime hero who disagreed with many of Hitler's policies and later joined a plot to assassinate him. For his part in the plot he was ordered to take poison. He died in 1944 as a result.

tide of battle surged in the North African desert. Great quantities of supplies, meanwhile, had been reaching the British army in Egypt. Finally the British, under General Montgomery, were ready for a grand series of assaults on Rommel's positions. In October, 1942, the first of the assaults was launched. Eventually Montgomery was successful. The Germans, unable to halt the British advance, were forced out of Egypt, across Libya, and into northern Tunisia.

Hitler's Attack on Russia

A startling event occurred on June 22, 1941, which gave considerable encouragement to the Allies. Unable to agree with Stalin about a division of territories in the Balkans, Hitler astonished the world by launching a ferocious attack on Russia, despite the nonaggression pact he had signed with Stalin in 1939. Believing that Hitler was likely to win, the government of the United States decided to send supplies to Stalin even though many Americans found it difficult to regard the Russian dictator as a dependable ally, mainly because he was a Communist.

Russia's Scorched Earth Policy. A few days after the attack started, Finland seized this opportunity to regain her lost lands and also attacked the Russians. At first there was little resistance to the German-Finnish attack. It was not long, however, before the Germans were able to occupy the rich Ukraine region and advance to the very gates of Moscow. As the Russians fell back they destroyed everything of value—oil wells, crops, factories, and even their own homes—so that the Nazi army could not use them.

The Winter Campaign. In spite of Hitler's tremendous early gains in Russia, his attack did not succeed as he had hoped. He had not been able to start as early as he had planned, because the unexpected resistance of the Yugoslavs led by Draja Mikhailovich had delayed the conquest of Greece. Hitler had not dared to start a second campaign until the first was over. With the onset of winter, Russian resistance increased. The Germans were not used to the bitter Russian winter, and they suffered much more than their enemies from the numbing cold and the deep snow. Bands of trained Russian civilians, daring guerrilla fighters, and mounted cossacks began to attack the German supply lines and small German detachments. Within sight of Moscow, the German attack came to a complete stop.

This was the moment for which the Russians had been waiting. A Russian army in the Ukraine suddenly launched a ferocious attack on the German forces in that region, and the Germans were forced to retreat. To correct this situation, the German leaders took troops from the north to reinforce their battered southern army. This was the signal for a strong Russian attack in the north. Slowly at first, but with increasing speed, the German forces gave ground as the Russians advanced. In desperation, Adolf Hitler discharged his generals on the Russian front and directed the war personally from the safety of Berlin. Still, the Russians, who were skilled winter

Winston Churchill was the inspirational war leader of Great Britain. Here he is shown giving his famous "V" for victory sign.

In 1941, Prime Minister Winston Churchill of Great Britain spoke on the radio, urging people in the conquered countries to join a "V for Victory" campaign against the Nazis. This was all the urging those opposed to the Germans needed, and a full-scale resistance movement went into operation. The letter "V" became the symbol of this secret opposition. Throughout the conquered lands, V's were scrawled on walls, on sidewalks, and in other conspicuous places. This victory symbol annoyed the Germans and encouraged those who opposed the Axis by showing them how widespread the secret opposition was. Radio stations broadcasting into the occupied lands opened their broadcasts with the heavy, ominous opening notes of Beethoven's Fifth Symphony—three short notes and one long note spelling out "V" in Morse code. By such signs and symbols as these did the enemies of Adolf Hitler gain courage and spread the idea of working always against the conquerors.

Hitler's Treatment of the Jews

Hitler was waging a tyrannical, brutal war on the home front as well as against the rest of the world. He used one particular group—the Jews—as a scapegoat, blaming the troubles of the German people on this group. His accusations were ridiculous, especially since German Jews had contributed greatly to cultural and economic successes in German history. However, Hitler caught the imagination of the German people with his accusations against the Jews, and he was able to persecute them without mercy. The horrifying fact is that before the war

fighters, continued to gain ground in this amazing winter campaign. When the spring of 1942 arrived, the Germans had been forced to give up a considerable part of the territory they had conquered during the preceding summer.

"V for Victory"

We have seen that Hitler had conquered most of western Europe by the end of 1941. His soldiers occupied the captive countries, and his dreaded secret police, the Gestapo, went to work hunting down those who opposed the Nazis. This was not an easy job. Large numbers of Poles, Norwegians, Frenchmen, Belgians, Dutchmen, and others in the conquered lands hated their Nazi oppressors and used every chance to do them harm.

In 1964, this group from the Auschwitz War Crimes Court inspected the Nazi Prison camp at Auschwitz, Poland; four million people, mostly Jews, were murdered here from 1940–1945.

was over, six million Jews had been marched into concentration camps where they were murdered or died of disease. This senseless slaughter and the destruction of liberty in Germany led many Americans to hate the Nazi regime.

The weapons Hitler used to persecute the Jews (and other minorities such as the Catholics) were name-calling, fear, and ignorance. The Nazi regime burned books which did not agree with their twisted beliefs about history. They condemned freedom of thought and action. They made illogical attacks on sincere patriots who did not agree with them. They reduced all issues to black and white, good and bad, true and false: there was no area in between. Inevitably, these practices sowed the seeds of their destruction.

Japanese Plans for Conquest

When World War I ended, Japan was given control of some of the islands and possessions of Germany in the Far East. The acquisition of these islands only increased Japan's appetite for more territory. During the twenty years until World War II began, Japan constantly tried to gain more possessions, hoping to establish herself as a world power. In 1931 she invaded Manchuria for the weakest of reasons. In 1934, Japan stated that she would allow no more Western expansion into Chinese affairs. By 1937, when the beginnings of war were stirring in Western Europe, Japan decided to launch a full-scale invasion of the mainland of China.

Chinese-Japanese Dispute. The American public generally favored the Chinese, and some groups campaigned for a trade embargo (stoppage) of war supplies to Japan. The United States government, however, did not wish to take such drastic action. It had maintained stable relations with Japan ever since the Japanese had bombed the *Panay*, a United States gunboat, in 1937. The Japanese had apologized profusely, and paid two million dollars to the U.S. government for damages. On the other hand, China had been accepting American aid against the Japanese since about 1937. By 1940, American aid to China had increased so much that Japan was in danger of being ousted from China altogether.

Changes in American Policy

American policy became directed strongly against Japan, however, when the Netherlands and France fell before the German onslaught. The rich Far East colonies of these two countries, French Indochina and the Dutch East Indies, now lay defenseless. In addition, the government of the United States was alarmed in September, 1940, when Japan signed an alliance with Germany and Italy. In that month, also, the Japanese brought pressure on the Hitler-dominated Vichy government of France to give them strategic bases in northern Indochina. In June, 1941, they demanded more bases in the southern part of Indochina.

Prelude to War. The Roosevelt administration finally took strong action. On September 26, 1940, it placed an embargo on all scrap metal shipments, except those to Western Hemisphere countries and Great Britain. In July, 1941, it froze all Japanese assets in the United States—that is, all property and money which could have been used to buy war materials was prevented from being utilized. The Netherlands and Great Britain did likewise. This was a severe blow to the Japanese militarists, since it cut off badly needed supplies, especially oil, which they had been getting from the United States.

The Japanese government now offered to make limited concessions to please the United States. President Roosevelt and Secretary of State Hull insisted, however, that Japan should withdraw from China and French Indochina. The Japanese rejected these terms in November, 1941. A secretly trained carrier force left a Japanese naval base and headed for the Hawaiian Islands, prepared to strike the first blow in a Pacific war between Japan and the United States.

Looking Back

1. How did the campaigns in Africa finally result in a British victory?
2. Why was Hitler's attack on Russia of the greatest benefit to the Allies?
3. Summarize the early military actions as the Nazis invaded Russia.
4. What were the significance and effects of the "V for Victory" operation?
5. How was the Rome-Berlin-Tokyo Axis viewed in America? in Europe?

The Chapter in Perspective

Who Are These People?
- Quisling
- Petain
- Churchill
- de Gaulle
- Willkie

Where Are These Places?
- Estonia
- Latvia
- Lithuania
- Belgium
- Netherlands
- Vichy

Denmark
Norway
Greenland
Yugoslavia
Greece

What Do These Dates and Terms Mean?

"phony war"
Maginot Line
Siegfried Line
Unoccupied France
Selective Service Act
"America Firsters"
Atlantic Charter
Lend-Lease Act

Free French
Dunkirk
1941

Questions for Study

1. Show that the fighting in 1940 and 1941 revealed an almost unstoppable Nazi war machine.

2. Why do many historians feel that Hitler's greatest blunder was the invasion of Russia?

3. What, in your opinion, caused Hitler to invade Russia?

4. For what reasons did isolationism grow in America? What factors prompted the growth of interventionism?

5. What were the main points of the Atlantic Charter?

6. Why, in your opinion, did the Nazis win such brilliant and strategic victories in the early campaigns of the war?

7. What factors prompted the Japanese desires for more territorial gains at this time?

8. Which side gained more from the "destroyer-for-bases" swap? Why?

9. How did the locations of the Maginot and Siegfried lines as well as the location and terrain of the "low countries" affect the role of these countries in World War II?

10. Locate the bases obtained by the United States in exchange for the destroyers. Of what value were these bases?

Place Yourself in History

France was beaten, but many Frenchmen were not. In the Occupied Zone, Nazi troops and officials are everywhere and you are governed by the invaders. One night, there is a discreet knock at your farmhouse door. With fear in your heart, you peer out. There stands an American flyer who has been shot down. He is exhausted—and the Nazis are on his trail. If you surrender him, you get an award and favored treatment by your conquerers and rulers. If you are caught assisting him, the penalty is death for you and your family.

What would you do? What role did the French Maquis, or underground, play in the war? How did its actions affect the German war effort? In what ways did it aid British and American flyers who had been shot down over France?

28

Days of Infamy and Victory

With the infamous attack on Pearl Harbor, the United States found itself engaged for the first time since its founding as a nation in a struggle for self-preservation. America's first efforts had to be directed toward winning the war in the Pacific. As the tide of that war shifted in America's favor, full-scale American participation in the European theater became possible. Following victory in Europe, allied efforts were concentrated on the defeat of Japan.

1. America Wages a Struggle for Life in the Pacific

Pearl Harbor

The attack on Pearl Harbor was successful beyond the wildest dreams of the Japanese. At 7:55 on Sunday morning, December 7, 1941, the first wave of carrier planes struck at the eight battleships anchored in the harbor. Within a half hour the battleships, three light cruisers, and a number of other vessels—the backbone of the Pacific Fleet—were sunk or crippled. One of the battleships, the *Arizona*, sank a few minutes after the attack started, carrying 1103 officers and men to their death.

Significantly, and fortunately, however, the American aircraft carriers were not in the harbor at the time. These ships, which were to play a most vital part in the war, were at sea on maneuvers. Not a single one of them was damaged in the least. Also, repair and storage facilities at Pearl Harbor were not badly damaged. Had carriers and storage facilities been destroyed, the base at Pearl Harbor would have become useless.

In addition to the ships, the Japanese destroyed almost half of the military planes on Oahu, the most heavily

The U.S.S. Oklahoma was badly damaged in the attack on Pearl Harbor. It later capsized.

populated of the Hawaiian Islands. When a second wave of enemy planes swept over the islands, they were met by antiaircraft fire and did little additional damage. At 9:45 all remaining Japanese planes, many of them riddled by bullets, returned to their carriers lurking far offshore out of sight. This attack—one of the most devastating in naval history—cost the Japanese twenty-nine planes and less than one hundred men. American casualties were heavy. The Navy lost 2000 officers and men killed and 710 wounded. The Army and Marine Corps lost 327 killed and 433 wounded. Among the civilian population of Oahu, some seventy were killed.

The Japanese strategy was not to seize Hawaii or to attack the American mainland. Their intention was to knock out American naval forces so as to win a free hand to conquer the Philippines and the British and Dutch possessions in the Far East. Their short-range strategy was successful, but in the long run they were doomed to defeat because Americans rose as one united country to punish the attackers.

War Declared

The next morning—December 8—President Roosevelt addressed Congress saying, "Yesterday, December 7, 1941—a date which will live in in-

U.S. military planes, like the one below, were "sitting ducks" during the Japanese attack. The Los Angeles Times announced the attack in huge headlines, listing damage and ships and planes lost.

famy—the United States of America was suddenly and deliberately attacked by the naval and air forces of the Empire of Japan." Within four hours Congress, by unanimous vote in the Senate and a vote of 388 to 1 in the House, declared that a state of war existed. Three days later Germany and Italy joined Japan in the war, and we officially accepted their challenge by declaring war on them. In a few months nearly all of the nations of the world were involved in war, either on one side or the other. In Europe only four—Switzerland, Portugal, Spain, and Sweden—remained technically neutral.

The Japanese Offensive in the Pacific

The attack on Pearl Harbor was followed almost at once by blows at other American positions in the Pacific. Guam and Wake Island fell quickly despite a gallant defense. In the Philippines, American and Filipino forces under General Douglas MacArthur took a stubborn stand on the narrow Bataan Peninsula, between Manila Bay and the open waters of the South China Sea. They also occupied rocky Corregidor and other fortified islands at the mouth of Manila Bay.

Fall of the Philippines. Early in April, 1942, defense lines on Bataan crumbled, and the defenders who had not been killed were taken prisoners. General MacArthur was not among the troops captured at Bataan. In February he had received orders from President Roosevelt to leave the Phil-

---

Our First Carrier Pilot

After the attack on Pearl Harbor, it became apparent that the carrier would replace the battleship as the backbone of the American Navy. Thirty years before the "day of infamy", the first successful carrier landing had been made, not by a Navy pilot but by a civilian flyer. In January, 1911, a young man named Eugene Ely landed a patched-up Curtiss biplane on a temporary wooden platform on the afterdeck of the armored cruiser *Pennsylvania*, anchored in San Francisco Bay.

It was a risky undertaking, but it succeeded—and it heralded the day when the mighty carrier would rule the seas.

The improvised platform on the Pennsylvania was only 119 feet long. The retarding gear consisted simply of two rows of sandbags with lines connecting the bags. Slung on the plane were three hooks which were designed to engage the lines and bring the plane to a halt.

Ely, protected by an inflated bicycle tube wound around his chest, gunned his eight-cylinder engine and made his approach. Lifeboats circled the ship, ready to pick him up if necessary. As the ship's company watched breathlessly, he cut his engine and settled down on the deck. The hooks hit the lines, which brought him to a smooth halt. After a brief time out for congratulations and refreshments, Ely made a successful take-off and landed at a nearby flying field.

ippines and proceed to Australia. In March, after careful preparations, he and a few other people escaped from the siege in a fast motor torpedo boat. They later changed to a bombing plane which carried them to Australia. His place was taken by General Jonathan Wainwright, who skillfully and bravely directed the defense of Bataan until forced to fall back on Corregidor. Here he and his remaining troops held out until May 6, when he was forced to surrender. The last American flag in the Far East was lowered.

In the meantime the Japanese had taken Hong Kong and the great British fortress of Singapore in Malaya, and Japanese forces were pouring into the East Indies and Burma.

The Battle of the Coral Sea. In March, 1942, the Japanese began to gather a huge fleet of warships and troop-carrying transports for an attack on Port Moresby, an important sea-

What American possessions were captured or endangered by the Japanese thrust in the Pacific?

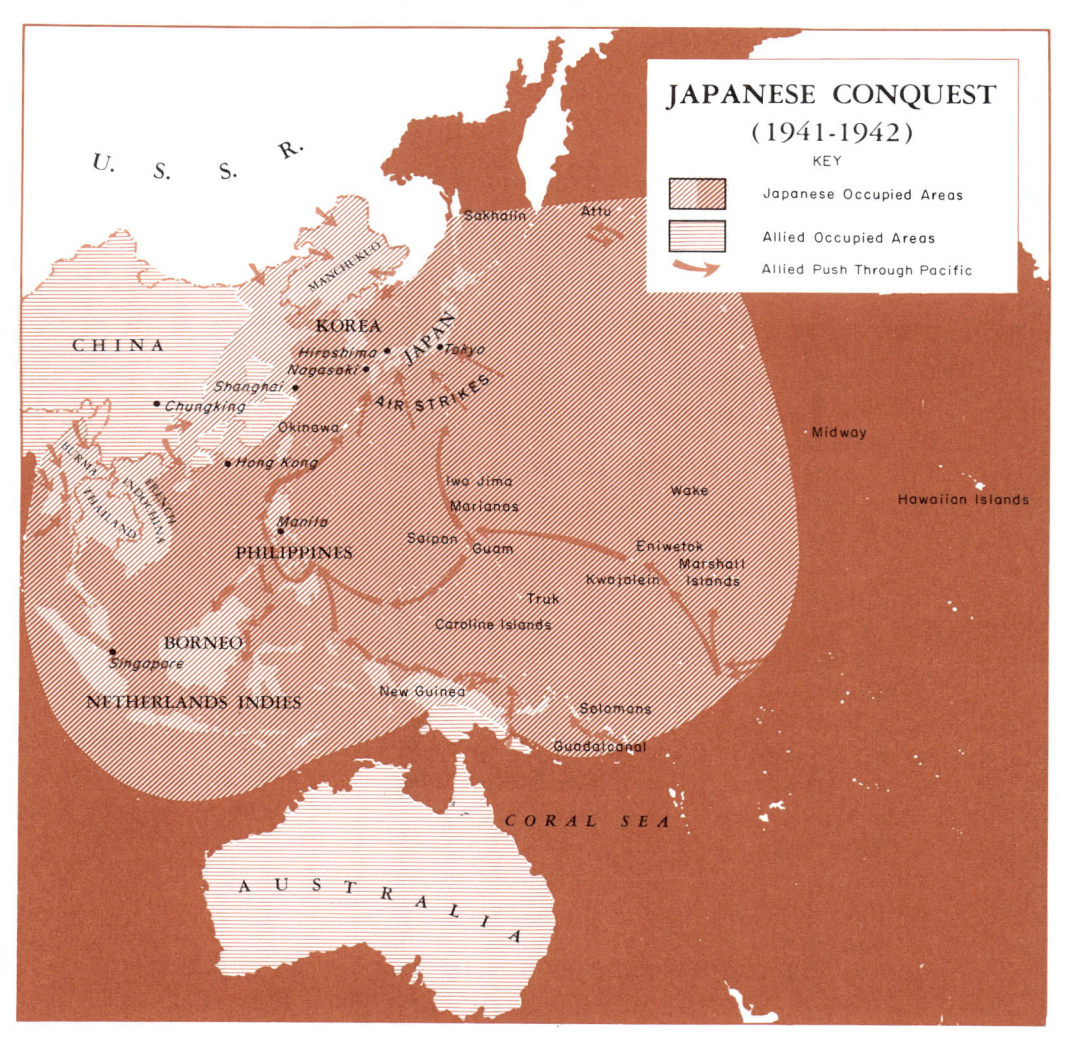

JAPANESE CONQUEST (1941-1942)

port in New Guinea from which attacks could be launched directly on Australia. While this Japanese invasion force was still being gathered and organized, Australian and American bombing planes suddenly struck at it. Twenty-three of the Japanese warships and transports were either sunk or seriously damaged, and the attack on Port Moresby had to be abandoned.

In early May, the Japanese planned to launch a strong attack directed at New Caledonia and the New Hebrides islands, east of Australia. If these islands were taken, the main supply route between the United States and Australia would be cut. In the Coral Sea, northeast of Australia, the advancing Japanese squadrons were pounced upon by American sea and air forces. Three American ships were sunk, including the giant aircraft carrier *Lexington*. The Japanese lost seventeen vessels, and their invasion force fell back and abandoned the attack on the islands.

The Battle of Midway

In June, 1942, Japan struck a blow in another theater of war. A small Japanese air force appeared over the American naval base of Dutch Harbor, in the Aleutian Islands, off the southwestern tip of Alaska. At the same time, small Japanese forces occupied the tiny and thinly-populated islands of Attu and Kiska at the extreme western end of the Aleutian group. Neither attack was serious, and the whole Alaskan move appears to have been a feint to send American defense forces rushing north from Midway Island and Hawaii. The Americans were not deceived, for they had

One of the most desperate weapons used by the Japanese in the war was the kamikaze suicide airplane. Japanese pilots crashed their planes on the decks of U.S. ships, doing great damage. The kamikaze aircraft above is attacking the *U.S.S. Missouri* in 1945.

discovered how to translate the secret Japanese radio code messages, and they knew exactly what to expect.

Within a few days after the Aleutian raids, American patrol planes spotted a large Japanese fleet approaching Midway Island. American planes and ships rushed to meet the threat. From June 3 to June 6 one of the most spectacular battles of the war took place. It ended in a crushing defeat of the Japanese invasion fleet. Had not this attack been beaten back, Midway would certainly have been taken, and the Hawaiian Islands would have been in danger of the same fate. Our whole Pacific coast would have been exposed to continuous attack, if these island bases had fallen into enemy hands.

American Counterattacks

In August, 1942, Allied forces in the Pacific area ceased fighting a purely defensive war and began to attack. A force of American warships appeared off the Solomon Islands, northeast of Australia, and marines landed on Guadalcanal and two other islands. The Japanese had seized these islands and had been industriously preparing them as bases for further operations. They defended them fiercely. Plainly, the conquest of the Solomons was to be a long, hard process.

Defeat at Savo Island. Two days after the first landings on Guadalcanal, our fleet suffered its worst disaster since Pearl Harbor. Five cruisers were surprised off Savo Island near Guadalcanal by a Japanese fleet which approached under cover of night. Before the American crews could locate the enemy and bring their guns to bear, four cruisers were disabled and sinking. The battle of Savo Island was a most disheartening defeat for the United States.

Victory at Guadalcanal. For several months a fierce struggle took place as American carriers, cruisers, and destroyers tried to prevent the Japanese from reinforcing their bases in the Solomons. Losses on both sides were heavy, but by November the victory was clearly in American hands. By February, 1943, all Japanese resistance on Guadalcanal was ended. For the remainder of the year American forces made landing after landing in the South and Central Pacific, penetrating the Japanese perimeter of defense and moving ever closer to the Japanese homeland.

Looking Back

1. How did the sneak attack on Pearl Harbor seriously damage but not wipe out American strength there?
2. By what steps did we find ourselves formally at war with Japan, Germany, and Italy?
3. Explain why the fall of the Philippines was a severe blow to the American cause.
4. Why were the victories in the battles of the Coral Sea and of Midway so important to the American cause?
5. Victory at Guadalcanal marked a shift in the tide of war. Explain.

2. Allies Move Toward Victory in Europe

Softening up the Axis

In the year 1942, the Axis Powers slowly but surely lost control of the air. Early in the war, the powerful German air force dealt paralyzing blows, smashing defenses of the Allies and spreading death, destruction, and terror throughout their cities. Warsaw, Rotterdam, London, and a host of other cities had been systematically blasted in order to frighten the victims into making peace. Herman Goering, commander of the German air force, proudly boasted that his planes and antiaircraft defenses would never permit enemy bombs to fall on German soil.

NORTH AFRICAN AND ITALIAN CAMPAIGNS (1942-1943)

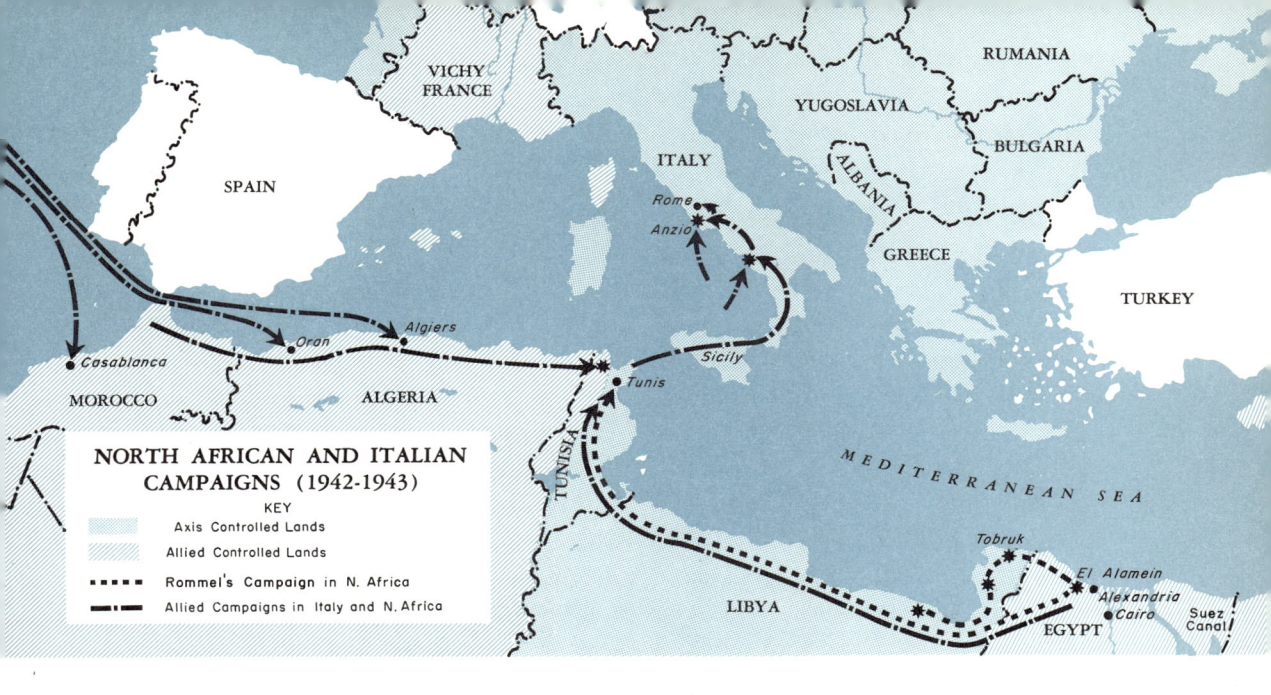

KEY
- Axis Controlled Lands
- Allied Controlled Lands
- ▪▪▪▪ Rommel's Campaign in N. Africa
- ▬▪▬ Allied Campaigns in Italy and N. Africa

It was an empty boast. Gradually the British and American aircraft production increased, and bombs began to rain on Germany. At first bombs fell in small, scattered raids and then in massive attacks of a thousand or more planes at a time. A deadly hail of huge bombs began to fall on German railroad centers, munition depots, submarine bases, and other military objectives. As the raids increased throughout 1943, German and Italian war production fell off and transportation systems were disrupted. The Axis nations were being "softened up."

Victory in North Africa

By the end of 1942 American forces were ready to help drive the Germans and Italians from North Africa. On November 8, Anglo-American forces under General Eisenhower landed at Casablanca on the Atlantic coast of French Morocco and at Oran and Algiers on the Mediterranean coast.

Eisenhower's forces landed so quickly and efficiently that there was little time to organize resistance. Algiers was quickly taken, as was Oran, but American troops met stern resistance at Casablanca. When the Hitler-appointed (Hitler conquered French possessions early in the war) French commander decided to shift his allegiance to the Allies, fighting in French North Africa ceased and the Allies had established an important base of operations.

German-Italian Surrender. By early 1943, a British army had driven Rommel's forces from Egypt and Libya back into Tunisia. When the Americans advanced from the west, the German forces were caught in a vise from which they could not escape. After weeks of bitter fighting, the Germans and Italians in Tunisia surrendered on May 12. Rommel himself managed to slip away and escape to Germany.

Italian Turnabout. In July, Americans and British troops landed in Sicily and before the end of August drove the Axis out of that great Italian island. Thereafter, Italian resistance

As soon as the Normandy beaches were secured on D-Day, supply ships rushed troops and equipment ashore. This photograph was taken from a captured Nazi trench.

weakened, although Germans occupied the country and kept fighting. A crisis in the Italian government forced Mussolini out of office. He was replaced by Marshall Badoglio, the conqueror of Ethiopia, who quickly made arrangements to surrender unconditionally to the Allies. On October 13, 1943, the new Italian government completed her turnabout and officially declared war on Germany.

The Turning Tide in Russia

German Advance. What in the meantime had been happening on the Russian front? In the summer of 1942, Hitler himself directed a great new assault upon the Russian lines. This time, the Germans, instead of striking all along the front, concentrated their attack upon the southern end of the Russian line in order to gain control of the wheat lands of the rich Ukraine region and the oil wells of the Caucasus mountain region. Little by little, the Russians were forced to fall back, losing the important cities of Kharkov and Rostov and the outer fringes of the steelmaking city of Stalingrad. Even some of the Caucasus oil fields fell to the invaders. For a time, Germany seemed to be on the verge of knocking Russia out of the war.

Russian Successes. Winter once more turned the tide. The German fighters withered under the freezing Russian wind. And the Russians, used to the winter, charged forward to defeat the frozen Germans. The defenders of Stalingrad, with their backs to the Volga River, not only held the Germans at bay but even forced them to retreat once more and at last captured or destroyed much of the army which had attacked Stalingrad. Rostov and Kharkov were recaptured. The German army in the Caucasus region was pushed against the eastern shore of the Black Sea.

Nor did the Russian successes halt this time with the coming of warm weather. The Russian tide continued to roll westward, driving the Germans out of Russia and across Poland. Late in 1944, Russian troops reached German soil, and in the early months of 1945 the Russian forces poured westward across Germany toward Berlin, the capital city. Germany's confident attempt to conquer Russia had turned into a disaster.

Invasion of Normandy

While the difficult campaign against the German forces in Italy was going on, the Allied forces under General Eisenhower were preparing for the great assault on western Europe. By May, 1944, Allied air power was judged capable of supporting the invasion properly. Bad weather delayed the operation until the morning of June 6: D-Day. On that fateful day a thunderous naval bombardment struck German defenses on the coast of Normandy, in northern France, while thousands of vessels landed troops and supplies. Within two weeks, a million men had landed and the seaport of Cherbourg had been captured.

After a slow advance, the Allies broke through the German lines at St. Lo in Normandy. Armored spearheads raced to free Paris late in August. The outmaneuvered Germans found themselves everywhere in wild retreat, while patriotic Frenchmen behind the lines added to their troubles by dynamiting roads, bridges, and railroads. By mid-September the Germans had been driven from most of France and Belgium.

The Collapse of Germany's Allies

In the late summer of 1944, the Axis forces in Europe began to fall apart. Rumania and Bulgaria, faced by the prospect of a Russian invasion, hastened to make peace with the Allies and turn against Germany. Finland, again beaten and invaded by Russians, changed sides and attacked the Germans. Hungary, invaded by Russians and Rumanians, was the last European ally to abandon Hitler, but it too

Much of the fighting in World War II was done in bombed cities like this one. Ruined buildings were hiding places for snipers, booby traps, and gun emplacements.

gave up the hopeless cause as the Russian armies closed around the capital city of Budapest.

"The Battle of the Bulge"

In December, 1944, the Germans on the western front made a last, desperate bid for victory. Aided by cold, stormy weather which kept Allied planes grounded, they drove furiously toward Antwerp along a seventy-mile front in the Ardennes Forest. Because of the way in which the German attack bent the Allied lines back, this operation is frequently referred to as "the Battle of the Bulge." At last the skies cleared, the air forces went into action, and the German attack was stopped. Soon the Germans were falling back, giving up the territory they had so recently taken.

A Fourth Term for Roosevelt

Despite the hazards of war, politics went on as usual in 1944. The Republicans, although they had been defeated in 1932, 1936, and 1940, hoped for a victory at last. At their convention in Chicago they nominated Governor Thomas E. Dewey of New York. The Democrats, meeting in Chicago a month later, renominated Roosevelt for a fourth term and chose Senator Harry S. Truman as his running mate.

In the election the popular vote was very close—about 25,500,000 to 22,000,000. Roosevelt, however, carried thirty-six states with 432 electoral votes, while Dewey carried only twelve states with 99 electoral vote. Franklin D. Roosevelt was not only the first but also the last President to serve for more than two terms. In 1951 the Twenty-second Amendment forbade the election of any president more than twice.

The Yalta Conference

Early in February, 1945, President Roosevelt and Prime Minister Churchill journeyed to Yalta, a town in southern Russia, to meet with Premier Stalin of Russia. This was not the first time the three had met. In November, 1943, they had conferred at Teheran, in Iran, where Stalin had promised to bring Russia into the Pacific War as soon as hostilities had ended in Europe. They had also discussed what course of action should be taken in regard to Japan, Germany, and Poland when the final victory was won.

At Yalta, Stalin again promised to enter the war in the Far East after the German surrender. In return, it was agreed that Russia would be given the Kurile Islands north of Japan, as well as territories and leases which the Russians had lost in the Russo-Japanese War, such as Manchukuo and rights to the port of Dairen. The division of Germany into zones of occupation was also discussed. It was agreed that the peoples of Europe should enjoy democratic government based on free elections. Plans were made for another conference, to be held at San Francisco in April, 1945, for the purpose of creating an international peace organization—the United Nations.

The Passing of a President

On April 12, 1945, the people of the United States were stunned to learn of the death of President Franklin D. Roosevelt. The President had been stricken suddenly while on a visit to

At Yalta, a tired and sick Roosevelt met with Churchill and Stalin to decide the fate of Germany and the future of the world. Roosevelt died two months later.

Warm Springs, Georgia, and death had occurred within a few hours. Late that same afternoon, Vice-President Harry S. Truman took the oath of office and became the new President of the United States. Facing him were many great unsolved problems. Almost at once, he announced that the war would be carried on as vigorously as ever. He further stated that the great United Nations peace conference would be held at San Francisco, as originally scheduled.

The Collapse of Germany

For some months after the smashing of the German attack in "the Battle of the Bulge," the American and British armies chipped away at the strong defenses of the Siegfried Line. Allied progress was slow but steady. Then, as one armored column after another smashed through the German fortifications, the German forces fell back to their next great defense barrier, the Rhine River.

Crossing the Rhine. The crossing of the Rhine promised to be an even harder operation than the taking of the Siegfried Line. The Rhine is a broad, fastflowing river, and the Germans had massed a large number of guns and men to defend it. One after another, the great bridges across the river were blown up, all except the Ludendorff bridge at Remagen. A column of American troops reached this bridge and took it before the Germans could destroy it. Pouring across the bridge, the Americans soon established a firm bridgehead on the east bank. Encouraged by this move, other British and American forces made crossings at other points, using hastily-constructed pontoon bridges and special assault boats operated by the sailors of the United States Navy. Frantic German counterattacks were thrown back, and the Rhine ceased to be a barrier to our troops.

Mussolini Executed. The end of the war and of Hitler's infamous regime was now near at hand as the Allied army cut across Germany from various directions, capturing thousands of Germans as they went. On the Italian front, British and American forces broke through the German lines in April. They were aided by bands of Italian patriots who succeeded in freeing the great cities of northern Italy as the Allies approached. One such group of Italians managed to capture Mussolini and a number of his Fascist followers, who were trying vainly to flee into Germany. The Italian dictator was quickly put to death by his enraged countrymen.

End of German Resistance. Late in April, 1945, units of the American

Arrows pointing eastward represent American activity. Those pointing westward represent Russian advances. Where do they meet? What contemporary issues were raised by their meeting?

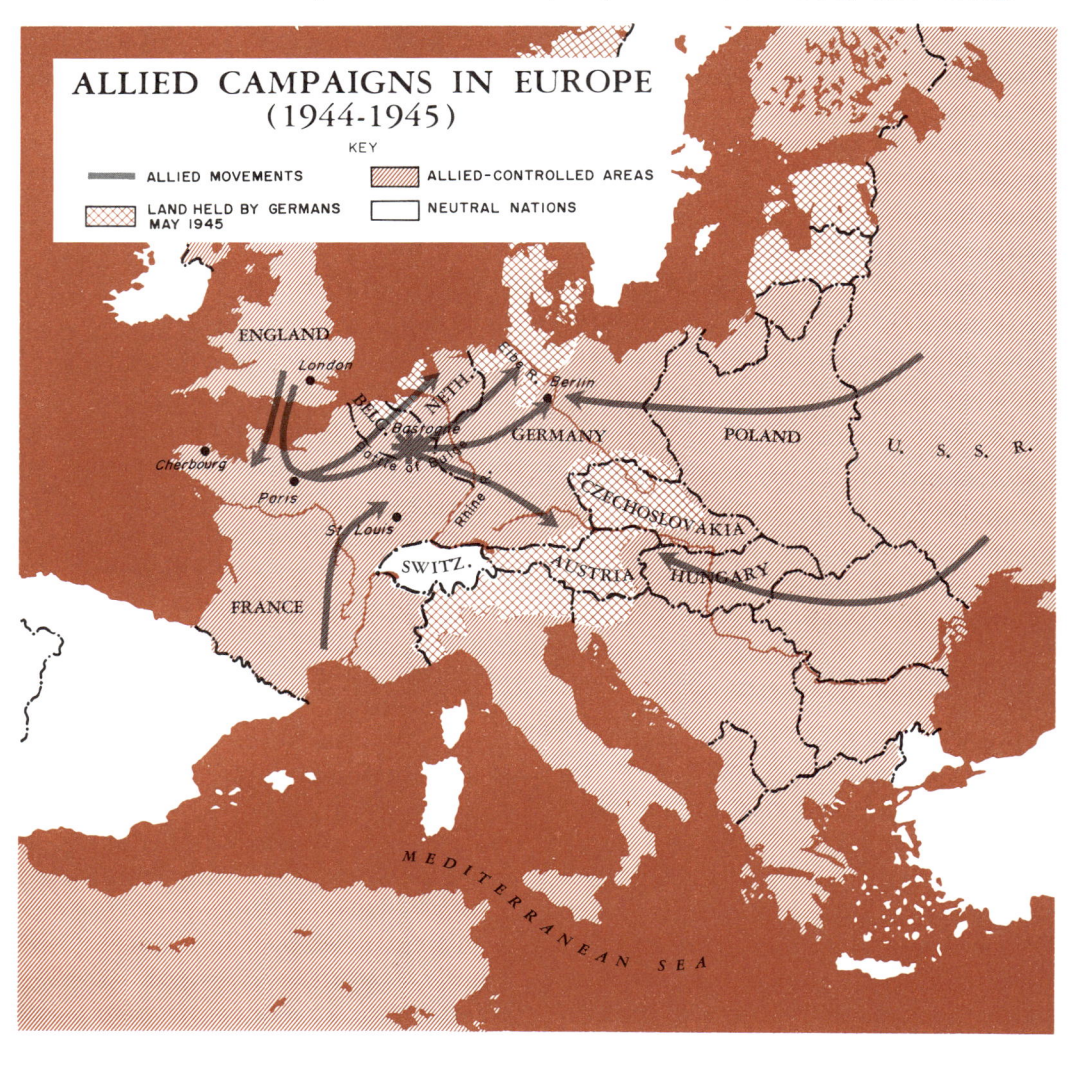

ALLIED CAMPAIGNS IN EUROPE (1944-1945)

and Russian armies met in friendship and victory south of Berlin near the Elbe River. Germany had been cut in two. Almost at once, organized German resistance went to pieces. The German armies in Denmark, the Netherlands, Norway, and many parts of Germany threw down their arms. Only scattered fighting continued.

Suicide of Hitler. In the midst of the confusion, the German radio reported that Hitler was dead. This bloodthirsty leader, guilty of the murder of 6,000,000 Jews, the most ghastly crime against mankind known to history, had committed suicide in an underground shelter in Berlin. With him fell the whole brutal Nazi regime—with its fearful concentration camps, its mass murder of innocent civilians, and its blindness to truth and justice.

On May 2, 1945, German forces in Italy surrendered completely. On May 8, 1945, all German forces surrendered unconditionally, amidst wild rejoicing in Europe and the United States. Now another great task had to be faced—the final defeat of Japan!

Looking Back

1. How did the winning of air superiority in Europe aid the Allied cause?
2. Why did the Italians prove to be a handicap to the Nazis?
3. How did the Germans first succeed and then fail in their Russian campaign?
4. Describe the Allied campaigns from D-Day to VE Day.
5. What agreements were reached at the Yalta Conference?

3. A Terrible Force is Loosed to End a Terrible War

An Ultimatum at Potsdam

In July, 1945, President Truman traveled to Potsdam, a suburb of Berlin, to confer with Stalin and Churchill. James F. Byrnes, the new Secretary of State, accompanied him. Later, Clement Attlee, the new British Prime Minister replaced Churchill at the meeting. Decisions were reached about the policing and administration of the various parts of Germany. It was agreed that Japan must surrender or be destroyed. Stalin promised that Russia would join in the war by August 15, though this provision was kept a secret until Russia actually did declare war on Japan on August 8.

Americans had another secret which they revealed only to Attlee and Stalin at this conference. The day before the conference began, scientists had exploded an experimental bomb near Los Alamos, New Mexico. It was a tremendously powerful device which American scientists, with the aid of British and Canadian technicians, had been working on since early 1940. Solemnly, in a Potsdam Declaration, they warned Japan to surrender. The Japanese leaders, to their sorrow, ignored the ultimatum.

Island-Hopping

While the Allies were pressing their attacks against Germany in 1944,

American submarines were taking a terrible toll of Japanese merchant shipping. Carrier-based planes were constantly bombing Japanese defenses in the Marshall and Mariana Islands. In February, 1944, successful landings were carried out on Kwajalein (Kwah-juh-LEEN') and Eniwetok (ehn-ih-wee'-tok) in the Marshalls. A few months later Saipan, Guam, and Tinian in the Marianas fell, after a stubborn resistance which cost heavily in American lives. This "island-hopping" was an extremely important operation, for it supplied good bases for future strikes against the Japanese homeland.

Battle of Leyte Gulf. Finally the way was cleared for an assault against the Philippines. General Douglas MacArthur, who in 1942 promised the Filipinos that he would return to liberate them, was in command of American forces. His plan was to separate the Japanese in Mindanao (mihn-dah-nah'-oh) from those in Luzon by landing on the island of Leyte (LAY'teh) in the central Philippines. Under cover of a tremendous naval bombardment and with a cloud of protecting planes overhead, American forces landed swiftly and efficiently on October 20, 1944.

The Japanese feared that their newly won empire in Southeast Asia was doomed. In a supreme effort to crush the American invaders by sinking their transports and supply ships, they decided to commit all of their remaining naval forces. The resulting conflict, known as the Battle of Leyte Gulf—in reality three separate battles—was the greatest naval engagement of all time. The Japanese fleet was virtually wiped out when four carriers, three battleships, and a score of cruisers and destroyers were sunk.

After a long and bitter struggle, the island of Leyte was secured. In December, a landing was made on the island of Mindoro, a short distance south of Manila. Another large-scale landing was then made at Lingayen Gulf, north of Manila on Luzon Island. The capital was now surrounded, and veteran armored forces and infantry began to converge on the city. Within a few weeks it was in American hands.

Iwo Jima. While mopping-up operations were still going on in the Philippines, the marines landed on Iwo Jima, a small volcanic island only 750 miles from Tokyo. From the middle of February to the end of March, 1945, they fought the fanatical Japanese garrison. The island, which was needed as a base for fighter planes and bombers, was taken at a very heavy cost in dead and wounded.

Unlike the war in Europe, the Pacific war was fought from island to island. Soldiers charged ashore under deadly fire.

The city of Hiroshima, Japan, was almost completely destroyed after an atomic bomb was dropped upon it. The two atomic bombs dropped on Japan are the only ones ever used in wartime.

Okinawa. The final island assault of the war was made at Okinawa, a large island about 370 miles south of Japan. Realizing that an iron ring was closing around them, the Japanese fought with great fury. Waves of *kamikaze* suicide planes came hurtling out of the skies to crash on the decks of American and British ships. Marine and army divisions suffered almost 50,000 casualties before the island was completely overrun in June. About 110,000 Japanese were killed and 7800 taken prisoner.

Surrender of Japan

Now the defeat of Japan became more and more certain. American bombers from captured airfields and from carriers dealt death and destruction from the skies over Japan. In desperation Emperor Hirohito replaced many of his military and government leaders with other men. Such moves could do no good. Japan was losing the war, and her leaders knew it.

The Atomic Attack on Hiroshima. Early in August, 1945, the war came to a dramatic climax. A single small bomb was dropped on the Japanese military center of Hiroshima. This terrible new weapon was the result of years of secret scientific experimentation by the most brilliant American, Canadian, and British scientists. The atomic bomb made use of a newly discovered force, vastly more powerful than any which man had ever used before—the liberated power of the atoms of which all matter is composed. Its power was equal to that of 20,000 tons of the most destructive high explosives previously known. In a single blinding flash and earth-shaking explosion, a large part of Hiroshima was blown to bits.

Not only the Japanese but people everywhere were tremendously shaken by the sudden knowledge that a new and terrific force had been unleashed in the world. The possibilities of atomic power, in war and in peace, were too enormous to be understood.

The Second Bomb. The people of Japan had no time to recover from their surprise and shock. On August 8, only two days after the first atomic bomb was dropped, Russia declared war upon Japan, and Russian troops invaded the Japanese puppet state of Manchukuo. The very next day, a second atomic bomb was dropped, and this one did even greater damage to the naval center of Nagasaki. Almost at once, the Japanese government began to ask for peace, and on August 14, after several days of trying to bargain, Japan agreed to surrender unconditionally. General Douglas MacArthur was placed in charge of the signing of the peace agreement and of the occupation of the Japanese homeland.

End of the War. On Sunday, September 2, 1945, Japan officially surrendered. The ceremony took place on the deck of the American battleship *Missouri* in Tokyo Bay. After the Japanese delegates signed the surrender document, General Douglas MacArthur signed in behalf of all of the Allied forces as a group. Then Admiral Chester Nimitz signed for the United States, and other representatives signed for the individual nations which had been fighting against the Japanese. The most terrible war in the history of the world was over.

Looking Back

1. What agreements were reached at the Potsdam Conference?

2. How did the American "island hopping" campaign lead to success in the Pacific?

3. Why did the Japanese risk everything at the battle of Leyte Gulf—and lose?

4. In what way did the use of the atom bomb affect the war?

5. The use of the atom bomb, while extremely destructive, saved countless lives. Explain.

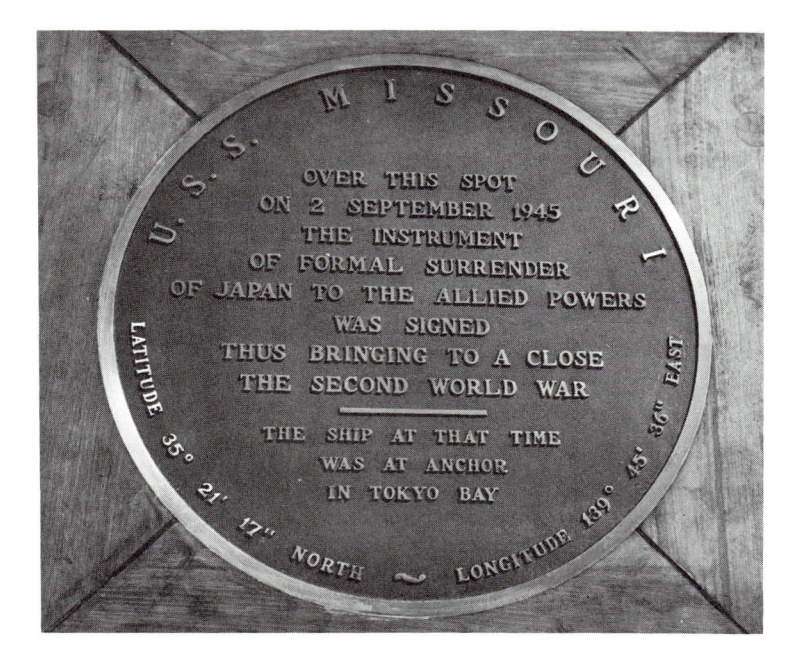

The battleship *U.S.S. Missouri* survived many attacks throughout the war. Therefore it seemed fitting that the Japanese surrender pact should be signed on its deck, September 2, 1945. This plaque remains in its deck today at the spot where the formal surrender was signed.

The Chapter in Perspective

Who Are These People?

MacArthur
Wainwright
Truman
Eisenhower
Dewey

Where Are These Places?

Pearl Harbor
Bataan
Corregidor
Hong Kong
Singapore
Coral Sea
Aleutian Islands
Solomon Islands
Nagasaki
Guadalcanal
French Morocco
Algiers
Stalingrad
Normandy
Leyte Gulf
Okinawa
Hiroshima

What Do These Dates and Terms Mean?

Dec. 7, 1941
VJ Day
May, 1942
June, 1942
D-Day
Battle of the Bulge
Battle of the Coral Sea
Battle of Savo Island
Battle of Midway
Yalta Conference
Potsdam Conference
June 6, 1944
Feb., 1943
May 8, 1945
VE Day
Aug. 14, 1945

Questions for Study

1. How did the American efforts for Lend-Lease eventually aid the "battle for production" at home?

2. Why were American losses at Guadalcanal so heavy?

3. Compare the effects of Napoleon's and Hitler's invasion of Russia.

4. Account for the rapid collapse of Germany's allies in the late summer of 1944.

5. On what grounds do critics of Yalta claim that the Russians received too much for too little?

6. Why did the Japanese fail to accept the Potsdam ultimatum?

7. The Battle of the Bulge has been called the last gasp of the once mighty Nazi war machine. Explain.

8. What technological advances were made in military weapons and types of warfare from World War I to World War II?

9. Trace the military campaigns in Europe that led to the collapse of the Nazis.

10. Trace the military campaigns in the Pacific that led to the surrender of Japan.

Place Yourself in History

Unexpected responsibilities have fallen upon your shoulders. In the midst of the greatest challenge your nation has ever faced, you have been suddenly projected into a position of trust, power, and decision. Word has come to you that an awesome, destructive weapon, has been secretly perfected at the cost of billions of dollars. Your warning to the enemy to surrender is disregarded. You wish to save lives—American as well as others. Your name is Harry S. Truman—and the atom bomb can be unleashed only upon your command.

What was the background under which Truman had to make his decision? What decision would you have made? Why? What were the immediate and long-range results of Truman's decision?

Expanding Your Outlook

Doing It Yourself

1. Write an eye-witness account of a "run" on a bank. Research reading and family or friends may help.
2. Imagine you were a member of the C.C.C. Write entries in a diary that show how you spent your time.
3. Prepare a report on "The Rise of the C.I.O."
4. Interview adult friends and neighbors to see how they feel about Social Security today. Report your findings to the class.
5. You are an American correspondent in Latin America. Write a report for your paper on how news of the "Good Neighbor" policy has been received.
6. Write a "letter to the editor," dated 1933, stating why you favor (or oppose) diplomatic recognition of Russia by the United States. Avoid hindsight!
7. On a map of Europe, number and color the nations that fell to the Nazi push for power.
8. Prepare an eyewitness radio broadcast covering the evacuation of Dunkirk.
9. Report to the class on the new weapons, methods of warfare, and strategy used in World War II. Compare these with World War I.
10. Write your own history of World War II by preparing fifteen newspaper headlines covering the major events.

Working with the Class

1. Organize committees to represent Germany, Italy, and Japan. Each committee is to tell why the nation it represents found itself at war with the United States in World War II.
2. A group may prepare a dramatic presentation concerning an "under-

ground" movement during World War II in a conquered European nation.
3. A committee of military strategists, using maps of the Pacific area, may summarize the fighting there from Pearl Harbor to the end of the war. Similar groups may wish to cover the European or African campaigns.
4. How and why the world stood silent while Hitler committed his atrocities might be a topic for a group discussion.
5. Organize a committee to prepare a bulletin board display featuring life in America during World War II. Ration stamps, draft cards, posters, war bond advertisements, patriotic slogans and other such items will be of interest.
6. Organize a committee to report to the class on the contributions made by American women to achieve victory in World War II.

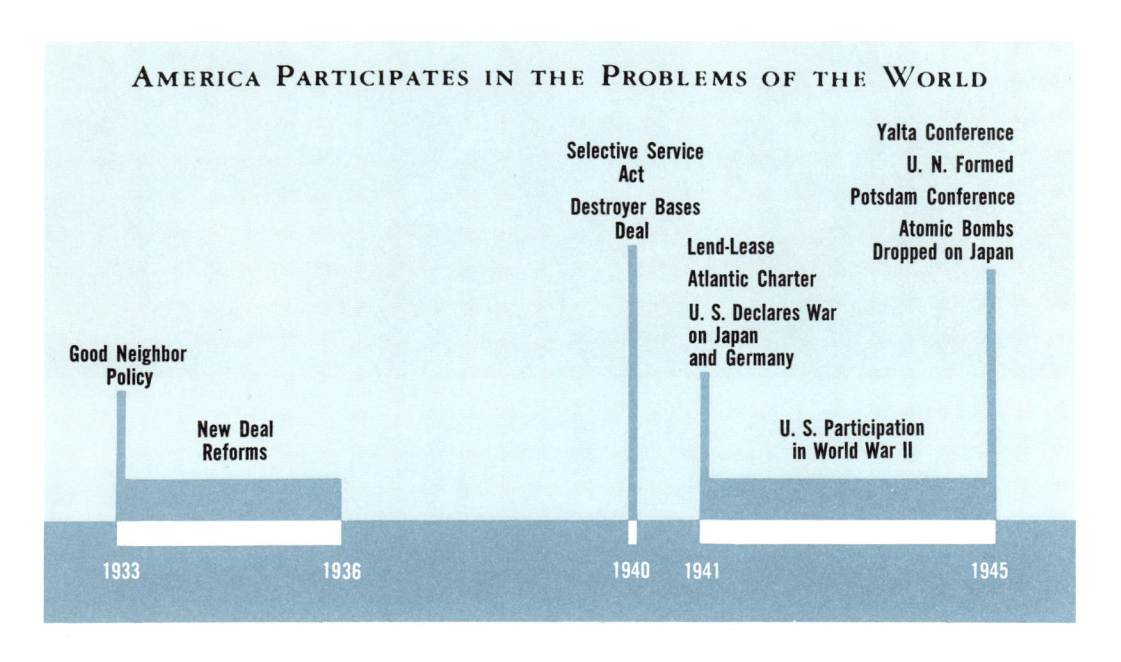

America Participates in the Problems of the World

- 1933 — Good Neighbor Policy
- 1936 — New Deal Reforms
- 1940 — Selective Service Act; Destroyer Bases Deal
- 1941 — Lend-Lease; Atlantic Charter; U. S. Declares War on Japan and Germany
- 1945 — Yalta Conference; U. N. Formed; Potsdam Conference; Atomic Bombs Dropped on Japan

U. S. Participation in World War II

Jackson Pollock's painting, Ocean Greyness, *is perhaps symbolic of a new age in art and culture. When the camera was invented, and it no longer was necessary for the artist to record things exactly as they were, artists turned to the expression of their feelings about what they saw. Also, when the world entered into the atomic age and then the space age, the limits of reality changed radically. Suddenly man's world expanded miles and miles into space; and, just as suddenly, man found his way into atoms, the tiniest specks of matter. New knowledge gave birth to great optimism and great confusion about the nature of life.*

The Solomon R. Guggenheim Museum Collection

ONE NATION INDIVISIBLE

UNIT 10

America Flourishes in a Shrinking World

29. The Problems and Challenges of Our Times

1. The Nations Organize for Peace. • **2.** The "Cold War" Begins • **3.** The "Cold War" Turns Hot in Asia • **4.** The Kremlin Changes Its Approach

30. The Uneasy Fifties

1. Domestic Concerns Dominate Eisenhower's First Term • **2.** Foreign Affairs Fill the Late Fifties

31. America Moves Ahead in the Sixties

1. National Affairs Concern Americans • **2.** Foreign Affairs Are a Continuing Problem • **3.** Science and Technology Shape the Modern World • **4.** Americans Continue to Build a Great Society

29 The Problems and Challenges of Our Times

The end of World War II was not the end of conflict. It merely ushered in a period of tension between the Western nations and the forces of communism. A great contest began between two systems of organizing human society: democracy and communism. This contest was fought not only on the military front but in the areas of economics and political strategy. It was mainly a "cold war"—a struggle for the minds of men. This chapter deals with the part played by our country in this "cold war."

1. The Nations Organize for Peace

In the fall of 1944, while the war was still being fought, delegates from Britain, Russia, China, and the United States met at an important conference at Dumbarton Oaks, a beautiful estate on the outskirts of Washington. Their purpose was to draft the outline for a new, more efficient international organization to replace the League of Nations.

The Founding of the United Nations

On April 25, 1945, as scheduled, the representatives of fifty nations gathered in San Francisco to complete the outline sketched out at Dumbarton Oaks. They were prepared to draw up the Charter of the United Nations. Both the Republicans and the Democrats were in warm support of the ideals of the United Nations, and President Roosevelt had shrewdly chosen members of both parties as delegates. The enthusiasm that greeted the United Nations proposals was quite different from the antagonism which the Senate had displayed toward the League of Nations in 1919.

The Veto Power. The *United Nations Charter* as finally approved bore many resemblances to the old League Covenant. There was one significant difference—any one of the five big powers (Russia, Great Britain, United States, France, Nationalist China: permanent members of the U.N. Security Council) could veto a United Nations action. This provision, which was insisted upon by the Americans and British as well as the Russians, was supposed to guarantee the *sovereignty* (freedom to act) of each of the great nations. As it turned out, the veto became a point of endless irritation and dispute. At San Francisco it was hoped that the veto would be used only when a nation's most important interests were involved. As time went on, however, the Soviets recklessly (about 100 times) used the veto anytime they felt their interests were even slightly threatened.

Ratification. After the historic conference at San Francisco closed on July 26, the Charter was submitted to the member nations for ratification. The United States was the first to ratify. The Senate gave approval on July 28 by a vote of 89 to 2. The Charter went into effect on October 24, 1945. In spite of the uncooperative attitude of the Russians, the world held high hopes that the United Nations would be an effective instrument for peace.

Flags of each of the members of the United Nations fly in front of its building in New York.

Representatives of each member nation gather in the General Assembly of the United Nations.

In April, 1946, the League of Nations held its final meeting and turned over to the United Nations all its equipment and records and the duty of maintaining the peace of the world. Late in the following year the United Nations gained a permanent home when John D. Rockefeller, Jr. donated a site in New York City to serve as its headquarters. Here beautiful buildings were erected, and in 1950 the United Nations organization moved into its new quarters.

Membership. Since its founding the United Nations has welcomed new members as soon as they have qualified for admission. To be a member, a nation must demonstrate that it is independent, that it believes in the Charter, and that it is able to carry out the duties required of it. By 1964 there were 111 member nations.

The Structure of the United Nations

According to the Charter, the United Nations is made up of six principal bodies.

The Security Council. (1) There is a *Security Council* of five permanent members (the United States, Great Britain, France, Nationalist China, and the Soviet Union) and six members elected in rotation by the General Assembly for two-year terms. This body is always in session, and its main function is to take action to prevent the outbreak of war.

The General Assembly. (2) The *General Assembly* meets once a year and consists of from one to five representatives from each member nation. Each nation has one vote, and a two-thirds vote of the Assembly is needed on important decisions. The Assembly acts as a world forum to discuss vital problems. It decides upon action relating to finances, membership, and operations, and it makes recommendations to the Security Council.

The Economic and Social Council. (3) The *Economic and Social Council* of eighteen members is elected by the General Assembly and has a wide range of duties concerning educational cooperation, higher living standards, better health, and human rights. To carry out these duties, it sets up special commissions and cooperates with a great number of international specialized agencies.

The Trusteeship Council. (4) The *Trusteeship Council* supervises colonies and undeveloped areas, either by itself or by appointing "trustees" for particular colonies. The "trustee" nations must report annually to the General Assembly about their progress in promoting the welfare of their trusteeship areas.

The International Court of Justice. (5) The *International Court of Justice* replaces the old World Court. Its fifteen members sit at the Hague in the Netherlands. They handle cases of international law which are submitted to them. The Security Council and the General Assembly may ask them for advisory opinions.

The Secretariat. (6) The *Secretariat* is headed by the Secretary-General of the United Nations. He is the chief administrative officer and is in charge of a large staff. He reports annually to the General Assembly and calls the attention of the Security Council to any situation which he thinks threatens world peace.

Looking Back

1. Explain the different reactions in the United States to the League of Nations and the United Nations.
2. How has the veto power hurt the effectiveness of the United Nations?
3. Name the six main divisions of the United Nations and tell the chief functions of each.

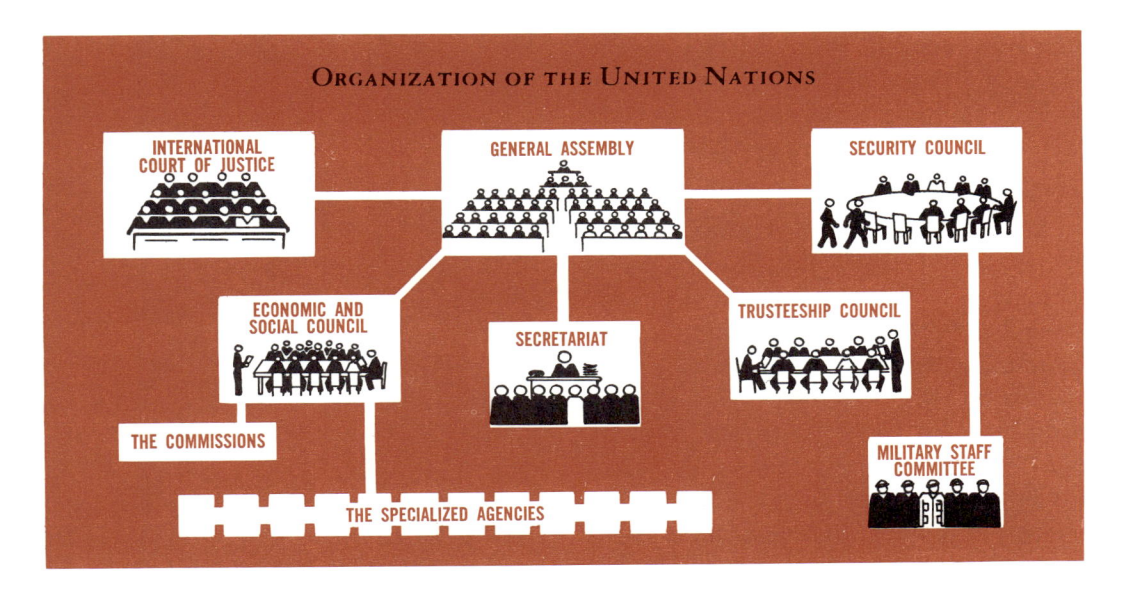

ORGANIZATION OF THE UNITED NATIONS

- INTERNATIONAL COURT OF JUSTICE
- GENERAL ASSEMBLY
- SECURITY COUNCIL
- ECONOMIC AND SOCIAL COUNCIL
- SECRETARIAT
- TRUSTEESHIP COUNCIL
- THE COMMISSIONS
- MILITARY STAFF COMMITTEE
- THE SPECIALIZED AGENCIES

2. The "Cold War" Begins

Unfortunately for the hopes of the world, the United Nations was unsuccessful in two very important respects. It was unable to form an effective permanent international police force or to bring about either disarmament or international control of atomic energy. In 1946 the United States generously agreed to share its atomic secrets with other nations, in return for a guarantee that atomic power would be used for peaceful purposes and not for weapons of war. But the Communist bloc refused to submit to international inspections as a guarantee. The armament race continued. Russia started a worldwide propaganda campaign against the United States, while at the same time busily developing its own research in atomic power.

A Propaganda Offensive

Even before the war ended, it could be seen that the Soviets had no intention of keeping all the promises they made at the Yalta Conference. Their aim was to impose Communist dictatorships wherever possible, to weaken the ties between the democratic nations, and to spread Red doctrines by means of propaganda and subversive activities. Their world offensive was conducted on all fronts—economic, political, and military. This great conflict is still going on. As the Soviets dropped an "iron curtain" around their smaller neighbors and built up a mighty army, the United States reluctantly prepared to meet the threat. The government took preventative measures both at home and abroad. The aim was to "contain" the spread of communism.

Measures Against Communism. As an answer to the deceitful stream of propaganda which the Soviets were beaming to the world, Washington prepared a radio counterattack of propaganda of its own directed by *The Voice of America*. Both the national and the state governments exercised renewed vigilance in detecting subversive organizations and individuals supporting the Soviet system.

The Truman Doctrine. In March, 1947, President Truman took measures to halt Russian aggression in Europe. He learned that the small minority of Communists in Greece were receiving encouragement in the form of military equipment from Yugoslavia and Albania in a plot to overthrow the British-supported monarchy. The British were also supporting Turkey against Soviet demands for Turkish territory. Upon being notified by Prime Minister Attlee that Britain could no longer keep up its support, Truman urged Congress to appropriate $400,000,000 to aid Greece and Turkey, and to send military advisers to help them strengthen their defenses. In this way the two countries were saved from being swallowed by communism.

When Harry Truman became President after the death of Roosevelt, some were unsure of his ability. Many now feel he was one of the country's finest chief executives.

Truman's decision to aid Greece and Turkey was a departure from former United States policy. Up to 1947, the United States had officially refrained from entangling itself in the affairs of any European country. Truman's new policy became known as the *Truman Doctrine*.

The Election of 1948

At home in America, people were preparing for the 1948 presidential election. The Democrats, after much argument, nominated President Harry Truman, with Senator Alben W. Barkley as Vice-Presidential nominee. Truman's party was weakened when a dissident group broke away and formed a Progressive party with former Vice-President Henry A. Wallace as its candidate. A Southern group also refused to accept Truman, formed a separate States' Rights Democratic party (known as *"Dixiecrats"*) and nominated Governor J. Strom Thurmond of South Carolina as its candidate.

The Republicans nominated Thomas E. Dewey, and they were confident of victory. Public opinion polls and the press predicted a Dewey landslide. Not at all shaken by these predictions, Truman fought a vigorous campaign, making speeches all over the country. The battle was so hard fought that the outcome was not known until the day after the polls closed. Truman won by a popular vote of 24,105,812 to 21,970,065 with an electoral vote of 303 to 189.

The Formation of Power Blocs

The Marshall Plan. In France, Italy, and West Germany strong Communist parties were taking advantage of hunger and economic weakness to spread their doctrines and disrupt the war-weakened, ineffective governments. As a result in June, 1947, the State Department completed a plan to bolster the economy of the European countries. This plan was presented by Secretary of State Marshall in a speech at Harvard University. He suggested that the European nations (including the Communist countries) work together to plan their recovery and raise production. Those who did so would receive American financial aid. Combined with the Truman Doctrine of 1947, the Marshall Plan gave the United States a two-pronged attack against communism.

The Soviet Union angrily denounced this plan, calling it "Yankee imperialism." It also prevented its *satellites* (nations which have communist gov-

In the election of 1948, Harry Truman showed himself to be an able campaigner. Here he is shown on his campaign train making one of his many "whistle stop" speeches. (Check the chart on Page 447 to see what percentage of people voted in 1948. What significance has the percentage?)

The Berlin Airlift was a great American success in the Cold War. Here American DC-3's unload needed supplies at Berlin's Tempelhof Airport.

ernments and are influenced by Russia) from participating in the Marshall Plan. The other European countries gladly accepted billions of dollars in American aid, which was administered by Economic Cooperation Administration (ECA) headed by Paul G. Hoffman, an American industrialist. The Marshall Plan proved to be a great success and a great help to European nations. By 1950 Europe's productivity had more than doubled, and it has been rising ever since.

The Warsaw Alliance. The Russians reacted strongly against the Marshall Plan. They formed their own plan, called the Warsaw Alliance, of nine satellite nations in 1947. In Western Europe, Communist parties in France and Italy tried to sabotage the Marshall Plan by ordering Communist-dominated unions to go on strike.

North Atlantic Treaty Organization headquarters at Paris, France, is shaped like a giant "A" which stands for Atlantic.

The Berlin Blockade

In June, 1948, the United States and Britain encouraged the formation of a new West German government which would share in the European recovery program. The Soviets who controlled the eastern part of Germany did not want a new Western capitalistic nation to be formed. To undermine Western influence in Germany, they decided in

June to try to force the Western nations out of Berlin, which was located in East Germany and administered by British, American, French, and Soviet authorities.

There was no written guarantee of land transit from West Germany across the Soviet zone to Berlin. Therefore, the Soviets reasoned, it would be easy to starve the Western allies out of Berlin by clamping down a blockade against road and rail traffic from West Germany. It was a dangerous plan which could have resulted in war. It failed when President Truman ordered a gigantic airlift to supply the city with food, coal, medical supplies, and other necessities. To the astonishment of the Soviets, the Air Force was able to carry in more supplies than had come overland. The Soviets gave up the blockade in May, 1949.

The North Atlantic Treaty Organization

The airlift was convincing evidence that the United States intended to resist Soviet aggression against the West. Together with the Marshall Plan, it encouraged the free nations to form a military alliance to supplement and protect the economic alliance.

France and Britain had formed a military alliance in 1947 and were joined the next year by Belgium, Luxemburg, and the Netherlands. In 1949 the *North Atlantic Treaty Organization (NATO)* came into being when these nations were joined by Italy, Portugal, Denmark, Norway, Iceland, Canada, and the United States. Greece and Turkey, although not "Atlantic" nations, were admitted in 1951. The West German Republic led by Chancellor Konrad Adenauer, was admitted in 1955.

The treaty signed by the fifteen nations declared that an attack on one would be regarded as an attack on all. The North Atlantic Treaty Organization then proceeded to form a defense force with headquarters near Paris. General Eisenhower was appointed as the first military commander of NATO early in 1951. It was now clear to all the world that the United States did not intend to withdraw from Europe as it had done after World War I.

Looking Back

1. What does the term "cold war" mean?
2. Show how the Truman Doctrine was a departure from former American policy. Give proof that it was effective.
3. In what ways was the election of 1948 an unusual one?
4. Give the purposes of the Marshall Plan. Would you have voted for it? Why?
5. List the purposes and member nations of NATO.

3. The "Cold War" Turns Hot in Asia

While the U.S. was attempting to contain the Communist drive in Europe, Russia was attempting to extend the Communist influence into the Far East. Communists were battling the French in Vietnam, the Nationalist Chinese all over China, and were making trouble in other places.

In Europe, Russians had occupied countries and set up puppet governments. This had happened in Hungary, Poland, Czechoslovakia, Albania and other countries. In the Far East they operated differently. Here, instead of occupying countries, the Russian Communists sent military and economic aid and advice. They trained native groups of Communists to start their own trouble with Russian-made tanks and guns.

Civil War in China

Communists vs. Nationalists. While NATO was being organized in Europe, the Chinese Nationalist government of Chiang Kai-shek was crumbling under the pressure of Chinese Communist armies. When Japan surrendered, American forces had helped the Nationalists return to power in eastern China. Stalin, although he had made a treaty of alliance with Chiang, secretly turned over great supplies of captured Japanese weapons to the Chinese Communists in western China.

Late in 1945 President Truman attempted to prevent a civil war in China. He believed that sending American troops to help the Nationalists would not be favored by the American people. Instead, he sent General George Marshall (later to be Secretary of State) to China to obtain a cease-fire and help the two Chinese parties to mend their quarrels. Marshall tried hard to promote peace and unity, but finally gave up when neither side would make concessions.

The People's Republic. In 1947 the Chinese Communists launched an all-out attack against the Nationalists. While the American government debated about what action should be taken, the Communists overwhelmed Chiang's demoralized and defecting armies. In April, 1949, with the aid of captured American weapons, the Communists captured Nanking, the Nationalist capital. In October they proclaimed a "People's Republic" with Mao Tse-tung (MAH'oat-SAY'-DOONG') as president. Chiang and his remaining supporters fled to the island of Formosa (Taiwan). It appeared that the millions in American aid to the Nationalists had been wasted.

The new Chinese regime was recognized by the Soviet Union, Great Britain, and some other countries. The United States refused to recognize Mao and consistently blocked the admission of Red China to the United Nations, where Chiang's Nationalist representative professed to speak for all of China. Mao soon proved that

General Douglas MacArthur, hero of World War II, later became a controversial figure when he challenged President Truman's authority.

WAR IN KOREA

EXTENT OF NORTH KOREAN ATTACK IN 1950

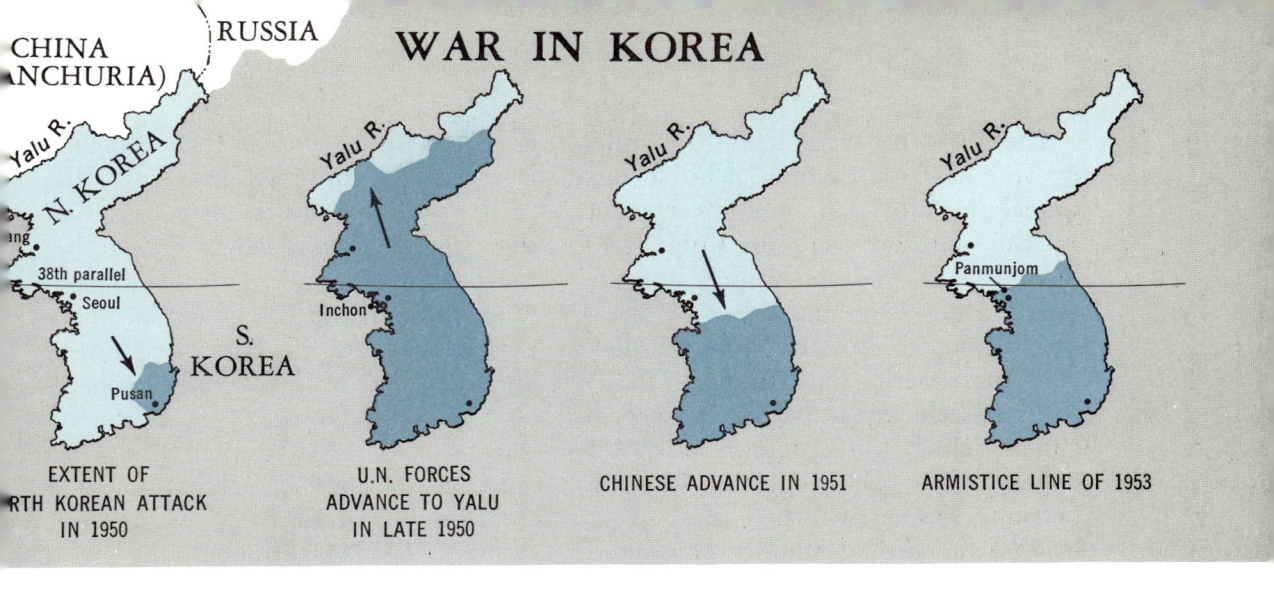

U.N. FORCES ADVANCE TO YALU IN LATE 1950

CHINESE ADVANCE IN 1951

ARMISTICE LINE OF 1953

his government was thoroughly Communist by signing a mutual assistance pact with Stalin in February, 1950.

The Occupation of Japan

In accordance with plans made at the Potsdam Conference in 1945, Allied troops were to occupy Japan until it was disarmed and educated in democratic principles. To accomplish this mission General Douglas MacArthur was appointed Supreme Commander of the Allied Powers (SCAP). Although Soviet officials protested loudly, MacArthur disregarded them and conducted the occupation in his own way. He was remarkably successful in winning the cooperation and even friendship of the Japanese people. He introduced many reforms of a democratic nature and set up a democratic form of government. The great industrial monopolies were broken up, land was distributed to the peasants, the educational system was improved, the rights of labor were safeguarded, and woman suffrage was granted. In order to assist industrial recovery, the United States gave up its demands for reparations.

With the exception of the uncooperative Russians, the Allied Powers went ahead with peace negotiations. The terms of the peace were very generous. Japan lost her foreign conquests, and American forces remained in the Ryukyu Islands south of Japan. However, her right of self-defense was recognized and no obstacles were placed in the way of her economic recovery. The treaty was signed in San Francisco in 1951 and was quickly ratified by the Senate. At the same time a treaty was signed permitting the United States to maintain armed forces in Japan.

War in Korea

When the Pacific war ended, the Americans occupied Korea up to the 38th parallel of latitude, and the Russians moved into the area north of that parallel. Unhappy Korea, which had been promised independence after thirty-five years of Japanese rule, soon learned that the Russians would not accept a unified and independent Korea unless it was governed by a native Communist regime.

The Two Koreas. The 38th parallel became an "iron curtain." The Soviets quickly installed a puppet government in the northern half of Korea and helped it to equip strong military forces. United Nations inspectors were not allowed to cross the 38th parallel.

In the south, the United Nations held free elections—a democratic procedure which the Communists would never permit. Dr. Syngman Rhee, a patriotic Korean who had lived as an exile in the United States, was elected to head the Republic of Korea. The United States recognized the republic as the legitimate government of the country. However, the United States government did not support Rhee in his desire to bring North Korea under his control. In June, 1949, American forces withdrew, leaving the South Koreans with inadequate equipment to defend themselves.

Aggression from North Korea. The North Koreans and their Russian advisers seized the opportunity given them by the departure of the Americans. On June 24, 1950, they launched a savage, two-pronged attack over the 38th parallel doubtless expecting that the United Nations would do nothing but protest. They were mistaken. President Truman and Congress placed the problem before the Security Council of the United Nations, which immediately branded North Korea as the aggressor and called upon the U.N. members to "furnish such assistance to the Republic of Korea as may be necessary to repel the armed attack." As it happened, the Russians were boycotting the Council at that moment and thus were unable to cast a veto which would have prevented action.

The United States and other U.N. members recognized the Communist attack upon South Korea for what it was—a brutal violation of the principles upon which the United Nations was founded. It was a severe test of the young organization. If, like the League of Nations, it failed to take action, it might, like the League, end in failure.

American troops in Korea fire covering shots at communist snipers in the hills so that an American convoy may cross the river safely.

U. N. "Police Action." On June 27, United States air and naval forces were on their way to help the South Koreans. Three days later President Truman ordered ground forces to start moving from Japan. The Seventh Fleet was directed to block Formosa from the Chinese mainland. On July 7, the Security Council requested those nations sending help to place their troops under American command. President Truman appointed General MacArthur as commander-in-chief.

This rapid succession of events plunged America into a *police action* which very much resembled a full-scale war. Although some fifteen nations besides the United States and South Korea contributed forces, about ninety per cent of the total were Americans and South Koreans.

The maneuver was brilliantly executed and caught the Communists completely by surprise. United Nations troops quickly recaptured Seoul, the capital of South Korea, and pursued the disorganized enemy up to the 38th parallel. Here they paused, waiting for a decision as to whether they should carry the war into North Korea and enable the United Nations to create a unified government for all of Korea. On October 1, the Red Chinese government warned that the Chinese would not tolerate the invasion of their North Korean neighbor by "imperialists." Was the Chinese premier, Chou Enlai, bluffing when he made this threat?

Invasion from Red China. After a series of indecisive battles, the Joint Chiefs of Staff in Washington on September 27, ordered MacArthur to pursue the North Koreans but not to penetrate Chinese territory. The United Nations Assembly approved this project on October 7. United Nations forces then crossed the border and headed for the Yalu River which marked the boundary with Manchuria. Later, they captured Pyongyang, the North Korean capital. MacArthur ordered a final offensive on November 24 to clear out the area as far as the river. Two days later a huge Chinese force crossed the Yalu River and attacked MacArthur's lines on the flank and rear. Chou Enlai was not bluffing.

The United Nations offensive was stopped. Through December the Chinese forced United Nations troops to withdraw from North Korea. Communist armies swept below the 38th parallel and occupied Seoul. In March, 1951, MacArthur's forces regrouped and launched a heroic counterattack. The Chinese were driven north and Seoul was recaptured for the second time. The two sides then dug in near the 38th parallel.

The Truman-MacArthur Controversy. Intervention by the Chinese caused a change in American public opinion. Although the majority of Americans had been in general agreement with the initial United Nations action in Korea, many of them now criticized the administration and demanded a withdrawal from what they called "Mr. Truman's War." Others took the opposite view and agreed with MacArthur's statement that "there is no substitute for victory," and they favored a direct attack on Communist China, even if it meant using the atomic bomb.

President Truman believed firmly that the greatest menace from communism lay in Europe, not in the Far East. He realized also that an all-out war with China would probably not be supported by the United Nations partners in Western Europe. He feared that Russia, bound by its alliance with China, might enter the conflict officially and provoke a third world war.

Consequently, Truman and the Joint Chiefs of Staff informed the outspoken MacArthur that it was American policy to secure South Korean independence and hold the line at the 38th parallel. General Omar Bradley, chairman of the Joint Chiefs, declared that an attack on China would be "the wrong war, at the wrong place, at the wrong time, and with the wrong enemy."

Recall of MacArthur. In March, 1951, MacArthur addressed a public statement to Joseph Martin, the House Republican leader. In it he demanded a general war against communism in the Far East. At this point the President lost patience with what he regarded as an attempt by a military leader to dictate government policy. Although he knew that the action against a popular hero would be severely criticized, he removed MacArthur from all command on April 11 and ordered him home. General Matthew B. Ridgway was ordered to take his place. In May the Senate Armed Forces Committee began an investigation of the conduct of the war and allowed MacArthur to state his views. Although they listened sympathetically, they ended by unanimously approving the administration's action and policy.

Back in Korea, the American forces under General Ridgway successfully beat off two Chinese offensives in April and May, inflicting terrible losses on the enemy. In June, 1951, the Russian delegate to the United Nations suggested that a cease-fire and armistice could be arranged. After the Chinese agreed, the President instructed Ridgway to open negotiations with the Communists.

Dwight D. Eisenhower served the U.S. as a general in World War II, as President from 1952–60, and as a political leader in the 1960's.

Armistice at Panmunjon. Peace talks began in July at Panmunjon, a neutralized spot near the 38th parallel. For two years exhausting negotiations with uncooperative Chinese and North Korean representatives continued. The armistice was finally settled in July, 1953. The boundary between the two parts of Korea was placed at the existing military line, somewhat south of the 38th parallel in the west, but considerably above it in the east. An exchange of prisoners was arranged, and means of enforcing the armistice were agreed upon. The Korean War ended in a stalemate, not a victory. The political future of Korea was not settled. Yet the intervention of the United Nations proved that the international organization could shoulder its responsibilities and stop aggression. This contrasted sharply with the power and responsibility of the League of Nations, which took no effective action to stop aggression anywhere.

In an effort to reassure the South Koreans that they would not be attacked again, the United States signed a mutual security treaty with them in October, 1953. Approved by the Senate in January, 1954, this treaty provided that each nation would consult with the other when danger threatened and that each would act in mutual support.

New Laurels for a General

As the presidential campaign of 1952 got under way, the Republicans were encouraged by the evident desire of the people for a change in the administration. Partly because of the unsatisfactory outcome of the Korean War and partly because the public distrusted some government officials, the voters were looking for new leaders.

At the Republican convention in Chicago the chief contenders for the presidential nomination were the able Senator Robert A. Taft and General Eisenhower. The general's personality and wartime reputation won him the nomination on the first ballot.

The Democratic convention saw a wide-open battle between a number of contenders since President Truman had announced that he did not wish to run again. After an exciting contest the Democrats nominated Governor Adlai Stevenson, an experienced and progressive administrator, the grandson of the Adlai Stevenson who had served as Vice-President in Cleveland's second administration.

The outstanding ability and high character of both candidates attracted voters to the polls in huge numbers. Eisenhower's personal popularity and his promise to go to Korea to help in achieving a quick and honorable peace won him the victory. He gathered approximately 33,824,000 votes against about 27,314,000 for Stevenson.

Divided Vietnam

One of the major problems facing the Eisenhower administration was the continuing war in Southeast Asia. In Indochina the French had been fighting since 1945 against the Communist Vietminh led by Ho Chi Minh. The ending of the Korean deadlock in 1952 enabled the Red Chinese to send aid across the border to the Vietminh.

Surrender at Dienbienphu. By the spring of 1954, Ho Chi Minh's forces were strong enough to attack the French and their Vietnamese allies at a frontier fortress named Dienbienphu (Dyen'byen'foo'). On May 7, 1954, the 12,000-man garrison surrendered and the Vietminh took over the northern part of the country.

The defeat of the French was also a blow to the United States, which had supported the French with money and materials, but not with troops. If the Communists won control of all of

Indochina, it was feared that eventually Burma, Malaya, Indonesia, and Thailand would succumb to the Reds.

Armistice in Southeast Asia. At a nineteen-nation conference in Geneva in July, 1954, an armistice was arranged. It provided for the independence of Cambodia and Laos, but permitted both the French and the Communists to keep small armed units in the latter country. Vietnam was divided near the 17th parallel, much as Korea had been divided at the 38th; the Communists occupied the north, the other side the south. As time went on the Americans gradually took over French responsibilities in South Vietnam.

A Network of Treaties

By the time Dienbienphu fell, the United States had signed a number of treaties aimed at containing communism in the Far East. In the fall of 1951, security treaties were concluded with Japan and the Philippines. In September, 1951, Washington made a defense pact with Australia and New Zealand. It was known as the ANZUS Pact, from the initials of the three countries. A mutual defense pact was made with Chiang Kai-shek's Nationalist government on Formosa at the end of 1954.

SEATO. The partial victory of the Communists in Indochina was a warning that the defense network needed further bracing. At a conference in Manila in 1954, Secretary of State Dulles succeeded in building a Southeast Asia Treaty Organization (SEATO). It was an Asian version of NATO but not as strong. Although it

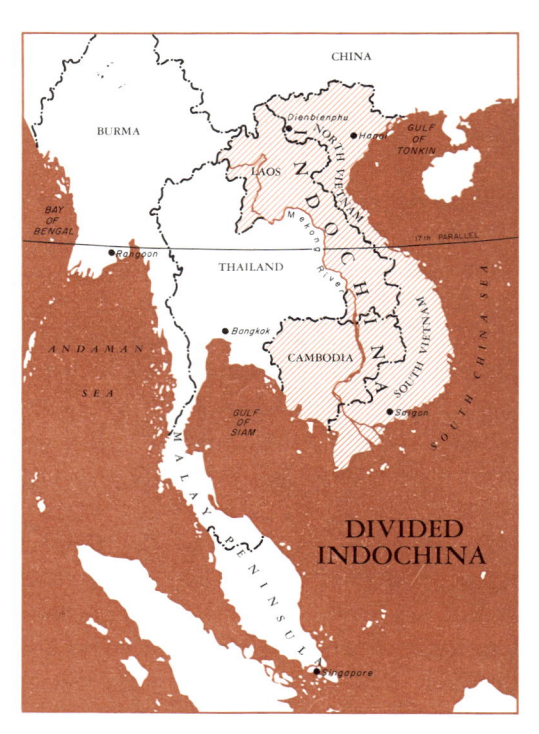

Southeast Asia has been a world "trouble spot" for several years. What problems exist there today? Have they been solved?

was designed for the protection of Southeast Asia, only three nations in that area joined it—the Philippines, Thailand, and Pakistan. Agreements made at the Geneva conference prevented Laos, Cambodia, and Vietnam from joining. India, Burma, Ceylon, and Indonesia insisted on remaining neutral. The five remaining members of the eight-nation organization were the United States, Great Britain, France, New Zealand, and Australia.

Communism on the March. Although SEATO paved the way for rendering military and economic aid, it did not stop the infiltrations of communism. Red China continued to make threatening gestures at Formosa. Communist guerrillas operated in the Malay peninsula, although they were suppressed by 1957, when Malaya won independence from Great Britain. In the Philippines the government had difficulty in crushing a Communist-led terrorist group known as the Huks. In Indonesia the Communists became powerful in the labor movement and were a constant threat to the stability of the government.

Looking Back

1. How did China fall to the Communists? Do you feel most Chinese wanted communism? Explain.
2. Compare the treatment of Japan at the end of World War II with that of Germany at the end of World War I.
3. What were the causes of the Korean War?
4. Give the background for and the results of the Geneva Conference of 1954 to settle affairs in Southeast Asia.
5. How did the United States act to "contain" communism by forming ANZUS and SEATO?

Summit Conference, Geneva, Switzerland, 1955. Hopes were high for peace. (left to right) Soviet Prime Minister Bulganin, President Eisenhower, French Premier Faure, Britain's Eden.

4. The Kremlin Changes Its Approach

After Stalin died in March, 1953, the Kremlin apparently intended to relax the tensions which were leading to war. Examples of the softening of Soviet policy were the decisions to make peace with Japan, to end the military occupation of Austria, and to admit limited numbers of Americans behind the Iron Curtain. Perhaps, too, the Russians feared an atomic war, since both the Soviet Union and the United States knew how to make deadly hydrogen bombs. In any case, conditions seemed ripe for a friendly meeting of the leaders of the Big Four (Great Britain, France, Russia, and United States) at Geneva in the summer of 1955.

A Meeting at the "Summit"

The whole world watched the "Summit Conference" (so named because the highest-ranking world leaders would attend), with great interest. Perhaps a way could be found to avoid the horrors of atomic warfare and bring peace to the world! President Eisenhower, by his straightforward and sincere manner, made a favorable impression on the Soviets when he arrived at Geneva. He astonished the delegates when he proposed that the United States and Russia exchange blueprints of their military establishments and take aerial photographs of each other's country.

Although the "spirit of Geneva" was friendly, the conference produced little of value. Important matters such as disarmament, trade relations, and the unification of Germany were left undecided. Not long afterwards, Nikita Khrushchev, the new Russian premier, was proclaiming that communism was bound to succeed and that "peaceful competition" with capitalism would end in a world-wide Communist victory.

Revolt in Hungary

In 1956 a wave of unrest arose in Poland and Hungary. In the latter country an October revolt of workers in Budapest displaced the Moscow-dominated government and put Prime Minister Imre Nagy in power. Washington was pleased by this development and offered to give economic aid to the new government. The liberty-loving Hungarians boldly told Moscow that they would withdraw from the Warsaw Pact which bound them to the Soviet Union. They also declared their neutrality in the "cold war."

In 1956, the Hungarian freedom fighters resisted the Soviets in any way they could, resorting to paving stones and homemade bombs.

The "Freedom Fighters." With typical brutality the Russians crushed this bid for freedom. In November thousands of Russian troops invaded the country under the protection of heavy tanks. Mercilessly they mowed down the unarmed patriots who opposed them and set up a puppet government which bowed to the will of Moscow. Later, they executed Imre Nagy.

U. S. Reaction. Americans were horrified by the cruelty of the Soviets and angrily questioned why the United States did not come to the rescue of the Hungarian "Freedom Fighters." Most of them came to realize, however, that armed intervention would almost certainly have led to a world war. Washington had to content itself with lifting the immigration bars in order to admit thousands of Hungarian refugees.

A Hollow Victory. The butchery in Hungary also caused the United Nations to lose prestige, for the Kremlin ignored the resolutions of the General Assembly which condemned the Russian action, and refused to admit U.N. investigators to enter the unhappy country. The Soviets, although they retained their hold on Hungary, won a hollow victory. All over the world, even in neutralist countries like India, there was a rising chorus of protest against this brutality by a nation which professed to believe in peace and democracy.

Trouble in the Middle East

Suez Crisis. In the same year as the Hungarian Revolution, Egypt's President Nasser decided that the time had come to take over the Suez Canal. The canal had been operated by a private company for many years, and was as important to trade between Europe and Asia as the Panama Canal was to trade between Pacific countries and Atlantic countries. Naturally, the countries who made much use of the Suez Canal were very distressed at this turn of events. They were accustomed to doing business with a private concern, and many wondered what would happen to their rights if Nasser took over the canal.

Border Dispute. At the same time, tempers were flaring between Israel and Nasser's country of Egypt. The border between the two countries was an area of extreme dispute. When the Suez Canal crisis was at its peak, Israel, seemingly supported by Great Britain, and France, launched an unexpected attack on Egypt. British and French troops rushed to the area to protect their interests, siding with Israel. The United Nations General Assembly decided it was time to act. Supported by United States policy, it requested Great Britain, France, and Israel to withdraw their troops, which they all did, and called for a cease-fire supervised by a United Nations security force. The U.N. practically settled the entire dispute.

Eisenhower's Aid. As a result of all this, Congress gave President Eisenhower in 1957 the right to help protect any Middle Eastern nation which asked for help against any nation controlled by international communism. It had been feared that Soviet Russia would use disturbances in the Middle East to spread communism throughout nations in trouble. American forces could ensure that this was not done by the Communists. For example, in 1958 they were sent to Lebanon to ensure the survival and independence of that little nation. Communist gains in the Middle East have been small ever since.

Looking Back

1. How did Russia show signs of a change in policy before the summit conference of 1955?
2. Why, in your opinion, did we fail to go to the aid of the Hungarian "Freedom Fighters"?
3. In what ways did the Russians both win and lose by putting down the revolt?
4. What were the causes for the attack on Egypt by Britain, France, and Israel in 1956?
5. Describe the action taken by the United Nations to end the fighting and by the United States to prevent future fighting in the Middle East.

The Chapter in Perspective

Who Are These People?

Wallace	Chou Enlai
Chiang Kai-shek	Ridgway
Mao Tse-tung	Eisenhower
MacArthur	Stevenson
Nasser	Khrushchev

Where Are These Places?

Dumbarton Oaks	Yalu River
San Francisco	Panmunjon
Formosa	Vietnam
38th Parallel	Geneva
Korea	17th parallel
Dienbienphu	Suez Canal

What Do These Dates and Terms Mean?

Charter of the United Nations	1949	Warsaw Alliance
Japanese Peace Treaty	1950	1954
1944	propaganda	1956
1945	"iron curtain"	Berlin Blockade
veto power	1951	NATO
Security Council	1952	Dixiecrats
Economic and Social Council	General Assembly	"police action"
1947	Trusteeship Council	ANZUS
1948	subversive activities	SEATO
International Court of Justice	Truman Doctrine	Secretariat
Geneva summit conference	Marshall Plan	Hungarian Revolt
"Cold War"	satellites	

Questions for Study

1. "We, the people of the United Nations, determined to save succeeding generations from the scourge of war. . . ." is part of the preamble to the Charter of the United Nations organization. Tell why you feel this aim has or has not been accomplished.

2. What steps has Russia taken to spread communism since World War II?

3. What steps has the United States taken to contain communism since World War II?

4. Opponents of the Marshall Plan state that we poured billions of dollars into Europe to rebuild competition for the United States. Tell why you agree or disagree.

5. What factors brought about the Berlin Blockade? How did the Allies gain their victory?

6. Why was the Korean situation the gravest challenge faced by the United Nations until that time?

7. What, in your opinion, would have been the course of events if Russia had been present in the Security Council to veto U. N. intervention?

8. What similarities can you find in the Vietnam situation that were present in Korea?

9. On a map of Asia, locate and name all the Asian countries mentioned in this chapter.

10. On a map of the world, color with different colors the members of NATO, SEATO, ANZUS, and the Warsaw Alliance.

Place Yourself in History

General Douglas MacArthur occupied a unique place in American history. He was an outstanding military leader who dedicated his life to serving his nation. In World War I, World War II, and the Korean War he performed many brilliant feats. And yet, in April, 1951, President Truman removed General MacArthur from his command and replaced him with General Ridgway. The "Great Debate" as to which policies to follow had been settled.

What policies were being debated? What were the arguments used by both sides? Whom would you have supported? Why?

30

The Uneasy Fifties

The 1950's and early 1960's saw progress and changes in the domestic life of America. It was a period of general prosperity and well being. Laws were passed to provide greater security for jobholders, to protect the rights of minority groups, and to care for health needs. Americans had more leisure to enjoy the material things of life that were being produced in great abundance. There were, of course, many improvements to be made in our society, but on the whole America looked forward with confidence and eagerness to the coming Age of Space. There was one great source of uneasiness—the fear that the tensions between the Communist World and the Free World might result in war.

1. Domestic Concerns Dominate Eisenhower's First Term

President Eisenhower was the thirty-third President of the United States, one of a number of military men to fill that post. An immensely popular hero of World War II, Eisenhower had been asked by both parties to become a candidate for President. In 1952, he made his choice; he ran as a Republican. Since he had been a military man all his life, he had, up until 1952, no strong party ties, and in general his administration reflected a bipartisan standpoint.

A Bipartisan Program

Some of President Eisenhower's programs were those that had been supported by Republican administrations in the past. For example, he wished to balance the budget and to reduce the number of federal employees. Like all Presidents, Democratic and Republican, he wished to prevent corruption or disloyalty in government. Also, some of his policies were associated with those of the Democratic party. He favored extending Social Security benefits to cover an additional ten million citizens. He wanted to increase unemployment compensation. He asked Congress to appropriate federal funds for highways, while most Republicans favored the use of state and local funds. Also, unlike the Republican administrations of the twenties, he favored lowering the tariff on imports, thus creating a more flexible trade between the United States and other nations. In most of his programs, Eisenhower exercised the powers of the federal government in the areas of welfare and foreign affairs. Also, he favored many of the reforms of the New Deal and he tried to improve upon them.

Labor Under Eisenhower

During Eisenhower's first term the country was generally prosperous, except for the farmers. Farming methods had become so efficient that great crop surpluses had piled up, resulting in lower prices. Thousands of small growers, unable to compete with their larger neighbors, left their farms and sought jobs in the cities. Industrial laborers, however, were able to better their lot. Several large industries made concessions to labor unions which helped to fatten the pay envelopes of the workers.

A. F. L. - C. I. O. Merger. In December, 1955, the American Federation of Labor and the Congress of Industrial Organizations patched up their quarrel, which had begun twenty years before, and merged in a vast "union of unions"—the A.F.L.-C.I.O. This resulted in a great increase in the power of organized labor.

Huge grain elevators, such as these in Nebraska, are necessary to store America's gigantic grain crops. These particular elevators have a capacity of 7.5 million bushels.

The Teamsters. The Teamsters Union, headed by David Beck, soon came under the fire of a Senate investigation of labor racketeering. Beck was charged with using union funds for his own private purposes. The evidence against him was so strong that he could not be re-elected as president of the union. The members elected James Hoffa, who was also under attack by the Senate committee.

Because of their refusal to clean house by getting rid of undesirable officers and because of their use of violence in labor disputes, the Teamsters were expelled from the A.F.L.-C.I.O. in 1957.

Objections to Taft-Hartley Act. In June, 1947, Congress had passed the *Taft-Hartley Act* over President Truman's veto. This act was designed to reduce the power of labor unions and prevent dishonesty in labor relations. It forbade the *closed shop* contract, which prevented employers from hiring non-union workers. It also forbade unions to charge unreasonably high initiation fees, to use union funds in political campaigns, or to elect officers who had refused to sign an oath that they were not members of the Communist party. The act also enabled the President to get an *injunction* (court order) to enforce an eighty-day "cooling-off" period whenever a strike threatened to do harm to the nation's economy.

It can be easily seen why labor leaders disliked the Taft-Hartley Act. They especially resented the requirement that they sign a non-Communist oath, since the employers were not required to sign such an oath. Those who defended the act argued that labor unions needed to be curbed in the same way in which the Wagner Act of 1935 curbed the anti-union policies of employers. In any case, Congress took no action to amend the Taft-Hartley

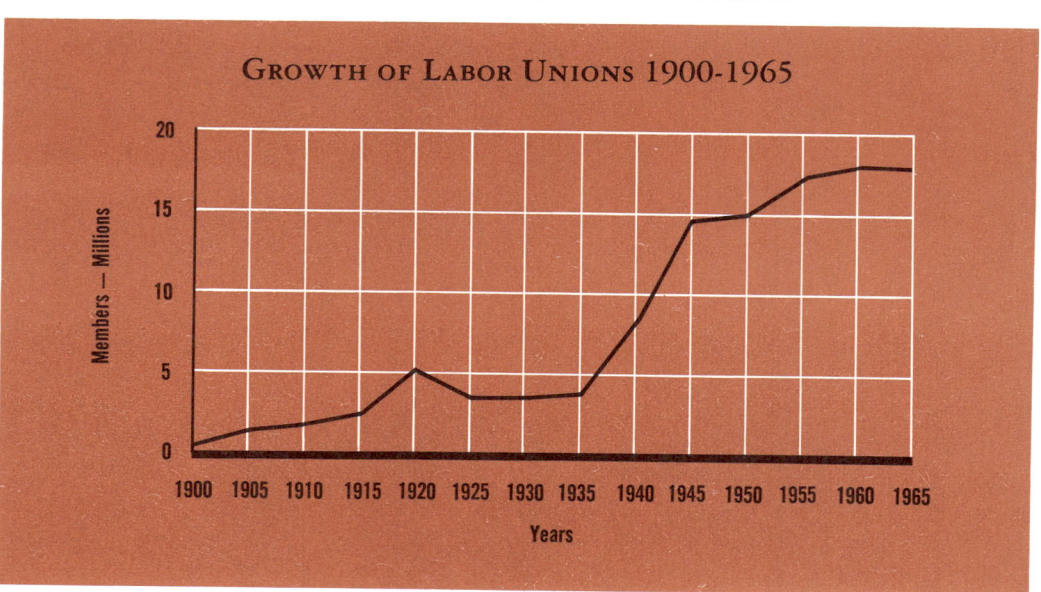

Why has union membership leveled off since 1955?

GROWTH OF LABOR UNIONS 1900-1965

Act, even though President Eisenhower thought it advisable.

Subversion and the Senator

It is important for any government to ensure that all of its officials are loyal and careful of the welfare of the country. It is just as important that no citizen be charged with disloyalty merely because he does not agree with the majority. The problem of protecting the nation from subversive activities was one which faced both the Truman and the Eisenhower administrations.

Security Checks. In 1946 President Truman set up a commission to investigate the loyalty of government employees and to plan a system of carrying on investigations and of providing fair hearings for accused persons. Early the following year, loyalty boards conducted widespread investigations of government employees, especially those in key positions. By 1951 more than three million employees had been cleared of any suspicion of subversive activity. About two hundred were dismissed as "bad security risks"—in other words, people who could not be trusted to serve the best interests of the United States.

McCarthy's Measures. As the "cold war" went on, it became apparent that extreme vigilance was needed to prevent Communist subversion. The Eisenhower administration continued the Truman program of investigation. A leader in the security program was Senator Joseph R. McCarthy of Wisconsin, who had figured in the loyalty investigations during Truman's administration and

Senator Robert A. Taft, 1889–1953, was a conscientious and brilliant senator from Ohio. He was known as Mr. Republican.

who continued to pursue the matter after Eisenhower was elected.

The methods of McCarthy and his agents were so violent and reckless that many Americans who had supported him began to turn away from him. In congressional hearings shown on television he accused the Secretary of War of "coddling Communists" and made unsupported accusations against other individuals and groups. Although most of McCarthy's accusations were emotional and without cause, many innocent people were permanently smeared. Had McCarthy not been a senator, his accusations would have carried little weight. However, he used his high office to give vent to his own personal feelings. By doing this he ignored his duty as a high official and a citizen.

Censure of McCarthy. Finally the Senate took the unusual action of

Senator Joseph McCarthy and his aide Roy Cohn listen to testimony in the *Army* vs. *McCarthy* hearing.

charging him with conduct that tended to bring the Senate into disrepute. In December, 1954, the Senate voted, 67 to 22, to condemn the conduct of a fellow member. McCarthy's influence then declined rapidly. There can be no defense of his unfair and undemocratic methods, other than that they did focus the attention of the nation on the problem of Communist infiltration and subversion.

Progress in Civil Rights

The decade following the end of World War II saw a marked attempt to improve racial relations in America, especially as far as educational opportunities for Negroes were concerned.

The "Separate But Equal" Doctrine. For years the National Association for the Advancement of Colored People (made up of both colored and white people) had tried to obtain a reversal of a Supreme Court decision made in 1896 (*Plessy* vs. *Ferguson*). This 1896 decision said that Negroes and white people should have school buildings and grounds which were equal, but that they need not go to school together. This decision interpreted a statement in the Fourteenth Amendment that no person should be denied "the equal protection of the law" to mean that "separate but equal" public facilities (such as schools and transportation) could be furnished to Negroes.

Finally, in May, 1954, the Supreme Court unanimously reversed the earlier decision. In the case of *Brown* vs. *Board of Education of Topeka* they ruled that "in the field of public education the doctrine of *separate but equal* has no place." In other words, they held that segregation of Negro school children violated the Fourteenth Amendment.

Integration of Schools. The decision in the case of *Brown* vs. *Board of Education of Topeka* was widely praised as an answer to Communist propaganda that American democracy did not extend to racial minorities. However, some people in the South and in several border states—as well as some in the North—protested that the federal government was interfering in education, a field in which the states should have authority. In some communities in the South, mob action took place against integration, and every possible legal maneuver was made to prevent integrated schools. Nevertheless, the process of desegregation went on, and the federal government wisely refrained from forcing the issue, hoping that respect for law and democratic ideals would gradually win. The problem has not yet been settled, and people on both sides continue to debate it.

Decreasing Discrimination. In areas other than education, efforts were made to lessen racial discrimination. The armed forces were desegregated. Anti-discrimination laws were passed dealing with segregated housing and unfair employment practices. In August, 1957, Congress passed a civil rights law to give federal protection to Negroes who wanted to register to vote. Gradually the promises of democratic rights and privileges made in the Constitution are being fulfilled.

A Second Eisenhower Triumph

In September, 1955, President Eisenhower suffered a heart attack while vacationing in Colorado. He recovered rapidly, however, much to the relief of the nation and particularly of Republican party leaders who believed that he was the only one who could lead them to victory in 1956. At their convention in August, the Republicans renominated Eisenhower and Vice-President Nixon, and offered a platform advocating what was called a "Modern Republicanism."

The Democrats, after a struggle between supporters of Senator Estes Kefauver and Adlai Stevenson, chose the latter as their standard-bearer. The party's platform called for repeal of the Taft-Hartley Act, expanded welfare programs, and aid for the farmers. It also called for integration of schools. After a contest with Senator John F.

Brown vs. Board of Education of Topeka; *excerpt from the opinion of the Supreme Court of the United States regarding segregation in the schools, delivered by Earl Warren, Chief Justice.*

[Education] is the very foundation of good citizenship. Today it is a principal instrument in awakening the child to cultural values, in preparing him for later professional training, and in helping him to adjust normally to his environment. In these days it is doubtful that any child may reasonably be expected to succeed in life if he is denied the opportunity of an education. Such an opportunity . . . is a right which must be made available to all on equal terms.

We come then to the question presented: Does segregation of children in public schools solely on the basis of race, even though the physical facilities and other 'tangible' factors may be equal, deprive the children of the minority group of equal educational opportunities? We believe that it does.

Dwight D. Eisenhower and his running-mate, Richard Nixon, during their 1952 Presidential campaign. They won easily.

Kennedy of Massachusetts, Kefauver was chosen as the Vice-Presidential candidate.

On November 6, the American people gave Eisenhower an overwhelming vote of confidence. His victory was even more decisive than in 1952, both in the popular and the electoral vote. The Republican triumph was a tribute to the President's personal popularity. However, it did not extend to other Republican candidates, since the Democrats won majorities in both houses of Congress.

Looking Back

1. What steps were taken by organized labor to increase its power and public image?
2. Explain organized labor's objections to the Taft-Hartley Act.
3. Why did most Americans consider "McCarthyism" worse than the evils it sought to eliminate?
4. How did *Brown* vs. *Board of Education of Topeka* affect American education?
5. For what reasons was Eisenhower's victory in 1956 called a "personal victory"?

2. Foreign Affairs Fill the Late Fifties

Changing Areas of Tension

In the spring of 1957 it became obvious that Communist and anti-Western elements were gaining ground in the Middle East. Fearing Russian aggression in this oil-rich area, President Eisenhower asked Congress for permission to extend military and economic aid to Middle East nations in order to help them maintain their independence. However, nations in the

Middle East who were powerful enough not to need American help resented American aid to their less fortunate neighbors. Led by President Nasser of Egypt these powerful countries opposed American attempts to guarantee the independence of the smaller nations, and war seemed imminent. Russia supported Nasser, and the major world powers were lining up against one another.

In the United Nations the Russians vetoed a British-American proposal that the U.N. undertake the task of protecting small Middle Eastern countries, and Khrushchev made his usual threats of war. Eventually this dangerous situation became stabilized. In August, the United Nations General Assembly unanimously adopted a resolution to the effect that no Arab state should attack or plot against its neighbors. Reassured by the U.N.'s arrangements to provide security for Lebanon and Jordan, the British and American troops were withdrawn two months later.

Quemoy and Matsu. The Middle East was not the only area of tension involving the United States. In August, 1958, the Red Chinese heavily bombarded the offshore islands of Quemoy and Matsu, where Chiang Kai-shek had stationed a strong Nationalist garrison. The U.S. Navy escorted Chiang Kai-shek's reinforcements to the islands, but took no further action. The Red Chinese guns quieted down after Secretary Dulles stated that the United States had made no promises to help Chiang Kai-shek recover the Chinese mainland.

Berlin Again. The Berlin crisis flared up again on November 17, 1958, when Khrushchev sent a note to Great Britain, France, and the United States stating that the three governments must get out of Berlin within six months or recognize and deal with the Communist East German government. The Russians also refused to permit the union of East and West Germany by means of free elections. As an added threatening gesture the

When Vice-President Nixon visited Venezuela in 1958, he was subjected to egg-throwing, hostile mobs. In this picture Venezuela troops prepare to protect his car.

Russians renewed their tests of nuclear weapons and refused to agree to international control of outer space explorations.

Troubled Neighbors to the South

In Latin America the people had been suffering from hunger and poverty since the end of World War II. Their raw materials did not command as high prices as they once did before the war; they had little capital for development of their industries; and their population was increasing at a dangerous rate.

Unfriendly Welcome for a Vice-President. Although the United States had tried to be a Good Neighbor and to aid Latin America, our neighbors to the south felt neglected as they watched billions of United States dollars flow into Europe and Asia. They began to blame Uncle Sam for many of their social and economic troubles. Well-trained Latin American Communists quickly took advantage of the hostility of the people toward the United States and promoted riots and disorders. In May, 1958, Vice-President Nixon, while on a friendly visit to eight Latin American countries, was given a hostile reception in many cities. In Caracas and Lima he and his wife were in considerable danger from angry mobs that surrounded them.

The Inter-American Bank. This treatment shocked the United States, and the State Department hastened to review its Latin American policy. The United States joined with Latin American countries to set up an Inter-American Bank to speed development and furnish credit. Ways were explored to increase the flow of trade among Western Hemisphere nations. The United States tried to gain more friends in Latin America.

Castro and Communism in Cuba. It was evident that new policies must be made to deal with rapidly changing Latin America, especially since Communist activities spread quickly among the masses of discontented people. Communists were particularly successful in the case of Cuba, where Fidel Castro and his followers overthrew the dictator Batista in January, 1959. A hint of Castro's later adoption of communism could be seen in the fact that he quickly made a trade pact with Russia and in 1960 invited Khrushchev to visit Cuba.

A Democratic Landslide in 1958

Toward the close of 1957 a noticeable recession took place in business.

The state of Alaska contributes much to the cultural mixture of the United States. The Sun Raven totem pole near Ketchikan is a fine example of Indian totem carving.

Industrial production dropped, and by the summer of 1958 about five million workers were unemployed. Several scandals in Washington involving members of the President's party were revealed. American foreign policy did not seem to result in significant gains. For these reasons the voters turned against the party in power and handed the Democrats a landslide victory, the most impressive since the Roosevelt landslide in 1936. Democrats won 13 Senate seats from Republicans and gained 47 seats in the House of Representatives.

Alaska and Hawaii

Two new states entered the Union in 1959—Alaska and Hawaii. The purchase of Alaska by Secretary of State William Seward in 1867 had been considered foolish by many. It was called "Seward's Folly" or "Seward's Icebox," because its only visible assets were snow and ice. However, when gold was discovered there in 1896, Alaska became a valuable possession. The Alaska fishing industry also became important to the American consumer.

On January 3, 1959, the President proclaimed Alaska the 49th state, and its two senators, Edward L. Bartlett and Ernest Gruening, and one representative, Ralph J. Rivers, prepared to take their seats in Congress.

Hawaii, once a kingdom, then an independent republic, then a territory of the United States, finally became the 50th state on August 21, 1959, just forty years after the first statehood bill was introduced in Congress. The islanders elected to the Senate a former territorial governor, Oren E. Long, and a lawyer and former legislator, Hiram L. Fong. Fong was the first Chinese-American ever to serve in the Senate. For their lone representative, the islanders chose Daniel K. Inouye, the first American of Japanese ancestry ever to hold membership in the House.

The Space Age

Sputniks and Luniks. The Age of Space began on October 4, 1957, when the Soviet Union launched the first man-made satellite, which they called Sputnik I. This 184-pound sphere circled the earth about every 1½ hours at altitudes ranging from about 140 miles to 560 miles above the earth. A month later the Russians launched Sputnik II, weighing 1120 pounds, and carrying the world's first space passenger—a live dog named Laika.

In the next four years the United States launched more than three times as many satellites as did the Soviet Union, but the Russians achieved more spectacular results. On January 4, 1959, Lunik I—the first man-made planet—was put into orbit around the sun by the Soviets. In September the Russian Lunik II hit the moon. In October their Lunik III circled the moon and radioed to earth photographs of the moon's dark side.

American Scientific Successes. In the meantime, the United States was moving ahead of the Soviet Union in perfecting intercontinental ballistic missiles (ICBM) and in constructing atomic-powered submarines which could launch missiles and cruise underwater for long periods of time.

The American space program is accomplishing wonders in weather

The *Alexander Hamilton*, a Polaris atomic submarine, can stay under water for great lengths of time, traveling at a higher speed than many surface vessels. In the sketch above, the location of the atomic reactor is shown. Nuclear submarines play an important role in the defense of the nation.

predicting and communications satellites. Its military research has aided the struggle for scientific control of space also, since Americans learned how to send increasingly larger amounts of weight (payloads) into space.

An Easing of "Cold War" Tensions

In early 1959, John Foster Dulles, Secretary of State under President Eisenhower, was forced by a serious illness to give up his duties. He died in May and Christian A. Herter, Acting Secretary of State, was selected by Eisenhower as Dulles' successor. Herter, an experienced diplomat and former governor of Massachusetts, worked closely with the President in an effort to solve the deadlock between the Russians and the West.

Cultural Exchanges. Although the heads of state in Russia and the United States found it difficult to come to any real agreement, both countries sponsored personal visits of individuals and groups. There was considerable interchange of students, artists, and musicians. These visits helped the people from each country to understand better the culture and problems of the other.

Top-Level Visits. In the summer of 1959, Anastas Mikoyan, a deputy premier of the Soviet Union, was invited to visit America, and Vice-President Nixon made a courtesy trip to Moscow. In both countries the distinguished visitors were well received by the people.

In August, 1959, President Eisenhower announced that there would be an exchange of visits between himself and Premier Khrushchev. The Russian leader appeared to enjoy his visit and was much interested in various aspects of American life. Eisenhower delayed his return visit while he made a good will tour of Western Europe, Latin America, and Southern Asia.

In the spring of 1960, a number of personal contacts and visits took place among Soviet and Western leaders in preparation for an East-West meeting. The meeting was scheduled to take place in Paris in May between American, Russian, English, and French heads of state.

The "U-2" Incident

On May 1, 1960, an American U-2 plane was shot down near Sverdlovsk in central Russia. It was later determined that the plane was making one of a series of very high altitude reconnaissance flights conducted by the United States over Soviet territory. The administration in Washington at first denied that the plane was on a spy mission, but on May 7, the State Department admitted that the plane was "endeavoring to obtain information now concealed behind the Iron Curtain"—in other words, spying. A few days later President Eisenhower defended the flight at a press conference, stating: "No one wants another Pearl Harbor. This means that we must have knowledge of military forces and preparations around the world, especially those capable of massive surprise attack."

The Soviet reaction to the incident was extremely violent. At the opening session of the Paris "summit" conference on May 16, Premier Khrushchev refused to take part until the United States apologized for the flight. Despite the efforts of Prime Minister Macmillan of Great Britain and President de Gaulle of France, the conference collapsed and the delegates left Paris. At the same time Khrushchev withdrew his invitation for the President's visit to Moscow, which had been scheduled for June.

Cooperation with Japan

After World War II, the defense of Japan became the responsibility of the United States, since the Japanese armed forces had been destroyed, and the new Japanese constitution prohibited the raising of regular military forces. The Korean War, however, led the Japanese to create a Self-Defense Force. This force was later made into a regular defense establishment as the Japanese economy became stronger. As the Red Chinese and the Soviets adopted a more hostile attitude in the Far East, the Japanese decided that they should strengthen their defenses in partnership with the United States.

A Mutual Security Treaty. A new treaty of mutual cooperation was signed by the two nations in January, 1960. It provided for a partnership to resist armed attack, for economic aid, and for the use of Japanese facilities by the American land, air, and naval forces. The Soviet Union protested strongly against the treaty, and radical and Communist groups in Japan led massive riots in an effort to prevent its signing.

Anti-U. S. Sentiment. As part of his tour of the Far East, President Eisenhower had planned to visit Japan when the treaty was ready for ratification by the Japanese Diet (parliament). When he reached Manila, however, he was warned that Japanese radicals had gotten out of hand and that the Japanese security forces could not control them. As a result, his visit was canceled. The administration of Premier Nobusuke Kishi was able to put the unpopular treaty into effect, but Kishi was forced to resign.

This development, together with the U-2 incident, led to a serious decline in American prestige abroad, and the "cold war" entered a new and uneasy stage.

Looking Back

1. For what reasons were Quemoy and Matsu projected into international prominence?

2. What factors caused a loss of American prestige in Latin America?

3. Show how the Russians won an early lead in the "race for space."

4. How did Khrushchev's visit to America help calm world tensions?

5. Discuss the factors that worked against a visit to Moscow by Eisenhower.

The Chapter in Perspective

Who Are These People?

McCarthy
Nixon
Herter
Castro

What Do These Dates and Terms Mean?

AFL-CIO
1896
closed shop
injunction
1954
integration
1956
1955
1959
civil rights
Sputnik
Lunik
U-2 incident
Taft-Hartley Act

Paris summit conference

Inter-American Bank

Plessy vs. *Ferguson*

Brown vs. *Board of Education of Topeka*

Questions for Study

1. In what ways did Eisenhower's policies indicate a bipartisan approach?

2. Discuss the causes for the Senate's unusual action in censuring Senator McCarthy.

3. Why, in your opinion, was the Supreme Court's decision in the *Brown* vs. *Board of Education* case unpopular in the South?

4. By what actions did the United States, Britain, and the United Nations seek to avoid warfare in the Middle East?

5. What significance would you attach to the admission of Alaska and Hawaii as states?

6. Do you believe that cultural exchanges help lessen international tensions? Why?

7. Locate the "hot spots" of the Cold War discussed in this chapter and discuss the importance of each.

Place Yourself in History

You are a member of the diplomatic corps of the United States in a major European capital. The U-2 incident has had great publicity. First denied by your government, the State Department and then President Eisenhower finally admitted that the plane was on a spying mission. Now you have been called to the foreign ministry for a report.

What would you say? How could you justify the actions taken by your government?

America Moves Ahead in the Sixties

31

The beginning of the 1960's saw the mood and direction of the American nation shift. The oldest president in American history, Dwight Eisenhower, was replaced by the youngest ever to be elected, John F. Kennedy. The new president was the first of the Roman Catholic faith to hold the post of chief executive. In many ways the bands of prejudice were slowly but noticeably being loosened throughout the nation. In American relationships with the rest of the world, the prospects of peace glowed more brightly. In a more peaceful world, Americans would have more freedom to explore man's newest frontiers, the depths of the ocean, and the far reaches of outer space.

1. National Affairs Concern Americans

The Election of 1960

The election of 1960, in which Senator John F. Kennedy defeated Vice-President Richard Nixon, was unique. There had been close elections in the past, when the United States had a smaller population and almost all elections were decided by a relatively small number of votes. However, in no election had the candidates run such a close race for the popular vote. President Kennedy won by only 119,000 votes, less than one fourth of one percent of sixty-eight million cast. Both candidates were under the age of fifty, another first in the history of presidential elections.

Television played a decisive role in the outcome of the presidential election. Meeting in a series of four face-to-face debates on national television, the two candidates outlined their positions on important questions of the day. It was generally felt that televi-

Senator Kennedy (left) and Vice-President Nixon (right) participated in a major "first" for a Presidential campaign. Millions of Americans watched them debate on television.

sion helped Senator Kennedy and hurt Vice-President Nixon. Before the debates, few Americans outside of his native New England had seen or heard Senator Kennedy speak, whereas all were familiar with the Vice-President of the preceding eight years. After the television debates, Senator Kennedy was as well-known as his opponent. In the debates, Senator Kennedy assumed the role of prosecutor; he asked many questions of Vice-President Nixon and managed to cast blame for many of the inevitable mistakes of the past on him. In addition, Senator Kennedy was a handsome and witty man, and this influenced many voters who hadn't seen him before. All these things contributed to an election victory for the Democratic candidate.

The New Frontier

Legislative Progress. During the period between his election and inauguration, President-elect Kennedy spelled out his proposals for legislative and presidential action, calling his program "The New Frontier." His proposed program included such items as additional Federal aid to education, a plan of medical care for the aged, a Peace Corps to aid emerging and backward nations, and an Alliance for Progress among North and South American nations. President Kennedy was also known to place Civil Rights for every American high on his list of necessary legislation.

Success of the New Frontier. President Kennedy was not entirely successful in getting his legislation through the Congress. The Peace Corps became a reality soon after his inauguration, but other proposals, such as medical care for the aged, did not pass the Congress in President Kennedy's lifetime. In foreign affairs, however, President Kennedy scored a number of triumphs.

He signed into law the first treaty in the history of the world banning the testing of nuclear weapons. He also stood as an example of courage to his countrymen in winning a showdown with Chairman Khrushchev of the Soviet Union during the Cuban missile crisis. He encouraged limited trade with the Soviet bloc, an event which many American businessmen welcomed.

History and the Arts. Aside from his interest in legislative matters, President Kennedy shared with his wife, Jacqueline, an interest in history and a deep and lasting attachment to the arts. Three years previously, while he was a senator, Mr. Kennedy had received the Pulitzer Prize for *Profiles in Courage,* a book of biographies of great Americans. It was natural, therefore, that he should have a sense of history in his new role.

Mrs. Kennedy set about revitalizing the historical values to be found in the White House and turning it into a great national home. She searched the cellars of the old building to find much of the furniture used by past presidents and their wives. She also conducted a country-wide search for antiques and art objects which had once had a place in the White House. Successful in this, she turned her attention to the social responsibilities of the President and herself, scheduling performances by leading musical and dramatic artists to entertain visiting dignitaries. An indication of President Kennedy's own interest in the arts was seen at his inauguration. There Robert Frost, a beloved American poet, recited one of his poems.

The Assassination of President Kennedy

President Kennedy's term of office came to a sudden and tragic end during a visit to Dallas, Texas, on November 22, 1963, when he was assassinated by a sniper using a high-powered rifle. Within a matter of minutes, he was pronounced dead at a nearby hospital. The assassination of the young, popular American President, survived by his wife and two young children, left the entire nation stricken with shock and grief.

World Reaction. From millions of Americans and from people all over

President Kennedy was the first President in more than fifty years to have a young, growing family living in the White House. His wife Jacqueline, his daughter Caroline, and his son John all won places of affection in the hearts of the nation. This picture was taken on Easter Sunday after the family had attended church services. The occasion was only six months before the young President was assassinated.

the world came messages of sympathy and regret. Kennedy's steadfast pursuit of a test-ban treaty earned him the respect and affection of people all over the world. On his visits to Europe, his charm and personality had captured the imagination of many Europeans. To them he was a symbol of all that America could be, and the embodiment of its strength, its youth, and its vigor. Chiefs of state from dozens of countries were present at his funeral in Washington, and throughout the United States and the world, people gathered about television sets to watch the ceremony and to pay their respect to a man they admired.

The Succession. Vice-President Lyndon Baines Johnson, who was present in Dallas and driving in the same procession on the day of the assassination, took the oath of office only two hours after Mr. Kennedy's death. The rapid and orderly succession demonstrated to the world the effective working of the Constitution and the solidarity of the American people. When Lyndon Johnson assumed the Presidency of the United States, he impressed everyone with his confidence and his determination to accomplish what his predecessor had not lived to finish. With deliberate calm, he set out to achieve a year of legislative accomplishments, among them a tax cut and a Civil Rights Bill, unequalled in American history.

The Election of 1964

At the Republican convention in July, 1964, the party selected Barry M. Goldwater, the junior senator from Arizona as their nominee for President. As vice-presidential nominee, the Republicans chose Representative William E. Miller of New York. The following month, the Democrats, as had been predicted, nominated Lyndon B.

In the crowded cabin of "Air Force I," the Presidential jet, Vice-President Johnson took the Presidential oath, flanked by Jacqueline Kennedy (right) and Mrs. Johnson.

Left: Dr. Martin Luther King, civil rights leader and minister, was the Nobel Peace Prize winner for 1964. Here King (left) accepts a plaque from the Mayor of his home town, Atlanta, Georgia, given at a dinner in honor of King's Nobel Prize award. Below: Dr. King and other civil rights leaders organized a Protest March in Washington, D.C. in the summer of 1963. The march was a disciplined success, attracting 200,000 sympathizers, both Negro and White. The size and sincerity of the crowd helped convince Congress to pass a comprehensive Civil Rights Bill the next summer.

Johnson by acclamation. President Johnson, with the approval of the convention, chose as his running mate Senator Hubert H. Humphrey of Minnesota. After what seemed to many to be a tiresome campaign, President Johnson was elected by the greatest popular majority in American history, winning 43 million votes to his opponent's 27 million. President Johnson had thus gained 61 percent of the total vote cast.

New Concern for Human Values

Civil Rights Bill. While President Kennedy was in office, he had urged the introduction of a Civil Rights Bill which would end discrimination on the basis of race and color in many areas of American life. Often frustrated in his relationship with the Congress, President Kennedy did not meet with much success in his civil rights recommendations. However, when President Johnson assumed office, the Congress supported the legislation partly because they were shocked by President Kennedy's death and partly because the injustice to Negro Americans had been made plain by demonstrations, some peaceful and some violent. President Johnson, himself a former Senate majority leader, secured cooperation between the legislative and executive branches of government. Under his guidance the Civil Rights Bill of 1964 became law.

The new bill ensured that no American could be denied the right to vote, or to obtain public accommodations, education, or a job, solely on the basis of his race or color. Sustained by the Supreme Court decision of 1954, which suggested that racially segregated schools violated the spirit of the Constitution, this bill legally ensured for the Negro American the rights which all citizens of the United States take for granted. The Civil Rights Bill was a giant step toward full equality under the law for twenty million American Negroes. The new law at last fulfilled the guarantees of the Constitution and the stated ideals of the Declaration of Independence for a significant element of the American population.

Looking Back

1. How did the electoral vote tally fail to reflect the closeness of the 1960 election?
2. How did the United States and the world react to President Kennedy's assassination?
3. Why do you think President Johnson won the election of 1964?
4. What provisions did the Civil Rights Bill of 1964 contain?

2. Foreign Affairs Are a Continuing Problem

Our Relations With the Soviet Bloc

Meeting at Vienna. Soon after his inauguration in 1961, President Kennedy traveled to Vienna to meet with Chairman Khrushchev of the Soviet Union. The young American President and the Soviet leader exchanged views and appraised each other's abilities. Although no great decisions were made at this meeting, each leader came away with a realistic view of the other. The meeting indicated that the two cold war adversaries were willing to continue to speak together about world problems.

Changes in Government. It appeared that President Johnson would adopt the same attitude of watchful hopefulness for world peace that President Kennedy had fostered. Then, late in 1964, Chairman Khrushchev was ousted from his position as Soviet Chief of State. Two Communist Party officials, Alexei Kosygin and Leonid Brehznev assumed control of the Soviet government. Brehznev and Kosygin, like President Johnson, seemed committed to "peaceful coexistence." Relations between the Soviet Union and the United States, which had been icy in the fifties, seemed to be thawing in the mid-sixties.

Other Communist Nations. Many of the so-called "satellites" of the Soviet Union seemed gradually to be changing their attitude toward the United States. Increased trade and better diplomatic relationships with Hungary, Czechoslovakia, Rumania and Bulgaria, all Soviet satellites, indicated that the Cold War in Europe was undergoing a change. These nations were showing more and more independence from Russian policies. The Soviet Union appeared to have learned from the Hungarian Revolt of 1956 that they could not choke their satellites to death. The Communist world no longer presented the simple unified picture it had immediately after World War II. It became increasingly apparent that the United States would have to deal with each Communist nation as a separate entity.

China-Soviet Split

During the first year of President Kennedy's term of office, a rift between the Soviet Union and Red China appeared to widen. Gradually these two countries, which had been firmly united by their belief in Communism, began to argue about the meaning of Communism. Since the two huge nations were different racially, culturally, and historically, the argument over the meaning of Communism probably reflected other, more serious differences. In any case, the split between the Soviet Union and China nudged the former into a position more closely aligned with that of western nations. This new attitude was demonstrated by Soviet approval in the test-ban agreement, signed by President Kennedy, which prohibited atmospheric testing of atomic weapons. When President Kennedy was assassinated, Khrushchev and his wife paid a visit to the American embassy in Moscow and expressed sincere sorrow. In stark contrast, the Red Chinese press reported the assassination with glee.

Communist Challenge

To say that affairs between the Soviet bloc and the United States became more friendly is not to say that the Cold War was ended. Trouble spots in the world continued to erupt. In 1961, Russians and East German communists erected a wall between East and West Berlin to prohibit traffic between the two zones. American and Russian troops glared at each other from time

On October 7, 1963, President Kennedy signed an agreement with the other countries possessing atomic weapons. It prohibited above ground nuclear testing, thus preventing contamination of the earth's atmosphere. President Kennedy said the pact was a "clear commitment to the cause of man's survival."

to time across that barricade. The Soviet Union continued to be dedicated to the spreading of world communism, and Americans were vigilant and determined to halt this movement. Communist groups, inspired by the Russian example, continued to cause trouble all over the world, in Latin America, in the Middle East, and in Europe itself.

Latin American Problems

Bay of Pigs. Before President Kennedy's inauguration in January, 1961, the United States broke diplomatic relations with Castro's Cuba. For some time, an invasion of the Cuban mainland had been planned by exiled Cubans living in this country. They had been encouraged, and aided to some extent, by agencies of the U.S. government. On taking office, President Kennedy decided not to prevent the invasion from taking place as planned. In April, 1961, the plan was put into action. It was poorly coordinated and ended in complete and dismal failure. The 1400 Cuban exiles who landed at the Bay of Pigs in Cuba were quickly routed by Castro's forces and many of them were killed. The attempt provoked loud cries of anger in Latin America and elsewhere. Many Americans questioned the wisdom of such clumsy intervention originating from the United States. An ominous note was added in succeeding months as the Soviet Union sent numerous military technicians to Cuba to bolster Castro's defenses.

The Cuban Missile Crisis

American concerns with Cuba were greatly increased in the fall of 1962. Aerial photography showed that Castro's government had armed the island with long range missiles of Soviet origin. President Kennedy acted quickly to consult with his advisors. He decided upon a course of action that would bring the United States into direct confrontation with the Soviet Union. He announced in a speech over national radio and television that American naval vessels would clamp a total blockade on ships carrying offensive weapons to Cuba. At the same time, he demanded that the Soviet Union remove any missiles which had already been placed in Cuba. All American armed forces were ordered on the alert.

President Kennedy's actions were a direct challenge to the Soviet leadership. The situation was very tense. Premier Khrushchev, recognizing that the United States meant business, ordered the Russian ships to return home. Then, a few days later, he ordered those missiles which had already arrived in Cuba to be dismantled and returned to the Soviet Union. President Kennedy and the United States had won a major strategic victory without bloodshed.

The Alliance for Progress

The United States has usually learned from its mistakes, and the government admitted it had made mistakes in its diplomatic policies toward Cuba in the 1940's and 1950's. In efforts to prevent situations similar to that in Cuba, the Kennedy administration tried to take constructive measures to improve relations with other Latin American countries. In the summer of 1961, these countries joined the United States in a program planned by President Kennedy and called the Alliance for Progress. The program suggested land reform, a Latin American Parliament, a Latin American Army, and a Latin American common market. If all of those things could come to pass, the fight against communism in Latin America might be won.

Unrest in Southeast Asia

Vietnam. The American nation encountered its most serious foreign policy problem in South Vietnam. This Southeast Asian country had been a French protectorate until, in 1954, Communist North Vietnam guerrillas forced the French to accept an unfavorable treaty and leave South Vietnam. At that time, the United States offered its aid to South Vietnam, and it was accepted by the government in power in 1955 headed by Ngo Dinh Diem. American influence became very great in South Vietnam, but the population, especially the Buddhists, became unruly. Finally, after years of dispute, a group of Air Force generals overthrew the Diem government in 1963. After that time governments rapidly succeeded one another in power as American influence waned. It was difficult for the American State Department to know what to do since from one day to the next the government might change. To add to the problem, the North Vietnamese guerrillas, the communist Viet Cong as they were called, were winning battle after battle. American troops and pilots, although only present in Vietnam in an advisory capacity, were being killed or wounded almost daily by 1965.

Other Southeast Asian Problems. Influenced by the Chinese Communists, other Southeast Asian nations

An American Peace Corps Volunteer (right) shows a young Chilean how to operate a band saw. Such voluntary help has made the United States more respected in the world.

were turning against the United States. Cambodia, Laos, and Indonesia, all seemed to be moving into the Communist camp. When President Sukarno of Indonesia, in January of 1965, removed his nation from the United Nations in protest against the seating of pro-Western Malaysia on the Security Council, the Southeast Asian problem was compounded.

The Brighter Side of U.S. Foreign Policy in the 1960's

Fortunately United States relations with the rest of the world were not as grim as those with Southeast Asia. The United States lost some friends and gained others in the early sixties, and in the main, she kept her old ties to her alliances, the North Atlantic Treaty Organization (NATO), the Australia-New Zealand-United States Pact (ANZUS), and the Southeast Asian Treaty Organization (SEATO).

The Peace Corps. The U.S. gained friends through one of the most unique foreign policy programs of the Kennedy administration, the Peace Corps. The purpose of this Corps was to recruit American specialists, many of them of college age, to train people in under-developed countries. Over ten thousand men and women joined the Corps and were sent to foreign countries where their services were requested. After learning the language and customs of a country, they gave aid in their own special fields, such as engineering, medicine, farming, and teaching.

Trade Expansion Act. One piece of legislation passed under President Kennedy which helped our relations with other nations was the Trade Expansion Act of 1962. This act authorized the President, over a five-year period, to reduce sharply the American duties on foreign goods from non-communist nations entering this country. It was hoped that these nations, finding it easier to sell their goods in the American market, would in turn buy greater amounts of American products and thus stimulate trade. Certain American companies, of course, would be hurt by this increased foreign competition and would be faced with the necessity of modernizing their plants, making new products, and finding new jobs for displaced workers. Congress decided, however, that the overall gain for American industry would justify the passage of the Trade Expansion Act.

A Growing UN

In the years following World War II, one of the most important changes which took place in the world was the growth of the United Nations. The most dynamic element in this growth was the emergence of the African nations. Held as colonies or "protectorates" by nations of Europe before World War II, these nations clamored for their freedom in the years following the war. As nations such as Somalia, Uganda, and Tanzania formed their own governments, other African nations followed suit. Each of these nations had an effect on United States foreign policy, and each, as they set up governments, was admitted to the United Nations. Twenty-five new African nations were admitted to the United Nations between 1945 and 1965. The organization could be said, by 1965, to represent practically the entire world. Exceptions were Red China, which has never been admitted to the United Nations, and Indonesia, which resigned.

Looking Back

1. Why would a change in Russian government be important to the United States?
2. How did President Kennedy meet the Cuban missile crisis?
3. Describe the problems faced by the United States in Vietnam.
4. What were the achievements of the administration of Kennedy and Johnson in foreign policy?

3. Science and Technology Shape the Modern World

World Space Progress

In both the United States and the Soviet Union, great strides were made in man's exploration of space. Throughout the late 1950's, both nations had accomplished wonders in orbiting small man-made planets and weather satellites. However, in the 1960's, man's dream of rocketing human beings into space was fulfilled. Only three months after President Kennedy was inaugurated, the Soviet Union sent a cosmonaut, named Yuri Gagarin into space. He orbited the earth for 108 minutes, reaching a top speed of 17,000 miles per hour. Gagarin was followed successfully by other Soviet spacemen, and later by a man and a woman who orbited at the same time in separate craft. Finally, in 1964, three Soviets orbited the earth in one capsule, and in March, 1965, a Russian pilot actually stepped from his capsule into the mysterious deep-freeze of outer space.

American Progress. On May 5, 1961, only one month after the Soviet Union's first manned space flight, the United States succeeded in firing a manned rocket into space. Navy Commander Alan B. Shepard became the first American astronaut when he was rocketed 116 miles above the earth in a 4000 pound capsule. Although he did not orbit the earth, landing 302 miles from his launch point, he proved that the United States had the capability to accomplish orbital flights.

In February, 1962, while most of America watched in fascination, Lieutenant Colonel John H. Glenn was rocketed into space to orbit the earth three times, becoming the first American to do so and gaining much ground in the space race. Then in March, 1965, two astronauts, Virgil I. (Gus) Grissom and John W. Young, "flew" their Gemini space craft in outer space.

Space Science

Americans have been concerned in the 1960's with much more than projecting men into space and retrieving them successfully. The composition of outer space, the surface of the moon and other planets, and the fascinating question of whether or not there is life on other planets, have all been matters that concern American space scientists.

One of the most successful American space probes was the Mariner II satellite which was sent toward Venus and

Astronaut John Glenn, first American to orbit the earth, spoke to numerous round-the-world stations on his journey through space. He also took pictures of himself (below).

onward to orbit about the sun. Mariner II was the first earth satellite to approach Venus, missing it by only 21,000 miles. It also set a new world record for communication when it sent scientific information about Venus back to the earth by radio. An American satellite was also sent towards Mars in 1964, in order to find out the composition of that planet's atmosphere and other information.

Communications Satellites. In addition to exploratory flights into outer space, the United States launched satellites to aid in communication. The Telstar Satellite launched July 10, 1962, enabled television programs to be transmitted in both directions between the United States and Europe. A second Telstar satellite, built by American Telephone and Telegraph Co., was launched by the National Aeronautic and Space Administration from Cape Kennedy, May 7, 1963. A much more complex instrument than the first Telstar, it could transmit live television programs. Many Europeans viewed President Kennedy's funeral ceremonies through the facilities of Telstar II.

Another type of communications satellite, Syncom II, was launched July 26, 1963. This satellite entered an orbit at the same speed as the rotation of the earth remaining at a fixed point above the surface of earth. Thus radio communications could be "bounced off" Syncom just as they could be bounced off a fixed mountain on the surface of the earth. Syncom made possible the transmission of telegraph and teletype messages between the United States and Nigeria, or other similar points.

The same principles had been followed in May of 1963, when the Air Force had launched four hundred million copper wires, called "needles" into space. The needles quickly spread into a ring around the earth. The purpose of this ring of needles around the earth was to determine whether or not radio communication could be bounced off the ring. It was found by Air Force scientists that coast-to-coast communication could be accomplished by the use of the needles.

Telstar II, communications satellite, circles the earth. It receives messages and relays them to other points on earth.

Medicine

It would be impossible to catalogue all the advances in medical science in the 1960's. New vaccines to cure diseases such as measles and polio were perfected during the early 1960's, as were multiple vaccines to control or cure a number of diseases at once.

Medicine is concerned with the prevention of disease as well as its cure. Basic research into the causes of disease is, therefore, important. To take only two examples of the concerns medicine has with the causative factors in disease, we can look at medical research into air pollution and its effects, and into smoking and health. When, in any American city, factories and automobiles discharge poisonous gases into the air, health and safety are endangered. The medical profession was concerned that poisons placed in the air by man could cause serious ailments to the lungs and blood. Therefore, medical centers were set up to examine the problem. The federal Public Health Service cooperated with the Los Angeles General Hospital and the University of Southern California School of Medicine in a long-term study of the effects of polluted air on human beings. Doctors could judge from this study what best can be done to combat diseases already caused by air pollution, and the Public Health Service could take steps to eliminate the causes of it. Means have been found already to reduce the poisons in automobile exhaust fumes.

Another example of medical concern with public health was the campaign based on a 1964 report by the Surgeon General of the United States to alert the public to the relationship between smoking and the incidence of lung cancer. In March, 1965, the Surgeon General released a supplementary report to the nation based on more conclusive research which sustained original conclusions. Such cooperation between the medical profession and the federal government has resulted in greater safeguards to the nation's health.

Other Medical Advances. One of the most fascinating medical developments to take place in the 1960's has been the invention of materials which can be used to replace human parts. A new plastic, known as silastic, has made possible the replacement of external and internal organs. A new method of treating animal bones has made it safe for human beings to undergo bone transplants which up to now have been impossible because of the body's tendency to reject any foreign matter. New materials have made possible the use of artificial kidneys and other organs and the "patching" of weak arteries and veins. If a human being becomes ill today, his chances of surviving are greater than they were even five short years ago.

Automation

One of the great opportunities and challenges for modern America is automation, or the use of machines which control themselves. Automation is not an entirely new concept. One of the first automatic machines, the spinning jenny, was invented two hundred years ago in England. However, in the last

Intricate automatic machines, such as this linear accelerator, typify our scientific age.

decade alone, self-regulating machines, computers, and computer-run heavy machinery have been invented which can accomplish phenomenal tasks.

Perhaps the most spectacular development in automation in the last few years is the perfecting of the computer, a machine which can react to certain facts supplied to it by men, and solve various problems. Computers cannot "think"; they do not have the power to invent ideas, but they can read and write and compare facts. The great value of computers is that they can store huge quantities of facts which can be utilized to perform tasks. Computers now can calculate payrolls, track satellites, guide various mechanical operations such as drilling or cutting, and determine the population of a given area in advance. A computer, when fed a barrage of facts, has designed an entire chemical plant which was later built on the West Coast of the United States, taking into account all the problems of material, cost, and labor time.

The Challenge of Automation

The work of computers and similar machines was formerly performed by men, and the fact that a man-made development has taken over is both a saving for industry and a problem for the men whose work has been taken over by the machine. In many cases, displaced workers, such as elevator operators, bookkeepers, unskilled laborers, heavy machinery operators and others have had to learn new skills directly related to the computers, such as electronics or computer service. Some companies which have saved money by using computers have offered to retrain their workers or to pass on the benefits of automation in other ways. The Federal government has also set up retraining centers to find use for men who are out of work as a result of automation. A good example of this is the training offered to West Virginia miners whose jobs have been eliminated by efficient coal mining machinery. Much remains to be done in this field.

Looking Back

1. Describe America's entry into the manned space race.
2. Name the scientific space projects in the 1960's.
3. What were the great advances in medical science in the 1960's?
4. Describe the challenge offered by automation.

4. Americans Continue to Build a Great Society

In a speech at Ann Arbor, Michigan, on May 22, 1964, Lyndon B. Johnson outlined his hope for America's future, calling it the "Great Society." ". . . in your time we have the opportunity to move not only toward the rich society and powerful society, but upward to the Great Society . . . where men are more concerned with the quality of their goals than the quantity of their goods." With the apparent easing of Cold War tensions, with the nation in the security of an economic boom, with tremendous scientific advances making life more pleasant, Americans did indeed have time to concentrate on the nature of their society. Like the farmer whose crops are planted, Americans could begin to patch up the chinks in their house, chinks which allowed the winds of poverty, ignorance, urban blight, polluted water and air to disturb the national life within.

Natural Resources

When the first colonists landed on American shores, they found a land in which they breathed clean fresh air, through which pure and clear water fit for drinking flowed, in which wild beasts, unafraid of man, abounded, and in which broad and beautiful vistas were uninterrupted by unsightly buildings. Almost two centuries later, in the time of Thomas Jefferson, the land had not changed very much. Jefferson himself felt that the United States would evolve into a land of small farms, spread across North America. When Jefferson was an old man in 1825, only ten percent of the American population lived in cities. Today seventy percent of the population lives in cities. Jefferson's dream of a nation of farms was dashed to pieces by 1890, 64 years after he had died, when the vast migration from farm to city was well under way. Today there are many areas where the air is not pure. In other areas, water is unusable for human consumption until it is passed through purification plants. Great herds of wild animals exist in safety only in "preserves" created by men. Many things about man's environment have changed in the three and a half centuries of settled America.

Air Pollution. With the beginning of the age of industrial growth and the use of steam and later of electric power came the problem of air pollution. First recognized as a problem by local authorities (the Pittsburgh city government is a good example), air pollution began to be thought of as a national problem in the 1950's.

When the automobile became a major mode of transportation in the United States, automobile exhaust systems added to the poisonous gases entering the atmosphere. As cities grew larger, and as highway systems stretched over vast expanses of America, air pollution became a national problem. No longer were people concerned only with the air over Pittsburgh or Los Angeles. By the mid-1950's the air covering vast areas such as the southern California coast, the southern shore of Lake Michigan or all of central Alabama was becoming polluted. Air pollution was no longer a local problem but a national one.

Water Resources. Water pollution became a national problem in the same way as did air pollution. At first in the 1940's, cities such as Cleveland, Ohio, or Detroit, Michigan, became concerned with the impurity of nearby bodies of water. Industrial wastes and raw sewage poisoned many rivers on which large cities are located. Then in the 1950's, when fish and plant life in all the Great Lakes and in many of our rivers and streams seemed in danger, it was obvious that such pollution affected many besides those who lived in any particular area. Insecticides sprayed on cotton fields in Tennessee and washed by rain into nearby streams found their way into larger rivers, taking their toll of fish and wildlife all along their path to the ocean.

The great economic strides taken by the United States in the last thirty years have allowed millions of Americans to enjoy more leisure time. In the scenes and activities on these pages, we see the great variety in American recreational opportunity. For people of every age and from every region, the United States provides a wealth of sports to play and watch. Museums, playhouses, *spectacular amusement parks, concerts, operas and a host of other things furnish Americans with a vigorous and interesting cultural setting. Television and the movies provide other forms of entertainment, while public and private libraries continue to flourish and grow. Crowded stadiums and crowded concert halls both indicate the avid participation of most Americans in recreation.*

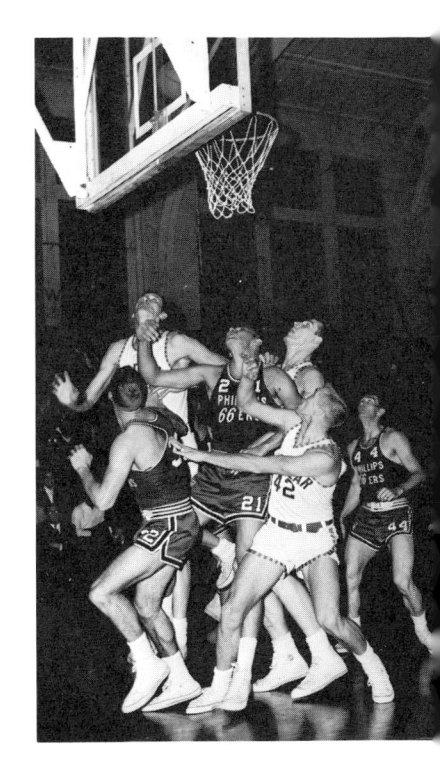

It was clear that something had to be done to educate Americans to the dangers of careless disposal of industrial waste and the dangers of untested pesticides. To this end, under the guidance of Stewart Udall, Secretary of the Interior under Presidents Kennedy and Johnson, the problems of water pollution were investigated.

Land Resources. It became apparent by the 1930's that Americans would have to change their attitudes about the use of land also. The days when a frontier farmer could vacate his wornout land for more productive pastures in the West vanished with the frontier. Land reclamation, such as that accomplished by the Tennessee Valley Authority, seemed to supply usable land when it was needed, but projects like TVA could not solve the problems of urban sprawl which cropped up after World War II. Unscrupulous builders erected dreary houses of inferior quality in fields near large cities. These poorly planned and located "housing projects" fulfilled a need for inexpensive housing, but some stood empty and uncared for, causing unsightly patches of wasteland near a city. Nothing could have been farther from Thomas Jefferson's dream of a well-kept, rural America in which land was used only as it was needed.

Education

Human resources are the most important held by the American nation. For some years Americans have been concerned about how best to conserve and develop those resources through better education for all. Late in the 19th century, such educators as John Dewey (see page 384) brought new ideas and ideals to education, advocating real democracy and education for everyone. His principles underlay the entire approach to American education

This small house in the German Village section of Columbus, Ohio is a fine, typical example of privately financed urban renewal. Using private funds and initiative, the residents of this inner city community have rebuilt and refurnished their homes to create a clean, orderly, and beautiful area.

Growth in Higher Education 1870-1960

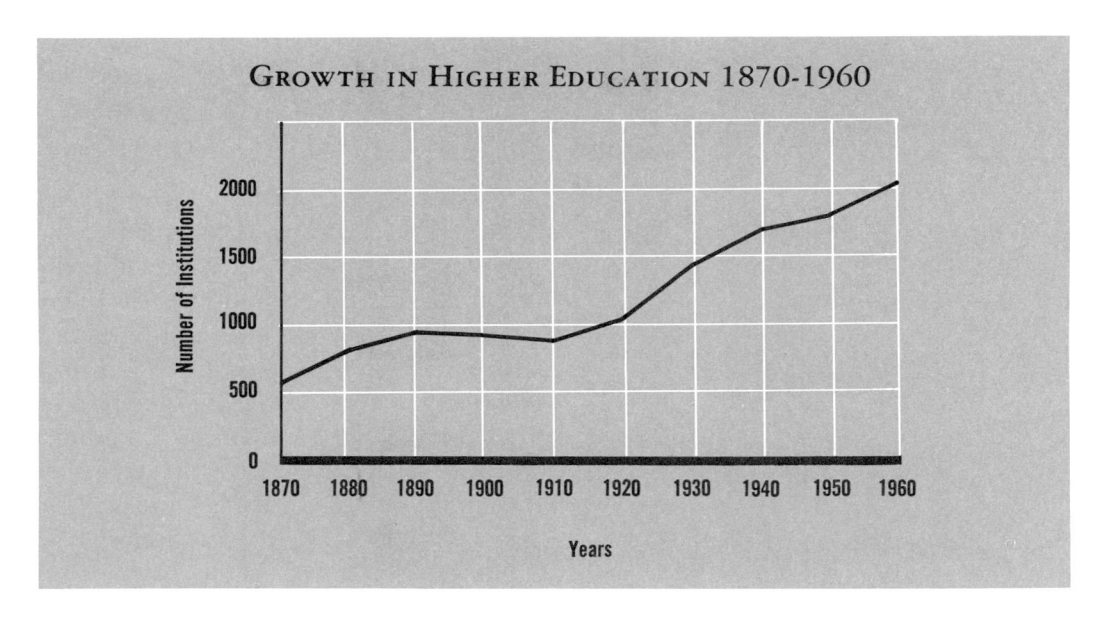

in the twentieth century, and in part were responsible for a great increase in school enrollment. In 1900, only ten million students regularly attended school in the United States. By the mid-1960's, the number had reached 40 million. School buildings had improved in quality as they grew in number. Teachers were better trained and better paid than formerly. Americans spent only 214 million dollars on education in 1900, approximately 21 dollars per pupil; today they spend nearly 20 billion—over 500 dollars per pupil—on airy and well-lighted classrooms, better teachers, modern textbooks, and equipment which would have seemed revolutionary in 1900. In the 1960's the

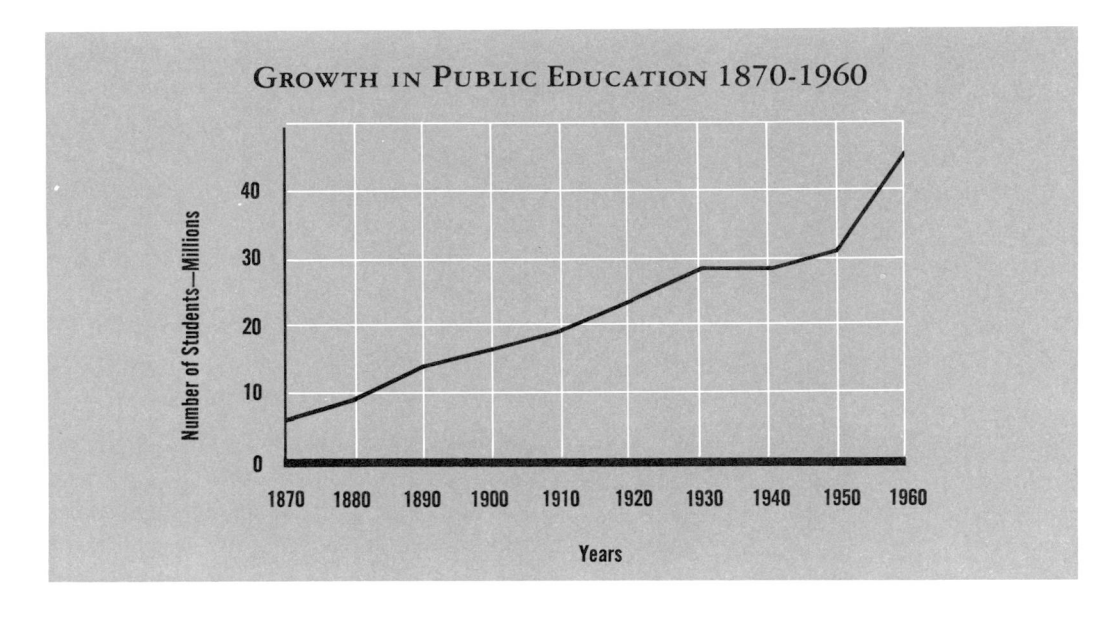

Growth in Public Education 1870-1960

Progress in Democracy

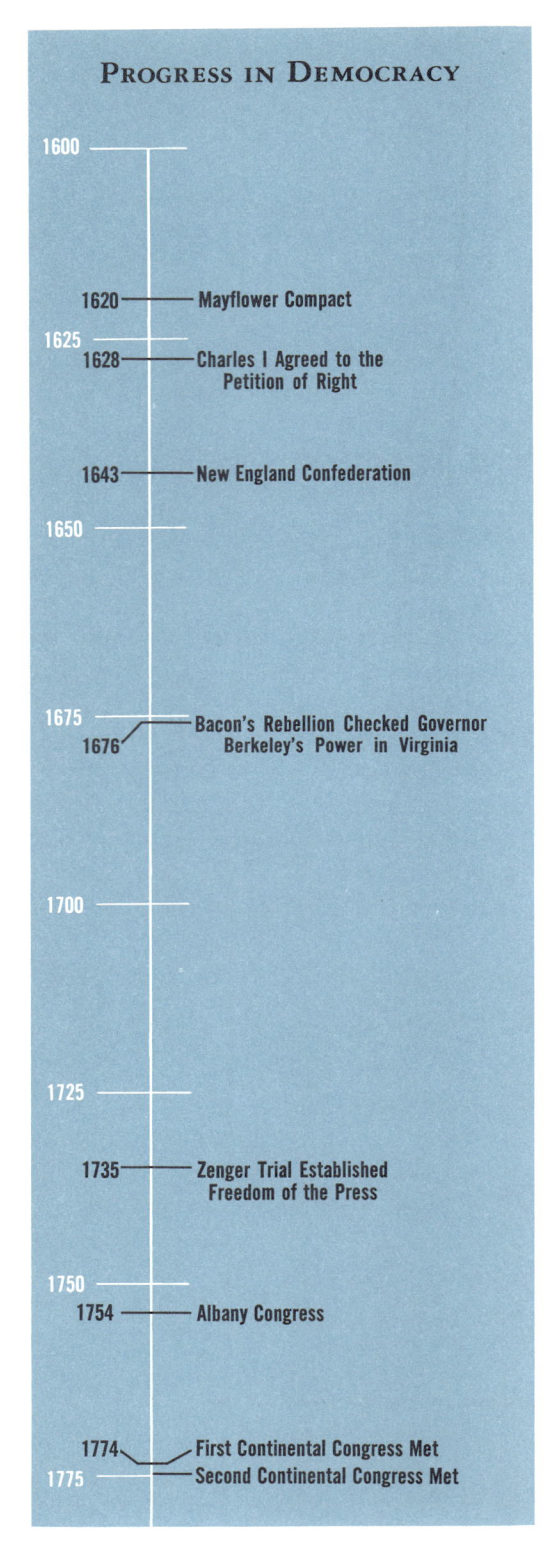

- 1600
- 1620 — Mayflower Compact
- 1625
- 1628 — Charles I Agreed to the Petition of Right
- 1643 — New England Confederation
- 1650
- 1675
- 1676 — Bacon's Rebellion Checked Governor Berkeley's Power in Virginia
- 1700
- 1725
- 1735 — Zenger Trial Established Freedom of the Press
- 1750
- 1754 — Albany Congress
- 1774 — First Continental Congress Met
- 1775 — Second Continental Congress Met

American system of education was brought to bear more firmly on the problem of conserving and developing the nation's human resources.

Population Explosion. The great increase in the birth rate which took place in the United States immediately after World War II—the so-called "baby boom"—made itself felt in school enrollment in the early 1950's. From 1950 to 1960 the school-age population increased from 30 million to 40 million. In that ten year period, therefore, innumerable new schools and classrooms had to be built to accommodate the increase. By the same token, new teachers had to be trained quickly and employed to teach the ten million newcomers. In contrast, during the preceding ten years, 1940–1950, the school-age population had increased less than one million.

New Accents. While the quantity of schools and teachers was increased, an increase in the quality of education had to be effected as well. The demands placed upon American education by space exploration and the age of automation, to mention two examples, were very great indeed. By 1955 it was thought that American education was weak in teaching the sciences and mathematics and that more verbal skills should be imparted to American students. As a result, the concentration on science and mathematics was increased, and new methods of teaching verbal skills were devised.

College Enrollment. The need for teachers, especially of science and mathematics, and the growing need for well educated technicians and writers, as well as men and women trained in all professions, led to a great increase in college enrollment. Also, a college education became a necessary prerequisite in responsible job employment. By 1963 the babies born after the war were ready to enter colleges, and higher education had to stretch itself to accommodate all who wished to enter college in the 1960's. College enrollment jumped by almost one million between 1960 and 1965, taxing the institutions already in existence and causing the formation of almost 100 brand new institutions. Junior colleges were founded to help take care of those who might only desire two years of higher education.

Educational Opportunities. The Supreme Court decision of 1954, suggesting that racially segregated schools were unconstitutional, gave rise to a drive for equal opportunities in education for all. American Negroes, especially in the Southern states, had been, up to 1954, condemned to overcrowded schools staffed by teachers who often were not permitted to obtain a competent education. Although the Supreme Court decision did not alter this overnight, it did give promise that this situation would be relieved. The Civil Rights Bill of 1964 went further in this direction, and the drive to grant all Americans the same educational opportunity was increased in intensity in the 1960's.

Another educationally deprived group was the poor in America's large cities. Often teachers desired to teach in suburbs rather than in schools of the poorer districts. Therefore, when shortages of teachers existed, the schools in poorer districts suffered. In the sixties, local and state governments took action

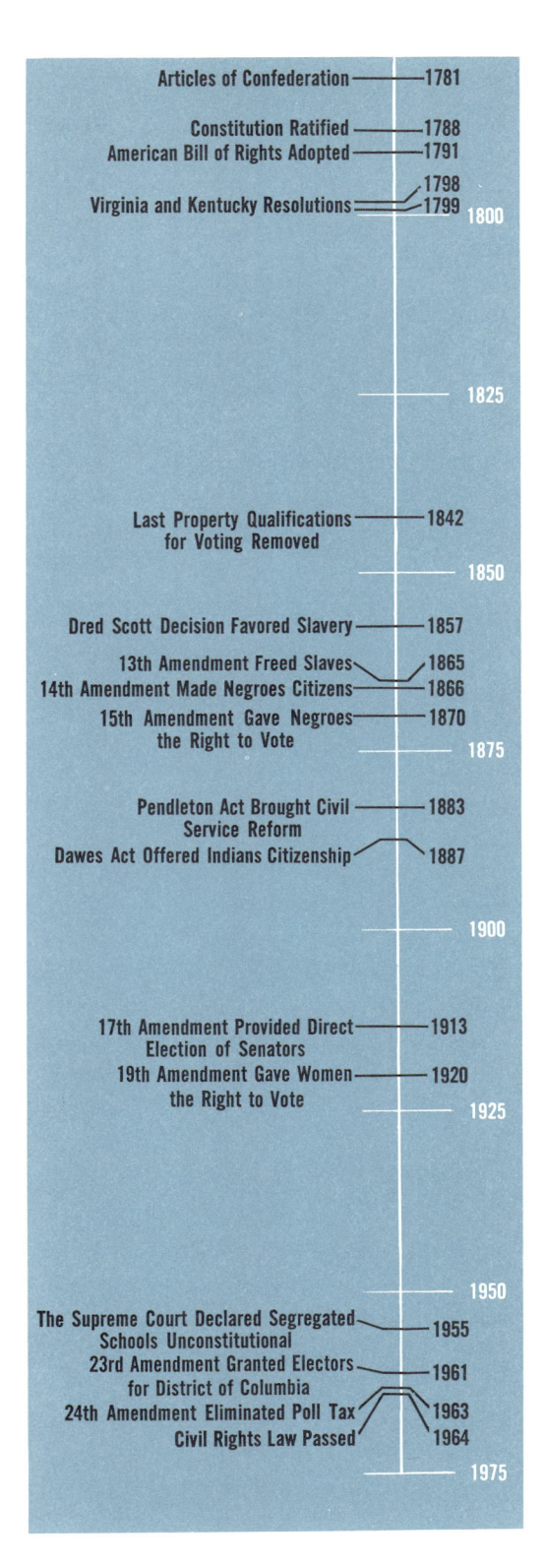

Articles of Confederation — 1781
Constitution Ratified — 1788
American Bill of Rights Adopted — 1791
Virginia and Kentucky Resolutions — 1798 / 1799
1800
1825
Last Property Qualifications for Voting Removed — 1842
1850
Dred Scott Decision Favored Slavery — 1857
13th Amendment Freed Slaves — 1865
14th Amendment Made Negroes Citizens — 1866
15th Amendment Gave Negroes the Right to Vote — 1870
1875
Pendleton Act Brought Civil Service Reform — 1883
Dawes Act Offered Indians Citizenship — 1887
1900
17th Amendment Provided Direct Election of Senators — 1913
19th Amendment Gave Women the Right to Vote — 1920
1925
1950
The Supreme Court Declared Segregated Schools Unconstitutional — 1955
23rd Amendment Granted Electors for District of Columbia — 1961
24th Amendment Eliminated Poll Tax — 1963
Civil Rights Law Passed — 1964
1975

URBAN AND RURAL POPULATION GROWTH 1790-1960

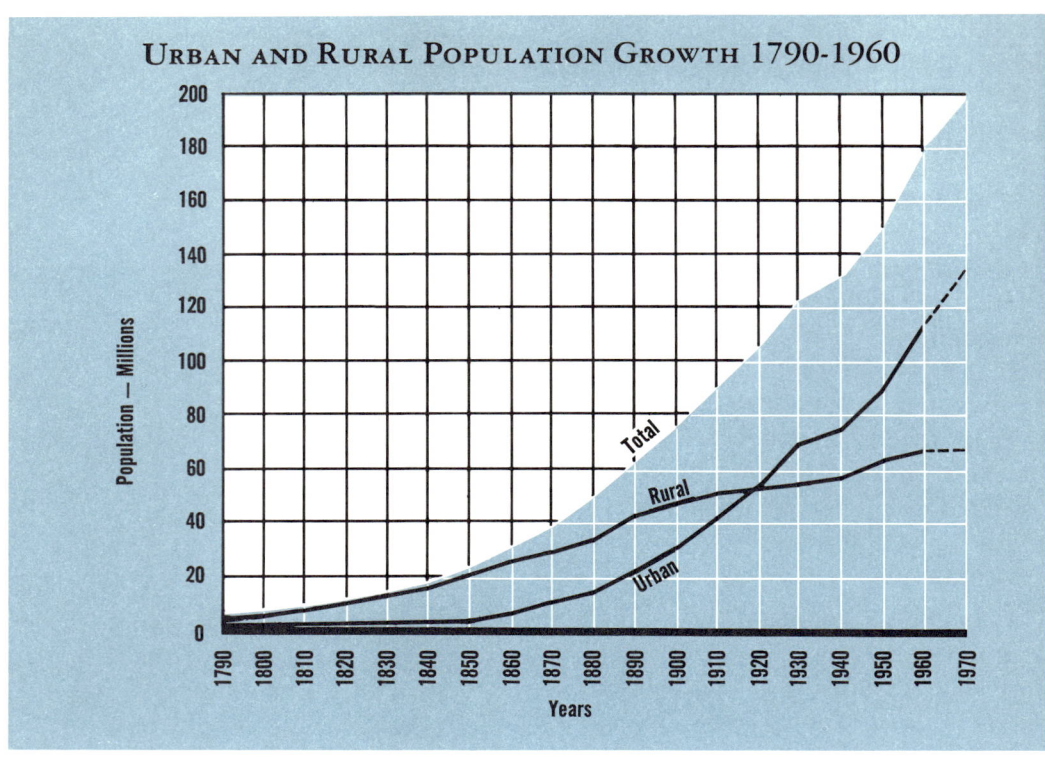

to insure good teaching in these districts. Also, schools and teachers in the "inner city" schools of many big cities began to realize that many children were "culturally deprived" at home. To combat this, programs of cultural education were started in city schools in order to acquaint children with objects and activities common to most American children.

Problems of City Life in the 1960's

In the 1960's, the American city began to evolve from gray, smoky oblivion to modern, clean usefulness. The hearts of old cities, founded in the middle of the 19th century and expanded by the Industrial Revolution, developed through the 20th century into overcrowded slums, unfit for anything but the automobiles which crowded their narrow streets. Like the frontier farmer who abandoned his land when it was no longer usable, the city dweller moved away from the heart of the city instead of rebuilding it. He moved to suburbs, farther and farther from the heart of town until often he had to travel for an hour by train, automobile, or bus to his place of employment. In the 1960's, the American city dweller began to realize, like the frontier farmer of an earlier age, that he could reclaim his city. By tearing down the old-fashioned, overcrowded structures that choked up the heart of the city and building new, high-rise dwellings and work areas, the city could once more serve a vital and useful function in American life. Land which had been wasted by urban sprawl could be turned into recreation areas for the city dwellers.

City Transportation. One result of the sprawling cities of the 1940's and 1950's was that transportation systems had to be developed to shuttle workers in and out of them. Subways, gigantic freeways to accommodate hundreds of thousands of automobiles, and buses were used for this purpose. Even with these improvements, traffic jams were common, and it became apparent that new answers had to be found to transportation problems. Studies were made to find efficient, low-cost means of carrying people to and from cities. One conclusion was that local mass transit problems could be eliminated almost completely if dwellings were built closer to places of employment. A new way of looking at city planning in America evolved from studies of transportation and urban renewal.

Urban Housing. When the slums of the inner cities were torn down, they left city planners with a problem of what to do with the people who had lived in them. Although the slums were ugly and wasteful, they still were the homes of those who lived there. Often in American cities these people were forgotten, left to fend for themselves in communities where they were not welcome or where they lacked the capital to pay higher rental costs. Some cities, however, remembered these forgotten people, providing low cost, clean housing near recreation areas for them. The necessary revolution in city planning could be cruel at times, and yet at other times it brought to the surface man's responsibility for his fellow man.

Conclusion

The United States accomplished a great deal in the 1960's. Most important, government leaders and people in general approached social problems with new understanding and new solutions. Many of the ideals of American democracy were more universally applied to all Americans during the 1960's. Many jobs were left to be done, but at last the decision had been made to try to do them. President Johnson's State of the Union message for 1965 aptly described the American nation at this point in its history as "free, restless, growing and full of hope."

Looking Back

1. Have America's natural resources been used or misused over the years? Explain.

2. List the changes and problems that have occurred in transportation methods in the past few years.

3. What important change is city life undergoing?

Stuyvesant Town, a low-cost housing development, was built to replace New York slums.

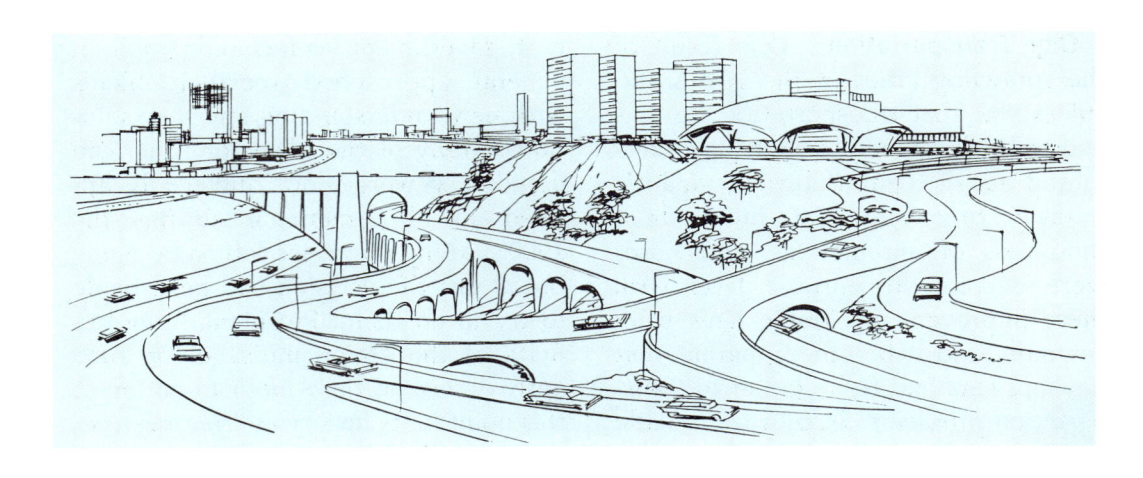

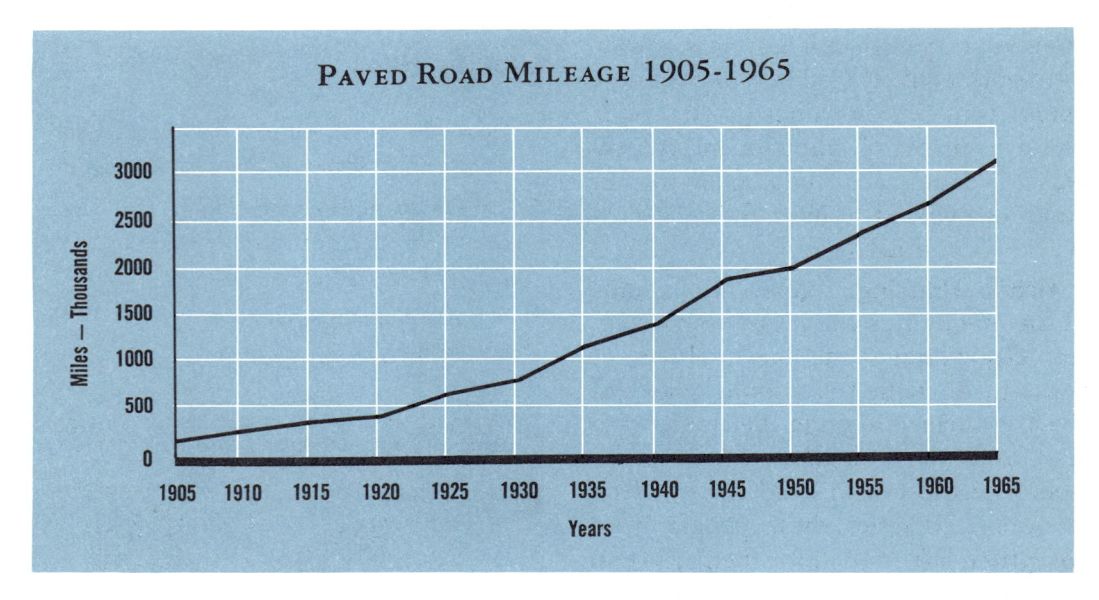

Paved Road Mileage 1905-1965

Miles — Thousands (vertical axis: 0 to 3000)
Years (horizontal axis: 1905 to 1965)

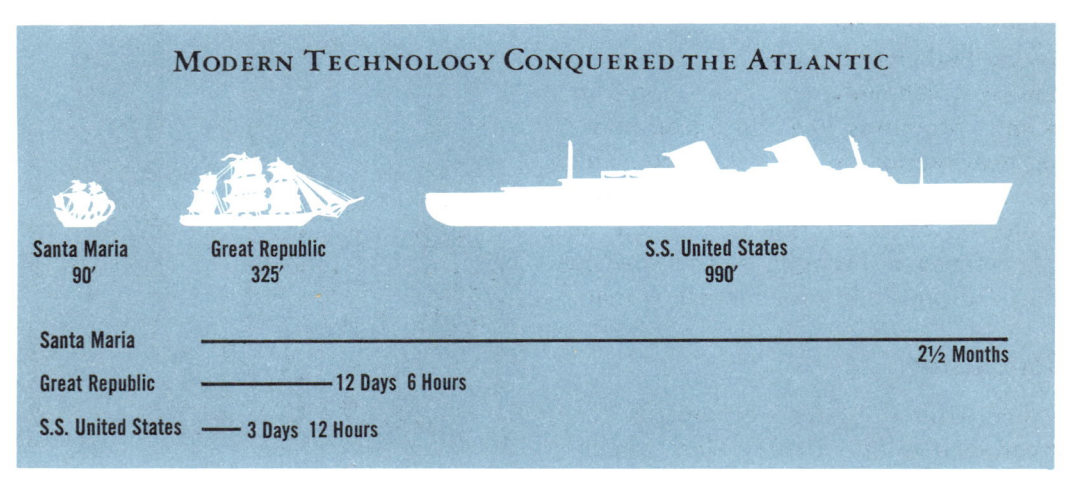

Modern Technology Conquered the Atlantic

Ship	Length	Crossing Time
Santa Maria	90′	2½ Months
Great Republic	325′	12 Days 6 Hours
S.S. United States	990′	3 Days 12 Hours

AIRLINE MILEAGE 1930-1965

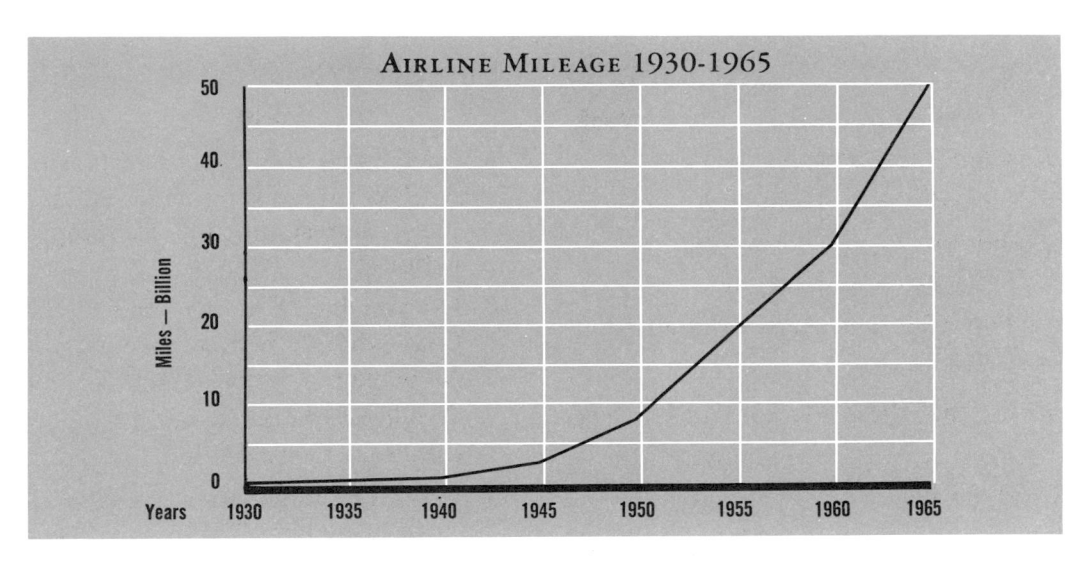

The age in which we live has been called, at various times, the Space Age, the Atomic Age, the Age of Technology, the Speed Age, and many other things. It might also be called the Age of Transportation, for in our own age, man has learned to transport himself more quickly and conveniently than ever before. A look at these graphs and charts will show you at a glance how man has advanced. Cars and trucks, ships, airplanes, and railroads, not to mention spacecraft such as the Atlas-powered Gemini, have shrunk the world to a convenient size for man. Magellan's crew took more than two years to sail around the world; Gus Grissom and John Young used approximately one and a half hours to travel the same distance. Transportation has truly come of age.

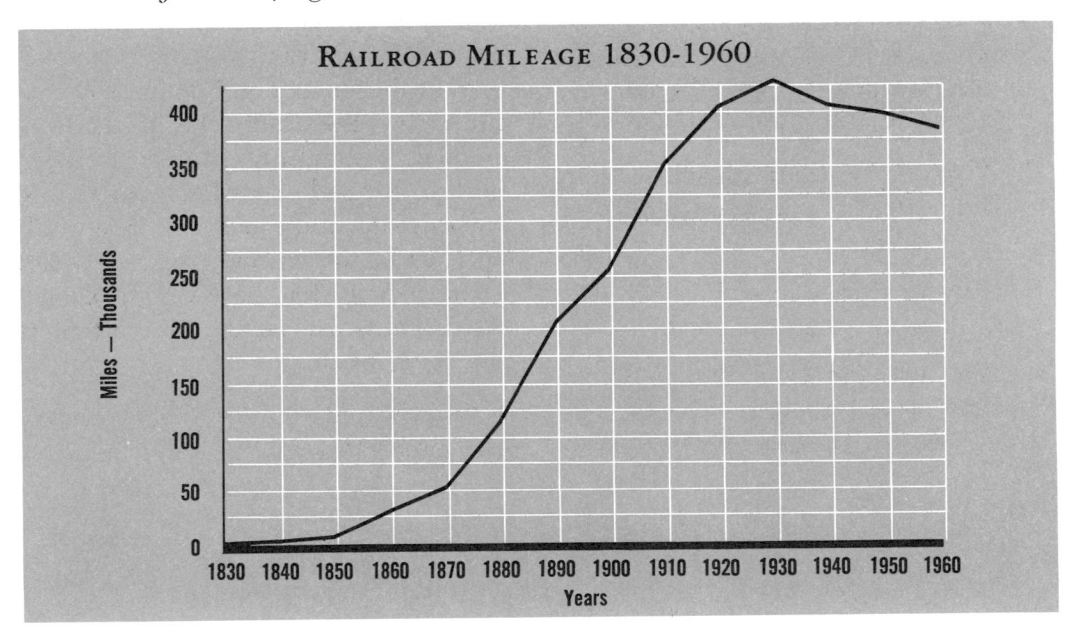

RAILROAD MILEAGE 1830-1960

The Chapter in Perspective

Who Are These People?

Kennedy
Johnson
Gagarin
Shepard
Glenn
Humphrey
Goldwater
Kosygin
Martin Luther King

Where Are These Places?

Guantanamo
Bay of Pigs
Laos
Congo

What Do These Dates and Terms Mean?

cosmonaut
astronaut
Berlin Wall
Peace Corps
Civil Rights
Trade Expansion Act
Population explosion, 1954
silastic
urban sprawl
air pollution
computer

Questions for Study

1. What arguments for changing our methods of electing a President may be found in studying the results of the election of 1960?
2. Why do you think President Kennedy called his program the "New Frontier"?
3. Why was the Bay of Pigs invasion a blow to American prestige?
4. Why was the Civil Rights Bill of 1964 a major step forward for American democracy?
5. How have the Communists succeeded in arousing political and social unrest in underdeveloped nations?
6. Do you feel that the United Nations will succeed in meeting the challenges it faces? Why?
7. Would you be interested in joining the Peace Corps? Why?
8. Why is automation a great challenge to mankind? Why is it also a great advantage?
9. How should the United States take steps to preserve its natural resources?
10. Which area in the world presented the greatest challenge to the maintenance of world peace in 1965?

Place Yourself in History

Your family has lived in Berlin for generations. With the division of the city after the war, you find yourself in East Berlin under Communist control. Now the Berlin Wall has been erected, preventing entrance to West Berlin. Armed sentries, barricades, barbed wire, and the threat of reprisals on your family are everywhere. Death is the penalty for those caught fleeing the Communist sector. Yet, attempts are being made.

What would you do? Would you try to escape? Why?

Expanding Your Outlook

Doing It Yourself

1. Make a chart illustrating the various groups within the U.N. and list the major responsibilities of each.
2. Prepare to debate for or against the inclusion of the veto power for the permanent members of the Security Council.
3. Write an editorial concerning the Truman Doctrine that might have appeared in London (or Moscow, Ankara, Athens).
4. Prepare an "on the spot" radio broadcast covering the airlift that helped break the Berlin Blockade.
5. Write a series of ten or more newspaper headlines that highlight the main events of the fighting in Korea.
6. Prepare a newspaper account of the U-2 incident for publication in Washington (or in Paris, Moscow, or Peking).
7. On an outline map of the world, indicate what you consider to be the five most "explosive hot spots." Support your choices before the class.
8. Draw a newspaper cartoon covering the construction of the Berlin Wall. Can your classmates guess in what paper the cartoon might have appeared?
9. Make a bulletin board display of banners, pins, slogans, pictures, and other materials relating to the presidential elections of 1960 and 1964.
10. Prepare a radio broadcast covering international reaction to either the removal of Khrushchev from power or the explosion of an atom bomb by the Red Chinese.

Working with the Class

1. Let assigned members of the class represent the current members of the Security Council and allow the class to observe a session of the Council.
2. Imagine that several members of the class represent top scientists of the world attending an international conference. What great changes, discoveries, and developments might they predict for the next ten years?
3. Assume members of the class represent the chief officials of the major powers. Hold a summit conference and try to resolve the problems facing the world today.
4. Set up a round-table discussion group for a TV program covering the successes and failures of the Kennedy-Johnson administration.

5. Let's peer into the future! Organize a committee to report on changes anticipated within the next ten years in foods, clothing, shelter, transportation, communication, education, manufacturing, and other areas.
6. Let each class member be a member of a "committee of the whole." Each should prepare a list of the ten most important contributions of the United States to the world. The class should then try to choose the one the majority feel most important.

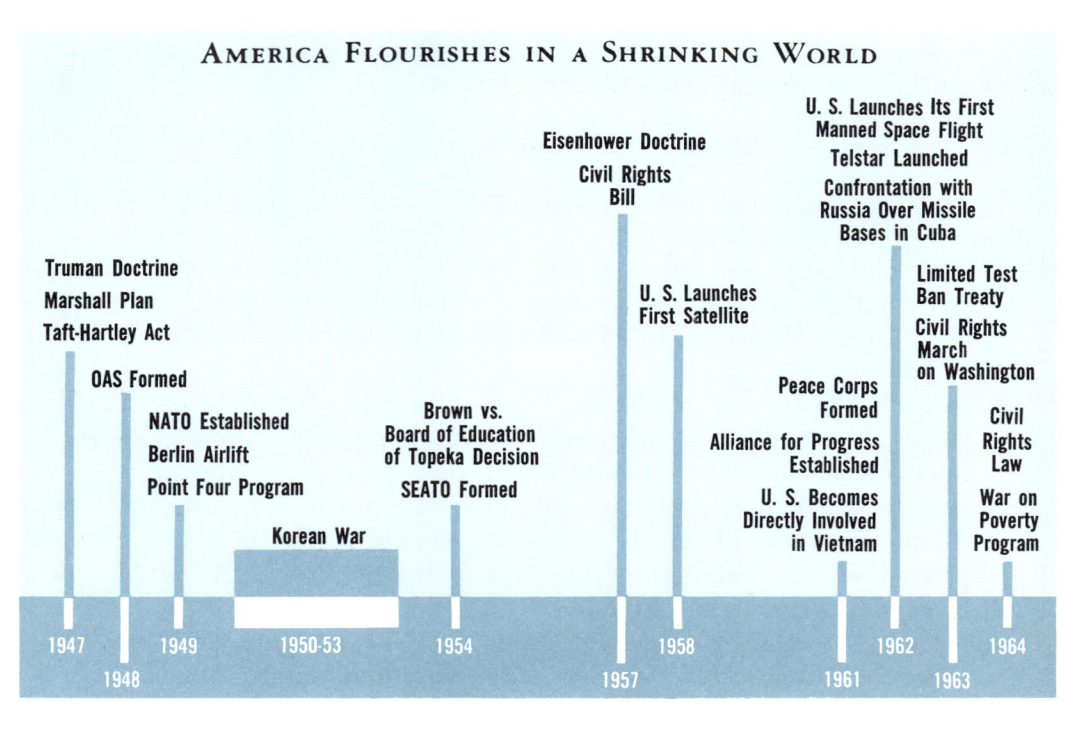

America Flourishes in a Shrinking World

Year	Event(s)
1947	Truman Doctrine; Marshall Plan; Taft-Hartley Act
1948	OAS Formed
1949	NATO Established; Berlin Airlift; Point Four Program
1950-53	Korean War
1954	Brown vs. Board of Education of Topeka Decision; SEATO Formed
1957	Eisenhower Doctrine; Civil Rights Bill
1958	U. S. Launches First Satellite
1961	Peace Corps Formed; Alliance for Progress Established; U. S. Becomes Directly Involved in Vietnam
1962	U. S. Launches Its First Manned Space Flight; Telstar Launched; Confrontation with Russia Over Missile Bases in Cuba
1963	Limited Test Ban Treaty; Civil Rights March on Washington
1964	Civil Rights Law; War on Poverty Program

APPENDIX

THE CONSTITUTION

The Preamble introduces, in very general terms, the purposes which The Constitution is intended to fulfill. It is argued that the phrase, "promote the general welfare," justifies the constitutionality of many types of welfare legislation.

PREAMBLE:

We, the people of the United States, in order to form a more perfect union, establish justice, insure domestic tranquility, provide for the common defense, promote the general welfare, and secure the blessings of liberty to ourselves and our posterity, do ordain and establish this Constitution for the United States of America.

THE CONGRESS:

ARTICLE I

Article I—defines the form and function of the legislative (or lawmaking) branch of the federal government.

SECTION 1

Section 1 divides this legislative branch into two houses: the House of Representatives (often called "The House") and the Senate. Sections 2 and 3 describe the qualifications for membership in these houses, methods of determining how many representatives each state shall have, how these representatives shall be chosen, and how vacancies shall be filled in a state's federal membership.

a. All legislative powers herein granted shall be vested in a Congress of the United States, which shall consist of a Senate and House of Representatives.

SECTION 2

This section provides that any voter (elector) qualified to vote for a member of his state's house of representatives (most numerous Branch) is qualified to vote for a member of the federal House of Representatives.

a. The House of Representatives shall be composed of members chosen every second year by the people of the several states; and the electors in each state shall have the qualifications requisite for electors of the most numerous branch of the legislature.

b. No person shall be a Representative who shall not have attained to the age of twenty-five years, and been seven years a citizen of the United States, and who shall not, when elected, be an inhabitant of that State in which he shall be chosen.

This section limited the power of Congress to tax a state with a small population even though its residents might be quite wealthy. It was modified by the XVI Amendment. The three-fifths reference to slaves was rendered obsolete by the XIII and XIV Amendments. This section also provides that a census (enumeration) shall be made every ten years to determine the number of federal representatives each state shall have.

c. Representatives and direct taxes shall be apportioned among the several States which may be included within this Union, according to their respective numbers, which shall be determined by adding to the whole number of free persons, including those bound to service for a term of years, and excluding Indians not taxed, three-fifths of all other persons. The actual enumeration shall be made within three years after the first meeting of the Congress of the United States, and within every subsequent term of ten years, in such manner as they shall by law direct. The number of Representatives shall not exceed one for every thirty thousand, but each State shall have at least one Representative; and until such enumeration shall be made, the State of New Hampshire shall be entitled to choose three; Massachusetts, eight; Rhode Island and Providence plantations, one; Connecticut, five; New York, six; New Jersey, four; Pennsylvania, eight; Delaware, one; Maryland, six; Virginia, ten; North Carolina, five; South Carolina, five; and Georgia, three.

d. When vacancies happen in the representation from any State, the executive authority thereof shall issue writs of election to fill such vacancies.

e. The House of Representatives shall choose their Speaker and other officers, and shall have the sole power of impeachment.

"Executive Officer" refers to the state governor. "Writs of election" are orders calling for an election.

"Sole power of impeachment" refers to the right of the House to charge federal officials with failure to fulfill their duties.

Section 3

a. The Senate of the United States shall be composed of two Senators from each State, chosen by the Legislature thereof, for six years; and each Senator shall have one vote.

b. Immediately after they shall be assembled in consequence of the first election, they shall be divided as equally as may be into three classes. The seats of the Senators of the first class shall be vacated at the expiration of the second year, of the second class at the expiration of the fourth year, and of the third class at the expiration of the sixth year, so that one-third may be chosen every second year; and if vacancies happen, by resignation or otherwise, during the recess of the Legislature of any State, the executive thereof may make temporary appointments until the next meeting of the Legislature, which shall then fill such vacancies.

c. No person shall be a Senator who shall not have attained the age of thirty years, and been nine years a citizen of the United States, and who shall not, when elected, be an inhabitant of that State for which he shall be chosen.

d. The Vice-President of the United States shall be President of the Senate, but shall have no vote unless they be equally divided.

e. The Senate shall choose their other officers, and also President *pro tempore* in the absence of the Vice President or when he shall exercise the office of President of the United States.

f. The Senate shall have the sole power to try all impeachments. When sitting for that purpose, they shall be on oath or affirmation. When the President of the United States is tried, the Chief Justice

The XVII Amendment cancels the phrase requiring Senators to be elected by state legislatures and provides that Senators shall be directly elected by the people.

Compare these qualifications to those of a member of the House as provided in Section 2 b.

"Equally divided" refers to the Senators being equally divided in their votes on a bill.

The Senate has the right to conduct the trials of those officials accused by the House under Section 2 e. "On oath or affirmation" refers to a solemn promise to be just. The Chief Justice of the Supreme Court shall preside over any impeachment trial of the President. Two-thirds of the Senate must find the accused guilty for conviction.

The Senate can only remove from office any person convicted under these proceedings. Regular courts may still prosecute him for any crimes he may have committed, including the crime which may have caused his impeachment.

Here the Constitution, while not listing any federal regulations of federal elections, provided that Congress may determine (and it has so determined) any such regulations at a future time.

The time of opening of the sessions of Congress was changed by the XX Amendment.

A quorum (over half of the members) must be present for the Congress to undertake any official business, though a smaller number may attend and postpone an official meeting until a later time.

While only a majority of a quorum is required for one of the houses to censure (criticize officially) one of its members, or deny him any of his congressional privileges (as distinct from his rights), a two-thirds majority of all the members of that house must agree to expel him.

While the voting records of the members of either house may be kept in a journal open to the public, no such record is required (a voice vote, not on the record, may be taken) unless one-fifth of the attending quorum votes that it shall be required for whatever bill or proposal is under discussion. This "Congressional Record" also includes many (but not all) of the speeches made in Congress, testimony at Congressional hearings, written evidence offered by Congressmen in support of their bills, and almost any material any Congressman submits to the keeper of the journal with request that it "be read into the record."

shall preside; and no person shall be convicted without the concurrence of two-thirds of the members present.

g. Judgment in cases of impeachment shall not extend further than to removal from office, and disqualification to hold and enjoy any office of honor, trust or profit under the United States; but the party convicted, shall, nevertheless, be liable and subject to indictment, trial, judgment and punishment, according to law.

Sections 4, 5 and 6 provide for the organizational procedures of the Congress.

SECTION 4

a. The times, places and manner of holding elections for Senators and Representatives shall be prescribed in each State by the Legislature thereof, but the Congress may at any time by law make or alter such regulations, except as to the places of choosing Senators.

b. The Congress shall assemble at least once in every year, and such meeting shall be on the first Monday in December, unless they shall by law appoint a different day.

SECTION 5

a. Each House shall be the judge of the elections, returns and qualifications of its own members, and a majority of each shall constitute a quorum to do business; but a smaller number may adjourn from day to day, and may be authorized to compel the attendance of absent members, in such manner and under such penalties as each House may provide.

b. Each House may determine the rule of its proceedings, punish its members for disorderly behavior, and with the concurrence of two-thirds, expel a member.

c. Each House shall keep a journal of its proceedings, and from time to time publish the same, excepting such parts as may, in their judgment, require secrecy; and the yeas and nays of the members of either House on any question shall, at the desire of one-fifth of those present, be entered on the journal.

d. Neither House, during the session of Congress, shall, without the consent of the other, adjourn for more than three days, nor to any other place than that in which the two Houses shall be sitting.

Section 6

a. The Senators and Representatives shall receive a compensation for their services, to be ascertained by law, and paid out of the treasury of the United States. They shall, in all cases except treason, felony and breach of the peace, be privileged from arrest during their attendance at the session of their respective Houses, and in going to and returning from the same; and for any speech or debate in either House they shall not be questioned in any other place.

Among the "compensations" provided members of Congress by law are their salaries, travel allowances, office expenses, and free mailing privileges, and the right to have the government printing office print up their various pamphlets and reports. Among their privileges is the freedom to speak in Congress without fear of being sued for libel or slander. Thus a slanderous statement, no matter how damaging, may be made by any Congressman against any other person and entered in the official Congressional Record. This privilege does not extend to member's remarks outside of Congress (including Congressional hearings), although their freedom from arrest will protect them if they stay out of the country between Congressional sessions.

b. No Senator or Representative shall, during the time for which he was elected, be appointed to any civil office under the authority of the United States, which shall have been created, or the emoluments whereof shall have been increased, during such time; and no person holding any office under the United States shall be a member of either House during his continuance in office.

The prohibition against appointment to certain civil offices does not apply to appointments to any military offices Congress may create and/or to the salaries (emoluments), which Congress may increase. Any Congressman holding a position in the government, such as a cabinet post, the Presidency or the Vice Presidency, shall resign his Congressional seat.

Section 7

Section 7 provides for the procedures necessary for Congress to make a law.

a. All bills for raising revenue shall originate in the House of Representatives; but the Senate may propose or concur with amendments as on other bills.

Any proposed laws to raise taxes must be first proposed in The House of Representatives.

b. Every bill which shall have passed the House of Representatives and the Senate shall, before it becomes a law, be presented to the President of the United States; if he approve, he shall sign it; but if not, he shall return it, with his objections, to that House in which it shall have originated; who shall enter the objections at large on their journal, and proceed to reconsider it. If, after such reconsideration, two-thirds of that House shall agree to pass the bill, it shall be sent, together with the objec-

The House and the Senate must agree upon a single bill. If they pass different bills on the same matter, their respective committees will attempt to write a compromise version based on the two bills and then submit this single version to a vote by both houses. If passed by both houses, the bill is then sent to the President who, as the Chief Executive, must then sign the bill into law. If he does not approve of the bill, he may "veto" it by sending it back unsigned to the house where it began. He cannot presently sign part of the bill into law and send the part of the bill he does not like back to the Congress. The Congress, upon receiving the bill, can try to agree on a version which will satisfy the President's objections, or, if two-thirds of both of the Congressional houses vote in favor of the bill, it may be made law without the President's signature. In such a case, the vote of each member of both houses shall be recorded in The Congressional Journal. If the President does not sign or return the bill within ten days, it automatically becomes law without his signature unless it was sent to him within ten days of the end of the Congressional session, in which case he can exercise a "pocket veto" by neither signing it nor returning it without fear that it will become law within ten days. This is to prevent Congress from sending the President many bills at the end of its session leaving him without enough time to study the bills and form his objections before the Congress would adjourn, leaving him with no group to which to return the vetoed bill.

Congress may issue an *order,* as distinct from a law, which is usually directed to a certain person or group, ordering them to do or cease doing a certain thing. Failure to follow this order is called "contempt of Congress" for which a person may be jailed for an indefinite period. *Resolutions* of Congress often take the form of a statement of praise for an individual or group or a statement that Congress is in agreement with some policy being pursued by the President, particularly in the field of foreign affairs.

tions, to the other House, by which it shall likewise be reconsidered; and, if approved by two-thirds of that House, it shall become a law. But in all such cases, the votes of both Houses shall be determined by yeas and nays, and the names of the persons voting for and against the bill shall be entered on the journal of each house respectively. If any bill shall not be returned by the President within ten days (Sundays excepted) after it shall have been presented to him, the same shall be a law in like manner as if he had signed it, unless the Congress, by their adjournment, prevent its return, in which case it shall not be a law.

c. Every order, resolution or vote, to which the concurrence of the Senate and House of Representatives may be necessary (except on a question of adjournment), shall be presented to the President of the United States; and, before the same shall take effect, shall be approved by him; or, being disapproved by him, shall be repassed by two-thirds of the Senate and House of Representatives, according to the rules and limitations prescribed in the case of a bill.

POWERS GRANTED:

SECTION 8

Section 8 lists the powers of the Congress. The last paragraph, giving Congress the power to make any law nesessary and proper for carrying out these powers, has been used to justify much Congressional law not specifically provided for in the Constitution. The "general welfare" clause in Section 8a has been similarly utilized.

Imposts are taxes on imports, often called tariffs. An *excise* is a tax on goods manufactured within the United States.

The Congress shall have power:
a. To lay and collect taxes, duties, imposts, and excises; to pay the debts and provide for the common defense and general welfare of the United

States; but all duties, imposts and excises shall be uniform throughout the United States.

b. To borrow money on the credit of the United States.

Congress can borrow money by issuing government bonds and bind the United States government to the repayment of such debts.

c. To regulate commerce with foreign nations, and among the several States, and with the Indian tribes.

Probably the most important power in the Constitution, the power to regulate commerce (trade) between the various states is a power of limitation on the rights of a state to try to limit other states' exports to it; thus it encouraged free trade among the states. It has also been used to justify such federal laws as Minimum Wage Legislation, The Civil Rights Law, and Child Labor Laws.

d. To establish an uniform rule of naturalization, and uniform laws on the subject of bankruptcies throughout the United States.

Naturalization is the procedure whereby a person not a citizen of the United States may become a citizen. Bankruptcy is a procedure whereby a company not able to pay its debts can sell all its assets to repay its creditors and, if the amount collected by such a sale is insufficient to pay all the bills, the officers of the company shall not be required to pay any of the remaining debt.

e. To coin money, regulate the value thereof, and of foreign coin, and fix the standard of weights and measures.

Fixing weights and measures means that Congress will determine the weight of a pound, the length of a foot, etc., for the entire country.

f. To provide for the punishment of counterfeiting the securities and current coin of the United States.

Securities include government bonds and various forms of paper money.

g. To establish postoffices and postroads.

Post roads were early federal highways for the transportation of mail.

h. To promote the progress of science and useful arts, by securing for limited times, to authors and inventors, the exclusive right to their respective writings and discoveries.

This section provides for the establishment of patents and copyrights assuring an inventor or writer that his work will not be copied during certain periods without his permission or compensation.

This provides for an unspecified number of federal courts to hear cases arising under federal law or Constitutional interpretation. Such courts are inferior to the Supreme Court, and can be overruled by it.

This law is primarily designed to define an area in which the federal government could act and a state government could not act. Thus a state could not prosecute one of its citizens for committing an act of war against a foreign nation. Only the federal government could prosecute in such a case.

Letters of Marque and Reprisal authorized private citizens to construct armed ships and capture enemy vessels at sea and, if caught, supposedly prevented the holder from being hanged as a pirate.

It is interesting to note that any money granted the Army had to be spent within two years. The Army could not undertake any long-range projects, payment for which would stretch over more than two years. No such restriction was applied to Navy appropriations.

No state can make any laws applying to Army or Navy troops without Congressional approval.

The militia is made up of state armies of private citizens, like the National Guard, which could be, and has been, ordered to enforce federal laws.

The officers of such militia units are determined by the state, without regard for any particular federal standards.

Congress alone can pass laws regulating the District of Columbia and areas purchased from states for the maintenance of federal forts, depots, ship yards, etc.

i. To constitute tribunals inferior to the Supreme Court.

j. To define and punish piracies and felonies committed on the high seas, and offenses against the law of nations.

k. To declare war, grant letters of marque and reprisal, and make rules concerning capture on land and water.

l. To raise and support armies; but no appropriation of money to that use shall be for a longer term than two years.

m. To provide and maintain a navy.

n. To make rules for the government and regulation of the land and naval forces.

o. To provide for calling forth the militia to execute the laws of the Union, suppress insurrections, and repel invasions.

p. To provide for organizing, arming and disciplining the militia, and for governing such part of them as may be employed in the service of the United States; reserving to the States respectively the appointment of the officers and the authority of training the militia according to the discipline prescribed by Congress.

q. To exercise exclusive legislation in all cases whatsoever, over such district (not exceeding ten miles square) as may, by cession of particular States, and the acceptance of Congress, become the seat of government of the United States; and to exercise like authority over all places purchased, by the consent of the Legislature of the State in which the same shall be, for the erection of forts, magazines, arsenals, dockyards, and other needful buildings; and

r. To make all laws which shall be necessary and proper for carrying into execution the foregoing powers, and all other powers vested by this Constitution in the government of the United States, or in any department or officer thereof.

POWERS DENIED:

Section 9

Section 9 denies the federal government certain powers.

a. The migration or importation of such persons as any of the States now existing shall think proper to admit, shall not be prohibited by the Congress prior to the year one thousand eight hundred and eight; but a tax or duty may be imposed on such importation not exceeding ten dollars for each person.

This is an agreement that the federal government would not prohibit the importing of slaves for a period of about twenty years after the ratification of Constitution.

b. The privilege of the writ of *habeas corpus* shall not be suspended, unless when, in cases of rebellion or invasion, the public safety may require it.

c. No bill of attainder, or *ex post facto* law, shall be passed.

A writ of habeas corpus provides that a prisoner shall have a hearing before a court and be charged with a specific crime or be released. A bill of attainder is a law providing that, when a person receives a sentence of death for certain crimes, all his property is forfeited to the state, thus punishing his widow and children for a crime they never committed. An *ex post facto law* seeks to punish a person for committing an act which was not a crime at the time the act was committed.

d. No capitation or other direct tax shall be laid unless in proportion to the census or enumeration hereinbefore directed to be taken.

A *capitation tax* is a tax paid for each person. This was modified by the XVI Amendment.

e. No tax or duty shall be laid on any articles exported from any State. No preference shall be given by any regulation of commerce or revenue to the ports of one State over those of another; nor shall vessels bound to or from one State be obliged to enter, clear or pay duties in another.

This clause seeks to make sure that the federal government does nothing to discourage trade between the states.

f. No money shall be drawn from the treasury but in consequence of appropriations made by law; and a regular statement and account of the receipts and expenditures of all public money shall be published from time to time.

No money shall be spent by the federal government unless the Congress has authorized such expenditure.

g. No title of nobility shall be granted by the United States; and no person holding any office of profit or trust under them shall, without the consent of the Congress, accept of any present, emolument, office, or title of any kind whatever, from any king, prince, or foreign state.

Bills of Credit are promissory notes designed to circulate as money. *Impairing contracts* refers to any act which makes a legal agreement between two persons of less value to one or both of them, such as declaring an existent contract void and not binding. There are many exceptions to this law.

Net produce refers to any money a state may have collected from imposts or duties in excess of what the state needs to operate the division charged with collecting such imposts or duties.

Duty of tonnage is a duty the amount of which is determined by the weight of the cargo being so taxed.

Section 10

Section 10 denies certain powers to the states. Most of these provisions are designed to prevent the states from setting up and operating counter-governments opposed to or in competition with the federal government.

a. No State shall enter into any treaty, alliance or confederation; grant letters of marque and reprisal; coin money; emit bills of credit; make anything but gold and silver coin a tender in payment of debts; pass any bill of attainder, *ex post facto* law, or law impairing the obligation of contracts; or grant any title of nobility.

b. No State shall, without the consent of the Congress, lay any imposts or duties on imports or exports, except what may be absolutely necessary for executing its inspection laws, and the net product of all duties and imposts laid by any State on imports or exports shall be for the use of the treasury of the United States, and all such laws shall be subject to the revision and control of the Congress. No State shall, without the consent of the Congress, lay any duty or tonnage, keep troops or ships of war in time of peace, enter into any agreement or compact with another State, or with a foreign power, or engage in war, unless actually invaded, or in such imminent danger as will not admit of delay.

THE PRESIDENCY:

ARTICLE II

Article II—defines the form and function of the executive (Presidential) branch of government.

Section 1

Section 1 defines the methods for the electing of the President and Vice President, his term, qualifications, salary and compensations.

Since our first President was elected in 1888, our Presidents are always elected in years divisible by four, although they don't take office until the following year.

Each party in a state appoints a number of electors equal to the number of that state's federal Representatives plus two. Whichever party wins the greatest number of Presidential votes in the election then is entitled to cast the votes of all its electors in the electoral college for its Presidential candidate. None of the electors, however, is bound to vote for his party's candidate.

a. The executive power shall be vested in the President of the United States of America. He shall hold his office during the term of four years; and, together with the Vice President chosen for the same term, be elected as follows:

b. Each State shall appoint, in such manner as the Legislature thereof may direct, a number of Electors equal to the whole number of Senators and Representatives to which the State may be entitled in the Congress; but no Senator or Representative, or person holding an office of trust or profit under the United States, shall be appointed an Elector.

c. The Electors shall meet in their respective States, and vote by ballot for two persons, of whom one at least shall not be an inhabitant of the same State with themselves. And they shall make a list of all the persons voted for, and of the number of votes for each; which list they shall sign and certify, and transmit sealed to the seat of government of the United States, directed to the President of the Senate. The President of the Senate shall, in the presence of the Senate and House of Representatives, open all the certificates, and the votes shall then be counted. The person having the greatest number of votes shall be the President, if such number be a majority of the whole number of Electors appointed; and if there be more than one who have such majority, and have an equal number of votes, then the House of Representatives shall immediately choose, by ballot, one of them for President; and if no person have a majority, then from the highest on the list, the said House shall, in like manner, choose the President. But in choosing the President, the vote shall be taken by States, the representation from each State having one vote; a quorum for this purpose shall consist of a member or members from two-thirds of the States, and a majority of all the States shall be necessary to a choice. In every case, after the choice of the President, the person having the greatest number of votes of the Electors shall be the Vice President. But if there should remain two or more who have equal votes, the Senate shall choose from them, by ballot, the Vice President.

The second paragraph was superseded by the XII Amendment.

d. The Congress may determine the time of choosing the Electors, and the day on which they shall give their votes, which day shall be the same throughout the United States.

e. No person, except a natural born citizen, or a citizen of the United States at the time of adoption of this Constitution, shall be eligible to the office of President; neither shall any person be eligible to that office who shall not have attained to the age of thirty-five years, and been fourteen years a resident within the United States.

A natural born citizen is a citizen born in the United States or born to United States citizens living outside the country or in one of the territories of the country.

f. In case of the removal of the President from office, or of his death, resignation, or inability to discharge the powers and duties of the said office, the same shall devolve on the Vice President; and the Congress may, by law, provide for the case of removal, death, resignation or inability, both of the President and Vice President, declaring what officer shall then act as President; and such officer shall act accordingly, until the disability be removed, or a President shall be elected.

No provision has yet been made as to who shall decide when the President is unable to discharge (or carry out) his powers and duties.

g. The President shall, at stated times, receive for his services a compensation which shall neither be increased nor diminished during the period for which he shall have been elected; and he shall not receive within that period any other emolument from the United States, or any of them.

h. Before he enter on the execution of his office, he shall take the following oath or affirmation:

"I do solemnly swear (or affirm) that I will faithfully execute the office of President of the United States; and will, to the best of my ability, preserve, protect and defend the Constitution of the United States."

THE EXECUTIVE POWER:

Sections 2, 3 and 4 define the powers and the duties of the President and provide for his removal from office.

SECTION 2

a. The President shall be commander-in-chief of the army and navy of the United States, and of the militia of the several States, when called into the actual service of the United States. He may require the opinion, in writing, of the principal officer in each of the executive departments, upon any subject relating to the duties of their respective offices; and he shall have power to grant reprieves and pardons for offenses against the United States, except in cases of impeachment.

The President is also the Commander-in-Chief of the Air Force, which was once a division of the Army. No military man can claim an authority equal to or greater than that of the President's. The Presidential power to require written reports on the duties of any of the executive departments, such as the department of the interior, of commerce, or of defense, is designed to enable the President to define and limit any department which may seek to over-extend its powers.

A *reprieve* delays a punishment.

A *pardon* releases a person from punishment.

While two-thirds of the Senate must consent to any treaties before the President can ratify (sign into law) them, his power to enter executive agreements with the heads of other governments without the Senate's consent has tended to weaken this limitation on Presidential power. While the Senate originally could require the President to submit all his appointments to them for approval, this is a power the Senate could, by law, deny itself. Not all Congressional powers can be delegated to others in this way, even if Congress wishes to do so.

b. He shall have power, by and with the advice and consent of the Senate, to make treaties, provided two-thirds of the Senators present concur; and he shall nominate, and by and with the advice and consent of the Senate shall appoint, ambassadors, other public ministers and consuls, judges of the Supreme Court, and all other officers of the United States whose appointments are not herein otherwise provided for, and which shall be established by law. But the Congress may, by law, vest the appointment of such inferior officers as they think proper, in the President alone, in the courts of law, or in the heads of departments.

c. The President shall have power to fill up all vacancies that may happen during the recess of the Senate, by granting commissions which shall expire at the end of their next session.

Section 3

a. He shall, from time to time, give to the Congress information of the state of the Union, and recommend to their consideration such measures as he shall judge necessary and expedient. He may on extraordinary occasions, convene both Houses, or either of them; and in case of disagreement between them, with respect to the time of adjournment, he may adjourn them to such time as he shall think proper. He shall receive ambassadors and other public ministers. He shall take care that the laws be faithfully executed; and shall commission all the officers of the United States.

Section 3—Duties of the President. The President can introduce bills to Congress for its consideration as possible laws. He can call Congress into a special session during a time when it might normally be recessed.

Faithful execution of the laws has come to mean very little. The President does not have to sign the laws. He can try to change them, or repeal them, or ignore them.

Section 4

a. The President, Vice President and all civil officers of the United States shall be removed from office on impeachment for, and conviction of treason, bribery or other high crimes and misdemeanors.

Section 4—To be removed, the President must be impeached by the House and convicted by the Senate of treason, bribery, or other serious crimes.

THE JUDICIAL POWER:

ARTICLE III

Article III—defines the form and function of the judicial branch of government, as headed by the Supreme Court.

Section 1

a. The judicial power of the United States shall be vested in one Supreme Court, and in such inferior courts as the Congress may, from time to time, ordain and establish. The judges, both of the Supreme and inferior courts, shall hold their offices during good behavior; and shall, at stated times, receive for their services a compensation, which shall not be diminished during their continuance in office.

This section confirms the right of Congress to set up lower courts for the hearing of federal cases. While Congress determines the number of justices on the Supreme Court bench, the President appoints the men to fill those positions, and their salary cannot be diminished while they are in office. Thus the justices may rule on the meaning of the Constitution without fear of temporary popular reprisals acting against them through the Congress or the Presidential office.

Section 2

Section 2 defines the powers of the Supreme Court.

a. The judicial power shall extend to all cases in law and equity arising under this Constitution, the laws of the United States, and treaties made, or which shall be made under their authority; to all cases affecting ambassadors, other public ministers and consuls; to all cases of admiralty and maritime jurisdiction; to controversies to which the United States shall be a party; to controversies between two or more States, between a State and citizens of another State, between citizens of different States, between citizens of the same State claiming lands under grants of different States, and between a

The court's first loyalty is to the Constitution. No Congressional law or Executive act can stand against the Constitution. Since all valid Congressional laws must be Constitutional, the Court hears all cases involving those laws, as well as all cases involving the Constitution itself.

The Court only rules on cases and controversies. Thus any persons seeking a Court ruling must be engaged in an actual, legal dispute with one of the parties seeking definite help, as distinct from two parties engaged in a theoretical dispute.

The jurisdiction of the court to hear controversies between a State and Citizens of another State was denied by the XI Amendment.

In the listed types of cases, the parties may come directly to the Supreme Court. In all other cases, the case is first heard by one of the lower federal courts and an appeal is made from there to the Supreme Court on the ground that the lower court made a mistake. With appellate jurisdiction, the Supreme Court may not try to change facts already decided by the lower court, but it may try to determine if the facts were properly collected and presented and if all the relevant facts were included.

State, or the citizens thereof, and foreign States, citizens or subjects.

b. In all cases affecting ambassadors, other public ministers and consuls, and those in which a State shall be a party, the Supreme Court shall have original jurisdiction. In all the other cases before mentioned, the Supreme Court shall have appellate jurisdiction, both as to law and fact, with such exceptions and under such regulations as the Congress shall make.

c. The trial of all crimes, except in cases of impeachment, shall be by jury, and such trial shall be held in the State where the said crimes shall have been committed, but when not committed within any State, the trial shall be at such place or places as the Congress may by law have directed.

Note that this section is referring to trials for crimes arising under the Constitution.

Section 3—defines treason because it is a serious offense frequently mentioned in the Constitution and because it is a crime the definition of which governments frequently like to expand. For instance, some leaders have claimed that any criticism directed against them or their government is treason. The Constitution limits treason to making war on the United States or supporting enemies of the United States. "Enemy" is a term that has in the past meant only those governments against which the United States has issued a declaration of war.

An overt act is an act seen by others.

Section 3

a. Treason against the United States shall consist only in levying war against them or in adhering to their enemies, giving them aid and comfort. No person shall be convicted of treason, unless on the testimony of two witnesses to the same overt act, or on confession in open court.

b. The Congress shall have power to declare the punishment of treason; but no attainder of treason shall work corruption of blood, or forfeiture, except during the life of the person attainted.

Congress can declare the punishment for treason after the treasonous act has occurred, but Congress cannot punish the children or heirs of the convicted party by seizing the guilty man's property or estate or by denying citizenship or other rights to those children, heirs or relations.

CONCERNING THE STATES:

ARTICLE IV

Article IV—defines the federal system—the relationship between the United States government and the state governments and the relationships between the various state governments.

Section 1

This section requires that each state accept as final the official acts and determinations of other states. This section most frequently involves judicial determinations of one state

a. Full faith and credit shall be given in each State to the public acts, records and judicial proceedings of every other State; and the Congress may, by general laws, prescribe the manner in which such acts, records and proceedings shall be proved, and the effect thereof.

which may have a bearing on the legal rights of two parties in another case in another state.

Section 2

a. The citizens of each State shall be entitled to all privileges and immunities of citizens in the several States.

b. A person charged in any State with treason, felony or other crime, who shall flee from justice, and be found in another State, shall on demand of the executive authority of the State from which he fled, be delivered up, to be removed to the State having jurisdiction of the crime.

c. No person held to service or labor in one State under the laws therof, escaping into another, shall, in consequence of any law or regulation therein, be discharged from such service or labor; but shall be delivered up on claim of the party to whom such service or labor may be due.

This section provides that people visiting in a state shall have the same privileges and freedoms as the residents of that state.

Section 3

a. New States may be admitted by the Congress into this Union; but no new State shall be formed or erected within the jurisdiction of any other State, nor any State be formed by the junction of two or more States or parts of States, without the consent of the Legislatures of the States concerned, as well as of the Congress.

b. The Congress shall have the power to dispose of, and make all needful rules and regulations respecting the territory or other property belonging to the United States; and nothing in this Constitution shall be so construed as to prejudice any claims of the United States or of any particular State.

This paragraph was made obsolete by the XIII Amendment.

Section 3—provides for the admission of new states to the United States and for the acquisition and control of territorial areas.

The only state carved out of an existent state in recent times is West Virginia, and this was done without the permission of Virginia which was claiming it was not part of the United States at the time and thus lost its right to complain.

Congress can sell and regulate all territories and no territories can use any of the rights of the Constitution to support a case against, or defend against a case by, the United States or any single state.

Section 4

a. The United States shall guarantee to every State in this Union a republican form of government, and shall protect each of them against invasion; and, on application of the Legislature, or of the executive (when the Legislature cannot be convened), against domestic violence.

This section provides that federal troops shall be used to put down violence in a state only if that state's legislature or governor asks them to come—unless the violence is acting to prevent the operation of federal laws or rulings.

FINAL PROVISIONS:

ARTICLE V

Article V—provides for the amending or changing of the Constitution.

This paragraph provides two alternative ways to propose and two alternative ways to adopt an amendment to the Constitution. Two-thirds of both the House and the Senate may propose an amendment, or Congress must call a Convention for the purpose of proposing an amendment if the legislatures of two-thirds of the states request it. Once proposed, the amendment must be approved by the legislatures of three-fourths of the states or by special convention in three-fourths of the states.

No amendment can deny a state its equal representation in the Senate.

a. The Congress, whenever two-thirds of both Houses shall deem it necessary, shall propose amendments to this Constitution; or, on the application of the Legislatures of two-thirds of the several States, shall call a convention for proposing amendments, which, in either case, shall be valid to all intents and purposes, as part of this Constitution, when ratified by the Legislatures of three-fourths of the several States, or by conventions in three-fourths thereof, as the one or the other mode of ratification may be proposed by the Congress; provided that no amendment, which may be made prior to the year one thousand eight hundred and eight, shall in any manner affect the first and fourth clauses in the ninth section of the first article; and that no State, without its consent, shall be deprived of its equal suffrage in the Senate.

ARTICLE VI

Article VI—further clarifies certain aspects of the Constitution.

The new government created by the Constitution would pay all debts of the old Confederation including the redemption of money issued by that government.

By providing that the Constitution is the Supreme Law of the Land, the Supreme Court, as the interpreter of that Constitution, becomes the final authority on all federal laws and no state can defy that authority, nor can any state choose which federal laws it will follow, which it will ignore.

a. All debts contracted and engagements entered into before the adoption of this Constitution shall be as valid against the United States under this Constitution, as under the Confederation.

b. This Constitution, and the laws of the United States which shall be made in pursuance thereof, and all treaties made, or which shall be made, under the authority of the United States, shall be the supreme law of the land; and the judges in every State shall be bound thereby, anything in the Constitution or laws of any State to the contrary notwithstanding.

c. The Senators and Representatives before mentioned, and the members of the several State Legislatures, and all executive and judicial officers, both of the United States and of the several States, shall be bound by oath or affirmation to support this Constitution; but no religious test shall ever be required as a qualification to any office or public trust under the United States.

ARTICLE VII

The ratification of the Conventions of nine States shall be sufficient for the establishment of this Constitution between the States so ratifying the same.

Done in convention, by the unanimous consent of the States present, the seventeenth day of September, in the year of our Lord one thousand seven hundred and eighty-seven, and of the independence of the United States of America the twelfth.

In witness whereof, we have hereunto subscribed our names.

GEORGE WASHINGTON,
President, and Deputy from Virginia

New Hampshire
John Langdon
Nicholas Gilman

Massachusetts
Nathaniel Gorham
Rufus King

Connecticut
William Samuel Johnson
Roger Sherman

New York
Alexander Hamilton

New Jersey
William Livingston
David Brearley
William Paterson
Jonathan Dayton

Pennsylvania
Benjamin Franklin
Thomas Mifflin
Robert Morris
George Clymer
Thomas Fitzsimmons
Jared Ingersoll
James Wilson
Gouverneur Morris

Delaware
George Read
Gunning Bedford, Jr.
John Dickinson
Richard Bassett
Jacob Broom

Maryland
James M'Henry
Daniel of St. Thomas Jenifer
Daniel Carroll

Virginia
John Blair
James Madison, Jr.

North Carolina
William Blount
Richard Dobbs Spaight
Hugh Williamson

South Carolina
John Rutledge
Charles C. Pinckney
Charles Pinckney
Pierce Butler

Georgia
William Few
Abraham Baldwin

Attest:
William Jackson, Secretary

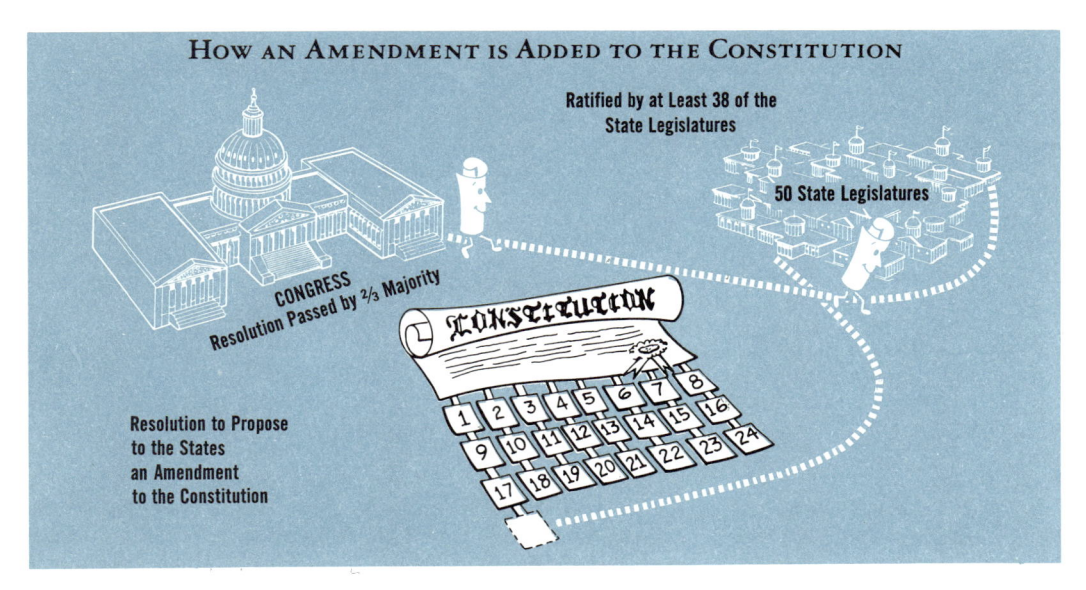

How an Amendment is Added to the Constitution

Resolution to Propose to the States an Amendment to the Constitution

CONGRESS
Resolution Passed by ⅔ Majority

Ratified by at Least 38 of the State Legislatures

50 State Legislatures

THE AMENDMENTS:

[The following ten amendments were proposed at the first session of the first Congress of the United States, which was begun and held at the city of New York on the fourth of March, 1789, and were ratified by December, 1791, by the requisite number of States. They are often referred to as the Bill of Rights.]

AMENDMENT I

Respecting an establishment of religion has been interpreted to apply to any act which would tend to aid or support a religious group.

Abridging (or restricting) the freedom of speech has been allowed out of consideration of public safety. *Petitioning the government for a redress of grievances* refers to the process of gathering and jointly requesting of the government a correction of some injustice.

Congress shall make no law respecting an establishment of religion, or prohibiting the free exercise thereof, or abridging the freedom of speech or of the press, or the right of the people peaceably to assemble, and to petition the government for a redress of grievances.

AMENDMENT II

It might be noted that this amendment states the right, in this case to keep and bear arms, and the purpose of this right. It is now debated whether the right should be maintained when the purpose of the right is no longer served.

A well regulated militia, being necessary to the security of a free State, the right of the people to keep and bear arms shall not be infringed.

AMENDMENT III

Quartering a soldier would involve keeping him in your home, feeding him and providing shelter, thereby relieving the government of this responsibility.

No soldier shall, in time of peace, be quartered in any house without the consent of the owner; nor in time of war but in a manner to be prescribed by law.

AMENDMENT IV

No federal agent can search or take evidence from a citizen, his house, or any of his property, without a warrant which will only be issued to the agent by a court after he has shown why he thinks he may find evidence of a crime with this warrant, stated the person or evidence he seeks, and described the place he intends to search. Any evidence collected without such a warrant shall not be allowed in any federal court as evidence of any crime.

The right of the people to be secure in their persons, houses, paper and effects, against unreasonable searches and seizures shall not be violated; and no warrants shall issue but upon probable cause, supported by oath or affirmation, and particularly describing the place to be searched, and the persons or things to be seized.

AMENDMENT V

No man shall be brought to trial for a serious crime unless he has first been charged with that crime by a grand jury, nor shall he be tried twice

No person shall be held to answer for a capital or otherwise infamous crime, unless on a presentment or indictment of a grand jury, except in cases arising in the land or naval forces, or in the militia, when in actual service in time of war or public danger; nor shall any person be subject for the same offense to be twice put in jeopardy of life or limb; nor shall be compelled, in any criminal case, to be a witness against himself, nor be deprived of life, liberty or property, without due process of law; nor shall private property be taken for public use without just compensation.

for a single crime, nor shall he be required to give information at his trial which might tend to prove his guilt.

Due process of law is a phrase, the meaning of which is unclear. It would exclude arbitrary, unjudicial, illegal procedures, and would include, in some cases, a right to a trial by jury.

AMENDMENT VI

In all criminal prosecutions, the accused shall enjoy the right to a speedy and public trial, by an impartial jury of the State and district wherein the crime shall have been committed, which district shall have been previously ascertained by law; and to be informed of the nature and cause of the accusation; to be confronted with the witnesses against him; to have compulsory process for obtaining witnesses in his favor, and to have the assistance of counsel for his defense.

Any man charged with a crime shall quickly be brought to trial, in public, before a fair jury, in the area where the crime took place. He shall be told of the crime with which he is charged, shall be able to see and question all those who claim to have evidence proving his guilt, can have the court force any witness who might help him to attend the trial and to testify, and can have the aid of an attorney.

AMENDMENT VII

In suits at common law, where the value in controversy shall exceed twenty dollars, the right of trial by jury shall be preserved; and no fact tried by a jury shall be otherwise re-examined in any court of the United States, than according to the rules of the common law.

In any case involving a dispute between two parties over their legal obligations to each other, as distinct from a case involving the violation of a written law, where one of the parties claims a right against the other, the value of which is greater than twenty dollars, there shall be a trial by jury unless such a jury is not wanted by either party. Any decision of the jury regarding the facts in dispute shall be final and, if the case is appealed to a higher federal court, that higher court cannot re-examine or change those facts, though it may add new facts or declare some of the facts inadmissible as evidence.

AMENDMENT VIII

Excessive bail shall not be required, nor excessive fines imposed, nor cruel and unusual punishments inflicted.

Bail is money which a person charged with a crime can promise to the court and consequently can be freed from jail until the time of his trial. Failure to appear at his trial would mean the money so promised would be given to the court.

Cruel and unusual punishments include torture and any practices outside the customary punishments of imprisonment, hard labor, and various forms of execution.

AMENDMENT IX

The enumeration in the Constitution of certain rights shall not be construed to deny or disparage others retained by the people.

The listing of individual rights in the Constitution does not mean that these are all the rights those individuals have.

AMENDMENT X

The powers not delegated to the United States by the Constitution, nor prohibited by it to the States, are reserved to the States respectively, or to the people.

> The United States government only has those powers listed in the Constitution. The States or the People have all other unlisted rights.

> Remember that the first ten amendments, when adopted, were considered to involve rights of citizens against actions of the federal government. They did not extend to state governments, which often violated these rights.

AMENDMENT XI

[Submitted by Congress to the State Legislatures in March, 1794, duly ratified, and proclaimed in January, 1798.]

The judicial power of the United States shall not be construed to extend to any suit in law or equity, commenced or prosecuted against one of the United States by citizens of another State, or by citizens or subjects of any foreign State.

> No person of another state can bring suit in court against a state without that state's permission. Without this legal immunity from suits by out-of-state residents as well as local residents, most states would be buried by lawsuits, since the exercise of their powers operates very close to the people.

AMENDMENT XII

[Submitted by Congress to the State Legislatures in December, 1803, duly ratified, and proclaimed in September, 1804.]

1. The Electors shall meet in their respective States, and vote by ballot for President and Vice President, one of whom at least shall not be an inhabitant of the same State with themselves. They shall name in their ballots the person voted for as President, and in distinct ballots the person voted for as Vice President; and they shall make distinct lists of all persons voted for as President, and of all persons voted for as Vice President, and of the number of votes for each; which lists they shall sign and certify, and transmit sealed to the seat of the government of the United States, directed to the President of the Senate. The President of the Senate shall, in the presence of the Senate and House of Representatives, open all the certificates and the votes shall then be counted. The person having the greatest number of votes for President shall be the President, if such number be a majority of the whole number of Electors appointed; and if no person have such majority, then from the persons having the highest numbers, not exceeding three, on the list of those voted for as President, the House of Representatives shall choose immediately, by ballot, the President. But in choosing the President, the votes shall be taken by States, the representation from each State having one vote; a quorum for this purpose shall consist of a member

> After casting and counting their ballots, the state electors shall swear that their count be accurate and shall send it to the President of the Senate (usually the Vice President of the United States). Before a joint session of the House and Senate, the President of the Senate shall count the electoral votes certified to him by the state electors. If no one of the candidates for President has a majority of the electoral votes, the three candidates with the most votes shall be offered to the House of Representatives which shall then vote to determine the winner, each state's group of representatives having one vote only. More than half of the states must agree on a single candidate.

or members from two-thirds of the States, and a majority of all the States shall be necessary to a choice. And if the House of Representatives shall not choose a President, whenever the right of choice shall devolve upon them, before the fourth day of March next following, then the Vice President shall act as President as in the case of the death or other constitutional disability of the President.

2. The person having the greatest number of votes as Vice President shall be the Vice President, if such number be a majority of the whole number of Electors appointed, and if no person have a majority, then from the two highest numbers on the list the Senate shall choose the Vice President. A quorum for the purpose shall consist of two-thirds of the whole number of Senators, and a majority of the whole number shall be necessary to a choice.

3. But no person constitutionally ineligible to the office of President shall be eligible to that of Vice President of the United States.

AMENDMENT XIII

[Submitted by Congress to the State Legislatures in February, 1865, duly ratified and proclaimed in December, 1865.]

1. Neither slavery nor involuntary servitude, except as a punishment for crime, whereof the party shall have been duly convicted, shall exist within the United States, or any place subject to their jurisdiction.

2. Congress shall have power to enforce this article by appropriate legislation.

This amendment, while abolishing slavery, has also acted to prevent the enforcement of any contracts involving personal services. For instance, if an opera singer promises to give a concert and then decides he doesn't want to, he cannot be forced to sing against his will.

AMENDMENT XIV

[Submitted by Congress to the State Legislatures in June, 1866, duly ratified, and proclaimed in July, 1868.]

1. All persons born or naturalized in the United States, and subject to the jurisdiction thereof, are citizens of the United States and of the State wherein they reside. No State shall make or enforce any law which shall abridge the privileges or immunities of citizens of the United States; nor shall any State deprive any person of life, liberty or property, without due process of law, nor deny to any person within its jurisdiction the equal protection of the laws.

This is probably the most important amendment to the Constitution. Section one prohibits states from abridging (denying) any of the privileges and immunities (or rights) of a United States citizen. What rights does a United States citizen have? Over a period of time the Supreme Court has decided he has those rights listed in the Constitution and its amendments. Thus the first ten amendments, which originally only restricted the federal government, now apply to the states as well. The section requiring "due process of law" has also been interpreted to protect a broad range of rights, as does the "equal protection of the laws" phrase which protects individuals from discriminatory state actions of any kind.

> This section was designed to prevent any state from attempting to deny the right to vote to any of its citizens. The penalty for doing so would be a reduction of that state's representation in the House. Curiously enough, this section has never been effectively utilized.

2. Representatives shall be apportioned among the several States according to their respective numbers, counting the whole number of persons in each State, excluding Indians not taxed. But when the right to vote at any election for the choice of Electors for President and Vice President of the United States, Representatives in Congress, the executive and judicial officers of a State, or the members of the Legislature thereof, is denied to any of the male inhabitants of such State, being twenty-one years of age, and citizens of the United States, or in any way abridged, except for participation in rebellion or other crime, the basis of representation therein shall be reduced in the proportion which the number of such male citizens shall bear to the whole number of male citizens twenty-one years of age in such State.

> This section was designed to deny any and all political positions to all supporters of the Confederacy who had previously held any federal or state position including positions in the Army. Note that they are not only denied any offices in the federal government but also in the state governments. Thus a large percentage of the white Southerners were denied any voice in their government.

3. No person shall be a Senator or Representative in Congress, or Elector of President and Vice President, or hold any office, civil or military, under the United States, or under any State, who having previously taken an oath as a member of Congress, or as an officer of the United States, or as a member of any State Legislature, or as an executive or judicial officer of any State, to support the Constitution of the United States, shall have engaged in insurrection or rebellion against the same, or given aid or comfort to the enemies thereof. But Congress may, by a vote of two-thirds of each House, remove such disability.

> This section operated to make all financial promises of the Confederate government worthless. Confederate soldiers who had been paid with Confederate money thus found their money to be worthless. Merchants, no matter where, who sold their goods to the Confederacy in exchange for Confederate money or bonds, could not collect their debts.

4. The validity of the public debt of the United States authorized by law, including debts incurred for payment of pensions and bounties for services in suppressing insurrection or rebellion, shall not be questioned. But neither the United States nor any State shall assume or pay any debt or obligation incurred in aid of insurrection or rebellion against the United States, or any claim for the loss or emancipation of any slave; but all such debts, obligations, and claims shall be held illegal and void.

5. The Congress shall have the power to enforce, by appropriate legislation, the provisions of this article.

AMENDMENT XV

[Submitted by Congress to the State Legislatures in February, 1869, duly ratified, and proclaimed in March, 1870.]

1. The rights of citizens of the United States to vote shall not be denied or abridged by the United

States or by any State on account of race, color, or previous condition of servitude.

2. The Congress shall have power to enforce this article by appropriate legislation.

AMENDMENT XVI

[Submitted by Congress to the State Legislatures in July, 1909, duly ratified, and proclaimed in February, 1913.]

The Congress shall have power to lay and collect taxes on incomes, from whatever source derived, without apportionment among the several States, and without regard to any census or enumeration.

This amendment made it possible for the federal government to tax a given income at a certain rate without regard to the state in which the tax payer might live. Prior to this amendment, a state with a small population, even if that population consisted entirely of millionaires, could not be required to pay a larger tax than another state of the same population.

AMENDMENT XVII

[Submitted by Congress to the State Legislatures in May, 1912, duly ratified, and proclaimed in May, 1913.]

1. The Senate of the United States shall be composed of two Senators from each State, elected by the people thereof, for six years; and each Senator shall have one vote. The Electors in each State shall have the qualifications requisite for Electors of the most numerous branch of the State Legislatures.

2. When vacancies happen in the representation of any State in the Senate, the executive authority of such State shall issue writs of election to fill such vacancies: Provided, That the Legislature of any State may empower the executive thereof to make temporary appointment until the people fill the vacancies by election as the Legislature may direct.

3. This amendment shall not be so construed as to affect the election or term of any Senator chosen before it becomes valid as part of the Constitution.

This amendment terminated the old practice of electing Senators representing the various states by their states' legislatures. Now the people themselves directly vote for the men who shall represent them in the Senate.

AMENDMENT XVIII

[Submitted by Congress to the State Legislatures in December, 1917, duly ratified, and proclaimed in January, 1919, as going into full force and effect January 16, 1920.]

1. After one year from the ratification of this article the manufacture, sale or transportation of intoxicating liquors within, the importation thereof into, or the exportation thereof from the United States and all territory subject to the jurisdiction thereof for beverage purposes is hereby prohibited.

2. The Congress and the several States shall have concurrent power to enforce this article by appropriate legislation.

Though directed against the distributors rather than the drinkers of intoxicating liquors, this amendment was designed to stop the practice of drinking alcohol. It did not achieve its end and was repealed by the XXI Amendment.

3. This article shall be inoperative unless it shall have been ratified as an amendment to the Constitution by the Legislatures of the several States, as provided by the Constitution, within seven years from the date of the submission hereof to the States by the Congress.

AMENDMENT XIX

[Submitted by Congress to the State Legislatures in June, 1919, duly ratified, and proclaimed in August, 1920.]

Many supported this amendment in the hope that politicians, if they had to appeal to women voters as well as men, might be more honest and moral.

1. The rights of citizens of the United States to vote shall not be denied or abridged by the United States or by any State on account of sex.
2. Congress shall have the power, by appropriate legislation, to enforce the provisions of this article.

AMENDMENT XX

[Submitted by Congress to the State Legislatures in March, 1932, duly ratified, and proclaimed in January, 1933.]

This amendment was designed to clear up several procedural problems in the operation of the government.

Sections one and two ended the earlier practice of having the new Congress in session almost three months before the President elected in the same election as that Congress could take office.

1. The terms of the President and Vice President shall end at noon on the 20th day of January, and the terms of Senators and Representatives at noon on the 3rd day of January of the years in which such terms would have ended if this article had not been ratified; and the terms of their successors shall then begin.

2. The Congress shall assemble at least once in every year, and such meeting shall begin at noon on the 3rd day of January, unless they shall by law appoint a different day.

Section three attempts to provide for the case when a President might die after his election but before his inauguration. This amendment does not provide for the interval between the time the Presidential candidate wins the popular election and the time the electoral college meets to cast its votes for him.

3. If, at the time fixed for the beginning of the term of the President, the President elect shall have died, the Vice President elect shall become President. If a President shall not have been chosen before the time fixed for the beginning of his term, or if the President elect shall have failed to qualify, then the Vice President elect shall act as President until a President shall have qualified; and the Congress may by law provide for the case wherein neither a President elect or a Vice President elect shall have qualified, declaring who shall then act as President, or the manner in which one who is to act shall be selected, and such person shall act accordingly until a President or Vice President shall have qualified.

Section four applies in cases when no Presidential candidate has received a majority of the electoral

4. The Congress may by law provide for the case of the death of any of the persons from whom the House of Representatives may choose a President

whenever the right of choice shall have devolved upon them, and for the case of the death of any of the persons from whom the Senate may choose a Vice President whenever the right of choice shall have devolved upon them.

5. Sections 1 and 2 shall take effect on the 15th day of October following the ratification of this article.

6. This article shall be inoperative unless it shall have been ratified as an amendment to the Constitution by the Legislatures of three-fourths of the several States within seven years from the date of its submission.

votes and the House of Representatives must decide the winner from among the three candidates with the most votes. If any of those candidates have died, the House can add replacement candidates.

AMENDMENT XXI

[Submitted by Congress to State Conventions in February, 1933, duly ratified, and proclaimed in December, 1933.]

1. The eighteenth article of amendment to the Constitution of the United States is hereby repealed.

2. The transportation or importation into any State, Territory, or Possession of the United States for delivery or use therein of intoxicating liquors, in violation of the laws thereof, is hereby prohibited.

3. This article shall be inoperative unless it shall have been ratified as an amendment to the Constitution by conventions in the several States, as provided in the Constitution, within seven years from the date of the submission hereof to the States by the Congress.

Section two provides that any state which wishes to prohibit intoxicating liquor within its boundaries shall have its wishes respected by neighboring states who may not send liquor into that state for the purpose of sale or consumption.

AMENDMENT XXII

[Submitted by Congress to the State Legislatures in March, 1947, duly ratified, and proclaimed in February, 1951.]

No person shall be elected to the office of the President more than twice, and no person who has held the office of President, or acted as President, for more than two years of a term to which some other person was elected President shall be elected to the office of the President more than once. But this Article shall not apply to any person holding the office of President when this Article was proposed by the Congress, and shall not prevent any person who may be holding the office of President, or acting as President, during the term within which this Article becomes operative from holding the office of President or acting as President during the remainder of such term.

Prior to the four Presidential terms of Franklin Delano Roosevelt, won in the elections of 1932 through 1944, no President had run for more than two terms. In reaction to Roosevelt's break with tradition, Republicans pushed this amendment only to have it take effect at a time when they had a candidate (Eisenhower) they would have liked to have had run for a third term.

This amendment enables the residents of the District of Columbia to vote for the President and Vice President. No matter what the population of the District may be, it cannot have more votes than the least populous state, which is presently Alaska with three electors (two Senators and one Representative). This amendment does not enable a resident of the District to have any representation in the Congress or any political voice in the operation of his local government (the District of Columbia is governed by the United States Congress).

AMENDMENT XXIII

[The following amendment was submitted to the Legislatures of the 50 states following approval by voice votes in both houses of the 87th Congress (House June 14, 1960; Senate June 16, 1960). Ratification by the required three-fourths majority of the states was completed March 29, 1961, when Kansas became the 38th state to ratify, 42 minutes before approval by the Ohio Legislature. Arkansas was the only state to reject the amendment. The amendment was formally declared a part of the Constitution on April 3, 1961.]

1. The District constituting the seat of Government of the United States shall appoint in such manner as the Congress may direct:
A number of electors of President and Vice President equal to the whole number of Senators and Representatives in Congress to which the District would be entitled if it were a State, but in no event more than the least populous State; they shall be in addition to those appointed by the States, but they shall be considered, for the purposes of the election of President and Vice President, to be electors appointed by a State; and they shall meet in the District and perform such duties as provided by the twelfth article of amendment.

2. The Congress shall have power to enforce this article by appropriate legislation.

AMENDMENT XXIV

[The following amendment was submitted to the Legislatures of the 50 states September 14, 1962, after approval by both houses of the 87th Congress. It became a part of the Constitution after ratification by the required 38 states was completed January 23, 1964; South Dakota was the 38th state to ratify.]

1. The right of citizens of the United States to vote in any primary or other election for President or Vice President, for electors or President or Vice President, or for Senator or Representative in Congress, shall not be denied or abridged by the United States or any State by reason of failure to pay any poll tax or other tax.

2. The Congress shall have the power to enforce this article by appropriate legislation.

IMPORTANT DATES IN AMERICAN HISTORY

1492	Columbus discovers America
1497	Cabot explores east coast of North America
1513	Balboa discovers the Pacific Ocean Ponce de Leon lands in Florida
1523	Verrazano explores east coast of North America
1534	Cartier discovers the St. Lawrence River
1539–42	DeSoto explores southeastern North America and discovers the Mississippi River
1540–42	Coronado explores southwestern North America
1585–87	Attempts to establish colonies on Roanoke Island fail
1607	Jamestown is founded
1608	Quebec is founded
1609	Hudson discovers the Hudson River
1610	Hudson discovers Hudson Bay
1614	Dutch establish first settlements in New Netherlands
1619	Virginia House of Burgesses meets for the first time The first Negroes arrive in Virginia
1620	Pilgrims land at Plymouth and draw up the Mayflower Compact
1630	Puritans establish the Massachusetts Bay Colony
1634	First settlement in Maryland
1636	Roger Williams founds Providence, the first settlement in Rhode Island Connecticut settlements founded
1638	Fort Christina in Delaware founded New Haven founded
1639	Fundamental Orders of Connecticut
1649	Act Concerning Religion in Maryland
1664	English capture New Netherland and rename it New York New Jersey becomes an English colony
1672	Charleston, South Carolina, is founded
1673	Marquette and Joliet explore the Mississippi River
1682	Penn and the Quakers found Pennsylvania LaSalle reaches the mouth of the Mississippi and claims Louisiana for France
1733	Oglethorpe founds Georgia
1754	French and Indian War begins
1754	Albany Plan of Union
1759	Fall of Quebec
1763	Treaty of Paris ends French and Indian War; France cedes New France to Great Britain Proclamation of 1763

1765	Stamp Act
1767	Townshend Acts
1770	Boston Massacre
1772	Committees of Correspondence organized
1773	Boston Tea Party
1774	Intolerable Acts First Continental Congress meets
1775	Battles of Lexington and Concord Second Continental Congress meets Battle of Bunker Hill
1776	Declaration of Independence Victory at Trenton
1777	Victory at Princeton Battle at Saratoga
1777–78	Winter at Valley Forge
1778	France allies itself with the Thirteen States
1778–79	George Rogers Clark captures British forts in the West
1781	Cornwallis surrenders at Yorktown Articles of Confederation go into effect
1783	Treaty of Paris ends the Revolutionary War and recognizes the independence of the Thirteen States
1785	Land Ordinance of 1785
1787	Constitutional Convention Northwest Ordinance
1789	Washington inaugurated as the first President
1790	Slater builds a spinning mill in Rhode Island
1791	Bill of Rights added to the Constitution
1793	Whitney invents the cotton gin
1794	Whiskey Rebellion put down
1797	Adams becomes President
1797–98	XYZ Affair
1798	Alien and Sedition Acts Virginia and Kentucky Resolutions
1801	Thomas Jefferson becomes President
1803	Louisiana Purchase
1807	Fulton's Steamboat a success
1808	Importation of slaves prohibited
1809	James Madison becomes President
1811	National Road is begun
1812–14	War of 1812
1813	Perry won the Battle of Lake Erie
1814	Hartford Convention Writing of the *Star Spangled Banner* Treaty of Ghent
1815	Battle of New Orleans

1817	James Monroe becomes President
1819	Florida ceded to U.S. by Spain
1820	Missouri Compromise
1823	Monroe Doctrine
1825	Erie Canal opened
1828	Baltimore and Ohio Railroad begun
1829	Andrew Jackson becomes President
1830	Webster-Hayne debate
1832	Nullification crisis
1834	McCormick invents the reaper
1836	Texas wins independence from Mexico
1838	Underground Railroad organized
1842	Webster-Ashburton Treaty
1844	Morse sends first telegraph message Goodyear patents his method of vulcanizing rubber
1845	James Polk becomes President
1846	Howe invents the sewing machine Oregon Boundary settlement
1846–47	Development of Hoe rotary press
1846–48	Mexican War
1848	Treaty of Guadalupe-Hidalgo
1848	Women's Rights Convention in New York State
1849	California gold rush Clayton-Bulwer Treaty
1850	Compromise of 1850
1852	*Uncle Tom's Cabin* published
1853	Gadsden Purchase
1854	Perry opens Japan Kansas-Nebraska Act Republican Party organized
1856	"Bleeding Kansas"
1857	Dred Scott decision
1858	Lincoln-Douglas debate
1859	First oil well drilled in Pennsylvania
1860	South Carolina secedes
1861	Abraham Lincoln becomes President Fall of Fort Sumter
1861	Civil War
1862	Battle of *Monitor* and *Merrimac* Homestead Act Morrill Act provides for land-grant colleges
1863	Emancipation Proclamation Battle of Gettysburg Siege of Vicksburg

1864	Sherman's march through the South
1865	Lee surrenders to Grant at Appomattox Court House Freedman's Bureau established Assassination of Lincoln Andrew Johnson becomes President Maximilian Affair Thirteenth Amendment abolishes slavery
1866	Atlantic cable successfully laid
1867	First Reconstruction Act Alaska purchased from Russia Beginning of Granger movement
1868	Fourteenth Amendment gives citizenship to everyone Impeachment proceedings against Johnson Fifteenth Amendment gives Negroes the right to vote
1869	Ulysses S. Grant becomes President Transcontinental Railroad completed Knights of Labor founded
1876	Telephone invented by Bell Disputed Hayes-Tilden Presidential election
1877	Reconstruction ends
1878	Bland-Allison Act
1879	Edison improves the incandescent lamp
1882	Chinese immigration restricted
1883	Pendleton (Civil Service) Act
1885	Grover Cleveland becomes President
1886	A.F. of L. founded Haymarket Riot
1887	Interstate Commerce Act Dawes Act
1889	First Pan-American conference
1890	Sherman Silver Act Sherman Antitrust law
1892	Populist Party holds its first national convention
1893	First successful automobile
1896	*Plessy* vs. *Ferguson* decision
1897	William McKinley becomes President
1898	Spanish-American War Annexation of Hawaii
1899	First Hague Peace Conference Open Door Policy
1900	Gold Standard Act
1901	McKinley assassinated Theodore Roosevelt becomes President Hay-Pauncefote Treaty
1903	Hay-Bunau-Varilla Treaty Wright Brothers make first successful airplane flight
1904	Roosevelt Corollary to the Monroe Doctrine

1906	Pure Food and Drug Act
1907	Second Hague Peace Conference Gentlemen's Agreement with Japan
1912	Progressive Party organized
1913	Woodrow Wilson becomes President Federal Reserve Act
1913	Sixteenth Amendment authorizes the income tax Seventeenth Amendment provides for direct election of Senators
1914	World War I begins Panama Canal opens Clayton Antitrust Act
1917	U.S. enters World War I
1918	Wilson announces the Fourteen Points End of World War I
1919	Treaty of Versailles
1920	U.S. refuses to join the League of Nations
1921	Washington Naval Conference
1924	Immigration Quota Act
1927	First talking movie
1928	Kellogg-Briand Pact
1929	Crash of '29
1933	Franklin Roosevelt becomes President
1933–36	Good Neighbor Policy New Deal Reforms
1935	C.I.O. formed
1940	Selective Service Act Destroyer-Bases Deal Roosevelt elected for a third term
1941	Lend-lease Atlantic Charter Attack on Pearl Harbor U.S. declares war on Japan and Germany
1942	Invasion of Africa Battle of the Coral Sea
1943	Invasion of Italy Conquest of Guadalcanal
1944	D-Day "Island-hopping" in the Pacific
1945	Yalta Conference Roosevelt died Harry Truman becomes President U.N. formed Potsdam conference Atomic bombs dropped on Japan End of World War II
1946	Philippines becomes independent

1947	Truman Doctrine Marshall Plan Taft-Hartley Act
1948	OAS formed
1949	NATO established Berlin airlift Point Four program
1950–53	Korean War
1951	Twenty-Second Amendment limits the terms of the President Peace treaty with Japan signed
1952	McCarran Immigration Act Television used in presidential campaign Hydrogen bomb tested
1953	Dwight D. Eisenhower becomes President Korean truce signed
1954	*Brown* vs. *Board of Education of Topeka* decision SEATO formed Censure of McCarthy
1955	A.F. of L.-C.I.O. Merger
1956	Suez Canal crisis
1957	Eisenhower Doctrine Civil Rights Bill Soviet Union launches first satellite
1958	U.S. launches first satellite
1959	Castro revolution in Cuba St. Lawrence Seaway opens
1960	U-2 incident
1961	John F. Kennedy becomes President Peace Corps formed Alliance for Progress formed U.S. becomes directly involved in Vietnam
1962	U.S. launches first manned space flight Telstar launched Confrontation with Russia over missile bases in Cuba
1963	Limited Test Ban Treaty halts nuclear tests in the atmosphere Civil Rights march on Washington Kennedy assassinated Lyndon Johnson becomes President
1964	Civil Rights Law War on Poverty Program Lyndon Johnson elected Nikita Khrushchev ousted
1965	Lyndon Johnson inaugurated

BIBLIOGRAPHY

Adams, James Truslow, ed. in chief, *Album of American History*, Vols. 1–5. Scribner's: 1944–1960. Original drawings, prints, and photographs illustrating American history from the Colonial Period to the inauguration of President Eisenhower.

Adams, James Truslow, ed. in chief, *Atlas of American History*. Scribner's: 1943. Chronology of United States geographic history from discovery to 1912; indexed.

Angle, Paul M., ed., *The American Reader*. Rand McNally: 1958; Premier Books: 1960. Well-selected source material dealing with U.S. growth as a world power.

Brown, Harriett M., and Guadagnolo, Joseph F., *America Is My Country*. Houghton Mifflin: 1955. Explication of the symbols of our country's democracy, national documents, monuments and shrines, patriotic songs, poems and holidays.

Butterfield, Roger, *The American Past*, rev. ed. Simon and Schuster: 1957. The story of American problems, personalities and politics from the birth of the nation to the nuclear age told in original pictures and prints.

Commager, Henry Steele, ed., *Documents of American History*, 7th ed. Appleton-Century-Crofts: 1962. Comprehensive, readily usable reference.

Findlay, Bruce and Esther, *Your Rugged Constitution: How America's House of Freedom Is Planned and Built*. Stanford University Press: 1950, 1952. Simplified, detailed explication.

Hays, William P., *Freedom*: reproductions of 26 significant documents from the Declaration of Independence through the United Nations charter. Coward: 1958. Valuable reference.

Hoff, Rhoda, *America: Adventures in Eyewitness History*. H. Z. Walck: 1962. Articles by historical figures from Governor William Bradford to Mary Antin, selected and edited to give the junior high reader an intimate view of history from the landing at Plymouth to the beginning of the twentieth century.

Hoyt, Edwin P., *Lost Statesmen*. Reilly and Lee: 1961. Sketches of great statesmen who lost elections.

Hornung, Clarence P., *Wheels Across America: A Pictorial Cavalcade Illustrating the Early Development of Vehicular Transportation*. A. S. Barnes: 1959. Mature but not difficult text profusely illustrated.

The Inaugural Addresses of the American Presidents From Washington to Kennedy. Annotated by Davis Newton Lott. Holt, Rinehart and Winston: 1961. Useful annotations and appended charts and documents, including the Declaration of Independence, Articles of Confederation, and the Constitution make this a valuable volume.

Kraus, Michael and Vera. *The Nation's Heritage: A Family Album for Americans*. Grosset & Dunlap: 1961. A pictorial history of America from its birth to the revolution of the automobile.

Morgan, James, *Our Presidents*, 2nd ed. Macmillan: 1958. Brief biographical sketches accompanied by a brief history of the presidency.

Morris, Richard B., ed., *Encyclopedia of American History*, rev. ed. Harper: 1961. Readable reference for the entire scope of American history from before Columbus to 1960; maps, charts, excellent index.

Morris, Richard B., and Noodress, James, *Voices from America's Past*, three volumes. Dutton: 1961. Diaries, letters, biographies, memoirs, essays, and narratives by the participants of history; edited, with notes. Volume I—Colonial Period; volume III—Twentieth Century.

Posell, Elsa Z., *American Composers*. Houghton Mifflin: 1963. Brief sketches of twenty-nine American composers and their influence.

Sickels, Eleanor M., *In Calico and Crinoline: True Stories of American Women, 1608–1865*. Viking Press: 1935. Interesting stories of women in colonial, Revolutionary, and Civil War days; contains some interesting background material on the South.

Stevens, William O., *Famous Humanitarians*. Dodd, Mead: 1953. Brief biographies of twenty great humanitarians, with photographs.

Tunis, Edwin, *Colonial Living*. World: 1957. Illustrated, interesting text. Some valuable material; oversize.

Wellman, Paul I., *Indian Wars and Warriors*. Houghton Mifflin: 1959. Two volumes, one on Indian wars in the Eastern United States, from Champlain's attack on the Iroquois to the defeat of the Seminoles, and one on the West, nearly a century of conflict with settlers.

BOOKS FOR UNIT ONE

American Heritage Junior Library, *Discoverers of the New World*. Narrative by Josef Berger. American Heritage: 1960. Profusely illustrated story of discovery and exploration from the late 15th to the late 18th century. A valuable series.

Averill, Esther, *King Philip*. Harper: 1950. The colonists and the Wampanog Indians.

Clark, Imogen, *Old Days & Old Ways*. Crowell: 1928. Representative seelction of manners and customs in colonial and revolutionary times; several short sketches of children who became or were associated with famous people.

Crouse, Anna, *Peter Stuyvesant of Old New York*. Random House: 1954. Easy reading, with a postscript, written with the intention of relating present-day New York and that of Peter Stuyvesant.

Dougherty, James H., *The Magna Charta*. Random House: 1956. Its relation to our own documents of freedom.

Dorian, Edith M., *Hodabey! American Indians Then and Now*. Whittlesey: 1957. Origin, culture, and history of the American Indian.

Elting, Mary, *First Book of Indians*. Watts: 1950. Discussion of the origin and location of tribes; contains useful maps.

Gray, Elizabeth J., *Penn*. Viking: 1938. Advanced reading biography of the Quaker founder of Pennsylvania.

Guerber, H. A., *Story of our Civilization*. Holt: 1926. Background on the contributions of other cultures to our own; good background.

Hodges, C. Walter, *Columbus Sailed*. Coward: 1939. The famous explorer from the point of view of those who knew him.

Hutton, Clarke, *Picture Story of Great Discoveries*. Watts: 1955. Ancient to modern.

Johnson, G. W., *America Is Born*. Morrow: 1959. Interesting, readable narrative of America from discovery to Constitutional Convention.

Long, J. C., *Maryland Adventure*. Winston: 1956. Reasons for the immigration found in England; personalities of George III and William Pitt.

Petry, Ann, *Tituba of Salem Village*. Crowell: 1964. Story of the Salem witch trials from the point of view of an accused slave; fictionalized biography based on actual records.

Putnery, W. K., *Team-Work in Colonial Days*. Wilde: 1938. The story of the social and economic helpfulness that made the settling of our country possible.

Quinn, Vernon, *The Exciting Adventures of Captain John Smith*. Stokes: 1928. Valuable material in this exciting book.

Shippen, Katherine B., *Lief Eriksson*. Harper: 1951. The story of the first voyage to America.

Starr, Frederick, *American Indians*. Heath: 1898. Itself an historic document, contains valuable information of the social and economic life of the American Indian.

Tharp, Louis H., *Champlain*. Little, Brown: 1944. The story of his life in France and his travels in America.

Weaver, R. B., *Amusements and Sports in America*. University of Chicago Press: 1939. Simplified, readable account of the games, sports, and social gatherings of the people in colonial America.

BOOKS FOR UNIT TWO

Bakeless, John and Katherine, *Spies of the Revolution*. Lippincott: 1962. Based on *Turncoats, Traitors, and Heroes*, emphasis is on new information, with reference to familiar spy stories only when necessary; special vocabulary glossary.

Bill, A. H., *Valley Forge: The Making of An Army*. Harper: 1952. A brief moment in detail, emphasizing the importance of Valley Forge to the overall result of the war.

Bliven, Bruce, *American Revolution, 1760–1783*. Random House: 1958. Overall picture of revolution.

Carmer, C. L., *Cavalcade of America*. Crown: 1956. Readable sketches of men and women who made our country great.

Carmer, C. L., *For the Rights of Men*. Hinds, Hayden & Eldridge: 1947. Short biographies from Zenger to Altgeld.

Carter, Hodding, *Marquis de Lafayette*. Random House: 1958. The contribution to the American war for independence of the "Bright Sword of Freedom."

Commager, Henry S., *The Great Declaration: A Book for Young Americans*. Bobbs-Merrill: 1958. Well-illustrated with selections from major documents; indexed.

Corse, Robert, *Go Away Home*. Norton: 1964. Novel of a boy and his dog on a trek to the Western Reserve.

Dalgliesh, Alice, *Fourth of July Story*. Scribner: 1956. Valuable material on an important point of American history.

Desmond, Alice Curtis, *Alexander Hamilton's Wife: A Romance of the Hudson*. Dodd, Mead: 1952. Intimate view of a critical period of American history.

Edmonds, Walter D., *Wilderness Clearing*. Dodd, Mead: 1944. Novel of teen-age romance in the wilderness of the Mohawk Valley, based on authentic history.

Ellsburg, Edward, *"I Have Just Begun to Fight!"* Dodd, Mead: 1942. Exciting story of John Paul Jones and American naval history.

Folsom, Franklin, *Beyond the Frontier*. Funk & Wagnalls: 1959. Based on the true adventures of Horatio Jones, young frontiersman, blood-brother and chieftain of the Seneca Indians, and Revolutionary patriot.

Holbrook, Stewart, *America's Ethan Allen*. Houghton Mifflin: 1949. Easy reading biography by the author of the adult biography *Ethan Allen*.

Hoyt, Edwin P., *John Quincy Adams*. Reilly & Lee: 1963. The story of the unpopular presidency of a man well-qualified to be President. Illustrated with photographs.

Nolan, Jeannette C., *Treason at the Point*. Messner: 1944. Teen-age adventure of Benedict Arnold's attempted betrayal at West Point.

Kenneth Roberts, *Rabble in Arms*. Doubleday: 1947. Advanced reading novel of the Revolution in New York and the defeat of Burgoyne.

Seton, Anya, *Washington Irving*. Houghton Mifflin: 1960. The story of this well-known author as an able diplomat.

Wilson, Hazel, *The Story of Mad Anthony Wayne*. Grossett & Dunlap: 1953. Story of one of the best and boldest colonial generals.

BOOKS FOR UNIT THREE

Basler, R. P., et al., *A Guide to the Study of the United States of America*. U.S. Library of Congress: 1960. Bibliography of "representative books reflecting the development of American life and thought."

Chase, Mary Ellen, *Donald McKay and the Clipper Ships*. Houghton Mifflin: 1959. Biography of the builder of the fastest ships of his day.

Criss, Mildred, *Abigail Adams: Leading Lady*. Dodd, Mead: 1952. Sympathetic account of the wife of one President and the mother of another, "a woman behind the men" during the birth of our nation.

Foster, Genevieve, *George Washington's World*. Scribner: 1941. Narrative of world events during Washington's lifetime.

Hough, Henry Beetle, *Great Days of Whaling*. Houghton Mifflin: 1958. True adventures of a most exciting profession.

Johnson, G. W., *America Grows Up*. Morrow: 1960. Interesting, well-written account of American history from 1776 to World War I. Written for his grandson.

Judson, Clara I., *Benjamin Franklin*. Follett: 1957. Emphasis is on his political activities as a leading statesman and politician of his day.

Latham, Jean Lee, *Young Man in a Hurry: The Story of Cyrus W. Field*. Harper and Brothers: 1958. Readable biography of the man whose determination lay the Atlantic cable.

Mason, F. van Wyck, *The Battles for New Orleans*. Houghton Mifflin: 1962. General Jackson as the dramatic defender of New Orleans.

Meigs, Cornelia, *Wind in the Chimney*. Macmillan: 1934. Easy reading novel of frontier life.

Moscow, Henry, and Malone, Dumas, *Thomas Jefferson and His World*. American Heritage: 1960. The many sides of one of our greatest leaders—legislator, scientist, architect, diplomat, farmer, inventor, patron of education and the arts.

Paine, Ralph D., *Fight for a Free Sea*. Yale University Press: 1921. Advanced reading on the American naval war.

Purdy, Claire L., *He Heard America Sing* (Stephen Foster). Messner: 1940. Instruction and entertainment, written especially for children, using originals from the Foster Song Book.

Schachner, Nathan, *Alexander Hamilton, Nation Builder*. McGraw-Hill: 1952. Sympathetic biography of one of our most controversial and able figures.

Sloane, Eric, *Diary of An Early American Boy, Noah Blake, 1805*. W. Funk: 1962. Many drawings and diagrams of early tools and the way they were used.

Sperry, Armstrong, *Danger to Windward*. Winston: 1947. Adventure in a Nantucket whaling ship by the author of several fast-moving historical novels for young people.

Tallant, Robert, *The Pirate Lafitte and The Battle of New Orleans*. Random House: 1951. A glimpse of the mysterious Lafitte through his feats during the struggle at New Orleans.

Vanderbilt, Cornelius, Jr., *The Living Past of America: A Pictorial Treasury of Our Historic Houses and Villages that Have Been Preserved and Restored*. Crown: 1955.

The White House: An Historical Guide. White House Historical Association: 1963. Photographs of current and historical interest of the building and the personalities who have lived there.

BOOKS FOR UNIT FOUR

Beebe, Lucius, and Clegg, Charles, *San Francisco's Golden Era: A Picture Story of San Francisco Before the Fire*. Howell-North: 1960. Some rare photos.

Boesch, Mark, *The Cross in the West*. Farrar, Straus, Cudahy: 1956. The story of Christian missionaries who explored from the Rio Grande to the Columbia rivers.

Cody, William F., *Autobiography of Buffalo Bill*. Rinehart: 1920. Advanced reading.

De Voto, Bernard, *The Journals of Lewis and Clark*. Houghton Mifflin: 1953. Advanced reading.

Dorian, Edith, *Trails West and the Men Who Made Them*. McGraw-Hill: 1955. Later French, Spanish, and English explorers.

Driggs, Howard R., *Westward America*. Lippincott: 1942. Epic of the New West.

Eifert, Virginia S., *Three Rivers South*. Dodd, Mead: 1953. The first volume of a Lincoln trilogy, dealing with Lincoln's formative years. The others are *Out of the Wilderness: Young Abe Lincoln Grows Up*. Dodd, Mead: 1956. and *With a Task Before Me: Abraham Lincoln, Leaves Springfield*. Dodd, Mead: 1958.

Garst, D. S., *Jim Bridger, Greatest of the Mountain Men*. Houghton Mifflin: 1952. Easy reading, fast moving excitement.

Horan, James D., *Mathew Brady: Historian With a Camera*. Crown: 1955. A picture album of excellent reproductions.

Hungerford, Edward, *Wells Fargo*. Random House: 1950. Exciting story of a chapter in the movement west.

Jones, Evan, *Trappers and Mountain Men*. Harper: 1961. Exciting story of the fur trade in the opening lands of the Louisiana Purchase and the Oregon Country.

Judson, Clara I., *Andrew Jackson, Frontier Statesman*. Follett: 1954. Our strong President as Indian fighter and a hero of the War of 1812.

Kane, Harnett T., *Gone Are the Days: An Illustrated History of the Old South*. Dutton: 1960. Profusely illustrated with drawings and photos.

Kjelgaard, James A., *The Coming of the Mormons*. Random House: 1953. Easy reading story of an American religious migration.

Kouwenhoven, John A., *Adventures of America, 1857–1900: A Pictorial Record From Harper's Weekly*. Harper and Brothers: 1938. Good contemporary history.

Murphey, Bill, *A Pictorial History of California*. Fearon: 1958. Very good; photographs illustrate California's colorful history from exploration to the beginning of World War II. Indexed.

Nathan, Adele, *Building of the First Transcontinental Railroad*. Random House: 1950. Easy reading.

The New York Times, *America's Taste, 1851–1959:* the cultural events of a century reported by contemporary observers in the pages of the New York Times. M. Longley, L. Silverstein, S. A. Tower, eds. Simon and Schuster: 1960.

Partridge, Bellamy, and Bettmann, Otto, *As We Were: Family Life in America, 1850–1900*. McGraw-Hill: 1946. Many rare reproductions.

Staffelbach, Elmer, H., *For Texas and Freedom*. Wagner: 1952. The Texan fight for independence.

Stevenson, Augusta, *Zeb Pike, Boy Traveler*. Bobbs: 1953. Story of a colorful Westerner.

BOOKS FOR UNIT FIVE

Adams, Julia, *Stonewall*. Dutton: 1931. Valuable information about a hero of the Confederacy.

Allen, Edward, *Informing a Nation: Horace Greeley*. Britannica Books: 1962. Sympathetic account of a political leader and molder of popular opinion in the late 19th century.

Bailey, Bernadine, *Abe Lincoln's Other Mother: The Story of Sarah Bush Lincoln*. Messner: 1958. Historically accurate story of an important influence in Lincoln's life.

Coit, Margaret, *The Fight for Union*. Houghton Mifflin: 1961. Great statesmen such as Webster, Clay, and Calhoun in the dramatic and critical years before the Civil War.

Commager, Henry S., *The Great Proclamation*. Bobbs-Merrill: 1960. Story of the Emancipation Proclamation told largely in the words of those who made it.

Commager, Henry S., and War, L., *America's Robert E. Lee*. Houghton Mifflin: 1951. An American who fought for what he believed to be right.

Donovan, Frank, *The Ironclads*. Barnes: 1961. Description of the battle between the Monitor and the Merrimack.

The Evening Star, Washington, D.C., *Mirror of War:* The Washington *Star* Reports the Civil War. Compiled and edited by John W. Stepp & I. William Hill. Prentice-Hall: 1961. Includes many original drawings and photos.

Fisher, Aileen, *My Cousin Abe*. Nelson: 1962. Abraham Lincoln's boyhood and youth from the point of view of his intimate companion Dennis Hawks.

Foster, Genevieve, *Abraham Lincoln's World*. Scribner: 1944. World events of the period from 1809–1865; advanced reading.

Hoehling, Mary, *Girl Soldier and Spy, Sarah Emma Edmundson*. Messner: 1959. The incredible true story of a woman of the Civil War—volunteer private in the Michigan Infantry, field nurse, dispatch rider, and secret agent.

Harnsberger, Caroline, *The Lincoln Treasury*. Wilcox and Follett: 1950. Selections from Lincoln's speeches, anecdotes, and addresses.

Hunt, Irene, *Across Five Aprils*. Follett: 1964. Novel of a family torn by loyalty to South and loyalty to country during the Civil War.

Jackson, Phyllis, *Victorian Cinderella: The Story of Harriet Beecher Stowe*. Holiday: 1947. Interesting biography, includes several portraits.

Lomask, Milton, *Andy Johnson: The Tailor who Became President*. Ariel Books: 1962. The dramatic story of Johnson's rise to the Presidency.

Merrill, J. M., *Rebel Shore*. Little, Brown: 1957. Union sea power in the Civil War.

Miers, E. S., *Billy Yank and Johnny Reb: How They Fought and Made Up*. Rand-McNally: 1959. Two Americans who fought for what they considered right.

Morrow, Honore, *With Malice Toward None*. Morrow: 1928. Second book of a Lincoln trilogy (*Forever Free; The Last Full Measure*), a novel of the last two years of the Civil War and the bitter political struggle over reconstruction between Lincoln and Sumner.

Nolan, Jeannette C., *The Story of Clara Barton of the Red Cross*. Messner: 1941. Complete and interesting biography.

Petry, Ann, *Harriet Tubman, Conductor on the Underground Railroad*. Crowell: 1955. Biography of the "Moses" of her people.

Norton, S., and Cournos, J., *Candidate for Truth: The Story of Daniel Webster*. Holt: 1953. Historically accurate story of a great American statesman and orator.

Redding, Jay S., *They Came in Chains; Americans from Africa*. Lippincott: 1950. Advanced reading.

Reeder, Russell Potter, *Sheridan, the General Who Wasn't Afraid to Take a Chance*. Duell, Sloan & Pearce: 1962. Story of a self-made military hero.

Sandburg, Carl, *Abe Lincoln Grows Up*. Harcourt Brace: 1926, 1956. Based on the original two-volume biography.

Sterling, Dorothy, *Captain of the Planter*. Doubleday: 1958. The story of Robert Smalls, the first Negro commissioned officer in the Union Navy and influential politician.

BOOKS FOR UNIT SIX

Andrist, Ralph K., and Hanna, Archibald, *The California Gold Rush*. American Heritage: 1961. The story of the California boom that attracted nearly 100,000 people in two years.

Bok, Edward, *The Americanization of Edward Bok*. Scribner: 1923. The story of a well-known journalist.

Buehr, Walter, *Railroads Today and Yesterday*. Putnam: 1958. The story of the changes railroads have made in American life.

Bontemps, Arna, *Frederick Douglass: Slave—Fighter—Freeman*. Knopf: 1959. Easy-reading story of a great statesman and writer.

Brown, M. H., and Felton, W. R., *The Frontier Years*. Holt: 1955. Illustrated by the photographs of L. A. Huffman, the renowned "photographer of the plains."

Chilton, Charles, *The Book of the West: An Epic of America's Wild Frontier and the Men who Created Its Legends*. Bobbs-Merrill: 1962. From before the white man to the present.

Dutton, William S., *Adventure in Big Business: A Stirring Account of America's Industrial Giants . . . How They Grew . . . How They Affect Your Life*. Winston: 1958. Explanation of the growth of American Big Business from the 19th century Industrial Revolution.

Havighurst, Walter, and Marion. *Song of the Pines*. Winston: 1949. Easy reading novel of Norwegian lumbering in Wisconsin.

Holbrook, Stewart H., *The Golden Age of Railroads.* Random House: 1960. Useful maps, charts and illustrations.

Horan, James D., and Sann, Paul, *Pictorial History of the Wild West:* A True Account of the Bad Men, Desperadoes, Rustlers and Outlaws of the Old West—And the Men Who Fought Them to Establish Law and Order. Crown: 1954. Good photos, reproductions of posters and drawings.

Komroff, Manuel, *Photographing History, Matthew Brady.* Encyclopedia Britannica Press: 1962. Pioneer photographer who covered the Civil War and whose gallery includes many famous people.

Lens, Sidney, *Working Men: The Story of Labor.* Putnam's: 1960. Colorful panorama of American labor and its great leaders.

McKown, Robin, *Painter of the West: Frederic Remington.* Messner: 1959. Exciting story of the painter who captured the fading spirit of the Old West.

Meadowcroft, Enid L., *The Story of Thomas Alva Edison.* Grosset & Dunlap: 1952. Easy reading biography of an American genius.

Moody, Ralph, *Riders of the Pony Express.* Houghton Mifflin: 1958. Exciting story of the race against time.

Paradis, Adrian A., *Labor in Action: The Story of the American Labor Movement.* Messner: 1963. Basis for discussion of labor-management problems through discussion of labor movements's growth to the present day.

Place, Marian T., *The Copper Kings of Montana.* Random House: 1961. Three personalities in the discovery and exploitation of the rich Southwestern copper deposits.

Reynolds, Quentin J., *Wright Brothers.* Random House: 1950. Easy reading biography.

Shippen, Katherine B., *Passage to America; The Story of the Great Migrations.* Harper: 1950. Account of the waves of European migrations to the U.S.

Shippen, Katherine B., *This Union Cause: The Growth of Organized Labor in America.* Harper: 1950. Labor unions as a force in American history.

Wellman, Paul I., *Gold in California.* Houghton Mifflin: 1958. Success and failure in the rush to California.

BOOKS FOR UNIT SEVEN

Burlingame, Roger, *Machines That Built America.* Harcourt, Brace: 1953. The history of American invention that has contributed to her growth.

Castor, Henry, *Teddy Roosevelt and the Rough Riders.* Random House: 1954. All of the colorful adventure of this dominant personality in United States history; America on its way to becoming a world power.

Curtis, Rosemary A., *Jennie, the Young Lady Churchill.* Chilton: 1963. Romance of the American mother of the colorful Winston Churchill, introducing Victorian England and her greatest figures from an American perspective.

Davis, Julia, *Ride with the Eagle: The Expedition of the First Missouri in the War with Mexico, 1846.* Harcourt Brace & World: 1962. Based largely on the actual diaries kept by six of the men in an incredible campaign.

Eliot, Alexander, *Three Hundred Years of American Painting.* Random House: 1957. Mature text and beautiful illustrations.

Faber, Doris, *Printer's Devil to Publisher: Adolph S. Ochs of* The New York Times. Messner: 1963. Factual biography of the man whose idealistic determination made the *Times* an internationally respected newspaper.

Follett, Helen, *Ocean Outposts*. Scribner: 1942. Our island possessions; maps and photos; the story of discovery and development.

Glad, Paul W., *McKinley, Bryan, and the People*. Critical Periods of History Series. Lippincott: 1964. Detailed discussion of the economic issues, personalities, rise of the Populist party, regional forces, rural-urban conflict, campaign strategy and voting patterns of the election of 1896.

Hahn, Emily, *Around the World with Nellie Bly*. Houghton Mifflin: 1959. Elizabeth Cochrane Seaman, one of America's earliest and ablest girl reporters, who visited factories and slums and described the conditions she saw.

Levine, I. E., *Electronics Pioneer, Lee De Forest*. Messner: 1964. Brilliant inventor of the triode vacuum tube, the basis for radio, television, guided missiles, rockets and modern computing machines.

Miner, Lewis S., *Mightier Than the Sword: The Story of Richard Harding Davis*. Whitman: 1940. Biography of a sensational and dramatic war correspondent.

Nolan, Jeannette, *The Gay Poet: The Story of Eugene Field*. Messner: 1940. Narrative story of a famous journalist and poet of his day.

Price, Willadene, *Gutzon Borglum, Artist and Patriot*. Rand McNally: 1961. Photographically illustrated biography of the interesting artist best-known for the Mount Rushmore monument.

Richardson, Mrya R., *Sophie of the Lazy B*. McBride: 1942. The story of a young girl caught in the conflict between cattlemen and sheepherders in Wyoming Territory.

Rikhoff, Jean, *Writing About the Frontier, Mark Twain*. Britannica Books: 1961. The story of his growth with the frontier from the Mississippi River of the steamboats to the California of the '49ers.

Shippen, Katherine B., *The Great Heritage*. Viking Press: 1949. Epic of American natural resources. Valuable bibliography of references—books, records, films.

Washington, Booker T., *Up from Slavery*. Doubleday: 1901. Dell: 1965. Autobiography of a man born in slavery who became a great educator and a leader in the American Negro's movement for equality.

Wilder, Laura Ingalls, *Long Winter*. Harper: 1953. The author's own experience of Dakota frontier life.

Winders, Gertrude H., *Robert Goddard, Father of Rocketry*. Day: 1963. Easy reading sympathetic biography, illustrated with photographs.

Wise, Winifred E., *Jane Addams of Hull House*. Harcourt: 1935. Biography based on Jane Addams own reminiscences, papers and letters; a page from American social history.

Zim, Herbert S., *Rolling Wheels: Fact and Fiction*. Spencer Press: 1959. Twenty-eight short stories about trains, horses, stagecoaches and cars.

BOOKS FOR UNIT EIGHT

Alexander, Roy, *The Cruise of the Raider "Wolf."* Yale University Press: 1939. Written by a man who was prisoner on the German "Wolf."

Army Times, the editors of, *The Yanks Are Coming: The Story of General John J. Pershing*. Putnam: 1960. World War I—America and her men in the war.

Barrett, Marvin, *The Years Between: A Dramatic View of the Twenties and Thirties.* Little, Brown and Company: 1962. Abundant photos illustrate interesting history at junior high school reading level.

Bishop, Joseph Bucklin, ed., *Theodore Roosevelt's Letters to His Children.* Scribner's: 1919, 1947. Letters from the Spanish-American War through his African travels.

Colby, Carroll B., *Fighting Gear of World War I;* equipment and weapons of the American doughboy. Coward-McCann: 1961. Rare and interesting photos.

Cook, Fred J., *Rallying a Free People: Theodore Roosevelt.* Kingston House: 1961. Story of his dynamic development from a frail boy to one of our most vigorous Presidents.

Crockett, Lucy H., *Capitan: The Story of an Army Mule.* Holt: 1948. The story of an Army mule that saw service for his country in Cuba, China, the Philippines, Mexico, and France.

Harlow, Alvin F., *Theodore Roosevelt: Strenuous American.* Messner: 1943, The story of our President who was rancher, soldier, and conservationist as well.

Hoyt, Edwin P., *Grover Cleveland.* Reilly and Lee: 1962. Historically accurate and interesting story of the President known for his fight against political corruption.

Lawson, Don, *The United States in World War I.* Ablard-Schuman: 1963. Fact-filled narrative of America in the War; photographs and maps.

Stallings, Laurence, ed., *The First World War: A Photographic History.* Simon and Schuster: 1933. Entirely photos; deals with the home front, preparation for war and training as well as actual war photos.

Vinton, Iris, *The Story of Edith Cavell.* Grosset and Dunlap: 1959. Thrilling story of the British nurse who helped many Allied soldiers escape occupied Europe in World War I, and who faced a firing squad for her courage.

Werstein, Irving, *The Many Faces of World War I.* Messner: 1963. Human approach to the leaders of the war; good maps; advanced reading.

BOOKS FOR UNIT NINE

American Heritage, *D-Day: The Invasion of Europe.* Narrative by Al Hine. American Heritage: 1962. Pictures and maps; glossary items of special terms.

Beach, Commander Edward L., U.S.N., *Submarine!* Holt: 1946. True story of the U.S.S. Trigger and submarine warfare in World War II.

Colby, Carroll B., *Fighting Gear of World War II.* Coward-McCann: 1961. Rare and interesting photos.

Derry, Sam, *The Rome Escape Line: The Story of the British Organization in Rome for Assisting Escaped Prisoners-of-War, 1943–44.* Norton: 1960. Wartime adventure directed by an escaped English officer and an Irish Monsignor hiding inside the Vatican.

Dupuy, Trevor Nevitt, *The Military History of World War II.* Watts: 1962— Several volumes, each dealing with a particular phase of the war; very interesting, with maps and photographs.

Hickok, Lorene A., *Reluctant First Lady: An Intimate Story of Eleanor Roosevelt's Early Public Life.* Dodd, Mead: 1962. Friendly portrait of a great First Lady.

Hickok, Lorena A., *The Road to the White House; FDR: The Pre-Presidential Years.* Chilton: 1962. Intimate biography of his formative years; good photographs.

Horan, James D., *The Desperate Years: A Pictorial History of the Thirties.* Crown: 1962. The struggle for survival, social revolution, experimentation in the arts and sciences, international and governmental change told in pictures.

Lawson, Don, *The United States in World War II.* Ablard-Schuman: 1963. Fact-filled narrative of America in the War; photographs and maps.

Loomis, Robert D., *Great American Fighter Pilots of World War II.* Random House: 1961. Exciting stories of important phase of resistance.

Miller, Francis T., *War in Korea and the Complete History of World War II.* Winston: 1952. Written in conjunction with a board of historical and military authorities, includes war photographs, official records and maps.

O'Neill, Hester, *Young Patriots.* Nelson: 1948. True stories of young people in World War II.

Peare, Catherine Owens, *The FDR Story.* Crowell: 1962. Interesting and personal story.

Savage, Katherine, *The Story of World War II.* Walck: 1958. Beginning with the rise of Hitler, the why and how of the war; photographs and maps.

Shirer, William L., *The Sinking of the Bismarck.* Random House: 1962. Recreation of the suspenseful week-long chase and final victory for the British; easy reading.

Steinberg, Alfred, *Harry S. Truman.* Putnam's: 1963. Sympathetic biography with "why Truman ranks among the ten greatest Presidents" as its motivating idea.

Turner, John Frayn, *Battle Stations: The U.S. Navy's War.* Putnam's: 1960. Maps and photographs.

Werstein, Irving, *A Nation Fights Back: The Depression and Its Aftermath.* Messner: 1962. Illustrated with photographs, an objective treatment of the causes and effects of the critical '30's.

Williams, Jay, *The Battle for the Atlantic.* Hale: 1959. From the American point of view.

BOOKS FOR UNIT TEN

Bailey, Stephen K., Samuel, Howard D., and Baldwin, Sidney, *Government in America.* Holt: 1957. Discussions of the expectations and instruments of government and of the obligations of citizenship.

Bingham, Jonathan B., *Shirt-Sleeve Diplomacy.* Day: 1954. The story of the Point Four program as it was implemented.

Blow, Michael, and Multhaus, Robert, *Men of Science and Invention.* American Heritage: 1961. American invention from colonial days to modern space exploration.

Boyd, Andrew, *An Atlas of World Affairs.* Praeger: 1957. Contemporary world problems explained by text and maps.

Colegrove, Kenneth, *Democracy Versus Communism,* 2nd ed. Van Nostrand: 1961. Comparative analysis of these political and economic opposites.

Donovan, Frank Robert, *Famous Twentieth Century Leaders.* Dodd, Mead: 1960. Sketches of twelve men of world importance in the twentieth century, including FDR.

Fenichell, Stephen S., *The United Nations: Design for Peace.* Winston: 1960. Man's movement toward an organization for the maintenance of world peace and how the U.N. has accomplished this.

Fribourg, Marjorie G., *Ports of Entry, U.S.A.* Little, Brown: 1962. True adventures of the United States Customs Bureau.

Galt, Tom, *How the United Nations Works,* rev. ed. Crowell: 1955. Handy guide for young people and adults on the organization and function of the U.N.

Galt, Tom, *Peace and War: Man-Made,* rev. ed. Beacon Press: 1962. Narrative of wars and man's efforts to resolve conflict by peaceable means.

Johnson, Gerald White, *The Presidency.* Morrow: 1962. Discussions of what the President does, how the Presidency has changed, and strong Presidents. Also volumes on the Supreme Court and Congress.

Kugelmass, J. Alvin, *Ralph J. Bunche, Fighter for Peace.* Messner: 1952, 1962. First biography of a famous American of the twentieth century; easy reading.

Roosevelt, Eleanor and De Witt, William, *UN: Today and Tomorrow.* Harper: 1953. Outlines the concrete work of the UN to maintain peace and raise the standard of living of the world; an intimate account.

Schechter, Betty, *The Peaceable Revolution: The Story of Nonviolent Resistence.* Houghton Mifflin; Riverside Press: 1963. Relation of the stories of Thoreau, Gandhi and American Negro-nonviolence in a world with the capacity to destroy itself.

Seegers, Kathleen Walker, *Alliance for Progress: The Challenge of the Western Hemisphere.* Coward-McCann: 1964. Pros and cons, but recognition of real accomplishment in the face of great difficulties; many photographs.

Shippen, Katherine B., *New Found World.* Viking: 1945. The story of developments in the Western Hemisphere in the first forty years of the twentieth century.

Woodson, Carter G., and Wesley, Charles H., *Negro Makers of History,* 5th ed., rev. Associated Publishers: 1958. Adaptation of *The Negro in Our History.* Includes many sketches and thought-provoking study questions.

REFERENCES USED IN COMPILATION

Historical Non-Fiction: An Organized, Annotated Supplementary Reference Book for the Use of Schools, Libraries, General Reader. Hannah Logaca, seventh edition, enlarged. McKinley: 1960.

Historical Fiction: similar.

The Reading of Young People, George W. Norvell. Heath: 1950.

Curriculum Guides from various states.

Librarian assistance and book reviews from the Children's and Junior High Room, Columbus Public Library.

PRESIDENTS OF THE UNITED STATES

ELECTION	PRESIDENTS AND VICE-PRESIDENTS	PARTY	CHIEF OPPONENT	PARTY
1788	George Washington (Va.) John Adams (Mass.)	none	none	
1792	George Washington (Va.) John Adams (Mass.)	none	none	
1796	John Adams (Mass.) Thomas Jefferson (Va.)	Fed. Dem.-Rep.	Thomas Jefferson	Dem.-Rep.
1800	Thomas Jefferson (Va.) Aaron Burr (N.Y.)	Dem.-Rep.	John Adams	Fed.
1804	Thomas Jefferson (Va.) George Clinton (N.Y.)	Dem.-Rep.	Charles Pinckney	Fed.
1808	James Madison (Va.) George Clinton (N.Y.)	Dem.-Rep.	Charles Pinckney	Fed.
1812	James Madison (Va.) Elbridge Gerry (Mass.)	Dem.-Rep.	DeWitt Clinton	Fed.
1816	James Monroe (Va.) Daniel Tompkins (N.Y.)	Dem.-Rep.	Rufus King	Fed.
1820	James Monroe (Va.) Daniel Tompkins (N.Y.)	Dem.-Rep.	none	none
1824	John Q. Adams (Mass.) John C. Calhoun (S.C.)	Nat. Rep.	Andrew Jackson	Dem.

Year	Winner (Pres. / VP)	Party	Opponent	Party
1828	Andrew Jackson (Tenn.) / John C. Calhoun (S.C.)	Dem.	John Q. Adams	Nat. Rep.
1832	Andrew Jackson (Tenn.) / Martin Van Buren (N.Y.)	Dem.	Henry Clay	Nat. Rep.
1836	Martin Van Buren (N.Y.) / Richard Johnson (Ky.)	Dem.	William H. Harrison	Whig
1840	William H. Harrison (Ohio) / John Tyler (Va.) John Tyler (Va.) President, Apr., 1841–45	Whig Whig	Martin Van Buren	Dem.
1844	James Polk (Tenn.) / George Dallas (Pa.)	Dem.	Henry Clay	Whig
1848	Zachary Taylor (La.) / Millard Fillmore (N.Y.) Millard Fillmore (N.Y.) President, July, 1850–53	Whig Whig	Lewis Cass	Dem.
1852	Franklin Pierce (N.H.) / William R. D. King (Ala.)	Dem.	Winfield Scott	Whig
1856	James Buchanan (Pa.) / John Breckinridge (Ky.)	Dem.	John C. Frémont	Rep.
1860	Abraham Lincoln (Ill.) / Hannibal Hamlin (Me.)	Rep.	John Breckinridge Stephen Douglas	Dem. Dem.
1864	Abraham Lincoln (Ill.) / Andrew Johnson (Tenn.) Andrew Johnson (Tenn.) President, Apr., 1865–69	Rep.	George McClellan	Dem.
1868	Ulysses S. Grant (Ill.) / Schuyler Colfax (Ind.)	Rep.	Horatio Seymour	Dem.
1872	Ulysses S. Grant (Ill.) / Henry Wilson (Mass.)	Rep.	Horace Greeley	Dem.

1876	Rutherford B. Hayes (Ohio) William A. Wheeler (N.Y.)	Rep.	Samuel Tilden	Dem.
1880	James A. Garfield (Ohio) Chester A. Arthur (N.Y.) Chester A. Arthur (N.Y.) President, Sept, 1881–85	Rep. Rep.	Winfield Hancock	Dem.
1884	Grover Cleveland (N.Y.) Thomas Hendricks (Ind.)	Dem.	James G. Blaine	Rep.
1888	Benjamin Harrison (Ind.) Levi P. Morton (N.Y.)	Rep.	Grover Cleveland	Dem.
1892	Grover Cleveland (N.Y.) Adlai E. Stevenson (Ill.)	Dem.	Benjamin Harrison	Rep.
1896	William McKinley (Ohio) Garret Hobart (N.J.)	Rep.	William J. Bryan	Dem. and Populist
1900	William McKinley (Ohio) Theodore Roosevelt (N.Y.) Theodore Roosevelt (N.Y.) President, Sept., 1901–05	Rep. Rep.	William J. Bryan	Dem. and Populist
1904	Theodore Roosevelt (N.Y.) Charles W. Fairbanks (Ind.)	Rep.	Alton Parker	Dem.
1908	William H. Taft (Ohio) James S. Sherman (N.Y.)	Rep.	William J. Bryan	Dem.
1912	Woodrow Wilson (N.J.) Thomas Marshall (Ind.)	Dem.	Theodore Roosevelt William H. Taft	Progressive Rep.
1916	Woodrow Wilson (N.J.) Thomas Marshall (Ind.)	Dem.	Charles E. Hughes	Rep.
1920	Warren G. Harding (Ohio) Calvin Coolidge (Mass.) Calvin Coolidge (Mass.) President, Aug, 1923–25	Rep. Rep.	James Cox	Dem.

1924	Calvin Coolidge (Mass.) Charles G. Dawes (Ill.)	Rep.	John W. Davis	Dem.	
1928	Herbert Hoover (Calif.) Charles Curtis (Kans.)	Rep.	Alfred E. Smith	Dem.	
1932	Franklin D. Roosevelt (N.Y.) John Garner (Texas)	Dem.	Herbert Hoover	Rep.	
1936	Franklin D. Roosevelt (N.Y.) John Garner (Texas)	Dem.	Alfred Landon	Rep.	
1940	Franklin D. Roosevelt (N.Y.) Henry Wallace (Iowa)	Dem.	Wendell Willkie	Rep.	
1944	Franklin D. Roosevelt (N.Y.) Harry Truman (Mo.)	Dem.	Thomas Dewey	Rep.	
	Harry Truman (Mo.) President, Apr, 1945–49	Dem.			
1948	Harry Truman (Mo.) Alben Barkley (Ky.)	Dem.	Thomas Dewey	Rep.	
1952	Dwight Eisenhower (N.Y.) Richard Nixon (Calif.)	Rep.	Adlai Stevenson	Dem.	
1956	Dwight Eisenhower (Pa.) Richard Nixon (Calif.)	Rep.	Adlai Stevenson	Dem.	
1960	John F. Kennedy (Mass.) Lyndon Johnson (Texas)	Dem.	Richard Nixon	Rep.	
	Lyndon Johnson (Texas) President, Nov., 1963–65	Dem.			
1964	Lyndon Johnson (Texas) Hubert Humphrey (Minn.)	Dem.	Barry Goldwater	Rep.	

THE STATES OF THE UNION

NO.	STATE NAME	DATE OF ADMISSION	POPULATION (1960 CENSUS)	AREA IN SQUARE MILES	CAPITAL	LARGEST CITY
1	Delaware	1787	446,292	2,057	Dover	Wilmington
2	Pennsylvania	1787	11,319,366	45,333	Harrisburg	Philadelphia
3	New Jersey	1787	6,066,782	7,836	Trenton	Newark
4	Georgia	1788	3,943,116	58,876	Atlanta	Atlanta
5	Connecticut	1788	2,535,234	5,009	Hartford	Hartford
6	Massachusetts	1788	5,148,578	8,257	Boston	Boston
7	Maryland	1788	3,100,689	10,577	Annapolis	Baltimore
8	South Carolina	1788	2,382,594	31,055	Columbia	Columbia
9	New Hampshire	1788	606,921	9,304	Concord	Manchester
10	Virginia	1788	3,966,949	40,815	Richmond	Norfolk
11	New York	1788	16,782,304	49,576	Albany	New York
12	North Carolina	1789	4,556,155	52,712	Raleigh	Charlotte
13	Rhode Island	1790	859,488	1,214	Providence	Providence
14	Vermont	1791	389,881	9,609	Montpelier	Burlington
15	Kentucky	1792	3,038,156	40,395	Frankfort	Louisville
16	Tennessee	1796	3,567,089	42,244	Nashville	Memphis
17	Ohio	1803	9,706,397	41,222	Columbus	Cleveland
18	Louisiana	1812	3,257,022	48,523	Baton Rouge	New Orleans

19	Indiana	1816	4,662,498	36,291	Indianapolis	Indianapolis
20	Mississippi	1817	2,178,141	47,716	Jackson	Jackson
21	Illinois	1818	10,081,158	56,400	Springfield	Chicago
22	Alabama	1819	3,266,740	51,609	Montgomery	Birmingham
23	Maine	1820	969,265	33,215	Augusta	Portland
24	Missouri	1821	4,319,813	69,686	Jefferson City	St. Louis
25	Arkansas	1836	1,786,272	53,104	Little Rock	Little Rock
26	Michigan	1837	7,823,194	58,216	Lansing	Detroit
27	Florida	1845	4,951,560	58,560	Tallahassee	Miami
28	Texas	1845	9,579,677	267,339	Austin	Houston
29	Iowa	1846	2,757,537	56,290	Des Moines	Des Moines
30	Wisconsin	1848	3,951,777	56,154	Madison	Milwaukee
31	California	1850	15,717,204	158,693	Sacramento	Los Angeles
32	Minnesota	1858	3,413,864	84,068	St. Paul	Minneapolis
33	Oregon	1859	1,786,687	96,981	Salem	Portland
34	Kansas	1861	2,178,611	82,264	Topeka	Wichita
35	West Virginia	1863	1,860,421	24,181	Charleston	Charleston
36	Nevada	1864	285,278	110,540	Carson City	Las Vegas
37	Nebraska	1867	1,411,330	77,227	Lincoln	Omaha
38	Colorado	1876	1,753,947	104,247	Denver	Denver
39	North Dakota	1889	632,446	70,665	Bismarck	Fargo
40	South Dakota	1889	680,514	77,047	Pierre	Sioux Falls
41	Montana	1889	674,767	147,138	Helena	Great Falls

42	Washington	1889	2,853,214	68,192	Olympia	Seattle
43	Idaho	1890	667,191	83,557	Boise	Boise
44	Wyoming	1890	330,066	97,914	Cheyenne	Cheyenne
45	Utah	1896	890,627	84,916	Salt Lake City	Salt Lake City
46	Oklahoma	1907	2,328,284	69,919	Oklahoma City	Oklahoma City
47	New Mexico	1912	951,023	121,666	Santa Fe	Albuquerque
48	Arizona	1912	1,302,161	113,909	Phoenix	Phoenix
49	Alaska	1959	226,167	586,400	Juneau	Anchorage
50	Hawaii	1959	632,772	6,424	Honolulu	Honolulu
	District of Columbia		763,956	69		
			179,323,175	3,615,211		

TERRITORIES OF THE UNITED STATES

TERRITORY	DATE OF ACQUISITION	POPULATION (1960 CENSUS)	AREA IN SQUARE MILES	CAPITAL, OR PRINCIPAL CITY
Puerto Rico	1899	2,349,544	3,435	San Juan
Guam	1899	67,044	212	Agaña
American Samoa	1900	20,051	76	Pago Pago
Panama Canal Zone	1904	42,122	553	Balboa
Virgin Islands	1917	32,099	133	Charlotte Amalie
Total		2,510,860	4,409	

INDEX

INDEX

A

Abolitionists, 269–270
Acadia (Nova Scotia), 18, 70, 71
Act Concerning Religion, 28–29
Adams, Charles Francis, 308
Adams, John, absence from Constitutional Convention, 151; representative of Continental Congress to Holland, 139; at Second Continental Congress, 110, 115; trade mission to London, 147
Adams (John) Administration, Adams serves in troubled times, 171–174; Alien and Sedition Laws, 172–173; election of 1800, 174; Kentucky and Virginia Resolutions, 173; new capital, 173–174; the XYZ affair, 171–172
Adams, John Quincy, 193, 203, 213, 214, 244, 277
Adams, Samuel, 99, 100, 108, 109, 151
Addams, Jane, 408
Adenauer, Konrad, 553
Administration of Justice Act, 101
The Adventures of Tom Sawyer (Twain), 398
Africa, in World War II, 519, 531–532
Agriculture, aid to farmers (New Deal), 495–496; expansion brings problems, 355–358; farm life, 358; farm mortgages, 357–358; farmers organize for self-improvement, 359–360; financial plight of farmers, 357–358; the Grange, 359–360; Granger Laws, 360; Interstate Commerce Act and, 360; lesson from industry, 356; National Farmers' Alliance, 360; one-crop system, 32, 46, 355–356; over production, 355–356; railroads and, 358; in South after Civil War, 313–314, 324; wasted resources, 356; western farmers demand cheap money, 360–362
Agricultural Adjustment Act, 495–496
Agricultural Adjustment Administration (AAA), 495–496
Aguinaldo, Emilio, 423
Air brake, 345
Air pollution, 591, 593
Alabama, statehood, 229
Alabama, 303–304, 308–309
Alamo, 242, 243

Alaska, statehood, 575; U.S. purchase of, 417
Albania, Italian attack on, 506
Albany Congress, 74
Aleutian Island raids, 529
Alexandria Convention, 148–149
Alfonso XIII, 506
Algeciras Conference, 445
Alger, Horatio Jr., 398
Algonquin Indians, 17
Alien Law, 173
Allen, Ethan, 111–112
Alliance for Progress, 586–587
Alsace, 456, 472
Altgeld, Governor John P., *p 368*, 369
Amendments, Constitutional, 158–159 (*see also* specific amendment number)
America First Committee, 517
American Association (baseball), 414
American Federation of Labor, accomplishments, 369–370; growth and split with CIO, 498–499; labor and the public, 370; merger with CIO, 567; Samuel Gompers, 369
American League (baseball), 414
American Red Cross, 464
American Revenue Act, 92–93
American Revolution: *see* Revolutionary War
American Telephone and Telegraph Co., 590
Amherst, General, 77
Anaconda Policy, 298–299
Anarchists, 368
André, Major, 130
Andros, Edmund, 33, 34, 60
Angell, James, 384
Anglicans, 36, 53
Annapolis Convention, 149
Anthony, Susan B., 411
Antietam, battle of, 295
Anti-Federalists, 154–155, 164, 171
Anti-Saloon League, 477
Appomattox Court House, 305
Apprentice Laws, 319
Arbitration, 368
Architecture, American, 395
Argonne Forest, 467
Arizona, 525
Armistice (1918), 467, 468

660

Army of the Potomac, 298
Arnold, Benedict, invasion of Canada, 114–115; treason of, 130
Art (painting), American, 394–395
Articles of Confederation, dissatisfaction with, 150–151; weak government under, 144–145 (*see also* Critical Period)
Artificial human organs, development of, 591
Ashburton, Lord, 241, 242
Asia, Southeast: *see* Southeast Asia
Associated Press, 391
Astor, John Jacob, 178
Atahualpa, 11–12
Atchison, Topeka and Santa Fe Railroad, 344
Atlantic Charter, 518
Atlantic Monthly Magazine, 391
Atomic bomb, 537, 539–540
Attlee, Clement, 537
Austin, Stephen, 243
Australia-New Zealand-United States Pact (ANZUS), 560, 588
Austria, assassination of Archduke Ferdinand, 457–458; German invasion of, 507–508; Triple Alliance, 456
Automation, 591–592
Axis Powers, 505–506, 508, 514, 516, 530–531
Aztec Indians, 11

B

Bacon, Nathaniel, 27, p 27
Badoglio, Marshall, 532
Bagot, Charles, 191
Bailey, James A., 412
Balboa, 9
Ballot, secret, 405
Baltic countries, in World War II, 511
Baltimore, Lord, 28, 29
Baltimore and Ohio Railroad, 203, 345
Bank holiday, 493
Bank of the United States, 166, 236–237
Banking, Hamilton's policy, 166; insured bank deposits, 493–494 (*see also* Banks; Currency; Federal Reserve System)
Banks, Federal Home Loan, 486; private, 237; reopened after Depression, 493; United States Bank, 166, 236–237
Barbary pirates, 147, 175

Barkley, Senator Alben W., 550
Barnard, Frederick, 384
Barnum, Phineas T., 412
Barry, Captain John, 132–133
Bartlett, Edward L., 575
Baseball, 414
Basketball, 415
Bataan, 527–528
"Battle of the Bulge," 534
Bay of Pigs, 586
Beauregard, General, 286, 289, 309
Beck, David, 568
Beecher, Henry Ward, 270
Belgians, 521
Belgium, German invasion (World War I), 458; German invasion (World War II), 512
Bell, Alexander Graham, 336
Belleau Wood, 466
Bellows, George, 394
Benton, Thomas Hart, 236
Berkeley, Governor William, 27, p 28, 60
Berlin blockade, 552–553
Berlin crisis (1958), 573
Berlin wall, 585
Beveridge, Albert J., 417
"Big Four," 471–472
Bill of Rights, 158–159
"Billy the Kid" (Bonney), 350
"The Birth of a Nation," 413
Blacklist, 367
Bland-Allison Act, 363
Bohemians, 372
Bolívar, Simón, 193
Bolsheviks, 502
Bon Homme Richard, 133
Books: *see* Libraries; Press
Boone, Daniel, 227–228, p 227
Boonesboro (Kentucky), 227–228
Booth, John Wilkes, 307
Booth, William, 408
Bootleggers, 477
Boston, in American Revolution, 108, 114
Boston Latin School, 54
Boston Massacre, 98–99
Boston Port Act, 101
Boston Tea Party, 100–101
Bowie, James, 243
Boxer Rebellion, 427–428

Boxers, 427
Braddock, General Edward, 74–75
Bradley, General Omar, 558
Bragg, General Braxton, 300
Breed's Hill, 112–114
Brest Litovsk Treaty, 465
Briand, Aristide, 475
Britain: *see* England; Great Britain
Britain, battle of, 514–515
Brooklyn, Civil War ship, 304; Spanish-American War ship, 425
Brown vs. Board of Education of Topeka, 386, 570
Brown, John, 282
Bruening, Heinrich, 375
Bryan, William Jennings, 362, 364, 420, *p 420*, 426, 446
Buchanan, James, 250, 278, 280, 287
Buddhists, 587
Buell, General, 295
Bulgarians, 459
"Bull Moose" Campaign, 448
Bull Run, first battle of, 288–289; second battle of, 295
Bulwer, Sir Henry, 254–256
Bunker Hill, battle of, 112–114
Burgoyne, General, 126–127
Burnside, General, 295
Burr, Aaron, 174, 175
Byllynge, 37
Byrd, William, 64
Byrnes, James F., 537

C

Cabot, John, 13
Cabot, Sebastian, 13
Cahokia, 228
Calamity Jane, 350
Calhoun, John C., 182, 213, 214, 273, 278
California, Mexican War in, 251; opposition to statehood, 253; slavery and, 272–273; statehood, 257 (*see also* Gold Rush)
Cambodia, independence of, 560
Camp, Walter, 414
Canada, American invasion of, 114–115
Canadian-U.S. boundary, 191, 240, 246
Canals, desire for, 200; era of building, 201–203; vs. railroads, 203–204 (*see also* Chesapeake and Ohio Canal; Erie Canal; Panama Canal)
Cantigny, 466
Cape of Good Hope, 5
Carnegie, Andrew, *p 332*, 384, 389
Carolina colonies, founding of, 29–30; the Grand Model, 29–30; political misfortune of, 30
Carpetbaggers, 315
Carranza, General Venustiano, 455
Carroll, Charles, 64, 203
Carter, Robert, 64
Cartier, Jacques, 16–17, 67
Cassatt, Mary, 394
Castro, Fidel, 574, 586
Catholics, 28, 29, 31, 55, 383, 408, 478, 483, 522, 579
Cattle industry, cattle kings, 347–349; the long drive, 347–348; from range to ranch, 348–349
Cayuga Indians, 130
Central Pacific Railway, 343–344
Central Powers, 459
Cervera, Admiral, 423
Champlain, 17–18
Chancellorsville, battle of, 297
Chapultepec, *p 249*, 252
Charles II, 30, 33, 34, 36
Charleston (South Carolina), fall to British, 134–135; founding, 30
Chase, Salmon P., 281
Château-Thierry, 466
Chattanooga, siege of, 300
Chautauqua, 413
Cherokee Indians, 276–277
Chesapeake, 179, 183
Chesapeake and Ohio Canal, 203
Chickamauga, battle at, 300
Child labor, 209, 210, 402, 497
China, Boxer Rebellion, 427–428; civil war in, 554–555; dispute with Japan, 522–523; Japanese invasion of, 504; People's Republic, 554–555; open door policy toward, 427; split with Soviet Union, 585; Washington Disarmament Conference, 474–475
Chinese, 343, 344, 373; (Nationalist) 554, 560; (Red) 557, 558, 573, 577, 585
Chisholm Trail, 348, 349
Chou En-lai, 557

Churchill, Winston, 516, 518, 521, *p 521*, 534, 537

Cincinnati Red Stockings, 414

Circus, 412

Cities, growth of, 208; housing problems in, 601; industrial revolution and, 209; problems in (1960's), 600–601; in South after Civil War, 312, 314; transportation problems in, 601

Civil Rights, decreasing discrimination, 571; early plea for, 316; integration of schools, 570–571; progress under Eisenhower, 570–571; "separate but equal doctrine," 570

Civil Rights Act (1865), 322

Civil Rights Bill (1964), 583–584

Civil Service, 409–410

Civil War, advance toward Richmond, 301–302; the *Alabama*, 303–304; the *Alabama* claims, 308–309; battle of Antietam, 295; battle at Chancellorsville, 297; battle of Gettysburg, 299–300; battle of Shiloh, 294–295; blockade of Southern ports, 290–291; bombardment of Fort Sumter, 285–286; call to arms, 286–288; comparison of North and South, 284–285; defeat of Hood, 303; election of 1864, 305; Emancipation Proclamation, 296–297; epilogue on, 309; Ericsson's *Monitor*, 292; fall of Savannah, 303; fifth year of war brings Union victory, 305–309; first battle of Bull Run, 288–289; first battle of the ironclads, 291–292; first year brings Confederate victories, 284–291; Fort Henry and Fort Donelson, 294; Grant leads Union forces in fourth year, 301–305; Lee's surrender to Grant, 305–306; loyal border states, 287; Mobile Bay Battle, 304–305; naval battles of, 303–305; a new Southern capital, 288; Northern confidence, 288–289; the Peninsular campaign, 289–290; Pickett's charge, 299; results of the war, 306; the Rock of Chickamauga, 300; second battle of Bull Run, 295; second year is indecisive, 291–295; Shenandoah Campaign, 302–303; Sherman's march through Georgia, 303; siege of Chattanooga, 300–301; siege of Petersburg, 302; siege of Vicksburg, 297–298; "Stonewall" Jackson holds ground, 289; support of Lincoln, 287; threat to Washington, 287–288; the "Trent" affair, 290–291; Union capture of New Orleans, 293–294; Union forges ahead in third year, 296–301; Union's Anaconda Policy, 298–299; the *Virginia*, 291–292; Wilderness Campaign, 301–302 (*see also* Confederacy; Secession)

Civil Works Administration (CWA), 494

Civilian Conservation Corps (CCC), 494

Clarendon, Lord, 29, 30

Clark, George Rogers, 131–132, 228

Clark, William, 177

Clay, Henry, Compromise of 1820, 192; Compromise of 1850, 272; Compromise Tariff Bill, 214; election of 1844, 245; and United States Bank, *p 232*, 236

Clayton, John M., 254–256

Clayton Act, 453–454

Clayton-Bulwer Treaty, 254–256, 441

Clemenceau, Georges, 471

Clermont, 199–200

Cleveland, Grover, 362, 364, 419

Clinton, General, 129

Clinton, Governor DeWitt, 201, *p 204*, 216

Closed shop, 568

Coal-grate invention, 207

Cody, Buffalo Bill, 412

Coke, development of, 207

Cold War, beginning, 549–553; Berlin blockade, 552–553; changing areas of tension, 572–574; China-Soviet split, 585; civil war in China, 554–555; Communism in Southeast Asia, 560–561; communist challenge, 585–586; easing of tensions, 576; Eisenhower's aid, 563–564; formation of power blocs, 551–552; Israel-Egypt border dispute, 563; Kremlin changes approach, 561–564; Marshall Plan, 551–552; measures against Communism, 550; meeting at the summit, Middle East trouble, 563–564; network of treaties, 560–561; North Atlantic Treaty Organization, 553; occupation of Japan, 555; propaganda offensive, 549–550; revolt in Hungary, 562–563; Southeast Asia Treaty Organization, 560; Suez crisis, 563; Truman Doctrine, 550; U.S. relations with Soviet bloc (1960's), 584–585; Vietnam divided, 559–560; war in Korea, 555–559; Warsaw Alliance, 552

Colfax, Schuyler, 346

College of William and Mary, founding, 27

Colleges: *see* Education

Colombia, Panamanian revolt against, 441–442; position with U.S. over Panama, 443

Colonies, thirteen, "American way" in the middle colonies, 55–56; the Boston Massacre, 98–99; Boston Tea Party, 100–101; Britain tightens control over, 98–102; British cost of protecting, 98–102; colonial character, 88–90; colonial communication, 58; colonial economy, 45–49; colonial life, 56–59; colonists voice their objections, 93–98; colonists at work and play, 56–59; Committees of Correspondence, 99; Declaration of Independence, 116–120; decline of English Governor's power, 60; educational beginnings, 53–55; England changes colonial policies, 88–93; environments mold different ways of life, 50–59; First Continental Congress, 102; growth of Americanism in, 88–90; the Intolerable Acts, 101–102; life in colonial South, 50–52; mercantile theory of trade, 91; nonimportation policy, 95–96; the Parson's Cause, 94–95; plantation system in South, 46–47; progress in self-government, 59–60; prosper and grow economically, 45–49; Puritan influences in New England, 52–53; Second Continental Congress, 109–111, 143–144; shipbuilding in, 65; Sons of Liberty, 96; Stamp Act Congress, 96–97; Stamp Act repeal, 97–98; Sugar and Stamp Acts, 92–93; taxation without representation, 93–98; theories of trade and development, 90–93; Townshend Acts, 99–100; unity begins to emerge, 59–60; Writs of Assistance, 92 (*see also* Middle colonies; New England colonies; Southern colonies; specific colonies)

Columbia Basin Project, 440

Columbia River, Lewis and Clark reached, 178

Columbia University, 384

Columbus, Christopher, later voyages, 8; letter to king and queen of Spain, 8; Marco Polo's book and, 5; a sailor's dream, 6; voyage of discovery (to North America), 6–8; youth of, 6

Committee to Defend America by Aiding the Allies, 517

Committee for Industrial Organization, 498

Committees of Correspondence, 99

Common Sense, 115

Communists, 465, 477–479, 573, 574, 577, 584–587

Company store, 209

Compromise of 1850, 272–273

Computer, 592

Comstock Lode, 349

Concert of Europe, 193

Concord, 107–109

Conestoga wagons, 230, *p* 230

Confederate States of America (Confederacy), capital of, 288; European support of, 290–291, 295, 297, 308–309; ex-Confederate leaders, 314–315; flag, 280; formation of, 280 (*see also* Civil War)

Congress, 292

Congress of Industrial Organizations (CIO), merger with A.F. of L., 567; rise of, 497–499; vertical vs. horizontal organization of, 498

Connecticut Plan (Compromise), 153

Constitution ("Old Ironsides"), 183

Constitution, Articles of, 156–158; Bill of Rights, 158–159; important rights guaranteed by, 153; interpretations of, 167; opinions about, 164; powers given in, 154; ratification by states, 154–155; slavery and, 264–265; sources used in writing, 153; Webster-Hayne debates on, 236 (*see also* Amendments, Constitutional; Constitutional Convention)

Constitutional Convention, commerce debate, 154; the Connecticut Compromise, 153; the Constitutional debates, 152–154; convenes at Philadelphia, 151–152; delegates to, 151–152; dissatisfaction with the Articles of Confederation, 150–151; framing a new constitution, 150–155; the New Jersey Plan, 153; three-fifths compromise, 153–154, 265; the Virginia Plan, 153; work of the convention, 152

Constitutions, state, 142–143

Continental Congress, First, 102

Continental Congress, Second, accomplishments, 143–144; adoption of the Articles of Confederation, 144; convened at Philadelphia, 109–111; a declaration and a proclamation, 111; George Washington takes command, 110–111

Convention of 1818, 191, 240–241

Coolidge, Calvin, 474, 479, 481

Coolidge Administration, business and the

country, 481–482; prosperity under, 480–482; succession to presidency, 480–481; victory at the polls, 481
Cooper, James Fenimore, 219, 398
Cooper, Peter, 203
Coral Sea, battle of, 528–529
Corbett, "Gentleman Jim," 415
Cornwallis, General Charles Earl, 122–125, 135–137
Coronado, 10
Corregidor, 528
Cortez, 10–11, 12
Cotton belt, 207, 228–229
Cotton gin, invention of, 228
Countess of Scarborough, 133
Court of Arbitration, 445–446
Cowpens, battle of, 136
Cox, James, 473, 479
Crane, Stephen, 399
Crazy Horse, 353
Crédit Mobilier, 345–346
Creek Indians, 249–250, 276
Crete, invasion of, 514
Crisis, The, 128
Crispus Attucks, *p* 99
Cristóbal Colón, 425
Critical Period, financial problems, 148; interstate jealousies, 147–148; new nation survives, 142–149; relations with other countries, 146–147; Second Continental Congress, 143–144; state constitutions, 142–143; two interstate conventions, 148–149; two significant laws, 145–146; weak government under Articles of Confederation, 144–145
Crittenden, Senator, 281
Crockett, Davy, 243
Crusades, 3–4
Cuba, adoption of constitution, 429; Bay of Pigs invasion, 586; becomes colony of Spain, 9; blockade of (1962), 586; Castro and communism in, 574; missile crisis, 586; Platt Amendment for, 429–430 (*see also* Spanish-American War)
Cultural exchanges (Russian-American), 576
Culture: *see* Social Revolution
Cumberland, 291–292
Cumberland Pass, 227, 228
Cumberland Road, 198, 230

Currency, Confederate, 314; Greenback party and paper money, 360–361; meeting money crisis during American Revolution, 125; paper money after American Revolution, 148; paper money from private banks, 237 (*see also* Banking; Banks; Gold Standard; Silver Question)
Custer, Colonel George A., 353
Czechoslovakia, 472, 508

D

D-Day, 533
da Gama, Vasco, 5
Dams, 500
Danzig (Poland), 508
Dare, Virginia, 23
Dartmouth College Case, 277
Davis, Jefferson, 280
Davis, John W., 481
Dawes, Charles, 108
Dawes Severalty Act, 353
de Gaulle, General Charles, 514, *p* 514, 577
De Grasse, Admiral, 137
De Kalb, 129, 135
de Leon, Ponce, 9
de Lôme, Dupuy, 421–422
de Soto, Hernando, 9–10
Decatur, Capt. Stephen, 190
Declaration of Causes for Taking up Arms, 111
Declaration of Independence, 116–120
Declaration of Lima, 503
Declaration of Rights, 96
Declaration of Rights and Grievances, 102
Declaratory Act, 97
Delaware, Lord, 36
Delaware colony, 36
Delaware Indians, 75, 147
Delaware River, Washington's crossing, 123
Democratic-Republicans (party), 167, 168, 171, 173, 174, 214, 276
Democrats (party), 214, 321, 327, 574–575
Denmark, in World War II, 512
Depression, Great, causes of 485–486; conditions during, 485; Hoover's relief measures, 486; schools in, 388; the tumbling stock market, 484–485 (*see also* New Deal)
Depression of 1921, 476–479

665

Detroit, 184, 230
Dewey, Commodore George, 422
Dewey, John, p 383, 384, 596–597
Dewey, Thomas E., 534, 551
Diaz, Bartholomew, 5
Díaz, Porfirio, 454
Diem, Ngo Dinh, 587
Dienbienphu, surrender at, 559–560
Dinwiddie, Governor, 73
District of Columbia, burning by British, 186; Civil War threat to, 287–288; naming of, 174; new capital, 171; slavery and, 272
Dix, Dorothea, 410–411
Dixiecrats, 551
Dodge, Grenville, 344
Dole, Sanford B., 419
Dominican Republic, U.S. intervention in, 444
Dominion of New England, 33–34
Dos Passos, John, 399
Douglas, Stephen A., 273–274, p 274, 278–279, 287
Drake, Col. Edwin, p 333
Drake, Francis, 13–14
Drama, 412
Dred Scott Case, 270–271
Drew, Daniel, 347
Du Bois, W. E. B., 385
Duke of York: see James II
Dulles, John Foster, 560, 573, 576
Dumbarton Oaks, 546
Dunkirk, rescue at, 513
Durant, T. C., 343
Dutch, 20, 32, 36, 55, 56, 63, 521
Dutch East India Co., 14
Dutch West India Co., 32

E

Early, General, 302–303
Earp, Wyatt, 350
Economic Cooperation Administration (ECA), 552
Economic and Social Council, 548
Edict of Toleration, 28–29
Edison, Thomas, 413
Education, American system, 382–384; booms in twentieth century 387–389; college enrollment, 598–599; colleges and universities, 384; development in America, 596–600; elementary, 382–383; growth of new schools, 388–389; high school, 383–384; higher, 387–388; more students attend more schools, 382–387; of Negroes, 385–387; new accents in, 598; opportunities of, 599–600; population explosion and, 598; schools in Depression, 388; war and, 388–389; of women, 384–385; (see also integration, school)
Edward, 132
Eighteenth Amendment (prohibition), 477
Einstein, Albert, 375
Eisenhower, Dwight D., p 558; commander of NATO, 553; invasion of Normandy, 533; landing in Africa, 531; oldest president, 579
Eisenhower Administration, Alaska and Hawaii statehood, 575; Berlin again, 573–574; bipartisan program, 566–567; Castro and communism in Cuba, 574; changing areas of tension, 572–574; cooperation with Japan, 577; cultural exchanges, 576; Democratic landslide in 1958, 574–575; divided Vietnam, 559–560; domestic concerns dominate first term, 566–572; easing of Cold War tensions, 576; election of 1952, 559; foreign affairs fill late fifties, 572–577; Inter-American Bank, 574; labor under, 567–569; meeting at summit, 562; network of treaties, 560–561; progress in civil rights, 570–571; Quemoy and Matsu, 573; second election, 571–572; space age, 575–576; subversion and the senator, 569–570; top-level visits, 576; troubled neighbors to the South, 574; U-2 incident, 577; unfriendly Latin American welcome for vice president, 574
Election, presidential, 1788, 164; 1792, 168; 1800, 174–175; 1828, 214; 1832, 236; 1836, 237; 1844, 245, 246; 1852, 273; 1856, 278; 1860, 278; 1864, 305; 1892, 362; 1896, 362, 420; 1900, 426; 1908, 446; 1912, 447–448; 1920, 473, 479–480; 1924, 481; 1928, 482–483; 1932, 486–487; 1940, 517; 1944, 534; 1948, 550–551; 1952, 559; 1956, 571–572; 1960, 579–580; 1964, 582–583
Elections, direct primary, 408
Eliot, Charles, 384
Eliot, T. S., 399
Elizabeth, Queen, 13, 22
Ely, Eugene, 527
Emancipation Proclamation, 296–297, 313

Embargo Act, 179, 211
Emergency Railroad Transportation Act, 500
Emerson, Ralph Waldo, 139, 219
Emigrant Aid Society, 274
Emma Willard School, 217
Empress of China, 147
England, colonization by companies, 23; discovery and exploration, 13–15; early attempts to found colonies, 22–23; looks to the New World, 22–23; monarchs of, *c 91;* stakes its claim in New World, 12–15 (*see also* English colonies; Great Britain)
English colonies, agricultural surplus in, 65; colonial charters, 23; England changes colonial polices, 88–93; fishing in, 66; French – Indian concern over expansion of, 64; fur trade in, 65–66; home manufacturing in, 66; increase in value of, 62–66; middle colonies develop middle way of life, 32–37; prosperity in, 64–66; rapid growth of population in, 62–63; religious motives bring settlers to New England, 37–43; settlers seek fortunes and freedoms in Southern colonies, 24–32; shipbuilding in, 65; westward territorial expansion of, 63–64 (*see also* Colonies, thirteen)
Eniwetok, 538
Entertainment: *see* Recreation
Era of Good Feeling, 190–194
Ericsson, John, 200, 292
Ericsson, Leif, 3
Erie Canal, 201, 230
Erskine, David, 181
Estonia, 465, 511
Ethiopia, Italian invasion of, 505
Europe, conflicting claims in New World, 19–20; the Crusades, 3–4; Dutch in the New World, 20; English in the New World, 20; French in the New World, 19–20; looks beyond its borders, 2–5; Marco Polo's travels, 4–5; the Norsemen, 3; outbreak of hostilities in World War I, 457–458; power struggle before World War I, 456–457; Prince Henry's School of Navigation, 5; rivalries on land and sea prior to World War I, 456–457; the Spaniards in the New World, 19 (*see also* World War II)
Executive Department, Federal government, 157

F

Farmers, farming: *see* Agriculture
Farragut, David G., 293–294, 304–305
Faulkner, William, *p* 388, 399
Federal Convention: *see* Constitutional Convention
Federal Home Loan Banks, 486
Federal Reserve Act of 1913, 452
Federal Reserve Board, 453
Federal Reserve System, 452–453, 463, 494
Federal Trade Commission, 453
The Federalist, 155
Federalists (party), 154–155, 164, 165, 167, 172, 173, 174, 188, 190–191, 276
Fenwicke, 37
Ferdinand VII, 193
Ferdinand, Francis, 456, 457
Ferguson, Major, 135–136
Field, James G., 361
Fifteenth Amendment (voting), 322
"Fifty-four Forty or Fight," 246
Filipinos, 426, 428–429, 527
Fillmore, Millard, 273
Finland, attack on Russia, 520
Finns, 511, 520
First Continental Congress, 102
Fisk, James, 347
Fisk University, 385
Fists of Universal Harmony (Boxers), 427
Fitch, John, 199
Fitzsimmons, Bob, 415
"Five-five-three ratio," 474
Five Power Treaty, 474
Flatboats, 198–199
Flatiron Building, 395
Fletcher vs. Peck, 277
Florida, 308–309
Florida, border raids, 249; cession of, 249; discovery and naming of, 9; disputed territory, 248–249; gained from Spain, 248–249; Jackson's Campaign in, 249; Seminole Indians, 249–250; statehood, 250
Foch, General, 466
Fong, Hiram L., 575
Food Control Act, 464
Football, 414–415
Forbes, General, 75–76

Forbes Road, 75
Ford, Henry, *p 339*
Ford's Theater, 307
Formosa (Taiwan), 554, 561
Fort Bedford, 75
Fort Christina, 36
Fort Donelson, 294
Fort Duquesne, 73, 76, 78
Fort Edward, 77
Fort Frontenac, 77–78
Fort Henry, 294
Fort Kaskaskia, 131
Fort Lee, 122
Fort McHenry, 186–187
Fort Moultrie, 134
Fort Necessity, 73, *p 73*
Fort Niagara, 76, *p 76*, 78
Fort Oswego, 76
Fort Pitt, 76
Fort Stanwix, 127
Fort Sumter, 285–286, 309
Fort Ticonderoga, 77–78, *p 77*, 111–112
Fort Washington, 122
Fort William Henry, 77
Forty-ninth parallel: *see* Canada-U.S. Boundary
Fountain of Youth, 9
Four Power Treaty, 474, 475
Fourteen Points (Wilson's), 470
Fourteenth Amendment (citizenship), 321–322, 570
France, aid to American Revolution, 129, 139; Americans and French attack Cornwallis, 137; areas claimed in New World, 67–68; concern over English colonial expansion, 64; declaration of war on Germany (1939), 509; disputed claims in New World, 67–68; exploration, 67; Germany declared war on (1914), 458; journeys of exploration, 16–18; London Disarmament Conferences, 475–476; recognition of American independence, 129; slavery and, 263; Triple Entente, 456; Washington Disarmament Conference, 474–475; in World War II, 511–512, 513–514
Francis I, 16
Franklin, Benjamin, the Albany Plan and, 75; at Constitutional Convention, 151; in Paris, 129, 133, 139

Freedmen's Bureau, 322
"Freedom Fighters," 563
Frémont, Captain John C., 251, 278
French colonies, farming and lumbering prove unprofitable, 69; grow more slowly than the English, 67–70; Huguenots settle in Florida, 18–19; King George's War, 71; King William's War, 70; Montreal fair, 69–70; population growth in, 68; Queen Anne's War, 70–71; wealth from furs, 68–70
French and Indian War, the Albany Congress, 74; battle on the Plains of Abraham, 79–80; Braddock's defeat, 74–75; British naval supremacy, 77–78; a cause of, 226; danger signals in Ohio Valley, 72–74; decides America's future, 72–80; early skirmishes, 73–74; fall of Ft. Duquesne, 76; fall of Quebec, 78–80; French advances under Montcalm, 76–77; George Washington's mission, 73; Indian raids, 75; power struggle in North, 76–78; second Ohio campaign, 75–76; Treaty of Paris, 80; Western campaigns, 74–76; year of decision (1759), 78
French and Indian wars, 70–71
French Republic, establishment of, 168
French Revolution, 140
Frolic, 183
Frost, Robert, 581
Fugitive Slave Law, 267
Fulton, Robert, 199
Fundamental Orders of Connecticut, 40

G

Gadsden, James, 257
Gadsden Purchase, 257
Gagarin, Yuri, 589
Gage, General, 107–108, 112–114
Gallatin, Albert, 240
Garfield, James A., 409
Garrison, William Lloyd, 269
Gates, General, 128, 135, 136
"Gay Nineties," 412
General Amnesty Act, 323
General Assembly (U.N.), 548
Genêt affair, 169
Geneva Summit Conference, 562
The Genius of Universal Emancipation, 269
George II, 31

George III, 90–91, *p 90*, 92, 98, 139
George, Lloyd, 471
Georgia, vs. Indians, 276–277; Sherman's march through, 303
Georgia colony, last of the thirteen, 30–32; Oglethorpe's Plan for, 30–31; rules and regulations of, 31–32; Spanish threat to, 31
Germans, 32, 35, 36, 63, 343, 511–521 (*see also* Nazis)
Germany, in Africa, 519–520; collapse of (World War II), 535–537; declares war (1914), 458; Hessian troops in American Revolution, 115; rise of Hitler, 506–507; road to World War II, 507–509; U.S. trouble with in Samoa, 430; Versailles Conference and, 472; in World War II, 530–537 (*see also* Axis Powers; World Wars I and II)
Gestapo, 521
Gettysburg, battle of, 299–300
Gettysburg Address, 298, 299–300
Ghent, Treaty of, 187–188
Gibbons vs. Oregon, 277
Gilbert, Sir Humphrey, 22
Glenn, Colonel John H., 589, *p 589*
Goering, Herman, 530
Goethals, Colonel George, 442
Gold Rush, discovery of gold, 253; gold fever, 253–254; routes of gold-seekers, 254
Gold Standard, adoption of, 363–364; end of, 493
Gold Standard Act, 364
"Golden Twenties," 479
Goldwater, Barry M., 582
Gompers, Samuel, 369, *p 369*
Goodyear, Charles, 207
Gorgas, William C., 429, 442
Gorges, Sir Ferdinand, 42
Gould, Jay, 347, 390
Government, colonial progress in self-, 59–60; corruption in city and state, 404–406; reform in election of senators, 454; reforms in city and state, 407–408; in South after Civil War, 315–316; weak under Articles of Confederation, 144–145 (*see also* Constitution)
Governor Dummer Academy, 216
Grand Canyon, discovery of, 10
Grand Model, 30

Grange, farmers organize for self-improvement, 359–360; fight for freight-rate controls, 347; growth of movement, 359; political activity, 359–360
Granger Laws, 360
Grant, Ulysses S., 294, 297–298, 300–306
Great Britain, the *Alabama* claims, 308–309; battle of (World War II), 514–515; declaration of war on Germany (1939), 509; entered World War I, 458; London Disarmament Conferences, 475–476; member of "Big Four," 471; pressing of American seamen into British service, 232; slavery and, 263; Triple Entente, 456; war with France, 181; Washington Disarmament Conference, 474–475; in World War II, 513–515; 519–520 (*see also* England; English colonies; Revolutionary War)
Great Depression: *see* Depression, Great
Great Lakes, trade route, 230
Great Law (Penn's), 35–36
Great Northern Railroad, 344
Great Society, 592
"The Great Train Robbery," 413
"The Greatest Show on Earth," 412
Greece, 472, 514, 520
Greeks, 372
Greeley, Horace, 197
Green, William, 369
Greenback party, 360–361
Greene, General, 136
Greenland, discovery of, 3; U.S. occupation of, 518
Griffith, D. W., 413
Gruening, Ernest, 575
Guadalcanal, 530
Guadalupe-Hidalgo, Treaty of, 252–253
Guam, 426, 527, 538
Guantanamo Bay naval base, 430
Guerriere, 183
Gulf of St. Lawrence, discovery, 17

H

Hague, *p 473*
Haiti, U.S. intervention in, 444
Hale, Nathan, *p 122*
Half Moon, 14
Halleck, General Henry W., 295
Hamilton, Alexander, at Annapolis Convention, 149; articles for *The Federalist*, 155;

at Constitutional Convention, 151; financial policy of, 165–166; first tariff act, 210; influence in Jefferson's election, 174; and Jay Treaty, 170; leader of Federalists, 276
Hamilton, Colonel Henry, 130–132
Hancock, John, 108, 109
Hanna, Mark, 420
Harper's Ferry, *p 281*
Harper's magazine, 391, *p 391*
Harding, Warren G., 473, 479, 480
Harding Administration, appointments, 480; corruption in high places, 480; election of 1920, 479–480; the 5-5-3 ratio, 474; importance of the Washington naval treaty, 474–475; Washington Disarmament Conference, 474–475; World Court, 473–474
Harrison, Benjamin, 362
Harrison, General, 229
Harrison, William Henry, 182, 184, 185, 237, 245
Hartford, 304
Hartford Convention, 188, 276
Harvard University (College), 53–54, *p 54*, 384
Hawaii, annexation of, 418–419; 50th state, 419; Pearl Harbor attack, 525–526; Republic of, 419; statehood, 575; sugar in, 418–419
Hawkins, General, 424
Hawthorne, Nathaniel, 398
Hay, John, 427, *p 427*, 428, 441
Hayes, Rutherford B., 323, 368, 409, 438
Haymarket Riot, 368–369
Hayne, Senator, 236
Headley Inn, *p 199*
Hearst, William Randolph, 390, 421
Hemingway, Ernest, 506
Henri, Robert, 394
Henry VII, 12, 13
Henry, Patrick, 94, 95, 102, 151
Henry, Prince, 5
Henry Street Settlement, 408
Herkimer, General, 127
Herter, Christian A., 576
Hessian troops, 115, 124
Hickok, "Wild Bill," 350
Hill, James J., 344
Hindenburg, von, 507
Hindenburg Line, 463, 467, 468
Hirohito, Emperor, 539

Hiroshima, bombing of, 539
Hitler, Adolph, 375, *p 505,* 506–509, 513, 520–522, 537
Ho Chi Minh, 559
Hoe, Richard, 220
Hoffa, James, 568
Hoffman, Paul G., 552
Holy Land, Crusades in, 3–4
Home Owners Loan Corporation, 500
Homer, Winslow, 394
Hood, General, 303
Hooker, General, 297, 301
Hooker, Thomas, 40
Hoover, Herbert, 464, 474, 480, 493
Hoover Administration, Depression relief measures, 486; election of 1928, 482–483; election of 1932, 486–487; Great Depression strikes America and the world, 484–487; London Disarmament Conferences, 475–476; problems upon entering office, 483; prohibition issue, 483
Hopkins, Johns, 384
Horn book, *p 54*
Hornet, 183
House of Burgesses, 26, 59–60
House of Representatives, Connecticut Plan for, 153
Housing, New Deal assistance in, 500–501; problems, 402; projects, 596
Houston, Sam, 244
Howard University, 385
Howe, Elias, 205
Howe, General, 112–114, 122, 126–128
Howe, Lord, 77
Howells, William Dean, 398
Hudson, Henry, 14–15
Hudson Bay, discovery of, 15
Hudson River, discovery of, 14
Hudson's Bay Co., 246
Hughes, Charles E., 474, 480
Huguenots, 18–19, 30, 36
Huks, 561
Hull, Cordell, 503, 523
Hull, Isaac, 183
Hull House, 408
Hull, General William, 184
Humphrey, Hubert H., 583
Hungarian Revolt (1956), 562–563, 584
Hungary, 472, 473
Huntington, Collis, 343

I

Iceland, discovery of, 3

Illinois, statehood, 229

Immigration, early restrictions, 373; employment of immigrants, 371–372; the "Gentlemen's Agreement," 373–374; immigrants in industry, 372–373; immigrants swell labor force, 370–376; influence of party machines on immigrants, 405; later laws on, 374–375; law aimed at Chinese laborers, 373; laws to control immigration, 373–375; the "new" immigration, 372; reasons for increase in, 371; recent, 375–376; surge of, 370–372

The Incas, 11–12

Income tax, 452

Independence Hall, 110, 151

Indiana, statehood, 229

Indians, and cattle drives, 347; Columbus' description of, 8; concern over colonial expansion, 64; and Connecticut colony, 40; and Delaware colony, 36; and early explorers, 9; and the fur trade, 65, 69–70; vs. Georgia, 276–277; Great Sioux uprising, 352–353; at Jamestown, 24; in Kentucky, 227; land reserved for, 226; make a last stand, 351–353; and Maryland colony, 28; massacres of American patriots, 130; missionaries to, 18; new way of life for, 353; and New York colony, 33; in Northwest Territory, 229; in Oregon Territory, 245; and the Pilgrims, 38; raids in French and Indian War, 75; and Rhode Island colony, 42; subduing the red man, 351–353; in Tennessee, 228; treaty with Penn, 34–35; uprising led by Pontiac, 91–92; at Vincennes, 132; and the Virginia colony, 27; and Western migration, 197; and westward territorial expansion, 63 (see also specific tribes)

Industrial Revolution, city life, 209; developments in textile industry, 205; formation of labor unions, 209–210; growth of cities, 208; growth of manufacturing, 205–207; increased cultivation, 207–208; reaches America, 204–210; results of, 207–209; working conditions in factories, 208–209

Industry, automation and, 592; cattle industry, 347–349; government encourages industrial growth, 210–214; growth of iron and steel industries, 207; immigrants in, 372–373; reforms in, 453–454; regulations of private industry (New Deal), 496; in South after Civil War, 318; textile industry, 205–206

The Influence of Sea Power Upon History, 1660–1783, 418

Injunction, 367, 568

Inouye, Daniel K., 575

Integration, school, 386–387, 570–571

Inter-American Bank, 574

The Interest of America in Sea Power, 418

International Bureau of the American Republics, 444

International Court of Justice (U.N.), 548

Interstate Commerce Act, 347, 360

Interstate Commerce Commission, 360, 446, 500

Intolerable Acts, 101–102

Irish, 32, 35, 36, 63, 343

Iron industry, 207

Ironclads (ships), 291–292, 308–309

Iroquois Indians, 17, 74, 127, 130

Irving, Washington, 219

Isabella, Queen, 6–7

Isolation, policy of, 431

Italians, 4, 372, 471, 513, 514

Italy, attack on Albania, 506; declared war on Germany, 531–532; entered World War I, 460; invasion of Ethiopia, 505; London Disarmament Conferences, 475–476; Mussolini's promises, 505; the Rome-Berlin Axis, 505–506; and Treaty of Versailles, 472; Triple Alliance and, 456 (see also Axis Powers; World War II)

Iwo Jima, 538

J

Jackson, Andrew, 187, 214, *p 234*, 244, 249

Jackson Administration, a backward glance at, 237; democracy gains under, 234–237; Jackson's inauguration, 234–235; nature of the Union, 236; new era begins with, 234; orderly government, 235; spoils system, 235; tariff controversy, 278; and United States Bank, 236–237; Webster-Hayne debates, 235–236; Western land sales, 235–236; Western problems, 233

Jackson, T. J. ("Stonewall"), 289, 290, 295, 297

James I, 23, 26

James II (Duke of York), 33–34, 36

Jamestown, 24–25

Japan, entered World War I, 459; invasion of Manchuria, 503; joined Axis Powers, 516; London Disarmament Conference and, 475–476; a mutual security treaty (1960), 577; occupation of, 555; plans for conquest, 522–523; Potsdam ultimatum to, 537; self-defense force, 577; surrender (World War II), 539–540; undeclared war on China, 504; U.S. cooperation with, 577; Washington Disarmament Conference and, 474–475 (*see also* World War II)

Java, 183

Jay, John, 139, 155, 165, 169, 170

Jay Treaty, 169–170

"The Jazz Singer," 413

Jefferson, Thomas, absence from Constitutional Convention, 151; appointed to write Declaration of Independence, 115; dream of rural society, 593; founder of Democratic-Republican party, 167; trade mission to Paris, 147; Washington's Secretary of State, 164; writings regarding unfair exploitation of man, 209

Jefferson Administration, authorized Cumberland Road, 198; Barbary pirates, 175; continuing problems in foreign affairs, 178–179; election of 1800, 174–175; Lewis and Clark Expedition, 177–178; Louisiana Purchase, 175–177; new party steers nation, 174–179

Jeffries, Jim, 415

Jews, 56, 372, 375, 408, 478, 521–522, 537

Joffre, General, 458

Johnson, Andrew, *p 318*

Johnson (Andrew) Administration, and Congress, 317, and Freedman's Bureau bill, 322; impeachment of the president, 320; opposition by Congress to Reconstruction plan, 319; Reconstruction plan, 318–319; Stevens and Sumner (leaders in Congress), 319–320

Johnson, Ban, 414

Johnson, General Hugh S., 497

Johnson (Lyndon) Administration, Americans build a great society, 592; changes in Soviet government, 584; Civil Rights Bill (1964), 583–584; election of 1964, 582–583; foreign affairs are continuing problem, 584–588; new concern for human values, 583–584; succession to presidency, 582; U. S. relations with Soviet bloc, 584–585; unrest in Southeast Asia, 587

Johnston, General Albert Sidney, 294–295

Johnston, General J. E., 289

Joliet, Louis, 18

Jolson, Al, 413

Jones, Captain John Paul, 133

Jones, Samuel M., 407

Journalism: *see* Press; "Yellow Press"

Judah, Theodore, 344

Judicial Department, Federal, 157

July 4, 1776, 115

The Jungle, 399, 440

K

Kai-shek, Chiang, 554, 573

Kamikaze planes, 539

Kane, John, 395

Kansas-Nebraska Bill, 273–275

Kansas Territory, 274

Kaskaskia, 228

Kearney, Colonel Stephen W., 251

Kearsarge, 304

Kefauver, Estes, 571–572

Kelley, Oliver H., 359

Kellogg, Frank, 475

Kellogg-Briand Treaty, 475

Kennedy, John F., 571

Kennedy Administration, Alliance for Progress, 586–587; assassination of the president, 581–582; Bay of Pigs invasion, 586; China-Soviet split, 584; communist challenge, 585–586; Cuban missile crisis, 586; election of 1960, 579–580; meeting with Khrushchev, 584; national affairs during, 579–584; New Frontier, 580–581; Peace Corps, 588; succession of president, 582; Trade Expansion Act, 588; unrest in Southeast Asia, 587

Kentucky, settlement of, 227–228; statehood, 228

Kentucky and Virginia Resolutions, 173

Key, Francis Scott, 186–187

Khan, Kubla, 4

Khrushchev, Nikita, 562, 573, 574, 576, 577, 581, 584, 585, 586

King, Martin Luther, *p 583*
King George's War, 71
King Ranch, 349
King William's War, 70
King's Mt., 135–136
Kishi, Premier Nobusuke, 577
Knights of Columbus, 464
Knights of Labor, 368
Knox, General Henry, 164
Korean conflict, aggression from North Korea, 556; armistice at Panmunjon, 558–559; invasion from Red China, 557; recall of MacArthur, 558; Truman-MacArthur controversy, 557–558; two Koreas, 556; U.N. "police action," 557
Kosciusko, 129
Kosygin, Alexei, 584
Ku Klux Klan, 323, 483
Kwajalein, 538

L

La Follette, Robert M., 407, *p 407*, 447, 481
La Salle, 18
Labor Day, 370
Labor unions, early obstacles, 366–367; formation of, 209–210; Haymarket Riot, 368–369; Knights of Labor, 368; labor under Eisenhower, 567–569; labor legislation (New Deal), 497; lockouts and yellow dogs, 367; rise of the American Federation of Labor, 369–370; rise of the Congress of Industrial Organizations, 497–499; strikes and violence, 367–368; Taft-Hartley Act, 568; the Teamsters, 568; union beginnings, 367–369; union gains, 210; workers band together to improve labor conditions, 366–370 (*see also* American Federation of Labor; Congress of Industrial Organizations)
Labrador, discovery, 13; U. S. fishing rights off, 241
Lafayette, 129, 137
Lake Champlain, 186
Lake Erie, 184–185, 230
Land Ordinance of 1785, 145
Laos, independence, 560
Latin America, Alliance for Progress, 586–587; Declaration of Lima, 503; hemispheric organizations, 444–445; Inter-American Bank, 574; Monroe Doctrine, 193–194; Panamanian revolution, 441–442; Pan-American Conference (1938), 503; Peru (Spanish colony), 12; Roosevelt Corollary to Monroe Doctrine, 444; troubled neighbors to the South (Eisenhower Administration), 574; U.S. intervention in Caribbean countries, 444 (*see also* Colombia; Cuba; Mexican War; Mexico; Panama Canal; Spanish-American War)
Latvia, 465, 511
Laurens, Henry, 139
Lawrence, 184–185
Lawrence, Captain James, 183
The League of Nations, 471, 472–473, 548
Lecompton Constitution, 275
Lee, General Charles, 122, 123, 128, 129
Lee, General Robert E., 295, 297, 299, 302, 305–306, *p 305*
Lee, Richard Henry, 115
Legislative Department, Federal, 156
Lend-Lease Bill, 517–518
Leopard, 179, 183
Leopold, King, 512
Letters of Marque, 133
Lewis, John L., *p 496*, 498
Lewis, Meriwether, 177
Lewis, Sinclair, 399
Lexington, 107–109
Lexington, 132, 529
Leyte Gulf, battle of, 538
The Liberator, 269
Liberty bonds, 464
Libraries, 389–390
Library of Congress, 389
Life on the Mississippi (Twain), 398
Liliuokalani, Queen, 419
Lincoln, Abraham, *p 279*
Lincoln Administration, assassination of president, 306–307; Confederate States of America, 280; election of 1860, 278–279; Emancipation Proclamation, 296–297, Gettysburg address, 298, 299–300; Lincoln enters office, 281–282; Lincoln's Reconstruction policy, 318, 320; secession and, 279–281; support at start of Civil War, 286; threat of war, 282 (*see also* Civil War)
Lincoln-Douglas debates, 278–279
Lincoln Memorial, 395
Lindbergh, Charles, 517

Literature, American, beginnings of, 219; "local color" in, 398–399; men of letters, 395–399; social protest in, 399
Lithuania, 508, 511
Livingston, Robert, 176, 256
Lockout, 367
Locomotive, 203
Lodge, Henry Cabot, 417
London, Jack, 399
London Company, 23, 24, 26, 27, 45
London Disarmament Conferences, 475–476
Long, Oren E., 575
Longfellow (poet), 219
Longstreet, General, 295
Lorraine, 456
Louis XIV, 18, 68
Louis XVI, 168
Louisbourg, 71, 77–78
Louisiana, discovery, 18; statehood, 229
Louisiana Purchase, 175–177, 240, 256–257
Loyalists, 105, 120, 121
Luce, Henry, 391
Lundy, Ben, 269
Luniks, 575
Lusitania, 461
Lutherans, 36
Lyon, Mary, 217, 385

M

MacArthur, General Douglas, 527, 538, 540, p 554, 555, 557–558
McCarthy, Senator Joseph, 569–570, p 570
McClellan, General George B., 289–290, 295, 305
McCormick, Cyrus, 207
McCulloch vs. Maryland, 277
Macdonald, Ramsay, 476
MacDonough, Commodore Thomas, 186
McDowell, Edward A., 414
McDowell, General, 289
Macedonian, 183
McKinley Administration, assassination of president, 436; election (1896), 362, 364, 420, (1900), 426; and gold standard, 364; Philippine insurrection, 428 (*see also* Spanish-American War)
McKinley Tariff, 418
McLoughlin, John, 246
Macmillan, Prime Minister, 577

Madison, James, at Constitutional Convention, 151; and *The Federalist*, 155
Madison Administration, freedom of the seas, 189–190; a growing sense of nationalism under, 189; new role for Supreme Court, 189; sent army into Florida, 248–249; U.S. moves ahead under, 189–190 (*see also* War of 1812)
Magazines: *see* Press
Magellan, Ferdinand, 10
Maginot Line, 511, 513
Mahan, Captain Alfred T., 418
Main Street, 399
Maine, boundary dispute, 239; statehood, 192, 229
Maine, sinking of, 421–422
Maine colony, 42–43
Manchukuo (Manchuria), 503, 540
Manchuria, Japanese invasion of, 503
Mann, Horace, 216–217
Mann, Thomas, 375
Manufacturing, colonial home, 66; iron and steel, 207; recovery in South after Civil War, 324; standardized parts, 206–207; steam power development, 207; textile, 205–206; vulcanized rubber, 207
Mao Tse-tung, 554
Marbury vs. Madison, 277
Marco Polo, travels, 4–5
Mariana Islands, 538
Marne River, 458, 466
Marquette, Father, 18
Marquis-of-Queensberry Rules (prizefighting), 415
Marshall, George, 551, 554
Marshall, John, 189, 277
Marshall Islands, 538
Marshall Plan, 551–552
Martin, Joseph, 558
Maryland colony, Act Concerning Religion, 28–29; an experiment in tolerance, 28–29; settlement, 28
Mason, Captain John, 42
Mason, George, 151
Massachusetts Bay colony, 39–40, 60
Matsu, 573
Maximilian, Archduke, 307–308
Mayflower, 38
Mayflower Compact, 38–39, 40
Meade, General, 299

674

Medicine, advances in, 590–591
Mein Kampf (Hitler), 506
Memel (Lithuania), 508
Mencken, H. L., 399
Mentally ill, treatment reforms, 410–411
Merit system (Civil Service), 409–410
Merrimac, 291
Mesabi Range, p 331
Metropolitan Opera House, 414
Mexican War, invasion of Mexico, 251–252; reason for war, 250–251; results of war, 253; Taylor's victories, 251; Texas border disputes, 250; Treaty of Guadalupe-Hidalgo, 252–253; war in California, 251
Mexico, Díaz era, 454–455; independence from Spain, 242; Maximilian in, 307–308; Mexican War, 250–253; rule over Texas, 242–243; U.S. boundary with, 252–253, 257; Villa and Pershing, 455; Wilson's policy toward, 455; the Zimmermann note to, 462
Middle colonies, balanced economy of, 49; Delaware, 36; New Jersey's complicated past, 36–37; New York under two nations, 32–34; Pennsylvania and the Quakers, 34–36; Revolutionary War battles in, c 124; Revolutionary War in, 120–130 (see also specific colony)
Middle East, area of tension (1957), 572; Suez crisis, 563–564
Midway Island, battle of, 529
Mikhailovich, Draja, 520
Mikoyan, Anastas, 576
Miller, William E., 582
Mining, 349–351 (*see also* Gold Rush)
Minutemen, 109
Missiles, intercontinental ballistic (ICBM), 575
Mississippi, statehood, 229
Mississippi River, discovered, 9; important trade route, 229; steamboats on, 200
Missouri, 540
Missouri, statehood, 192, 229
Missouri Compromise, 192; (repeal) 274
Missouri Pacific Railroad, 347
Mobile Bay, battle in, 304
"Molly Maguires," 367
Monitor, 292
Monmouth, battle of, 129
Monroe Administration, international agreements, 191–192; Louisiana Purchase, 176, 256; Missouri Compromise, 192; nation enters "era of good feeling" under, 190–194; national prosperity, 190–191; ordering of General Jackson into Florida, 249; sectional differences, 191
Monroe Doctrine, Concert of Europe and, 193–194; effect of, 194; European reaction to, 239; Maximilian in Mexico and, 308; Roosevelt Corollary to, 444; statement of, 193–194
Montcalm, General, 76–80
Montezuma, 11, 12
Montgomery, General, 520
Montgomery, Richard, 114
Morgan, J. P., 364
Mormons, 247
Morocco, French-German dispute, 445
Morrill Land Grant Act of 1862, 384
Morris, Robert, 125
Moses, Anna Mary ("Grandma"), 395
Moslems, 3–4
Mount Holyoke Seminary (College), 218, 385
Mount Vernon Convention, 148–149
Movies, 412–413
"Muckrakers", 407
Music, 413–414
Mussolini, Benito, 504–505, p 505, 508, 513, 514, 532, 536

N

Nagasaki, bombing of, 540
Nagy, Imre, 562–563
Naismith, Dr. James, 415
Napoleon III, 307–308
Napoleon Bonaparte, 172, 173, 175–176, 182, 256
Narragansett Indians, 42
Nasser, President (Egypt), 563, 573
Nast, Thomas, 405
National Association for the Advancement of Colored People, 385–386, 570
National Farmers' Alliance, 360
National Grange: *see* Grange
National Labor Relations Act, 403, 497
National Labor Relations Board, 497
National Labor Union, 367
National League (baseball), 414
National Recovery Administration (NRA), 496–497

675

National Republicans, 214
National Road, 198, 230
National Woman Suffrage Association, 411
National Youth Administration (NYA), 495
Natural resources, 438–440, 593–596
Navigation Laws, 90
Nazis (National Socialists), 506, 521, 522
Nebraska Territory, 274
Negroes, 25, 37, 46, 50–52, 56, 63, 187, 219, 315–317, 319–324, 385–387, 395, 478, 570–571, 584, 599 (see also Civil Rights; Integration, school; Slavery)
Netherlands, conquered by Germany (World War II), 512; in New World, 14, 20; New York colony, 32–33; World Court at the Hague, 474
Neutrality Acts, 502, 516
Nevada, statehood, 287
New Deal, Agricultural Adjustment Act, 495–496; alphabetical work agencies, 494–495; banks reopened, 493; Civilian Conservation Corps (CCC), 494; economic recovery, 501; end of gold standard, 493; farmer-aid measures, 495–496; helping the railroads, 500; housing and slum clearance, 500–501; insured bank deposits, 494–495; meeting the financial crisis, 492–494; new labor legislation, 497; public utilities, 499–500; putting water to work, 499–500; regulating private industry, 496–497; relief of jobless, 494–495; social security, 501
New England colonies, Connecticut, 40–42; diversified economy of, 47–49; Massachusetts Bay colony, 39–40; New Hampshire and Maine, 42–43; non-Puritan influences on, 53; Pilgrims of Plymouth, 37–38; Puritan influences on, 52–55; religious freedom in Rhode Island, 42; religious motives bring settlers to, 37–43
The New England Primer, 54–55
New France, 77, 80
New Freedom, 450–451
New Frontier, 580–581
New Hampshire colony, 42–43
New Jersey colony, 36–37
New Jersey Plan (Constitution), 153
New Mexico Territory, 257, 272
New Orleans, battle of, 187; British capture of, 293–294; mission to Paris for purchase of, 176

New World, discovery of, 7; Dutch in, 14, 20; England stakes its claim, 12–15; English discovery and exploration in, 13–15; European conflicts over, 19–20; France takes interest in, 16–19; French explorations in, 16–18; Spanish conquerors in, 10–12; further Spanish explorations in, 8–10, (see also English colonies; French colonies)
New York, boundary settlement, 241
New York Assembly, 98
New York Bay, discovery of, 14
New York Central Railroad, 345
New York City, attack on, 122–123
New York colony, Dutch settlement of, 32; English settlement in, 33; growth and progress, 34; ratification of Constitution by, 155; surrender to British, 32–33
New York Journal, 390, 421
New York World, 390, 421
The New Yorker, 391
Newfoundland, 241
Newspapers: see Press
Niagara, 185
Nicaragua, U.S. intervention in, 444
Nickelodeons, 413
Nimitz, Chester, 540
Niña, 7
Nine Power Treaty, 474, 475
Nineteenth Amendment (suffrage), 411, 477
Nixon, Richard, election of 1956, 571; election of 1960, 579–580; trip to Russia, 576; unfriendly welcome in Latin America, 574
Nonimportation Policy, 95
Nonintercourse Act, 179, 211
Normandy invasion, 533
Norris, Frank, 399
Norsemen (Vikings), 3
North Atlantic Treaty Organization (NATO) 553, 588
North-South controversy, balance of power, 271–272; "bleeding Kansas," 274; Clay's Compromise, 272; Compromise of 1850, 272–273; debate in Congress, 273; Kansas-Nebraska Bill, 273–275; land additions heighten, 271–275; Lecompton Constitution, 275; Northern demands, 272; passage of Omnibus Bill, 273; "popular sovereignty," 273–274; power struggle, 275; repeal of Missouri Compromise, 274; Southern demands, 272; violence, 275

676

Northern Pacific Railroad, 344
Northern Securities Co., 437
Northwest Ordinance, 145, 217, 229–230, 264
Northwest Territory, boundary dispute, 239; Northwest Ordinance, 229–230; opening of, 229–230; states formed from, 145
Norway, in World War II, 512
Norwegians, 521
Nullification, 214

O

Oberlin College, 385
Oglethorpe, James, 30, 31
Ohio, statehood, 229
"Old Guard," 448
Old North Church, 108
Omnibus Bill, 273
One-crop system, 32, 46, 355–356
O'Neill, Eugene, 399
Open door policy, 427–428
Orchestras, 413–414
Oregon, 423, 425
Oregon Territory, "54° 40′ or fight," 246; missionaries to Indians in, 245; peaceful settlement of boundary dispute, 246–247; the Whitmans and settlement of, 245–246
Organization of American States (OAS), 445
Oriskany, 127
Orlando, Vittorio, 471

P

Pacific Fur Co., 178
Pacific Ocean, Lewis and Clark reached, 178; search and discovery by Balboa, 9
Packets, 198–199
Pago Pago (Samoan Islands), 419
Paine, Thomas, 115, 128, 151
Painting (art), 394–395
Pakenham, Sir Edward, 187
Palmer, General A. Mitchell, 478
Panama, revolution for independence, 441–442
Panama Canal, construction of, 442; importance of, 443; need for, 440–441; protecting, 442–443; revolt in Panama, 441–442; route chosen, 441
Panama Canal Zone, 443
Pan-American Conference, 503
Pan-American Union, 444

Panay Incident, 504, *p 504*, 522
Panic of 1893, 364
Panmunjon, armistice at, 558–559
Panzer divisions, 513
Paris, summit conference in, 577
Paris, Treaty of (1763), 80, 139, 146
Parker, Captain, 108, 111
Parker Ranch, 349
"Parsons' Cause," 94–95
Party (political) machines, 404–405
Paterson, William, 153
Patronage, 408–410
Patterson, General, 288
Peace Corps, 580
"Peaceful coexistence," 584
Peacock, 183
Pearl Harbor, attack on, 525–526; U.S. rights for naval base, 418
Pemberton (Confederate commander), 298
Pendleton Act, 409–410
Peninsular Campaign, 289–290
Penn, William, 34, 36
Pennsylvania, 527
Pennsylvania colony, the Great Law of, 35–36; a home for Quakers, 34–36; treaty with Indians, 34–35; William Penn, 34, 36
Pennsylvania Railroad, 345, 406
People's Republic of China, 554–555
Pepperell, Colonel, 71
Permanent Court of International Justice, 473–474
Perry, Oliver Hazard, 184, *p 185*
Pershing, General, 455, *p 455*, 463, 466
Peru, colony of Spain, 12
Petain, Marshal Henri, 513
Petersburg, siege of, 302
Philadelphia, establishment of, 34; Howe's capture of, 127–128; U.S. capital, 174
Philippines, fall of (World War II), 527–528; insurrection in (1899), 428–429; MacArthur's return, 538; U.S. acquisition of, 426–427
Phillips Academy at Andover, 216
Phillips Exeter Academy, 216
Phips, Sir William, 70
Phonograph, 413
Pickett, General, 299
Pierce, Franklin, 273, 274, 275, 287
Pilgrims, 37, 38–39, 40, 47

Pinchot, Gifford, 439
Pinckney, Charles, 172, 213
Pinta, 7
Pippin, Horace, 395
The Pit, 399
Pitt, William, 75, 98
Pizarro, 11–12
Plains of Abraham, battle on, 79–80
Plantation system (South), 32, 46–47, 266
Platt Amendment, 429–430
Plessy vs. Ferguson, 386, 570
Plymouth (Massachusetts), Pilgrims landed at, 38
Plymouth colony, arrangements to found, 37–38; Mayflower Compact, 38–39; progress in self-government, 60; struggle for survival, 38
Plymouth Company, 23
Poe, Edgar Allan, 219
Poland, in World War II, 508, 511
Poles, 129, 521
Polish "Corridor," 472, 508
Politics, on frontier, 232; party machines, 404–405; rise of political parties, 167–168; in South after Civil War, 318–320
Polk, James K., 245, 251
Pontiac, 91–92
Pope, General John, 295
Populist (People's) Party, 361–362
Port Royal, 70, 71, *p 71*
Postal savings system, 447
Potsdam Declaration, 537
Powderly, Terence V., 368
Presbyterians, 36
Presidential administrations: *see* specific president's name
Presidential elections: *see* Election, presidential
Press, expanding power of, 390–391; growth of newspapers, 391; new interest in books, 390; newspapers, 219–220; periodical magazines, 391; pioneers in journalism, 390–391 (*see also* "Yellow Press")
Princeton, victory at, 123–125
Printing press, rotary, 220
Prizefighting, 415
Proclamation of 1763, 91–92
Proclamation for Suppressing Rebellion and Sedition, 111
Profiles in Courage, 581

Progressive party, 481, 550
Prohibition, Eighteenth Amendment, 477; issue of, 483; Twenty-first Amendment (repeal), 483; Volstead Act, 477, 483
Protestants, 31, 35, 36, 53, 408 (*see also* Huguenots; Pilgrims; Puritans; Quakers)
Providence (Rhode Island), establishment, 42
Prussia, 456
Public utilities, 499
Public Works Administration, 494
Puerto Rico, governing of, 430; Ponce de Leon and, 9; U. S. acquired possession of, 426
Pulaski, 129
Pulitzer, Joseph, 390, 421
Pullman, George, 345
Pure foods and drugs, 440
Puritans, advantages of Puritan discipline, 53; educational beginnings, 53–55; influence in New England, 52–55; living earned from the sea, 47; of Massachusetts Bay, 39–40; role of Puritan Church, 52–53; unusual punishments of, 53 (*see also* Pilgrims)

Q

Quadruple Alliance, 193
Quakers, 34–36, 37, 55, 120, 218
Quebec (Canada), American failure at, 114; fall of, 78–80; first town in French territory (New World), 68; founding of, 17; *p 68*
Quebec Act, 101
Queen Anne's War, 70
Quemoy, 573
Quisling, 512

R

Railroads, advances in, 345; vs. canals, 203–204; the Central Pacific, 343–344; corrupt practices, 345–347; Crédit Mobilier, 345–346; driving the "golden spike," 343; an expanding network, 344–345; and the farmer, 358, 360; iron horse spans a continent, 342–347; linking the oceans, 344; need for government control, 346–347; New Deal help for, 500; rails, 345; regulation laws, 438; system in South after Civil

War, 314; Transportation Act (1933), 500; Union Pacific, 342–343; "wedding of the rails," 342–344

Raleigh, Sir Walter, 22

Randolph, Edmund, 153, 165

Reader's Digest, 391

Reaper, mechanical, 207

Reciprocal Trade Agreements Act (1934), 502

Reconstruction, Andrew Johnson and, 318–320; carpetbaggers and scalawags, 315; Civil Rights Act, 322; Congress and the president wage own war, 317–320; Congressional reconstruction brings bitterness, 321–324; Constitutional amendments, 321–322; corrupt government, 315–316; effects of war on economy in South, 312–314; emancipated whites, 317; end of, 323; ex-Confederate leaders, 314–315; farms and crops, 313–314; freed Negroes, 316–317; homes and cities, 314; industry in South, 314; Lincoln's reconstruction policy, 318, 320; military occupation of South, 322; military reconstruction, 322; new way of life, 316–317; problems in politics and voting, 314–316; railroads in South, 314; Reconstruction Acts, 322; recovery of South, 323–324; Southern resistance ("solid South"), 323; South's condition in 1865, 312–317

Reconstruction Acts, 322

Reconstruction Finance Corporation (RFC), 486

Recreation, Americans find time to enjoy life, 412–415; Chautauqua, 413; circus, 412; drama, 412; movies, 412–413; music, 413–414; sports, organized, 414–415; theatrical entertainment, 412–413, 594–595

The Red Badge of Courage (Crane), 399

"Red Scare," 477–479

Reforestation, 351

Reforms, twentieth century, in city and state governments, 407–408; ending the spoils system, 408–410; new roles for women, 410–411; workers for social justice, 408; writers attacking corruption, 407 (*see also* Civil Rights)

Remington, Frederic, *p 197*, 394

Republicans (party), 278, 317, 321

Revere, Paul, 108

Revolutionary War (American Revolution) advantages of Americans, 105–107; advantages of British, 104–105; American independence becomes a reality, 138–140; American occupation of Boston, 114; American victories at Trenton and Princeton, 123–125; Americans advance on land and sea, 130–133; armed resistance begins, 104–111; attack on New York City, 122–123; Barry's naval successes, 132–133; battle of Cowpens, 136; battle of Monmouth, 129; battles of, *c 124;* British strategy, 120–122; Bunker Hill costly to British, 112–114; Burgoyne's expedition, 126–127; the campaign in the West, 131–132; changing tides of battle, 129–130; defeat of Gates in South Carolina, 135; "divide and conquer," 121–122, 125–129; effects of, 139–140; England carries war into middle colonies, 120–130; European army officers join Washington's army, 129; fall of Charleston, 134–135; final victory at Yorktown, 136–137; Gage's plan against resistance, 107–108; Hessian troops in, 115, 124; Howe's capture of Philadelphia, 127–128; importance of "bread colonies" in, 121; independence declared, 115–116; Indian and Tory massacres, 130; invasion of Canada, 114–115; jealousy of Washington's command, 128–129; Lexington and Concord, 107–109; meeting a money crisis during, 125; in New England and middle colonies, *c 124;* patriot preparations, 108; patriot victory at Ticonderoga, 111–112; redcoats surrender at King's Mt., 135–136; resistance to rebellion, 111–116; rout of redcoats by minutemen, 109; St. Leger's Campaign, 127; Second Continental Congress, 109–111; shots "heard round the world," 108–109; surrender of Cornwallis, 137; treason of Benedict Arnold, 130; Treaty of Paris (1783), 139; war on the sea, 132–133; war in the South, 134–137; Washington's retreat across New Jersey, 122–123; widening American-British rift, 115–116; winter at Valley Forge, 128

Rhee, Syngman, 556

Rhine River, 535–536

Rhode Island colony, 42

Richmond (Virginia), capital of Confederacy, 288; Grant entered city, 305; Grant's advance on, 301–302

Ridgway, General Matthew B., 558

Rio Grande River, 245, 253
The Rise of Silas Lapham, 399
Rivers, Ralph J., 575
Roanoke Island colony ("lost colony"), 23
Robertson, James, 228
Roberval, Jean Francois, 17
Rochambeau, General, 137
Rockefeller, John D., 383, 384
Rockefeller, John D. Jr., 548
Rome-Berlin Axis: *see* Axis Powers
Rommel, General Erwin, 519, *p 519,* 531
Roosevelt, Franklin D., vice-presidential candidate, 479
Roosevelt (Franklin) Administration, aggressive militarism leads world into war, 503–509; America wages struggles in Pacific, 525–530; American defensive measures, 516; America's war role debated, 516–517; Atlantic Charter, 518; changes in American policy (World War II), 523; Civil War in Spain, 506; destroyers to Britain for bases, 516; election of 1932, 486–487; fireside chats, 493; fourth term, 534; gold standard and, 364; the "good neighbor" (Canada), 503; Japan on the march, 503–504; lend-lease—end of neutrality, 517–518; Neutrality Acts, 502; New Deal 492–501 (*see also* New Deal); new Italian empire, 504–506; passing of president, 534–535; prelude to World War II, 523; reciprocal trade agreements, 502; recognition of Soviet Russia, 502; rise of Hitler, 506–507; road to World War II, 507; Selective Service, 516; steered middle course in foreign policy, 502–503; third term, 517; war declared by U.S., 526–527; and World Court, 474; Yalta Conference, 534 (*see also* World War II)
Roosevelt, Theodore, Assistant Secretary of Navy, 422; "Bull Moose" Campaign, 448; leader of "Rough Riders," 424; Vice-president, 427
Roosevelt (Theodore) Administration, canal to link the oceans, 440–443; conservation of nation's resources, 438–440; contributions to world peace, 445–446; Corollary to Monroe Doctrine, 444; faces domestic issues, 436–440; "Gentlemen's Agreement," 374; the man and the leader, 436–437; Nobel Peace Prize, 446; pure foods and drugs, 440; railroad regulation laws, 438; "Square Deal," 437–438; trouble in coal fields, 438; U.S. intervention in Caribbean countries, 444; wields the "big stick" in foreign affairs, 440–446
Root, Elihu, 446
Rosecrans, General, 300, 301
"Rough Riders," 423–424
Roughing It, 350
Rubber, vulcanized, 207
Rumania, 460, 472
Rumsey, James, 199
Rush, Richard, 191, 240
Rush-Bagot Agreement, 191
Russia: *see* Soviet Union
Russian revolution, 464–465
Russo-German Nonaggression Pact (1939), 508–509
Russo-Japanese War, 446

S

Sacajawea, 178
St. Augustine (Florida), establishment, 19
St. Croix Island, 443
St. John Island, 443
St. Lawrence River, discovery of, 17
St. Leger's Campaign, 127
St. Mihiel Salient, 466–467
St. Thomas Island, 443
Saipan, 538
Salomon, Haym, 125
Salvation Army, 408, 464
Samoa, U.S. Protectorate of, 419
Sampson, Admiral, 423
San Jacinto, battle of, 244
San Juan Hill, battle of, 424
San Martín, José de, 193
Santa Anna, 242–244
Santa María, 7
Santiago, battle of, 425–426
Sarajevo, 457–458
Saratoga, 126
Sargent, John Singer, 394
Satellites, man-made, 575–576, 589–590
Saturday Evening Post, 391
Savannah, fall of (to British), 135; (in Civil War), 303; founding, 31
Savo Island, battle of, 530
Scalawags, 315
Schley, Commodore, 423
Schools: *see* Education

Schurz, Carl, 409
Schuyler, General Philip, 126
Science, 589–592
Scots, 36, 56, 63
Scott, Dred, 270–271
Scott, General Winfield, 251
Secession, causes of, 262; by default, 280–281; further, 286–287; Lincoln's election and, 279–281
Second Continental Congress: *see* Continental Congress, Second
Second Hague Conference, 446
Secretariat (U.N.), 548
Securities and Exchange Commission (SEC), 494
Security Council (U.N.), 547, 548
Sedition Law, 173
Selassie, Haile, 505, 519
Selective Service Act (1917), 463
Selective Training and Service Act (1940), 516
Seminole Indians, 249–250
Senate (U.S.), Connecticut Plan for, 153
Seneca Falls Convention, 411
Seneca Indians, 130
Separatists, 37, 39
Serapis, 133
Serbia, 457–459
Settlement houses, 408
Seventeenth Amendment (election of senators), 447, 454
Sevier, John, 228
Seward, William H., 273, 281, 308, 417, 575
Sewing machine, 205
Shannon, 183
Shawnee Indians, 75
Shays, Daniel, 148
Shays' Rebellion, 148
Shenandoah, 308–309
Shenandoah Valley Campaign, 302–303
Shepard, Alan B., 589
Sheridan, General, 302-303, 305, 308
Sherman, General, 301, 303
Sherman Antitrust Act, 437
Sherman Silver Act, 363–364
Shiloh, battle of, 294–295
Shreve, Henry M., 200, 229
Sicily, in World War II, 531
Siegfried Line, 512, 535

Silastic (medical plastic), 591
Silver Question, adoption of gold standard, 363–364; Bland-Allison Act, 363; Cleveland's solution, 364; free coinage of silver, 362–363; new discoveries (silver) in the West, 363; panic of 1893, 364; politics and the single standard, 364; Sherman Silver Act, 363–364; 16:1 ratio, 362–363
Sinclair, Upton, 399, 440
Sioux Indians, 352–353
Sitting Bull, 353
Sixteenth Amendment (Income Tax), 447, 452
Skyscrapers, 395
Slavery, abolitionists, 269–270; background of, 263–264; Compromise of 1850, 272–273; and Constitution, 153–154, 264–265; Constitutional Convention compromise, 265; Dred Scott Case, 270–271; early disagreements, 264–265; Emancipation Proclamation, 296–297, 313; end of, 320; freedom for slaves, 263–264; Fugitive Slave Law, 267; issue draws sectional lines, 262–271; Kansas-Nebraska Bill, 273–275; Missouri Compromise, 192, (repeal) 274; under Northwest Ordinance, 146; in South, 46–47, 50–52, 265–267; in Texas, 244; Thirteenth Amendment, 321; Underground Railroad, 268–269
Slidell, John, 250
Sloat, Commodore, 251
Slovaks, 372
Smith, Alfred E., 483
Smith, Captain John, 24–25
Smith, Joseph, 207
Smoking, and health, 591
Social Revolution, beginning of American literature, 219; educational advances, 215–218; extension of suffrage, 218–219; Horace Mann's reforms, 216–217; newspapers, 219–220; public and private schools, 216; religious freedom, 218; schools for girls, 217–218 (*see also* Education; Literature; Press)
Social Security, 501
Soil Conservation and Domestic Allotment Act, 496
Solomon Islands, 530
Sons of Liberty, 96
The South: *see* Civil War; Confederacy; North-South Controversy; Reconstruction; Slavery; Southern colonies

South Carolina, secession, 279–280; and tariff laws, 214, 278
Southeast Asia, armistice in, 560; communism on the march, 560–561; unrest in (1960's), 587 (*see also* Vietnam)
Southeast Asian Treaty Organization (SEATO), 588
Southern colonies, the Carolinas, 29–30; Georgia, 30–32; life in, 50–52; Maryland, 28–29; plantation system in, 46–47; Revolutionary War in, 134–137, (battles of) *c 124;* Virginia, 24–28 (*see also* specific colonies)
Southwest territory, 228
Soviet Union, cultural exchanges with U.S., 576; Germany declared war on (1914), 458; Hitler's attack on, 520–521; revolution in, 464–465, 471; Russo-German Nonaggression Pact, 508–509; Russo-Japanese War, 446; Triple Entente, 456; turning tide in World War II, 532–533; U.S. recognition of, 502 (*see also* Cold War; Communists)
Space Age, American progress in, 589; American scientific successes in, 575–576; communications satellites, 590; Mariner II (Venus probe), 589–590; space science, 589–590; sputniks and luniks, 575
Spain, Christopher Columbus' voyage, 6–8; Civil War in, 506; further explorations in New World, 8–10; the New World conquerors, 10–12; turns westward to New World, 6–12; U.S. gained Florida from, 248–249 (*see also* Spanish-American War)
Spalding, Eliza and Henry, 246
Spaniards, 19, 31
Spanish-American War, American "yellow press" in, 421; battle of San Juan Hill, 424; battle of Santiago, 425–426; declaration of war, 422; de Lôme letter, 421–422; end of hostilities, 426; Manila Bay battle, 422–423; naval blockade of Santiago, 423; pro-Cuban sympathies, 421–422; results of, 426; the "Rough Riders," 423–424; sinking of the *Maine,* 421–422; Spanish rule in Cuba, 420–421
Specie Circular, 237
"Spheres of Influence," 427
Spinning mill, 205–206
Spoils system, 235, 408–410
Square Deal, 437–438

Stagecoaches, 58; 230
Stalin, Joseph, 509, 520, 534, 537, 554, 555, 561
Stamp Act, 92–93, 96–98
Stamp Act Congress, 96–97
Standard Oil Co. of Ohio, 406
Standardized parts, 206
Stanford, Leland, 343, 344, 384
Stanton, Edwin, 307, 309, 320
"Star Spangled Banner," 187
Stark, Colonel John, 126
States' Rights, 214, 236, 276–282
Steamboats, 199–200, 229–230
Steel industry, 207
Steffens, Lincoln, 407
Steinbeck, John, *p 398,* 399
Stephens, Urich, 368
Stephenson, George, 203
Steuben, Baron von, 129
Stevens, John L., 419
Stevens, Thaddeus, 319–320
Stevenson, Adlai, 559, 571
Stock-market tumble (1929), 484–485
Stowe, Harriet Beecher, 270
Straits of Magellan, discovery, 10
Strikes, 367–368
Stuyvesant, Peter, 33
Submarine warfare, 460, 461
Subversion, security checks, 569; Senator McCarthy, 569–570
Suez Canal crisis, 563–564
Suffrage: *see* Voting
Sugar Act, 92–93
Sukarno, President, 587
Sullivan, General John, 130
Sullivan, John L., *p 408,* 415
Sullivan, Louis, 395
Sumner, Charles, 319–320
Supreme Court, change under John Marshall, 189
Sussex, 461
Sutter, Johann, 253
Swedes, 36
Swiss, 63

T

Taft, Senator Robert A., 559, *p 569*
Taft, William Howard, mission to Philippines, 428

Taft Administration, attempts to follow Roosevelt's policies, 446–448; election of 1912, 447–448; Taft's progressivism, 446–447
Taft-Hartley Act, 568–569
Tallmadge amendment, 192
Tamiami Trail, *p 250*
Tammany Hall, 405
Taney, Chief Justice, 271
Tarbell, Ida M., 407
Tariff, of Abominations, 213, 278; Bill of 1816, 211; Bill of 1824, 211–213; Bill of 1832, 214; Bill of 1833 (Clay's Compromise), 214; doctrine of states' rights and, 214; first American, 210–211; Hamilton's measures, 210–211; McKinley Tariff, 418; opposition to tariff, 211–214; party split over tariff, 213–214; protecting infant industries, 211; sectional differences on, 211; Underwood-Simmons Act, 451–452
Taxation: *see* Income tax; Stamp Act; Sugar Act
Taylor, General Zachary, 250–251, 254, 273
Teachers College of Columbia University, 384
Teamsters Union, 568
Technology, modern, 589–592
Tecumseh, 182, 197, 229
Tecumseh, 304
Teller Amendment, 422
Ten Years War (Cuban rebellion), 420
Tennessee, settlement of, 228; statehood, 228
Tennessee Valley Authority (TVA), *p 498*, 499–500, 596
Tenochtitlan, 11
Tenure of Office Act, 320
Territorial expansion: *see* westward expansion
Texas, the Alamo, 242, 243; annexation of, 242–245; border disputes, 250; boundaries, 272; under Mexican rule, 242–243; Polk and annexation, 245; statehood, 245; Texan independence (Republic of Texas), 243–244; (*see also* Cattle industry)
Textile industry, Howe's sewing machine, 205; power loom, 205; spinning and weaving, 205; Whitney's cotton gin, 205
Thirteenth Amendment (slavery), 306, 321
Thirty-eighth parallel (Korea), 558–559
Thomas, General, 300, 301, 303

Three-fifths Compromise (Constitution), 153–154
Thurmond, J. Strom, 551
Tinian Island, 538
Tippecanoe, 182, 197, 229
Tonnage Act, 165
Tories, 105, 125, 127, 130, 135
Touro Synagogue, *p 29*
Townshend Acts, 99–100
Trade, colonial, 90–93; decline (War of 1812), 211; early American (1785), 147; early internal, 233; effect of Embargo and Nonintercourse Acts on, 179, 211; Far Eastern, 4–5; fur, 27, 65–66, 226; Trade Expansion Act (1962), 588 (*see also* Tariffs)
Trade Expansion Act (1962), 588
Transportation, city, 601; colonial, 58; flatboats and packets, 198–199; railroads vs. canals, 203–204; steamboats, 199–200, 229–230 (*see also* Canals; Railroads)
Travis, William Barret, 242, 243
Treaties: *see* specific treaty name
Tredegar Iron Works, 288, 328
Trent affair, 290–291
Trenton, victory at, 123–125
Triple Alliance, 456
Triple Entente, 456
Truman, Harry S., vice-presidential candidate, 534; *p 550*
Truman Administration, Berlin blockade, 552–553; civil war in China, 554–555; election of 1948, 550–551; Marshall Plan, 551–552; North Atlantic Treaty Organization (NATO), 553; occupation of Japan, 555; Potsdam ultimatum, 537; security checks, 569; succession to presidency, 535; Truman Doctrine, 550; Truman-MacArthur controversy, 557–558; war in Korea, 555–559 (*see also* Korean conflict; World War II)
Truman Doctrine, 550
Trustbusting, 437–438, 447
Trusteeship Council (U.N.), 548
Truth in Securities Act (1933), 494
Tryon Palace, *p 29*
Tubman, Harriet, 269
Tulane, Paul, 384
Turkey, 472
Tuskegee Institute, 385

Twain, Mark (Samuel Clemens), 350, 398
Tweed, William "Boss," 405–406
Twelfth Amendment (voting), 174–175
Twenty-first Amendment (prohibition repeal), 483
Twenty-second Amendment (tenure), 534
Tyler, John, 245

U

U-2 incident, 577
Udall, Stewart, 596
Uncle Tom's Cabin, p 269, 270
Underground Railroad, 268–269
Underwood-Simmons Act (tariff), 451–452
Union (U.S.), Union Army: *see* Civil War
Union Pacific railroad, 342–343, 345
United Nations, founding of, 546–548; growth of, 588; Korean "police action," 557; membership, 548; permanent members of Security Council, 547; ratification of charter, 547–548; resolution on Arab states, 573; structure of, 548; veto power in, 546–547
United Press, 391
United States, 183
United States Bank, 166, 236–237
Universities: *see* Education
Urbanization, causes of, 401; corruption and injustice accompany, 401–406; problems of, 402–403; urban government corruption, 404–406 (*see also* Cities)
Utah Territory, 247, 272

V

Vaccines, 590
Vagrancy Laws, 319
Valley Forge, winter at, 128
Van Buren Administration, annexation of Texas and, 244; election of 1836, 237; Western problems during, 233
Vanderbilt, Cornelius, 345
Vassar College, 385
Vaudeville, 412
Vermont, northern boundary settled, 241; statehood, 229
Verrazano, Giovanni, 16, 63, 67
Versailles, Treaty of, 470–472
Vespucci, Amerigo, 8–9
Vichy (France), 513

Vicksburg, siege of, 297–298
Viet Cong, 587
Vietnam, American assistance to, 587; division of, 559–560; surrender at Dienbienphu, 559–560
Villa, "Pancho," 455
Vincennes, 131–132, 228
Vinland, 3
Virgin Islands, U.S. purchase of three islands in, 443
Virginia colony, Bacon's Rebellion, 27; Captain John Smith, 24–25; expansion and progress, 27–28; government of, 26–27; growth of, 25–26; House of Burgesses, 26, 59–60; land included in charter, 64; settlement, 24
Virginia Company, 28, 37–38
Virginia and Kentucky Resolutions, 173, 276
Virginia Plan (Constitution), 153
Voice of America, 550
Volstead Act, 477, 483
Voting, extension of suffrage, 218–219; Fifteenth Amendment (right to vote), 322; Nineteenth Amendment (women's suffrage), 411, 477; secret ballot, 405; in South after Civil War, 314–316; Twelfth Amendment (separate vote for president and vice president), 174–175

W

Wages and Hours Act (1938), 497
Wagner Act, 403, 497
Wainwright, General Jonathan, 528
Wake Island, 527
Wald, Lillian, 408
Walk-in-the-Water, 230
Walker, Robert J., 275
Wallace, Henry A., 550
War of 1812, American sea successes, 183; American success on Lake Champlain, 186; battle of New Orleans, 187; British blockade, 184; British plan of attack, 185–187; coastal attack, 186–187; declaration of war, 182–183; Hartford Convention, 188; loss of Detroit, 184; Treaty of Ghent, 187–188; trouble on high seas, 181–182; victory on Lake Erie, 184–185; war on the sea, 183–184; war in the West, 184–185
"War Hawks," 182, 232
Warren, Earl, 386, 571

Warsaw Alliance, 552

Washington, Booker T., 385, *p 386*

Washington, George, accompanied General Braddock, 74–75; and Alexandria Convention, 149; commander of Revolutionary patriot forces, 110–111, 114; at Constitutional Convention, 151–152; crossed Delaware River, 123; death of, 173; escape from Cornwallis, 125; and Howe's troops on way to Philadelphia, 127–128; jealousy of his command, 128–129; led army to New York City, 122; and massacres of patriots, 130; mission to French for Governor Dinwiddie, 73; retreat across New Jersey, 122–123; Trenton and Princeton victories, 123–125; at Valley Forge, 128

Washington, D.C.: see District of Columbia

Washington Administration, foreign affairs, 168–170; the Genêt affair, 169; Hamilton's financial policy, 165–166; Jay Treaty, 169–170; proclamation of neutrality, 168–169; reelection of Washington, 168; rise of political parties, 167–168; upheaval in Europe, 168; Washington's advisers (cabinet), 164–165; Washington's Farewell Address, 170–171

Washington-on-the-Brazos, (Texas), 243

Washington Disarmament Conference, 474–475

Washington Naval Treaty, 474–475

Wasp, 183

"Watchful Waiting" policy, 455

Water pollution, 593–596

Water power plants, 500

Wavell, Sir Archibald, 519

Weaver, James B., 361, 362

Webster, Daniel, 236, 241, 253, 273

Webster-Ashburton Treaty, 241–242

Wesleyan College, 385

West Indies, discovery and naming, 7–8

West Virginia, statehood, 287

Westinghouse, George, 345

Westward expansion, American-British Convention of 1818, 240–241; American know-how goes into operation, 196–204; annexation of Hawaii, 418–419; annexation of Texas, 242–245; Clayton-Bulwer Treaty (1850), 254–256; colonial viewpoint on, 64; demands of Westerners, 232; effects on economy, 232–233; flatboats and packets, 198–199; Florida gained from Spain, 248–249; Gadsden Purchase, 257; the gold rush and, 253–254; gold, silver and copper strikes and, 349–350; land purchases complete continental borders, 256–257; Louisiana Purchase, 175–177, 256–257; lumbering and, 350–351; man-made waterways, 200–203; migration routes, 230; natural wealth helps to populate the West, 349–351; opening of the Northwest, 229–230; the Oregon territory, 245–247; pathways into the wilderness, 227–228; the protectorate of Samoa, 419; purchase of Alaska, 417; railroads vs. canals, 203–204; roads to the West, 198; settling the Southwest, 228–229; spirit of imperialism leads to, 417–419; steamboats and, 199–200; territory acquired through war, 248–256; U.S. acquires Puerto Rico, Guam, and the Philippines from Spain, 426; U.S. grows through treaties, 239–247; Webster-Ashburton Treaty, 241–242; western land sales, 235–236; western migration, 197–198; western movement affects nation, 231–233; western settlement poses new problems, 226–230; Westerners, 232; the Wild West, 350

Weyler, General Valeriano, 421

Whigs, 107, 237

Whiskey Rebellion, 165–166

Whistler, James MacNeill, 394

White, John, 23

White, William Allen, 517

White House, 171, 581

Whitman, Dr. Marcus, 245–246

Whitman, Narcissa, 246

Whitney, Eli, 205, 206, 228

Whittier (writer), 219

Wickersham, George, 483

The Wild West, 350

"Wild West" shows, 412

Wilderness Campaign (Civil War), 301–302

Wilderness Road, 227

Wilhelmina, Queen, 512

Wilkins, Roy, 386

Willard, Emma, 217

Williams, Roger, 42

Williamsburg (Virginia colony), 27

Willkie, Wendell L., 517, *p 517*

Wilmot, David, 271

Wilmot Proviso, 271

Wilson, Woodrow, impression of, 453

Wilson Administration, American response to League of Nations, 472–473; the "Big Four," 471–472; election of 1912, 448; financial program, 451–453; financing the war, 464; Fourteen Points, 470; intervention in Dominican Republic, 444; League of Nations, 471–473; neighbor to south (Mexico), 454–455; New Freedom, 450–451; reforms in government and industry, 453–454; Treaty of Versailles, 470–472; U.S. declaration of war, 462–463; U.S. drawn into World War I, 461–468; vetoed immigration laws, 374; a victors' treaty, 472; wartime measures, 463–464; Wilson's inauguration, 451; Wilson's war message to Congress, 461; world disarms for peace, 470–476 (see also World War I)

Winthrop, John, 39–40, 60

Wolfe, General, 78–80

Wolfe, Thomas, 399

Women, education of, 384–385; new roles for, 410–411; women's suffrage, 411, 477

Women's Christian Temperance Union (W.C.T.U.), 477

Wood, Leonard, 424, 429

Works Progress Administration (WPA), 495

World Court, 473–474

World War I, the armistice, 468; arrival of Americans in Europe, 466; attempts at neutrality, 461–463; British blockade of American ships, 461; the eastern front, 459; first years of war, 458–460; German invasion of Belgium, 458; German submarines, 461; Germany's final drives, 465–466; new allies, 459–460; outbreak of hostilities, 457–458; power struggle in Europe before, 456–457; progress of the war, 464–468; rivalries on land and sea, 456–457; submarine warfare, 460; Treaty of Versailles, 470–472; U.S. declaration of war, 462–463; U.S. wartime measures, 463–464; war declarations in Europe, 458; Western front, 458–459; Zimmerman note to Mexico, 462

World War II, air-borne invasion of Crete, 514; allies move toward victory in Europe, 530–537; America increases aid to allies, 516–519; American effort in the Pacific, 525–530; atomic attack on Hiroshima, 539; Axis attack on Greece and Yugoslavia, 514; battle of Britain, 514–515; "battle of the Bulge," 534; battle of Coral Sea, 528–529; battle of Leyte Gulf, 538; battle of Midway, 529; changes in American policy during, 523; Chinese-Japanese dispute, 522–523; collapse of Germany, 535–537; collapse of Germany's allies, 533–534; collapse of the low countries, 512–513; crossing the Rhine, 535–536; declarations of war, 509; defeat at Savo Island, 530; end of German resistance, 536–537; end of the war, 540; fall of France, 513; fall of the Philippines, 527–528; the free French, 513–514; help for Mussolini, 514; Hitler's attack on Russia, 520–521; Hitler's treatment of the Jews, 521–522; invasion of Denmark and Norway, 512; invasion of Normandy, 533; island-hopping, 537–539; Italy declares war on Germany, 531–532; Iwo Jima, 538; Japanese offensive in Pacific, 527–529; Japanese plans for conquest, 522–523; most of Europe falls to aggressors, 511–515; Mussolini executed, 536; Okinawa, 539; Paris abandoned, 513; Pearl Harbor, 525–526; rescue at Dunkirk, 513; road to war, 507–509; Russian advances, 511; second atomic bomb, 540; softening up the Axis, 530–531; suicide of Hitler, 537; surrender of Japan, 539–540; turning tide in Russia, 532–533; ultimatum at Potsdam, 537; U.S. declares war, 526–527; "V for Victory," 521; victory at Guadalcanal, 530; victory in North Africa, 531–532; war in Africa, 519; western front, 511–514

Wright, Frank Lloyd, 395

Wright brothers, p 337

Writs of Assistance, 92

X Y Z

XYZ Affair, 171–172

Yale University, 384

Yalta Conference, 534, p 535

"Yellow dog contract," 367

Yellow fever, conquer of, 429

"Yellow press," 390–391

Yorktown, victory at, 136–137, 142

Young, Brigham, 247

Young Men's Christian Association, 464

Young Men's Hebrew Association, 464

Young Women's Christian Association, 464

Yugoslavia, after World War I, 472; in World War II, 514, 520

Zimmermann note, 462

Picture Sources

Alaska Economic and Tourist Development: 574
American Airlines: vi (desert, Jefferson Memorial, Chinatown in San Francisco); vii (Grand Canyon); 11; 254; 372; 396 (top r.); 397 (center)
American Forest Products Industries: 351
American Iron and Steel Institute: 331
Association of American Railroads: Library of Congress, 314; Bessemer and Lake Erie Railroad, 373
Bell Telephone Laboratories, Incorporated: 590
Helen Breaker, Paris: Courtesy of Charles Scribner's Sons, 506
Brookhaven National Laboratory: xii; 591
Brown Brothers: 204
Caribbean Gardens, Naples, Florida: 7
Carnegie Corporation of New York: 332
The Chase Manhattan Bank Money Museum: 96; 361; 363
Chicago Historical Society: 95; 219; 279; 308; 318; 319; 496
Colorado Advertising and Publicity Department: viii
CBS Television: 580
Columbus Area Chamber of Commerce: Ohio State University Photo, 595 (bottom l.)
Columbus Dispatch: 596
Commonwealth of Kentucky: 227 (top); Kentucky Historical Society, 232
Charles Phelps Cushing: 75; 90; 99; 110 (both); 113; photo by Sawders, 188; 201 (top); 249; 297; 305; 343; 495
Documentary Photo Aids: 269 (top); Library of Congress, 281; 337 (top); 375; 413; 414; 424; 459; 526 (bottom r.); National Archives, 529
Duke University Photo: 397 (top l.)
Florida Development Commission: 248; 250; 595 (top)
Florida Southern College: 397 (top r.)
Ford Motor Company: 339
French Embassy Press & Information Division: 514
Ewing Galloway: 369; 437
Philip Gendreau: 173; 500; photo by A. F. Sozio, 601
General Dynamics Corporation: 576
Goodyear International Corp.: 595 (center r.)
Harvard University News Office: 54
Howard University: 385
Richard W. Hume: 48; 263 (both)
Illinois Historical Society and Information Service (Division of Parks): 230; 368
Indianapolis Motor Speedway Official Photos: 594 (center r.)
John Hancock Mutual Life Insurance, Freedom Trail Committee: xv
S. C. Johnson & Son, Inc.: 397 (bottom l.)
Kansas State Historical Society, Topeka: 294; 299
Keystone View Co.: 234; 427; 483; 550
Donald L. Knapp: vii (World's Fair)
KLM Royal Dutch Airlines: 473
Leviton-Atlanta: 583 (top)
Library of Congress: Reproduced from the collections of, 54; 134
Massachusetts Department of Commerce: 57; 107
Mergenthaler Linotype Company: 334
Meston's Travels, Inc., El Paso, Texas: ii–iii; vii (schoolhouse); 17; 37; 242; 246; 384; 389; 397 (bottom r.); Cover
Missouri Resources Division: photo by Massie, 594 (center l.)
Mount Holyoke College: 384
NASA Photo: xii; 589
National Archives: U.S. Office of War Information, 386; Navy Department, 422; U.S. War Department General Staff, 455, 467; U.S. Strategic Bombing Survey, 539
NAACP: 386
National Film Board of Canada: photo by Gar Lunney, 23; photo by Atlantic Guardian (1949), 66; photo by Chris Lund, 68; photo by Legault, NFB Production "Columbia River," 192
National Grange: 359
National Park Service Photo: 102
New Brunswick Travel Bureau Photo: 594 (top)
The New York Public Library: State of Rhode Island, 206; 390; 391; Theatre Collection, 412
New York State Department of Commerce: 76; 77; 114; 595 (bottom r.)
North Carolina Department of Archives and History: ix
North Carolina Department of Conservation and Development: x; xi; 29; 135; 595 (center l.)
Norwegian Information Office: 3
Nova Scotia Information Service: 71 (both)
Ohio Development Department: vi (bridge); 185; 199; 201 (bottom)
Ohio Historical Society: 269 (bottom)
Ohio University: 217
Pacific Area Travel Association Photo: 418
Panama Canal Company: 443
Peace Corps: 587
Pennsylvania Department of Commerce: 73; 128; 129

Pennsylvania Historical and Museum Commission: 333
Phillips Academy, Andover, Massachusetts: 216
Puerto Rico, Government of: photo by Rotkin, 430
Rhode Island Development Council: 29; Rhode Island Historical Society, 43
Roland W. Richardson: 462
H. Armstrong Roberts: 139
Franklin D. Roosevelt Library: 535
The Salvation Army: 408
Sarah M. Siegenthaler: 396 (top l.)
Singer Sewing Machine Co.: 205
Stanford University: 383
State Historical Society of Missouri: 227 (bottom)
Taft, Stettinius & Hollister of Cincinnati: 569
Telephone Historical Collection, Montreal: 337
Union Pacific Railroad Photo: vi (skyline); xii; 352; 353; 594 (bottom r.)
United Air Lines Photo: 547 (top)
United Nations: 547 (bottom)
United Press International: (Acme) 505; 552
United States Coast Guard Official Photo: vii (lighthouse); 532
United States Department of Agriculture: 357; 567
United States Forest Service: 439
United States Navy Official Photo: 183; 526 (top and bottom l.); 540
United States Steel Corporation: 16
Vermont Development Department: 594 (bottom l.)
Virginia Chamber of Commerce: 25; photo by Flournoy, 26, 27; 28; photo by Flournoy, 166, 170, 396 (center and bottom)
The White House: Robert L. Knudsen, 172; Cecil Stoughton, 582
Wide World Photos: 374; 398; 399; 407; 460; 471; 472; 486; 512; 517; 519; 521; 522; 554; 556; 558; 561; 570; 572; 573; 581; 583 (bottom); 585
Eileen Young: x